Baedeker's

GERMANY

Imprint

219 colour photographs
34 town plans, 4 general maps, 5 special plans, 3 ground-plans, 1 large map of Germany

Text: based on Baedeker/Allianz guides to the Federal Republic of Germany and German Democratic Republic

Editorial work: Baedeker-Redaktion (Peter M. Nahm, Vera Beck)

Cartography: Gert Oberländer, Munich; Franz Kaiser, Sindelfingen; Mairs Geographischer Verlag, Ostfildern-Kemnat (large map of Germany)

General direction:
Dr Peter Baumgarten, Baedeker Stuttgart

English language edition:
Alec Court

English translation:
James Hogarth

To make it easier to locate the various sights listed in the "A to Z" section of the Guide, their coordinates on the large map of Germany are shown in red at the head of each entry.

Following the tradition established by Karl Baedeker in 1844, sights of particular interest are distinguished by either one or two stars.

The symbol   on a town plan indicates the local tourist office from which further in-

formation can be obtained. The post-horn symbol indicates a post office.

In a time of rapid change it is difficult to ensure that all the information given is entirely accurate and up to date, and the possibility of error can never be completely eliminated. Although the publishers can accept no responsibility for inaccuracies and omissions, they are always grateful for corrections and suggestions for improvement.

1st English edition

© Baedeker Stuttgart
Original German edition

© 1992 The Automobile Association
United Kingdom and Ireland

© 1992 Jarrold and Sons Ltd
English language edition worldwide

US and Canadian edition
Prentice Hall Press

Distributed in the United Kingdom By the Publishing Division of the Automobile Association, Fanum House, Basingstoke, Hampshire RG21 2EA

Licensed user:
Mairs Geographischer Verlag GmbH & Co., Ostfildern-Kemnat bei Stuttgart

The name *Baedeker* is a registered trade mark
A CIP catalogue record of this book is available from the British Library

Printed in Italy by G. Canale & C.S.p.A – Borgaro T.se –Turin

ISBN 0–13–059510–1 US and Canada
      0 7495 0575 3 UK

Contents

The Principal Sights at a Glance

Continued on page 634

Preface

This guide to Germany is one of the new generation of Baedeker guides.

These guides, illustrated throughout in colour, are designed to meet the needs of the modern traveller. They are quick and easy to consult, with the principal places of interest described in alphabetical order, and the information is presented in a format that is both attractive and easy to follow.

This guide, covering the whole of the reunited country of Germany, is in three parts. The first part sets the background, with a general account of the topography and history of the country. In the second part places and features of tourist interest – towns, regions, mountains, river valleys, lakes – are described. The third part contains a variety of practical information. Both the sights and the practical information are listed in alphabetical order.

The new Baedeker guides are noted for their concentration on essentials and their convenience of use. They contain numerous specially drawn plans and colour illustrations; and at the end of the book is a large map making it easy to locate the various places described in the "A to Z" section of the guide with the help of the co-ordinates given at the head of each entry.

Facts and Figures

General

Since the reunion of the two parts of the country in 1990 Germany lies between 6° (Aachen) and 15° (Görlitz) of eastern longitude and between 47°16′ (south of Oberstdorf) and 55° (the island of Sylt) of northern latitude.

Situation

Germany has a total area of some 357,000sq.km/137,800sq.miles, extending for some 875km/545 miles from north to south and 640km/400 miles from east to west. It has a population of some 79 million. The country is divided into sixteen *Länder* or provinces: see pages 9–12.

Area and extent

Germany, a founder member of the European Community, lies in northern Central Europe. As a result of its central situation within Europe it has more common frontiers with other countries than any other European state. On the east it is bounded by Poland, on the south-east by Czechoslovakia, on the south by Austria and Switzerland, on the south-west by France, on the west by Luxembourg and Belgium, on the north-west by the Netherlands and on the north by Denmark. It has natural frontiers on the Baltic to the north and the North Sea on the north-west.

Germany is a tourist country of inexhaustible variety, with an everchanging pattern of scenery extending from the sea to the mountains, from the lowland regions along the Baltic and North Sea coasts by the way of rolling forest-covered uplands to the Bavarian Alps.

The patterns of human settlement show a similar variety – isolated farmhouses, the clustered houses of large villages, frowning medieval castles, old walled towns and modern industrial cities with their well planned residential areas. Many small towns have preserved the aspect of past centuries, many cities have brought new life into the old town centres. In the north handsome old brick-built houses bear witness to the wealth of the Hanseatic towns which once ruled the seas. Farther south the old free imperial cities, princely capitals and episcopal cities have their magnificent cathedrals, palaces and town halls to proclaim in the stone language of architectural styles the changes in human attitudes and in economic importance which time has brought, while great expanses of open country and countless holiday and health resorts offer relaxation and recreation to those seeking relief from the strains and stresses of modern life.

The German *Länder*

LAND	CAPITAL
Schleswig-Holstein Area: 15,729sq.km/6073sq.miles. Population: 2,567,000 (163 per sq.km/422 per sq.mile) Main elements in economy: agriculture, tourism	**Kiel**
Freie und Hansestadt (Free Hanseatic City) Hamburg Area: 755sq.km/292sq.miles. Population: 1,606,300 (2128 per sq.km/5512 per sq.mile) Main elements in economy: industry, commerce, services	**Hamburg**

◀ *Goethe and Schiller in front of the German National Theatre in Weimar*

Germany: the *Länder*

SCHLESWIG-HOLSTEIN

Kiel

Lübeck

Bremerhaven

Rostock

MECKLENBURG-VORPOMMERN

Schwerin

FREIE UND HANSESTADT HAMBURG

Oldenburg

FREIE HANSESTADT BREMEN

NIEDERSACHSEN

BRANDENBURG

Hannover

Braunschweig

SACHSEN-ANHALT

Potsdam

BERLIN

Münster

Bielefeld

Magdeburg

Dessau

Cottbus

NORDRHEIN-WESTFALEN

Dortmund

Göttingen

Halle (Saale)

Leipzig

Düsseldorf

Kassel

FREISTAAT SACHSEN

Aachen

Köln

HESSEN

Erfurt

Jena

Dresden

Bonn

Gera

Chemnitz

Koblenz

THÜRINGEN

Zwickau

RHEINLAND-PFALZ

Wiesbaden

Frankfurt

Mainz

Darmstadt

FREISTAAT BAYERN

SAARLAND

Ludwigshafen

Mannheim

Saarbrücken

Heidelberg

Nürnberg

Karlsruhe

BADEN-WÜRTTEMBERG

Stuttgart

Regensburg

Ulm

Augsburg

München

Freiburg

Former boundaries between the Federal Republic of Germany and the German Democratic Republic and between West and East Berlin

HESSEN — Names of *Länder*

——— Boundaries of *Länder*

Wiesbaden — Capitals of *Länder*

© Baedeker

Mecklenburg-Vorpommern (West Pomerania)   Schwerin
Area: 23,838sq.km/9204sq.miles. Population: 1,964,000
(82 per sq.km/212 per sq.mile)
Main elements in economy: agriculture, shipbuilding, tourism

Freie Hansestadt (Free Hanseatic City) Bremen   Bremen
Area: 404sq.km/156sq.miles. Population: 662,000
(1638 per sq.km/4242 per sq.mile)
Main elements in economy: foodstuffs and tobacco industries, shipbuilding, commerce, shipping

Niedersachsen (Lower Saxony)   Hannover
Area: 47,439sq.km/18,316sq.miles. Population: 7,191,000
(157 per sq.km/407 per sq.mile)
Main elements in economy: agriculture, industry, mining

Sachsen-Anhalt (Saxony-Anhalt)   Magdeburg
Area: 20,445sq.km/7894sq.miles. Population: 2,965,000
(145 per sq.km/376 per sq.mile)
Main elements in economy: agriculture, mining, chemical industry

Brandenburg   Potsdam
Area: 29,059sq.km/11,220sq.miles. Population: 2,641,000
(91 per sq.km/236 per sq.mile)
Main elements in economy: agriculture, forestry, mining

Berlin   Berlin
Area: 883sq.km/341sq.miles. Population: 3,410,000
(3862 per sq.km/10,003 per sq.mile)
Main elements in economy: commerce and services (particularly education), industry, tourism

Nordrhein-Westfalen (North Rhine-Westphalia)   Düsseldorf
Area: 34,071sq.km/13,155sq.miles. Population: 16,901,000
(496 per sq.km/1285 per sq.mile)
Main elements in economy: mining, agriculture, forestry, industry, commerce, services

Hessen (Hesse)   Wiesbaden
Area: 21,114sq.km/8152sq.miles. Population: 5,577,000
(264 per sq.km/684 per sq.mile)
Main elements in economy: agriculture, industry, tourism

Thüringen (Thuringia)   Erfurt
Area: 16,251sq.km/6275sq.miles. Population: 2,684,000
(165 per sq.km/427 per sq.mile)
Main elements in economy: agriculture, mining, industry

Freistaat Sachsen (Free State of Saxony)   Dresden
Area: 18,337sq.km/7080sq.miles. Population: 4,901,000
(267 per sq.km/692 per sq.mile)
Main elements in economy: agriculture, mining, chemical industry

Rheinland-Pfalz (Rhineland-Palatinate)   Mainz
Area: 19,849sq.km/7664sq.miles. Population: 3,657,000
(184 per sq.km/477 per sq.mile)
Main elements in economy: agriculture, forestry, industry, tourism (mineral springs)

Saarland   Saarbrücken
Area: 2570sq.km/992sq.miles. Population: 1,054,000
(410 per sq.km/1062 per sq.mile)
Main elements in economy: industry, mining, agriculture, forestry

Baden-Württemberg   **Stuttgart**
Area: 35,751sq.km/13,803sq.miles. Population: 9,460,000
(265 per sq.km/686 per sq.mile)
Main elements in economy: industry, foodstuffs and tobacco products, agriculture (wine), tourism

Freistaat Bayern (Free State of Bavaria)   **Munich**
Area: 70,554sq.km/27,241sq.miles. Population: 11,068,000
(157 per sq.km/407 per sq.mile)
Main elements in economy: tourism, industry, foodstuffs and tobacco products (brewing), agriculture (wine), forestry

---

Topography

North Sea Coast

The life of the North German coastal regions is conditioned by the sea. The sea deposited the material which formed the *marschen* (salt-marshes, fenlands), and consumed the land it had created in wild storm tides which in earlier centuries carved out the Dollart and Jade Bay; it tempted man to embark on its waters and range over the oceans; and sea fishing and sea-borne trade still play the major part in the economy of these regions.

Tides

Along the North Sea coast the tides raise and lower the water level by between 2m/6½ft and 3.5m/11½ft, and, advancing up the funnel mouths of the Elbe and the Weser, allow ocean-going vessels to sail some 100km/65 miles inland to Hamburg and 70km/45 miles inland to Bremen. In the port of Hamburg the difference between high and low tide is still of the order of 2m/6½ft. The wind carries the moisture and the almost frost-free winter temperatures of the sea deep inland, and when it rises into a storm it dominates the scene both at sea and inland.

Watt

The flat North Sea coast is protected by dykes, on the seaward side of which extends the *watt*, an expanse of mud-flats between 5km/3 miles and 30km/20 miles wide which is above sea level only at low tide. Some stretches of the *watt* have been dyked to form polders of new fenland.

North Frisian Islands

The ancient coastline is marked by the North Frisian Islands, mainly consisting of expanses of sandy heathland (*geest*), on which the wind has piled the sand up into great dunes, and the Halligen – islands, now partly dyked, which are the surviving fragments of a larger area of fenland. The East Frisian Islands have extensive beaches and dunes. Some 70km/45 miles off the mouth of the Elbe is Heligoland, its red cliffs rearing out of the sea to a height of almost 60m/200ft.

Lowlands

The lowlands between the Ems and the Elbe reach a height of barely 40m/130ft at a distance of 100km/60 miles from the coast, with only the occasional hill. There are numerous shipping canals which carry heavy traffic. North-east of the Elbe the edge of the glaciers moving westward in the last ice age left a terminal moraine of boulder clay which now runs across Schleswig-Holstein from north to south-east as a range of hills partly covered by forest. To the west of these hills is a sandy and unproductive expanse of *geest*, while to the east is a fertile region of clayey detritus. Here the ice gouged out long troughs which are now occupied by lakes.

Fenland and *geest*

The landscape pattern is set by the contrasts between the fenlands, the *geest* and the expanses of bog. The flat fenlands form an almost continuous strip up to 20km/12½ miles wide along the North Sea coast and the estuaries of the rivers. Dark-coloured clays deposited by the sea and the rivers form a fertile soil which now mainly supports grazing for the black-and-white cattle. The farmhouses and villages lie along the edge of the *geest* or on artificial mounds, *warften* or *wurten*, which provide protection from storm tides. The *geest* is the undulating land whose green and yellow slopes rise above the fenlands. It consists of glacial sands and provides grazing for sheep and arable land, with some areas of sparse woodland and fields of grain.
In the low-lying depressions there are large areas of bog, parts of which have been

brought into cultivation. Straggling villages extend along the countless canals, used for transporting the peat which is cut here for fuel. The austere beauty of this region was discovered only at the end of the 19th century by the Worpswede school of artists.

The Low German dialect (Plattdeutsch) is used both in conversation and in writing. The distinctive old Frisian language was for many years in danger of dying out, but is now deliberately cultivated, particularly on Sylt and Heligoland. The traditional farmhouses are long single-storey buildings under a high-pitched roof thatched with straw or reeds. The rooms are laid out round the hall in a pattern which varies between Lower Saxony and East Friesland, with a parlour (*pesel*) which is often very handsomely furnished.

Village types vary from place to place. East of the Weser large irregularly laid out villages predominate, west of the river separate farms. In the fenland and bog regions long straggling villages are the normal pattern, in East Holstein small circular villages.

Schleswig-Holstein, the most northerly of the German *Länder,* is washed by two seas, with its principal coastline facing the Baltic. Here deep inlets (*förden*) cut far into the land between ridges of wooded hills, forming excellent natural harbours. Along the flat west coast new land is continually being wrested from the sea by the construction of dykes. The North Sea islands lie in a wide arc off the coasts of Schleswig-Holstein (the North Frisian Islands) and East Friesland (the East Frisian Islands). The fashionable island of Sylt (linked with the mainland by a causeway carrying a railway line), Föhr and Amrum, Norderney and Borkum, the Halligen and numerous smaller dune-fringed islands are filled with life and activity by the holidaymakers who flock there in summer.

Schleswig-Holstein

The Hanseatic towns of Hamburg and Bremen are the most important German commercial ports handling overseas trade. Hamburg, Germany's "gateway to the world", lying more than 100km/60 miles from the North Sea, fascinates visitors not only with its port installations and the busy shipping on the Elbe but also with its townscape around the Alster basin, its imposing business houses, its carefully restored old districts and its great range of cultural activities. From here there are attractive trips to the Altes Land with its springtime profusion of blossom, the fertile Vierlande, the Saxon Forest (Sachsenwald) and the Lüneburg Heath.

Bremen, whose overseas trade is handled mainly by Bremerhaven, still preserves the dignified air of an old Hanseatic town.

Baltic Coast

Germany's coastline on the Baltic extends for some 720km/450 miles from the Flensburger Förde and the island of Usedom. Between Lübeck Bay and Kiel Bay is the "Switzerland of Holstein" (Holsteinische Schweiz), a hilly region with many lakes which is the remnant of an Ice Age ground and terminal moraine. The moraines which were formed during the last glaciation are covered with areas of woodland and arable land and fall down to the sea in sheer cliffs. Farther east there is frequent alternation between cliffs, stretches of flat coast and broad sandy beaches, but there are none of the wide inlets reaching far inland which are found to the west.

Characteristic of this stretch of the Baltic coast are the drowned depressions known as *bodden*. They are the result of a series of geological processes – the shaping of the earth's surface by the glaciers of the last ice age and their melt-waters, which in some cases found an outlet along ice-margin trenches but were sometimes dammed up, the stage-by-stage rise in the level of the Baltic after the last ice age and the consequent phases of marine transgression, small shifts in the upper earth's crust and a slight regression some 3000 years ago, the damming up of rivers flowing from the interior to the coast and the steady silting up of the shallower waters.

Bodden and *haffs*

On the east side of Wismar Bay, at the west end of the German Baltic coast, is a typical *bodden* formation, in the form of the salt *haff* (lagoon) which is separated from the open sea by the Wustrow peninsula. The Breitling, the enlarged lower course of the river Warnow, at the south end of which is Rostock, is closed off from the sea at Warnemünde. There are striking examples of *bodden,* originally formed in the Pleistocene epoch, between the Fischland–Darss–Zingst peninsula and the mainland, between the islands of Hiddensee and Rügen, and within Rügen. In the eastern section of this stretch of coast are the three largest *bodden:* the Greifswalder Bodden and, between the island of Usedom and the mainland, the Achterwasser and the Oderhaff.

Mountains, hills and rivers

Lowlands

Low hills

Uplands

Mountains

14

The landscape of the Baltic coast is by no means entirely flat and low-lying. This is true only of the sandy plains between the morainic ridges. The moraines themselves rise to some height particularly where they have been considerably compressed, reaching over 100m/330ft round Wismar Bay, 128m/420ft in the Kühlung ridge to the west of Bad Doberan, 161m/528ft on the Jasmund peninsula on Rügen, over a foundation of chalk, with chalk cliffs rising to a height of 117m/384ft in the Königsstuhl.

The rivers flowing into the Baltic are relatively small – the Warnow at Rostock, the Recknitz at Ribnitz-Damgarten, the Ryck at Greifswald, the Peene at Anklam. None of these rivers flows directly into the open sea: they all reach it after passing through a *bodden*. The Peenestrom, the western arm of the Oder, flows through the Oderhaff and the Achterwasser and then, north of Wolgast, through the Greifswalder Bodden before finally reaching the sea. In the past the lack of waterways reaching far inland considerably hampered the development of the ports on the Baltic coast.

Mecklenburg · West Pomerania

Extending inland from the coastal regions as far as an imaginary line from Rostock by way of Demmin to Pasewalk are the north-eastern Mecklenburg lowlands, an area mainly occupied by ground moraines, with few lakes. Beyond this again is the Mecklenburg lake district, with the towns of Güstrow, Malchin, Neubrandenburg and Prenzlau, where the massive thrusts of the glaciers during the late ice age gouged out troughs and formed compressed moraines. In this region are some of the largest lakes in the lowland regions – the Kummerower See, the Malchiner See, the Tollensesee, the Ueckersee. Here too are areas with considerable differences in level, for example in the "Mecklenburg Switzerland", between Teterow and Malchin. While the steep-sided moraines have preserved their forest cover, in the rest of the north-eastern lowlands and in the basin areas arable land predominates.

The predominant geomorphological feature, however, is the Northern Morainic Ridge, a tract of higher land some 25–30km/15–20 miles wide, bounded on the north and south by two parallel terminal moraines, which extends from the Klützer Winkel (west of Wismar) and the uplands west of the Schweriner See to the Oder valley between Schwedt and Oderberg. The highest points lie in the northern outliers of the ridge – the Hohe Burg (144m/472ft) at Bützow, the Helpter Berge (179m/587ft) at Woldegk and the Brohmer Berge (149m/489ft) between Friedland and Pasewalk.

Within the Northern Morainic Ridge lie the Mecklenburg lakes. Some of them, like the two largest, Lake Müritz and the Schweriner See, extend from the northern to the southern terminal moraine. Others are affected by intermediate features between the two lines of moraines.
West of the Schweriner See round-topped ground moraines predominate, between Schwerin and the larger lakes (Plauer See, Fleesensee, Kölpinsee and Müritz) gently undulating ground moraines.
To the east of the large lakes the patches of outwash sand increase considerably in size and here – for example in the area of the small lakes around Neustrelitz–Weserberg–Mirow and Lychen/Templin – determine the pattern of the landscape. In these areas there are extensive stretches of heath and woodland (pine, beech and oak). With its varied pattern of relief, its numerous lakes and expanses of forest the Northern Morainic Ridge attracts large numbers of visitors.
To the south of the Northern Morainic Ridge is a foreland area, characterised by the melt-water channels of varying width which run from north to south towards the Elbe and the Berlin or Eberswald *urstromtäler* ("ice-margin trenches" formed by melt-water from the glaciers). One of these channels extends from the Schweriner See by way of the Stör valley and the Lewitz depression to the lower Elde valley and the Elbe valley. In this foreland area are the Ruhner Berge, which rise to 178m/584ft near Parchim.

Ice-Margin Trenches and Morainic Plateaux

To the south of the Northern Morainic Ridge and its foreland is the most southerly belt of late morainic formations – an area of morainic plateaux and large ice-margin trenches, extending eastward from the Elbe between Burg (near Magdeburg) and Wittenberg by way of the Elbe–Oder lowlands (taking in the Havelland, the Berlin conurbation, the Spreewald and the Oderbruch) to the Neisse and the Oder between Forst and Oderberg. This area is bounded on the north by the Eberswald trench and on the south by the Baruth trench. Between them, running in the same direction, broadly from east-south-east to west-north-west, is the Berlin trench.

These three *urstromtäler*, formed by melt-water during the last ice age, are linked by various transverse valleys running from north to south. The Eberswald trench joins up with the Berlin trench, and all three finally join in the Elbe *urstromtal*. The result is to produce a confused pattern of arable land on morainic plateaux, expanses of pasture-land in the sandy soil of the valleys, areas of outwash sand covered with inland dunes and pine forests, and rivers, mostly now canalised, which frequently form chains of lakes.

North-east of Berlin the Eberswald trench cuts off the Barnim plateau – the largest of the morainic plateaux in Brandenburg, rising to 150m/490ft – from the terminal moraine to the north. To the east of the Barnim plateau and its easterly neighbour the Lebus plateau is the Oderbruch, which was brought into cultivation in the 18th century; to the south is the Berlin *urstromtal*, with the lower course of the Spree. Between this and the Baruth trench, in which is the Spreewald, are the Beeskow, Teltow, Nauen, Zauche and some other plateaux. In the Havelland and Rhinluch area, where the three *urstromtäler* join, the plateaux are of very small size.

Southern Morainic Ridge (Südlicher Landrücken)

To the south of the area of morainic ridges and *urstromtäler* the Southern Morainic Ridge runs north-west to south-east from the Altmark by way of the Fläming Heath to the Lusatian Hills. From north to south it is cut by three rivers: the Elbe, to the north of Magdeburg, between the Letzlingen Heath and the Hoher Fläming; the Spree; and the Neisse, in the Lusatian Hills.

The Southern Morainic Ridge is an early formation which came into being in the second-last ice age, the Saale/Riss glacial but was altered during the last ice age (the Vistula/Würm glacial) by solifluxion, drifting and dissection by valleys. As a result the surface pattern is much gentler than in the later morainic formations. The Southern Morainic Ridge lacks the covering of loess characteristic of the foreland of the uplands to the south. To this area belongs the Magdeburg *urstromtal*, which extends from Bad Muskau by way of Hoyerswerda, Senftenberg, the valley of the Black Elster and the middle Elbe valley to Magdeburg and is continued by the Ohre valley to the north-west. Apart from the Fläming Heath, which rises to 201m/659ft, the landscape pattern around Cottbus and north of Magdeburg is determined by the Southern Morainic Ridge and its foreland areas.

Altmark

The Altmark, an agricultural region lying to the north of Magdeburg, is part of the loess-free lowland area, along with the forest-covered Letzlingen Heath to the north of the Ohre valley, through which runs the Mittelland Canal. The relief pattern of the Altmark is characteristic of an early morainic formation, though – like the late morainic region to the east – it is broken up into a series of plateaux and depressions.

North-Western Lowlands

The North-Western Lowlands were covered during the ice age by massive deposits of boulder clay. They consist of three very different parts – the coastal region, Lüneburg Heath and the area of heath and moorland to the west, between the Weser and the Ems.

Lüneburg Heath

Taken in its widest sense, the name of Lüneburg Heath applies to the ridge of *geest* which extends between the lower Elbe and the valley of the Aller and Weser. The real Lüneburg Heath, however – an infertile expanse of *geest* with great stretches of heather and juniper bushes and areas of beautiful deciduous and coniferous forest – lies west of the town of Lüneburg from which it takes its name. The best impression of this rather sombre landscape in its natural state is to be found in the nature reserves round the

Wilseder Berg (169m/554ft: the highest point on the Heath, with magnificent wide-ranging views), at Hermann Löns's grave near Fallingbostel and in the Südheide round Hermannsburg.

The economy of the Lüneburg Heath has changed in recent years. Much of it has now been brought into agricultural use, and to the traditional sheep-farming and horse-breeding, now practised on a much smaller scale, have been added bee-keeping and the rearing of carp and trout. Industry and the holiday and weekend tourist trade are now increasing in importance, and large tracts of the Heath are used as military training areas.

The eastern part of Lüneburg Heath is occupied by the Wendland area, which consists partly of fertile fenland and partly of sandy hills such as the Göhrde (noted for its mushrooms) and the Drawehn.

To the south-west of the Lüneburg Heath is the lower Aller/Weser valley with its fertile river fens.

On the edge of the Heath are the old salt-working and trading town of Lüneburg, with fine old brick buildings which bear witness to its Hanseatic days, and the former ducal residence of Celle, with its many-gabled Schloss and its old half-timbered houses.

To the west of Lüneburg Heath, between the Weser and the Ems, is a great expanse of heath and moorland, a flat landscape varied only by low *geest* hills like the Dammer Berge and the ridge of the Hohe Geest. Once a fifth of this area was covered by bog, but much of it has now been brought into cultivation. There are two different kinds of country here – the low moorland *niedermoore),* with expanses of stagnant water like the Stein-huder Meer and the Dümmer which are gradually drying out round the edges, and the high moorland *(hochmoore),* on which bog mosses establish themselves on beds of sand, absorb great quantities of water and spread in all directions. The moor landscape is bleak and featureless. In the drier parts there are frequently a few isolated birch-trees as well as heather, and in the low-lying areas an occasional windmill relieves the monotony of the scene. A particularly fine stretch of the Heath is to be seen near Ahlhorn.

The farmhouses of Lower Saxony bring the living quarters and the farm offices together under one roof, round a central hall. West of the Weser the isolated farmhouse pre-dominates, east of the river the large irregular village. The Wendland has small circular villages, huddled together for protection; the fenlands have long strip villages.

In Lower Saxony, the lowland region between the Elbe and the Ems which extends from the coast to the verges of the uplands, the larger towns have also much to attract the tourist. Hannover, capital of the *Land* of Lower Saxony, is an entirely modern city, as a result mainly of its boldly conceived reconstruction after heavy war damage. The famous Herrenhausen gardens recall its great days as a princely capital. Two towns used to vie with one another in their wealth of well preserved Late Gothic and Renaissance half-timbered buildings and Romanesque and Gothic churches – the old ducal residence of Braunschweig (Brunswick), the town of Henry the Lion, with consummate examples of Romanesque architecture in its Cathedral, Gothic in the Town Hall and Renaissance in its Gewandhaus, and Hildesheim, where Romanesque church art achieved a flowering hardly equalled anywhere else in Germany.

Lower Saxony

The Harz and its Foreland

The Harz and its foreland lie along the north-western edge of the German uplands, consisting of both sedimentary (sandstone and limestone) and igneous rocks (granite and basalt) which were folded in a north-westerly to south-easterly direction, eroded into an undulating plateau and finally carved up by rivers into a number of separate groups of hills.

The northern foreland is an area of great geological interest. Here the folded and eroded hills lie deep under the surface, overlaid by deposits of salt left by the ancient Permian sea and massive beds of rock belonging to the following Mesozoic era, including the extensive reserves of iron ore in the Salzgitter industrial area. Between troughs of arable land extend wooded ridges of harder rock such as the Lappwald, the Elm and the Asse. At Helmstedt is a large field of lignite.

Topography

The Harz thrusts out like a bastion from the northern edge of the central uplands into the lowlands. It is made up of slates, greywackes and limestones which have been penetrated and altered by volcanic rocks (granites, porphyry, etc.). In the Western Harz or Upper Harz (Oberharz) the old eroded landscape has survived as a gently undulating plateau between 600m/2000ft and 700m/2300ft in height not much broken up by valleys. Above this rise a few flat-topped hills and ridges of harder rock, the highest points in the range, reaching 1142m/3747ft in the Brocken. The fringes of the hills are deeply indented by valleys, some of which have impressive rock formations and sheer cliff faces.

Apart from mining and tourism the economy of the region depends mainly on forestry, since two-thirds of the Harz are covered by forest. Important also are cattle-farming (the brown Harz breed) and dairying (Harz cheese).

Mining

Mining of silver, copper, lead, zinc and iron was at one time of predominant importance in the economy of the Harz. As early as 968 a large lode of silver was discovered on the Rammelsberg near Goslar, and from about 990 this was properly worked. By the 16th century mining had spread to more than thirty places in the western Harz, and this period saw the establishment of the seven free mining towns of Grund, Wildemann, Lautenthal, Clausthal, Zellerfeld, St Andreasberg and Altenau as well as other mining villages. After a period of decline during the Thirty Years' War mining developed again in the early 18th century, and in 1775 a School of Mining (later a Mining Academy; now the University of Technology) was founded in Clausthal. In the 19th century the mines of the Upper Harz began to be worked out, and nowadays only the Rammelsberg and the Bad Grund area are of any importance.

In addition to the large irregular villages found in narrow valleys the straggling linear village is common in the Harz. The farmhouses follow the pattern of the Franconian half-timbered house: in this well wooded region timber construction was the norm.

Of the many river valleys in the Harz the rocky Oker valley, with the Oker Dam, is the most beautiful. There is an attractive trip from Braunlage through the charming Oder valley to the Oder Dam, framed in wooded hills, and from there to Kerzberg. On the south-eastern fringes of the Harz are the beautiful Bode valley and the Rappbode Dam.

Leinebergland

West of the Harz, to the north of a line from Herzberg to Holzminden, lies the Leinebergland, a region of varied scenery mainly given up to agriculture, centred on the interesting town of Einbeck. To the west of the lower Leine is the circular Hils basin, enclosed by three hills – the sandstone massif of Hils, Ith with its picturesque limestone crags, and Külf. On the north side of the basin extends the Osterwald, a range of hard white sandstone hills in the Weserbergland, to the north-west the broad Deister ridge with its coal-mines. To the west of this are the Bückeberge, which also contain coal, and to the south of both the Deister ridge and the Bückeberge is Süntel, the beginning of the long chain of Weser hills, the northern ridge of which, the Weser-Wiehengebirge, peters out in the lowlands near Bramsche, north-west of Osnabrück.

To the east of the river Leine rise the limestone uplands of the Sieben Berge, covered with deciduous forest, and north of this is the Hildesheim Forest, with the town of Hildesheim on its northern fringes.

South of the Herzberg–Holzminden line is the southern Hannover plateau, a region of Bunter sandstone and Muschelkalk limestone, horizontally bedded, extending to the Weser. Within the bend in the upper Leine lies the gently rolling Unteres Eichsfeld, an agricultural area at a height of around 300m/1000ft. To the north of this the Göttingen Forest, with the university town of Göttingen, extends above the fertile valley of the middle Leine, and farther west are the wooded Solling and Bramwald hills.

Kyffhäuser Hills

Beyond the loess-covered lowland known as the Goldene Aue ("Golden Meadow") rise the Kyffhäusergebirge (477m/1565ft), with the ruins of Burg Kyffhausen and a conspicuous monument commemorating the establishment of the German Empire in 1871. On the south side of the hills can be seen karstic formations covered by Permian deposits – dry valleys, swallowholes, caves, disappearing streams, karstic resurgences, etc. The warm, dry southern slopes support an abundant flora of Pontic-Mediterranean type, with mixed oak forests and expanses of wooded steppe and treeless steppe heathland.

Loess country

The loess country consists of the Magdeburger Börde, the eastern and south-eastern Harz foreland, the central Thuringian basin, the southern part of the Saxon Lowland

(Leipzig basin), the loess-covered area in northern and central Saxony between the Mulde and the Elbe, and part of Upper Lusatia. In this tract of country north of the upland region the loess overlies Pleistocene sediments in some areas and older rocks in others. The loess country is predominantly arable (sugar-beet, wheat), with only occasional remains of woodland.

Weserbergland

At Münden (Hannoversch Münden) the Weser valley turns north, forming the eastern boundary of Westphalia. At the Porta Westfalica near the cathedral city of Minden it passes through the northern range of hills into the open lowlands. The picturesque winding valley, with its wooded slopes rising to 300m/1000ft above the valley bottom, has a unifying character which is reflected in the ancient little towns and monastic houses (the most important of which is the Benedictine abbey of Corvey) and in the architectural forms of the "Weser Renaissance".

Weser valley

The Weserbergland encloses the Münster lowlands on the east and north-east. At its eastern end is Velmerstot (468m/1536ft), the highest peak in the Teutoburg Forest, whose wooded ridges extend north-west for 100km/60 miles to end in the lowlands of the Ems valley. On the east side of these ridges, with the pleasant former princely capital of Detmold and the old linen-weaving town of Bielefeld, is a hilly region which, under various names, extends east beyond the Weser. The southern part of the region is of varied character, partly forest and partly arable land; its northern edge, under the name of Wiehengebirge, runs west from the Weser at Minden to taper away in the plain north-west of the old episcopal and Hanseatic city of Osnabrück. In this hilly region are numerous spas, among them Bad Pyrmont, Bad Salzuflen and Bad Oeynhausen.

Münsterland

The Münsterland, within the *Land* of North Rhine-Westphalia, is a wide expanse of lowlands extending south-east between the Teutoburg Forest and the Sauerland. This level region, interspersed only by a few groups of low hills, is a country of fertile soil, mainly devoted to agriculture, which has given Westphalia such delicacies as its pumpernickel bread, its hams, its Münsterland *Korn* (corn brandy) and its *Steinhäger* (juniper brandy). Many old moated castles (Nordkirchen, Raesfeld, Gemen, etc.) and manor-houses belonging to noble families have been preserved.
In the western Münsterland there are patches of bog and heath; in the eastern part, to the north of the old episcopal city of Paderborn, is the Senne, formerly an area of wind-blown sand.

In the centre of the Münsterland lies its chief town, Münster, an episcopal city and an important traffic junction. The importance of this old provincial capital as a spiritual centre is shown by its many churches, and the Baroque town houses of the country nobility reflect an atmosphere of gracious living.
The town of Soest is an architectural gem, with its well preserved and unspoiled old town centre and its beautiful old churches.
The 272km/169 mile long Dortmund-Ems Canal provides a navigable waterway from the industrial area to the port of Emden.

Sauerland

The Sauerland (the "south" land – the southern part of Westphalia) occupies the most northerly part of the Rhenish Uplands. The predominant rocks are slates and grey-wackes, with occasional occurrences of Devonian limestones containing remarkable caves such as the Attahöhle and the Dechenhöhle.

The landscape pattern of the eastern Sauerland is set by the Rothaargebirge, a range of low round-topped hills which reaches its highest point in the Kahler Asten (841m/2759ft) near Winterberg. To the west the land – half of it forest-covered – falls; it is broken up by

Rothaargebirge

picturesque winding valleys, the largest of which are the Ruhr valley in the north and the Sieg valley in the south.

Bergisches Land

The most westerly ridges of hills, historically belonging to the Rhineland, are known as the Bergisches Land. With its wooded countryside the Sauerland is a popular recreation area (Arnsberg, Brilon, Winterberg), particularly for the population of the industrial area, both in summer and in winter.

Westphalia and the Lower Rhineland occupy the area between the Weser (from Münden to Minden) in the east and the Dutch frontier in the west. They lie partly in the North German lowlands, with their great expanses of arable land and their stretches of moorland and heath, partly in the uplands, with their wooded hills and picturesque well watered valleys, and partly in the wide valley of the mighty Rhine. In sharp contrast to these landscapes of tranquil charm with their ancient little towns is the industrial region of Rhineland-Westphalia, which within a relatively small space in the west central part of the area overlies all three of these natural landscapes and forces its own imprint on them.

Rhineland-Westphalia Industrial Region

The Rhineland-Westphalia industrial region, long one of the largest concentrations of industry in Europe, extends over the south-western edge of the Münsterland, the northwestern part of the Sauerland and the adjoining Rhine valley almost to the Dutch frontier. In the centre of the region is a landscape of urban type covering some thousands of square kilometres, within which there is room not only for mighty industrial complexes, housing for a population of some millions and a dense network of busy traffic routes but also for a surprising amount of natural scenery.

Economy

The basis for the large-scale development of industry was provided by the availability of coal as a source of energy. At first the coal was worked by opencast methods in the seams which outcropped in the Ruhr valley; then from the 18th century onwards the seams had to be followed northward at ever greater depths. From the middle of the 19th century, with large mining companies increasingly dominating the industry, output rose rapidly. Fierce competition and economic crises led to amalgamations which produced very large industrial concerns.

The iron and steel industry was closely bound up with coal. Smelting with coal began in 1784, and about 1830 the seams of black-band ironstone between the coal measures began to be worked. From the end of the 1960s iron-ore from the Lahn, Sieg and Dill area was also used; from 1878 it was brought in from Lorraine; and finally increasing demand led to the import of ore from many different countries. The output of the iron- and steelworks is still processed by large numbers of different firms, ranging from heavy industry to small hardware producers. Other industries less directly dependent on the mines and steelworks include the textile industry, based in Wuppertal and west of the Rhine, and the chemical industry, for which coal is an important raw material. In recent decades coal-mining has been in decline. It is planned, however, to increase the use of coal for the production of energy in thermal power stations.

The towns in the industrial region, having developed rapidly in relatively recent times, present an almost entirely modern aspect; and the townscape is no longer dominated by blast furnaces, pithead gear and factory chimneys as it was in the past.

Lower Rhineland

The Lower Rhineland is a down-faulted basin between the Belgian and Dutch frontiers and the north-western edge of the Rhenish Uplands, a gently undulating region of loess soils with towns and villages of some size. In the western part of the region is the important coal-mining and industrial area around Aachen.

In the northern half of the Lower Rhine basin is that part of the Rhineland-Westphalia industrial region which lies on the left bank of the river, with coal-mines at Homberg and Moers and a varied range of industry, notably the textile industry of Krefeld and Mönchengladbach.

Lower Rhine

The Lower Rhine in the strict sense is the continuation of the Lower Rhineland basin to the north-west and the Münsterland to the south-west. It is an area of sandy soil and pine forests; only the immediate river valley has fertile water-meadows. Settlement takes the form of individual farmsteads and small and ancient towns.

Hesse

The *Land* of Hesse, established after the Second World War, extends from the Rhine in the west to the borders of Thuringia in the east and from the Neckar valley at Heidelberg in the south to the Weser bend at Bad Karlshafen in the north. It is a region of very varied character falling within the central uplands of Germany. The close juxtaposition of barren and largely forest-covered uplands and fertile depressions gives the country an intimate and attractive character which is also reflected in the varied patterns of life and culture of its population.

From time immemorial the Hessian depression, lying between the Rhenish Uplands and the hills around the Fulda and Werra valleys, has been a major traffic route between North Germany and the Upper Rhine, and it was largely on this account that during the Middle Ages the territorial rivalries of the ruling princes focused on this region. In our own day Hesse, apart from the higher areas of forest-covered hills, makes a major contribution to the German economy.

Hessian Uplands

The western part of Hesse is occupied by the Taunus and Westerwald hills, which form part of the Rhenish Uplands. After being upfolded at an early stage of geological history in a south-westerly and north-easterly direction these hills were then eroded into a rolling plateau area. The main ridge of the Taunus, a range of isolated hills of grey and white quartzites with a steep scarp to the south, rears above the Rhine-Main plain, reaching its highest point in the Grosser Feldberg (881m/2891ft). To the north the hills slope gradually down, forming a plateau which is slashed by numerous tributaries of the Lahn.

Taunus

North of the Lahn the Taunus joins the Westerwald, a rolling plateau mainly composed of Palaeozoic slates, with a few rounded basaltic hills rising to a slightly greater height. This region, bounded on the north by the industrialised Sieg valley and on the south by the Lahn valley, which is particularly attractive between Limburg and Bad Ems, has an average height of between 300m/1000ft and 600m/2000ft, reaching its highest point in the Fuchskauten (675m/2215ft). The western part has extensive stretches of forest; the eastern part is sparsely wooded and has a fairly raw climate. In the Kannenbäckerland to the south-west rich deposits of clay gave rise to a famous pottery industry. The Westerwald is a region of small agricultural holdings, with the working of basalt, clay and lignite also making their contribution to the subsistence of the population (who are not all of Hessian origin). In the north-east the Westerwald merges into the Rothaargebirge, within the Westphalian Sauerland, while its most easterly hills jut into the Wittgensteiner Land and the Upland area.

Westerwald

Between the Rothaargebirge with its northern foothills and the Hessian depression are the Burgwald, the Kellerwald, the Wildungen Hills and the Waldeck uplands, an abundantly forested region which offers little scope for agriculture. The valleys are deeply indented, a feature which made possible the construction of the Eder Dam.

To the east of the Taunus, separated from it by the Hessian depression, rears up the almost isolated Vogelsberg, whose conical form betrays the former volcano. This is a remote hill-farming region, with fertile but thin and stony soil. The austere and solitary landscape has a certain charm, particularly in the Oberwald area. The highest peaks are the Taufstein (772m/2533ft) and the Hoherodskopf (767m/2517ft).

Vogelsberg

From the Vogelsberg a ridge of high ground leads east to the Rhön, an upland region of very distinctive scenery, composed of a sharply articulated massif of Bunter sandstone to which volcanic flows of basalt have given rounded summit forms. The Rhön forms the ancient boundary between Hesse and Franconia; its highest peak, the Wasserkuppe (950m/3117ft), a favourite resort of gliding enthusiasts, lies in Hessian territory. The High Rhön (Hochrhön), with its sombre coniferous forests and great expanses of mountain pasture, is one of the remotest of Germany's upland regions.

Rhön

To the north the Vorderrhön runs into the Seulingswald. Farther north still is the Meissnerland, with the most varied scenery in Hesse. Its central features are the legendary

Hoher Meissner (750m/2461ft), a steeply scarped tabular hill of basalt, Knüll, north of the Vogelsberg, and the Habichtswald west of Kassel. The northern part of the Meissnerland is occupied by the Kaufunger Wald, which, like the Reinhardswald to the north-west beyond the river Fulda, is a continuation of the Bunter sandstone plateau of southern Hannover.

The most important parts of Hesse from the economic point of view are the fertile valleys and basins through which run the main traffic routes. The Lahn and the Fulda are the most important rivers whose catchment areas lie entirely within Hesse. At Hannoversch Münden the Fulda joins with the Werra, whose valley forms the north-eastern boundary of the *Land*, to form the Weser. The Fulda's best known tributary is the Eder, with one of the largest dams in Europe. The Eder in turn has as one of its tributaries the Schwalk, which flows through one of the most fertile parts of Hesse.

Hessian Depression
(Hessische Senke)

The Hessian Depression, which extends from Frankfurt am Main to Bad Karlshafen on the Weser, is a chain of low-lying basins and river valleys, whose warm and sheltered situation makes them one of Hesse's principal agricultural regions. The southern part of the depression is occupied by the Wetterau, a particularly fertile area between the Taunus and the Vogelsberg, with Bad Nauheim on its eastern slopes. To the north of this is the Lahn valley, between Giessen and Marburg. Thereafter the depression becomes gradually narrower and bears north-east into the Schwalm valley, which it follows into the Fulda valley and the rich agricultural area around Kassel, and then continues between the Reinhardswald and the Habichtswald to reach the Weser valley at Bad Karlshjafen. Frankfurt am Main and Kassel are the principal centres of economic life and communications in northern and southern Hesse respectively.

Hesse shows wide variations in population density, the north being much more thinly populated than the south. The difference is due to the very different economic structure of the two regions. In the north, which is basically agricultural, more than half the population live in small towns or villages of under 2000 inhabitants, while in the highly industrialised south more than a third of the population live in towns of between 20,000 and 100,000 inhabitants. Since the last war, however, the rural population has been considerably increased by the influx of people who had lost their homes in other parts of Germany.

The normal settlement pattern in Hesse is the large irregular village, with isolated farmhouses and small hamlets in the hill regions with a poorer climate. The predominant house type, particularly in southern Hesse, is the Franconian (Central German) farmstead, in which the two-storey dwelling-house with its trim half-timbered gable, the barn and the stalls or stables are built round a central courtyard entered through a gateway. In northern Hesse the Low German house type was formerly normal but has now become rare. The many small and medium-sized towns in Hesse, with their charming half-timbered buildings, are laid out on a regular plan, often with a wide main street which serves as market-place.

Economy

Hesse is an old farming region in which large areas are still predominantly agricultural. About a fifth of the population gain their subsistence from agriculture, with a predominance of small holdings. In the basins and valleys intensive arable farming is practised; grassland and pasture are found mainly in the hills. Forestry also plays an important part in the economy, a third of Hesse being wooded.
Most of the industry is concentrated in the Rhine-Main plain, the Kassel basin, the district of Hersfeld and the Lahn-Dill area, but there are also industrial establishments in many rural areas. Roughly half the population is employed in industry and craft production. The main industrial centres are Frankfurt am Main, Wiesbaden, Kassel, Fulda, Offenbach and Hanau, whose metalworking industry, engineering plants, optical works, leather goods and jewellery have an international reputation.
The most important minerals in Hesse are iron ore (Lahn-Dill area), potash (Werra valley) and lignite (Hessian Depression). There are also numerous mineral springs (e.g. Selters).

Thuringia

Thuringian Basin
(Thüringer Becken)

The long spur of the Thuringian Forest, extending and gradually broadening from north-west to south-east, is separated from the Harz by the Thuringian Basin. Like the southern foreland of the Thuringian Forest, the Elbe Sandstone Hills and the Zittau Hills, the Thuringian Basin is part of a subsidence area in the German uplands. The central part of this extensive depression, north of Erfurt, lies at an altitude of only 150–200m (500–650ft), while the edges lie between 400 and 500m (1300 and 1650ft).

In the interior of the Thuringian Basin are expanses of loess-covered Keuper (Upper Triassic) sediments and low-lying areas subject to the danger of flooding, such as the Unstrut valley. Farther out there are outcrops of older rocks including Muschelkalk, isolated hills which have resisted erosion (Bleicherode Hills, Ohmgebirge), Bunter sandstones and Upper Permian rocks.

The Thuringian Basin is climatically favoured, with moderate rainfall. The Keuper areas, with no forest cover, are intensively cultivated, while the hills of Bunter sandstone are covered with coniferous forest.

The geological structure of the Thuringian Forest bears the marks of the Hercynian orogeny, but the present form of this range of hills, 60km/40 miles long by 7–14km (4½–9 miles across), dates from the later Alpine earth movements, and has been much dissected by the formation of valleys. The highest peaks rise above 900m/3000ft: Grosser Beerberg (982m/3222ft), Schneekopf (978m/3209ft), Grosser Inselsberg (916m/3005ft).

Thuringian Forest (Thüringer Wald)

In the southern foreland of the Thuringian Forest the landscape pattern is set by Upper Permian formations, Bunter sandstone, Muschelkalk and Keuper rocks, and to the south-west, in the Rhön, by Tertiary volcanic activity (basalts).

The Werra valley, for much of its length a wide, open valley, runs through the whole of southern Thuringia from south-east to north-west.

With their low temperatures and relatively abundant precipitation the higher levels of the Thuringian Forest (above 500m/1650ft) offer ideal conditions for winter sports, with guaranteed snow, and as a result the area between Eisenach and Oberhof attracts visitors throughout the year. A considerable section of the Rennsteig, a popular long-distance trail, runs along the ridge of the Thuringian Forest.

Erzgebirge

The Erzgebirge range, running from south-west to north-east, has a different alignment from the Harz, the Thuringian Forest and the Thuringian Hills but is in line with the Hercynian massif, now levelled down. It reaches a height of 1214m/3983ft in the Fichtelberg.

The name Erzgebirge (Ore Mountains) recalls the time, 800 years ago, when the discovery of rich silver deposits near Freiberg brought prosperity to this hitherto undeveloped forest region and led to the steady clearance of the forest, beginning in the valleys and extending up the slopes of the hills. This is reflected in the pattern of settlement, with linear forest villages straggling up the valleys, flanked by broad strip fields, and the mining towns lying close to the mine workings in the valley and on the plateau.

Mining

Elbe Sandstone Hills · Lusatian Uplands · Zittau Hills

The hills lying close to the frontier with Czechoslovakia – the Elbe Sandstone Hills, the Lusatian Uplands and the Zittau Hills – have the same general structure as the German upland regions (Mittelgebirge).

The Elbe Sandstone Hills, lying lower than the Lusatian Uplands to the north and the Erzgebirge to the south-west, were formed as a result of erosion by the Elbe. The characteristic features of these hills, with their regularly bedded but much weathered sandstones, are the deep canyon-like valley of the Elbe as it cuts through the hills at a height of 120–130m (390–425ft), the eroded plateaux at heights of around 200m/650ft and the tabular hills rising to over 400m/1300ft.

Elbe Sandstone Hills (Elbsandsteingebirge)

The German part of the Elbe Sandstone hills has been known since the Romantic period as the "Saxon Switzerland", the most attractive tourist area in the vicinity of Dresden.

Saxon Switzerland (Sächsische Schweiz)

Topography

Lusatian Uplands
(Lausitzer Bergland)

The Lusatian Uplands, formed by an upthrust between two parallel faults, consist of granites of varying age. As a result it is a region of gentle curves, with relatively shallow valleys. In the eastern part of the region the relief is varied by volcanic intrusions and dykes; the most northerly of these is the Landeskrone (420m/1378ft) near Görlitz.

Zittau Hills

The development and structure of the Zittau Hills, lying at the eastern tip of Germany between the upper Neisse and the Lusatian Uplands, are similar to those of the Elbe Sandstone Hills.

Rhine Valley

One of Europe's great tourist attractions has long been the Rhine valley, a cheerful wine-producing region which combines scenic beauty with architectural masterpieces and a historic past.

The area where the Rhine forces its way through the Rhenish Uplands is of great geological interest. At Mainz the natural barrier formed by the hills of the Rheingau forces the river to turn west, but beyond Bingen, in what is known as the "Bingen Hole" (Binger Loch), it cuts its way through the hills and resumes its northward course. The conflict between the river and the hard rock of its bed has produced a gorge-like valley with irregularities of gradient which create hazards for shipping. The depth of the river at this point is due to the upthrust of the local rock, which in the Tertiary era had lain at a lower level, making it necessary for the Rhine to carve its way through this rock in successive stages when it rose as a result of upthrusts during the later Tertiary. The results of this process can be clearly seen in the raised terraces of river-borne rock debris on the banks of the Rhine.
Farther downstream the Rhine encounters softer rock, in particular slate, which allows the valley to open out. It narrows again at certain points where harder greywackes occur, for example at the legendary Loreley Rock and at St Goar. In the more open parts of the valley deposits of loess have provided fertile soil for the development of thriving towns and villages, vineyards and orchards. All this, combined with the castles perched above the steeply scarped banks and the occasional islands, creates an ever-changing landscape pattern.

Neuwied Basin

Below Koblenz, where the Mosel flows into the Rhine, the valley opens out into the little Neuwied Basin, formed by a downfaulting of the slates in Tertiary times, with subsequent infilling by river-borne deposits and volcanic lava flows. The towns on this stretch of the Rhine have developed active industries (blast furnaces, iron and steel works), while the hinterland on the left bank, together with the Maifeld, which forms a transition to the Eifel, is the great potato-growing area of the Rhineland.

Siebengebirge

Shortly before the river enters the Lower Rhine plain it passes on the right an outlier of the Westerwald, the Siebengebirge (460m/1509ft), a shapely group of seven hills mainly composed of volcanic debris. It provides a magnificent finale to the Middle Rhine, with the most northerly of the Rhine vineyards growing on its flanks.

Cologne Lowland
(Kölner
Tieflandsbucht)

Beyond Bonn is the Lower Rhineland or Cologne Lowland, a gently undulating region resulting from the downfaulting of a range of hills. Only in the area south of Cologne is there more variety in the topographical pattern. The deposits of lignite in this region, laid down in the middle Tertiary to a depth of over 100m/330ft and covered with only a thin layer of earth, so that they can be worked by opencast methods, are the largest so far discovered anywhere in the world. On this stretch of the Rhine have developed a number of important towns which have played major roles in the cultural and economic life of Germany – Bonn, Cologne, Neuss, Düsseldorf and Duisburg, where the real Lower Rhine begins. Farther downstream the wide river valley is covered with fertile fenland meadows. The towns in this area are smaller, but preserve the aspect of a long past. At Elten the Rhine reaches the frontier with the Netherlands.

Passenger shipping

Mainz, capital of the *Land* of Rhineland-Palatinate, is the starting-point of the passenger shipping services on the Rhine, Germany's most beautiful river. Along the banks of the river lie the wine towns of the sunny Rheingau, the steep rock faces lining the passage through the Rhenish Uplands, old castles, ruins and picturesque little townships. Many celebrated beauty spots tempt the tourist to linger – Rüdesheim in the shadow of the Niederwald memorial commemorating the establishment of the German Empire, Bingen, Assmannshausen, Bacharach, Kaub with the Pfalz in the middle of the Rhine, St Goar and St Goarshausen with the Loreley Rock, Boppard or Braubach with the Marksburg and Koblenz with the Deutsches Eck and the fortress of Ehrenbreitstein. Farther downstream are the old-world town of Andernach, the Siebengebirge, from the summits of which the view extends to Cologne Cathedral, Bad Godesberg (Bonn's diplomatic quarter) and finally the university town of Bonn itself, birthplace of Beethoven and seat of the German government (now due to be displaced by Berlin).

Mosel Valley · Eifel

In the lateral valleys opening off the Rhine and the neighbouring upland regions the landscape is quieter, less touched by modern developments. The Rhine's most famous tributary is the beautiful Mosel (Moselle), which was given its name by the Romans (Mosella, the Little Mosa or Meuse). It rises in the southern Vosges and flows into the Rhine at Koblenz after a course of over 500km/310 miles.

The most attractive part of the Mosel is between Trier and Koblenz. After passing through the Trier basin the river begins its winding course through the Rhenish Uplands, between the Hunsrück and the Moselberge, outliers of the Eifel. The ever-changing scenery is given additional attraction, particularly between Bernkastel and Cochem, by numbers of old castles on the slopes above the river and in side valleys and by a succession of old-world little towns and wine villages. The development of towns of any size was inhibited by the river's meandering course and the narrowness of the valley; but this had the great benefit of leaving the Mosel to its more contemplative way of life, in contrast to the busy activity of the Rhine valley. Large-scale river regulation works, however, have now made possible the development of an active shipping traffic. And still, as in Roman times, the sun warms the slaty soil which produces the long-famed wines of the Mosel.

The Mosel valley is caught between two ranges of hills, the Eifel and the Hunsrück. The Eifel – the eastern part of the Ardennes – was formerly one of the remotest and most inaccessible areas in Germany but is now served by a network of excellent roads. This austere and lonely region of wooded uplands and winding valleys, suitable only for forestry and cattle-farming, has a special charm of its own.

In geological terms the Eifel is a range of residual hills some 70km/45 miles long by 30km/20 miles across, with an average altitude of some 600m/2000ft, in which numerous volcanoes erupted in Tertiary and Pleistocene times. The lava flows from these volcanoes can still be recognised in the present-day landscape, particularly around the Nürburg Ring, the world-famous racing circuit, and in the neighbourhood of Daun and Manderscheid. The *maare* so characteristic of the Eifel are funnel-shaped volcanic craters, now mostly containing small lakes. A typical example is the Laacher See, 52m/171ft deep, which is surrounded by over forty volcanic vents and four extinct volcanoes.

In the north-western Eifel there are a number of beautiful artificial lakes formed by dams across the valleys, such as the Schwammenauel Dam on the river Rur.

To the north of the Eifel is the Ahr valley, which offers great attractions in its beautiful scenery, its fragrant wine and the medicinal springs of Bad Neuenahr.

South of the Eifel, bounded by the Rhine, the Mosel, the lower course of the Saar and the Nahe, is the Hunsrück, the most southerly part of the Rhenish Uplands on the left bank of the Rhine. This upland region lies between 400 and 500m (1300 and 1650ft), traversed by a long ridge of quartzite hills reaching their highest point in the Erbeskopf (816m/2677ft). The undulating plateau has been cleared of much of its forest cover and has many small settlements; the hills are one of the largest forested areas in Germany, mainly beautiful deciduous forest.

The Nahe valley offers the visitor its picturesque old towns, in particular Bad Kreuznach and Idar-Oberstein with its jewellery and precious stones and its rock church.

Eifel

Ahr valley

Hunsrück

Nahe valley

25

Topography

Pfälzer Wald

The most beautiful part of the Palatinate (Pfalz), which lies between the Nahe and the Rhine, is the Pfälzer Wald (Palatinate Forest), most of it now protected as a nature reserve, the western part of which is also known as the Haardt. On the steep eastern face of the hills there are numerous old castles.

Saarland

The industrial Saarland can be reached either through the Pfälzer Wald or on the road up the Nahe valley from Bingen. The capital, Saarbrücken, is a lively town with a number of fine buildings, and the surrounding area with its coal-mines and factories has much natural beauty as well.

Upper Rhine Plain (Oberrheinische Tiefebene)

The Upper Rhine Plain, a depression between 30 and 40m (10 and 25 miles) wide, was created by faulting in the Oligocene period. It is bounded on the east by the Black Forest, the Kraichgau and the Odenwald, on the west by the Vosges, the Haardt and the uplands of the northern Palatinate. The underlying rock which outcrops on the borders of the plain is overlaid in the plain itself by Pleistocene deposits of loess, which form a fertile soil for the growing of fruit and vines.

On the Upper Rhine the hills with the vineyards and orchards on their slopes draw back and give place to a fertile plain. From the former Hessian grand-ducal capital of Darmstadt the Bergstrasse – where spring first comes to Germany – runs along the foot of the Odenwald by way of the picturesque little towns of Zwingenberg, at the foot of Melibokus, Bensheim, Heppenheim and Weinheim to the famous old university town of Heidelberg.

Black Forest (Schwarzwald)

The Black Forest extends for some 160km/100 miles from north to south between Pforzheim and Lörrach, with a breadth of some 20km/12½ miles in the north and 60km/40 miles in the south. With its dark forest-covered hills, its hilltop meadows and its valleys watered by abundant mountain streams, it is of all German upland regions the one which offers the richest variety of scenery both grandiose and charming.
On the west the Black Forest falls down to the Upper Rhine plain, some 800m/2600ft below, in a steep scarp, slashed by valleys well supplied with water by the rain-bringing west winds, some of them narrow and gorge-like. The highest peaks are on this side. To the east the hills slope down more gently, with broader valleys and lower ridges, to the upper Neckar and Danube valleys, both of which are some 250m/820ft higher than the Rhine plain.
The main ridge of the Black Forest is an undulating plateau with round-topped hills rising to a somewhat greater height. The plateau is broken up by numerous valleys, so that it does not form a continuous ridge but is irregularly shaped, with the watershed following a rather tortuous course. Between Freudenstadt and Offenburg the Kinzig valley cuts across the whole of the Black Forest range.

Northern Black Forest

The northern Black Forest, beyond the Kinzig valley, is made up of broad ridges of Bunter sandstone, and almost two-thirds of its area are covered by forest. The settlements are strung out along the deep valleys, many of them still showing the pattern of the linear villages of the early medieval period of forest clearance. Only in modern times have roads been built along the high ground.

Attractive features of the landscape are the little mountain lakes such as the Mummelsee and Wildsee, nestling in hollows gouged out by glaciers, particularly around the Hornisgrinde (1166m/3826ft), the highest peak in the northern Black Forest.

Central Black Forest

The central Black Forest, between the Kinzig valley and the Höllental road, is – like the southern Black Forest – mainly composed of granites and gneisses, with frequent intrusions of Permian porphyries. On the west side downfaulted beds of younger rock form foothills, such as the Bunter sandstone hills north of Emmendingen. To the east horizontally bedded Bunter sandstones and Muschelkalk limestones form a fringe of lesser scenic attraction which along with the exposed but fertile Baar plateau runs into the Swabian Jura.

The lower parts of the valleys in the central Black Forest are wide and favourable to human settlement. Higher up there is usually a steeper stretch, cut deeply into the rock, which may form beautiful waterfalls, as at Triberg. In a wider section of the valley above this there may be fields and meadows reclaimed from the forests which cover the plateau. The highest peak in the central Black Forest is Kandel (1241m/4072ft), between the Elz, Simonswald and Glotter valleys.

The southern Black Forest, with the finest scenery, is dominated by the 1493m/4899ft high Feldberg. From here a ridge extends west to Belchen (1414m/4639ft), the most beautifully shaped hill in the Black Forest, and Blauen (1165m/3822ft), projecting farthest into the Rhine plain. Around the Feldberg deeply indented valleys radiate in all directions: the Höllental, the Wiesental, the Abtal and the Gutachtal or Wutachtal, whose beauty is enhanced by lakes like the Titisee, Schluchsee and Feldsee, occupying depressions carved out by Ice Age glaciers. In this region forest covers barely half of the total area, and villages and fields reach up to greater heights (Blasiwald, 1190m/3904ft). The mountain meadows on the summits have a pre-Alpine aspect, providing good pasturage which on the Feldberg and Belchen is used for summer grazing.

Southern Black Forest

To the east of Lörrach extends the Dinkelberg plateau, an area of down-faulted Muschelkalk limestones with some karstic formations. Between the Wutach and the Rhine is a tabular hill of Jurassic date, Randen (926m/3038ft), which forms a bridge between the Swabian and the Swiss Jura, with its southern half actually in Switzerland. From Randen there is a road through the striking scenery of the Hegau, with its volcanic cones, to Lake Constance, Germany's largest lake.

The typical Black Forest house, found south of the Kinzig valley, is a variant of the Alpine type of house: a timber-built house on stone foundations with numerous small windows, which seeks protection from the long winter with its abundance of snow by bringing the living quarters and farmstead together under a single overhanging roof covered with shingles or thatch (though this is becoming increasingly rare). Often a gallery, usually decked with flowers, runs round the upper storey.

House type

Iron-mining once played an important part in the economy of the Black Forest but has now almost completely disappeared. Its decline in the 16th century turned the population towards agriculture. On account of the altitude, however, there is little arable farming, and the predominant activity is cattle-rearing, using the mountain pastures above the tree-line for summer grazing. Fruit-growing is also of importance, mainly in the valleys to the west. The types of fruit most commonly grown are cherries (which produce the famous Black Forest liqueur, kirsch) and plums (the Bühl area being famous for its early plums).

Economy

A major contribution to the economy is made by forestry and woodworking. Formerly the finest trunks were floated down the Rhine to Holland; but after the coming of the railways the floating of logs down the Black Forest rivers (the Kinzig, the Nagold, the Enz) gradually died out. The old small-scale crafts of the Black Forest including glass-making, charcoal-burning and pitch-boiling have likewise disappeared, giving place to large sawmills and woodworking plants.

The industry of the region developed out of a widespread cottage industry, which to some extent still exists. The famous Black Forest clock-making industry, introduced about the middle of the 17th century, was originally a craft solely for wood-carvers, but by about 1750 the wheels were also being made from brass. The best-known clock factories are at Schramberg and Villingen-Schwenningen. The manufacture of musical boxes and of radio and television sets has developed alongside this industry.

Trossingen is famed for its mouth-organs and accordions. Other local crafts are brush-making and straw-plaiting. There is also some textile industry (particularly ribbon manufacture), mainly in the Wiesental. In recent years there has been some development of hydroelectric power; the most notable hydroelectric power stations are on the Murg at Forbach and on the Schluchsee.

Swabia (Schwaben)

The great attraction of Swabia for visitors lies in the diversity of its scenery, the alternation of hills and valleys, forests and fields, orchards and vineyards. To the attentive eye, however, these changing scenes fall into a logical sequence of natural landscapes, reflecting, more clearly than anywhere else in Germany, the constitution and structure of the soil. Entering Swabia from the Upper Rhine plain or travelling south-east from the lower Main valley, we pass from older into ever younger geological formations, climbing up a series of great steps in the scarplands of South Germany.

Odenwald

In the Odenwald, which together with the Black Forest forms the western boundary of these scarplands, the underlying granites and gneisses are still exposed on the west side of the hills. This region, broken up by a dense network of valleys into a landscape of round-topped hills and covered with a patchwork of forests, fields and villages, contrasts with the extensive eastern part in which the coherence of the old residual hills has been preserved in spite of the deeply indented valleys. The thin soils of the reddish-brown Bunter sandstone, unsuitable for arable farming, are covered with magnificent beech forests. The Neckar flows through the southern tip of the Odenwald in a deeply slashed valley, its romantic charm scarcely affected by its development into a major waterway.

Neckarland

The Neckarland or Unterland of Württemberg and Baden, which lies immediately south-east of the Odenwald, consists mainly of Muschelkalk and Keuper (Middle and Upper Triassic) formations. This is the old heartland of Swabia, rich in historical associations and monuments of art and architecture. Starting from the south-western corner between the Black Forest and the Swabian Alb, it broadens out towards the north-east and merges imperceptibly into Lower Franconia. The extensive Muschelkalk plains are fertile arable land, with their covering of loess and their mild climate in the rain shadow of the hills to the west. It is a bright and smiling landscape, with trim villages set amid orchards of apples and pears. The valleys of the Neckar and its tributaries (Enz, Kocher, Jagst) and of the Tauber form sharp angular indentations which divide the land into a series of *gaus* – to the west of the Neckar the Oberes Gäu, the Strohgäu, the Zabergäu and the Kraichgau, which provides a passage from the Upper Rhine into Swabia through the wide gap between the Odenwald and the Black Forest; to the east the Hohenlohe plain, the Bauland and the Taubergrund.

Wherever the eye travels to the south or east of these plains it encounters the dark forest-covered slopes of the Keuper (Upper Triassic) hills. The resistant beds of middle Keuper rock everywhere form sharp "steps" in the landscape. In contrast to the continuous scarp of the Jurassic hills farther south, the Keuper scarp in Württemberg is much broken up, projecting here, retreating there, and thus giving the Unterland its varied landscape pattern. The Keuper hills are carved up by the intervening valleys into narrow tabular formations, buttresses and ridges. As in the Bunter sandstone region, almost the whole area is occupied by forests. Only in those areas where the fertile Lias (Lower Jurassic) is found, as in the Filder area south of Stuttgart and the Alb foreland, does open arable farming develop.

In earlier times the Keuper hills, being so much broken up, had no name applying to the whole range; more recently the term Swabian Forest has come into use, but the various separate parts are still known by their own names. Thus to the south-west, between Stuttgart and Tübingen, is the old ducal hunting reserve of Schönbuch; to the east of the Neckar are the Schurwald and Welzheimer Wald and, projecting far to the north-west, the Löwenstein Hills, the Mainhardter Wald and the Waldenburg Hills; and beyond these the Ellwangen Hills form a transition to the Frankenhöhe range in which the Keuper scarp turns northward into Franconia. Far to the west are two Keuper outposts in the Kraichgau, the Heuchelberg and Stromberg.

However diverse these landscape patterns may be, they nevertheless have many features in common, reflecting the Swabian traditions of peasant farming and small holdings of land (on which farming is only a part-time occupation). Characteristic features of the landscape are the orchards on the gently rolling hills and the vineyards on the slopes of the valleys. Everywhere picturesque old towns bear witness to the vicissitudes of a long past.

The Unterland has a varied range of industries, covering almost every kind of industrial activity but heavy industry, which provides an appropriate balance to the region's agriculture and a safeguard against the effects of economic crises.

The boundary of the Unterland is formed by its most striking feature, the impressive escarpment of the Swabian Alb. Here the geological structure is reflected with particular clarity in the landscape pattern. Out of the Lias plains of the Lower Jurassic in the foreland area gently rolling slopes of Middle Jurassic rock, traversed only at some points by a preliminary scarp, climb 200–300m (650–1000ft) to the Albtrauf, the rim of the escarpment, composed of resistant Upper Jurassic limestones. From a distance the escarpment appears to be a continuous wall, which seems particularly massive when seen against the light of the midday sun; but on a closer approach the hill face, covered with beech forests, breaks down into a number of separate buttresses of varying width separated by short but deeply indented valleys. Evidence of the scarp which once extended farther north-west is provided by isolated outliers including the Hohenstaufen and Hohenzollern hills, the ancestral seats of two great imperial dynasties.

Swabian Alb
(Schwäbische Alb)

In sharp contrast to the mild and smiling fruit-growing district below is the bleak and austere plateau of the Swabian Alb, which slopes down gradually in a gently undulating plain, covered with arable fields and pastureland but with little forest and little water, to the Danube and the Alpine Foreland. The permeable limestone shows many karstic features – dry valleys, caves and swallowholes, seepage from rivers (the Danube) and underground watercourses which surface again as abundant springs like the Blautopf at Blaubeuren.

The few large villages lie widely separated from one another, mostly in the valley bottoms; their long-standing shortage of water was made good only by large-scale water supply works in the last quarter of the 19th century. From a height of some 700m/2300ft in the north-east the Swabian Alb rises gradually to 1000m/3300ft in the south-west, reaching its greatest height in the Lemberg, on the Heuberg plateau. Between Tuttlingen and Sigmaringen the Danube cuts its way through the Alb in an impressive rocky gorge.

In Upper Swabia – part of the Alpine Foreland which falls within Württemberg – the scenery changes once again. The wide plain is covered by sediments deposited by a shallow sea of the Tertiary era, debris left by the Alpine glaciers, which thrust far out into the foreland area during the Ice Age, and boulders and sand deposited by the rivers. In the northern part of Upper Swabia these deposits have produced a fairly uniform surface pattern, but there is greater diversity in the southern part. Here the terminal moraine landscape, of relatively recent geological date, has been preserved almost unchanged – round-topped hills covered by dark stretches of forest extending in wide arcs or in contorted patterns, small lakes or bogs filling depressions, intricately winding valleys and narrow gullies. Scattered over this unruly and apparently random landscape are isolated farmsteads, the normal pattern of settlement in this area. Stock-rearing begins to predominate over arable farming in many parts of the area.

Upper Swabia
(Oberschwaben)

Lake Constance (Bodensee)

From Upper Swabia, whose scenic beauties and art treasures may tempt the visitor to linger, the road runs south to Lake Constance, the "Swabian sea". The smiling and fertile landscape of Swabia is here given additional attraction by the atmosphere of the south and the views of the majestic mountains.

The friendly resorts on the shores of Lake Constance, Germany's largest lake, have long attracted visitors, with their vineyards and orchards, their bathing beaches and their views across the great expanse of the lake, dotted with sailing boats, to the jagged blue line of the Alps. Also within easy reach is the Hegau, with the Hohentwiel and other conical hills, the weathered remains of extinct volcanoes.

Franconian Scarpland (Fränkisches Stufenland)

The geologically interesting Franconian scarpland owes its origin to the erosional work of rivers over many millions of years. It consists of interbedded Triassic and Jurassic rocks of varying hardness which were given a slight eastward tilt in the Middle Tertiary, during the uplifting of the Upper Rhine area and the down-faulting which produced the Rhine rift valley. Thereafter the action of the Rhine river system in the west and the

Topography

Danube in the east carved prominent scarps from the hard rock. During this process erosion was most active in the areas of greatest upthrust, and the Rhine moved its catchment area steadily farther east. Travelling from west to east, we pass from older to ever younger rocks. This clearly marked rhythm gives the scenery of Franconia an attractive diversity and great charm.

Spessart

The most westerly of the Franconian scarps is the Spessart, which is bounded on the south by the Mainviereck (the stretch of the Main between Lohr and Aschaffenburg) and on the north by the rivers Kinzig and Sinn. It is mainly composed of Bunter sandstones, which abut on the basement rock in the western Spessart. The tabular sandstone is of little use for agriculture but is covered by extensive beech forests. It also makes an admirable building stone whose beautiful flesh-coloured tones contribute to the beauty of the Franconian towns. The Spessart sandstone formations continue beyond the Sinn into the southern Rhön, to the north of which, in Hesse, is the Hochrhön (High Rhön), covered with basaltic lava from Tertiary volcanoes.

Eastern Franconian Plateau (Mainfränkische Platte)

A completely different picture from the Spessart and the Rhön, with their relatively sparse population, is presented by the limestone scarp of the Eastern Franconian Plateau, immediately east of the Mainviereck and along the Franconian Saale, which abuts on the Bunter sandstone scarp, with a less sharply defined edge. This area of loess and clay – with the Marktheidenfelder Gau in the west, the Grabfeld in the north, the Gerolzhofener Gau in the east, the Ochsenfurter Gau in the south-east and the Würzburger Gau in the centre – is fertile agricultural land. The villages are ringed by large orchards, and excellent wines are produced on the limestone slopes of the Main valley and in the Steigerwald on the edge of the scarp.

To the east of the Eastern Franconian Plateau is another prominent scarp, the Franconian Terrace, composed of sandstones of the middle Keuper period, which begins in the north with the Hassberge, continues south of the wide Main valley in the Steigerwald, and then forms a transition, by way of the Windsheim embayment and the Frankenhöhe, to the Keuper scarp of the Black Forest. On the Frankenhöhe the sandstone cover is dissected into a series of separate tabular formations; in the Steigerwald there are still intact areas of some size; and in the Hassberge the sandstone survives substantially unbroken as a ridge projecting towards the Grabfeld.

Middle Franconian Basin (Mittelfränkisches Becken)

The Franconian Terrace, mostly forested and broken up by broad valleys, slopes down very gradually eastward to merge into the Middle Franconian Basin, which is drained by the Regnitz and the Redwitz. Here again arable land predominates over forest, though not to the same extent as on the Franconian Plateau. Among the main agricultural areas are the Bamberger Gau (fruit-growing) and the hop-growing Redwitz area in the Rangau south of Nuremberg. Only on the sandy soils round Nürnberg are there areas of woodland interspersed with heath. Bee-keeping, which has been practised here for many centuries, provides the basis for the manufacture of the famed Nürnberg gingerbread, while the local timber long supplied the raw material for the equally well known Nürnberg toy industry. The Middle Franconian Basin is the most populous part of Franconia.

Franconian Jura (Fränkischer Jura)

The most easterly, and with a relative altitude of some 250m/820ft the most pronounced, of the scarps is the Franconian Jura or Franconian Alb, with light-coloured limestone cliffs of Upper Jurassic date, visible from afar, rearing up above a narrow lower scarp of the Middle Jurassic. With an altitude of some 600m/2000ft, the Franconian Alb, and particularly the area known as the "Franconian Switzerland" in its northern part, has all the characteristics of a karstic landscape – large-scale clefting and leaching away of the carbonate limestone, with the formation of caves and swallowholes, underground watercourses and dry valleys on the surface – giving it some of the most attractive scenery in the whole of the Alb. That this scarp once extended farther west is shown by a number of outlying hills like the Hesselberg (689m/2261ft), north of the Ries basin, and the Hahnenkamm (644m/2113ft), at the point where the river Altmühl enters the Jura. In the picturesque gorge of the Altmühl to the south the famous limestone flags of Solnhofen are worked.

Ries

West of this lies the Ries around Nördlingen, a circular basin formed by the impact of a large meteorite on the boundary between the Franconian and the Swabian Jura.

To the north-east the "Franconian Switzerland" gives place along the line of several fault scarps to the very fertile Upper Main uplands, built up from rocks of Triassic and Jurassic date, with the former princely residences of Bayreuth and Kulmbach as its principal towns.

Beyond this, in the extreme north-eastern corner of Bavaria, is the Franconian Forest, dissected by the river system of the Rodach and White Main and displaced below the Upper Main uplands by a series of faults. This plateau covered with coniferous forest forms a bridge between the Thuringian Forest and the East Bavarian border hills to the south-east. The slate worked in numerous quarries makes a valuable contribution to the economy of this unproductive forest region.

Franconian Forest
(Frankenwald)

Along the southern edge of the Alb flows the Danube (Donau), whose valley opens out several times into wide flood plains and areas of marshland, now brought into cultivation, such as the Donauried at Dillingen, now meadowland, and the boggy Donaumoos near Ingolstadt. Only to the east of Donauwörth, in the Neuburg narrows, do the hard Jurassic limestones come closer to the river.

Danube Valley

South of the Danube extends the Swabian-Bavarian Plateau. The northern part of this is a fertile upland region of Tertiary marls and sands, in which is the Holledau or Hallertau hop-growing district. In the western part, between the rivers Lech and Iller, is a zone of Ice Age river gravels with tracts of pine forest, heathland and bog. To the north of Munich are the Dachauer Moos and the Erdinger Moos; to the south the area merges into the hilly Alpine Foreland. In the south Swabian territory extends as far east as the river Lech, taking in the old imperial city of Augsburg.

Swabian-Bavarian
Plateau
(Schwäbisch-
Bayerische
Hochebene)

The usual settlement pattern is the old Germanic type of large irregular village; only on the Franconian Terrace and in the Franconian Jura are separate farms and small hamlets commonly found. The Franconian or Central German type of farmhouse extends as far as the Franconian Jura. In this type the trim half-timbered gable of the two-storey dwelling-house faces on to the street, with the barn and animal stalls forming part of the same building, all enclosing a rectangular courtyard entered through a gateway.
The numerous small and medium-sized towns with their charming half-timbered houses are regularly laid out, often with a broad main street which serves as a market square.

In the agriculture of Franconia small and medium-sized holdings predominate. Almost two-thirds of the land is cultivated, mostly with grain. The production of hops is vital to the brewing industry, and the major part of the Bavarian crop comes from the Holledau (Hallertau) area. Other important hop-growing areas are the Rezat valley (Spalt) and between Nürnberg and Bamberg, where hops of good quality have been grown since the 14th century. In the lower Regnitz basin, around Bamberg, tobacco is grown, while the Main valley produces fruit and excellent wine.

Agriculture

There has been a considerable development of industry and crafts in Franconia. It has a number of major industrial centres – Nürnberg, Fürth, Erlangen, Augsburg and Schweinfurt – and in the Franconian Forest, between Hof and Bayreuth, a varied range of textile industries has developed out of the old Upper Franconian hand-weaving trade.
Franconia has no minerals apart from the Solnhofen limestone worked in the Altmühl valley. It has, however, numerous mineral springs.

Industry and
crafts

Franconia (Franken)

In Franconia, the most northerly part of the Free State of Bavaria, the scarped landscape of Württemberg continues, but here the plains are more extensive, the edges of the scarps smoother, the hills lower. A number of handsome towns punctuate the winding course of the Main in Lower Franconia.

Between Franconia and Bohemia extends a tract of secluded forest country – a region of more austere character which seems almost out of place amid the smiling and varied landscapes of southern Germany. The western slopes and foreland of the hills on the Bavarian–Bohemian frontier form a natural unit and a continuous stretch of attractive tourist country, but they are divided up by administrative boundaries, so that most of the Fichtelgebirge falls within Upper Franconia, the Bavarian Forest with its foreland extending across the Danube to the south belongs to Lower Bavaria, and the Upper Palatinate –

Topography

the central core of the region – stretches from the plateau of the Franconian Alb by way of the Naab depression to the East Bavarian border hills.

Franconian Alb (Fränkische Alb)

The Franconian Alb turns its face, with its steep and furrowed brow, towards Franconia; to the rear it slopes imperceptibly down to the east and south-east, falling from 600m/2000ft to 500m/1650ft in a plateau of limestones and dolomites of the Upper Jurassic, merges on its northern flank, roughly between Bayreuth and Schwandorf, into the Naab depression and at the bend on the Danube at Regensburg dips under the Tertiary uplands of the Bavarian plateau. The rolling and inhospitable Jurassic plateau has a covering of short grass over most of its area, with some stretches of forest. Cultivated fields and pastureland are found only at certain places, particularly in the valleys, where the barren limestone has a covering of clay.

The finest scenery in this region is to be found in the sharply indented river valleys – the Pegnitz valley at Hersbruck (the Hersbruck Alb), the Altmühl valley between Beilngries and Kelheim, the Danube valley at Weltenburg.

There are no towns of any size apart from Amberg, once the chief place in the Upper Palatinate. The large towns lie outside the hills: Nürnberg in the western foreland and Regensburg at the south-east corner, where the Alb, the Bavarian Forest and the Alpine Foreland meet.

Upper Palatinate (Oberpfalz)

The central element in the Upper Palatinate is the Naab valley, a depression of moderate depth between the Franconian Alb and the East Bavarian border hills. The geological substructure in this area is complex. Little is to be seen on the surface, since all earlier formations have been overlaid by the gently undulating surface of Tertiary deposits. The underlying rocks can, however, be detected in vegetation and crop patterns – the impervious Tertiary clays being revealed by the countless little lakes and ponds, the Keuper and Cretaceous sandstones by forests, the New Red Sandstone by arable fields.

Naab valley

The river Naab, formed by the junction of the Fichtelnaab, coming from the Fichtelgebirge, and the Waldnaab, coming from the Upper Palatinate Forest, flows down at a moderate gradient through a valley which varies in width – now narrow, now opening out to form a basin – to join the Danube above Regensburg. Weiden and Schwandorf, both situated in wide basins, are important as traffic junction points and market towns as well as for the production of ceramics. Characteristic features of this area, once a major route between Central Germany and Czechoslovakia, are the numerous castles, many of them watching over ancient little towns.

The Upper Palatinate and Lower Bavaria are decisively terminated by the East Bavarian border hills, which extend south-east from the Fichtelgebirge into Austria for a distance of some 300km/185 miles. Here the underlying gneisses and granites form rounded ridges and wide plateaux which have been broken up by longitudinal valleys and wide pass-like transverse valleys. The residual hills, thrust upwards and sideways, present steep escarpments to the south-west and fall away more gently to the north-east to merge into the Bohemian plateaux in Czechoslovakia. Although the character of this long range of hills changes several times and each part has, very properly, its own particular name, the whole range nevertheless has an overall unity. These lonely expanses of forest are an impressive sight when seen from one of the peaks.

Fichtelgebirge

The Fichtelgebirge, although at the northern end of the East Bavarian border hills, does not properly form part of that range. The Saale, the Eger, the Main and the Naab all rise in these hills. The meeting of two differently aligned ranges of hills (the Thuringian Forest, running from north-west to south-west, and the Erzgebirge, running from north-east to south-west) led to the upthrusting of horsts almost at right angles to one another and gave the Fichtelgebirge a horseshoe-shaped form. Above a gently undulating residual plateau forest-covered granite ridges rear up to a height of some 300m/1000ft, reaching 1000m/3300ft in the Schneeberg and Ochsenkopf. The extensive spruce forests, beautiful river valleys, tumbles of boulders and weathered granite crags hold great attractions for visitors. The area within the horseshoe is mainly arable land and pasture, but also has active industries (ceramics, woodworking, textiles). The chief town of the Fichtelgebirge is Wunsiedel, but the largest place is the porcelain town of Selb.

Since there are wide gaps between the ridges of hills, the Fichtelgebirge presents no great obstacles to traffic: only the west side falls steeply down into the valley basin in which lies Bayreuth.

The broad Tirschenreuth plateau, glittering with numerous little lakes, forms a transition between the Fichtelgebirge and the Upper Palatinate Forest, which extends for a distance of some 90km/55 miles to the Furth depression. It consists of a series of graduated residual ridges whose flat gneiss summits rarely rise higher than 900m/3000ft. Large-scale clearance has removed more of the forest cover here than in other parts of the border hills, but the thin soil and harsh climate yield only a modest subsistence to the sparse population who live from agriculture – though forestry work, glass-blowing and the porcelain industry to some extent make up for this.

Upper Palatinate Forest (Oberpfälzer Wald)

The Furth depression (470m/1540ft), the old gateway between Bohemia and Bavaria, is a 15km/9 mile wide gap in the East Bavarian border hills, traversed by the little river Chamb, which rises on the Bohemian side.

Bavarian Forest (Bayerischer Wald)

The Bavarian Forest is the last, the highest and the most impressive part of the East Bavarian border hills. It begins beyond the Furth depression and is bounded on the north-west by the rivers Chamb and Regen and on the south-west by the Danube valley. To the south-east it extends to the Linz basin in Austria and on the north merges into the Bohemian Forest (Böhmerwald) in Czechoslovakia.

Here too the underlying rocks are gneiss and granite, and here too the hills are broken up by longitudinal valleys, with individual hills presenting steeply scarped slopes to the south-east. From extensive level areas of drift emerge broad step-like formations in which the rivers have carved out narrow gorges since the further upthrust of the hills. Evidence of these tectonic processes is given by the Pfahl, a long quartz dyke which can be clearly recognised only at those points where it has been exposed by erosion and has resisted the effects of weathering longer than the softer neighbouring rocks. It marks the boundary between the two principal ranges in the Bavarian Forest, the Vorderer Wald and the Hinterer Wald.

The Vorderer Wald (Einödsriegel, 1126m/3694ft), also known as the Donaugebirge or Danube Hills, is an undulating residual plateau which rises above the Danube depression in two stages of 500m/1640ft and 700m/2300ft. Above these two stages the summit region attains 1000m/3300ft, broken up into smaller ranges of hills by the numerous gorges carved out by rivers flowing down to the Danube. The very varied countryside in the western part of the range – a mingling of forests, meadows and arable fields, round-topped hills and valleys – is dotted with small hamlets and isolated farms.

Vorderer Wald

The Hinterer Wald is also made up of a number of ranges of hills extending from north-west to south-east – the Hoher Bogen (1081m/3547ft), south of the Furth depression; the Künisches Gebirge (Osser, 1293m/4242ft); the ridge running from the Kaitersberg (1134m/3721ft) to the Grosser Arber (1457m/4780ft), the highest peak in the whole of the range; the massif including Rachel (1452m/4764ft) and Lusen (1371m/4498ft), within the Bavarian Forest National Park; and the Dreisesselgebirge, with the Dreisessel (1312m/4305ft) and Plöckenstein (1378m/4521ft). The massive ridges and steep flanks of the Hinterer Wald have a continuous cover of magnificent natural forest, much of it with the aspect of unspoiled primeval woodland. On the northern and eastern slopes, just below the summit region, dark-surfaced lakes in glacier-hewn hollows bear witness to the action of the ice, here on a relatively small scale. Over the broad summit ridges extend areas of moorland or, above the tree-line, hill pastures with dark clumps of dwarf pines and, here and there, weathered granite crags or tumbles of boulders. Human settlement is confined to some longitudinal valleys (Kötzting, Viechtach, Zwiesel) and to the lower levels below the main summit ridge where clearance has produced sizeable gaps in the forest cover, particularly around Grafenau and Freyung and along the Goldener Steig ("Golden Path") leading into Bohemia.

Hinterer Wald

Given the harsh climate and thin soil, agriculture produces only modest yields of rye, oats and potatoes. Since there are no minerals the only other sources of income for the local people – some of whom still live in simple timber houses – are to be found in exploiting the resources of the forest and, more recently, in the tourist trade.

Lower Bavaria (Niederbayern)

Scenery of a very different kind is to be found to the south of the Bavarian Forest in the Danube depression and the Tertiary hills of Lower Bavaria. The valley of the Danube between Regensburg and Vilshofen, here some 30km/20 miles wide, was the original area of settlement of the Bajuwari after their movement westward from Bohemia. In this region the villages lie close to one another amid fertile fields of wheat, barley and sugar-beet. The market town for the agricultural produce is Straubing. The city of Regensburg, at the western end of the depression, enjoys a particularly favourable situation and has had a correspondingly successful development.

The Tertiary uplands, falling gently away into the Danube depression, are broken up into long ridges of hills by numerous rivers (the Laaber, the Isar, the Vils, the Rott) and their tributaries, producing a landscape which is basically uniform but offers an attractive variety of detail. Along the larger rivers lie the market villages and a few towns, of which only Landshut rose to major importance as the residence of the Dukes of Lower Bavaria. The rural population live in small hamlets or individual farms scattered about in the upland countryside. The main crop is wheat; the Holledau (Hallertau) district to the west is noted for its hops.

Alpine Foreland

The Alpine Foreland reached its present form at a late stage, as a result of glacier action during the Ice Age. The glaciers surged out of the large valleys from the Iller to the Salzach and spread out over the foreland area in great sheets of ice, carrying with them the rubble they had scoured off the mountains and depositing it along their edges in the form of moraines. The basins gouged out by the arms of the glaciers are now filled by lakes (Ammersee, Starnberger See, Chiemsee) or bogs, or have been drained by rivers. At the end of the glacial period the ice sometimes paused for a considerable period during its retreat or made a minor advance, creating smaller basins on the fringes of the mountains such as the Tegernsee, the Kochelsee and the Walchensee.

Thus the Alpine Foreland is by no means a featureless plain. The varied land-forms, the alternation of forests, rivers and lakes and the snug little towns and villages with their onion-domed churches combine to produce a very attractive landscape pattern with a distinctive character.

Bavarian Alps

In the Bavarian Alps the oldest and most resistant rocks (Triassic limestones of Wetterstein and Dachstein type) are in the south, where they form the highest peaks, the Zugspitze (2963m/9722ft) and the Watzmann (2714m/8905ft). To the north of these jagged limestone mountains are less rugged sandstone hills such as the Zwiesel at Bad Tölz. When the primeval sea developed into a fresh-water bog in the middle Tertiary the molasse (post-tectonic sediments) was deposited in the form of conglomerates (nagelfluh), clays and coal. West of the Iller these rocks form such hills as the Stuiben; farther east only foothills in the plain like the Auerberg and the Hoher Peissenberg.

Allgäu Alps

In the Allgäu Alps the hard limestone forms only the highest peaks, so that the valleys are wider and have less steeply sloping sides than farther east.
In the central Bavarian Alps the alternation of hard and soft strata led to regular folding and the development of longitudinal valleys and ridges running east and west.

Berchtesgaden Alps

In the Berchtesgaden Alps the Dachstein limestones, up to 2000m/6500ft thick, resisted folding, so that massifs including the Reiter Alpe and the Untersberg were left standing as we see them today. The solubility of the limestone in water, however, led to the creation of karstic forms, with pavements of clefts and ridges, swallowholes and larger cavities (for example in the Steinernes Meer, the "Stone Sea").
In general, variations in height are the result of folding movements; the formation of the valleys, on the other hand, was the work of running water, the carrying power of which is amply demonstrated by the debris deposited on many valley bottoms. The detailed

shaping of the landscape, however, was due to the action of ice. Local glaciers carved out of the rounded mountain forms steep and rugged peaks like the pyramids of the Watzmann and the Schönfeldspitze in the Steinernes Meer, and gouged out of the flanks of the summit ridges recesses or depressions (*kare*) which now contain small mountain lakes or have developed into large rounded corries (for example the Obersee, above the Königssee). From the Central Alps came great flows of ice which filled up the valleys on the edge of the hills to a height of 1500m/4900ft above sea level and scoured them out (for example the Leisach valley near Garmisch and the Isar valley at Mittenwald). This also gave rise to steep-sided valleys, their lower slopes covered with rock debris and above them the flatter region of Alpine meadows.

Traditional costumes are still worn to a greater extent in Upper Bavaria than anywhere else in Germany, and even in Munich have not been entirely displaced by modern dress. The characteristic features of men's dress are leather shorts, a cloth waistcoat with silver buttons, a jacket of heavy woollen material (loden) with stag-horn buttons and a green hat with a chamois beard or other hunting trophy, while the women wear a black bodice laced with silver and a kerchief or tucker on the bosom; there are, however, many local variations.

Costume

Folk art, too, is still vigorously alive, interacting fruitfully with the artistic life of Munich. Among its characteristic manifestations are the painted biers used in funerals, the memorial tablets set up at the scene of an accident, the decorated domestic utensils and the painted house-fronts. Oberammergau is noted for its wood-carving, Berchtesgaden for its wooden caskets, while Mittenwald has been famed for more than two centuries for its violin-making.

Folk art

Bavaria is a land of religious processions, with its various "St George's rides" and "St Leonard's cavalcades" and its Corpus Christi processions. In autumn there is the "Almabtrieb", when the cattle, gaily decorated, are driven down from their mountain pastures. At weddings the decorated "Kammerwagen" containing the bride's trousseau is often to be seen. And everywhere visitors will encounter the old Bavarian folk songs and dances, with the traditional zither accompaniment. In this field a special place is occupied by the yodellers and the "Schnaderhüpferl", a four-lined verse, often in satirical vein, which may be improvised on the spot. The "Schuhplattler" dance represents a lover's wooing. There are, too, a variety of dramatic performances, including the famous Oberammergau Passion Play, which carried on the tradition of the medieval mysteries, and the plays performed in the peasant theatres of Tegernsee and Schliersee and the folk theatre of Kiefersfelden.

Customs

In the mountains the typical house type is the so-called "Alpine house", which has a flat roof weighted with stones and incorporates the cow-stalls on the ground floor. In the Alpine Foreland the houses have steeply pitched roofs and the dwelling-house and farm buildings are separate, often laid out round a square courtyard. The towns on the Inn and Salzach have distinctive Italian-style houses with straight-ended roofs and arcades.

The settlement pattern shows a predominance of separate farms, particularly in the morainic zone in the foreland. The villages tend to avoid the lowest parts of the valley, which are exposed to flooding and in winter are cold and misty. In the mountains the favoured sites are the upper edge of the valley bottom and the detrital cones of tributary streams; in the foreland the morainic hills and the middle terraces.

The Bavarian Alps achieve their effect by their great variety of land forms and scenery. The Allgäu Alps are given their specific character by their steep mountain meadows and beautifully shaped peaks, while the Wetterstein range has its sheer rock faces and Germany's highest mountain, the Zugspitze, now made accessible even to the non-climber by its mountain railways. Farther east the gentle contours of the Tegernsee hills are juxtaposed with the mighty limestone massifs of the Berchtesgaden Alps (National Park).

History

Prehistory and the Early Historical Period

500,000–150,000 B.C.	The oldest known human remains on German soil are the lower jaw of *Homo heidelbergensis* found at Mauer, near Heidelberg, the skull from Steinheim an der Murr and the skeleton of Neanderthal man from the Neander valley near Düsseldorf.
60,000–10,000	During the Palaeolithic period (*c.* 60,000–10,000 B.C.) men live in large groups by hunting, gathering and fishing, fashioning implements and weapons from stone, wood or bone and dwelling in tents, huts or caves.
8000–1800	Transition towards the establishment of settlements; log-built houses, pile dwellings (Lake Constance) and towards agriculture and stock-rearing; beginnings of trade and intercommunication; "Hunengräber" (megalithic tombs) on Lüneburg Heath.
1800–750	Bronze Age in Central Europe; the most highly prized materials are bronze, amber and gold. Tumulus tombs.
c. 1000	Beginning of the Iron Age in Europe.
800–400	First Central European culture (La Tène) developed by the Celts (at first in southern Germany, then extensive migrations in Europe); construction of hill forts (e.g. the Heuneburg, near Sigmaringen).
800–70	The Germanic peoples thrust into Celtic territory from Schleswig-Holstein, advancing to the Oder and the Rhine and into southern Germany.
c. 58 B.C.	In a succession of military campaigns the Romans make the Rhine the north-eastern frontier of the Roman empire. Romanisation of the left bank of the Rhine.
from 40 B.C.	Construction of forts at Cologne, Trier, Koblenz, Mainz, etc., to secure the Rhine frontier.
A.D. 9	A Roman army led by Varus is defeated by the Cheruscan leader Arminius (Hermann) in the Teutoburg Forest. Germany as far as the Rhine and the Danube is freed.
from A.D. 90	Construction of the Limes, a 550km/340 mile long defensive line from the Rhine to the Danube designed to check German advances over the frontier, and of numerous forts (Wiesbaden, Augsburg, Regensburg, Passau, etc.).
from 200	Emergence of a number of large West Germanic tribes – Alemanni, Franks, Chatti, Bajuwari, Saxons, Frisians, Thuringians, Langobardi.
c. 260	The Germans break through the Limes and the Danube frontier.

From the Great Migrations to the End of the Carolingian Empire (300–918)

	The period of the great migrations, which change the whole map of Europe, begins with the advance of the Huns into Europe (*c.* 375). The Eastern Germanic peoples destroy the Western Roman Empire (476), but the states they found do not last. The Western Germans move into the territory of the Roman Empire without losing contact with their own ancestral lands. The mingling between Germanic traditions and the Christian church (which also embodies the cultural traditions of antiquity) gives rise to the pattern of life of the medieval West.
481–511	By unifying the Franks and conquering Gaul the Merovingian king Chlodwig (Clovis) becomes the founder of the Frankish kingdom. Strengthening of the common feeling between Germans and Romans.

The Franks defeat the Alemanni, accept the Catholic faith and so gain the support of the Church.	496

Christianisation of the Germans by Iro-Scottish monks; foundation of monasteries at Würzburg, Regensburg, Reichenau, etc. — from 600

Missionary activity in the Merovingian kingdom by the Anglo-Saxon monk Boniface; foundation of monasteries at Fritzlar, Fulda, etc.; establishment of bishoprics under Papal authority. — from 720

Pépin, mayor (controller) of the palace under the Merovingian king, himself assumes the title of king and is anointed by the Church. The Frankish kings now set up as protectors of the Pope, and begin to take an interest in Italian affairs. — 751

Charlemagne extends the Carolingian empire into northern Italy and the territories of all the West Germanic peoples (the Saxons and Bajuwari or Bavarians). — 772–814

Charlemagne's authority in Western Europe is confirmed by his coronation as Emperor in Rome; re-establishment of the Roman Empire. — 800
The Frankish empire is divided into counties, and its frontiers are protected by border Marches. Imperial strongholds (*Kaiserpfalzen*) at Aachen, Ingelheim, Worms, Nijmegen, etc., become economic and cultural centres. The "Carolingian Renaissance": revival of Greek and Roman culture, promotion of education and scholarship.

The German Empire in the Middle Ages, down to the Reformation
(c. 919–1517)

In the struggle which now begins between the Pope and the Emperor, between the supreme spiritual and the supreme secular power, the Emperor is compelled to give way; but at the same time the foundations of ecclesiastical authority are undermined, since the Popes bring about a secularisation of the Church.

Successive partitions of the Carolingian empire; the German Empire develops out of the East Frankish kingdom. — 843–880

The Germanic peoples (Franks, Saxons, Swabians and Bavarians) are united under Duke Henry of Saxony, who takes the title of king. The term Kingdom (Empire) of the Germans ("Regnum Teutonicorum") is applied for the first time to the Frankish kingdom. — 919–936

Otto the Great, crowned king at Aachen in 936, strengthens the royal authority by appointing bishops and abbots as princes of the Empire (Reichsfürsten); establishment of a national church (Reichskirche). — 936–973

Otto wins the Langobardic (Lombard) crown by marrying the widowed queen Adelheid. — 951

Decisive victory over the Hungarians in the Lechfeld, near Augsburg; submission of the Slavs between the Elbe and the Oder. — 955

Otto I is crowned Emperor in Rome; strong German influence on the Papacy. — 962
First flowering of German culture, with women playing a large part (Otto's mother Mathilde, his wife Adelheid, his daughter-in-law Theophano, Hrotsvitha of Gander-sheim, etc.); monasteries as cultural centres; flowering of Romanesque architecture (Mainz, Speyer, Worms, Hildesheim, etc.).

Revival of monasticism and founding of new monasteries, daughter houses of Cluny (the principal foundation in Germany being at Hirsau in the Black Forest). — c. 1000

The kingdom of Burgundy is incorporated in the German Empire. — 1033

During the reign of Henry III Germany supports the Cluniac reform of the Church; the Peace of God, prohibition of simony (the purchase of clerical offices) and of the marriage — 1039–56 of priests. Imperial authority over the Pope reaches its peak. Construction of an imperial stronghold (*Pfalz*) at Goslar.

from 1075	Investiture dispute between Henry IV and Pope Gregory VII over appointments to ecclesiastical offices.
1077	Henry IV submits to the Pope at Canossa.
1096–1291	The Crusades. Establishment of knightly religious orders (Templars, Knights of St John, Teutonic Order). Emergence of a European nobility with common aims and ideals, expressed particularly in the ideas of chivalry. Cultural and commercial exchanges with the East.
from 1100	Foundation of new towns around imperial strongholds, castles, bishops' palaces and monasteries. The towns begin to establish municipal rights and liberties, while the rural population remain in a state of serfdom. Strict control of markets. The towns are ruled by patricians (merchants carrying on long-distance trade); the craftsmen form guilds, governed by strict rules, which seek to obtain control of the towns. Intensification of long-distance trade with the east and the north; the trading towns come together in the Hanse (Hanseatic League), under the leadership of Lübeck; action against pirates. Decline of the Hanse in the 15th century. Colonisation movement in the east: German settlers (peasants, townspeople, the Teutonic Order) move into the thinly populated Slav territories east of the Oder (Bohemia, Silesia, Pomerania, Poland), establishing towns and villages governed by German law.
1122	Temporary reconciliation between Henry V and the Pope in the Concordat of Worms. Consequences of the investiture dispute: weakening of the Ottonian Reichskirche, strengthening of the German secular princes.
1152–90	Emperor Frederick I (Barbarossa), of the Hohenstaufen dynasty. An accommodation is reached with the rival Guelph party by the grant of the duchy of Bavaria to Henry the Lion, Duke of Saxony. Austria becomes a separate duchy. Return to the Italian policies of the Ottonian emperors and their successors the Salians. Resumption of German colonisation in the east.
1177	Reconciliation between the Emperor and the Pope in Venice.
1180	Henry the Lion is outlawed; Bavaria is given to Otto von Wittelsbach (founder of a dynasty which was to rule in Bavaria until 1918) and Saxony is divided. Setback for the colonisation movement in the east.
1184–86	The Hohenstaufen empire under Barbarossa reaches its peak in the "Reichsfest" (imperial celebrations) held at Mainz and the marriage of his son Henry in Milan to the Norman princess Constance of Sicily. The power of the feudal lords is undermined by the appointment of "ministerials" (unfree servants of the Emperor) as officials. Flowering of chivalry (practices of knighthood, courtly love, court life in castles) and of epic poetry and the Minnesang ("Nibelungenlied", Wolfram von Eschenbach, Gottfried von Strassburg, Hartmann von der Aue, Walther von der Vogelweide).
1212–50	Frederick II establishes a modern, professionally administered state in Sicily. Grant of extensive sovereign powers to ecclesiastical and secular princes, leading to the rise of independent territorial states. The struggle with the Papacy saps the Empire's strength. Fall of the Hohenstaufen dynasty after Frederick II's death, followed by an interregnum during which there is no Emperor.
1250–1450	Gothic cathedrals built at Freiburg im Breisgau, Marburg, Strasbourg, Cologne, etc.
between 1220 and 1235	Eike von Repgau composes the "Sachsenspiegel" ("Mirror of the Saxons"), the oldest German law-book of the Middle Ages (first in Latin, later in Low German).
1226	Conquest and Christianisation of Prussia by the Teutonic Order.

Foundation of universities at Prague, Vienna, Heidelberg, Cologne, Leipzig and Rostock.	1300–1500
The Empire loses territory on all its frontiers (Switzerland, Schleswig-Holstein, West Prussia, the Low Countries).	1300–1648
Emperor Charles IV (of Luxembourg) seeks to restore the imperial authority by establishing a strong dynastic power. Policy of expansion in the east.	1346–78
Europe is ravaged by the Black Death. Persecution of the Jews, on religious and economic grounds.	c. 1350
The Golden Bull: in future the Emperor is to be chosen by seven Electors (the Archbishops of Mainz, Trier and Cologne, the King of Bohemia, the Count Palatine of the Rhine, the Duke of Saxony and the Margrave of Brandenburg).	1356
The modern world comes into being as a result of far-reaching intellectual, economic and political changes. Beginnings of natural science; Copernicus founds modern astronomy.	from 1400
The knightly classes are impoverished by the introduction of mercenary armies and foot soldiers; predatory activity by "robber knights".	from 1400
Gutenberg invents the art of printing with movable type in Mainz. Humanism in Germany: rediscovery of ancient literature, concern with the world and with nature. German humanists: Ulrich von Hutten, Johannes Reuchlin, Jakob Wimpheling, Philip Melanchthon.	c. 1450
The Renaissance: rebirth of ancient art (architecture and sculpture); discovery of beauty in nature and the individual qualities of human personality. German painters: Albrecht Dürer, Hans Holbein the Younger. Increasing particularism of the territorial princes in face of the preponderant power of the Habsburgs. Social discontents of the knights and peasants as a result of the establishment of a money economy. Changes in the art of war with the increasing use of firearms. Economic power of the towns. The beginnings of capitalism. Rise of the Fugger family through commerial and financial activities; they become financiers to both ecclesiastical and secular rulers.	
Reform of the Empire by Maximilian I: establishment of Imperial Supreme Court (Reichskammergericht), levying of imperial taxes, increasing power of the Imperial Diet (Reichstag). The reforms are, however, frustrated by the territorial fragmentation of the Empire.	1493–1519

From the Reformation to the End of the Holy Roman Empire (c. 1517–1815)

The Reformation destroys the unity of the Roman Church, while at the same time the increasing power of the state constricts the liberty of the nobility and the townspeople. The system of absolutism gradually develops in the territorial states, so that the Emperor's authority is confined to his own dynastic possessions, and the German Empire (now known as the "Holy Roman Empire of the German Nation") falls apart into a multiplicity of separate states.

There is much criticism in Germany of abuses in the Church and a desire for reform. Popular piety mingled with superstition.	c. 1500
Beginning of the Reformation: Luther nails his 95 "theses" against the abuse of indulgences to the church door in Wittenberg.	1517
Luther is outlawed at the Diet of Worms. The Reformation spreads rapidly, helped by the Emperor Charles V's wars with France and the Turks. Luther's translation of the Bible establishes the basis of modern German.	1521
Luther in conflict with Anabaptists and Iconoclasts. Unsuccessful rising of discontented imperial knights (Reichsritter) led by Franz von Sickingen.	1522

History

1524–25	Peasant wars in Swabia, Franconia (Götz von Berlichingen, Florian Geyer) and Thuringia (Thomas Müntzer) against ruling princes and lords; repressed by the territorial princes.
from 1545	Beginning of the Counter-Reformation in Germany, the main motive force being provided by the Jesuit order, founded by the Spaniard, Ignatius de Loyola. Central and north-eastern Germany almost wholly Protestant, western and southern Germany predominantly Catholic.
1546–47	War of the League of Schmalkalden between the Emperor Charles V and Protestant rulers.
1555	Peace of Augsburg: recognition of the Lutheran faith; the religion of a state to be that of its ruler ("Cuius regio, eius religio").
1556	Charles V abdicates; the Habsburg Empire is divided.
1608–09	Formation of the Protestant Union and the Catholic League.
1618–48	Thirty Years War. Causes: the conflicts between Catholics and Protestants, the efforts by the various states within the Empire to increase their power and the Habsburg Emperor's attempt to achieve the religious and political unity of the Empire. The immediate occasion for the war is the rising of the Protestant nobility of Bohemia against the Emperor ("Defenestration of Prague"), but the conflict is widened into a European war by the intervention of King Christian IV of Denmark, the Spaniards, Gustavus II Adolphus of Sweden and France under Cardinal Richelieu. Germany becomes the main theatre of war and the scene of the final conflict between France and the Habsburgs for predominance in Europe. Large areas of Germany are laid waste, and it loses something like a third of its population; general impoverishment.
1640–88	Rise of Brandenburg-Prussia under the Great Elector, Frederick William. Establishment of absolutism.
1648	Peace of Westphalia (signed in Münster and Osnabrück): cessions of territory to France and Sweden; the Low Countries and Switzerland are lost to the Empire. Decline of imperial power; rise of Brandenburg-Prussia.
1678–81	Louis XIV of France conquers parts of Alsace and Lorraine.
1683	The Turks are defeated outside Vienna by a German-Polish army commanded by Prince Eugene of Savoy. Reconquest of Hungary; German settlement in the Banat. Austria under the Habsburgs develops into a great power.
1688–97	Louis XIV wages an unsuccessful war in the Palatinate; great devastation (Heidelberg Castle, Speyer, Worms). French language and culture are adopted by the German courts and nobility.
1701	Elector Frederick of Brandenburg is crowned "king in Prussia".
1713–40	Establishment of a highly centralised state by King Frederick William I, the "Soldier King".
18th century	Baroque and Rococo art and architecture (Schloss, Berlin; Zwinger, Dresden; great composers – Bach, Handel, Telemann, Haydn, Mozart). The Age of Enlightenment: belief in progress, tolerance, rights of man. Writers of the German classical period (Herder, Goethe, Schiller).
1740–48	War of the Austrian Succession. Maria Theresa fights for recognition of her succession to the throne. Loss of Silesia to Frederick II, the Great, of Prussia (1740–86) in the Silesian Wars and the Seven Years' War (1756–63).
1763	Peace of Hubertsburg between Austria, Prussia and Saxony: Prussia becomes a European great power. Beginning of rivalry between Prussia and Austria for the leadership of Germany.

Establishment of "enlightened absolutism" in Prussia and Austria (the ruler as "the first servant of the state"), against resistance from the nobility and citizenry. Economic development; legal reforms (abolition of torture, improvement in the status of Jews); first emancipations of the peasants; promotion of education.	from 1763
Peace of Basle between France and Prussia: left bank of the Rhine ceded to France; Prussia to be neutral. Austria continues the struggle.	1795
Under the "Reichsdeputationshauptschluss" (a resolution of a committee of the Imperial Diet meeting in Regensburg) Napoleon abolishes almost all the ecclesiastical and the smaller secular states and most of the free imperial cities. New medium-sized states established in south-western Germany; expansion of Prussia.	1803
Establishment of the Confederation of the Rhine under Napoleon's protection; dissolution of the Holy Roman Empire. Prussia defeated at Jena and Auerstedt.	1806
Peace of Tilsit: cession to France of all Prussian possessions west of the Elbe; establishment of the kingdom of Westphalia under Napoleon's brother Jérome.	1807
Reconstruction and reform in Prussia: regulation of municipal government, liberation of the peasants, freedom to practise trades, emancipation of the Jews, reform of the army (Freiherr vom Stein, Hardenberg, Scharnhorst, Gneisenau).	1808–12
Beginning of the Wars of Liberation, following the destruction of Napoleon's army in Russia (1812). Germany is liberated after the Battle of the Nations at Leipzig. End of the Confederation of the Rhine.	1813
Final defeat of Napoleon at Waterloo by Wellington and Blücher.	1815
Congress of Vienna for the regulation of European affairs, under the leadership of Prince Metternich (Austria). Political principles: the restoration, legitimacy and solidarity of rulers for the repression of revolutionary and nationalist ideas. Foundation of the German Confederation (Bund) of 39 states (35 ruling princes and 4 free cities) under Austrian leadership, with a Federal Diet (Bundestag) meeting at Frankfurt am Main.	1814–15

From the Restoration to the First World War (1815–1914)

The history of the 19th century is principally determined by the effects of the French Revolution and the developing Industrial Revolution. Liberal and nationalist ideas are fostered by the middle classes. The conditions of the bourgeois-capitalist world give rise to the difficulties and discontents of the working classes.

The "Wartburg festival", organised by student organisations; burning of reactionary books.	1817
Karlsbad Decrees: introduction of censorship, supervision of universities. "Persecution of the demagogues" (Arndt, Jahn, Görres).	1819
First steamship on the Rhine.	1825
Gauss and Weber construct the first telegraph.	1833
Establishment of the Zollverein, a customs union between Prussia and most other German states, but excluding Austria.	1834
First German railway line, between Nürnberg and Fürth.	1835
Marx and Engels draw up the Communist Manifesto (though it does not acquire significance until later).	1847/48
March Revolution in the German states. In May the German National Assembly meets in the Paulskirche in Frankfurt to draw up a national German constitution.	1848

History

1849	The 1848 revolution proves abortive: King Frederick William IV of Prussia refuses the imperial crown, the Frankfurt parliament is dissolved, the ruling princes repress the risings by military force and the German Confederation is re-established.
from 1850	Increased rate of capital formation (joint-stock companies). Rise of the middle classes, economically, politically and socially. Formation of a propertyless proletariat.
1857	The Norddeutscher Lloyd shipping line established in Bremen.
1862	Prince Bismarck becomes chief minister of Prussia.
1864	Prussia and Austria at war with Denmark over Schleswig-Holstein.
1866	Austro-Prussian War; Prussian victory at Königgrätz. Siemens constructs the first dynamo.
1867	Establishment of the North German Confederation under the leadership of Prussia; offensive and defensive alliances between Prussia and the South German states. Exclusion of Austria.
1870/71	Franco-Prussian War. After the French defeat at Sedan Alsace and Lorraine are ceded to Germany, creating an obstacle to Franco-German understanding.
1871	The German Empire is proclaimed in the Palace of Versailles as a federal state (a "Little German" solution).
1872–78	"Kulturkampf" between the state and the Catholic church in Prussia and the German Empire.
1875	Foundation of the Socialist Workers' Party of Germany (the "Gotha Programme").
1878	Unsuccessful efforts by Bismarck to repress social democracy. Congress of Berlin to secure the maintenance of peace in Europe, with Bismarck as "honest broker".
1879	Dual Alliance of Germany and Austria-Hungary.
1882	Triple Alliance (Germany with Austria-Hungary and Italy).
1883–89	Introduction of social insurance
1884–1885	The Emperor William II seeks to make Germany a world power ("a place in the sun"); establishment of German colonies in South-West Africa, the Cameroons, Togo, East Africa, etc.
1885	Gottlieb Daimler and C. F. Benz each construct a petrol engine independently of one another.
1887	"Reinsurance Treaty" between Germany and Russia.
1890	Bismarck is dismissed by William II on account of policy and personal differences (the "dropping of the pilot").
1893	Rudolf Diesel develops the diesel engine.
1895	Opening of the Kiel Canal between the North Sea and the Baltic.
from 1898	Negotiations for an alliance between Germany and Britain break down as a result of Admiral Tirpitz's programme of warship construction. Increasing isolation of Germany.
1900	Promulgation of Code of Civil Law (Bürgerliches Gesetzbuch).
1907	First flight of the dirigible airship built by Graf Zeppelin at Friedrichshafen.

From the First World War to the Division of Germany (1914–49)

Imperialist power politics and the determined pursuit of national interests lead to the outbreak in 1914 of the First World War, the consequences of which hold the germ of renewed political tensions between the states of Europe. Under pressure of economic hardship new ideologies come to the fore, particularly in Italy and Germany, and as a result of the reckless policies pursued by the authoritarian powers lead to the Second World War, the catastrophic consequences of which bring about even more profound and far-reaching changes in the world political situation than the first war. The political centre of gravity shifts towards the United States and the Soviet Union, and Europe declines in importance. The unbridgeable differences between the world powers prevent the creation of a new political order and peaceful cooperation between the peoples.

First World War. The incident which sparks off the war is the assassination of the Austrian heir apparent and his wife at Sarajevo in Serbia (July 28th 1914). The causes are the opposing policies of the European states, the armaments race, German-British rivalry, the difficulties of the Austro-Hungarian multinational state, Russia's Balkan policy and over-hasty mobilisations and ultimatums. Germany declares war on Russia on August 1st, and on France on the 3rd; Britain declares war on Germany on August 4th.
Fighting in western, southern and eastern Europe, in the Near East and the German colonies. In the west a war of position with bloody battles; no decisive victories in the east; the British blockade has crippling effects on Germany's supplies of raw materials and foodstuffs. — 1914–18

The entry of the United States into the war marks a decisive turning-point. — 1917

Peace treaty of Brest-Litovsk between Russia and Germany. — 1918
Revolution in Germany (Nov. 9th); abdication of the Emperor and all German ruling princes; proclamation of a Republic by the Social Democrat Philipp Scheidemann. Armistice signed at Compiègne (November 11th).
Foundation of the German Communist Party (December 1918) and the German Workers' Party (January 1919), which becomes in 1920 the National Socialist German Workers' Party (NSDAP).

Treaty of Versailles. Germany loses Alsace-Lorraine, Eupen-Malmédy, North Schleswig, Posen, West Prussia, the Memel area, Upper Silesia and all its colonies; the Rhineland and Saar are occupied; limits on the size of the German army (100,000 men) and navy; no German air force; Germany accepts sole responsibility for the war; reparations (amount not stated) to be paid. — July 28th 1919

The Weimar Constitution comes into effect, with Friedrich Ebert as first President (until 1925). — Aug. 11th 1919

Kapp Putsch and Communist disturbances in Central Germany and the Ruhr. — 1920

Treaty of Rapallo between Germany and the Soviet Union; resumption of diplomatic relations. — 1922

Passive resistance to French occupation of the Ruhr. — 1923
Inflation: loss of confidence in the democratic regime.
Hitler's Munich putsch; the National Socialist Party is banned (until 1925).

Field Marshal Hindenburg elected President. Locarno treaty: guarantee of peace with France. — 1925

Germany is admitted to the League of Nations. — 1926

Beginning of the world economic crisis. — 1929

Presidential government under Heinrich Brüning; emergency decrees. Growth of unemployment (over 6 million) and of the radical parties. — 1930–32

End of the Weimar Republic. Hindenburg appoints Adolf Hitler Chancellor. The Reichstag fire (February 27th). Abrogation of basic rights under the Emergency Decree for the — Jan. 30th 1933

43

Protection of the People and the State. Enabling law (March 24th) giving Hitler's government full legislative power. A centralised totalitarian state is established (dissolution of the *Länder* and of all parties and trade unions), no longer based on the rule of law (hostility to religion and the Church, persecution of Jews, repression of all opposition, concentration camps established).
Germany leaves the League of Nations (October).

1934	Shooting of Ernst Röhm and political opponents (June); establishment of the "SS state".
1935	"Nuremberg race laws" directed against Jewish citizens (ban on marriage between Germans and Jews; loss of German citizenship). Universal military service; open rearmament.
1936	German troops march into the demilitarised Rhineland. German-Italian treaty (the "Rome-Berlin axis") in October. Anti-Comintern Pact with Japan (November). Olympic Games in Berlin and Garmisch-Partenkirchen.
1938	The Anschluss: Austria is annexed to Germany (March). Munich Agreement: Sudeten German territory in Czechoslovakia is ceded to Germany (September).
1939	Germany takes over the rest of Czechoslovakia as the "Protectorate of Bohemia and Moravia" (March). Military alliance between Germany and Italy (May). Non-Aggression Pact between Germany and the Soviet Union (August).
1939–45	Second World War. Blitzkrieg against Poland (September 1st 1939).
1940	German occupation of Denmark, Norway, the Netherlands, Belgium, Luxembourg and France. Beginning of the Battle of Britain.
1941	German troops in North Africa (February). Conquest of Yugoslavia and Greece (April). Attack on the Soviet Union (June). The United States enter the war (December).
1941–45	Systematic murder of some 6 million Jews (412 concentration camps); killing of the mentally ill and political opponents.
1943	The German 6th Army surrenders at Stalingrad (February); German withdrawal from Russia and North Africa; air attacks on German towns.
1944	Allied landings in North Africa (June). Unsuccessful attempt on Hitler's life by Count Stauffenberg (July 20th). Germany occupied by American, British, French and Russian forces.
1945	Germany surrenders (beginning of May) and is divided into four occupation zones (June). German territory east of the Oder-Neisse line is incorporated in Poland and the Soviet Union (Potsdam conference, August).
1945–46	Over 11 million Germans are evacuated from the eastern territories. Trials of war criminals at Nuremberg.
1948	Beginning of Marshall Aid. Currency reform in the occupation zones.
1948–49	The Berlin blockade; division of the city into two. Foundation of the Free University in West Berlin.

From the Division of Germany to Reunification (1949–90)

1949	**Federal Republic of Germany** Foundation of the Federal Republic of Germany. Temporary Basic Law (May 23rd). President Heuss, Chancellor Adenauer. Rapid economic development (the "German economic miracle") in a "social market economy" promoted by Ludwig Erhard.

German Democratic Republic
Foundation of the German Democratic Republic (GDR; Oct. 7th), with Wilhelm Pieck as President and Otto Grotewohl as prime minister.

German Democratic Republic   1950
Agreement between GDR and Poland on Oder-Neisse frontier line.
GDR becomes a member of Comecon.

German Democratic Republic   1951–52
Beginning of first five-year plan; establishment of large industrial combines and agricultural cooperatives.
Local government reorganisation into 14 regions.

German Democratic Republic   June 17th 1953
Rising in Soviet sector of Berlin and in GDR.

Federal Republic of Germany   1955
The Federal Republic joins NATO.
Adenauer visits Moscow and secures the liberation of German prisoners of war and the resumption of diplomatic relations with the USSR.

German Democratic Republic
Warsaw treaty of friendship, cooperation and mutual assistance (May).
Treaty with USSR on promotion of economic, scientific and cultural relations (September).

Federal Republic of Germany   1956
Building up of army (Bundeswehr); introduction of universal military service.

German Democratic Republic
Law on establishment of a People's Army. Development of craft cooperatives and trading organisations with state participation. Opening of Semper Gallery, Dresden.

Federal Republic of Germany   1957
Foundation of the European Economic Community and Euratom.

German Democratic Republic
First nuclear reactor in GDR, at Rossendorf, near Dresden, comes on stream.

Federal Republic of Germany   1958
Berlin crisis.

German Democratic Republic
Opening of Buchenwald Memorial near Weimar.

German Democratic Republic   1960
Socialist production relationships established in agriculture. Formation of Council of State under chairmanship of Walter Ulbricht.

Intensification of the Berlin crisis by the building of the Berlin Wall (August 13th).   1961

Federal Republic of Germany   1963
Franco-German friendship treaty signed in Paris.
State visit by US President Kennedy to the Federal Republic and West Berlin.

German Democratic Republic
Development of new industries (electronics, petrochemicals, manufacture of scientific apparatus, data processing).

German Democratic Republic   1964
Treaty of friendship, mutual assistance and cooperation with USSR.

History

<table>
<tr><td>1966</td><td>

Federal Republic of Germany
Economic crisis (rising prices); structural crisis in Ruhr mining industry.
Coalition government under K. G. Kiesinger.

</td></tr>
<tr><td>1967</td><td>

Federal Republic of Germany
Formation of an extra parliamentary opposition.

German Democratic Republic
Measures for improvement of working and living conditions (5-day week, increase in minimum wages and holiday entitlements).

</td></tr>
<tr><td>1968</td><td>

Federal Republic of Germany
Emergency powers law.

German Democratic Republic
Referendum on socialist constitution of GDR.

</td></tr>
<tr><td>1969</td><td>

Federal Republic of Germany
"Social-liberal" coalition government under Willy Brandt, which pursues a policy of improving relations with the Communist states.

</td></tr>
<tr><td>1970</td><td>

Federal Republic of Germany
A treaty with the Soviet Union renouncing the use of force is signed in Moscow (August).
An agreement is reached with Poland in Warsaw (December).

</td></tr>
<tr><td>1971</td><td>

Four-power agreement on Berlin.
Agreement on transit traffic between the Federal Republic and West Berlin.

</td></tr>
<tr><td>1972</td><td>

Federal Republic of Germany
Summer Olympics in Munich.

German Democratic Republic
Nationalisation of firms with state participation, private firms and many craft cooperatives.

</td></tr>
<tr><td>1973</td><td>

Treaty between the Federal Republic and the Democratic Republic. Both states become members of the United Nations.

</td></tr>
<tr><td>1974</td><td>

Federal Republic of Germany
Willy Brandt resigns as a result of the Guillaume affair (espionage on behalf of GDR) and is succeeded by Helmut Schmidt. Fall in inflation rate.

German Democratic Republic
A new constitution comes into force on the GDR's 25th anniversary (October 7th).

</td></tr>
<tr><td>from 1974</td><td>

Federal Republic of Germany
Steep increases in the price of oil lead to a world-wide energy crisis and economic recession.
Political radicalism escalates into terrorism.

</td></tr>
<tr><td>1976</td><td>

Federal Republic of Germany
Decree banning the employment of political extremists in the public service.

German Democratic Republic
Erich Honecker becomes chairman of the Council of State.

</td></tr>
<tr><td>1977</td><td>

Terrorists murder the Federal Attorney-General, Bubeck (April), and a leading banker, Ponto (July). German commandos free hostages in highjacked plane at Mogadishu (Somalia). Kidnapping and murder of German Employers' Federation chairman, Schleyer.

</td></tr>
</table>

Federal Republic of Germany   1978
Controversial law against terrorism (February).

German Democratic Republic
First German into space: GDR cosmonaut Sigmund Jähn a crew member of the Soviet space-craft "Soyuz 31".

Federal Republic of Germany   1979
Karl Carstens elected President (May 23rd).

Federal Republic of Germany   1980
After a general election Helmut Schmidt is re-elected Chancellor in a coalition government.

Federal Republic of Germany   1982
Economic stagnation; rapid rise in unemployment.
NATO summit in Bonn (June 10th).
The coalition government breaks up over differences of view on the economy (September). Helmut Kohl elected interim Chancellor.

Federal Republic of Germany   1983
President Carstens dissolves the Bundestag (January). After an election on March 6th a coalition government is formed, with Kohl as Chancellor.
First "Green" members of Bundestag.

Federal Republic of Germany   1984
Richard von Weizsäcker succeeds Carstens as President.

Federal Republic of Germany   1985
The Federal government agrees, from the political point of view, to the US Strategic Defence Initiative.

German Democratic Republic
The Warsaw treaty of 1955 is extended.

The West German Social Democratic Party and the GDR Socialist Unity Party draft an agreement on the establishment in Europe of a chemical-weapons-free zone (June).

Federal Republic of Germany   1986
After the accident at the Chernobyl reactor a ministry of the environment is established.

German Democratic Republic
Mikhail Gorbachev, General Secretary of the USSR Communist Party, visits the GDR (April).
The Synod of Evangelical (Protestant) Churches declares in favour of giving citizens more responsibility.
Opening of train ferry between Mukran on the island of Rügen and Klaipeda in the USSR (Lithuania).

Federal Republic of Germany   1987
An election in January returns the coalition government to power; Helmut Kohl continues as Chancellor.
Hans-Joachim Vogel succeeds Willy Brandt as chairman of the Social Democratic Party.
Erich Honecker, chairman of the GDR Council of State, visits the Federal Republic (September).

German Democratic Republic
Amnesty for offenders; abolition of death penalty.

Federal Republic of Germany   1988
Death of Franz Josef Strauss, prime minister of Bavaria and chairman of the CSU (Christian Social Union) party.

German Democratic Republic
Erich Honecker is received by President Mitterand in Paris (January).
On the 69th anniversary of the murder of Karl Liebknecht and Rosa Luxembourg there are clashes in East Berlin between party officials and members of peace and human rights groups (January).

1989

Federal Republic of Germany
40th anniversary of the Federal Republic.
Increased damage to forests by pollution; many seals die on North Sea coast; sea-water increasingly polluted by algae.

German Democratic Republic
After protests against alleged ballot rigging in local government elections more than 100 people are arrested in Leipzig (May).

During the summer large numbers of GDR citizens take refuge in West German embassies in Eastern European countries in the hope of emigrating to the West. Thousands of people cross the frontier intp Hungary and Austria, and later into Czechoslovakia.

German Democratic Republic
The East German government allows refugees in Poland (Sept. 30th) and Czechoslovakia to travel to the West, but introduces a visa requirement for entry to Czechoslovakia (Oct. 3rd); disturbances in Dresden when the railway station is closed during the transit of refugees from Prague to the West (Oct. 4th).
On Nov. 9th the government, unexpectedly, allows East German citizens to enter West Berlin and the Federal Republic.
Hundreds of thousands of people take advantage of the opportunity; new crossing points are opened in the Berlin Wall and along the frontier with the Federal Republic.

Since Reunification (from 1990)

1990

The achievement of economic, currency and social union between the two German states (July 1st), with the introduction of the D-mark in East Germany, prepares the way for the full union of the two states.
The reunification of the two Germanys comes into force on October 1st, which is declared a national public holiday. The occasion is celebrated, particularly in Berlin, with various political and cultural events.
144 members of the former Volkskammer, the East German parliament, join the Bundestag in Bonn as representatives of East Germany pending a general election to be held in December. Five new *Länder* are established in the former territory of the GDR – Mecklenburg-West Pomerania, Brandenburg, Saxony, Saxony-Anhalt and Thuringia.

The first all-German parliamentary election is held on December 2nd.

Ramsau, near Berchtesgaden ▶

Germany from A to Z

N.B.   Since the reunion of the two Germanys many place-names and street names have been changed in the former German Democratic Republic, and further changes are to be expected. This should be borne in mind when using the town plans in this Guide.
The list of topographical terms on page 600 may be found useful in interpreting German place-names.

Aachen   G 1

Land: North Rhine-Westphalia
Altitude: 125–410m/410–1345ft
Population: 245,000

Situation and characteristics

Aachen (formerly known by its French name of Aix-la-Chapelle), Germany's most west-erly city and historically one of Europe's most important towns, lies near the Dutch and Belgian frontiers in a forest-ringed basin in the foothills of the Eifel (see entry) and the Ardennes. The hot brine springs of Bad Aachen are particularly effective in the treatment of gout, rheumatism and sciatica.
The equestrian stadium in the Soers district is the venue of international riding, jumping and driving tournaments, held every year.

History

Aquae Granni, the hottest springs in Europe (37–75°C/99–167°F), were already fre-quented in Roman times for their curative properties. In the Middle Ages Aachen was one of the leading towns in Germany, a frequent residence of the Frankish kings, a stronghold much favoured by Charlemagne, and from the time of Otto I (936) to that of Ferdinand I (1531) the place of coronation of 32 German kings and the meeting-place of numerous Imperial Diets and church assemblies. In the 18th and 19th centuries it was the "watering-place of kings".

Marktplatz

Town Hall

In the Marktplatz is the Town Hall (Rathaus), built about 1350 on the foundations of the Carolingian imperial stronghold (helm roofs of towers rebuilt in 1979 to a design by Dürer), with its fine Coronation Hall (frescoes on the life of Charlemagne by A. Rethel) and copies of the imperial regalia (orb, sword, crown; originals now in Vienna). To the south of the Town Hall is the Katschhof, marking the site of the Carolingian palace courtyard.

Couven Museum

Nearby, in an old burgher's house at Hühnermarkt 17, is the Couven Museum (Aachen domestic interiors from 1740 to 1840).

Newspaper Museum

At Pontstrasse 13 is the International Newspaper Museum (Zeitungsmuseum; first and most recent issues of some 100,000 titles).

**Cathedral

The Cathedral (Dom) consists of a central octagon built about 800 as Charlemagne's palace church and the Gothic choir, completed in 1414. Under the dome is a cande-labrum presented by Frederick I Barbarossa; in the gallery is Charlemagne's marble throne; and in the choir is the golden reliquary containing his remains. The Treasury contains many precious things.
Near the Cathedral, where now stands a reproduction of a Roman portico, the remains of Roman baths and temples were brought to light in 1967–68.

Grashaus

South-west of the Cathedral is the so-called "Grashaus" (1267), Aachen's earliest town hall, which now houses the municipal archives.

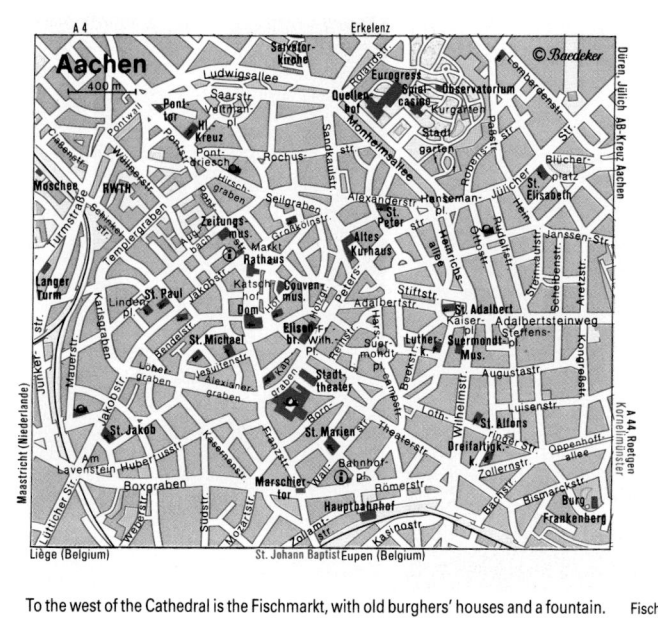

To the west of the Cathedral is the Fischmarkt, with old burghers' houses and a fountain.

Fischmarkt

In Friedrich-Wilhelmplatz is the Elisenbrunnen, the emblem of Aachen's role as a spa, with the drinking fountain and a colonnade designed by K. F. Schinkel. A few paces away is the Municipal Theatre (Stadttheater; 1825; opera, operettas, plays).

Friedrich-Wilhelm-Platz
Elisenbrunnen

Some 500m/550yds north-east of the Elisenbrunnen, in Komphausbadstrasse, is the Old Kurhaus (Altes Kurhaus), which now houses the New Gallery and Ludwig Collection (mainly 20th century art; special exhibitions).

Ludwig Collection

At the east end of the pedestrian zone is the Kaiserplatz, with St Adalbert's Church. A little way south of this is the Suermondt Museum (sculpture, paintings).
To the east of the railway station (Hauptbahnhof), in Burg Frankenberg, is the Municipal Museum.

Suermondt Museum

Spa District (Kurbezirk)

In the north of the town are the Eurogress (conference and congress centre), the International Casino, housed in the New Kurhaus, and the Kurpark. To the west, at the end of the Ludwigsallee, rises the frowning Ponttor (town gate) with its barbican (c. 1320).
There are other spa facilities in the southern district of Burtscheid.

On the south-eastern outskirts of the town, in the Drimborner Wäldchen landscape reserve, is Aachen's Zoo.

Zoo

On the Lousberg (340m/1116ft) stands the Belvedere revolving tower restaurant, with fine panoramic views.

Lousberg

6km/4 miles south-east of the town centre lies the suburb of Kornelimünster, with the Stefanskirche (St Stephen's Church), which dates from Carolingian times, and an old monastery (14th–15th century church).

Kornelimünster

51

Aachen Cathedral   The Octagon

Ahr Valley   G 2

Land: Rhineland-Palatinate

Situation and characteristics	The Ahr valley (Ahrtal) in the northern Eifel, famed for its wines, is one of the most beautiful of the Rhine's tributary valleys. The river, 89km/55 miles long, rises at Blankenheim and flows into the Rhine below Sinzig.
Ahrtal wines	

In the narrow valley nestle a succession of wine towns and villages – Altenahr, Mayschoss, Rech, Dernau, Marienthal, Walporzheim, Bachem and Ahrweiler.

The wines are mainly red (Spätburgunder). Wine has been produced in this most northerly wine-growing region in Germany since Roman times, from around A.D. 260. For walkers there is a 30km/20 mile long "Red Wine Trail", which runs through a delightful landscape of vineyards from Lohrsdorf to Altenahr.

The finest part of the valley is the romantic stretch between Altenahr and Bad Neuenahr-Ahrweiler, where the river forces its way in a winding course between rugged slate crags. Particularly impressive is the high rock face known as the Bunte Kuh at Walporzheim. The hills are crowned with ruined castles, and their slopes are covered with woodland and vineyards.

Bad Neuenahr-Ahrweiler

The little medieval town of Ahrweiler, amalgamated with Bad Neuenahr in 1969, a well-known centre of the red wine trade and a popular spa, has the only alkaline springs (36°C/97°F) in Germany. The spa facilities lie on the right bank of the Ahr; the two most important springs are the Grosser Sprudel (90m/295ft deep) and the Willibrordussprudel (376m/1234ft deep). In the south of the town is the 18th century St Willibrord's Church (R.C.). Above Neuenahr is Neuenahr Castle (Burg Neuenahr).

Alfeld an der Leine

Land: Lower Saxony
Altitude: 93m/305ft
Population: 23,000

Alfeld, the chief place in the Leinebergland (see entry), lies on the right bank of the river Leine at the foot of the Sieben Berge (Seven Hills). The beautiful old part of the town has preserved its medieval character. Alfeld is noted for its flower nurseries (cyclamens) and has a varied range of industry.

Situation and characteristics

Old Town (Altstadt)

The old town is dominated by the twin towers of the parish church of St Nicholas, a 15th century Gothic hall-church. Notable features of the interior are the Triumphal Cross group, the font and the tabernacle.

St Nicholas's Church

On the Kirchhof are the Old Latin School (Alte Lateinschule; 1610), with rich figural decoration, which now houses the Heimatmuseum, and the Municipal Museum (prehistoric material, regional history; dioramas). Nearby is the Shoemakers' Guild-House, a handsome half-timbered building of 1570. The town's oldest half-timbered building (1490) is at Seminarstrasse 3.

* Latin School

To the north of the church is the Town Hall (Rathaus; 1584–86), with a picturesque staircase tower. To the left of the entrance can be seen the "Blue Stone", which features in a local legend about the daughter of a burgomaster of Alfeld who was abducted by the robber knight Lippold von Rössing.

Town Hall

Lippoldshöhle (Lippold's Cave)

Some 1.5km/1 mile south-west of the suburb of Brunkensen (zoo) is the Lippoldshöhle, a cave in the depths of the forest. It consists of a number of chambers and passages which once (c. 1300) formed part of the castle of the robber knight Lippold von Rössing.

Allgäu

Länder: Baden-Württemberg and Bavaria

The Allgäu is an attractive upland and mountain region (ridges of post-tectonic sediments, moraines) in the Alpine Foreland. It occupies the southern part of Bavarian Swabia between Lake Constance and the Lech valley and extends north-west into Württemberg.
The Allgäu is traversed by the Deutsche Alpenstrasse (see entry) and, farther north, a branch of the Upper Swabian Baroque Highway (see Upper Swabia).

Situation and characteristics

The high Alpine chain of the Allgäu Alps, part of the Northern Calcareous Alps, forms with its bizarrely shaped peaks the boundary between Bavaria and the Austrian provinces of Vorarlberg and Tirol. The highest point is the Grosser Krottenkopf (2657m/8718ft) in northern Tirol.

Allgäu Alps

* Landscape

The landscape of the Allgäu, with its tiers of steep foothills, magnificent lakes (Alpsee, Grüntensee, Weissensee, Hopfensee, Forggensee, etc.), quiet ponds and moors, extensive forests, lush mountain meadows and trim villages set against an imposing backdrop of mountains, is strikingly beautiful and attracts large numbers of visitors both in summer and for winter sports.

Characteristic of the region are the "grass hills" (e.g. Höfats, 2258m/7408ft), whose steep slopes hold potential hazards for hill walkers.

Noted for its intensive cattle-rearing (the famous Allgäu breed) and highly developed dairying industry (milk, butter, cheese), the Allgäu is also a region of spas and medicinal springs. The well-known Kneipp water cure was first devised in Bad Wörishofen (see Landsberg, Surroundings), and is now applied in many other spas. There are also mud baths and various mineral springs. Sunshine and mountain air also have their health-giving effect.

See Augsburg, Kempten, Kleinwalsertal, Memmingen, Oberstdorf, Pfronten, Sonthofen and Wangen.

Alsfeld G 4

Land: Hesse
Altitude: 268m/879ft
Population: 17,000

Situation and characteristics

This charming little town on the upper course of the river Schwalm, between Vogelsberg and Knüll, was chosen as European model town for the preservation of the architectural heritage on account of its well preserved old town with its half-timbered houses. Its economy centres on the textile and woodworking industries.

* Townscape

* Town Hall

The central feature of the old town is the Marktplatz, on the east side of which, standing alone, is the Late Gothic Town Hall (Rathaus; 1512–16), with its oriel windows topped by helm roofs. This is one of the finest half-timbered buildings in the whole of Germany, with a handsome council chamber and court room.

Other historic buildings

On the north side of the Marktplatz, on the right, is the Weinhaus (1538), stone-built, with a stepped gable; to the left is the Bückingsches Haus (late 16th c.), with a fine oriel; on the west side of the square, opposite the Town Hall, is the Stumpfhaus (1609), with rich carved and painted decoration; and on the south side the Hochzeitshaus (Wedding House), a handsome Renaissance building of 1564–71 (wine cellar, etc.).

Regional Museum

In Rittergasse, which leads west from the Marktplatz, are the Regional Museum and Tourist Information Office, housed in two restored 17th century houses (fine Renaissance doorway).

Walpurgiskirche

Just north of the Town Hall, at the near end of Fuldergasse (many half-timbered houses), is the Walpurgiskirche (St Walburga's Church; 13th–15th c.), with Late Gothic wall paintings and fine monuments. At the end of the street is the Leonhardsturm (1386).

Trinity Church

In the Rossmarkt can be found the 14th century Trinity Church (Dreifaltigkeitskirche), adjoining which are the remains of an Augustinian monastery.

Altenburg

On a hill above the Schwalm, 2km/1¼ miles south of the town, is the 18th century Schloss Altenburg.

Altenberg G 9

Land: Saxony
Altitude: 750–905m/2460–2970ft
Population: 3000

Situation and characteristics

The old mining town of Altenberg lies on the Geisingberg in the eastern Erzgebirge, on the road from Dresden via Zinnwald to Prague (E 55), only 4km/2½ miles from the frontier with Czechoslovakia.

Sights

The town's main tourist attraction is the Pinge, a huge crater formed in 1620 by the simultaneous collapse of a number of small mining shafts. Originally with an area of 1.25 hectares/3 acres, it now covers 22 hectares/55 acres and is steadily being extended by further mining.

*Pinge

The Mining Museum (Bergbaumuseum), housed in a 400-year-old washery, illustrates the techniques for processing tin ore in earlier times. Features of the museum include a stamp mill, a water-wheel and a permanent exhibition on "500 Years of Tin-Mining in Altenberg". Adjoining the museum is the Neubeschert-Glück shaft, illustrating the method of opening up and consolidating mine shafts.

Mining Museum

Surroundings of Altenberg

From the Kahleberg (905m/2969ft), the highest peak in the eastern Erzgebirge, there are fine views of Altenberg, the Galgenteiche ("Gallows Ponds") and the Geisingberg.

Kahleberg

The Georgenfeld Moor, a tract of 18,000 year old moorland 11 hectares/27 acres in extent, can be traversed on a log road. The flora includes sundews, northern bilberries, cranberries, purple moor-grass and other rare plants.

Georgenfeld Moor

At Schellerhau is a fine botanic garden with 2000 characteristic mountain plants.

Schellerhau

Schmiedeberg has one of the finest churches in Saxony, built by Georg Bähr (1666–1738), architect of the Frauenkirche in Dresden.

Schmiedeberg

Dippoldiswalde, the economic centre of the eastern Erzgebirge, has a number of notable buildings – a Renaissance house in the Markt, the Town Hall, the Schloss and the Town Church.

Dippoldiswalde

A few kilometres north-east of Altenberg in the Müglitz valley are Burg Lauenstein, an old frontier fortress, and the little town of Lauenstein, with its Schloss (old pharmacy), burghers' houses and Falknerbrunnen (fountain) as reminders of its medieval past. The church contains fine sculpture and relief carving, including works by the Pirna sculptor Michael Schwenke (1563–1610).

Lauenstein

Altenburg

Land: Thuringia
Altitude: 180–230m/590–755ft
Population: 53,000

The town of Altenburg, 35km/22 miles south of Leipzig, a former ducal residence once notable for its fine buildings and art treasures, is now famed as the home of skat (a popular German card game which originated in this area).

Situation and characteristics

Castle

The Castle (Schloss) stands on a porphyry crag rearing picturesquely above the town. A curving drive (1725) with two obelisks leads up to a gateway with a triumphal arch (1742–44). In the spacious courtyard, entered through the Bell-Tower, is an open-air theatre (performances in summer). On the site of the Hausmannsturm is a Slav defensive wall dating from around 800. The Mantelturm (once the castle dungeon), known as the "Flasche" ("Bottle"), dates from the 11th century, the Renaissance gallery from 1604. Otherwise the castle in its present form is the result of 18th century rebuilding.

The Castle Museum (Schlossmuseum) has a large collection of playing cards and a playing-card-maker's workshop of 1600.

Castle Museum
(*playing cards)

Notable features of the interior are the Banqueting Hall, with a ceiling painting by K. Moosdorf of "Cupid and Psyche", and the Bach Room, with ceiling paintings on the history of the Wettin family.

Castle Church

The Castle Church (Schlosskirche; after 1444) has an organ by H. G. Trost (1738), on which Johann Sebastian Bach played in 1739.

Schlosspark

Notable features of the Schlosspark, landscaped by Peter Joseph Lenné in the 19th century, are the Tea-House and the Orangery (1712).

* Lindenau Museum

At the lower end of the park is the Lindenau Museum (1873–75), housed in a building in Italian Renaissance style, with a varied collection – casts of antique sculpture, medieval German sculpture, Italian Renaissance and neo-classical sculpture, Greek and Etruscan vases, Italian painting of the 13th–15th centuries, and paintings, graphic art and sculpture of the 19th and 20th centuries.
Also in the park is the Mauritianum, a natural history museum.

Old Town

Brühl

Below the castle is the Brühl, the town's original market square. On the south side stands the Seckendorff Palace (1724–25), and opposite this is a building of 1604 which formerly housed the ducal administration, with the finest moulded stucco ceiling (restored) in Saxony and Thuringia.
Also in the square is the Skat Fountain, the only monument to a card game.

St Bartholomew's Church

The Late Gothic Bartholomäuskirche (St Bartholomew's Church) has a Romanesque crypt (12th c.).

* Town Hall

The spacious Markt is dominated by the handsome Renaissance Town Hall (Rathaus; by N. Grohmann, 1562–64). Also in the square can be seen a number of fine burghers' houses.

Other Districts

Rote Spitzen

The Rote Spitzen ("Red Points") – a Romanesque brick-built structure with one pointed and one curving tower – are a remnant of a 12th century church belonging to a house of Augustinian canons. The building now houses a collection of wood-carving ranging from medieval to Baroque.

Nikolaiviertel

The Nikolaiviertel is a picturesque old quarter, with the 12th century Nikolaiturm (views).

Windischleuba   G 7

Location:
7km/4½ miles N

In Windischleuba, on the site of a 14th century moated castle, is a later Schloss (much rebuilt), once occupied by the poet and ballad-writer Börries von Münchhausen (1874–1945).

Kohrener Land   G 7

The Kohrener Land, north-east of Altenburg, is a popular recreation area with small patches of woodland (Streitwald, Stöckigt) and a number of features of interest.

Kohren-Salis

In Kohren-Salis, which first appears in the records in 974, are a Pottery Museum (Töpfermuseum), a Potters' Fountain (by K. Feuerriegel, 1928) and remains of an old fortification (originally Slav).

Rüdigsdorf

In the district of Rüdigsdorf is an Orangery with a music room (fine frescoes of "Cupid and Psyche" by Moritz von Schwind, 1838).

Potters' Fountain, Kohren-Salis

On the Lindenwerk is a Mill Museum.

In Gnandstein stands a well preserved Romanesque stronghold, with a museum, Romanesque residential quarters, a 33m/110ft high keep, an outer ward, women's apartments and defensive ramparts. The museum contains three altars by P. Breuer (1502/03).

∗ Gnandstein

Borna

On the north side of the Markt is the 15th century St Catherine's Church, with a fine carved altar by Hans Witten. The Reichstor (Imperial Gate; 1753) is a relic of the town's old fortifications (museum).

Situation:
18km/11 miles N

Altes Land

C 5

Land: Lower Saxony

The Altes Land ("Old Land"), on the lower Elbe between the Süderelbe (within the city limits of Hamburg) and Stade, is the richest and most beautiful of the Elbe fenlands (Elbmarschen), 32km/20 miles long and 2–7km/1¼–4½ miles across (area 157 sq.km/61 sq. miles). It is Germany's most northerly fruit-growing region, at its most enchanting when the cherry-trees are in flower, turning the orchards into a sea of blossom. This is the time for a walk along the high dykes of the dark fenland rivers or the Elbe, looking down on the fruit-orchards below. Apples, pears and plums are grown as well as cherries.

Striking features of the Altes Land are its handsome and colourful farmhouses, with high thatched roofs and tiles between the white timber framing. The gables are decorated with elegant finials in the form of swans' necks. Here and there can be seen, beyond the bridge spanning the ditch in front of the house, richly carved entrance doorways.

Situation and
∗ landscape

Altmark

Obstmarschenweg	The beautiful Obstmarschenweg ("Fenland Fruit Trail") runs over the plain with its network of canals.

Sights

Jork	The chief place in the Altes Land is Jork, situated near the junction of the Este with the Elbe, with handsome old farmhouses, a church of 1709 and an experimental fruit-growing station.
Lühe	From Lühe, a popular weekend resort on the south bank of the Elbe, there is a ferry to Schulau ("ship-greeting station": see Hamburg, Surroundings). Between Lühe, Schulau and St Pauli ply the ships of the HADAG line.
Stade	See entry

Altmark   D–E 6–7

Land: Saxony-Anhalt

Situation	The Altmark is the low-lying area between the Middle Elbe depression on the east and north-east, the Ohre valley with the Mittelland Canal on the south and the Elbufer-Drawehn Nature Park on the west and north-west.
Topography	The Altmark is flat in some areas and gently undulating in others, with terminal moraines (the Hellberge, near Wiepke, 160m/525ft), tracts of outwash sand (Colbitz-Letzlingen Heath, 139m/456ft) and extensive depressions (Wische, Drömling).
Agriculture and forestry	The light sandy soils of the Altmark are suitable for agriculture and forestry. Fields of rye and potatoes alternate with areas of woodland, and there are large areas of forest in the southern part of the region, on Letzlingen Heath.

Sights

Access	The Altmark can be reached on good roads from the Berlin-Magdeburg-Marienborn motorway via Haldensleben (equestrian statue of Roland in Markt; numerous megalithic tombs in Haldensleben Forest) or Wolmirstedt, from the B 5 by way of the bridge over the Elbe at Wittenberge or from the east by way of the Elbe bridge at Tangermünde. The chief towns in the Altmark are Stendal (see entry), an old Hanseatic town and an important traffic junction, Salzwedel and Tangermünde (see entries), two attractive little medieval towns, and Gardelegen (pop. 13,000), famed for its Garley beer. Gardelegen has a Heimatmuseum (local museum; collection of cast-iron oven panels of the 17th–19th centuries).
Arendsee	The Arendsee, known as the "pearl of the Altmark", is a lake with an area of some 540 hectares/1350 acres, one of the most popular recreation areas, with beautiful wooded scenery, in a region which apart from this has few lakes. The little town of Arendsee, a much frequented altitude resort, has a former Benedictine nunnery with a Romanesque church and half-timbered houses of the early 19th century.

Altötting   L 8

Land: Bavaria
Altitude: 402m/1319ft
Population: 11,000

Situation and characteristics	Altötting, the oldest and most celebrated pilgrimage centre in Bavaria, with the mother house of the Capuchin order, lies on a hill on the right bank of the Inn, roughly half way between Munich and Passau.

Altötting first appears in the records in 748, the Holy Chapel in 877. The pilgrimage to the Virgin of Altötting began in 1489 and reached its highest point in the reign of Elector Maximilian I (1598–1654). The town still attracts over 500,000 pilgrims a year. It was visited by Pope John Paul II in 1980.

Holy Chapel

The Holy Chapel in Kapellplatz was originally an octagonal structure built in Carolingian times, to which a nave was added in the late 15th century. Housed in a silver tabernacle of 1645 is the famous carved wooden image of Our Lady of Altötting, a black Madonna dating from around 1300. Round it, in silver urns, are the hearts of 21 Bavarian rulers and of Tilly, the celebrated Imperial general of the Thirty Years' War. In the ambulatory are numerous ex-votos.

* Image of the Virgin

The Pilgrimage and Heimatmuseum in Kapellplatz contains material recovered by excavation, a model of the Baroque square, objects expressing popular piety, votive offerings, etc.

Museum

On the west side of the square is the Altöttinger Marienwerk, where visitors are shown films on the life of the Virgin and of Brother Conrad (see below) and on the Pope's visit, and can see dioramas on the history of the pilgrimage.

Marienwerk

Stiftskirche

On the south side of the square stands the twin-towered Stiftskirche (collegiate church of SS Philip and James), a hall-church built about 1500. It contains the grave slab of the Frankish king Carloman (d. 880). The Treasury is richly endowed with precious objects, including the famous Goldenes Rössl (Golden Horse) of 1404, a masterpiece of French goldsmith's art. At the south-east corner of the cloister is the Tilly Chapel or St Peter's Chapel, with a vault containing the remains of General Count Tilly (d. 1632).

* Treasury

To the north-west of Kapellplatz is the Brother Conrad Church, with a reliquary containing the remains of the saint of that name. To the east of the square can be seen the Panorama, a colossal painting of the Crucifixion (by Gebhard Fugel, 1903). Near the Panorama, at Kreszentiaheimstrasse 18, is a "mechanical Nativity scene", with wooden figures from Oberammergau.

Other sights

Burghausen

On a hill above the town is the imposing Burg, one of the largest castles in Germany, fully 1km/³⁄₄ mile long from end to end. At the entrance is the Municipal Museum of Photography (Städtisches Fotomuseum). Within the castle itself are the Municipal Historical Museum and an outstation of the Bavarian State Galleries (Late Gothic painting from Bavaria).

Situation:
17km/10½ miles SE
Burg

With its handsome burghers' houses, the old town of Burghausen, which is almost completely preserved, is very typical of the towns of the Inn and Salzach valleys.

Old town

Around the Wöhrsee lies a landscape reserve and recreation area (bathing station).

Amberg   17

Land: Bavaria
Altitude: 374m/1227ft
Population: 46,000

Amberg, formerly capital of the Upper Palatinate, lies in the eastern part of the Franconian Jura, nestling in the valley of the Vils, which flows through the old town.

Situation

Sights

The old medieval and Baroque town is still ringed by walls, with towers and gates. The line of the old ramparts is now marked by a succession of parks and gardens.

Town Hall
*St Martin's Church

The hub of the old town within its oval circuit of walls is the Marktplatz, with the Town Hall (Rathaus, 14th–16th c.; Great Council Chamber and Lesser Council Chamber, with beautiful coffered ceilings) and the Late Gothic hall-church of St Martin (1421–83), the most important Gothic church in the Upper Palatinate after Regensburg Cathedral. The 91m/299ft high west tower was built in 1534. The church contains the imposing monument of Count Palatine Ruprecht Pipan (d. 1397).

Altes Schloss

Electoral Palace

Behind the church stands the Altes Schloss (Old Castle, 13th–14th c.), now housing the Prehistoric Museum (still in course of development). To the south-west of the Marktplatz is the 17th century Electoral Palace (Kurfürstliches Schloss), now occupied by local government offices. From the palace the town walls are carried over the river Vils on two arches, known as the Stadtbrille (the town's "spectacles").

Schrannenplatz

In Schrannenplatz, in the north-west of the old town, are the Schulkirche (School Church), with a Rococo interior, and the Municipal Theatre, housed in a former Franciscan church.

Maltesergebäude

From the Marktplatz Georgenstrasse (pedestrian zone) leads to the Maltesergebäude, a former Jesuit college, with a fine meeting hall.
Adjoining the Maltesergebäude is the Gothic church of St George, with stucco work by J. B. Zimmermann.

Municipal Museum

In Baustadelgasse, south-east of the Marktplatz, is the Municipal Museum (opened in 1989).

Mariahilf church

3km/2 miles north-east of Amberg, on a hill commanding extensive views, stands the pilgrimage church of Mariahilf, with stucco decoration by Giovanni Battista Carlone and ceiling paintings by Cosmas Damian Asam.

Ammersee   L 6

Land: Bavaria
Area: 47 sq.km/18 sq. miles

Situation and characteristics

The Ammersee lies 35km/22 miles south-west of Munich in the Alpine Foreland. It came into existence in the last ice age, when a mighty glacier thrust northward from the Loisach valley. The lake was originally almost twice its present size, but silt deposited by the river Ammer has steadily encroached on its northern and southern shores.
The lake, surrounded by forest-covered morainic hills, is 16km/10 miles long by 3–6km/2–4 miles across, with a depth of up to 81m/266ft. All round its shores are attractive resorts, with bathing stations and facilities for rowing and sailing, as well as for cycling. There is also good fishing (whitefish, vendace, pike-perch). In spite of these attractions the Ammersee is less crowded at weekends than the nearby Starnberger See (see entry).

Boat services

The larger places on the shores of the lake are linked by regular boat services.

Round the Ammersee

The road round the Ammersee runs at some distance from its shores for most of the way, with views of the lake only at the points indicated below.
It is recommended to include the Wörthsee and Pilsensee (both to the north-east of the Ammersee) in the round trip.

Inning

At the northern tip of the Ammersee, easily reached from Munich on A 96 and B 12, is Inning, with a beautiful Rococo church (1765). From here the route continues either

Andechs Monastery

Ceiling painting

direct to Herrsching or (taking in the Wörthsee and Pilsensee) via Seefeld. From the direct road, beyond Breitbrunn, there is a fine view of the whole of the Ammersee.

The popular resort of Herrsching lies in the Herrschinger Winkel, the only bay in the Ammersee, which here reaches its greatest breadth of 6km/4 miles.

Herrsching

A short distance south of Herrsching rises the "sacred hill" of Andechs (711m/2333ft), on which is the Benedictine monastery of Andechs, famed as a place of pilgrimage since 1455. The church (by J. B. Zimmermann, 1754) is in sumptuous Rococo style, with the much venerated 15th century image of the Virgin on the high altar. The monastery has its own brew-house.

Andechs

In Diessen, at the south end of the lake, is a masterpiece of Bavarian Rococo, the church belonging to a house of Augustinian canons, built by Johann Michael Fischer in 1732–39. Heimatmuseum.

Diessen

South of Diessen, at Raisting, is a ground station for satellite communications, with huge parabolic dishes. More than 2500 channels for telephone, telex and data transmission services provide links with some fifty different countries.

Raisting

Farther south the Ammergebirge and Benediktenwand form a backdrop to the beautiful lake scenery. In clear weather the view extends to the Zugspitze in the Wettersteingebirge.

The road north from Diessen soon turns away from the western shore of the Ammersee to return to Inning by way of the commandingly situated little town of Utting and Schöndorf with its 12th century "lake chapel".

Anklam
B 8

Land: Mecklenburg-West Pomerania
Altitude: 5m/16ft
Population: 20,300

Annaberg-Buchholz

Situation	The old Hanseatic town and port of Anklam lies on the south bank of the river Peene near the point where it flows into the Peenestrom, which runs north into the Baltic. Anklam was the birthplace of Otto Lilienthal (1848–96), one of the pioneers of flying, who after observing the flight of birds built what would now be called a hang-glider.

Sights

*St Mary's Church	The town is dominated by the 13th century Marienkirche (St Mary's Church), which has fine Gothic wall paintings.
Pulverturm	To the south of the Markt stands the 20m/65ft high Pulverturm (Powder Tower), a relic of the town's fortifications. On the south side of the Markt is the Lilienthal Memorial, erected in 1982.
Steintor	A prominent landmark is the 32m/105ft high Steintor (14th c.), with a stepped gable and blind arcading.
Museum	In Ellbogenstrasse, near the railway station, is the Otto von Lilienthal Museum, which illustrates the history and development of the town and the life and work of its most famous son.

Surroundings of Anklam

Relzow	To the north of the town, in Relzow, can be found the Rohrpott (now protected as a national monument), a half-timbered building with a thatched roof and a large open chimney.
Murchin	In the Seeholz in Murchin, 7km/4½ miles north of Anklam, can be seen a monument to the troops led by Ferdinand von Schill, a Prussian officer who tried to bring the Prussian king into Austria's war with Napoleon.
Spantekow	15km/9 miles south-west of Anklam is Spantekow, with a 16th century Renaissance-style moated castle in the form of an irregular square. Over the gate is a relief of the knight Ulrich von Schwerin and his wife.
Stolpe	10km/6 miles west of Anklam, on the Peene, lies the village of Stolpe, with an old ferryman's house, a smithy, the village church and the ruins of a Benedictine abbey founded in 1153.
Quilow	Quilow has a 16th century moated castle, a two-storey building in Renaissance style.

Annaberg-Buchholz   G 8

	Land: Saxony Altitude: 350–700m/1150–2300ft Population: 26,200
Situation	Annaberg-Buchholz, the economic and cultural centre of the eastern Erzgebirge, lies some 30km/20 miles south of Chemnitz on the slopes above the river Sehma, between the Schottenberg and the Pöhlberg.

Sights in Annaberg

*St Anne's Church	In Grosse Kirchgasse is the Late Gothic St-Annen-Kirche (St Anne's Church; 1499–1525), the largest hall-church in Saxony, built of the local gneiss. Notable features of the interior are the Bergaltar (Miners' Altar; by Hans Hesse, 1521), with representations of miners at work in the silver-mines; the Schöne Tür ("Beautiful Door"); the font (by Hans Witten, 1515); and the Münzeraltar (Coiners' Altar; by Christoph Walter, 1522).

Opposite the church, at Grosse Kirchgasse 16, is the Erzgebirge Museum, with exhibits and documents illustrating the history and economy of the Upper Erzgebirge and the town.

Erzgebirge Museum

In the Markt are the Town Hall (Rathaus; rebuilt 1751) and old burghers' houses. In Münzergasse is the Bergkirche (Miners' Church; 1502).

Town Hall

At Johannesgasse 23 is the Adam-Ries-Haus, home of the arithmetician Adam Ries, who was involved in mining, coining and land surveying around 1523.

Adam-Ries-Haus

Sights in Buchholz

The main feature of interest in Buchholz is St Catherine's Church, begun in 1504 but completed only in 1872–77.
In Katharinenstrasse is the Stiefelmühle, an old half-timbered building.

St Catherine's

Pöhlberg

To the east of Annaberg-Buchholz rises the Pöhlberg (831m/2727ft; restaurant, Pöhlberghaus, outlook tower). On the road to the summit, at 760m/2495ft, is a skiing area. There are two other skiing areas on the hill, the Andreasabfahrt (piste; ski-lift) at an old quarry (basalt columns known as the "Butter Kegs"), and another at 760m/2495ft (ski-jump).

Surroundings of Annaberg-Buchholz

In Frohnau, north of Buchholz, is the Frohnauer Hammer (Frohnau Forge) Museum of Technology, housed in a building which was originally a flour-mill and later was used as an oil-mill and from 1621 to 1904 for forging copper and iron.

Frohnauer Hammer

North-west of Annaberg-Buchholz are the Greifensteine, a group of hills (Kreuzfelsen, Gamsfelsen, Seekofel, Kleiner Brocken, Stülpnerwand, Turnerfelsen) much frequented by climbers. Rising to a height of 731m/2399ft, they are the remnants of a mighty granite massif. Greifenstein Museum; open-air theatre; Stülpnerhöhle and Ritterhöhle (old mining adits).

* Greifensteine

These two villages on the road to Marienberg have fine 15th century fortified churches.

Mauersberg Grossrückerswalde

Ansbach

I 6

Land: Bavaria
Altitude: 409m/1342ft
Population: 40,000

Ansbach, in the valley of the Rezat, is the chief town of Central Franconia and an important traffic junction. Once the residence of the Margraves of Brandenburg-Ansbach, it is famed for its Rococo architecture.

Situation and characteristics

* Margrave's Palace

On the edge of the old town, at the end of the Promenade, stands the former Margrave's Palace (Schloss), one of the most important 18th century palaces in Franconia, with 27 state apartments (Great Hall and Mirror Room in early Rococo style). It now houses the Bavarian State Collection of Ansbach faience and porcelain and the Staatsgalerie (17th and 18th century pictures).

63

Apolda

Hofgarten | South-east of the palace is the Hofgarten (Court Garden), with the 102m/335ft long Orangery (1726–34; now used for conferences and other events) and a stone commemorating the enigmatic foundling Kaspar Hauser who was stabbed to death here in 1833. (There is also a commemorative monument in Platenstrasse in the town centre).

Old Town

Gambertus Church | In Johann-Sebastian-Bach-Platz is the three-towered Gambertus Church (Protestant; occasional concerts and recitals), with the Schwanenritterkapelle (Chapel of the Swan Knight), a Romanesque crypt and the burial vault of the Margraves (25 sarcophagi). In Martin-Luther-Platz is the Late Gothic Johanniskirche (St John's Church; Protestant).

Markgrafenmuseum | In Schnaitbergstrasse, to the north of Martin-Luther-Platz, the Markgrafenmuseum (Margravial Museum), has material on the history of the town and a Kaspar Hauser Collection.

Synagogue | In Rosenbadstrasse, to the south of the town centre, is the Baroque Synagogue, which once served the town's large Jewish community.

Surroundings of Ansbach

Wolframs-Eschenbach | 20km/12½ miles south-east of Ansbach lies the little town of Wolframs-Eschenbach, still surrounded by its old walls and moat. This was the home town of the medieval poet Wolfram von Eschenbach (c. 1170–c. 1220), author of "Parsifal". There is a monument to him in the Markt.
Also in the Markt are the old half-timbered Town Hall (Rathaus), the former House of the Teutonic Order and the Liebfrauenmünster (Minster of Our Lady).

Apolda

G 7

Land: Thuringia
Altitude: 175m/574ft
Population: 28,700

Situation and characteristics | Apolda lies some 30km/20 miles east of Erfurt on the eastern edge of the Thuringian Basin. Its main industries are bell-founding and the manufacture of knitwear.

Sights

Town Hall | In the Markt stands the Town Hall (Rathaus), a two-storey Renaissance building (1558–59).

*Bell Museum and Knitwear Museum | The Bell Museum (Glockenmuseum) at Bahnhofstrasse 41 illustrates the history of bells over 3000 years. The collection includes Oriental, early European and Chinese bells as well as those made in Apolda.
The Knitwear Museum (Wirker- und Strickermuseum), at the same address, documents the development of the local textile industry down to the present day.

Kapellendorf

Situation: 7km/4½ miles SW | In Kapellendorf is a moated castle (12th–16th c.), one of the finest and best preserved buildings of its kind. Pentagonal in plan, it is a particularly fine example of a Gothic stronghold of the type built in flat country, defended by a water-filled moat. In 1806 it was the headquarters of the Prussian army commanded by Prince von Hohenlohe (skirmishes at Kapellendorf and Vierzehnheiligen; Prussian defeats at Jena and Auerstedt). On the nearby Sperlingsberg an outlook tower commemorates the Prussian and Saxon troops who fell in the battle.

Arnstadt

Land: Thuringia
Altitude: 285m/935ft
Population: 30,000

Arnstadt, 20km/12½ miles south of Erfurt, known as the "gateway to the Thuringian Forest", is famed for its associations with Johann Sebastian Bach and its rich art collections.

Situation and characteristics

Sights

In the Markt is the three-storey Renaissance Town Hall (Rathaus; 1581–83), showing the influence of Dutch models. On the east side of the square are galleries in Renaissance style, built in the late 16th century as a cloth hall.

Town Hall

Near the Town Hall, in the Haus zum Palmenbaum (Palm-Tree House), are a collection of mementoes of Bach's stay in Arnstadt and the Municipal Museum.
A modern monument to Bach (by Bernd Göbel, 1985) shows the composer as a young man.

Bach Memorial House
Municipal Museum

Johann Sebastian Bach was organist in this church (originally known as the New Church). In front of the church is the Hopfenbrunnen (Hop Fountain; 1573).

Bach Church

The Liebfrauenkirche (Church of Our Lady; 1180–1330) is the finest 13th century church in Thuringia after the cathedral in Naumburg (see entry). In a style transitional between Romanesque and Gothic, it contains numerous works of art, including a Late Gothic altar.

Liebfrauenkirche

In front of the church is an old paper-mill (16th c.; enlarged in 1633), a handsome half-timbered building.

Papermill

In the Schlossplatz stands the Neideckturm (Neideck Tower), all that remains of a once splendid Renaissance palace.

Neideckturm

The Neues Palais (New Palace), a Baroque building erected in 1728–32, now houses a museum, with the famous Mon Plaisir collection of 400 dolls, displayed in 84 rooms. The dolls, made by ladies of the court and by craftsmen at the behest of Princess Augusta Dorothea, give a faithful picture of life at a German princely court of the early 18th century and of the living and working conditions of ordinary people.
The palace also contains a valuable collection of Brussels tapestries of the Renaissance period, including the two famous "Monkey Tapestries", and a collection of East Asian and Meissen porcelain of the first half of the 18th century and Dorotheenthal faience. In the south wing is a Baroque porcelain cabinet.

Neues Palais
*Doll Collection

Surroundings of Arnstadt

North-west of Arnstadt, in a landscape reserve extending on both sides of the motorway, is the group of three castles known as the Drei Gleichen: the ruined Mühlburg (first mentioned in the records in 704), probably the oldest castle in Thuringia; Burg Gleichen, also ruined, the subject of many legends; and the Wachsenburg, now a hotel.

*Drei Gleichen

Arolsen

Land: Hesse
Altitude: 290m/950ft
Population: 17,000

Aschaffenburg

Situation and characteristics

The Baroque town of Arolsen lies 40km/25 miles west of Kassel in the Waldecker Land. Formerly the seat of the Princes of Waldeck and Pyrmont, it was from 1918 to 1929 the chief town of the Free State of Waldeck. Developed as a princely residence from the early 18th century onwards, Arolsen has preserved the aspect and atmosphere of the Baroque period, even though the original plan was never completely carried out. The town now has a variety of industry (electrical appliances, woodworking, synthetic materials, tools). Arolsen was the birthplace of the sculptor Christian Daniel Rauch (1777–1857) and the painter Wilhelm von Kaulbach (1804–74).

Sights

Town Church

In the Kirchplatz is the Town Church (Stadtkirche, 1735–87; Protestant), a building in late Baroque and early neo-classical style designed by the court architect L. J. Rothweil. The altar has marble figures of Faith, Love and Hope by C. D. Rauch.

At No. 6 in Rauchstrasse, which opens off the Kirchplatz, can be seen the birthplace of C. D. Rauch (museum). In Kaulbachstrasse, which crosses Schlosstrasse, is the home of the Kaulbach family of artists (No. 3), now also a museum, devoted particularly to the work of the painter Wilhelm von Kaulbach.

Palais Schreiber

In the Baroque Palais Schreiber (1717), at Schloss-strasse 24, is an exhibition illustrating with the help of models the building of the Baroque town under the direction of L. J. Rothweil. The palace has an imposing Great Hall.

*Schloss

On the east side of the old town stands the Schloss (Palace), a harmoniously proportioned building built between 1710 and 1729 on the model of Versailles, with two wings projecting from the main block. Notable features of the interior are the Steinerner Saal (Stone Hall), with stucco decoration, the staircase hall and the Alhambra Room. To the south and south-east of the palace are various offices (stables, barn). Beyond the beautiful Grosse Allee (Grand Avenue; 1676) is the Neues Schloss (New Palace), built between 1764 and 1778 and remodelled in neo-classical style in 1853.

Twiste Lake

In the eastern district of Wetterburg lies a lake created by the damming of the river Twiste, now a popular recreation area (bathing stations, water-skiing, wind-surfing, rowing, sports grounds, endurance sport centre).

Arolsen-Landau

Wasserkunst

In the south-eastern district of Landau (Schloss; Early Gothic church), beyond the lake, is the Wasserkunst, a waterworks established in 1535 which continued to operate until 1981.

Mengeringhausen

The south-western district of Mengeringhausen has many old half-timbered buildings. Particularly notable are a 14th century moated castle, the handsome Town Hall and the birthplace of the hymn-writer Philipp Nicolai (1556–1606).

Aschaffenburg   H 4

Land: Bavaria
Altitude: 130m/427ft
Population: 59,000

Situation and characteristics

Aschaffenburg lies in Lower Franconia on the hilly right bank of the Main, on the edge of the Spessart (see entry). The old town is dominated by the massive bulk of the Renaissance palace once occupied by the Electors of Mainz.

*Schloss Johannisburg

On the west side of the old town, on the banks of the Main, stands Schloss Johannisburg (1605–14), a palace in late Renaissance style which was a subsidiary residence, after Mainz itself, of the Electors of Mainz. It now houses the State Art Gallery (Dutch and early German painting), the Palace Museum and the Palace Library. Magnificent state apartments.

Museums

North-west of the palace are the Palace Gardens (Schlossgarten), beyond which is the Pompejanum, a reproduction (1842–49) of the Villa of Castor and Pollux in Pompeii; fine view of the Main.

Schlossgarten

*Stiftskirche

From the palace the Schlossgasse runs south-east to the Stiftskirche, the collegiate church of SS Peter and Alexander (12th and 13th c.). The church contains a number of important works of art, including a "Lamentation" by Matthias Grünewald. Late Romanesque cloister. In the former chapterhouse is the Stiftsmuseum (church art, collection of faience).

To the east of the Stiftskirche, in Wermbachstrasse, is the Schönborner Hof, now housing the Natural History Museum and an information centre on the Czech town of Kraslice, with which Aschaffenburg is twinned.

Schönborner Hof

From the Town Hall Freihofgasse and Sandgasse run east. At the near end of Würzburgerstrasse, the continuation of Sandgasse, is the Sandkirche, a Rococo church built in 1756 (sumptuous interior; ceiling painting, restored 1986). Just north of this is Schöntal Park, laid out in 1780.

Sandkirche
Schöntal

On the southern outskirts of the town, at Obernauerstrasse 25, is the Rosso Bianco Collection, with numerous racing cars, rally cars and veteran and vintage cars.

**Racing Car Museum

Schloss Johannisburg

Surroundings of Aschaffenburg

*Schönbusch | 3.5km/2 miles south-west of Aschaffenburg we come to Schönbusch, a park landscaped in the English style, with a little neo-classical palace, a lake and various pavilions and restaurants.

*Mespelbrunn | 20km/12½ miles south-east of Aschaffenburg, picturesquely situated in a side valley of the Elsava, stands the moated castle of Mespelbrunn, which is open to the public. The ancestral home of the Echter family, it passed in 1665 to the Counts of Ingelheim-Echter.

Attendorn   F 3

Land: North Rhine-Westphalia
Altitude: 255m/837ft
Population: 22,000

Situation and characteristics | The old Hanseatic town of Attendorn lies near the Biggesee in the southern Sauerland, between the Rothaargebirge and the Ebbegebirge. The town was devastated by fire on six occasions during the 18th century, and in consequences most of its historic buildings date from after 1783.

Sights

District Museum | The Old Town Hall (14th c.) in the Alter Markt now houses the District Museum (geology, prehistory, history of the town, hunting collection, collection of tin figures). Facing it, to the north, is the parish church of St John the Baptist (14th c.), the "cathedral of the Sauerland".
There are some remains of the old fortifications, particularly on the north side of the old town (Pulverturm, Bieketurm).

Fire Service Museum | South-west of the town centre, at St-Ursula-Strasse 5, is the Fire Service Museum (Feuerwehrmuseum), opened in 1986. Open May–Oct. on second Sat. in month.

Attahöhle | East of the town on the Finnentrop road is the Attahöhle, a stalactitic cave discovered in 1907 (open to the public).

Schnellenberg | Above the town to the south-east is Burg Schnellenberg, a large 17th century castle which is now a hotel. Renaissance chapel; Castle Museum (open only in summer).

Biggesee

South-west of Attendorn lies the Biggesee, a lake formed in 1964 by the construction of a 640m/700yd long dam on the river Bigge. The lake, which is spanned by two two-level bridges for road and rail traffic, and the neighbouring Listersee are now a popular recreation area (boat services).

Elspe

Elspe Festival | Elspe, 20km/12½ miles north-east of Attendorn, is famed for the Karl May Festival (named after the popular 19th century author of adventure stories), which is held annually in June and July; open-air theatre.

Augsburg   K–L 6

Land: Bavaria
Altitude: 496m/1627ft
Population: 249,000

Augsburg, the third largest city in Bavaria (after Munich and Nürnberg), lies north of the Lechfeld at the confluence of the Wertach and the Lech. This ancient and famous imperial city, home of the two great medieval merchant dynasties of the Fuggers and the Welsers, is now the chief town of the administrative region of Bavarian Swabia (Bayerisch-Schwaben).

In Roman times Augsburg was connected with Verona by the Via Claudia, and its favourable situation promoted the development of commerce and industry. Its present-day industries include large textile and engineering firms. The city has a very active cultural life, and the new University of Augsburg opened its doors in 1970. One of the most popular tourist routes in Germany, the Romantic Highway (Romantische Strasse: see entry), runs from the Main valley via Augsburg to Füssen on the Austrian frontier.

Situation and characteristics

*Cathedral

From the Rathausplatz Karolinenstrasse and the Hoher Weg lead north to the Cathedral (Dom; 9th–14th c.). The bronze doors of the south aisle (11th c.) have 35 relief panels. The five windows on the south side of the nave have the

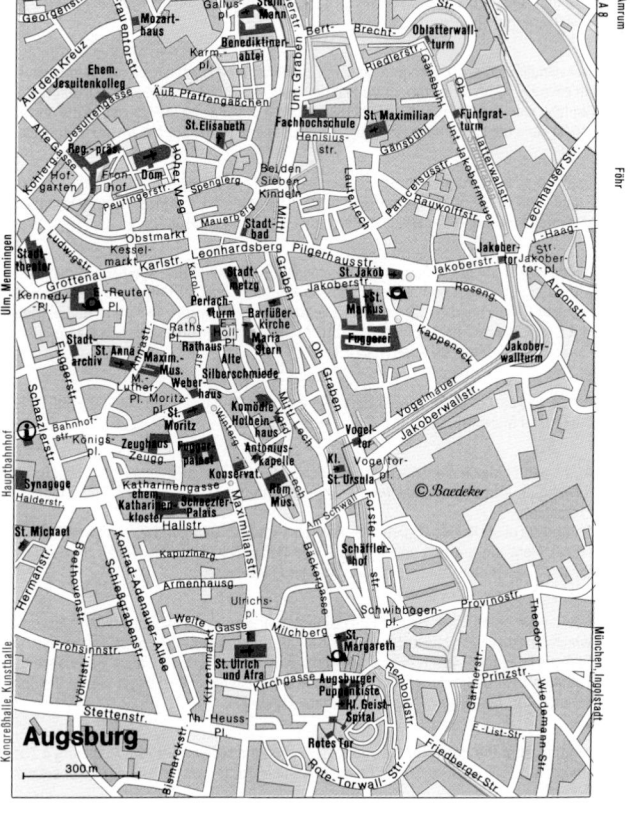

oldest figural stained glass in Germany, probably dating from before 1100. Four of the side altars have altarpieces by Hans Holbein the Elder.

Diesel House Mozart House	To the east of the Cathedral, in Springergässchen, can be seen a house once occupied by Rudolf Diesel (1858–1913), inventor of the diesel engine. North of the Cathedral, in Frauentorstrasse, is the Mozart House, birthplace of Leopold Mozart, the composer's father (memorial museum).

Central Area

* Town Hall	In the centre of the town, the main axis of which is Karolinenstrasse/Maximilianstrasse, stands the Town Hall (Rathaus; 1615–20), a massive Renaissance building designed by the municipal architect, Elias Holl. Nearby are the 78m/256ft high Perlachturm (panoramic views) and the Augustus Fountain (1589–94).
Fuggerei	To the east of the Rathausplatz, in the Jakobusvorstadt, is the Fuggerei, a little "town within the town", with its own four gates, founded by the Fugger family in 1519 to provide homes for poor citizens of Augsburg. This is the oldest social housing scheme in the world, and the occupants still pay an annual rent of only 1 Rhenish guilder (= DM1.71) for a 2½-roomed house.
Maximilianstrasse	In Maximilianstrasse (the beginning of the old Roman road between Germany and Italy), which runs south from the Town Hall, is the Gothic St-Moritz-Kirche (St Maurice's Church), with the Mercury Fountain 1599) in front of it. Facing the church, to the north, can be seen the Weberhaus (Weavers' House), one of Augsburg's many guild-houses.
Fugger House	To the south is the Fugger House (Fuggerpalast; 1512–15), the town house of the Princes Fugger von Babenhausen, who rose in the 15th and 16th centuries from apprentice weavers to the world's wealthiest merchants (Damenhof, 1516).
* Schaezler-Palais	A little way south of the Fugger House stands the Schaezler-Palais, a Rococo mansion with a large banqueting hall, now housing the Municipal Art Collection (the German Baroque Gallery) and the State Gallery (early German masters, including Holbein the Elder, Hans Burgkmair the Elder and Albrecht Dürer). In front of the palace is the Hercules Fountain (by Adriaen de Vries, 1602).
Roman Museum	A little way east of the Schaezler-Palais, in a former Dominican church (16th–18th c.) is the Roman Museum.
* St Ulrich's Minster	At the end of Maximilianstrasse is St Ulrich's Minster (SS Ulrich and Afra; 1500; R.C.), forming an attractive architectural ensemble with the little St Ulrich's Church (1458; Protestant). South-east of St Ulrich's Church rises the Rotes Tor (Red Gate), with a tower by Elias Holl (1622). Here too are two water towers, the Heilig-Geist-Hospital (1631), an open-air theatre and a puppet theatre, the Augsburger Puppenkiste.
* Maximilian Museum St Anne's Church	South-west of the Town Hall, in Philippine-Welser-Strasse, is the Maximilian Museum, which offers a vivid picture of the history, art and culture of Augsburg. In Annastrasse is St Anne's Church (14th–17th c.; Protestant), with the Lutherhöfle, which was visited by Luther in 1518. In the church can be seen the burial chapel of the Fugger family, the first considerable Renaissance work in Germany (1509–12).
Zoo Botanic Garden	South-east of the Rotes Tor (see above), beyond the railway line, are Augsburg's Zoo (more than 1900 animals) and its beautiful Botanic Garden, on the fringes of Siebentisch Forest.

Augustusburg

See Chemnitz, Surroundings

Aurich   C 3

Land: Lower Saxony
Altitude: 6m/20ft
Population: 35,000

Aurich lies on the Ems-Jade Canal, some 25km/15 miles from the East Frisian coast. Its origins go back to around 1200, and for centuries it was the chief place in East Friesland. Peat is still cut in the surrounding moorlands.   Situation and characteristics

South-west of the Schloss, on the Ems-Jade Canal, is the town's harbour, the starting-point of cruises in small boats on the canal.   Canal cruises

Sights

In the centre of the town lies the Marktplatz, first laid out in 1517. On the west side of the square is the Baroque Knodtsches Haus, now occupied by a school.   Marktplatz

In Burgstrasse, to the south of the Marktplatz, are other Baroque gabled house-fronts and the Historical Museum, housed in the former chancery of the Counts and Princes of East Friesland.   Historical Museum

Farther west is the Lambertshof, with the Lambertikirche (St Lambert's Church; 1832–35), which has a carved Gothic altar from Antwerp (c. 1510).   Lambertshof

To the south-west of the town centre stands the Schloss, a palace built in 1851–55 on the foundations of a much older castle and now occupied by government offices. Attached to the Schloss are the court stables (Marstall; 1732).   Schloss

To the east of the Schloss extends the Georgswall, on which are the low Pingelhus, whose bell used to announce the departure of ships, and the meeting-place of the East Frisian Landschaft (a rural credit association established to assist nobles ruined by the Seven Years' War); rebuilt around 1900 in Renaissance style, it has a sumptuously appointed interior (portraits of Counts and Princes of East Friesland).   Pingelhus East Frisian Landschaft

To the west of the Schloss is the Stiftsmühle, a windmill which is still in working order; Mill Museum.   Stiftsmühle

Outside the town, to the north, is Wallinghausen, with the Gulfhof, which now houses a Coach Museum.   Coach Museum

Baden-Baden   K 3

Land: Baden-Württemberg
Altitude: 183m/600ft
Population: 50,000

Baden-Baden, situated in the Oos basin on the western slopes of the northern Black Forest, within the Upper Rhine plain, is a very popular international health resort, thanks to its favourable situation, its mild climate and its radioactive brine springs (temperature 68°C/154°F; 800,000 litres/176,000 gallons daily). The incorporation of the little town of Steinbach into Baden-Baden has also made it a wine-producing town.
The Schwarzwald-Hochstrasse (Black Forest Ridgeway: see Black Forest) skirts the extensive forests within the municipal boundaries.   Situation and characteristics

Kurgarten

The hub of fashionable life in Baden-Baden is the Kurgarten, laid out in front of the Kurhaus (spa establishment) built by Friedrich Weinbrenner in 1821–24 (café-restaurant, casino; conducted tours). The main road is now carried under the gardens in a tunnel. In the Kurpark, north of the Kurhaus, is the Trinkhalle or Pump Room (frescoes illustrating Black Forest legends). On the Michaelsberg, above the Trinkhalle to the north-west, is the Greek-Romanian Chapel (views), built by Leo von Klenze in 1863–66, with the tombs of the Stourdza boyar family. To the south of the Kurhaus are the Little Theatre and the Kunsthalle. To the east, beyond the Oos, are the Haus des Kurgastes ("Visitors' House") and the Kongresshaus (Congress Centre).

*Lichtentaler Allee — From the Kunsthalle the famous Lichtentaler Allee runs south along the left bank of the Oos, passing tennis courts, the Bertholdbad (indoor and outdoor pools) and the Gönne-ranlage (gardens in Art Nouveau style), to the Cistercian abbey of Lichtental (founded 1245), with the Princes' Chapel. Near the abbey is the Brahms House, in which the composer lived between 1865 and 1874.

Old Town

The closely packed old town is built on the slopes of the Schlossberg. Half way up is the Gothic Stiftskirche (R.C.), with the tomb of Margrave Ludwig Wilhelm, known as "Türkenlouis" (d. 1707), and a sandstone crucifix by Nicholas of Leyden (1467).

Thermal springs — To the north-east, on the slopes of the Schlossberg, are the thermal springs, which supply the Friedrichsbad (1869–77). In the Römerplatz can be seen the 17th century Convent of the Holy Sepulchre (Kloster zum Heiligen Grab). Under the square are the remains of Roman baths.

Toy Museum — In Gernsbacherstrasse is the Toy Museum (Spielzeugmuseum), a private collection.

*Caracalla Baths — To the east are the Caracalla Baths (Caracalla-Thermen; water up to 69°C/156°F), a modern bathing and therapy centre with two circular pools and a "mushroom fountain" in the centre.

Paradies — To the south of the Caracalla Baths is the Paradies ("Paradise"), a complex of fountains and cascades constructed in 1925.

Neues Schloss

On top of the hill (access road), at a height of 212m/696ft, stands the Neues Schloss (New Castle), built by Margrave Christoph I in 1479 and occasionally used as a residence by the former grand-ducal family, now housing the Zähringen Museum. In the old court stables (Marstall) is a museum on the history of the town.

Surroundings of Baden-Baden

Merkur — 4km/2½ miles east rises Merkur (670m/2198ft; cableway), a hill affording magnificent views, with a nature trail and waymarked footpaths.

Hohenbaden — 4.5km/3 miles north is the Altes Schloss (Old Castle) of Hohenbaden (403m/1322ft), a former residence of the Margraves of Baden, now in ruins. Fine views from the tower. Nearby lies the Battertfelsen nature reserve (climbing school).

Badenweiler   L 3

Land: Baden-Württemberg
Altitude: 450m/1475ft
Population: 3500

Badenweiler, a much frequented spa and climatic resort, lies on the south-western edge of the Black Forest (see entry), commandingly situated on a terrace 210m/689ft above the Upper Rhine plain. The town is closed to through traffic.

The Town

Above the town to the west is the Schlossberg, with the ruins of a castle of the Dukes of Zähringen, built in the 11th century and destroyed in 1678 (view). On the slopes of the hill are the Kurpark, with subtropical vegetation, and the Kurhaus (1972), built on terraces on the hillside. To the east of the park can be seen the remains of Roman baths (2nd and 3rd c. A.D.). Nearby is the Markgrafenbad (Margrave's Baths; thermal water, indoor and outdoor pools, treatment facilities).
On the northern outskirts of the town is a recreational open-air swimming pool with water chutes, white-water channels, play areas, sports facilities, etc.

*Kurpark

Ascent of the Belchen

From Badenweiler take the road which runs east along the Klemmbach to Wembach, and from there follow B 317 north to Schönau. 1.5km/1 mile beyond this the road to the Belchen branches off on the left. It climbs at a moderate gradient for 11.5km/7 miles (fine views) to the Belchenhaus, from which it is a 10 minutes' climb on foot to the summit (1414m/4639ft; superb panoramic views).

Ballenstedt   F 6

Land: Saxony-Anhalt
Altitude: 220m/722ft
Population: 8600

The little town of Ballenstedt, once the residence of the Princes of Anhalt-Bernburg, lies some 70km/45 miles north-west of Halle on the northern edge of the Lower Harz. With its many tourist attractions, it is now a popular holiday resort.

Situation and characteristics

Schloss

The town's principal attraction is the Schlossberg, with the Schloss, the Baroque ducal palace. The palace occupies the site of a religious house founded in the 11th century which became a Benedictine abbey in 1123 and was converted into a residence for the Princes of Anhalt in the 16th and 17th centuries. Of the monastic church there remain the west end and part of the crypt, now incorporated in the north wing of the palace, and there are also remains of the Romanesque conventual buildings in the west wing. In the south wing is the Roman Room, with an 18th century wall covering of painted linen depicting Roman ruins.

On one side of the open courtyard is the palace theatre, in neo-classical style (1788). Among those associated with the theatre were Franz Liszt and Albert Lortzing.

Theatre

Below the palace, to the south, are the Court Stables (Marstall; 1821). A short distance away, in a very handsome mansard-roofed house (1765) at Wilhelm-Pieck-Allee 37, is the Heimatmuseum (finds from Burg Anhalt, etc.).

Court Stables Museum

The Schlosspark (area 52 hectares/130 acres) is famed for its impressive fountains and cascades (designed in their final form by P. J. Lenné in the second half of the 18th century). At the south-west corner of the park, on the Röhrkopf, stands a hunting lodge of 1770.

Schlosspark

Old Town

The old town has numerous two-storey half-timbered houses of the 17th and 18th centuries and remains of the 16th century fortifications, with three towers (Oberturm,

Roseburg Park, Ballenstedt

Unterturm, Marktturm). A particularly fine example of half-timbering is the Old Town Hall (Altes Rathaus; 1683), a plain two-storey building which is now an old people's home.

The Oberhof is a 16th century Renaissance mansion with two wings projecting from the main block.

The Late Gothic parish church of St Nicholas (15th c.) was burned down in 1498, leaving only the tower still standing, but was subsequently rebuilt.

Surroundings of Ballenstedt

Roseburg

North-west of the town is the Roseburg, with remains of the original castle of that name (mentioned in the records in 964) and the little park laid out between 1907 and 1925 by the Berlin architect B. Sehring. In the park are several towers and smaller structures, fountains, cascades and bridges.

Ermsleben

7km/4½ miles north-east of Ballenstedt is Ermsleben, with the church of St Sixtus (remains of Romanesque tower, otherwise mainly Gothic and Baroque). In the Konrads-burg district can be found remains (choir and crypt) of a Late Romanesque Benedictine abbey church.

Aschersleben

Aschersleben (14km/9 miles north-east on B 185) has preserved large sections of its old town walls, with towers, the outer ward and the moat, as well as two outworks, the Westdorfer Warte and the Stassfurter Warte. A former freemasons' lodge at Markt 21 (Zu den drei Kleeblättern, the House of the Three Clover-Leaves) is now occupied by the Heimatmuseum. Of the Renaissance burghers' houses in the town some are particularly notable for their elaborately decorated oriels (Krukmannsches Haus, in Markt; Über den Steinen 5; Hohe Strasse 7).

Baltic Coast   A 5 – B 9

Länder: Schleswig-Holstein, Mecklenburg-West Pomerania

The Baltic coastline of Germany extends for some 720km/450 miles from Flensburg to
the island of Usedom. Bights and fjord-like inlets penetrate far inland – the Flensburger
Förde, the Schlei, Eckernförde Bay, the Kieler Förde, Lübeck Bay, Wismar Bay, the Saaler
Bodden, the Greifswalder Bodden, the Stettiner Haff. The islands of Fehmarn, Rügen and
Usedom are linked with the mainland by bridges.

The Baltic is linked with the North Sea only by the Skagerrak and Kattegat, so that there is   Ecology
little exchange of waters between the two seas. The fresh water flowing into the Baltic
from the mainland gives it a considerably lower salt content than other seas. The inflow
of polluted river water, however, has led to a considerable concentration of harmful
substances in the Baltic and endangered its ecological system. Efforts have been made
to halt this development, but so far it has not been possible to achieve a consensus
between the states bordering the Baltic on a programme of action.

In contrast to the treeless fen landscapes of the North Sea coast (see entry), much of the   Landscape
Baltic coast is attractively wooded (mostly beech forests). Characteristic features of the
eastern part of the coast are the shallow *bodden* – depressions carved out by glaciers
during the Ice Age which over the millennia have been drowned by the gradual rise in sea
level. The Baltic has scarcely any tides.

Flensburg to Lübeck Bay

The string of resorts along the Baltic coast begins with Glücksburg on the Flensburger
Förde, which also has a picturesque moated castle.
In Eckernförde Bay are the Damp 2000 holiday centre, Eckernförde itself and Schwede-
neck with its sandy beaches at Dänisch Nienhof and Surendorf.
In the Kieler Förde are Schilksee with its Olympiahafen and the neighbouring little resort
of Strande, the sailing centre of Maria Wendtorf, Laboe (see Kiel, Surroundings) and
Heikendorf.
Below the steep wooded slopes at Hohwacht are attractive bathing beaches. At Olden-
burg is the Weissenhäuser Strand holiday centre.

On the island of Fehmarn there is a beautiful stretch of beach at Burg-Südstrand. On the   Fehmarn
west coast, in the Wallnau bird sanctuary, there are a number of natural beaches. On the
mainland opposite Fehmarn lies the Heiligenhafen holiday centre, with beaches on
the Steinwarder peninsula.

In Lübeck Bay are a whole series of resorts – Dahme, Kellenhusen, Grömitz, Rettin and
Pelzerhaken (within the territory of Neustadt in Holstein), Sierksdorf (with the Hansaland
leisure park), Haffkrug-Scharbeutz, Timmendorfer Strand and the fashionable resort of
Travemünde.

See also Lübeck, Kiel, Schleswig, Flensburg and Holsteinische Schweiz

Wismar Bay

In Wismar Bay, between the morainic hills of the Klützer Winkel in the west (Heidberg,
near Grevesmühlen, 113m/371ft; Hoher Schönberg, 90m/295ft) and Kühlung in the east
(Diedrichshagener Berge, 130m/425ft), are not only the old Hanseatic town of Wismar
(see entry) but a number of much frequented bathing areas. The most westerly is at
Boltenhagen, which became popular in the 19th century. More recently the shallow
Wohlenberger Wiek has come into favour. The Salzhaff at Rerik is popular with water
sports enthusiasts.

See Wismar, Surroundings   Island of Poel

Mecklenburg Bay

On the open coast of Mecklenburg Bay, just to the east of Wismar Bay, are two resorts   Kühlungsborn
lying close together: Kühlungsborn (pop. 8000), with the second highest number of   Heiligendamm

visitors among the resorts on the Baltic coast, and Heiligendamm, the oldest German seaside resort, founded in 1793 near Doberan, then the summer residence of the Dukes of Mecklenburg.

Bad Doberan   See Rostock, Surroundings

Warnemünde   See Rostock, Surroundings

*Fischland–Darss–Zingst

The Fischland–Darss–Zingst peninsula (see Darss), which lies between a string of *bodden* to the west (Ribnitzer See, Saaler Bodden, Bodstedter Bodden, Barther Bodden and Grabow) and the open Baltic, is one of the most unspoiled areas of natural scenery on the Baltic coast. It can be reached by way of Ribnitz-Damgarten or Barth.

Strelasund

The Strelasund, which separates Rügen from the mainland, links the western chain of *bodden* with the Greifswalder Bodden, which in turn is linked by the Peenestrom with the Achterwasser and Oderhaff.

The Greifswalder Bodden, which is separated from the open sea by an underwater sill with the little islands of Ruden and Greifswalder Oie, is the principal approach to the old Hanseatic town of Stralsund (see entry).

Greifswalder Bodden

Near the southernmost tip of the Greifswalder Bodden, the Dänische Wiek, is the town of Greifswald (see entry), founded at some time before 1248 by monks from the Cistercian monastery of Eldena.

The principal resorts on the Greifswalder Bodden are Lubmin and Loissin as well as several on the Mönchgut peninsula on Rügen.

Rügen (see entry) is the largest of the islands lying off the coast here.

Off Rügen to the west, serving as a kind of breakwater, is the island of Hiddensee.

The island of Usedom (see entry) is smaller than Rügen, but scarcely inferior to it in scenic beauty.

Bamberg   H 6

Land: Bavaria
Altitude: 231–386m/758–1266ft
Population: 70,000

Situation and characteristics

Bamberg, the old imperial and episcopal city and the most important town in Upper Franconia, lies on the western edge of a wide basin in the valley of the Regnitz, here divided into two arms, which flows into the Main 7km/4½ miles downstream. The oldest part is the episcopal town on the high west bank of the left arm of the river, with the Cathedral and the old Benedictine abbey of Michaelsberg. The "Bürgerstadt" (borough) which grew up from the 12th century onwards lies on the flat ground between the two arms of the Regnitz. Bamberg is a university town, and its symphony orchestra has an international reputation. The town has a river port on the Rhine–Main–Danube Canal. The industrial zone (principally engineering, textiles, electrical apparatus and appliances) lies to the east of the town. Bamberg also has numerous breweries; a local speciality is Rauchbier (to be had at the brewery's own Schenkerla bar and elsewhere in the town).

The Bürgerstadt

In the centre of the Bürgerstadt, the borough which grew up between the two arms of the Regnitz, is the long Grüner Markt (pedestrian zone), with the Baroque church of St Martin

Old Town Hall   *Alte Hofhaltung*

(1686–91) and, to the north of this, the New Town Hall (Neues Rathaus; 1733–36). Nearby, at Fleischstrasse 2, is the well-stocked Natural History Museum (Naturkunde-Museum).

South of the Grüner Markt by way of the Obstmarkt is the Obere Brücke (Upper Bridge), with an attractive views to the right of Klein-Venedig (Little Venice; old fishermen's houses). In the middle of the bridge is the Old Town Hall (Altes Rathaus; rebuilt by J. M. Küchel in 1744–56). Its unusual situation reflects the fact that it served both the Bürgerstadt and the episcopal town on their different sides of the river.   *Old Town Hall*

On the island in the Regnitz, to the south of the Old Town Hall, stands the old castle of Geyersworth (1585–87), once a stronghold of the Prince-Bishops.   Schloss Geyersworth
At Schillerplatz 26 is the E.-T.-A.-Hoffman-Haus, in which the writer lived from 1809 to 1813. On the south-east side of the town centre is the Karl May Museum, commemorating the 19th century writer of adventure stories.

The Episcopal Town

In the commanding Domplatz stands the early 13th century Cathedral (Dom) with its four   ** Cathedral
towers. On the north side is the Fürstentor (Prince's Doorway), the principal entrance, with figures of apostles and prophets and a relief of the Last Judgment in the tympanum. On the south side of the east choir is the Adamspforte (Adam's Doorway; statues now in the Diocesan Museum), on the north side the Marienpforte or Gnadenpforte (Virgin's Doorway), with the Cathedral's oldest sculpture (c. 1210).

In the interior of the Cathedral, in front of the east choir (Georgenchor, St George's   ** Bamberger Reiter
Choir), is the tomb (by Tilman Riemenschneider, 1499–1513) of the Emperor Henry II (d. 1024) and his wife Kunigunde (d. 1039). On the left-hand pier of the choir is the figure of the famous Bamberger Reiter or Bamberg Horseman (c. 1240), who is traditionally identified as King Stephen of Hungary (St Stephen), Henry's brother-in-law. On the

77

outside of the stone choir screen are figures of the twelve apostles and twelve prophets; on a pillar between the prophets are Mary and Elizabeth; and on the side with the apostles are allegorical figures of Church and Synagogue (by the sculptor who carved the Horseman). In the east crypt is the modern sandstone sarcophagus of King Conrad III (d. 1152 in Bamberg). In the west choir (St Peter's Choir) can be seen the marble tomb of Pope Clement II (d. 1047), previously Bishop of Bamberg – the only Papal tomb in Germany (c. 1235). On the west wall of the south transept is the Bamberg Altar (1520–23), by Veit Stoss.

Diocesan Museum	The Diocesan Museum, in the chapterhouse, contains the rich cathedral treasury, precious vestments (including Henry II's imperial robes) and the statues from the Adamspforte.
*Alte Hofhaltung	On the west side of the Domplatz is the Alte Hofhaltung or Alte Residenz, one of the finest creations of the German Renaissance, built as the Bishop's palace in 1571–76. It now houses the Historical Museum (applied and decorative art, etc.). The Calderón Festival is held in the courtyard.
*Neue Residenz	On the north side of the square stands the Neue Residenz (1695–1704), J. L. Dientzenhofer's greatest work, with the Prince-Bishop's residential apartments, the Gallery of German Art (Heisterbach Altar; painting of the 15th–18th c.) and the State Library (temporary special exhibitions). In the courtyard is a beautiful rose-garden with a magnificent view.
*Michaelsberg	On top of the hill is the former Benedictine abbey of Michaelsberg (1009–1803), with St Michael's Church (12th–15th c.; ceiling paintings of medicinal herbs). To the north and west of the church are the new abbey buildings erected by J. L. Dientzenhofer (1696–1702) and Balthasar Neumann (1742).
Upper Parish Church	On the Kaulberg, in the southern part of the old town, stands the Upper Parish Church (Obere Pfarrkirche), Bamberg's finest Gothic building (14th–15th c.). A little way east is the Böttingerhaus, a distinguished Baroque building of 1707–13. Beyond this, on the banks of the Regnitz, is Concordia, a handsome Baroque palace of 1716–22.
Carmelite Convent	South-west of the Upper Parish Church is the Carmelite Convent (Karmelitenkloster; 12th c., altered about 1700), with a beautiful Late Romanesque cloister.

Surroundings of Bamberg

*Pommersfelden	Schloss Pommersfelden (Weissenstein; 20km/12½ miles south-west) is a sumptuous Baroque palace by J. L. Dientzenhofer (1711–18), with a famous staircase hall and a picture gallery.

Barth

See Darss

Bautzen   F 9

Land: Saxony
Altitude: 219m/719ft
Population: 51,700

Situation and characteristics	Bautzen (in Sorbian Budysin), the thousand-year-old chief town of Upper Lusatia, lies on a granite plateau on the upper course of the Spree, some 50km/30 miles east of Dresden. The imposing silhouette of this many-towered town, particularly on the side facing the Spree, reflects its long history. Bautzen is now the principal centre of Sorbian cultural and political life.

Hauptmarkt

The town's traditional centre is the Hauptmarkt, with seven streets and lanes opening off it. On the north side of the square is the Town Hall (Rathaus; 1729–32), a three-storey Baroque building incorporating some Gothic work.
On the east and west sides of the square are a number of patrician houses (Nos. 6, 7, 8).

Town Hall

At the corner of the Hauptmarkt and Innere Lauenstrasse stands the Gewandhaus (Cloth Hall), in neo-Renaissance style (1882–83), with a Ratskeller of 1472.

Gewandhaus

There are numbers of handsome burghers' houses in the streets opening off the Hauptmarkt, particularly in Reichenstrasse (Nos. 4, 5, 12).
The Reichenturm, a tower leaning 1.44m/4ft 9in off the vertical (1490–92), has a Baroque top and lantern added in 1715–18; on it is a monument to Emperor Rudolph II (1577).

Reichenstrasse

South of the Reichenturm, at Kornmarkt 1, is the Museum on the History of Bautzen (Stadtmuseum).

Museum

There are a number of fine burghers' houses in Innere Lauenstrasse (Nos. 2, 6, 8, 10). Also in this street is the Lauenturm (1400–03), with a Baroque top and lantern of 1739.

Innere Lauenstrasse

On the north side of the Town Hall lies the Fleischmarkt, with a monument to Elector Johann Georg I of Saxony (1865). On the east side of the square are two notable Renaissance houses (Nos. 2 and 4) and a number of Baroque houses.

Fleischmarkt

*Cathedral

The Fleischmarkt is dominated by the Cathedral (Dom) of St Peter, a Gothic hall-church (1213–1497) with a tower almost 85m/280ft high and a ground-plan which is curiously off the straight. It is now Co-Cathedral of the diocese of Dresden-Meissen.
The Cathedral has been used in common by Catholics and Protestants since 1524. The most notable features of the Catholic part (the choir) are the high altar (by G. Fossati, 1722–24), with an altarpiece ("Peter receiving the keys") by G. A. Pellegrini, sandstone sculpture by B. Thomae, a pupil of Balthasar Permoser, and a life-size crucifix by Permoser himself (1714). Of particular interest in the Protestant part are the Fürstenloge (the Elector's box; 1673–74) and the reredos (1644).

The Domstift (Chapterhouse) is a horseshoe-shaped Baroque building (1683) with the coat of arms of the cathedral chapter over the main entrance (1755).

Domstift

Burgstadt

The street called An der Petrikirche and Schloss-strasse, with the old House of the Estates (Ständehaus; 1668) and the Castle Pharmacy (Schlossapotheke; 1699), lead into the Burgstadt ("Castle Town"), the oldest part of the town, which grew up around the castle in Bautzen's early days in an entirely unregulated way – unlike the planned layout around the Hauptmarkt.

On the edge of the Burgstadt can be seen the ruins of the Mönchskirche (Monks' Church; c. 1300; destroyed by fire 1598), all that remains of the monastery which once stood here.

Mönchskirche

Schloss Ortenburg

The thousand-year-old castle of Ortenburg, once the seat of the royal governor of Lusatia, has lost much of its architectural unity as a result of destruction during the Thirty Years' War and rebuilding at various times during its history. The tower (1486) at the north-east entrance dates from a rebuilding in the Late Gothic period; it bears a seated figure of King Matthias Corvinus of Hungary (of which Lusatia was a province from 1469 to 1490).
The massive main block of the castle, also Late Gothic, was altered in the mid 17th century and embellished with three Renaissance gables in 1698. On the first floor is the

Audience Chamber, with fine figural stucco decoration on the ceiling (by Vietti and Comotan, 1662).

Sorbian Museum

In one of the buildings within the castle is the Museum on the History and Culture of the Sorbs (Museum für Geschichte und Kultur der Sorben; see Lusatia).

Round the Town Walls

Many of Bautzen's historic old buildings can be seen on a walk round the town walls, which are almost completely preserved on the Spree side of the town. Among them, on the north, are the Schülerturm (Schoolboys' Tower), which dates from before 1515; the Gerberbastei (Tanners' Bastion; 1503), now a youth hostel; the Nikolaiturm (St Nicholas's Tower), built at some time before 1522; and the ruins of the Nikolaikirche (St Nicholas's Church; 1444), burned down after two bombardments during the Thirty Years' War (1620 and 1634).

On Oster-Reymann-Weg (from the sally-port onwards) are the ramparts of the Ortenburg, with the castle's water-tower (Burgwasserturm; probably 10th c.), which also contains a prison.

*Alte Wasserkunst

Passing the Mühlbastei (Mill Bastion; c. 1480) and going through the Mühltor (Mill Gate; rebuilt 1606), we come to the Wendischer Kirchhof (Wendish Churchyard), with St Michael's Church (1498; the church of the Protestant Sorbs) and the Alte Wasserkunst (Old Water-Tower; by W. Röhrscheidt the Elder, 1588), which served both for the town's protection and for water supply. The very emblem of Bautzen, it now houses a Museum of Technology.

Neue Wasserkunst

Beyond the Friedensbrücke (Peace Bridge; 1908–09, rebuilt 1946–49) is the Neue Wasserkunst (New Water-Tower; by W. Röhrscheidt the Younger, 1606–10).

Surroundings of Bautzen

Grosswelka

At Grosswelka (5km/3 miles north) is the "Urzoo" (Primeval Zoo), with life-size models of numerous species of dinosaur.

Wilthen

In Wilthen (10km/6 miles south), near the church and manor-house, are examples of an old Lusatian house type, the (*umgebindehaus)*, with external posts and beams supporting the upper storey and roof. From the nearby Mönchswalder Berg there are magnificent views of the surrounding countryside.

Neukirch

Neukirch (15km/9 miles south-west) has a Pottery and Regional Museum. This is a convenient base from which to climb the Valtenberg (588m/1929ft), the highest peak in the Lusatian uplands.

Schirgiswalde

Schirgiswalde (15km/9 miles south), the "Pearl of Upper Lusatia", is a popular holiday resort with a fine Baroque parish church (1739–41; richly decorated interior), a neo-classical Town Hall (1818), two arcaded houses on the Markt and a number of *umgebindehäuser*.

Bischofswerda

Features of interest in Bischofswerda (18km/11 miles south-west) are the neo-classical Town Hall (1818), with an external staircase; St Mary's Church (originally Gothic, rebuilt in neo-classical style 1815–16), now known as the Christuskirche; and numerous neo-classical burghers' houses. The Begräbniskirche (Late Renaissance, 1650), now known as the Kreuzkirche, has an over-lifesize sandstone crucifix (c. 1535) and a pulpit with figural reliefs.

Rammenau

Rammenau (4km/2½ miles north-west of Bischofswerda), birthplace of the great German philosopher Johann Gottlieb Fichte (1762–1814), has one of the finest Baroque palaces in Saxony (by J. C. Knöffel, 1721–35; occasional concerts), with a Fichte Memorial Room.

On the summit of the Zugspitze ▶

Bavarian Alps

Land: Bavaria

Situation and
characteristics

The Bavarian Alps (Bayerische Alpen), with their foreland, extend south from Munich to
the Austrian frontier and from Lake Constance in the west to the neighbourhood of
Salzburg in the east. They are part of the Northern Calcareous Alps, behind which, after a
zone of slate with rounded landscape forms, the higher Central Alps tower up.
The Deutsche Alpenstrasse (see entry) runs through the area.

**Landscape

The mountains reach a height of almost 3000m/10,000ft in the Zugspitze; the main
valleys lie between 700m/2300ft and 1000m/3300ft. The foreland consists of a high
plateau with numerous lakes, sloping down to the north from some 700m/2300ft at the
foot of the mountains to around 500m/1640ft and slashed by valleys ranging in depth
from 50m/165ft to 200m/650ft.

The Calcareous Alps are relatively young mountains, having been formed by folding in
the Tertiary era (some 70 million years ago). The deeply indented valleys which separate
the mountain masses from one another were carved out by Ice Age glaciers, which also
patterned the Alpine 'foreland with their moraines and deposits of rock debris. The
numerous lakes were formed when the ice melted.

The Alps offer endless scope for excursions of all kinds. The Pre-Alps – which take in the
Ammergau Alps, the hills of the beautiful Isarwinkel between Bad Tölz and the Walchensee, the charming Tegernsee Hills and the Schliersee Hills – offer magnificent forest
walks, easy climbs and rewarding views of the plain and the mountains. On a larger scale
are the Allgäu Alps, where the retreat of the forests has revealed more clearly the variety
of form of the mountains, and the limestone masses of the Berchtesgaden Alps (National
Park), whose plateaux (Untersberg and Steinernes Meer) are a paradise for hill walkers.
The most impressive mountain scenery is to be found in the Wettersteingebirge, with
Germany's highest peak, the Zugspitze (2963m/9722ft), and in the wild and rugged
Karwendelgebirge.

See also Ammersee, Berchtesgaden, Deutsche Alpenstrasse, Ettal, Füssen, Garmisch-
Partenkirchen, Kleinwalsertal, Mittenwald, Oberammergau, Oberstdorf, Bad Reichenhall and Bad Tölz

Bavarian Forest

Land: Bavaria

Situation and
characteristics

The Bavarian Forest (Bayerischer Wald) is the name given to the great expanse of
wooded hills in eastern Bavaria which is bounded on the south by the Danube valley (see
entry) between Regensburg and Passau. In the north-east it merges into the Bohemian
Forest (in Czechoslovakia and Austria) and continues beyond the Furth depression into
the Upper Palatinate Forest (Oberpfälzer Wald). Here as elsewhere the forests are
suffering from the effects of pollution.

*Landscape

Near the Danube lies the Vorderer Wald, a rolling upland region at altitudes of up to
around 1100m/3600ft in which only the highest parts and the steeper slopes are still
wooded. Behind this is the Hinterer Wald, the main part of the range, reaching its highest
point in the Arber (1457ft/4780ft), near Bayerisch Eisenstein. Other major peaks are
Osser (1293m/4242ft), near Lam; Rachel (1452m/4764ft) and Lusen (1371m/4498ft), near
Grafenau, in the Bavarian Forest National Park (area 120 sq.km/45 sq. miles); and the
Dreisessel (1378m/4521ft), in the south-east of the range.

Between the Vorderer and the Hinterer Wald is the Pfahl, a quartz dyke between 50m/165ft and 100m/330ft wide which has been weathered out of the granite and gneiss and can be followed for a distance of 140km/90 miles.

The particular beauty of these hills lies in their natural woodland, which in certain nature reserves (on the Arber, Falkenstein, Dreisessel, etc.) preserves the appearance of primeval forest (beech, fir, spruce). Below the Arber lie solitary mountain lakes, occupying basins gouged out by Ice Age glaciers.

Bodenmais

Perhaps the most popular holiday resort in the Bavarian Forest is Bodenmais (alt. 700m/2300ft; pop. 3400). In the 15th century silver-mining brought the town prosperity. Another craft developed at the same time was glass-making, which still contributes to the town's economy, promoted by an influx of glass-blowers from Bohemia after the Second World War; many glass-works can be visited.

On the north side of the town are the Kurhaus and Kurpark, an open-air swimming pool and various sports facilities.

South-east of the town rises the Silberberg (Silver Mountain, 955m/3133ft; chair-lift; panoramic views), with a summer toboggan-run, game enclosure, a children's play area and a zoo where the animals can be handled. There are a number of old mine shafts in the hill, some of them used for the treatment of asthma sufferers; one of them, the Barbarastollen, is open to the public.

Silberberg

*Grosser Arber

To the north of Bodenmais is the Grosser Arber (1457m/4780ft), the highest peak in the Bavarian Forest. At its foot are the Arber Lakes (boat rental), from which it is a 2-hour climb to the summit (magnificent panoramic views; skiing area).

Bayerisch Eisenstein

15km/9miles north-east of Bodenmais is Bayerisch Eisenstein, on the Czechoslovak frontier (crossing point). Features of interest in the little town are a local museum, a number of glass-works and an open-air swimming pool (artificial waves).

Zwiesel

South of Bayerisch Eisenstein we come to Zwiesel (alt. 585m/1919ft; pop. 11,000), the chief town in the Bavarian Forest, with an interesting Forest Museum. In nearby Lindberg is a Farmhouse Museum.

Half way along the road from Zwiesel to Bayerisch Eisenstein a side road goes off to the Zwieseler Waldhaus, from which it is a 2-hour climb to the summit of the Grosser Falkenstein (1315m/4315ft; views).

Grosser Falkenstein

See also Passau, Regensburg and Straubing

Bayreuth

H 7

Land: Bavaria
Altitude: 342m/1122ft
Population: 72,000

Bayreuth lies in the wide valley of the Roter Main between the Fichtelgebirge and the "Franconian Switzerland" (see entries). Its Baroque buildings and Rococo palaces recall its former status as residence of the Margraves of Brandenburg-Kulmbach. It now has a University, founded in 1975. It is world-famed as a festival city dedicated to the operas of Wagner.

Situation and characteristics

Bayreuth

Wagner Festival
The Bayreuth Festival, founded by Wagner in 1872, is devoted exclusively to performances of his operas. After his death the festival was directed by his widow Cosima, then
by his son Siegfried and later by Siegfried's widow Winifred. When the festival started
again after the Second World War, in 1951, it was directed by Wagner's grandsons
Wieland and Wolfgang, and after Wieland's death in 1966 by Wolfgang alone.

Sights

*Opera House
A little way south-east of the Josephsplatz, the hub of the town's traffic, is the Margravial
Opera House (1745–48), with a sumptuous Baroque interior (Franconian Festival).
Nearby, in Münzgasse, is the Iwalewa-Haus (contemporary art of the Third World).

Altes Schloss
In Maximilianstrasse is the 17th century Altes Schloss (Old Palace; burned down in 1945
and subsequently rebuilt). In the former palace church (1753–54; Protestant) is the tomb
of Margrave Frederick and his wife Wilhelmine.

To the south-west is the Town Parish Church (Stadtpfarrkirche; Protestant), with the
burial vault of the Margraves.

Jean-Paul-Haus
At Friedrichstrasse 5 is the house in which the Romantic writer Jean Paul (Jean Paul
Friedrich Richter, 1763–1825) lived and died.

Neues Schloss
In Ludwigstrasse stands the Neues Schloss (New Palace; 1753–59), with the residential
apartments of the Margraves, several museums (including the State Picture Gallery, the
Municipal Museum and the "Klingendes Museum") and a Wagner Memorial Room.
Nearby is the Jean Paul Museum. To the rear of the palace is the Hofgarten (Museum of
Freemasonry; Zoo).

Haus Wahnfried
At Richard-Wagner-Strasse 48 is Wagner's Haus Wahnfried (1873; now a museum).
Behind the house can be seen the tomb of Wagner and his wife Cosima, daughter of
Franz Liszt (Grabstätte Richard Wagners).
At the corner of Wahnfriedstrasse and Lisztstrasse is the house in which Liszt (1811–86)
died.

Festspielhaus

On the Grüner Hügel, a low hill at the north end of the town (1km/¾ mile from the station),
is the Festspielhaus (Festival House; 1800 seats), built in 1872–76 to house the Wagner
Festival which is held almost every year in July and August.

Surroundings of Bayreuth

*Eremitage
5km/3 miles east is the Eremitage (Hermitage), with the Altes Schloss (1715–18), the
Neues Schloss (1749–53) and a beautiful park (fountains).

Kulmbach   H 6

23km/15 miles north-east of Bayreuth, on the Weisser Main, is Kulmbach, noted for its
numerous breweries (Strong Beer Festival at the beginning of Lent; Beer Festival in
July/August).

Old town
In the Markt stands the Town Hall, with an elegant Rococo façade (1752). On the
Burgberg (Castle Hill) is the Langheimer Klosterhof, a richly decorated Baroque monas-
tery (1694). To the east is the Late Gothic St Peter's Church (15th c.).

Plassenburg
Above the town rears the massive Plassenburg, which passed to the Hohenzollern family
in 1340 and until 1604 was the seat of the Margraves of Brandenburg-Kulmbach. The
present building dates mainly from 1560–70; its finest feature is the Renaissance
courtyard, the Schöner Hof.

In the Plassenburg can be found the Tin Figures Museum (Zinnfigurenmuseum), with a remarkable collection of over 300,000 tin figures, displayed in more than 220 dioramas (tin figure exchange held in alternate, odd-numbered years), and a collection of hunting weapons.

*Tin Figures Museum

Berchtesgaden   M 8

Land: Bavaria
Altitude: 573m/1880ft
Population: 25,500

Berchtesgaden, at the end of the Deutsche Alpenstrasse (see entry), is perhaps the best known tourist town and one of the most popular climatic resorts in the Bavarian Alps. It is surrounded by mountains – the Hoher Göll, Watzmann, Hochkalter and Untersberg.

Situation and characteristics

Sights

In the centre of the town is the handsome palace of the Wittelsbachs, originally a house of Augustinian canons founded about 1100 which was secularised in 1803. It now houses a museum (weapons, furniture, porcelain, pictures).

Schloss

Beside the Schloss stands the Romanesque and Gothic Stiftskirche (monastic church), with a beautiful cloister.

Stiftskirche

To the south of the Schloss is the Kurgarten (Hofgarten), with the Kurhaus (used also for congresses).

Kurgarten

North-east of the town centre, in Schroffenbergallee, is Schloss Adelsheim (1640), now occupied by the Heimatmuseum (local woodcarving; showroom for sale of craft products).

Heimatmuseum

Also to the north-east of the town is the Salt Mine (Salzbergwerk; conducted tour in miners' clothes), with a Salt Museum.

Salt Mine

3km/2 miles north of Berchtesgaden stands the pretty pilgrimage church of Maria Gern.

Maria Gern

Berchtesgadener Land

The Berchtesgadener Land, once held directly from the Emperor by the Augustinian canons of Berchtesgaden, lies in the south-eastern corner of Bavaria, driving a wedge into Austrian territory. It is enclosed by high Alpine peaks with precipitous rock faces.

Obersalzberg

South-east of Berchtesgaden is the Obersalzberg (cableway), with a park-like landscape and superb views. Hitler's mountain retreat, which stood here, has been largely destroyed.

On the Obersalzberg is the starting-point of the 6.5km/4 mile long Kehlsteinstrasse, a private road built by Hitler to give access to his "tea-house" on the Kehlstein. It has five tunnels and gradients of up to 28%, and can be used only by special buses (mid May to mid October). From the parking place at the end of the road a tunnel leads to a lift up to the Kehlsteinhaus (1834m/6017ft; restaurant; magnificent panoramic views).

*Kehlsteinstrasse

Another scenic road is the Höhenringstrasse, a toll road from Berchtesgaden by way of Oberau to the 1551m/5089ft high Rossfeld.

*Rossfeld-Ringstrasse

**Königssee

The Königssee (alt. 602m/1975ft) is one of the great beauty spots of the Berchtesgadener Land. There is an attractive footpath along the east side of the lake to the Malerwinkel

St Bartholomä, in the Berchtesgadener Land

("Painters' Corner"; superb views of the lake and the mountains). Another equally attractive possibility is a boat trip to the pilgrimage chapel of St Bartholomew (17th c.) at the south end of the lake and a walk from there to the Obersee (alt. 613m/2011ft).

Jenner

From the village of Königssee (German Heraldic Museum; seen by appointment) a cabin cableway ascends the 1874m/6149ft high Jenner (magnificent views; skiing area).

Berchtesgaden National Park

Berchtesgaden National Park (area 210 sq.km/81 sq. miles) takes in the southern tip of the Berchtesgadener Land, including the Königssee, and the Watzmann group, and extends northward to near Bad Reichenhall (see entry).

Ramsau

From Berchtesgaden the Deutsche Alpenstrasse runs west to Ramsau (altitude resort; brine inhalation treatment) and the Hintersee (boat hire).

Bergisches Land   F 2

Land: North Rhine-Westphalia

Situation and characteristics

The Bergisches Land, formerly the County of Berg, lies between the Ruhr and the Sieg, the Rhine and the Sauerland region, with a landscape patterned by hills, forests, meadows and rivers. In earlier times water power provided the motive force for ironworks and mills, resulting in the development of a small-scale ironworking industry. Many rivers in this area have now been harnessed by dams, leading to the formation of a series of artificial lakes (Bever, Neye, Sengbach, Wupper).

The typical local house has black and white half-timbering, with green shutters and a slated roof; often the side walls are also clad with slates.

See Cologne, Surroundings

See also Remscheid, Solingen and Wuppertal

Bergstrasse   H–I 4

Länder: Baden-Württemberg and Hesse

The Bergstrasse, the Roman *strata montana,* runs alongside the rift valley of the Upper Rhine, on the western slopes of the Odenwald, from Darmstadt to Heidelberg. The region is famed for its mild climate, and in spring – which comes here earlier than in the rest of Germany – it is a sea of blossom. The influx of visitors reaches its peak in late March and early April. In addition to fruit, wine and vegetables the region also produces figs and almonds, and exotic trees grow in the parks.

Situation and characteristics

Sights

From the hilltops, crowned by old castles, there are magnificent views. The finest of the hills is Melibokus (515m/1690ft), near Zwingenberg. In the picturesque little town of Bensheim the Bergstrasse cuts across the Nibelungenstrasse. Not far away is Lorsch, with its Carolingian gatehouse, one of the oldest buildings in Germany. Heppenheim has a charming market square surrounded by half-timbered buildings; above the town can be seen the ruined Starkenburg (11th c.; observatory). The old town of Weinheim is dominated by the ruins of Burg Windeck (12th–13th c.); in the park belonging to the castle of the Berckheim family are rare plants and old cedars. A short distance east is Birkenau, the "village of sundials". Above the little wine town of Schriesheim are the ruins of the Strahlenburg.

Berlin   D–E 8

Capital of Germany
Altitude: 35–50m/115–165ft
Population: 3.4 million

In this guide the description of Berlin has been deliberately kept short, since fuller information is provided in the "Berlin" volume in the same series.

Berlin, Capital of Germany

Berlin, capital of the reunited Germany (though the timing for the transfer of the seat of government from Bonn has not yet been settled), lies on the navigable river Spree, which flows into the Havel at Spandau. It is a focal point of political, cultural and economic life and Germany's principal industrial city.

Berlin has all the flair of an international city, pulsating with life. The Berlin Opera and Berlin Philharmonic Orchestra are world-famous. The museums in Dahlem, Charlotten-burg and the Tiergarten and on Museum Island are of international standing. The Film Festival and Radio Exhibition, the "Green Week" in the Trade Fair Halls and the sporting contests in the Olympic Stadium are only a few of the most important events in the city's calendar.

Berlin

The city and its Wards

Borders of *Land*
Borders of Wards
Former course of Berlin Wall

SIGHTS

Charlottenburg

* Gedächtniskirche

In the east of the Charlottenburg district, in busy Breitscheidplatz, stands the emblem of West Berlin, the ruined tower of the neo-Romanesque Kaiser-Wilhelm-Gedächtniskirche (Emperor William Memorial Church; 1891–95). Adjoining it is the new church, a flat-roofed octagonal structure designed by Professor Eiermann (1959–61).

Europa-Center

To the east is the Europa-Center (1963–65), a shopping and business complex with a 22-storey tower block 86m/282ft high (shopping malls, restaurants, planetarium, water-clock, roof swimming pool, casino, etc.).

From this point two of the city's major shopping and commercial streets begin. Tauentzienstrasse, lined with shops, runs south-east to Wittenbergplatz, with the large KaDeWe department store ("Kaufhaus des Westens", the "shopping centre of the West"; notable particularly for its food department). To the east, at Kleiststrasse 13, is the Urania building, with lecture and exhibition rooms and the Berlin Postal Museum. (There is another Postal Museum in the eastern part of the city: see page 100).

* Kurfürstendamm

The other major street is the Kurfürstendamm, which leads west from the Gedächtniskirche for 3.5km/2 miles. With its shops, restaurants and cafés, its many cinemas and theatres, it is a magnet for all visitors to Berlin. At No. 227 is the Berliner Panoptikum, a wax museum.

Zoo

To the north of Breitscheidplatz are the Kunsthalle and, in Budapester Strasse, the Berlin Zoo, with 10,900 animals and an aquarium.

University Quarter

From the Gedächtniskirche Hardenbergstrasse runs north-west, passing the Zoo Station, to the extensive University quarter, with the University of Technology and the

Victory Column in the Grosser Stern ▶

Großer Stern

Kurfürstendamm and Memorial Church

College of Art. At the north-east end of Hardenbergstrasse is the attractively laid out Ernst-Reuter-Platz (fountains). Just off the square, at the near end of Bismarckstrasse, stands the Schiller Theatre (1950–51), and beyond this, farther west, is the Berlin Opera House (Deutsche Oper Berlin), opened in 1961.

*Schloss Charlottenburg

In the heart of the Charlottenburg district is Charlottenburg Palace (restored), a long range of 17th and 18th century buildings dominated by a tall dome. In the grand courtyard is an equestrian statue of the Great Elector, Frederick William of Brandenburg (by Schlüter and Jacobi, 1697–1700). The historical apartments are in the central range of buildings (the Nehringbau and Eosanderbau).

*Gallery of the Romantic Period

On the ground floor of the the east wing, the Knobelsdorff Wing, is the Gallery of the Romantic Period (a branch of the New National Gallery), with 19th century paintings. On the upper floor are the apartments occupied by Frederick the Great and the "Golden Gallery". In front of the Knobelsdorff Wing can be seen a statue of Frederick I (by Schlüter, 1698; cast).

Museum of Prehistory

The Langhansbau houses the Museum of Prehistory and the Early Historical Period. In the Schlosspark is the mausoleum of Queen Luise (d. 1810) and her husband King Frederick William III (d. 1840), which also contains the remains of the Emperor William I (d. 1888) and his wife the Empress Augusta (d. 1890). The marble figures were the work of C. D. Rauch and E. Enke.
In the Belvedere is a collection of Berlin porcelain from the Royal Porcelain Manufactory.

Opposite Charlottenburg Palace can be found the building known as the Stülerbau (1850). In the western section of this is the West Berlin Collection of Antiquities (Antikenmuseum); in the eastern section, on the other side of Schloss-strasse, is the Egyptian Museum (Ägyptisches Museum), a department of the State Museums, with the world-famous limestone bust of Queen Nefertiti (c. 1360 B.C.).

*Egyptian Museum

Westend

In the Westend district (part of Charlottenburg) are the Trade Fair and Exhibition Grounds (Messe- und Ausstellungsgelände), with a range of exhibition halls and pavilions which house all the major Berlin exhibitions.

Trade Fair Grounds

In this area too is one of Berlin's landmarks, the Funkturm (Radio Tower), popularly known as "Langer Lulatsch". Erected in 1924–26 for the Radio Exhibition, it is 138m/453ft high (150m/492ft to tip of aerial), with a restaurant at 55m/180ft and a viewing platform at 125m/410ft (lift). At the foot of the tower is the German Radio Museum.

Funkturm

On the Messedamm the International Congress Centre (ICC), opened in 1979, has seating for 20,300.

*ICC

*Olympic Stadium

North-west of Theodor-Heuss-Platz lies the Olympic Stadium, one of Europe's largest and finest sports installations, built in 1936 to the design of Werner March for the 11th Olympic Games. The oval stadium, 300m/330yds long by 230m/250yds across, can seat some 90,000 spectators. Immediately north-west is the popular Waldbühne, an open-air theatre with seating for 25,000.

Waldbühne

To the south of the Olympic Stadium, at the Heilsberger Dreieck, is the 17-storey Corbusierhaus, a huge block of flats built in 1957.

Charlottenburg Palace

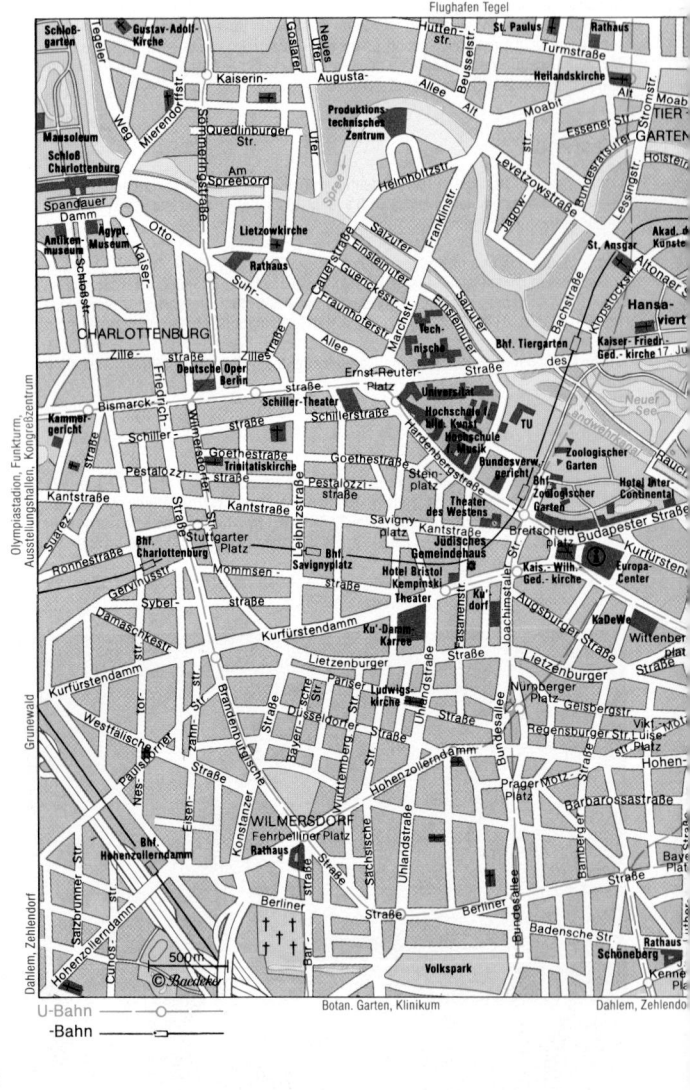

Tiergarten

Grosser Stern

In the Tiergarten district to the north lies the park of that name, traversed from west to east by the Strasse des 17. Juni. On the Grosser Stern, a roundabout half way across the park, rises the 67m/220ft high Victory Column (Siegessäule), commemorating the campaigns of 1864, 1866 and 1870–71 (extensive views from the platform at the top).

Bellevuepark
Hansaviertel

In the northern half of the park is Bellvuepark, laid out in the style of an English landscaped park, with Schloss Bellevue, the Berlin residence of the President of the

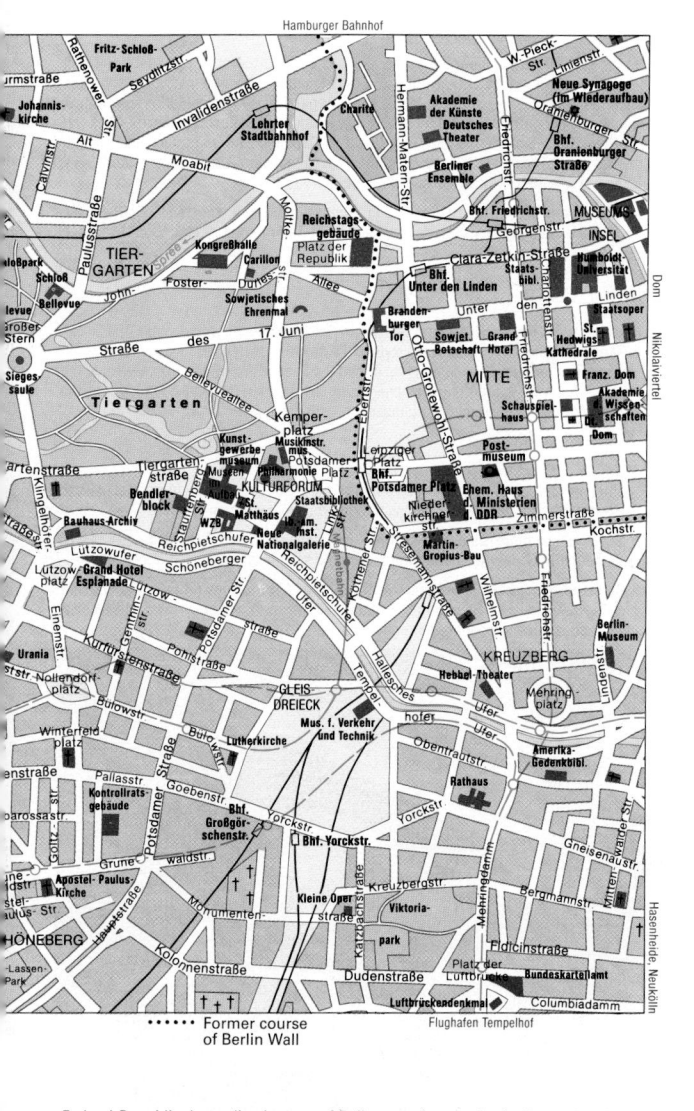

Federal Republic. Immediately west of Bellevuepark extends the Hansaviertel, developed between 1955 and 1957 as a model residential district by leading architects of the day (including Aalto, Düttmann, Eiermann, Gropius and Niemeyer), with some interesting examples of modern church architecture (e.g. the Kaiser-Friedrich-Gedächtniskirche and St-Ansgar-Kirche).

To the south of Tiergartenstrasse, on the Herkulesufer, is the Bauhaus-Archiv (Museum of Design; exhibitions).

Philharmonic Hall

Round Kemperplatz, at the south-east corner of the Tiergarten, are the Philharmonic Hall (Philharmonie; by H. Scharoun, 1960–63), the Museum of Musical Instruments (Musikinstrumentenmuseum) and the Museum of Applied Art (Kunstgewerbemuseum). A short distance south, at Potsdamer Strasse 50, are the New National Gallery (by Mies van der Rohe, 1965–68; painting and sculpture of the 19th and 20th centuries) and, facing it, the National Library (1978; 3 million volumes) and the Ibero-American Institute (1976). To the west is the German Resistance Memorial.

Soviet Memorial

At the east end of the Strasse des 17. Juni stands the Soviet Memorial (1945). Close by, beyond the old boundary between East and West Berlin, is the Brandenburg Gate (see page 97).

Reichstag Building

In the Platz der Republik can be seen the old Reichstag Building (Reichstagsgebäude), built by Paul Wald in 1884–94 in the style of the Italian High Renaissance and restored in 1969 after suffering severe destruction during the Second World War. To the west of the Platz der Republik is the Kongresshalle (Congress Hall; 1957), popularly known as the "pregnant oyster"; the building collapsed in 1980 but was rebuilt in 1987.

Kreuzberg

South-east of Kemperplatz is Kreuzberg, the smallest but most densely populated ward in West Berlin (some 42,000 Turks), with numerous street-corner bars.

Gropiusbau

In Stresemannstrasse is the Renaissance-style Gropius Building (Gropiusbau; 1877–81), with the Berlin Gallery (painting, graphic art and sculpture since the 19th century).

Museum of Transport and Technology

In Trebbiner Strasse is the Museum of Transport and Technology (Museum für Verkehr und Technik; Industrial Revolution, road and rail transport, air travel, domestic technology, production engineering, printing, etc.).

Congress Hall

Farther east, housed in the old Supreme Court (Kammergericht; 1734–35) in Linden-strasse, is the Berlin Museum, illustrating the historical and cultural development of Berlin since the mid 17th century (pictures, graphic art, applied art, domestic interiors, toys, etc.). It is planned during the nineties to amalgamate this museum with the Märkisches Museum (see page 104).

Berlin Museum

Tempelhof

Immediately south of Kreuzberg is the Tempelhof ward. The extensive area known as the Tempelhofer Feld was the parade ground of the Berlin garrison from the 18th century onwards. From 1923 to 1974 Tempelhof was Berlin's main airport, and until 1970 it was used by the American forces in Berlin. In front of the large airport building is the Air-Lift Memorial (by Professor Ludwig, 1951), commemorating the aid given by the Western allies during the Soviet blockade of West Berlin (June 28th 1948 to May 11th 1949). There is a corresponding memorial at Frankfurt Airport.

Airport

To the north of the airport lies Hasenheide Park, with an open-air theatre and the Rixdorfer Höhe, a hill built up of rubble from buildings destroyed during the Second World War.

Hasenheide

Schöneberg and Steglitz

South-east of Charlottenburg are the Schöneberg and Steglitz districts, with busy shopping and commercial streets such as Schloss-strasse.

Schöneberg Town Hall (Rathaus) in J.-F.-Kennedy-Platz is the seat of the Chief Burgomaster of Berlin. In the tower is the Freedom Bell presented by the United States in 1950.

Town Hall

In Steglitz are two new and eye-catching buildings, the Steglitzer Turm (north of Schloss-strasse; restaurant) and the controversial Steglitzer Kreisel (south of Schloss-strasse).

Steglitzer Kreisel

A short distance south-west of the Steglitzer Kreisel can be found the Botanic Garden (area 42 hectares/105 acres; Victoria Regia House, tropical houses, botanical museum).

Botanic Garden

To the east of the Steglitzer Kreisel and the urban motorway is the Insulaner, a hill built up from rubble from buildings destroyed during the Second World War. On top of the hill is the Wilhelm-Foerster-Sternwarte (Observatory, with Planetarium; 1963).

Observatory

Zehlendorf

**Dahlem Museums

In Zehlendorf ward is the district of Dahlem, with the Auditorium Maximum of the Free University of Berlin, various institutes run by the Max Planck Society and the Dahlem Museums: the Picture Gallery (with world-famed masterpieces, including 26 Rembrandts), the Sculpture Gallery, the Print Cabinet, the Museum of Ethnography, the Museum of Indian Art, the Museum of Islamic Art and the Museum of East Asian Art.

Wannsee

Zehlendorf, with attractive rural housing developments, extends along the Schlachtensee and Nikolassee to the river Havel, which here swells out to form the Wannsee, a favourite resort of Berlin water sports enthusiasts.

One of the most attractive spots in the Havel area is the 1500m/1650yd long Pfaueninsel ("Peacock Island"), with a "ruined castle" built in 1794 and a beautiful English-style park.

*Pfaueninsel

To the east of the Wannsee and the motorway intersection known as the Zehlendorfer Kleeblatt ("Zehlendorf clover-leaf") can be found the Düppel Museum Village (Museumsdorf), a reconstruction of a medieval settlement.

Düppel
Museum Village

Berlin

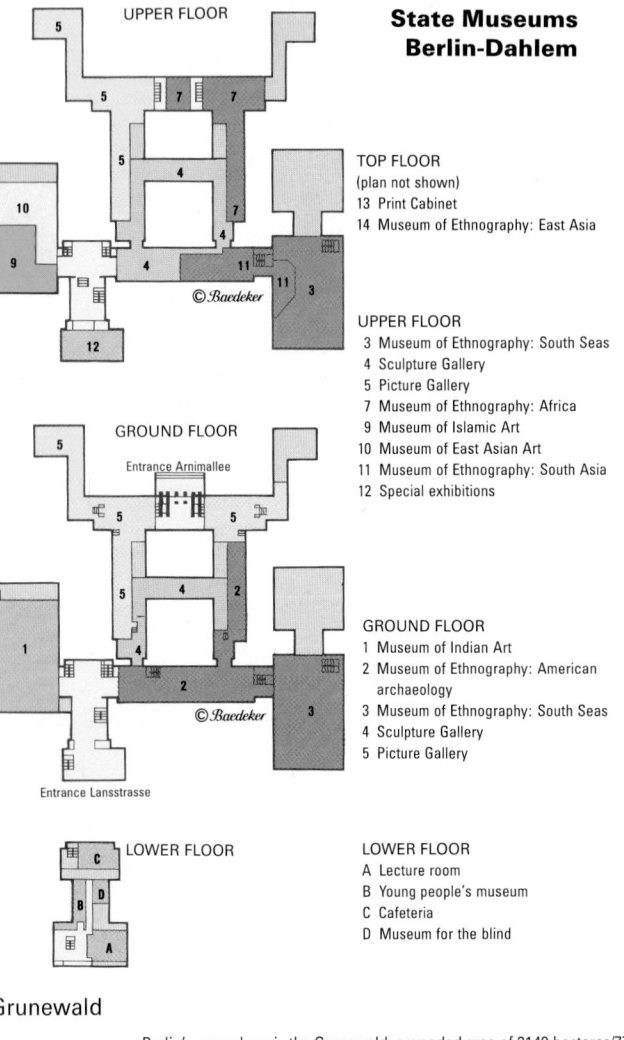

UPPER FLOOR

State Museums
Berlin-Dahlem

GROUND FLOOR

Entrance Arnimallee

© Baedeker

Entrance Lansstrasse

LOWER FLOOR

TOP FLOOR
(plan not shown)
13 Print Cabinet
14 Museum of Ethnography: East Asia

UPPER FLOOR
3 Museum of Ethnography: South Seas
4 Sculpture Gallery
5 Picture Gallery
7 Museum of Ethnography: Africa
9 Museum of Islamic Art
10 Museum of East Asian Art
11 Museum of Ethnography: South Asia
12 Special exhibitions

GROUND FLOOR
1 Museum of Indian Art
2 Museum of Ethnography: American archaeology
3 Museum of Ethnography: South Seas
4 Sculpture Gallery
5 Picture Gallery

LOWER FLOOR
A Lecture room
B Young people's museum
C Cafeteria
D Museum for the blind

Grunewald

Berlin's green lung is the Grunewald, a wooded area of 3149 hectares/7778 acres, with the Grunewaldsee, the Krumme Lanke, the Schlachtensee, the Hundekehlensee and the Teufelssee. The Teufelsberg, the highest point in West Berlin (115m/377ft), was built up after the war from the rubble of demolished buildings.
Here too is Jagdschloss Grunewald, a hunting lodge originally built in Renaissance style in 1542 which was given its present form in the 18th century (Hunting Museum; collection of pictures).

Tegel

The most northerly of the Havel lakes is the Tegeler See (area 408 hectares/1008 acres).   Tegeler See
The neo-classical Schloss Tegel, a conversion of an earlier hunting lodge, was built by   Schloss Tegel
Karl Friedrich Schinkel in 1821–23 for the scholar and statesman Wilhelm von Humboldt.
It contains mementoes of Humboldt; in the park can be seen the Humboldt family tomb.
Not open to the public.

Tegel Airport, with a hexagonal ring of gates, replaced Tempelhof (see above) for civil   *Airport
traffic in 1976.

Berlin-Mitte

Berlin-Mitte was one of the eight wards of East Berlin.

**Unter den Linden

The famous avenue known as Unter den Linden ("Under the Lime-Trees"), some
1400m/1530yds long and 60m/200ft wide, runs from Pariser Platz in the west to Marx-
Engels-Platz in the east.

Immediately east of the Tiergarten (see page 92), beyond the former boundary between   **Brandenburg Gate
West and East Berlin, is the Pariser Platz, in which stands the Brandenburg Gate (Brandenburger Tor), the very emblem of Berlin. The Gate, modelled on the Propylaea on the
Acropolis of Athens, was built in 1788–91 by C. G. Langhans; the flanking colonnades
were added in 1868 by J. H. Strack. On top of the Gate is the 6m/20ft high quadriga
(four-horse chariot) of the goddess of Victory. The original, in copper, by Johann
Gottfried Schadow (1793) was destroyed during the Second World War and replaced by
a new one in 1958 after the restoration of the war-damaged Gate. One of the original
horses' heads is now in the Märkisches Museum (see page 104).

Farther east, at the corner of Friedrichstrasse and Behrenstrasse, is the Comic Opera   Comic Opera
(Komische Oper).
Beyond the Lindencorso, an office block built in 1965, are the Altes Palais (Old Palace; by
C. F. Langhans, 1834–36) and the old Governor's House (by G. C. Unger, 1721), on the site
of the earlier Dutch Palace. Adjoining is the Old Library (Alte Bibliothek; known as the
"Kommode"), also by Unger (1774–88), a copy of a design by J. B. Fischer von Erlach for
the Michaelertrakt of the Hofburg in Vienna.

At the corner of Charlottenstrasse stands the National Library (Deutsche Staats-   National Library
bibliothek; by E. von Ihne, 1903–14), with an imposing entrance courtyard. This
important scholarly library has more than 5.5 million books, manuscripts, musical
scores, prints and maps.

On the central promenade, at the end of the trees, is an equestrian statue of Frederick the   *Statue of
Great by Christian Daniel Rauch (1851), The statue, 13.50m/44ft high, which stood for   Frederick the Great
many years in the park at Sanssouci, was restored to its original place in 1980.

The Humboldt University building was originally erected by J. Boumann the Elder in   Humboldt
1748–53 as a palace for Prince Henry, Frederick the Great's brother. In 1809, on the   University
initiative of Wilhelm von Humboldt (1767–1835), it was converted into a University, the
first Rector of which was J. G. Fichte. Scholars who have taught at the University (known
since 1946 as the Humboldt University) include the philosophers Hegel and Schleier-
macher, the Grimm brothers, Hermann von Helmholtz, Max Planck, Albert Einstein, C. F.
von Graefe, Rudolf Virchow, Robert Koch and Ferdinand Sauerbruch.

The Neue Wache (New Guard-House; by K. F. Schinkel, 1816–18) was modelled on a   *Neue Wache
Roman fort. The relief on the pediment was the work of A. Kiss (1842). Since 1960 the
building has been a memorial to the victims of Fascism.

The Opera House (Deutsche Staatsoper), opposite the Old Library ("Kommode"), was   *Opera House
designed by G. W. von Knobelsdorff in 1741–43 as the first building in a "Forum

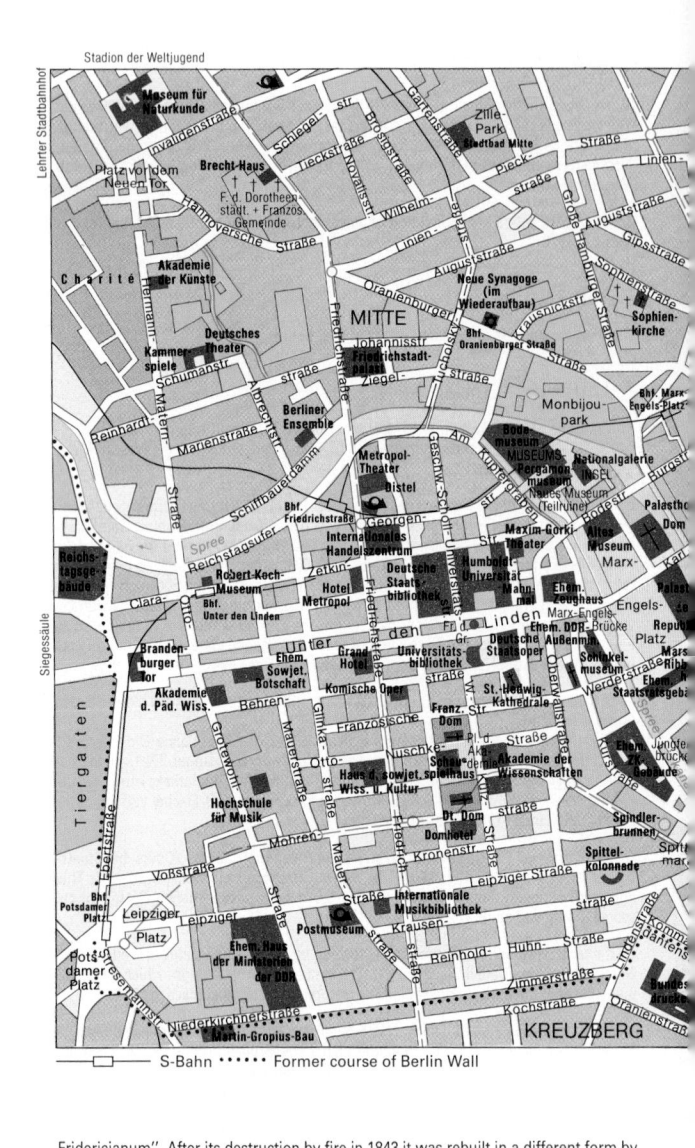

———□——— S-Bahn ••••• Former course of Berlin Wall

Fridericianum". After its destruction by fire in 1843 it was rebuilt in a different form by C. F. Langhans, with a pediment relief (1844) by Ernest Rietschel. Completely destroyed in 1944, the Opera House was rebuilt in 1955 and thoroughly restored in 1986.

*St Hedwig's Cathedral

South of the Opera House is St Hedwig's Cathedral (1747–73; by J. G. Büring and J. Boumann, after J. L. Legeay), which was modelled on the Pantheon in Rome. (St Hedwig was the patron saint of Silesia, which was conquered by Frederick the Great during the Seven Years' War, bringing large areas with a Catholic population into Prussia).

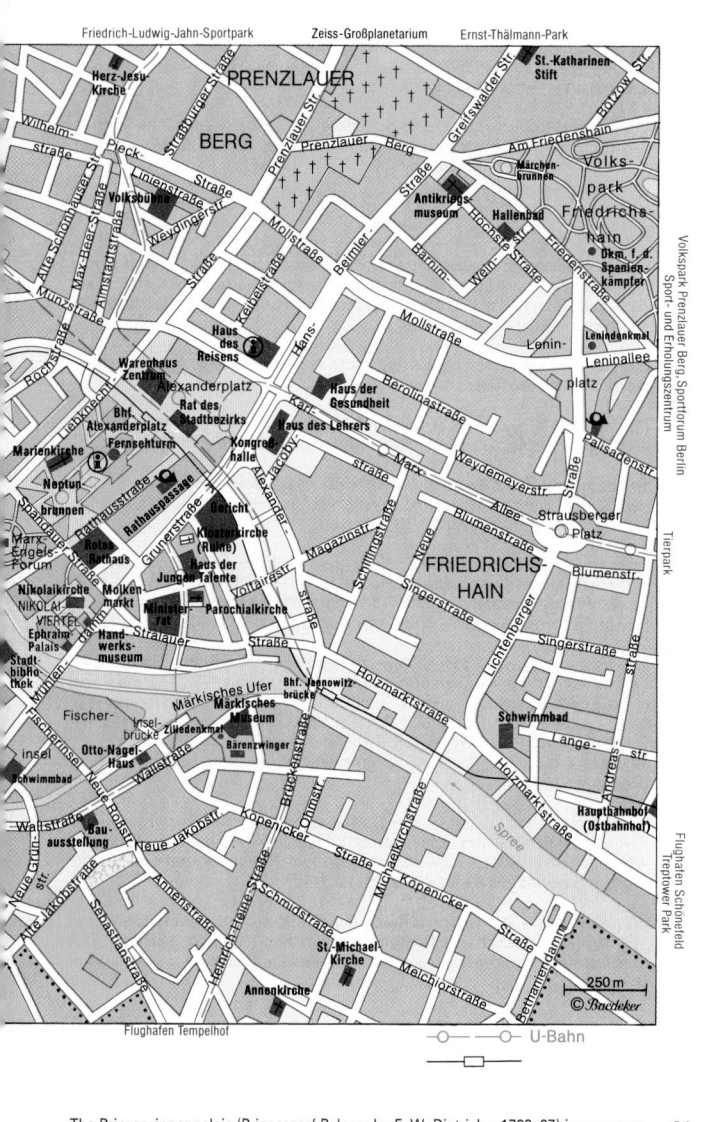

The Prinzessinnenpalais (Princesses' Palace; by F. W. Dietrichs, 1733–37) is now occupied by the Operncafé. In front of it are over-lifesize statues (by C. D. Rauch and pupils, 1822–26 and 1853–55) of four great Prussian generals of the War of Liberation: Scharnhorst, Blücher, Yorck and Gneisenau.

Prinzessinnen-palais

The Palais Unter den Linden (1732), a Baroque palace built by P. Gerlach for the Crown Prince of Prussia, was rebuilt and extended in 1968–69. In front of it is a monument to the Prussian reformer Freiherr vom Stein (by H. Schievelbein, 1875).

Palais Unter den Linden

Arsenal — The oldest building in Unter den Linden is the Arsenal (Zeughaus; by J. A. Nering, A. Schlüter and J. de Bodt, 1695–1706), one of the finest Baroque buildings in Germany. It now houses the German Historical Museum.

Schlossbrücke — At the Arsenal the Schlossbrücke (Palace Bridge) leads over an arm of the Spree to Marx-Engels-Platz and the Marx-Engels Forum (see page 103). On its piers are eight sculptured groups in white marble by K. F. Schinkel (1845–57).

Friedrichstrasse

The 3.5km/2 mile long Friedrichstrasse runs north–south at right angles to Unter den Linden from the Oranienburg Gate in the north to the street intersection at the Halle Gate in the south. From 1961 to 1990 it was cut at Zimmerstrasse by the Berlin Wall, at the site of the legendary Checkpoint Charlie.

The features of interest described in this section lie on or near the section of Friedrichstrasse to the north of Unter den Linden.

Metropol-Theater — The old Admiral's Palace (by H. Schweitzer and A. Diepenbrock, 1910) has been occupied since 1955 by the Metropol-Theater and a cabaret, Die Distel ("The Thistle").

Theater am Schiffbauerdamm — In Bertolt-Brecht-Platz is the world-famed Theater am Schiffbauerdamm (by H. Seeling, 1891–92), the home from 1954 of the Berliner Ensemble, founded and directed by Bertolt Brecht and his wife Helene Weigel.

Friedrichstadt-palast — Beyond the Weidendammerbrücke (1895–96; fine wrought-iron railings) over the Spree, to the right, stands the new Friedrichstadtpalast (opened 1984), a variety and revue theatre of international standing, with all the refinements of modern stage techniques. In front of it is a monument to the variety artiste Claire Waldoff (1884–1957).

*Dorotheenstadt Cemetery — In Chausseestrasse, which leads north-west from the north end of Friedrichstrasse, is the Dorotheenstadt Cemetery (Dorotheenstädtischer Friedhof; from 1762), with the graves of many famous people, including J. G. Fichte, G. W. F. Hegel, C. W. Hufeland, C. D. Rauch, J. G. Schadow, K. F. Schinkel, F. A. Stüler, Heinrich Mann, Arnold Zweig, H. Eisler, Bertolt Brecht and Helene Weigel, L. R. Becher and Anna Seghers.
Adjoining is the French Cemetery, with the tomb of the painter and etcher Daniel Chodowiecki (d. 1801).

Brecht-Haus — In the Brecht-Haus at Chausseestrasse 125, the last home of Bertolt Brecht and Helene Weigel, is the Bertolt Brecht Centre (opened 1978), with the archives of Brecht and his wife, the rooms in which they lived and worked, rooms for lectures, readings and other events, a bookshop and the Brecht-Keller restaurant.

*Natural History Museum — At Invalidenstrasse 34 is the Natural History Museum (Museum für Naturkunde; opened 1890), a centre of research and education with collections of material on the history of the earth and of man, an interesting collection of minerals and a collection of giant dinosaur skeletons.

Potsdamer Platz and Leipziger Strasse

Before the Second World War Potsdamer Platz, laid out in 1741 by Frederick William I, was the busiest square in Europe, forming a link between the eastern and western parts of Berlin. With the building of the Berlin Wall it became a no man's land between two lines of walls, designed to ensure that no one could find his way to the West through the maze of underground passages associated with Hitler's last retreat, the "Führerbunker". Since the union of the two Germanys the Potsdamer Platz and the adjoining Leipziger Platz are destined to become the hub of thr reunited city of Berlin.

Postal Museum — At the intersection of Leipziger Strasse and Mauerstrasse is the second of Berlin's two Postal Museums (see page 88), the old Postal Museum of the German Democratic

Republic, originally founded in 1872. It is now in process of reorganisation, and only a small part of the collection is on show.

To the north of Leipziger Strasse is the Gendarmenmarkt (former called Platz der Akademie), one of Berlin's finest squares. It takes its name from the fact that a regiment of the Gendarmerie had stables here from 1736 to 1782. In the square is a monument to Schiller (by R. Begas), unveiled in the presence of Emperor William I in 1871, later removed and finally returned to its original position in 1988.

*Gendarmenmarkt

The square is dominated by the old Schauspielhaus (Theatre), built by K. F. Schinkel in 1818–21. It was reopened in 1984, after careful restoration to its original form, as a concert hall.

Schauspielhaus

On the south-west side of the square is the German Cathedral (Deutscher Dom), built in 1701–08 for the Lutheran community. The dome is topped by a gilded figure 7m/23ft high. After restoration the Cathedral is to become a museum.

German Cathedral

On the north side of the square stands the French Cathedral (Französischer Dom), built for the French Reformed community. Like the German Cathedral, it has a handsome dome. Both domes, by K. von Gontard, were later additions to the churches.
The Cathedral now houses the Huguenot Museum (history of the Huguenots in France and Prussia).

French Cathedral

From the Gendarmenmarkt Französische Strasse and Werderstrasse lead north-east to the twin-towered Friedrichswerder Church on the north-west side of the Werderscher Markt. This 19th century church (aisleless, with stellar vaulting), designed by K. F. Schinkel, was badly damaged during the Second World War. Since restoration in 1987 it has housed the Schinkel Museum, which documents the life and work of the great 19th century architect Karl Friedrich Schinkel (1781–1841).

Friedrichswerder
Church
(Schinkel Museum)

**Museum Island

The world-famed Museum Island (Museumsinsel) extends from the Old Museum (Altes Museum) to the confluence of the Spree and the Kupfergraben. Designated by royal order in 1841 as a "precinct devoted to art and the study of antiquity", it was developed from 1843 onwards, and reached its final form with the building of the Pergamon Museum between 1909 and 1930.
It is planned to restore the Museum Island to its pre-war state. An important element in the plan is the rebuilding of the New Museum.

Beside the ruins of the New Museum is the National Gallery, originally built as a festival hall by J. H. Strack in 1866–76 to the design of F. A. Stüler and subsequently enlarged to house a museum of contemporary art. During the Nazi period some 300 modern works were removed from the museum as "degenerate", and another 900 were destroyed during the Second World War. The collection includes German painting and sculpture of the 19th and early 20th centuries (particularly works by Berlin artists) and pictures by French Impressionists.

*National Gallery

The Pergamon Museum contains several important collections: the Collection of Antiquities and the West Asian Collection on the main floor, the Islamic Museum and East Asian Collection on the upper floor and the Museum of Ethnography on the lower floor. The Collection of Antiquities includes valuable works of ancient sculpture, pride of place being taken by the reconstructed Pergamon Altar. The altar, built around 180–160 b.c. as a votive offering to Zeus and Athena (tutelary goddess of the city of Pergamon in Asia Minor), was brought to Berlin in 1902.
Other notable items are some fine examples of Hellenistic architecture from Priene, Magnesia and Miletus (Roman market gate from Miletus, 165 b.c.) and sculpture from Miletus, Samos, Naxos and Attica.
The West Asian Museum possesses many fine examples of Late Babylonian architecture, including some notable architectural elements from the reign of Nebuchadnezzar II (603–652 b.c.). Other examples of monumental architecture from Western Asia are a

**Pergamon
Museum

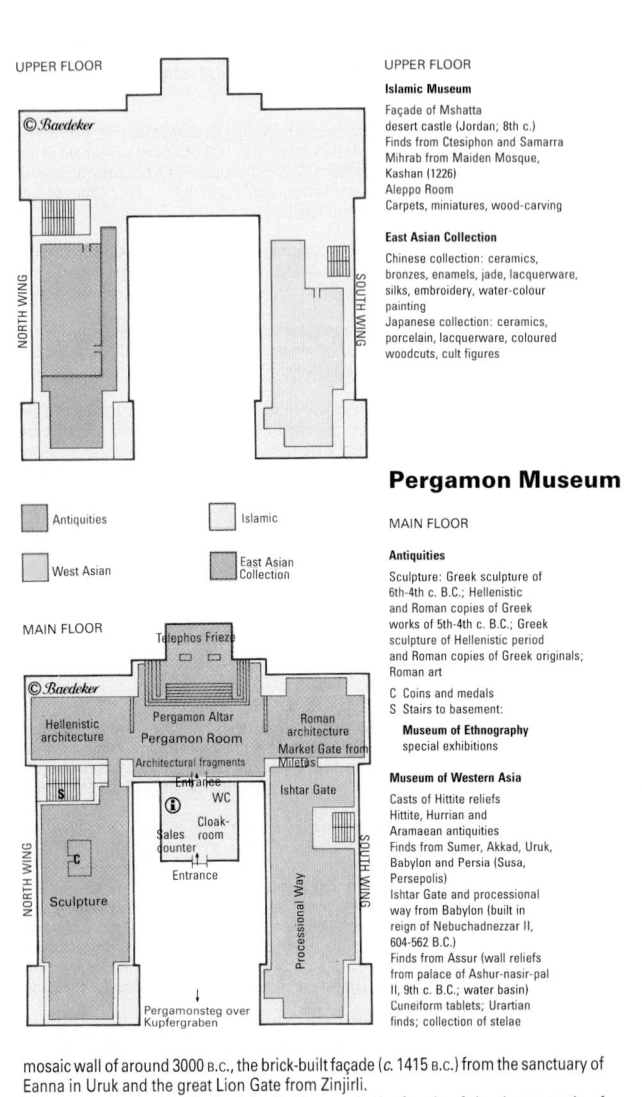

UPPER FLOOR

© Baedeker

NORTH WING

SOUTH WING

UPPER FLOOR

Islamic Museum

Façade of Mshatta
desert castle (Jordan; 8th c.)
Finds from Ctesiphon and Samarra
Mihrab from Maiden Mosque,
Kashan (1226)
Aleppo Room
Carpets, miniatures, wood-carving

East Asian Collection

Chinese collection: ceramics,
bronzes, enamels, jade, lacquerware,
silks, embroidery, water-colour
painting
Japanese collection: ceramics,
porcelain, lacquerware, coloured
woodcuts, cult figures

Antiquities

West Asian

Islamic

East Asian
Collection

Pergamon Museum

MAIN FLOOR

Antiquities

Sculpture: Greek sculpture of
6th-4th c. B.C.; Hellenistic
and Roman copies of Greek
works of 5th-4th c. B.C.; Greek
sculpture of Hellenistic period
and Roman copies of Greek originals;
Roman art

C Coins and medals
S Stairs to basement:

Museum of Ethnography
special exhibitions

Museum of Western Asia

Casts of Hittite reliefs
Hittite, Hurrian and
Aramaean antiquities
Finds from Sumer, Akkad, Uruk,
Babylon and Persia (Susa,
Persepolis)
Ishtar Gate and processional
way from Babylon (built in
reign of Nebuchadnezzar II,
604-562 B.C.)
Finds from Assur (wall reliefs
from palace of Ashur-nasir-pal
II, 9th c. B.C.; water basin)
Cuneiform tablets; Urartian
finds; collection of stelae

MAIN FLOOR

© Baedeker

Telephos Frieze

Hellenistic
architecture

Pergamon Altar

Pergamon Room

Roman
architecture

Market Gate from
Miletus

Architectural fragments

Entrance

WC

Cloak-
room

Sales
counter

Entrance

Roman
architecture

Ishtar Gate

Processional Way

NORTH WING

SOUTH WING

C

Sculpture

S

Pergamonsteg over
Kupfergraben

mosaic wall of around 3000 B.C., the brick-built façade (c. 1415 B.C.) from the sanctuary of
Eanna in Uruk and the great Lion Gate from Zinjirli.
The most valuable item in the Islamic Museum is the façade of the desert castle of
Mshatta in Jordan (8th c.), a gift from Sultan Abdul Hamid to Emperor William II.

*Bode Museum

The Bode Museum, a neo-Baroque building by Ernst von Ihne (1897–1904), lies at the
north end of the Museum Island. Originally opened in 1904 as the Emperor Frederick
Museum, it was renamed Bode Museum in 1956 in honour of Wilhelm von Bode
(1845–1929), founder of the museum and its director from 1872 to 1929.
The Bode Museum contains a number of different collections – the Egyptian Museum
(Egyptian history from prehistoric times to the Greco-Roman period), the Papyrus
Collection (30,000 papyri), the Early Christian and Byzantine Collection (icons, Coptic art,

funerary stelae, pottery), the Sculpture Collection, the Picture Gallery, the Museum of Prehistory and the Early Historical Period and the Coin Cabinet.

Old Museum and Berlin Cathedral

Adjoining the Lustgarten is the Old Museum (Altes Museum), Schinkel's finest work (1824–30), a neo-classical building with a portico. A wide staircase flanked by bronze sculptures leads up to the portico, which has 18 Ionic columns. The Museum houses a variety of collections belonging to the State Museums in Berlin, including the Print Cabinet and a collection of drawings. In front of the museum is a large granite basin (diameter 6.90m/22½ft, weight 76 tons) hewn from the famous Markgrafenstein, a huge erratic boulder from the Rauensche Berge near Bad Saarow-Pieskow.

*Old Museum

Berlin Cathedral (Dom) stands on the banks of the Spree south-east of the Old Museum. The neo-Baroque building (by J. Raschdorff, 1894–1905) occupies the site of an earlier cathedral of 1750.

*Cathedral

Marx-Engels-Platz and Marx-Engels Forum

Mark-Engels-Platz occupies the site of the old Stadtschloss (Town Palace), the ruins of which were demolished in 1950 to provide (together with part of the Lustgarten) a spacious square for demonstrations and parades. All that remains of the palace is a doorway incorporated into the former Council of State building (see below) on the south-east side of the square.

Marx-Engels-Platz is dominated by the former Palace of the Republic (Palast der Republik, built in 1973–76 by an architects' collective led by H. Graffunder, which until 1990 was the meeting-place of the Volkskammer (People's Chamber, the old East German parliament) and a cultural centre.

Palace of the Republic

Berlin Cathedral

Berlin

Marx-Engels Forum	Beyond the Palace of the Republic lies the Marx-Engels Forum, inaugurated in 1986, with the Marx-Engels Monument (by L. Engelhardt, 1986), two bronze relief plaques, eight stelae of high-grade steel (with engraved photographs illustrating events in the class struggle) and a five-section marble wall, with symbolic representations of exploitation by W. Stötzer. On the south-east side of Marx-Engels-Platz stands the former Council of State building (by R. Korn and H. Bogatzky, 1962–64). Built into the façade is a doorway from the old Stadtschloss (by E. von Göthe, 1707–13).
Marstall	South-east of Marx-Engels-Platz is the Alter Marstall (Old Court Stables; by M. M. Smids, 1665–70), an Early Baroque building now concealed by the Neuer Marstall (by E. von Ihne, 1896–1902), which is used for exhibitions.
*Ribbeckhaus	Adjoining the Alter Marstall, at Breite Strasse 35, is the Ribbeckhaus, a four-gabled building erected in 1624 for the Ribbeck family, a noble Brandenburg family. It is Berlin's only surviving Renaissance building.
Municipal Library	Next to the Ribbeckhaus is the Municipal Library (by H. Mehlan, E. Kussat and G. Lehrmann, 1964–66), with a handsome entrance wing bearing 117 steel plaques with different forms of the letter A (by F. Kühn, 1967). On the Friedrichsgracht and Gertraudenbrücke lies a little corner of old Berlin (restored), with old-style bars and shops selling jewellery and craft products.

Märkisches Ufer

The street known as the Märkisches Ufer ("Brandenburg Shore") runs along the south bank of the Spree to the east of the Fischerinsel ("Fishermen's Island"). This part of the town was developed as a residential area from the late 17th century onwards.

Ermeler-Haus	At Nos. 10–12 can be seen the Ermeler-Haus, moved here in 1966 from its former position in Breite Strasse. This old burgher's house, later restored and rebuilt in Rococo style, belonged from 1824 to 1918 to the family of the tobacco merchant Ferdinand Ermeler.
Otto-Nagel-Haus	At Märkisches Ufer 16–18 are two 18th century houses which in 1973 were converted into a museum commemorating the painter Otto Nagel (1894–1967).
Köllnischer Park	The Köllnischer Park, to the south of the Märkisches Ufer, is an attractive place of relaxation, with sculpture, reliefs and a bronze monument (by H. Drake) commemorating the humorous and satirical artist Heinrich Zille. The bear-pit (Bärenzwinger), with Berlin's heraldic animals, is a popular attraction.
*Märkisches Museum	The Märkisches Museum (Brandenburg Museum) was founded in 1874 on the initiative of R. Virchow and E. Friedel and is housed in a building (by L. Hoffmann, 1899–1908) in traditional Brandenburg style. It has collections of material on the history of Berlin and the surrounding area, the arts, the theatre and literature. There are regular demonstrations of mechanical musical instruments.

**Nikolaiviertel

The Nikolaiviertel (St Nicholas quarter) – a recent development – lies to the south, between the Rotes Rathaus (Red Town Hall: see below) and the banks of the Spree. It occupies the eastern half of the old double town of Cölln-Berlin, the site of the earliest settlement. In the development of this area after the war the emphasis was on creating small and compact neighbourhood units. There was very little restoration of older buildings: what resulted was a planned reconstruction of a quarter of old Berlin, incorporating a few old buildings, some of them moved here from other parts of the city.

St Nicholas's Church	The Nikolaikirche (St Nicholas's Church), a Late Gothic church (14th–15th c.) remodelled in the 19th century, was badly damaged during the Second World War but has recently

been rebuilt. During excavations in the ruined church remains of a 13th century Romanesque basilica were found, and below this a well preserved 12th century burial ground.
From 1657 to 1666 Paul Gerhardt, a well known Protestant hymn-writer, was pastor of
the church. The tower with its twin steeples is the landmark and emblem of the Nikolaiviertel. The church is now a branch of the Märkisches Museum.

On the Mühlendamm can be found the interesting Craft Museum (Handwerksmuseum),   Craft Museum
which is also a branch of the Märkisches Museum (crafts and craft products from the 13th
to the 19th century).

The Knoblauch-Haus at Poststrasse 25, which was owned by the prosperous Knoblauch   Knoblauch-Haus
family for 150 years, is an 18th century burgher's house remodelled in neo-classical style
at the beginning of the 19th century. It now contains an exhibition on family history.

Alexanderplatz

Alexanderplatz, so named in 1805 in honour of Tsar Alexander I of Russia, has been   *Alexanderplatz
much altered in the course of its history, most recently in 1968. It is a busy traffic
intersection and shopping area, with numerous public buildings.

At the south-west corner of the square is East Berlin's most conspicuous landmark, the   *Television Tower
365m/1200ft high Television Tower (Fernsehturm). Two high-speed lifts take visitors up
to the viewing platform at 207m/680ft. In the Tele-Café the tables and chairs are on a
revolving ring which makes one complete turn every hour.

In the centre of the square can be seen the Friendship of the Peoples Fountain (by W.   Friendship of the
Womacka, 1969), a spiral composition of seventeen fountain basins.   Peoples Fountain

A popular rendezvous point in Alexanderplatz is the Urania World Clock (Urania-Welt-   Urania World Clock
zeituhr). It occupies the site of an earlier monument, the figure of "Berolina" by Emil
Hundrieser.

Alexanderplatz, with the World Clock

Berlin

The oldest buildings in Alexanderplatz are the Berolinahaus and Alexanderhaus (by P. Behrens, 1928–30). Of more recent date is the Zentrum department store (by J. Kaiser and G. Kuhnert, 1967–70). At the south-east corner of the square stands the Kongresshalle.

Red Town Hall
The new Berlin Town Hall, known as the Rotes Rathaus (Red Town Hall) because of its red brick walls, is a three-storey neo-Renaissance building with a 74m/243ft high tower (by H. F. Waesemann, 1861–69). A terracotta frieze depicting scenes from the history of Berlin (by Geyer, Schweinitz and Calandrelli).

In front of the Town Hall are two statues by F. Kremer – the "Trümmerfrau" (a woman clearing rubble) and the "Aufbauhelfer" (a worker helping in the rebuilding of Berlin). A little way east of the Town Hall, in Klosterstrasse, is the Baroque Palais Podewils (by J. de Bodt, 1701–04)

Parish church
Near the Palais Podewils is the parish church (Parochialkirche; by J. A. Nering and M. Grünberg, 1695–1703).

Klosterkirche
The ruins of a Franciscan church (Franziskaner-Klosterkirche) have been used since 1973 for exhibitions of various kinds.

Towards Waisenstrasse extends a stretch of the old town walls, with a typical old Berlin restaurant, "Zur letzten Instanz".

Neptune Fountain
The open space between the Television Tower, the Town Hall, the Marienkirche and Spandauer Strasse, together with the large flight of steps at the Television Tower, the terraces in front of it, the fountains and gardens, is a pleasant area of recreation in the heart of the city. At the south-west end can be seen the Neptune Fountain (Neptunbrunnen; by Reinhold Begas, 1891), depicting Neptune enthroned on a shell and surrounded by female figures symbolising the Elbe, the Oder, the Rhine and the Vistula.

*St Mary's Church
On the west side of the gardens is Berlin's oldest surviving church, the Marienkirche (St Mary's Church). This brick-built Gothic hall-church (begun 1270, enlarged 1380) has a helm-roofed tower (by C. G. Langhans, 1484). Below the tower is a fresco of the "Danse Macabre", accompanied by verses in Low German (1484). The interior is richly furnished, with an Baroque pulpit in alabaster (by A. Schlüter, 1703), a bronze font and a Late Gothic winged altar.

Friedrichshain

Friedrichshain Park
Friedrichshain Park, on the slopes of the Mühlenberg, is one of the largest parks in central Berlin, laid out in 1846 to the design of Gustav Meyer. In the park are the neo-Baroque Fairytale Fountain (Märchenbrunnen; by L. Hoffmann, 1913), various memorials and a cemetery containing the graves of those who died in the 1848 revolution.

Prenzlauer Berg

Jewish Cemetery
In Schönhauser Allee, in the Prenzlauer Berg ward, is the Jewish Cemetery (Jüdischer Friedhof; 1827). Among those buried here are the opera composer Giacomo Meyerbeer (d. 1864), the publisher Leopold Ullstein (d. 1899) and the painter Max Liebermann (d. 1935).

Outside Kollwitzstrasse 25, once the home of the painter and sculptress Käthe Kollwitz, can be seen a copy of her sculpture "The Mother".

*Husemannstrasse
Husemannstrasse has been restored in the style of the Wilhelmine period (late 19th century).

*Planetarium
One great attraction in this area is the large Planetarium north-east of the Ernst-Thälmann-Park (S-Bahn station Prenzlauer Allee), conspicuous with its gleaming silver dome, 30m/100ft high.

Pankow

Schloss Niederschönhausen (by E. von Göthe, 1704) is set in an attractive park, originally laid out in 1764 as a Rococo pleasure garden, which J. P. Lenné later converted into an English-style landscaped park, with rare trees.

Schloss Niederschön-hausen

The Bürgerpark (1856–64) is a popular place of recreation, with a restaurant. Adjoining is the Schönholzer Heide park.

Bürgerpark

Buch

In the Buch district are the Buch Clinik and the Baroque Schlosskirche, a church in the form of a Latin cross (by F. W. Dietrichs, 1731–36).

Lichtenberg

In the park (laid out by J. P. Lenné) of Schloss Friedrichsfelde is the Tierpark (opened 1955; area 160 hectares/400 acres), with some 1000 species of animals. Notable features are the Alfred Brehm House (with Tropical Hall), in which the large felines are housed, the bear house and the penguin pool.
Schloss Friedrichsfelde (by M. Böhme, c. 1719), the handsome Baroque palace at the entrance to the park, has been thoroughly restored.

*Tierpark (Zoo)

Treptow

Treptow Park was laid out in 1876–82, in the style of an English landscaped park, for the recreation of the people of East Berlin. The Great Industrial Exhibition of 1896 was held here.
In the park is the Soviet Memorial (Sowjetisches Ehrenmal; 1947–49), commemorating the Soviet troops who fell in the battle for Berlin in 1945.

*Treptow Park

In the south-east of the park, at Alt-Treptow 1, is the Archenbold Observatory (Stern-warte), built in 1896 on the occasion of the Industrial Exhibition and extended by Konrad Reimer and Friedrich Körte in 1908–09.

Archenbold Observatory

Köpenick

The Town Hall of Köpenick is remembered for the story of the "Captain of Köpenick", a shoemaker named Wilhelm Voigt who dressed up in military uniform, took charge of a squad of soldiers and arrested the burgomaster of the town.

Town Hall

On the Schlossinsel is Köpenick's Baroque Schloss (by R. von Langerfeld, 1647–85), with a sumptuous interior. It houses a Museum of Applied Art (Kunstgewerbemuseum), the first of its kind in Germany, founded in 1867, with a collection of European applied and decorative art over a thousand years.

*Schloss (Museum)

The Müggelsee and Müggelberge are frequented by Berliners throughout the year. Particular attractions in summer are the Müggelturm, the Spree Tunnel and the bathing station on the Lake.

*Müggelsee

Altglienicke

In the Altglienicke district is a garden suburb (around Akazienweg and Gartenstadtweg) laid out to the design of B. Taut in 1913–14 in a colourful style showing the influence of Expressionism. It is popularly known as the "Tuschkasten-Siedlung" ("Paintbox Town").

Bernburg   E 7

Land: Saxony-Anhalt
Altitude: 85m/279ft
Population: 40,900

Situation and characteristics	Bernburg, once the residence of the Princes and Dukes of Anhalt-Bernburg, lies some 30km/20 miles north of Halle. It is now an important industrial town and a popular tourist centre.

Sights

*Schloss	Bernburg's principal landmark is the Schloss (1538–70), a Renaissance palace on the banks of the Saale, with its richly decorated Baroque doorway, its "Blue Tower", its Romanesque keep ("Eulenspiegel Tower"; outlook tower) and its Renaissance features (nave by A. Günter and N. Hoffmann). The Schloss now houses the District Museum; of particular interest is the exhibition, "Mills and Millers". Within the Schloss are the old court theatre, in neo-classical style (by J. A. P. Bunge, 1826–27), now the Carl Maria von Weber Theatre, and lodgings for members of the court.
Schlosskirche	In the castle church of St Ägidien or St Giles (1752; Baroque, with Romanesque elements) is the three-storey ducal burial vault, with sumptuous Baroque sarcophagi.
Notable houses	Of the old houses in the town, mostly Renaissance and Baroque, the following are particularly notable: in Thälmannplatz No. 28 (1746) and No. 2 (Late Gothic, c. 1530), with benches in the entrance doorway; in Breite Strasse No. 25 (c. 1600; the old Ducal Chancery), No. 103 (1550; half-timbered) and No. 115 (1775), in Late Baroque styele, with a richly decorated façade.
Town walls	The walls round the old town and new town (15th–17th c.) are almost completely preserved, but only a few of the towers have survived (Nienburger Torturm, with Renaissance gable; Hasenturm). The Augustinian convent in the new town (c. 1300) is incorporated in the town walls.
Churches	Bernburg has a number of important churches: the parish church of St Mary (13th c.), with a richly sculptured choir (c. 1420); the unfinished Late Gothic hall-church of St Nicholas, with parts of an Early Gothic basilica; in the Dröbel district a cruciform church with a tower and dome (by J. A. P. Bunge, 1827–29); and in the Waldau district the parish church of St Stephen (12th c.), an aisleless Romanesque church with a flat roof.
Neustädter Brücke	The Neustädter Brücke (New Town Bridge), with several arches, was renovated in 1787. On the banks of the Saale can be found the Krumbholz recreation area, with a zoo, a Red Indian village, a Fairytale Garden and a miniature railway. Boat trips on the Saale.

Surroundings of Bernburg

Nienburg	Nienburg (5km/3 miles north-east) has a church which originally belonged to a Benedictine monastery. A masterpiece of German High Gothic, it was begun in 1242 as a basilica and completed after 1282 as a hall-church. Notable features of the interior are a Late Romanesque column with representations of the months, a painting by Lucas Cranach the Younger (1570) and a number of 14th century grave slabs.
Plötzkau	In Plötzkau (8km/5 miles south) is a Renaissance palace (1566–73) built on the foundations of a medieval castle, with 21 dormers and four main gables.
Calbe	Features of interest in Calbe (13km/8 miles north-east) are the Renaissance and Baroque houses in the Markt and the parish church of St Stephen, a Late Gothic hall-church (15th c.) with a brick-built porch, two low towers and a Late Gothic winged altar, pulpit and font (by U. Hachenberg, 1561–62). The interior of the 12th century St Laurence's church was modernised in 1964–65.

Biberach an der Riss   L 5

Land: Baden-Württemberg
Altitude: 524–653m/1719–2142ft
Population: 28,000

Biberach an der Riss lies in hilly moraine country in Upper Swabia, on the Upper Swabian Baroque Highway (see Upper Swabia). Now a considerable industrial town, it still preserves something of an old-world aspect.
The writer Christoph Martin Wieland, a native of Biberach, served as town clerk from 1760 to 1769.

Situation and characteristics

The Town

In the centre of the old town is the attractive Marktplatz, at the east corner of which is the Town Hall, a half-timbered building of 1432, with the New Town Hall (1503) beside it. In the Untere Schranne (1593) is a Wieland Museum. On the east side of the square stands the parish church of St Martin (remodelled in Baroque style in 1746–48).

Marktplatz

South-east of the church is the 16th century Heiliggeist-Spital (Hospital of the Holy Ghost; 15th century Gothic church), which now houses the Municipal Museum.

Hospital of Holy Ghost

On the south side of the old town is the house occupied by Wieland, with a permanent exhibition, "Gardens in Wieland's World".

Wieland-Gartenhaus

Ochsenhausen

15km/9miles east of Biberach on the Upper Swabian Baroque Highway is Ochsenhausen Abbey, a Benedictine house founded in 1093 and secularised in 1802. The conventual buildings (now occupied by a school) mainly date from the 17th and 18th centuries; the original church is richly decorated and furnished in Baroque style. The Library is now used for concerts.

Abbey

The Öchsle old-time railway runs between Ochsenhausen and Warthausen, near Biberach, at weekends in summer.

Old-time railway

In the quiet valley of the Rot, 5km/3 miles north of Ochsenhausen, is the walled Cistercian monastery of Gutenzell, with a beautiful Baroque church by Dominikus Zimmermann.

Gutenzell

10km/6 miles south-east is the Premonstratensian abbey of Rot an der Rot, with a Baroque church.

Rot an der Rot

Bad Wurzach

In the Wurzacher Ried, a protected area of marshland 20km/12½ miles south-east of Biberach, lies Bad Wurzach, a spa (mud baths) situated on the Upper Swabian Baroque Highway, with a Baroque palace built between 1723 and 1728.

Schloss

Bad Waldsee

The little medieval town of Bad Waldsee, also on the Upper Swabian Baroque Highway, has a church (originally Gothic, remodelled in Baroque style in 1766) which belonged to a house of Augustinian canons (façade and high altar by Dominikus Zimmermann).

Stiftskirche

Bad Schussenried

At Bad Schussenried the Swabian Poets' Highway (Schwäbische Dichterstrasse), coming from Biberach, 15km/9 miles north-east) intersects the Upper Swabian Baroque Highway. The most notable feature of the town is the Premonstratensian abbey (Baroque), with a fine church and a sumptuous library.

Abbey

2km/1¼ miles south-east of Bad Schussenried is the Kürnbach Open-Air Museum (farmhouses of the 15th–18th centuries).

Kürnbach Open-Air Museum

Bielefeld

**Steinhausen
pilgrimage church

In Steinhausen, an outlying district of Bad Schussenried (5km/3 miles north-east), is the pilgrimage church of SS Peter and Paul (by Dominikus Zimmermann, 1728–33), which has been called "the most beautiful village church in the world". Built on an oval ground-plan, it has a magnificent ceiling painting in the dome.

Bad Buchau

Nunnery

Bad Buchau, situated on the edge of the Federsee basin, also lies on the Upper Swabian Baroque Highway. On the northern outskirts of the town is a former house of Augustinian nuns. The church (originally Romanesque; remodelled in Baroque style 1774–76) now serves as the town's parish church.

**Federsee

To the north of the town is the Federsee, fringed by beds of reeds (nature reserve). The area is famed for the Stone Age remains found here (now in the nearby Federsee Museum).

Riedlingen

Heiligkreuztal

North-west of Bad Buchau on the Upper Swabian Baroque Highway is the little town of Riedlingen (pop. 9000), 6km/4 miles west of which is the old monastic house of Heiligkreuztal (beautiful Gothic tracery in windows).

Zwiefalten

*Minster

From Riedlingen the Upper Swabian Baroque Highway continues north-west to Zwiefalten, with a twin-towered Baroque minster (sumptuous interior).

Obermarchtal

*Monastic church

From Zwiefalten the Upper Swabian Baroque Highway runs east to Obermarchtal, situated above the Danube, with the extensive range of buildings of a house of Premonstratensian canons. The church has fine stucco decoration of the Wessobrunn school.

Bielefeld   E 4

Land: North Rhine-Westphalia
Altitude: 115m/377ft
Population: 304,000

Situation and
characteristics

Bielefeld, situated at an important pass through the hills of the Teutoburg Forest (see entry), is the economic and – with a recently founded university, a vocational college, a theatre and concert and other halls – also the cultural centre of Eastern Westphalia and Lippe. To the south of the old town centre with its half-timbered houses is the well planned modern residential district of Sennestadt. For many centuries the manufacture of linen was the mainstay of the town's economy; nowadays the principal industry is engineering, followed by electrical apparatus and appliances, car manufacture, foodstuffs and clothing.

Old Town

Alter Markt

The central feature of the old town is the Alter Markt (Old Market Square), on the south side of which stands the Batig-Haus (1680), with a Renaissance gable. Opposite it is the Theater am Alten Markt.

To the east of the Alter Markt are the Art Nouveau Municipal Theatre (Stadttheater; 1904) and the Old Town Hall (Altes Rathaus; neo-Renaissance and neo-Gothic), also built in 1904.

Municipal Theatre

To the west, at the near end of Obernstrasse, one of the town's principal shopping and commercial streets, is the Crüwell-Haus (c. 1530), with a magnificent stepped gable.

Crüwell-Haus

North of the Markt is the Altstädter Kirche (Old Town Church of St Nicholas; 1340), which has a fine carved altar from Antwerp. To the east of the church is the Linen-Weavers' Fountain (1909).

Altstädter Kirche

In Obernstrasse (south-west of the Alter Markt), half concealed, stands the Late Gothic church of St Jodokus (1511), with a Black Virgin of 1220. To the south of the church, at Welle 61, is the Waldhof Historical Museum.

St Jodokus

The Kunsthalle (1966–68), in Artur-Ladebeck-Strasse, has an important collection of 20th century art; in front of it can be seen Rodin's "Thinker".

Kunsthalle

In Kreuzstrasse is Spiegels Hof, a 16th century noble mansion with a fine clover-leaf gable. It is occupied at present by the Natural History Museum, for which a new building is planned.
Nearby is the twin-towered Late Gothic Marienkirche (St Mary's Church; 14th c.), with a number of fine monuments.

Spiegels Hof

Farther south is the Sparrenburg (c. 1240), the old castle of the Counts of Ravensberg (underground defensive works, 37m/121ft high tower), with a restaurant. The Sparren-burg has a festival with knightly tournaments and medieval plays with music.

Sparrenburg

South-west of the Sparrenburg are the Bethel Homes, founded by the Lutheran pastor Friedrich von Bodelschwingh (1831–1910).

Bethel

Western District

The central area of Bielefeld is bounded on the west by the Ostwestfalendamm (express-way) and the railway line. Beyond these are the Botanic Garden and Olderdissen Zoo (Tiergarten; over 1000 European animals).

Botanic Garden
Zoo

A little way north of the Zoo can be found the Farmhouse Museum (Bauernhaus-Museum), an open-air museum with old houses and domestic equipment, a windmill, traditional costumes, etc.

Farmhouse Museum

Oerlinghausen

15km/9 miles south-east of Bielefeld, at the foot of the Teutoburg Forest, is Oerling-hausen (pop. 16,000), with the Archaeological Open-Air Museum (dwellings and crafts of the prehistoric and early historical period).

Open-Air Museum

Stukenbrock Safariland: see Paderborn, Surroundings

Stukenbrock

Black Forest (Schwarzwald)

K–L 3–4

Land: Baden-Württemberg

The Black Forest, with its dark forest-covered hills one of the most visited upland regions in Europe, lies in the south-western corner of Germany, extending for 160km/100 miles from Pforzheim in the north to Waldshut, on the High Rhine, in the south. At the northern end it is some 20km/12½ miles wide, at the southern end 60km/40 miles. On the west side it descends to the Rhine valley (see entry) in a steep scarp which is slashed by well

Situation and characteristics

watered valleys; on the east it slopes more gently down to the upper Neckar and Danube valleys (see entries). The main ridge is broken up by numerous valleys, with flat-topped summits rising to only a moderate height above it.

**Landscape

Northern Black Forest	The northern Black Forest – the part lying north of the Kinzig valley, which cuts through the whole range from Freudenstadt to Offenburg – is made up of broad ridges of Bunter sandstone and reaches its highest point in the Hornisgrinde (1166m/3826ft, on whose slopes romantic little lakes such as the Mummelsee and Wildsee nestle in corries. The main tourist attractions of this region are the magnificent spa facilities of Baden-Baden, the valleys of the Murg with the interesting Murg hydroelectric installations, the Alb with the spa of Bad Herrenalb, the Enz with Wildbad, the Nagold with the attractive resort of Bad Liebenzell, picturesque Hirsau with its ruined abbey and the forests around Freudenstadt.
Central Black Forest	The central Black Forest, between the Kinzig valley and the Höllental, consists mainly of granite and gneiss, and reaches its highest point in the Kandel (1241m/4072ft), between the beautiful Simonswald, Elz and Glotter valleys. The area most popular with tourists is the stretch along the Schwarzwaldbahn (Black Forest Railway), centred on Triberg with its famous falls. To the east the central Black Forest merges into the Baar plateau, which in turn leads into the Swabian Alb (see entry).
Southern Black Forest	The southern Black Forest, scenically perhaps the most magnificent part of the range, is dominated by the 1493m/4899ft high Feldberg, from which a ridge runs west to the beautifully shaped Belchen (1414m/4639ft) and Blauen (1165m/3822ft), the peak reaching farthest towards the Rhine plain. Among the most striking beauty spots in this region are the two large lakes carved out by glaciers on the slopes of the Feldberg, the Titisee and Schluchsee, and the valleys which radiate from the Feldberg, in particular the romantic Höllental, and the Wiese and Alb valleys which run down to the High Rhine.

Spas and Health Resorts

There are so many spas and health resorts in the Black Forest that only the most important can be mentioned here. In the northern Black Forest, in addition to the well known spas of Baden-Baden and Wildbad, there are Freudenstadt, Bad Herrenalb, Gernsbach, Schönmünzach, Bad Liebenzell, Hirsau, Bad Teinach and the resorts in the Rench valley. In the central Black Forest there are Triberg with the neighbouring resorts of Schonach and Schönwald, Konigsfeld, St Märgen, the Glotter valley and Europe's highest brine spa, Bad Dürrheim (700–850m/2300–2800ft). In the southern Black Forest there are Titisee, Hinterzarten and the area around the Feldberg, St Blasien, Menzenschwand, Schönau and the thermal resort of Badenweiler.

Winter Sports Resorts

Popular winter sports centres in the Black Forest, Germany's oldest skiing area (the first "snowshoe club" having been founded at Todtnau in 1891) are the Kniebis plateau, Dobel, Baiersbronn, Triberg and surrounding area, Furtwangen, Neustadt-Titisee, Lenzkirch and the Feldberg and surrounding area. The northern Black Forest is more suited for langlauf skiing, while the best areas for Alpine skiing are around the Feldberg, Belchen and Herzogenhorn.

Tourist Routes

*Schwarzwald-Hochstrasse	The famous and very popular Schwarzwald-Hochstrasse (Black Forest Ridgeway) follows the crest of the hills through magnificent fir forests, with extensive views, from Baden-Baden along the Hornisgrinde to the Kniebis plateau at Freudenstadt. The southward continuation of the road runs from Triberg to Waldshut.

View towards Kandel ▶

| Schwarzwald-Tälerstrasse | The Schwarzwald-Tälerstrasse (Black Forest Valley Road) begins at Rastatt and ascends the Murg valley, passing the imposing Schwarzenbach Dam, and then continues by way of Freudenstadt, where it meets the Black Forest Ridgeway, to Alpirsbach. |

Schwarzwald-Bäderstrasse The Schwarzwald-Bäderstrasse (Black Forest Spa Route) is a 270km/170 mile long circuit which takes in a series of spas between Pforzheim and Freudenstadt (Bad Liebenzell, Bad Teinach, Freudenstadt, Bad Rippoldsau, Wildbad, Bad Herrenalb, Baden-Baden, Waldbronn).

See also Baden-Baden, Badenweiler, Freiburg, Freudenstadt, Karlsruhe, Pforzheim and Wildbad

Blankenburg

See Wernigerode

Blaubeuren   K 5

Land: Baden-Württemberg
Altitude: 519m/1703ft
Population: 12,000

Situation and characteristics Blaubeuren is picturesquely situated on the southern edge of the Swabian Alb (see entry) in a rocky valley in the upper reaches of the Danube, now drained by the little river Blau. The town grew up around a Benedictine monastery founded in the 11th century.

*Blautopf

The great sight of Blaubeuren is the Blautopf, one of the largest karstic resurgences in Germany. This funnel-shaped depression, 21m/69ft deep, filled with shimmering bluish-green water, is linked with a water-filled cave system which has been explored for a distance of some 1300m/1400yds. On the edge of the Blautopf can be seen a historic old ironworks.

Blaubeuren Monastery *High altar The monastery has recently been well restored. The church has a high altar (1493) of the Ulm school, with panel paintings by B. Zeitblom and B. Strigel, and fine choir-stalls. A beautiful cloister adjoins the church. In the monks' bath-house is an interesting little local museum.

Museum of Prehistory In the south-east of the old town is the Museum of Prehistory (Urgeschichtliches Museum), with material dating back to Neanderthal times, including a 33,000-year-old ivory miniature which is the oldest known representation of the human figure.

Bochum   F 2

Land: North Rhine-Westphalia
Altitude: 104m/341ft
Population: 408,000

Situation and characteristics Bochum, in the heart of the Ruhr, between the rivers Emscher and Ruhr, offers a textbook example of the structural change which is taking place in the economy of this region. This town which owed its rise to coal and steel no longer has any mines and has acquired new industrial and commercial interests. In addition to its traditional steel industry it now manufactures cars (Opel) and radio and television sets. In the scientific and cultural field it has the Ruhr University (opened 1965), the Institute of Environmental Research and Futurology and its Schauspielhaus (Theatre). It is also the home of the German Shakespeare Society.

Town Centre

In the town centre are the Town Hall (Rathaus; 1931; carillon) and the 14th century Propsteikirche, with the Romanesque shrine of St Perpetua.

In the north of the town (Am Bergbaumuseum 9) is the German Mining Museum (Deutsches Bergbau-Museum), with a demonstration pit, a winding-tower and a geological collection.

*Mining Museum

South-east of the Mining Museum, at Kortumstrasse 147, is the Art Collection of the Bochum Museum (mainly art since 1945). The museum's collection of material on the history of the town is in Haus Kemnade (see below).

Bochum Museum

Farther south-east, at Castroper Strasse 67, the Planetarium illustrates the movements of heavenly bodies and the orbits of artificial satellites.

Planetarium

To the north of the Planetarium lies the Municipal Park (Stadtpark), with the Zoo (Tierpark; 1000 animals of 235 species) and an outlook tower.

Zoo

The Geological Garden, on the site of an old pit in the south of the town in Querenburger Strasse, gives a clear picture of the local rock structures.

Geological Garden

Ruhr University

South-east of the town is the campus of the Ruhr University, with a well known art collection (antiquities, coin collection, modern art).

Art collection

Within the University grounds lies the Botanic Garden (designed for research but also open to the public).

Botanic Garden

South-Western Districts

In the Sevinghausen district can be found Helfs Hof, a farmhouse dating from about 1560 which is now the Wattenscheider Heimatmuseum (furniture, craft tools, documents).

Helfs Hof

In the Dahlhausen district is the Railway Museum (Eisenbahnmuseum; old steam, electric and diesel locomotives, rolling-stock, signalling systems, etc.).

Railway Museum

Surroundings of Bochum

10km/6 miles south-east is Stiepel, with the Late Romanesque Marienkirche (St Mary's Church; frescoes) of around 1200. On the left bank of the Ruhr stands Haus Kemnade, a moated house of 1664 which now contains the Bochum Museum's collection of material on the history of the town, a Farmhouse Museum and a collection of musical instruments.
On Lake Kemnade, formed by a dam on the Ruhr, are a boating harbour and a regatta course.

Stiepel
Haus Kemnade

Bode Valley

See Thale

Bonn   G 2

Land: North Rhine-Westphalia
Altitude: 64m/210ft
Population: 290,000

Bonn

Situation and characteristics

Bonn lies on both banks of the Rhine, which here enters the Cologne lowlands after its passage through the Rhenish Uplands. The pattern of the city's life is set by its old and famous University, its role as the seat of government (now due to be transferred to Berlin), its busy commercial life and its attractive setting (particularly on the river side, with its view of the nearby Siebengebirge). Since the incorporation of Beul and Bad Godesberg into the city it has also possessed a renowned spa resort within its boundaries. Bonn was the birthplace of Beethoven.

Town Centre

In the centre of the old town is the Markt, with the Old Town Hall (Altes Rathaus; 1737–38). At Rathausgasse 7 is the Municipal Art Collection (20th century German painting and sculpture). A little way north stands the church of St Remigius (Remigiuskirche; 13th and 14th c.).

*Beethovenhaus

At Bonngasse 20 is the house in which Beethoven was born, now a museum, with a concert hall for chamber music.

*Minster

South-west of the Markt, in Münsterplatz, stands the venerable Minster (dedicated to SS Cassius and Florentinus), one of the finest Romanesque churches on the Rhine (11th–13th c.; east crypt 11th c.). On the south side of the church is an attractive 12th century cloister.

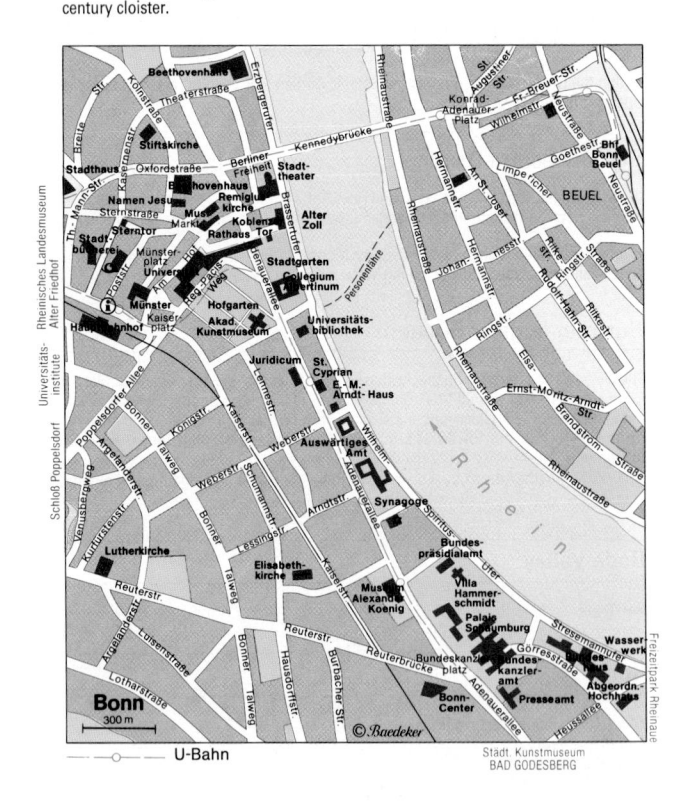

Marktplatz and Old Town Hall

At the near end of Adenauer-Allee stands the Koblenzer Tor (Koblenz Gate) which gives access to the east wing of the long range of buildings of the University built by Enrico Zuccali and Robert de Cotte between 1697 and 1725 as the Electoral palace. To the south lies the Hofgarten.

University

To the east of the Koblenzer Tor, on the banks of the Rhine, are the Stadtgarten (Municipal Park) and the Alter Zoll (Old Custom House), on a former bastion with views of the Rhine and the Siebengebirge. Here too is a monument to the patriotic writer Ernst Moritz Arndt (1769–1860), whose house at Adenauer-Allee 79, upstream, is now a museum.

Stadtgarten

To the north of the Alter Zoll, just before the bridge over the Rhine, is the Stadttheater (Municipal Theatre; 1963–65). Downstream from the bridge, on the left bank of the Rhine, is the Beethovenhalle (1957–59; damaged by fire in 1983).

Theatre

Beethovenhalle

To the west of the railway station (Hauptbahnhof) can be found the Rhineland Museum (Rheinisches Landesmuseum), with a rich collection of antiquities (Roman and Frankish art), medieval works of art and pictures.

Rhineland Museum

Government District

To the south, along Adenauer-Allee, are numerous government and public buildings: at No. 135 the Villa Hammerschmidt, official residence of the President of the Federal Republic; at Nos. 139–142 the Palais Schaumburg and the Federal Chancellor's Office (Bundeskanzleramt; 1975–77), with a monument (1981) to Konrad Adenauer in front of it; at No. 150 the Alexander Koenig Zoological Museum. On Bundeskanzlerplatz is the Bonn-Center. To the east, in Görresstrasse, stands the parliament building, the Bundeshaus (at present in course of reconstruction), with its rear front facing the Rhine. Adjoining is a 30-storey tower block, the Abgeordneten-Haus (members' offices). Beyond this lies the Rhineaue Park.

Poppelsdorf

Schloss
To the south-west of the town, at the end of the Poppelsdorfer Allee (around which are handsome houses built between 1860 and 1914), is the Poppelsdorfer Schloss (1715–30), with the Botanic Garden beyond it.

Kreuzberg
South-west of the Poppelsdorfer Schloss (20 min.) rises the Kreuzberg (125m/410ft), with a Franciscan friary and a conspicuous Baroque church (1627–37), built on to the east end of which is the "Heilige Stiege" (Scala Santa; by Balthasar Neumann, 1746–51).

Bad Godesberg

To the south lies Bad Godesberg (now part of Bonn), with many diplomatic missions. Its main features of interest are the ruined Godesburg (keep of 1210; hotel), the Redoute (a Rococo Electoral palace, now used for official receptions) and the Deutschherrenkommende, a former house of the Teutonic Order, now an embassy.

Schwarzrheindorf

In the Schwarzrheindorf district, on the right bank of the Rhine, is a unique Romanesque double church (12th c.).

Surroundings of Bonn

Brühl
*Schloss
20km/12½ miles south-west of Bonn, in Brühl, is Schloss Augustusburg (1725–28; begun by J. C. Schlaun), a gem of Rococo architecture, with a famous staircase hall by Balthasar Neumann. The palace is now used for government receptions and other state occasions.

To the south of Brühl can be found a large amusement park, Phantasialand, with a Wild West town and a variety of attractions, sideshows, etc.

Bad Honnef
15km/9 miles south-east of Bonn on the right bank of the Rhine, at the foot of the Siebengebirge, is Bad Honnef, once the residence of Konrad Adenauer (1876–1967), first Chancellor of the Federal Republic. His house in the Rhöndorf district is now a memorial museum.

Siebengebirge
See Rhine Valley

Bottrop   F 2

Land: North Rhine-Westphalia
Altitude: 28m/92ft
Population: 118,000

Situation and
characteristics
The town of Bottrop, on the northern edge of the Ruhr industrial area, owes its origin to a village named Borgthorpe which first appears in the records in the 11th century. It developed rapidly when coal began to be mined here in 1863. It claims to be the mining town with the largest area of parks and gardens.

The Town

Stadtgarten
Quadrat
In the centre of the town is the peaceful Stadtgarten (Municipal Park), in which is the Quadrat, a modern media centre with the Museum of Prehistory and Local History (good Ice Age collection), the Modern Gallery (exhibitions) and a large collection of works by the Bottrop painter Josef Albers (1888–1976).

Traumland
In the northern district of Kirchhellen-Feldhausen can be found the Traumland ("Dreamland") theme park.

Also in Feldhausen is Schloss Beck, a moated house by Johann Konrad Schlaun (1766–71), with an interior in early neo-classical style.

Schloss Beck

Brandenburg

E 7

Land: Brandenburg
Altitude: 31m/102ft
Population: 94,000

Brandenburg, once an episcopal city and a town with extensive trading connections, lies 50km/30 miles south-west of Berlin on the lower Havel, surrounded by the Beetzsee, the Plauer See and the Breitlingsee.

Situation and characteristics

Dominsel (Cathedral Island)

The Cathedral of SS Peter and Paul (begun 1165), on the Dominsel, is a Romanesque basilica with extensive alterations in Gothic style. In the crypt (1235) is a memorial chapel (1953) commemorating Christians murdered during the Second World War.
The "Bunte Kapelle" ("Painted Chapel") has Late Romanesque wall paintings. Notable features of the richly furnished interior are the 13th century stained glass, the Romanesque crucifix, the 14th century Bohemian Altar (showing the influence of Bohemian panel painting), the Lehnin Altar (1518), the Marienaltar (c. 1430), the Wagner Organ, the Angel Candelabrum (1441) and grave-slabs of bishops and canons. In the conventual buildings, parts of which have been preserved, are the cloister, the Cathedral Archives (valuable manuscripts) and the Cathedral Museum, with fine medieval vestments and the Brandenburg Lenten Veil (c. 1290). In front of the Cathedral is the Burghof, with the Cathedral offices.

*Cathedral

In Burgweg stands the Gothic Petrikapelle (St Peter's Chapel), which has been the parish church of the Cathedral parish since 1320, with cellular vaulting of 1520. A Slav king named Pribislaw-Heinrich is said to have been buried in 1150 in an earlier church on the site.

St Peter's Chapel

Old Town

The old town lies west of the Dominsel on the banks of the Havel. Its main feature of interest is the Town Hall (Rathaus; 1470), a two-storey Late Gothic brick building with a stepped gable, a tower and doorway with rich brick tracery and a large pointed-arched doorway in the east gable.
In front of the Town Hall can be seen a figure of Roland (1474; a symbol of municipal authority), over 5m/16ft high, which originally stood in front of the Town Hall in the new town (destroyed in 1945). Adjoining the Town Hall is the Ordonnanzhaus (13th–15th c.).

*Town Hall

To the north of the Town Hall is the parish church of St Gotthardt (12th c.), the oldest building in Brandenburg, with a Late Gothic nave (15th c.) and a Baroque crest to the tower. Notable features in the interior are the bronze font (Romanesque, 13th c.), a Triumphal Cross group (15th c., Late Gothic), a tapestry of around 1463 depicting a unicorn hunt, a Renaissance altar (1559) and 16th and 18th century epitaphs.

St Gotthardt's Church

The Municipal Museum, in the Freyhaus (Hauptstrasse 96), a Baroque building of 1723 with a fine staircase hall, has much material illustrating the history of the town and an important collection of European graphic art of the 16th–20th centuries, including an almost complete representation of the work of Daniel Chodowiecki.

Municipal Museum

In the south of the old town can be found the ruined parish church of St John (St Johannis), an Early Gothic brick church (13th c.; part restored 1951), with a rose window over the north doorway and a slender tower (1500).

St John's Church

Parts of the town walls still survive, with four gate towers – the Rathenower Torturm (Gothic blind arcading), the Plauer Torturm (topped by an openwork crown), the Mühltorturm and the Steintorturm – and the Wasserpromenade and Annenpromenade.

Town walls

Brandenburg Cathedral	Roland, outside the Old Town Hall

<table>
<tr><td>St Nicholas's
Church</td><td>South-west of the old town is the Nikolaikirche (St Nicholas's Church), a brick-built Late Romanesque basilica (1170–1230; damaged 1945).</td></tr>
</table>

New Town

St Catherine's Church

The new town lies to the south of the Dominsel. In the centre stands the parish church of St Catherine (Katharinenkirche; 1395–1401), an outstanding example of brick-built Gothic architecture and the masterpiece of Hinrich Brunsberg. It is a vaulted hall-church in what is called the Rich style; particularly fine is the gable of the Fronleichnamskapelle or Marienkapelle (Corpus Christi or St Mary's Chapel). Notable features of the interior are a Late Gothic double winged altar (1474), St Hedwig's Altar (1457), in the South Chapel, the font (1440), in the North Chapel, the pulpit (1668) and numerous epitaphs.

Gymnasium

Near St Catherine's is the former Gymnasium (Grammar School; 1797), a three-storey Baroque building with a coat of arms below the mansard roof. There is a reference to a church school on this site as early as 1386.

Burghers' houses

There are interesting 18th century burghers' houses at Steinstrasse 21, Neustädtischer Markt 7 and 11, Gorrenberg 14, Kleine Münzstrasse 6 and Kurstrasse 7.

Marienberg

On the Marienberg (69m/226ft) is the Marienberg Park. Here a Germanic tribe, the Semnones, worshipped the goddess Freya, and in the 11th and 12th centuries there was also a Slav sanctuary on the hill. In 1220 a church dedicated to the Virgin, with a wonderworking image, was built here; it was destroyed during the Thirty Years' War, and the ruins were finally pulled down in 1772.

Brandenburg-Plaue

In Plaue (10km/6 miles west on B 1) are a Baroque palace (1711–16), now occupied by a school, and a brick-built Late Romanesque church with Gothic wall paintings (15th c.) and a Renaissance pulpit.

Surroundings of Brandenburg

Lehnin Abbey (20km/12½ miles south-east) was the first Cistercian house in Branden-burg, founded in 1180 by Margrave Otto I. The church, an Early Gothic basilica dedicated to the Virgin, begun in 1190 and consecrated in 1262, is one of the earliest and most important examples of North German brick-built architecture. Of the conventual build-ings there remain the monks' cells, the royal lodgings, the granary, the falconer's house and the abbey walls, with a triple-arched gatehouse.

*Lehnin Abbey

The village of Ketzür (10km/6 miles north-east) has an Early Gothic church (14th–18th c.) with fine 17th century wall paintings and an early 17th century epitaph.

Ketzür

Rathenow (32km/20 miles north-west on B 102) has a Romanesque parish church (renovated 1517) with a Late Gothic winged altar and the monument (by J. G. Glume, 1738) of Elector Frederick William, depicted in the garb of a Roman emperor. At Rhi-nower Strasse 12B is the Heimatmuseum (history of the town's optical industry, etc.).

Rathenow

Braunschweig (Brunswick)   E 6

Land: Lower Saxony
Altitude: 72m/236ft
Population: 252,000

The old Guelph town of Braunschweig (better known in English as Brunswick), the second largest city in the *Land* of Lower Saxony, lies on the Oker in a fertile plain in the north of the Harz foreland area. In the old town a few "islands of tradition" bear witness to the rich history of the town, which suffered severe destruction in the Second World War. Braunschweig's Technical College (now the University) was the earliest in Germany (founded 1745).

Situation and characteristics

Central Area

In the heart of the town lies the Burgplatz, with Burg Dankwarderode (restored), built about 1175 by Henry the Lion (with a two-storey wing of 1887). In the centre of the square is a magnificent bronze lion, set up here by Henry the Lion in 1166 as a symbol of his power.

Burgplatz
*Lion

On the north side of the square can be seen the Huneborstelsches Haus (1536), which was moved to its present position in 1902; it is now a guild-house.

*Huneborstelsches Haus

The Romanesque and Gothic Cathedral (Dom) of St Blasius (Blaise), the earliest large vaulted building in Lower Saxony, was built in 1173–95 during the reign of Henry the Lion. In the nave is the tomb of Henry and his wife Mathilde (*c.* 1250), a masterpiece of Late Romanesque sculpture of the Saxon school. In front of the choir, under a brass of 1707, are buried Emperor Otto IV (d. 1218) and his wife Beatrix. In the high choir, which, like the south aisle, has Romanesque wall paintings, is a seven-branched candelabrum 4.5m/15ft high, presented by Henry the Lion. The oldest and most important item in the furnishings of the Cathedral is the Imerward Crucifix (1150), from the first cathedral.

**Cathedral

To the north of the Burgplatz is the large Hagenmarkt, with a fountain commemorating Henry the Lion (1874) and the Katharinenkirche (St Catherine's Church; 12th–14th c.; Protestant), with an organ installed in 1980, incorporating parts of a Baroque organ of 1623. A little way west is the 12th century Andreaskirche (St Andrew's Church; Roma-nesque, with Gothic alterations).

Hagenmarkt

To the north of the town centre is the University of Technology, founded in 1745 as the Collegium Carolinum. Nearby is the Natural History Museum.

University

The Markt, south-west of the Burgplatz, forms the heart of the old Hanseatic commercial town. It originated as a street market in the 11th and 12th centuries. On the west side of

Markt

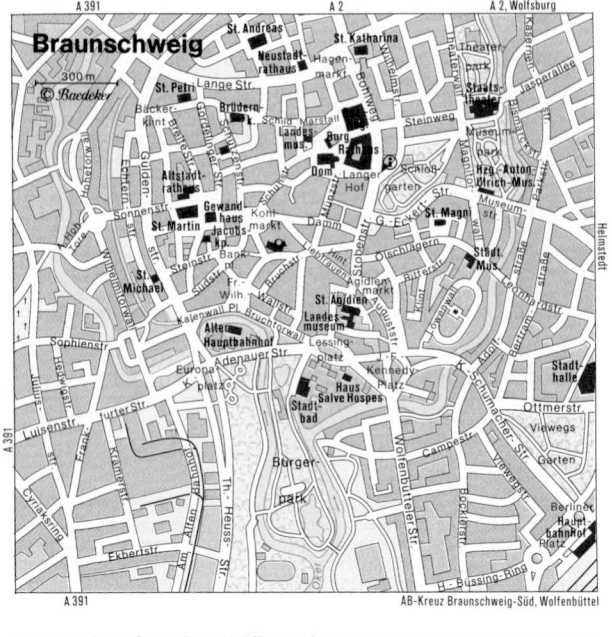

A 391   A 2   A 2, Wolfsburg

A 391   AB-Kreuz Braunschweig-Süd, Wolfenbüttel

the square is the Gothic Town Hall (Rathaus), originally a 14th century banqueting hall, with a two-tier arcade in front. Opposite it is the Martinikirche (St Martin's Church; 12th–14th c.; Protestant).

Gewandhaus

On the south side of the square can be seen the medieval Gewandhaus (Cloth Hall; restored), now occupied by a restaurant. Its east gable (1591) is the finest example of Renaissance architecture in Braunschweig.

St Michael's Church

South-west of the Markt can be found the little Michaeliskirche (St Michael's Church; Protestant), which was consecrated in 1157; in its present form it is a 14th century Gothic hall-church. At Alte Knochenhauerstrasse 11 is Braunschweig's oldest half-timbered house front. At Güldenstrasse 7 can be seen the handsome Haus der Hanse (1567).

Ottilienteil

To the south of the Burgplatz, around the Gothic church of St Ägidien or St Giles (R.C.; choir 13th c., nave 14th c.), is the picturesque Ottilienteil quarter, with many half-timbered houses. Adjoining the church, in the old Dominican monastery, is the Braunschweig Provincial Museum (Landesmuseum; history, folk traditions).

St Magnus's Church

South-east of the Burgplatz is the finely restored Magnikirche (St Magnus's Church), consecrated in 1031 (Protestant; modern sculpture). Behind the church there remains a corner of old Braunschweig, with fine half-timbered houses. In the churchyard of St Magnus's (700m/750yds south-east) can be seen the tomb of the writer and philosopher G. E. Lessing (1729–81: see Wolfenbüttel). On the east side of the churchyard is the Stadthalle (1965).

Museumspark

On the eastern edge of the town centre, beside the Museumspark, stands the Herzog-Anton-Ulrich-Museum (Museumstrasse 1), with a collection of art and applied art (imperial robes of Otto IV; Rembrandt's "Family Group", c. 1668). 200m/220yds south, on the Löwenwall, is the interesting Municipal Museum (Städtisches Museum).

Bürgerpark

On the southern edge of the town centre lies the beautiful Bürgerpark, with a swimming pool (the Stadtbad) and a recreational and educational centre. Adjoining is the elegant Schloss Richmond (1768–69).

Burgplatz

Altstadtmarkt

Braunschweig-Riddagshausen

In the suburb of Riddagshausen to the east of the town, beyond the Prinz-Albrecht-Park, can be found a notable church belonging to a former Cistercian monastery (13th c.). To north and south are the Riddagshausen nature reserve and the Buchhorst landscape reserve.

Bremen   D 4

Capital of the *Land* of Bremen
Altitude: 5m/16ft
Population: 526,000

The Free Hanseatic City of Bremen, on the lower Weser (57km/35 miles from Bremer-haven), capital of the *Land* of Bremen, is one of the largest seaports and centres of sea-borne trade in Germany, carrying on a considerable trade in grain, cotton and tobacco. The *Land* consists of the city of Bremen and the port of Bremerhaven (see entry), which are separated from one another by a stretch of territory in Lower Saxony.

Situation and characteristics

City Centre

The old town is bounded on the east and north-east by the town moat and the line of the old town walls (now laid out in gardens). Near Bürgermeister-Smidt-Strasse can be seen a windmill, the Mühle am Wall.

Town walls

In the picturesque Markt, in front of the Town Hall, stands a famous 5.4m/18ft high figure of Roland (1404), the symbol of the city's freedom and independent jurisdiction.

*Markt
*Roland

The Town Hall (Rathaus) is a brick-built Gothic structure (1405–10), with a sumptuous Renaissance façade added in 1609–12. On its east side is the New Town Hall (1912). The

*Town Hall

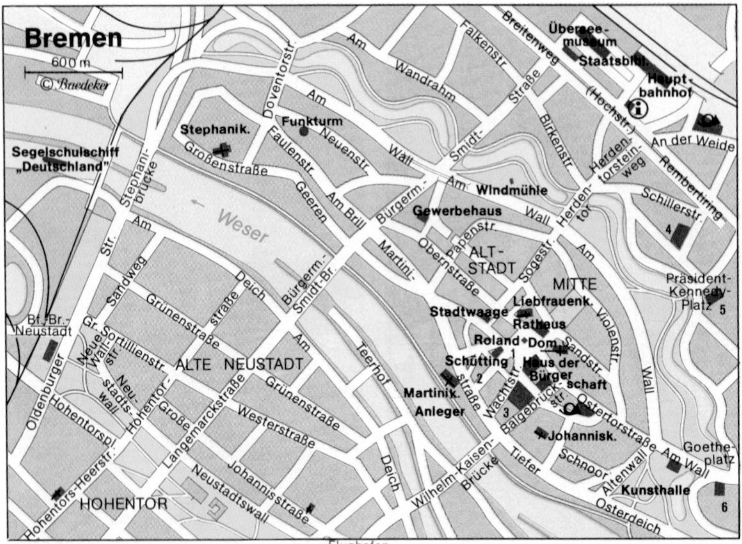

Häfen · Stadthalle

1 Markt 2 Böttcherstraße 3 Baumwollbörse 4 Zentralbad 5 Stadtarchiv 6 Theater am Goetheplatz

Old Town Hall has one of the most elegant banqueting and reception halls is Germany (40m/130ft long, 13m/43ft wide, 8m/26ft high), with a large mural painting of the "Judgment of Solomon" (1537). This is the scene of the annual Schaffermahlzeit, a traditional meal for ship-owners and seamen. On the side facing the market is a richly carved spiral staircase.

*Ratskeller

On the west side of the Old Town Hall is the entrance to the Ratskeller, famed for its well stocked wine-cellar. The Hauff Room is decorated with frescoes by Max Slevogt (1927) illustrating Wilhelm Hauff's "Fantasies in the Bremen Ratskeller" (1827). Under the north-west tower can be seen a bronze group (by Gerhard Marcks, 1953) of the "Bremen Town Musicians" (a donkey, a dog, a cat and a cock who feature in an old folk tale).

Cathedral

The Cathedral (Dom) of St Peter (Protestant) dates from the 11th, 13th and 16th centuries. The exterior, with its twin towers (98m/322ft high), was restored between 1888 and 1898. The richly decorated Baroque pulpit (1638) was a gift from Queen Christina of Sweden. In the Bleikeller ("Lead Cellar") are a number of leathery mummified bodies.

Opposite the Cathedral is the modern Haus der Bürgerschaft (Citizens' House; 1966). To the west is the Schütting (1537–38), the old merchant guild-house, occupied since 1849 by the Chamber of Commerce.

Liebfrauenkirche
Gewerbehaus

North-west of the Markt stands the 13th century Liebfrauenkirche (Church of Our Lady), with medieval wall paintings and modern stained glass (by A. Manessier, 1966–73). Farther north-west, at the end of the pedestrian zone, is the Gewerbehaus (Trades House; 1618–19, restored), now occupied by the Chamber of Crafts.

*Böttcherstrasse

Beyond the Schütting is the entrance to the narrow Böttcherstrasse, which in 1926–30 was transformed from a street of mean dwellings into a "museum street" at the expense of a wealthy Bremen coffee dealer, Dr L. Roselius. On the left is the Paula-Becker-Modersohn-Haus, with works by the Worpswede painter of that name (d. 1907), on the

Roland, outside Bremen Town Hall ▶

right the Hag-Haus, then on the left the Roselius-Haus (1588; examples of Low German art from Gothic to Baroque), the Haus des Glockenspiels (House of the Carillon), the Bremen Casino and the Robinson Crusoe House.

°Schnoorviertel

Beyond the Cotton Exchange (Baumwollbörse) in Wachtstrasse is the charming Schnoorviertel, the oldest part of Bremen, now the haunt of artists, with burghers' houses of the 15th–18th centuries and old beer-houses. Also in this area is the 14th century Johanniskirche (St John's Church; brick-built Gothic).

°Kunsthalle

In the south-east of the old town, at the Ostertor, is the Kunsthalle (17th century Dutch paintings, old German masters, French and Dutch painting of the 19th and 20th centuries, works by painters in the Worpswede artists' colony).

°Overseas Museum

To the north of the old town, on the west side of Bahnhofsplatz, can be found the interesting Overseas Museum (Überseemuseum), with collections of material on natural history, trade and ethnography (South Seas, Australia, Asia) and an exhibition on Bremen's import and export trade.
To the north-east lies the Bürgerpark (area 200 hectares/500 acres), laid out in 1866 in the style of a landscaped English park.

Bremen-Schwachhausen

Focke Museum

In the north-eastern suburb of Schwachhausen, at Schwachhausener Heerstrasse 240, is the Focke Museum, the Bremen Museum of Art and Culture, with Bremen bygones, material illustrating the Low German way of life and a seafaring section (with a Hanseatic "kogge" or merchant ship).
To the east are the large Rhododendron Park (azalea museum) and the Botanic Garden.

Port

To the north-west of the old town is Bremen's port (15 docks capable of taking ocean-going vessels). The most important docks are the Überseehafen, the Europahafen and the Neustädter Hafen (container terminal), all with freeport facilities. There are harbour tours from the Martinianleger (landing-stage) by the Wilhelm Kaisen Bridge.

Surroundings of Bremen

Worpswede

23km/14 miles north-east is Worpswede, famed as an artists' colony (Vogeler, Modersohn, Mackensen, Hans am Ende, etc.; permanent art exhibitions), on the Teufelsmoor.

Bremerhaven   C4

Land: Bremen
Altitude: 3m/10ft
Population: 135,000

Situation and
characteristics

Bremerhaven lies 57km/35 miles north of Bremen at the junction of the Geeste with the Weser, just before the Weser flows into the North Sea. It is part of the *Land* of Bremen, though separated from Bremen itself by a stretch of Lower Saxon territory. Bremerhaven is a thriving port, with the largest fishing harbour in mainland Europe and extensive docks handling ocean-going vessels, as well as an institute of marine research.

The Port

Fishing harbour

The most southerly part of the port installations which extend along the Weser is the fishing harbour, where about half the whole German catch of fish is landed. It is interesting to watch the fish auctions held when the boats come in with their catches.

Bremerhaven Harbour

Between the fishing harbour's double sluice-gates and the landing-stage of the Weser ferry is the North Sea Museum (Nordsee-Museum; marine flora and fauna), run by the Alfred Wegener Institute of Polar and Marine Research.

North Sea Museum

In the eastern district of Geestemünde, at Kaistrasse 6, is the Morgenstern Museum (prehistory, history of the town, local traditions).

Morgenstern Museum

To the north, beyond the Geeste, lies the Old Harbour, with the German Shipping Museum (Deutsches Schiffahrtsmuseum), housed in a building designed by Hans Scharoun. Notable among the exhibits is a Bremen "kogge" (a Hanseatic merchant ship). Among the historic old ships in the harbour are a Mark XXI submarine and a four-master, the "Seute Deern" (restaurant).
On the harbour stands a 112m/367ft high radar tower (viewing platform). On the east side is the Columbus-Center (tower blocks; 1978).

**German Shipping Museum

Still farther north, on the Weserdeich, is the Zoo am Meer ("Sea Zoo"; seals, polar bears, etc.; aquarium).

Zoo am Meer

At the north end of the port is the container terminal, the largest of its kind in Europe (viewing platform on the main building).

Container Terminal

Bremerhaven-Speckenbüttel

In the northern district of Speckenbüttel is the Speckenbüttel Open-Air Museum, with 17th century farmhouses from Lower Saxony.

Open-Air Museum

Bruchsal   I 4

Land: Baden-Württemberg
Altitude: 115m/377ft
Population: 22,000

Brunswick

Situation and
characteristics

The town of Bruchsal, north-east of Karlsruhe, lies in the Upper Rhine plain on the borders of the Kraichgau, at an important road and rail junction.

*Schloss

The town's principal attraction is the 18th century Baroque palace of the Prince-Bishops of Speyer. It was begun by Maximilian von Welsch in 1722, and Balthasar Neumann was also involved in its design. It is an elaborate complex of some fifty separate buildings set in a beautiful park. The palace suffered severe damage during the Second World War but has been excellently restored.

Interior

The interior of the palace is one of the most brilliant achievements of German Rococo; particularly fine is the staircase hall by Balthasar Neumann, with a large ceiling painting in the dome (originally by Januarius Zick). The church was rebuilt in modern style to the design of Professor Götz of Heidelberg (crucifix, tabernacle and holy water stoup by Fritz Wotruba; Stations of the Cross by HAP Grieshaber).

Museums

The Corps de Logis houses a branch of the Baden Provincial Museum (pieces of original furniture from the palace, porcelain and faience, tapestries; hunting collection).

There is an unusual and interesting Museum of Mechanical Musical Instruments (with demonstrations).

Among the exhibits in the Bruchsal Municipal Museum are Ice Age animals, archaeological finds from prehistoric and early historical times, coins and medals.

St Peter's Church

In the south-east of the town stands St Peter's Church (by Balthasar Neumann, 1742–49), with the tombs of the last Prince-Bishops of Speyer. There are occasional concerts and recitals in the church.

Brunswick

See Braunschweig

Celle   D 5

Land: Lower Saxony
Altitude: 40m/130ft
Population: 73,000

Situation and
characteristics

This old ducal town on the Aller, on the southern fringe of Lüneburg Heath, has preserved its character as a princely capital down to our own day. The rectangular layout of the picturesque half-timbered streets of the old town is aligned on the palace.

Schloss

The Schloss, built partly in the Late Gothic period and partly in the Baroque style of the second half of the 17th century, was the residence of the Dukes of Brunswick and Lüneburg from 1292 to 1866. It has fine state apartments and the oldest court theatre in Germany (1674); the chapel has a sumptuous Renaissance interior. A short distance away, to the north, is the Provincial Supreme Court (Oberlandesgericht).

Museum

Opposite the palace is the Bomann Museum, with a rich collection of material on the history of Hannover, including a Lower Saxon farmhouse of 1571.

Old Town

The old town, with its picturesque half-timbered streets and lanes, lies to the east of the palace. Particularly fine is Kalandgasse, with the old Latin School. At its south end is the Stechbahn, once the scene of knightly tournaments. *‌*Half-timbered buildings

In the Markt stands the Town Church (Stadtkirche; 14th and 17th c.), with epitaphs and grave slabs of the last Dukes of Celle and a princely burial vault (tomb of the Danish Queen Caroline Mathilde, d. 1775). Town Church

The Town Hall (Rathaus) is in Late Renaissance style (1530–81). Other notable buildings in the old town are the Hoppener-Haus (1532) at Poststrasse 8 and the Stechinelli-Haus (17th c.) at Grosser Plan 14. Town Hall

Farther south, straddling the river Fuhse, is the Provincial Stud Farm (Landgestüt), founded in 1735 by the Elector of Hannover, who was also George II of Britain (breeding of stallions; stallion parades in autumn). Stud Farm

Surroundings of Celle

Kloster Wienhausen, a former Cistercian nunnery (13th–14th c.) 10km/6 miles south-east, is now a Protestant house of retreat for women (nuns' choir; 14th century wall and ceiling paintings and a Holy Sepulchre of 1445; famous 14th and 15th century tapestries, shown only once a year at Whitsun). *‌*Kloster Wienhausen

North-west of Celle (north-east of Wietze) is Winsen an der Aller, with an open-air Farmhouse Museum. Winsen a.d. Aller

25km/15 miles north of Celle is the town of Bergen (Heimatmuseum in Römstedthaus). In Bergen-Belsen, 7km/4½ miles south-west, was the Nazi concentration camp of Belsen, now razed to the ground; its site is marked by a commemorative obelisk. Bergen

Hoppener-Haus

Old-time railway	An old-time railway, the Celler Land Express, runs north from Celle to Müden and north-east to Hankensbüttel; the journey takes 75 minutes in each direction.

Chemnitz G 8

Land: Saxony
Altitude: 300m/1000ft
Population: 300,000

Situation and characteristics	The industrial city of Chemnitz (known from 1953 to 1990 as Karl-Marx-Stadt) lies in a wide stretch of the valley of the river Chemnitz, in the Erzgebirge Basin. In the 16th century an important textile centre in the Electorate of Saxony, Chemnitz developed in the 19th century into a major industrial town, its economy centred on engineering.

Town Centre

* Roter Turm	Pre-war Chemnitz had preserved only a few buildings from earlier centuries, and after the war these were carefully rebuilt. Among them is the Roter Turm (Red Tower), the lower part of which dates from the 12th century. In the surrounding gardens are various pieces of sculpture ("Hymns of Praise" after Bertolt Brecht).
New Town Hall	From the Red Tower it is only a few steps to the Markt and the New Town Hall (Neues Rathaus; 1907–11), with a fine Art Nouveau interior (P. Perks, M. Klinger, R. König, etc.). In the tower is a carillon of 48 bells.
* Old Town Hall	Immediately adjoining is the Old Town Hall (Altes Rathaus; 1498, originally Late Gothic), which was completely destroyed in 1945 and subsequently rebuilt. In the centre of the market front is the tower, with a richly decorated Renaissance doorway (1559). In the west part of the building can be seen a reconstruction of the old Councillors' Room (Ratsherrenstube), with Late Gothic vaulting. On the rear front rises the Hoher Turm (High Tower), probably a 13th century defensive tower which was incorporated in the Town Hall in the 14th century and later much altered.
Town Church	In the Markt stands the Town Church, dedicated to St James (St Jakobi), a Late Gothic hall-church (much restored) originally founded about 1165, with an Art Nouveau west front and a 17th century font.
Siegertsches Haus	Diagonally opposite the Town Hall is the Siegertsches Haus, with the town's only surviving Baroque house front (1741). Adjoining the Markt is the Rosenhof (pedestrian zone).
Theaterplatz	In Theaterplatz can be seen an imposing group of buildings – the Opera House (1906–09), a neo-Romanesque church and the Museum. The Museum displays the city's art collection, which includes well known works by Impressionists and Expressionists.
Sterzeleanum ("Petrified Forest")	The Sterzeleanum is a geological collection of international reputation: a "petrified forest" of tree stumps some 250 million years old, partly in Theaterplatz and partly in the Museum.

Schlossberg

Schlosskirche	On the Schlossberg (Castle Hill) are a number of historic buildings. The Schlosskirche (Castle Church; founded 1136) of St Mary, a Late Gothic hall-church which originally belonged to a Benedictine abbey, has a main doorway with Late Gothic tracery (by F. Maidburg and H. Witten), Late Gothic wall paintings and a "Scourging of Christ" by H. Witten. Only parts of the old conventual buildings survive. The Schlossberg Museum has a collection of material on the history of the town.

Ebersdorf

Stiftskirche	In the northern district of Ebersdorf is the 15th century Stiftskirche. Originally built around 1400 as a fortified village church, it became a pilgrimage centre in the 15th

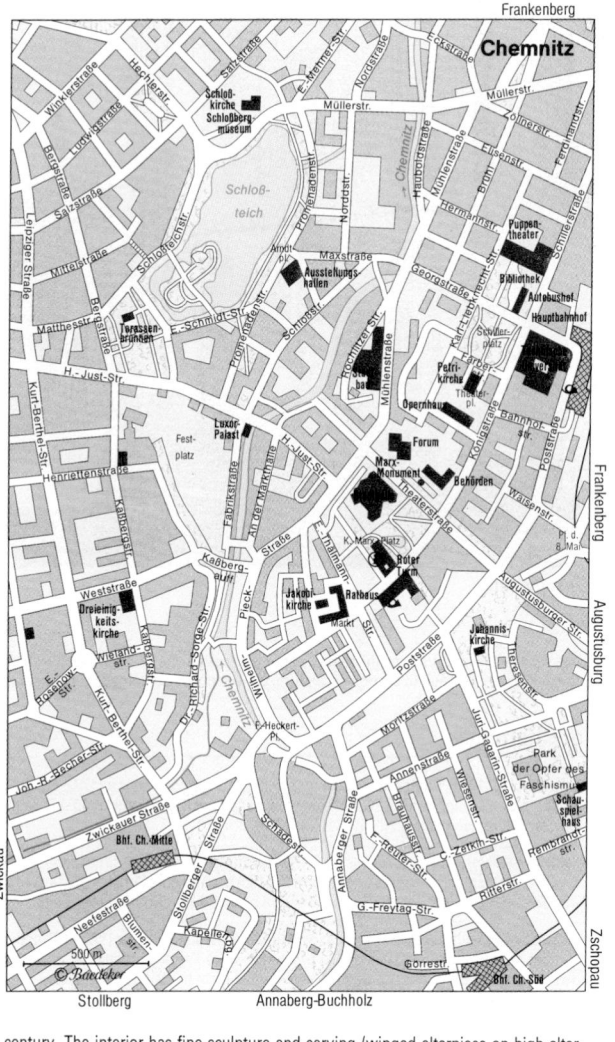

century. The interior has fine sculpture and carving (winged altarpiece on high altar, 1513).

Niederrabenstein

In Niederrabenstein are the interesting Felsendome ("Rock Cathedrals") – an old limestone quarry with cathedral-like chambers hewn from the rock, magnificent limestone crystals and underground pools. Adjoining are the old lime-kiln and the manager's house.

"Petrified Forest", Theaterplatz

Oberrabenstein

Oberrabenstein has preserved the remains of an old castle (living quarters, keep), which now houses a collection of Baroque sculpture, old weapons and domestic equipment.

Surroundings of Chemnitz

Lichtenwalde

Lichtenwalde (10km/6 miles north-east on F 169) has a Baroque palace (1722–26; now occupied by a school), with a 15th century chapel and a Baroque park (1730–37; pavilions, sculpture, fountains).

Hainichen

Hainichen (22km/14 miles north-east on F 169) has an interesting Heimatmuseum, with a collection of material on the life and work of the 18th century poet Christian Gellert, who was born in Hainichen. The parish church has a beautiful Late Gothic winged altar.

Hohenstein-Ernstthal

Hohenstein-Ernstthal (20km/12½ miles west) has a Baroque church (1756–57) and a number of old burghers' houses. Also of interest are a Karl May memorial museum, dedicated to the 19th century author of adventure stories; the Municipal Museum, with material illustrating the history of ore-mining in Hohenstein; and two 19th century weavers' houses.

Augustusburg

Situation and characteristics

Augustusburg, a charming little holiday resort in the central Erzgebirge, above the Zschopau valley, lies 13km/8 miles east of Chemnitz. Its chief attraction is its Renaissance Schloss on the Schellenberg.

Funicular

From Erdmannsdorf station in the Zschopau valley a funicular (1911) runs up to Augustusburg (length of track 1200m/1300yds, height difference 168m/551ft, time 8 minutes).

Schloss Augustusburg

The main feature of the town is the Renaissance Schloss (1567–72; now a museum and *Schloss
youth hostel), the largest in the Erzgebirge, originally built as a hunting lodge for Elector
Augustus I of Saxony. Of particular interest are the North Doorway, the "Heraldic
Doorway" and the well-house, with the 130m/425ft deep well and wooden windlass.
Only fragments of the interior decoration have been preserved. In the Hasensaal (Hare
Room) are a series of paintings (by H. Göding) of the "War of the Hares against the City of
the Hunters and Hounds" (one of the popular "world turned upside down" themes). In
the Venus Room there are also wall paintings by Göding.

The Schlosskapelle (by Erhard van der Meer, 1572) is an aisleless, barrel-vaulted chapel   Schlosskapelle
with two- and three-storey galleries round three sides. It has a carved and gilded altar
(probably from the Salzburg workshop of W. Schreckenfuss, 1571), an altarpiece by
Lucas Cranach the Younger on which Elector Augustus and his family are depicted in
front of Christ crucified, and a fine Baroque organ (by G. Reukewitz, 1758).

Within Schloss Augustusburg are a museum on the game animals and birds of the   Museums
Erzgebirge and a motorcycle museum. In the stables behind the palace can be seen a
collection of coaches (mainly from the royal court at Dresden).
In the tower of the Lindenhaus is a collection of material on the architectural history of
the palace. There are also periodic special exhibitions in the tower.

Surroundings of Augustusburg

In the valley of the Flöha is the Hetzdorfer Schweiz ("Switzerland of Hetzdorf"). In the   Hetzdorfer
villages of Hohenfichte and Hennersdorf are two old covered wooden bridges, of which   Schweiz
very few survive.

There are pleasant walks through the Sternmühlental to the Adelsberg (504m/1654ft;   Adelsberg
outlook tower).

133

Zschopau

Situation and characteristics	Zschopau lies 10km/6 miles south of Chemnitz in the valley of the river Chemnitz in the central Erzgebirge.
Schloss Wildeck	Above the old town centre (restored) rears Schloss Wildeck (12th c.; rebuilt in 16th and 19th c.), an irregular complex of buildings with a 35m/115ft high keep known as Dicker Heinrich ("Fat Henry").
*Town Hall Edelhaus	In the Markt is the Town Hall (Rathaus; 16th c., altered in 1749–51), with a clock-tower and a carillon of Meissen porcelain. The Edelhaus (1561) is a handsome Renaissance building, now occupied by local government offices.
Parish church	The Late Gothic parish church of St Martin (1495) has a fine Baroque interior (after 1751), an organ of 1755 and a neo-classical altar (1859).

Surroundings of Zschopau

*Zschopau valley Wolkenstein	The most beautiful stretch of the Zschopau valley begins at Wolkenstein, where the lower parts of the wooded hillsides fall steeply down to the valley bottom, with outcrops of the local slate rocks visible in the walls of the valley. Agricultural land begins only between 80m/260ft and 130m/425ft above the valley bottom.

Chiemsee   L 7–8

	Land: Bavaria
Boat services	Regular services (including services to islands) from Prien, Gstadt, Seebruck and Chieming.
Situation and characteristics	With an area of 82 sq.km/32 sq. miles, the Chiemsee is the largest of the Bavarian lakes, measuring between 5km/3 miles and 15km/9 miles across and up to 73m/240ft in depth. It occupies the central part of a basin carved out by an Ice Age glacier, and once extended southward as far as Grassau, over an area which has since been silted up by deposits from the Tiroler Ache. In summer the lake is dotted with sailing boats.

*Landscape

*Herreninsel *Fraueninsel Krautinsel	There are three islands in the lake: the Herreninsel (250 hectares/625 acres, mostly wooded), with Schloss Herrenchiemsee, built between 1878 and 1885 for King Ludwig II of Bavaria on the model of Versailles (magnificent state apartments, including a 98m/322ft long Hall of Mirrors; King Ludwig Museum); the Fraueninsel (8 hectares/20 acres), with a Benedictine nunnery, set amid lime-trees, founded by Duke Tassilo III in the 8th century (church with Late Romanesque wall paintings) and a picturesque little fishing village; and, lying between the other two, the little uninhabited Krautinsel, the kitchen garden of the nunnery on the Fraueninsel.

Circuit of the Chiemsee

	This route round the lake is described in a clockwise direction, starting from the Bernau motorway exit.
	From the Felden district in Bernau the lakeside road runs north to Prien-Stock.
Prien	Prien, the most popular of the lakeside resorts, has an interesting Heimatmuseum and a picture gallery (in the Old Town Hall). 2km/1¼ miles east (reached by the old Chiemsee

Chiemsee, with the Fraueninsel

railway, opened in 1887, as well as by road), in Stock, is the harbour (boat services to the islands). The route continues via Rimsting.

Directly opposite the Fraueninsel (boat service), on the shores of the lake, is the beautifully situated little resort of Gstadt. From here the road continues close to the shores of the lake.   Gstadt

Seebruck, at the northern tip of the lake, has Roman origins (Museum Römerhaus Bedaium). From here a rewarding detour can be made to Seeon (5km/3 miles north), with a former Benedictine monastery (12th c. church) and the Schanzenberg Motor Museum (veteran and vintage cars).   Seebruck

Chieming has a beautiful bathing beach. In the outlying district of Ising is a Horse Museum.   Chieming

Grabenstätt is also a settlement with Roman origins (small Roman Museum). The Johanniskirche (St John's Church) has Late Gothic frescoes. To the west is a nature reserve (herons, etc.).   Grabenstätt

At Grabenstätt we can return to the motorway.

Chiemgau

The Chiemgau is the area of the Alpine Foreland lying to the south of the lake. With its green moraine hills set against the backdrop of the Chiemgauer Berge, it is a favourite holiday area.

The principal resorts in the Chiemgau are described from west to east.

Aschau, in the Prien valley, is a popular winter sports centre as well as a summer resort. Above Hohenaschau is the picturesque castle of that name. Close by is the lower station of the Kampenwand cableway (upper station at 1460m/4790ft; magnificent views).   Aschau
Kampenwand

Marquartstein	The lively holiday village of Marquartstein lies in the forest-fringed valley of the Tiroler Ache. There is a rewarding climb of the Hochfelln.
Reit im Winkl	Reit im Winkl, lying close to the frontier with Tirol (Austria), has developed into a popular winter sports resort. There are good pistes on the Winklmoosalm (1160m/3800ft).
Bergen	Near the Bergen motorway exit is the village of that name, at the foot of Hochfelln (1670m/5479ft; cabin cableway; fine panoramic views).
Ruhpolding	The neat village of Ruhpolding lies in a basin in the valley of the Weisse Traun, on the Deutsche Alpenstrasse (see entry). Late Baroque parish church; Heimatmuseum.
Traunstein	Traunstein, beautifully situated on a hill above the Traun, offers visitors brine baths, mud baths and the Kneipp cure. It has a beautiful parish church of 1696. There are fine panoramic views from the Hochberg (775m/2543ft) and the Teisenberg (1333m/4374ft).

Coburg H 6

Land: Bavaria
Altitude: 297m/974ft
Population: 46,000.

Situation and characteristics	This former ducal capital lies on the southern slopes of the Thuringian Forest, on the river Itz, a tributary of the Main, with a massive fortress looming over it.

Old Town

Markt	In the attractive Markt are the Town Hall (Rathaus; 1579) and the former Regierungsgebäude (government offices; now the Stadthaus), a richly decorated Late Renaissance building of 1599.
Morizkirche	South-east of the Markt stands the Morizkirche (St Maurice's Church; 14th–16th c.; in the choir the 12m/30ft high tomb of John Frederick of Saxony, d. 1595). Opposite the church is the Gymnasium Casimirianum, a grammar school in Renaissance style (17th c.) founded by Duke John Casimir.
Ehrenburg	On the east side of the old town is the Schlossplatz, with the Ehrenburg (formerly the ducal palace), rebuilt by Schinkel in 1816–38, which contains interesting state and private apartments as well as the Coburg Provincial Library. In the west wing is the Baroque Hofkirche (court church).
Hofgarten	Beyond an arcade which came from the former ballroom building lies the beautiful Hofgarten (Court Garden), extending up the hill to the castle. Half way up is the Natural History Museum (animals from all over the world; fossils and minerals; ethnography).

*Coburg Castle (Veste Coburg)

Coburg Castle (Veste Coburg; alt. 464m/1522ft) is one of the largest castles in Germany, dating mainly from the 16th century (restored in the 19th and 20th centuries). In the Fürstenbau are the former residential apartments of the ducal family. Luther Room, in which the reformer sought refuge during the Diet of Augsburg in 1530; Luther Chapel. Collections of works of art, weapons and coins.

Surroundings of Coburg

Neustadt	In Neustadt (15km/9 miles north-east) is the Museum of the German Toy Industry, with a collection of dolls wearing traditional costumes. In front of the Museum is the Harlequin Fountain.

Coburg, with its Castle

Staffelstein

25km/15 miles south of Coburg by way of Lichtenfels, in the Main valley, we come to the ancient little town of Staffelstein, birthplace of the 16th century arithmetician Adam Riese. Above the town rises the Staffelberg (539m/1768ft), from which there are far ranging views.

North-east of the town, half way to Lichtenfels, is Grundfeld-Vierzehnheiligen, dom-   ** Vierzehnheiligen
inated by the great pilgrimage church of Vierzehnheiligen, the finest achievement of Franconian Baroque architecture, perched high above the left bank of the Main (alt. 387m/1270ft). The church was built between 1743 and 1772 to the design of Balthasar Neumann. The name reflects its dedication to the Fourteen Holy Helpers.
The plan of the church is unique, with its interplay of ovals and circles, and the spatial concept of the interior (decorated by J. M. Feuchtmayr and J. G. Übelherr) is bold and imaginative. The sumptuous Gnadenaltar stands on the spot where the "Fourteen Helpers in time of need" are said to have appeared to a shepherd in 1445.

Opposite Staffelhausen, high above the right bank of the Main, is the palatial Benedictine   * Banz
monastery of Banz. Begun by Johann Leonhard Dientzenhofer in 1695, the massive rectangular complex was completed by the addition of a gatehouse wing by Balthasar Neumann. The magnificent twin-towered church, built by Dientzenhofer in 1710–19, has a richly decorated interior, with stucco ornament and ceiling paintings, and a high altar by Balthasar Esterbauer (1714). Notable features of the conventual buildings are the Abbot's Chapel and the Imperial Hall. There are also a small Egyptian collection and a collection of fossils from the local Jurassic rocks.

Cologne (Köln)   G 2

Land: North Rhine-Westphalia
Altitude: 36m/118ft
Population: 974,000

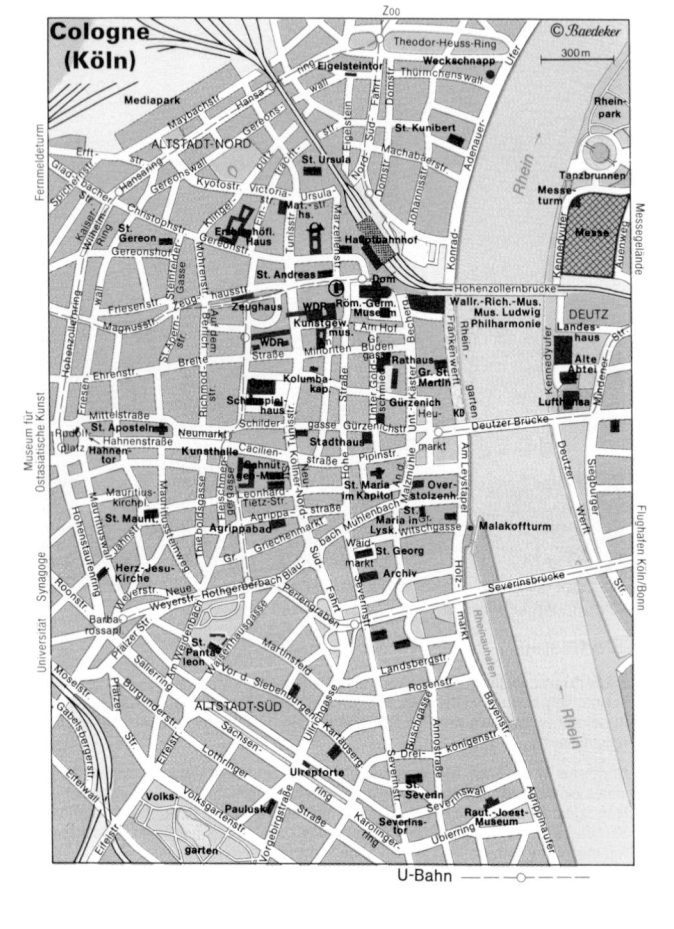

Cologne
(Köln)

U-Bahn — — —○— — —

In this guide the description of Cologne has been deliberately kept short, since fuller information is provided in the "Cologne" volume in the same series.

Situation and characteristics

This old cathedral city on the Rhine (which is spanned by eight bridges within the city limits) is one of the the most important traffic junctions and commercial centres in western Germany. The motorway encircling Cologne provides a link between ten motorways; numerous international trade fairs are held in the city; and there is a busy shipping traffic between its river port and the North Sea. Cologne is the see of an archbishop and a university town, with several higher educational establishments in addition to its University.

** Cathedral

Near the left bank of the Rhine stands Cologne's towering landmark, the Cathedral (Dom) of St Peter and St Mary, a masterpiece of High Gothic architecture and one of the largest

Cologne Cathedral

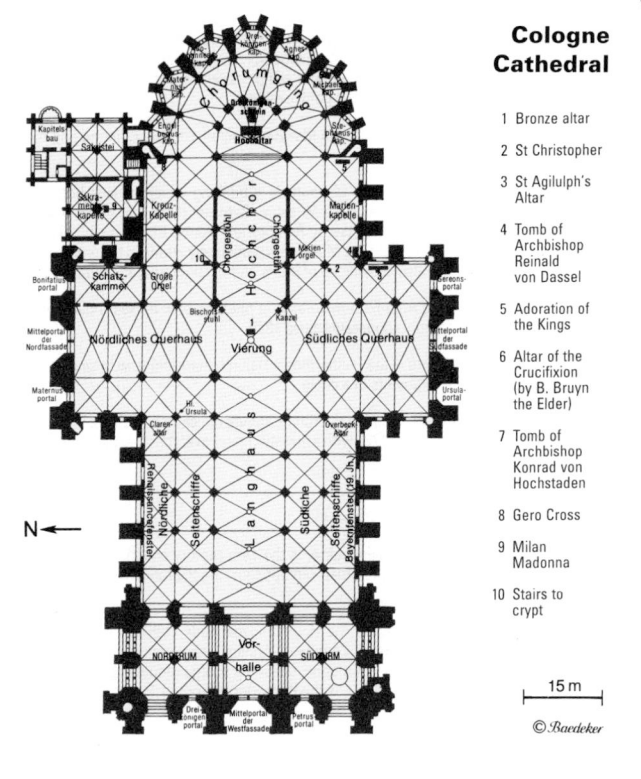

1 Bronze altar

2 St Christopher

3 St Agilulph's Altar

4 Tomb of Archbishop Reinald von Dassel

5 Adoration of the Kings

6 Altar of the Crucifixion (by B. Bruyn the Elder)

7 Tomb of Archbishop Konrad von Hochstaden

8 Gero Cross

9 Milan Madonna

10 Stairs to crypt

15 m

© Baedeker

cathedrals in Europe. Begun in 1248, it was the most ambitious building project of the Middle Ages; but work came to a halt at the beginning of the 16th century, and the cathedral was not completed until 1842–80.

The interior of the cathedral is imposing, with an area of 6166 sq.m/7375 sq.yds and a total of 56 pillars. Above the high altar is the Reliquary of the Three Kings (Dreikönigen-schrein), a masterpiece of the goldsmith's work of the Rhineland, made in the 12th/13th century to the design of Nicholas of Verdun to house relics of the Three Kings brought to Cologne from Milan. In the ambulatory is the famous relief of the Adoration of the Kings (c. 1440), wrongly known as the Dombild. On the pillars of the choir are fine Early Gothic statues (14th c.). In the Kreuzkapelle (Chapel of the Cross) can be seen the Gero Cross, and in the Treasury are many other precious objects (reliquaries, Gospel books, monstrances, etc.).

*Interior

From the south tower (over 500 steps), in which are the cathedral bells, there are panoramic views.

Domhügel (Cathedral Hill)

Between the Cathedral and the Rhine is Cologne's Cultural Centre, inaugurated in 1986 with the opening of the new Wallraf-Richartz Museum, Ludwig Museum and Philharmonic Hall.

Cultural Centre

On the south side of the Cathedral is the Roman-Germanic Museum (Römisch-Germanisches Museum). Exhibits of particular interest are the Dionysus Mosaic (2nd c.

**Roman-Germanic Museum

139

A.D.) and the 15m/50ft high funerary monument of Poblicius (1st c. A.D.), both of which were discovered in the course of excavations in the city. The museum also displays other mosaics, Roman glass, domestic pottery and sculpture, and much else besides. The Treasury contains Roman and Germanic gold jewellery.

Diocesan Museum

Nearby, at Roncalliplatz 2, is the Diocesan Museum (sacred art from Cologne and the Lower Rhineland).

**Wallraf-Richartz
Museum and
Ludwig Museum

To the east of the Roman-Germanic Museum is a building which houses both the Wallraf-Richartz Museum and the Ludwig Museum. Between them they cover a wide range of European painting, with works by Rembrandt, Manet, Renoir, Leibl, Liebermann and Slevogt. The Wallraf-Richartz Museum is particularly strong in the work of the Cologne school. There are also collections of prints and of contemporary painting.

In the same building is the Agfa-Foto-Historama, a photographic museum displaying photographs and photographic apparatus since 1840.

Philharmonic
Hall

Below the level of the square is the Philharmonic Hall (Philharmonie), with seating for 2000 rising in concentric segments of a circle.

Gross St Martin

To the south of the Cathedral, close to the Rhine, stands the church of Gross St Martin (Great St Martin's; consecrated 1172), with a massive tower over the crossing, a trilobate choir and richly articulated walls.

Central Area

St Andrew's
Church

West of the Cathedral, in Komödienstrasse, is the 15th century church of St Andreas (Andrew). In the crypt, in a re-used Roman sarcophagus, are the remains of St Albertus Magnus.

Municipal
Museum

In the adjoining Zeughausstrasse is the Regierungsgebäude (1951–52; government offices), opposite which is the rebuilt Zeughaus (Arsenal), now housing the Municipal Museum (material on the history of Cologne, including a large model of the town). At the end of Zeughausstrasse, on left, is the Römerturm (Roman Tower; 1st c. A.D.), a relic of the Roman town walls.

*St Gereon's
Church

To the north-west is St Gereon's, the city's most unusual Romanesque church, with a long choir (11th c.) built on to a ten-sided domed structure dating from Roman times (enlarged in 1227).

Museum of
Applied Art

South-west of the Cathedral, in the street called An der Rechtschule, is the Museum of Applied Art (Museum für Angewandte Kunst), with a collection of applied and decorative art from the medieval period onwards. The museum moved to these premises, previously occupied by the Wallraf-Richartz Museum, in 1988.

Town Hall

To the south of the Cathedral stands the Old Town Hall (Altes Rathaus), with a Renaissance portico. In the Hansasaal (Hanseatic Hall) are Gothic figures of eight prophets and the nine "good heroes" (pagan, Jewish and Christian). There is a carillon in the tower. South-west of the Town Hall is a 12th century Jewish ritual bath (*mikve*). Under the

Praetorium

Spanischer Bau are remains of the Roman Praetorium (Governor's Palace; open to visitors).

Gürzenich

Farther south is the Gürzenich, the city's most important old secular building (1437–44), originally a warehouse and banqueting hall; it has been restored and is now used for a variety of events and occasions.

St Maria im Kapitol

Near the south end of the Hohe Strasse is the church of St Maria im Kapitol (11th–13th c.), built on the site of a Roman temple. In the nave are two beautifully carved early medieval doors (1050–65). Under the choir is a large crypt.

Church of
Holy Apostles

From the Hohe Strasse, near the Gürzenich, Schildergasse (pedestrian zone) runs west to the Neumarkt, on the far side of which is the Late Romanesque church of the Holy Apostles (St Aposteln; 11th–13th c.).

South-east of the Neumarkt, in the old church of St Cecilia, is the Schnütgen Museum (sacred art). On the west side of the museum is the Josef Haubrich Kunsthalle (exhibitions).

*Schnütgen Museum

In the extreme south-west of the central area stands the church of St Pantaleon (10th–17th c.; restored), with the tomb of the Empress Theophano (d. 991), wife of Otto II.

St Pantaleon's Church

The "Ring"

Round the old town runs a ring of streets on the line of the old town walls, recently replanned as a series of gardens and promenades. Of the old fortified town gates there remain the Eigelsteintor in the north, the Hahnentor in the west and the Severinstor in the south.

A little way north of the Severinstor we come to the well restored church of St Severinus (St Severin; 11th–15th c.), with an interesting Roman and Frankish burial ground.

St Severinus

Near here, on the Ubierring, is the Rautenstrauch-Joest Museum of Ethnography (pre-Columbian cultures of America; Oceania and Africa).

Rautenstrauch-Joest Museum

On the west side of the central area, at Universitätsstrasse 100, is the Museum of East Asian Art (Museum für Ostasiatische Kunst), designed by the Japanese architect Kunio Mayekawa and opened in 1977. Only part of the collection, which covers Chinese, Korean and Japanese art, can be shown at any one time. Beautiful Japanese garden.

Museum of East Asian Art

North-west of the central area, beyond the railway, rises the Telecommunications Tower (Fernmeldeturm), known as "Colonius". It is 243m/797ft high, with a viewing platform at 170m/558ft and a revolving restaurant.

Telecommunications Tower

North of the Theodor-Heuss-Ring and the Zoobrücke (Zoo Bridge) are the Florapark, which was laid out by P. J. Lenné in 1862 and extended in 1914 to form the Botanic Garden, and the Zoo (with aquarium, terrarium and insectarium).

Botanic Garden Zoo

Deutz and Mülheim

On the right bank of the Rhine is the district of Deutz, linked with the left bank by the Severinsbrücke (1959; a road bridge 691m/755yds long), the Deutzer Brücke (1948; road bridge), the Hohenzollernbrücke or Dombrücke (rail and pedestrian bridge) and the Zoobrücke (1966; road bridge), and by a cableway, the Rheinseilbahn, between the Zoo and the Rheinpark (see below).

Bridges Cableway

The district of Mülheim, to the north, is reached by way of the Mülheimerbrücke, a suspension bridge built in 1949–51 (road bridge; 315m/345yds long).

In Deutz are the Trade Fair Grounds, the Kongresszentrum Ost (congress and conference centre) and the beautiful Rheinpark "Dancing Fountain"; mineral baths.

Trade Fair Rheinpark

Bergisch Gladbach

15km/9 miles north-east of Cologne lies Bergisch Gladbach (pop. 104,000), the main feature of interest in which is the Bergisches Museum (mining, industry, craft production), with displays illustrating country life and buildings, a reconstruction of a mine shaft, traditional craft techniques, etc.

Bergisches Museum

6km/4 miles north is Altenberg Cathedral (Altenberger Dom; also known as the Bergischer Dom), one of the finest examples of the Early Gothic of the Rhineland (1255–1379). It has a richly furnished interior (Gothic stained glass, tombs of princes and abbots, a beautiful "Annunciation").

*Altenberg Cathedral

Brühl

15km/9 miles south of Cologne is Brühl, with Schloss Augustusburg, the 18th century palace of the Archbishop of Cologne. Sumptuously decorated and furnished, this is one

*Augustusburg

of the most charming palaces in the transitional style between Late Baroque and Rococo (magnificent staircase hall by Balthasar Neumann; large park; concerts in palace).

* Phantasialand

Near Brühl is the Phantasialand amusement park, one of the largest of its kind in Europe, with a wide variety of attractions – a cableway, a white water run, a Viking boat trip, a Casa Magnetica in which the law of gravity is apparently suspended, a monorail, a reproduction of old Berlin, Chinatown (with pagodas and rickshaws), a Wild West town, a tiger enclosure, a dolphin show and a computer-controlled electronic show (a journey round the world represented by puppets).

Lake Constance (Bodensee)   L–M 4–5

Länder: Baden-Württemberg and Bavaria

Situation

Lake Constance (the Bodensee in German) lies on the southern border of Germany, bounded on the south by Switzerland and, at its south-eastern tip, by Austria. The town of Konstanz lies in latitude 47°39' north and longitude 9°10' east; Bregenz, at the south-east end of the lake, in latitude 47°30' north and longitude 9°44' east.
Mean water level: 395m/1296ft. Area: 545 sq.km/210 sq. miles (Obersee and Überlinger See together 480 sq.km/185 sq. miles, Untersee 65 sq.km/25 sq. miles).

Frontier lines

The national frontier lines in Lake Constance are largely undemarcated. Only the Untersee has a clearly established boundary line along the middle of the lake, laid down under a treaty of 1855 between the Grand Duchy of Baden and the Swiss canton of Thurgau. The Überlinger See, which is bounded on three sides by German territory, falls with the *Land* of Baden-Württemberg as far as a line from Meersburg to Eichhorn (Konstanz). In the Obersee the international boundary is fixed only for the small inlet at Konstanz, roughly along the middle of the Konstanzer Bucht, under an agreement between Baden and Switzerland.
For the whole of the rest of the Obersee there is no international agreement defining areas of sovereignty; but since the end of the First World War there has been fairly general tacit agreement about frontier lines.

General

Lake Constance, lying below the northern edge of the Alps, is by far the largest lake in Germany, the third largest lake in Central Europe (after Lake Balaton in Hungary and Lake Geneva) and the second largest of the lakes bordering the Alps. From south-east to north-west it is divided into the Obersee, the largest and deepest part of the lake, extending from Bregenz Bay to Eichhorn (Konstanz), and two much narrower, shorter and shallower branches, the Überlinger See between the Bodanrück and Linzgau and the Untersee, separated from the main lake by a strip of land traversed by the Rhine at Konstanz. At its northern end the Untersee splits into the Gnadensee, between the island of Reichenau and the Bodanrück, and the Zeller See, between the Höri and Mettnau peninsulas in Radolfzell Bay.

**Landscape

Lake Constance offers scenery of striking beauty, with its majestic expanse of water and its fringe of old lakeside towns and attractive villages.
Along the south side of the lake is an imposing backdrop of wooded hills and, beyond these, the Appenzell Alps (Säntis, 2504m/8216ft); to the east, beyond the wide valley of the Alpine Rhine, the Vorarlberg Alps and above them Rätikon, with the Schesaplana (2964m/9725ft); and, farther east still, the Bregenzer Wald (Pfänder, 1064m/3491ft) and the Allgäu Alps.
The Upper Swabian foreland to the north of the lake, with the Linzgau to the west, is an upland region with numerous rivers, rising to its highest point at 837m/2746ft – a region of scattered villages, woodland, arable fields and orchards.
The shores of the Obersee are mainly flat, with a number of large bays, particularly at the delta of the Rhine, the Dornbirner Ach and the Bregenzer Ach. The long-settled land around the western end of the lake, patterned by the Bodanrück, the Mettnau and Höri peninsulas and the fjord-like Überlinger See, continues to the west without any in-

terruption in the Hegau, which with its boldly shaped hills ranks among the most attractive volcanic landscapes in Germany.

Various areas on the shores of the lake, particularly near the mouths of the larger tributary rivers, have been declared landscape or nature reserves in order to maintain them in their relatively unspoiled condition. The most important nature reserves are the Wollmatinger Ried, where the Rhine flows from the main lake into the Untersee; the south-eastern part of the Mettnau peninsula; various sections of the shores of the Höri peninsula; the Mindelsee and the marshland around its shores; the area around the mouth of the Stockacher Aach; the north shore of the Bodanrück, around the Marienschlucht and between Litzelstetten and Wallhausen; the area around the mouth of the Seefelder Aach between Seefelden and Unteruhldingen; and the Eriskircher Ried around the mouth of the Old Rhine.

Protection of nature

The Lake Constance Trail (Bodensee-Rundwanderweg)

Walkers are catered for by the Lake Constance Trail (Bodensee-Rundwanderweg), which encircles the lake at varying distances from its shores and at varying heights for a distance of 272km/169 miles, marked by a black arrow curving round a black dot. Within German territory it frequently follows the paths waymarked (blue and yellow lozenge) by the Schwarzwaldverein; on the south side of the lake it coincides with the European long-distance trail No. 5 (Lake Constance to the Adriatic; marked by white signs).

Art and Architecture

There are numerous historic buildings round Lake Constance on which much restoration work has been carried out, and excellent work has also been done in cleaning up and improving the towns and villages. The region offers examples of the artistic achievement of every period and style, and visitors interested in art and architecture may therefore find it helpful to have some notes about the outstanding sights.

The finest examples of Romanesque are to be found on the monastery island of Reichenau (Minster, Mittelzell; St George's, Oberzell; SS. Peter and Paul, Niederzell) and in Konstanz (Minster) and Lindau (St Peter's).

Romanesque

Gothic buildings, both religious and secular, are much more numerous: Konstanz (St Stephen's, Mauritziusrotunde; Kaufhaus/Council Building), Meersburg (Grethgebäude), Überlingen (Minster), Lindau (Diebsturm), Eriskirch (parish church), Radolfzell (Minster), Markdorf (St Nicholas's, Stadtschloss), Salem (monastic church), Ravensburg (St Jodok's, Town Hall, Weigh-House).

Gothic

Impressive Renaissance buildings are the palaces of Heiligenberg and Wolfegg and the town halls of Lindau and Konstanz. The early Baroque period is represented by the Altes Schloss in Meersburg, the Schlosskirche in Friedrichshafen and the Ritterschaftshaus in Radolfzell. The outstanding examples of High Baroque and Rococo are Weingarten Abbey and the pilgrimage church at Birnau; others are the Neues Schloss in Meersburg, the Imperial Hall in Salem monastery, the Neues Schloss in Tettnang, the old monastic church at Weissenau (near Ravensburg), St Martin's Church in Langenargen and St Mary's in Lindau, and the Schloss and Schlosskirche on the island of Mainau.

Renaissance and Baroque

Boat Services on Lake Constance

Boat services on Lake Constance run from the middle of April to the middle of October. (Passport or equivalent document required for entry to Switzerland or Austria.) The main routes are the following (with numerous other intermediate calls, and additional services between some of the intermediate statyions):
Konstanz–(Mainau)–Meersburg–Friedrichshafen–Lindau–Bregenz
Konstanz–Meersburg–(Mainau)–Überlingen
Überlingen–Ludwigshafen–Bodman

Regular services

Kreuzlingen–Konstanz–Reichenau–Radolfzell or Schaffhausen
Lindau–Bad Schachen–Wasserburg–Rohrschach

Ferries
There are ferry services (passengers and cars) all year round between Friedrichshafen and Romanshorn and between Konstanz-Staad and Meersburg (the latter a 24-hour service).
There are also local passenger ferries between Allensbach station and the island of Reichenau (Mittelzell) and across the Rhine at Konstanz.

Excursions
During the summer there are numerous excursions of various kinds (sometimes subject to weather conditions) from the larger towns on the lake (whole-day or half-day trips, shorter breakfast or coffee trips, evening dancing parties, mystery excursions, special trips for particular events).

Boating
Like all shipping on the lake, pleasure craft are subject to the Lake Constance shipping regulations, which everyone in charge of a boat must know.
Persons in charge of a motorboat of over 5 HP or a sailing boat with a sail area over 12 sq.m/130 sq.ft must have a driving or sailing licence.

Sailing on the lake is not for the novice. Although the wind usually blows steadily from east or west it is often gusty near the shore. Danger may arise from the storms which blow up suddenly, and attention should be paid to the storm warning lights on the shore.

See also Friedrichshafen, Konstanz, Lindau, Meersburg, Ravensburg and Überlingen

Cottbus   E 9

Land: Brandenburg
Altitude: 64m/210ft
Population: 129,000

Situation and characteristics
Cottbus (Sorbian Chosebuz), the political, economic and cultural centre of Lower Lusatia and the south-eastern gateway to the Spreewald (see entry), lies on the banks of the Spree.

Sights

Altmarkt
Situated at the intersection of old long-distance trade routes, the Altmarkt was ideally situated for the business of the town's merchants. After a great fire in 1671 it was surrounded by new buildings in Saxon Baroque style. The whole square is now protected as a national monument. Particularly notable buildings are No. 21, No. 22 (an old butcher's shop, now a wine bar) and the Löwenapotheke (Lion Pharmacy, established 1586), which now houses the Lower Lusatian Pharmacy Museum.

Oberkirche
To the east of the Altmarkt is the Oberkirche (Upper Church), a brick-built hall-church with a Renaissance altar by A. Schultze of Torgau.

Wendish Church
To the north of the Altmarkt stands the Wendish Church (formerly a Franciscan church) in which services were held in the Sorbian language for the Sorbian population of the area.

Schlosskirche
The Baroque Schlosskirche (Palace Church), in Spremberger Strasse, was built by Huguenots in 1707–14.

Spremberger Turm
At the south end of the street rises the Spremberger Turm, a relic of the old town walls. The battlements round the top were added by K. F. Schinkel.

*Municipal Theatre
In Schillerplatz is the Municipal Theatre (Stadttheater; by B. Sehring, 1908), in Art Nouveau style.

Parks

Carl Blechen Park
To the east of the Altmarkt, beyond the Sandower Brücke, lies the Carl Blechen Park, with an open-air theatre. Near the bridge are the Münzturm (Mint Tower) and the Tuchmacherbrunnen (Clothworkers' Fountain).

Schloss Branitz

Goethe Park, south-west of the Carl Blechen Park, has a small lake and a swan enclosure. Beyond this is the Cosmos Planetarium, the first of its kind in Europe (opened 1974).

Goethe Park

In the Elias Park, farther south, is a miniature railway. Here too there is a zoo, with large numbers of waterfowl.

Elias Park

The Branitzer Park is a masterpiece of German landscape gardening, laid out by Prince Hermann von Pückler-Muskau from 1846 onwards, with two pyramids, one of them containing Pückler-Muskau's tomb.

*Branitzer Park

On the east side of the park stands Schloss Branitz, a Baroque palace (1772) which was remodelled by Gottfried Semper around 1850. It now houses the Cottbus Regional Museum (Bezirksmuseum), with a collection of drawings and paintings by the Cottbus painter Carl Blechen (1798–1840) and interesting displays on the history of the town.
In the old court stables (Marstall) can be found the natural history section of the museum (geology, flora and fauna, lignite mining).
The old smithy (also built by Semper) was opened in 1986, after extensive reconstruction, as a technical exhibit.

*Schloss Branitz
(Regional Museum)

At Spremberger Strasse 1 is the Cottbus State Art Gallery (contemporary art: photography, painting, graphic art, sculpture).

Art Gallery

Surroundings of Cottbus

Features of interest in Peitz (10km/6 miles north on B 97) are the old fort, the neo-classical Town Hall (1804) and the ironworks, with the Ironworking Museum. There is lively activity here during the carp-fishing season in autumn.

Peitz

In Bad Muskau (39km/24 miles south-east) is a large landscaped park designed by Prince Hermann von Pückler-Muskau. The Schloss (16th century) was rebuilt between 1863 and

Bad Muskau

1866 and suffered severe destruction in the Second World War (reconstruction planned). In the Upper Park is a ruined 13th century church (Gothic) built of undressed stone.

Kromlau

In the neighbouring village of Kromlau lies a large Schlosspark (c. 1850), modelled on Muskau and Branitz, with a Kavaliershaus (lodgings for members of the court) and Schloss (1845).

Cuxhaven   B 4

Land: Lower Saxony
Altitude: 3m/10ft
Population: 60,000

Situation and characteristics

Cuxhaven, much favoured as a health resort on the North Sea, lies at the west end of the Elbe estuary, here 15km/9 miles wide. From 1394 to 1937 the town belonged to Hamburg. It is one of Germany's most important fishing ports.

Old Town

Schloss Ritzebüttel

In the oldest part of the town, to the south, is Schloss Ritzebüttel, a defensive tower built about 1300 and enlarged in 1616. It now houses the Heimatmuseum (at present closed during restoration of the Schloss).

Reyersches Haus

Near the Schloss, at Südersteinstrasse 38, is the neo-classical Reyersches Haus (c. 1780), with the Municipal Museum (prehistory and early historical period; shipping and seafaring).

Harbours

In the east of the town are the fishing harbour and the fish market (interesting fish auctions at 7am; guided tour). Farther east lies the Amerikahafen, built in 1892–1902 especially for the HAPAG Line and enlarged in 1922, but now little used; large passenger liners now moor at the outer mole (Steubenhöft).

Alte Liebe

At the northern tip of the harbour is the Alte Liebe ("Old Love"), the landing-stage used by boats sailing on the Elbe and to the coastal resorts and Heligoland (see entry), with a 34m/112ft high radar tower, a signal station, a wind semaphore and a basin for model ships.

Döse

Kurpark
Beacon

At the northernmost tip of land, in the district of Döse, is the Kurpark, with a sealion pool and a bird meadow. To the east, at the end of a 250m/275yd long pier, stands a large wooden spherical beacon, the landmark and emblem of the town.

Duhnen

5km/3 miles west of the town centre, beyond Döse, we come to the seaside resort of Duhnen, which was incorporated in Cuxhaven in 1835, with a beautiful beach (promenade), a spa establishment and an indoor swimming pool (artificial waves).

Museums

At Wehrbergsweg 7 is the Lütt Shipping Museum (Schiffsmuseum; nautical equipment, local types of boat, etc.) and at Wehrbergsweg 28 the Puppet Museum (theatre puppets from all over the world).

Stickenbüttel

Wreck Museum

In the Stickenbüttel district, at Dorfstrasse 80, can be found the interesting Wreck Museum (Wrackmuseum; objects recovered from wrecked ships; history of sea rescue service).

Lüdingworth

In the south-eastern district of Lüdingworth stands a church known as the Bauerndom   Bauerndom
("countryfolk's cathedral"; 13th and 16th c.), with a richly decorated Baroque interior
and an organ by A. Wilde and Arp Schnitger.

Neuwerk and Scharhörn

In the shallow coastal waters north-west of Cuxhaven, at a distance of 12km/7½ miles
and 17km/10½ miles respectively, are the islands of Neuwerk (area 3 sq.km/1¼ sq. miles;
pop. 36) and Scharhörn (2.8 sq.km/1 sq. mile). Administratively both islands belong to
Hamburg, but they are most easily reached from Cuxhaven (by boat, or at low water in a
horse-drawn carriage or on foot over the mud-flats: check the time of the tide!).

Roughly a third of the island's area is dyked arable land; the rest is mostly grazing. The   Neuwerk
landmark of Neuwerk is the 35m/115ft high lighthouse, originally a defensive tower of
the 13th or 14th century which was converted to its present function in 1814; from the top
there are fine all-round views. Nearby is the "cemetery of the nameless ones" (with the
graves of unknown seamen).

5km/3 miles farther out (reached from Neuwerk by walking over the mud-flats: guide   Scharhörn
essential) is the lonely sandy island of Scharhörn, with a 28m/92ft high beacon and a
seabird sanctuary.

Danube Valley   L 3–K 9

Länder: Baden-Wurttemberg and Bavaria

With a total course of 2840km/1765 miles, the Danube (Donau) is Europe's second   General
longest river (after the Volga). Along its course runs an ancient traffic route, followed by
the Nibelungs on their way to the court of King Etzel (Attila) and their own destruction.
The Romans built forts and settlements along its banks, and in later centuries these were
followed by monastic houses and princely residences.

The present-day tourist can see the beauties of the Danube valley on the motor-ships   Boat services
which travel down the river from Regensburg to Passau (and from there on to the Black
Sea).

From Donaueschingen to Passau

At Donaueschingen (see entry) two little Black Forest streams, the Brigach and the Breg,
join to form the Danube, the real source river being the Breg.

A few miles downstream some of the water seeps away through the permeable limestone and re-emerges 12km/7½ miles farther south as the source of the Aach.

At Kloster Beuron (a monastery founded in the 11th century which fostered choral   Beuron
singing, scholarship and the arts; fine Baroque church) the river cuts its way through the
Swabian Alb (see entry) in numerous bends – the first of the major beauty spots on its
course.
At Sigmaringen (see entry) the imposing Hohenzollern castle rears above the river.

Between Riedlingen and Ehingen are two magnificent Baroque churches: Zwiefalten (by   Zwiefalten
Johann Michael Fischer) and Obermarchtal (by Michael Thumb, with rich stucco orna-   Obermarchtal
ment by Josef Schmuzer). Soon afterwards comes the old cathedral city of Ulm (see
entry), and beyond this Günzburg with its Frauenkirche (see Ulm, Surroundings).

Neuburg an der Donau is a trim little princely capital, perched on a high Jurassic crag   Neuburg
above the river.

Danube Valley

Donaudurchbruch, near Weltenburg

Ingolstadt	Ingolstadt (see entry), a former residence of the Dukes of Bavaria and university city, is now also a considerable industrial town.
*Donau-durchbruch	Another scenic high spot is at Weltenburg, where the Danube breaks through the Jurassic limestones between bizarrely shaped rock faces: this is the famous Donaudurchbruch.
Weltenburg	Weltenburg has a monastic church (1717–21) built by Cosmas Damian Asam, one of the great masters of South German Baroque. At Kelheim (see Regensburg, Surroundings) can be seen the Befreiungshalle (Hall of Liberation), built by King Ludwig I of Bavaria to commemorate the Wars of Liberation of 1813–15. At the cathedral city of Regensburg (see entry), the Roman Castra Regina, the Danube reaches the most northerly point on its course.
Walhalla	At Donaustauf can be found the Walhalla, a marble temple modelled on the Parthenon, built by Ludwig I in 1830–42 as a German Temple of Fame.
	The river now traverses, with numerous bends, the low-lying country on the south side of the Bavarian Forest (see entry). Straubing (see entry) has associations with Agnes Bernauer, daughter of an Augsburg barber, who became the wife of Duke Albrecht II of Bavaria: whereupon his enraged father had her accused of witchcraft and drowned in the Danube.
Metten Niederalteich	Metten and Niederalteich, near Deggendorf, are old and famous Benedictine abbeys with fine Baroque churches.
	At the old episcopal city of Passau (see entry) the Inn and the Ilz flow into the Danube, which just east of the town leaves German territory to enter Austria.

Darmstadt

Land: Hesse
Altitude: 146m/479ft
Population: 138,000

The former capital of the Grand Duchy of Hesse lies at the end of the Upper Rhine plain amid the foothills of the Odenwald. From here the Bergstrasse (see entry) runs south to Heidelberg.

Situation

Central Area

In the centre of the town is the Luisenplatz, with the 33m/108ft high Ludwigssäule (Ludwig Column), topped by a bronze statue of Grand Duke Ludwig I (by Schwanthaler, 1844). On the north side of the square can be seen the former Kollegiengebäude (1780), now occupied by the Regierungspräsidium (district administrative offices). On the south side is the New Town Hall (Neues Rathaus), with the Congress Centre.

Luisenplatz

To the west, in Steubenplatz, is the Kunsthalle (1957; exhibitions).

Kunsthalle

To the south, in Wilhelminenplatz, stands the neo-classical Ludwigskirche, modelled on the Pantheon in Rome. In front of it is an obelisk commemorating Princess Alice, wife of Grand Duke Ludwig IV.

Ludwigskirche

To the east of Luisenplatz is the Schloss, an extensive range of buildings dating from the 16th, 18th and 19th centuries. In the complex are the Provincial and University Library and the Schlossmuseum. To the south of the Schloss are the White Tower (Weisser Turm), a relic of the town's fortifications, the rebuilt Old Town Hall (Altes Rathaus; Renaissance, with a staircase tower on the façade) and the Town Church (Stadtkirche; 15th–18th c.), with a burial vault containing the tombs of Landgraves of Hesse.

Schloss

North of the Schloss, in Friedensplatz, is the Hessian Landesmuseum, with a picture gallery, collections of sculpture and graphic art, a department of applied art, a rich Art Nouveau collection and a mineralogical section. Beyond the museum is the Herrngarten, with the burial mound of Landgravine Henriette Caroline (1721–74). On the east side of the gardens is the College of Technology (Technische Hochschule), on the north side the

*Landesmuseum

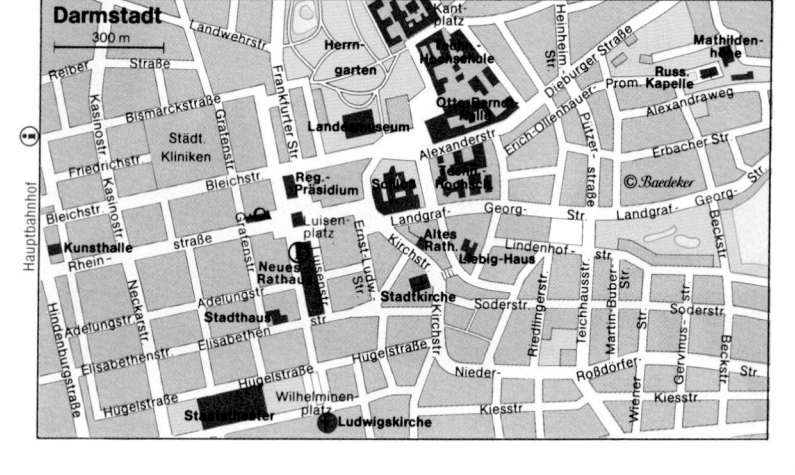

Prinz-Georg-Palais

Prinz-Georg-Palais (17th c.), with a valuable collection of porcelain and a Rococo garden, and on the south side the neo-classical Old Theatre (Altes Theater; 1819), now housing the State Archives.

Pädagog

In Pädagogstrasse, in the southern part of the central area, can be seen the Pädagog (restored), a Renaissance building of 1629 which originally housed the first Latin School (grammar school) in Hesse; it is now occupied by various educational institutions.

Orangery

In Bessunger Strasse, in the south of the town, is the Orangery (1719), now used for conferences and social occasions.

*Mathildenhöhe

In the east of the town is the Mathildenhöhe, on which Grand Duke Ernst Ludwig established an artists' colony (Art Nouveau houses and artists' studios) in 1899. In the centre of the settlement are an exhibition building (temporary art exhibitions) and the 48m/157ft high Hochzeitsturm (Wedding Tower; views).

Adjoining are the Russian Chapel and, a short distance away, the Ernst-Ludwig-Haus (German Academy of Language and Literature; Art Nouveau Museum).

Vivarium

In Heinrichstrasse, on the eastern outskirts of the town, are the Vivarium (Zoo) and the Botanic Garden.

Steinbrücker Teich

To the north-east of the town (reached by way of Dieburger Strasse) lies the Steinbrücker Teich recreation area (Wild West village; mini-golf; boat hire, etc.).

Surroundings of Darmstadt

Kranichstein

5km/3 miles north-east is the old hunting lodge of Kranichstein, an imposing Renaissance building with an interesting Hunting Museum (at present closed). There is a Railway Museum at the railway station.

Mathildenhöhe

In the northern district of Wixhausen can be found a Village Museum (country life).

Wixhausen
Village Museum

Darss (Fischland-Darss-Zingst Peninsula)   B 7–8

Land: Mecklenburg-West Pomerania

Fischland, Darss and Zingst, like the rest of the *bodden* country (see page 13) of North Mecklenburg, form a very popular recreation and holiday area, reached from B 105 by way of Ribnitz-Damgarten (pop. 16,000) or Barth. The various seaside resorts are linked by a road following the coast.

Situation and
characteristics

*Landscape

Darss – an area formerly difficult of access – is a tract of wooded country, rich in game, some 6000 hectares/15,000 acres in extent, with a mile-long sandy beach, which forms the central section of the Fischland-Darss-Zingst peninsula on the Baltic coast. Originally the three parts of the peninsula were separate islands – Fischland into historical times, Darss until the 15th century, Zingst until 1874, when the Prerowstrom was closed off by a dyke. Darss and Zingst form the greater part of the West Pomeranian Bodden National Park.

*Darss

Fischland, the most westerly section of the peninsula, is a morainic ridge up to 18m/60ft in height, the steep seaward scarp of which, the Hohes Ufer (between the Baltic resorts of Wustrow and Ahrenshoop), has been battered for centuries by breakers and storm tides and is cut back every year by about half a metre (20 inches). The material broken off by the waves during all these centuries has been carried north-eastward by the coastal current and deposited – as fan-shaped dunes on Altdarss, with its 7m/23ft high coastal cliffs, as ridges of sand and lines of dunes on Neudarss, as the Bernsteininsel (Amber Island) at the northern tip of Darss (Darsser Ort), which has been linked with the mainland only in recent times.

Fischland

Barth   B 8

The little town of Barth, on the Barther Bodden, is the gateway to the seaside resorts on the Darss and Zingst peninsula.

Situation and
characteristics

The Marienkirche (St Mary's Church), a massive brick-built Gothic church, first appears in the records in 1314; the interior was restored by F. A. Stüler in 1856. The tower has been for centuries a well known seamark. The church has an important collection of material on church history, including one of the last copies of the Low German Bibles printed in Barth (1588).

*St Mary's Church

Of the town's former circuit of walls with four gate-towers there remains only the Dammtor (14th c.), a brick-built structure with small dormer windows in the roof. The Fangelturm (16th c.) was used for a time as a prison; it how houses an astronomical station run by the local secondary school.

Remains of
fortifications

In Mauerstrasse is the former Stift, a house of retreat for women of noble birth founded by King Frederick I of Sweden in 1733. This charming Baroque house, built on the site of the old ducal castle, is now divided into flats.

Stift

In the Markt can be seen a fountain with three bronze fishes, the town's coat of arms.

Markt

Zingst, 13km/8 miles north on the other side of the Meiningenstrom, has a beautiful bathing beach and a towerless village church (by F. A. Stüler, 1862).

Zingst

A few kilometres west of Zingst, on the Prerowstrom, is the seaside resort of Prerow, with the Darss Heimatmuseum, an old seamen's church (1726) and numbers of old seamen's houses with elaborately carved doors.

Prerow

Dessau

Land: Saxony-Anhalt
Altitude: 61m/200ft
Population: 103,800

Situation and characteristics

Dessau, once capital of the Free State of Anhalt, lies at the junction of the Mulde with the Elbe. The Princes of Anhalt fostered literature and the arts, and the town developed into a considerable cultural centre. The Bauhaus, the 20th century's most celebrated school of design, was based in Dessau from 1925 until its closure in 1932.

** Bauhaus

As a building, the Bauhaus (by Walter Gropius, 1925–26) enjoys international reputation as one of the outstanding achievements of 20th century architecture. It is equally famous as the home, until 1932, of a school of design covering all artistic disciplines. Since 1977 the Bauhaus has been an important cultural centre, with international exhibitions of architecture, graphic art and design; it is also the home of the Dessau Landestheater, the "Theater im Bauhaus". The building was restored in 1976–79. Its most striking external features are the large suspended glass curtain wall (area 1400 sq.m/15,000 sq.ft), the Bauhaus Bridge and the entrance. Features of the interior are the Aula (Great Hall, with stage), the Mensa (Refectory), the vestibule and the exhibition and lecture room.

* Bauhaus-Siedlung

The Bauhaus-Siedlung in Dessau-Törten (by Walter Gropius, 1926–28) is a settlement of 316 villas designed to demonstrate the idea of mechanising the construction of houses. The Stahlhaus (by Georg Muche and Richard Paulick, 1926) stands on steel piles and is clad with sheet steel. The five Laubenganghäuser (by Hannes Meyer, 1930), three-storey buildings with 21 flats in each, have staircases borne on arcades leading to the flats. The Meisterhäuser (by Gropius, 1926–28) in Ebertallee are examples of modern functional architecture.

Bauhaus, Dessau

The Museum of Natural History and Prehistory (Museum für Naturkunde und Vorgeschichte; 1746–50) is a reproduction of the Santo Spirito Hospital in Rome; its angular tower, 40m/130ft high, was added in 1847. The collection covers geology, mineralogy, botany, palaeontology and zoology, with prehistoric material from the districts of Dessau, Rosslau and Köthen.

Town Centre

Natural History Museum

The Georgenkirche (St George's Church; 1712–17) is in Dutch Baroque style; one of the architects involved was Carlo Ignazio Pozzi. Its most notable features are the three-storey onion-domed tower and the mansard roof on an elliptical plan.

St George's Church

Georgengarten

In the English-style Georgengarten is the neo-classical Schloss Georgium (by Friedrich Wilhelm von Erdmannsdorff, 1781), with a notable picture gallery (works by Dürer, Lucas Cranach the Elder and Tischbein; Dutch, Flemish and German painting of the 12th–20th centuries).

Schloss Georgium
* Picture gallery

In the adjoining Lehrpark (16 hectares/40 acres; a zoological and botanical "study park") can be seen almost 500 animals of 110 different species and 125 species of tree. The park was established in the 19th century by August Hooff.

Lehrpark

* Schloss Mosigkau

9km/6 miles south-west of Dessau is Schloss Mosigkau, a gem of Late Baroque architecture (designed by Georg Wenzeslaus von Knobelsdorff), which since 1951 has housed the State Museum (Staatliches Museum). The collection includes Dutch, Flemish and German painting of the 17th and 18th centuries (with works by Rubens, Pesne, Jordaens, van Dyck, Moreelse and Fyt) and 17th and 18th century applied and decorative art. In the park (laid out in 1755–57 by C. F. Brose and J. G. Schoch in the French style, with Japanese gardens) are a variety of rare and exotic plants and a maze.

* Luisium

The Luisium is an intimate English-style garden (by Johann Friedrich Eyserbeck, 1780), with a house in the style of an Italian villa (by Friedrich Wilhelm von Erdmannsdorff, 1774–77). It is lavishly decorated with arches, colonnades, temples, statues, monuments, grottoes, a Chinese bridge and an orangery.

Surroundings of Dessau

23km/14 miles south-east of Dessau is Gräfenhainichen, birthplace of the greatest Protestant hymn-writer Paul Gerhardt (1607–76), with the neo-classical Paul Gerhardt Chapel (1844) and the Paul Gerhardt House (1907–09; monument to Gerhardt by Friedrich Pfannenschmidt).

Gräfenhainichen

Rosslau, 6km/4 miles north, on the Elbe, has a castle built in 1215. Other features of interest are the cemetery gateway (1822) and the Innungsbrauhaus (Guild Brewhouse; 1826), both by Gottfried Bandhauer.

Rosslau

20km/12½ miles north is Zerbst, which has an almost completely preserved circuit of walls (4km/2½ miles long, up to 7m/23ft high), with a wall-walk (half-timbered roof) and three 15th century town gates. The Museum, housed in an Early Gothic monastic church (1252), has a valuable collection including faience, incunabula, manuscripts and a Cranach Bible of 1541. The Trinity Church (by Cornelis Ruckwaert, 1683–96), in Dutch Baroque style, has fine sculpture by Giovanni Simonetti.

Zerbst
* Town walls

Thiessen, 16km/10 miles north, boasts a water-powered copper-works of around 1600, one of the oldest and best-preserved of its kind (now a museum).

Thiessen

Detmold   E 4

Land: North Rhine-Westphalia
Altitude: 134m/440ft
Population: 68,000

Situation and
characteristics

The old residence and garrison town of the former principality of Lippe-Detmold lies in the valley of the Werra on the northern slopes of the Teutoburg Forest (see entry). The picturesque old town still preserves many 16th and 17th century half-timbered houses.

The Town

Markt

The central feature of the old town is the Markt, with the neo-classical Town Hall (Rathaus; 1830), the 16th century Erlöserkirche (Church of the Redeemer; Protestant), with an organ of 1795, and the Donop Fountain (1901).

Schloss

To the north is the Hofgarten (entrance in Lange Strasse), with the Schloss, a palace in Weser Renaissance style (by Jörg Unkair and Cord Tönnis, 1548–57) with four wings laid out round a central courtyard, incorporating an older tower of 1470. It contains valuable collections of tapestries and porcelain.

Landesmuseum

Farther north stands the Landestheater (1914–18). To the north-west of the Hofgarten, on the Ameide, is the Landesmuseum (Provincial Museum; natural history, ethnography, local material).

Neues Palais

On the south side of the town, in the beautiful Allee, is the Neues Palais (New Palace; 1708–17), now occupied by the North-West German Academy of Music. Behind the palace is the beautiful Palaisgarten.

* Westphalian
Open-Air Museum

500m/550yds south, on the Königsberg, lies the Westphalian Open-Air Museum (Landesmuseum für Volkskunde), covering an area of 80 hectares/200 acres, with 90 build-

Schloss, Detmold   *Hermannsdenkmal*

ings brought here from different parts of Westphalia (demonstrations of old craft techniques; special exhibitions).

Surroundings of Detmold

In the Heiligenkirchen district, 4km/2½ miles south, is a bird park (Vogelpark) with 320 different species of birds.

Bird Park

In the Berlebeck district, 5km/3 miles south, can be found the Adlerwarte (Eagle Observatory), with 80 birds of prey from all over the world.

Adlerwarte

8km/5 miles south-west, on the Grotenburg (386m/1266ft), rises the Hermannsdenkmal (by Ernst von Bandel, 1838–75), a huge monument commemorating the battle in the Teutoburg Forest in A.D. 9 in which the Cheruscan chieftain Hermann (Arminius) inflicted a crushing defeat on the Roman army. The total height of the monument, including the base, is 53m/174ft.

Hermannsdenkmal

12km/7½ miles south of Detmold (2km/1¼ miles west of Horn-Bad Meinberg) are the Externsteine, a group of fissured sandstone rocks, the highest rising to 37.5m/123ft, originally a pagan shrine and later a Christian place of pilgrimage (monumental stone carving of the Descent from the Cross, c. 1120).

*Externsteine

Deutsche Alpenstrasse (German Alpine Highway)   M 5–M 8

Land: Bavaria

The Deutsche Alpenstrasse, the development of which began in 1933, runs for some 500km/310 miles from Lake Constance in the west through the Allgäu and Bavarian Alps to the Königssee in the Berchtesgadener Land, remaining within German territory all the way. It follows existing roads so far as possible, with some new sections of road at gradients never exceeding 15%. Two sections still to be improved are between Wallgau and the Sylvenstein-Stausee (at present a forestry road subject to toll) and between Tatzelwurm and the Inn valley (the Tatzelwurmstrasse). The route is still not completely signposted.

Along the Deutsche Alpenstrasse

From Lindau (see entry) the road runs north-east into the Allgäu (see entry), climbing steadily, with many bends. Off the road to the left is Lindenberg (see Wangen im Allgäu); then follow little holiday resorts such as Weiler-Simmerberg and Oberstaufen and the popular holiday area around Sonthofen (see entry), with Immenstadt and the large Alpsee. From Sonthofen a detour can be made to Oberstdorf and the Kleinwalsertal (see entries) to the south.

From Sonthofen the road runs east via Hindelang and the winding Jochstrasse to the winter sports resort of Oberjoch, where it turns north, passing a side road on the right leading into the Jungholz enclave of Austrian territory within Germany (and within the German customs area). Beyond Wertach the road skirts the beautiful Grüntensee, passes Oy-Mittelberg, turns east again and after passing through Pfronten (see entry) runs close to the Austrian frontier and comes to Füssen (see entry), around which are the magnificent castles of Kings Ludwig II and Maximilian II of Bavaria and several beautiful lakes.

From Füssen the Deutsche Alpenstrasse coincides with the Romantische Strasse (see entry) as it runs north-east into the Alpine foreland. At Steingaden is a former monastic church with a sumptuous Baroque interior, and a few kilometres away the world-famed Wieskirche (see Füssen, Surroundings).

At Schönegg the Romantische Strasse turns north, while the Deutsche Alpenstrasse heads south and continues by way of Oberammergau (see entry) and the Benedictine monastery of Ettal (see entry; rewarding detour to Schloss Linderhof) to the leading winter sports resort of Garmisch-Partenkirchen (see entry), at the foot of Germany's highest mountain, the Zugspitze.

Beyond Krün (where a road runs south to the violin-makers' town of Mittenwald: see entry) and Wallgau the route follows a forestry road (toll) to the Sylvenstein-Stausee which branches off B 11 on the right. This follows the edge of a large nature reserve and then skirts the long Sylvenstein artificial lake (road on left running north to Bad Tölz: see entry). Beyond the end of the lake is a junction where a road branches off on the right and leads south into Austria. The road to the north crosses the Achenpass (941m/3087ft) and continues to the Tegernsee (see entry), Schliersee, Spitzingsee and Bayrischzell. Beyond this is the Tatzelwurmstrasse (still to be improved), which descends into the Inn valley.

In the Inn valley the Alpenstrasse follows A 93 (the Inntal motorway) northward to the junction known as the Inntal-Dreieck and then turns east on the A 8 motorway, sign-posted to Salzburg. At Bernau it leaves the motorway (attractive detour north and round the Chiemsee: see entry) and reaches the Chiemgauer Berge, passing the well known holiday resorts of Reit im Winkl, Ruhpolding and Inzell. On the river Saalach, which farther north forms the frontier with Austria, is Bad Reichenhall (see entry). Then the Alpenstrasse comes to an end in the extreme south-eastern corner of Germany at Berchtesgaden (see entry), with the Königssee, the Rossfeldstrasse and the Kehlsteinstrasse.

Deutsche Weinstrasse (German Wine Highway)　　　　　　　　　　I 3

Land: Rhineland-Palatinate
Length: 83km/52 miles

The Deutsche Weinstrasse follows the east side of the Pfälzer Wald (Palatinate Forest), with its many old castles, through one of the largest continuous wine-producing regions in Germany (some 21,000 hectares/52,500 acres). It begins at Bockenheim, a few kilometres west of Worms (see entry), and ends at the Weintor ("Wine Gate") at Schweigen, near the frontier with France.

*Along the Deutsche Weinstrasse

The Deutsche Weinstrasse is marked by special signs with a stylised bunch of grapes (on the southern section a wine-flagon). It traverses an almost uninterrupted succession of vineyards and orchards and numerous picturesque little wine towns and villages.

Bockenheim

Bockenheim, at the beginning of the main wine-producing district, is the starting-point of the Weinstrasse. From here it runs south down the east side of the Pfälzer Wald nature reserve to the little town of Grünstadt, a centre of the wine trade, and the vine-growing villages of Kirchheim and Kallstadt.

Bad Dürkheim

Bad Dürkheim (pop. 15,000) is held to be the largest German wine town, with an annual vintage festival in September, the Wurstmarkt ("Sausage Market"). It is also a health resort, to which many visitors come for its "grape cure" and its sodium chloride medicinal spring (Kurhaus, with casino, and Kurgarten; spa treatment establishment; indoor pool and outdoor pool, the Salinarium). An unusual feature is the Dürkheimer Fass, the Great Tun of Dürkheim (capacity 1.7 million litres/374,000 gallons), now fitted out as a wine bar. In the Schlosskirche can be seen the Renaissance tomb (restored in the 19th century) of Count Emich XI of Leiningen and his wife. In Haus Catoir is the Heimatmuseum, in the former ducal mill the Palatinate Museum of Natural History (Pfalzmuseum für Naturkunde).
3km/2 miles west are the imposing ruins of the Benedictine abbey of Limburg.

Wachenheim

Over the old-world little town of Wachenheim loom the ruins of the Wachtenburg. South-west of the town lies the Kurpfalz-Park (big game; amusements).

Deidesheim (pop. 3500) is another important wine-growing town. Handsome Town Hall with an external flight of steps; Ceramic Museum; Wine-Growing Museum in the Old Town Hall.

Deidesheim

Neustadt an der Weinstrasse (pop. 53,000) is one of the great centres of the Palatinate wine trade. In the Marktplatz stands the twin-towered Stiftskirche (1368–1489), with the "Imperial Bell", one of the largest cast steel bells in the world. Opposite the church is the handsome Town Hall (18th–19th c.). There is an interesting Railway Museum (trips on the "Cuckoo Line").

Neustadt an der Weinstrasse

In the district of Hambach, to the south-west, is the Hambacher Schloss (the Maxburg), which was destroyed in 1688; the interior was restored from 1979 onwards. This was the scene of the "Hambacher Fest" in 1832, a demonstration in favour of democracy and republican government.

Hambacher Schloss

The Alsterweiler Chapel in Maikammer has a Late Gothic triptych.

Maikammer

It is worth making a detour to the picturesque village of St Martin, a few kilometres west, which is scheduled as a national monument.

St Martin

Edenkoben is another attractive little town. 3km/2 miles west can be found the palatial Villa Ludwigshöhe, built in 1846–52 for King Ludwig I of Bavaria. Above it are the ruins of the Rietburg (chair-lift).

Edenkoben

Off the Weinstrasse to the east is Landau (pop. 37,000), with a Late Gothic Augustinian church (beautiful cloister) and the Early Gothic Stiftskirche. Remains of fortifications built by Vauban in 1687; Festhalle in Art Nouveau style; beautiful parks (particularly the Goethe Park); Zoo.

Landau

From the junction with the road to Landau the road to the west leads to Annweiler am Trifels, with handsome half-timbered houses. Above the town stands the old imperial stronghold of Trifels (fine panoramic views), in which Richard Coeur-de-Lion was held prisoner in 1193.

Annweiler

The Weinstrasse continues to Leinsweiler. Above the village is the Slevogthof, once the summer residence of Max Slevogt (1868–1932), with mural paintings by the artist. His grave is in the garden.

Leinsweiler

The spa of Bad Bergzabern (pop. 6000) has a 16th century Schloss. Modern thermal pools, indoor and outdoor; Kneipp cure.

Bad Bergzabern

From Bad Bergzabern an attractive detour can be made to Dörrenbach, 2km/1¼ miles west (fortified church, half-timbered Town Hall).

Dörrenbach

In Schweigen stands the Weintor (Wine Gate; 1936–37), marking the end of the Deutsche Weinstrasse. There is an instructive Wine Trail.

Schweigen

Dinkelsbühl

Land: Bavaria
Altitude: 440m/1444ft
Population: 11,000

With its completely preserved circuit of walls (14th–15th c.) and its old gabled houses, the old Franconian imperial city of Dinkelsbühl is the very picture of a little medieval town.

Situation and characteristics

* Townscape

In the Marktplatz stands the Late Gothic church of St George (1448–99; R.C.), one of the finest hall-churches in Germany, with a beautiful interior. On the high altar can be seen a

* St Georg

Bad Doberan

"Crucifixion" of the school of Hans Pleydenwurff; tabernacle of 1480. In the west tower is a Romanesque doorway (13th c.).

House of
Teutonic Order

The House of the Teutonic Order, to the south of the Marktplatz (Deutschordenshaus; 1761–64), has a fine chapel.

*Deutsches Haus
Schranne

In the Weinmarkt, immediately north of the Marktplatz, is the Deutsches Haus, a beautiful half-timbered building of the 16th century. Adjoining it on the right is the old Schranne (Granary), in which the pageant play of the "Kinderzeche" (commemorating an occasion in 1632 when the children of the town, then under siege by the Swedish army, saved it from destruction by begging the Swedes for mercy) is performed every year.

Segringer Strasse

Segringer Strasse, which runs west from the Markt, is particularly charming with its continuous succession of old gabled house-fronts.

Town gates

There are four gates in the town walls: the Segringer Tor on the west, the Rothenburger Tor on the north, the Wörnitztor on the east and the Nördlinger Tor on the south.

Museums

In the Nördlinger Tor is the "Dritte Dimension" ("Third Dimension") Museum (photography, optics, holographs, etc.) and nearby, in Nördlinger Strasse, the Kabinett der Geheimnisse (Cabinet of Secrets), with figures representing scenes from detective literature. In Lutherstrasse, near the Rothenburger Tor, is the Historical Museum (history of the town).

Crailsheim

20km/12½ miles north-west, in the Jagst valley, is Crailsheim (in Baden-Württemberg), with the Johanniskirche (St John's Church; Romanesque and Gothic), with a 15th century high altar. In the old Spitalkapelle (Hospital Chapel) is the Hohenlohe Heimatmuseum.

Feuchtwangen

11km/7 miles north of Dinkelsbühl is the little town of Feuchtwangen, once an imperial city, with an attractive Marktplatz; Romanesque church, formerly collegiate, with old craftsmen's workshops in the cloister (dramatic performances in summer); Museum of Folk Art (faience).

Bad Doberan

See Rostock, Surroundings

Donaueschingen   L 3

Land: Baden-Württemberg
Altitude: 675m/2215ft
Population: 18,000

Situation and
characteristics

Donaueschingen lies on the eastern fringe of the Black Forest (see entry), on the river Brigach, which together with the Donauquelle ("Source of the Danube") in the Schlosspark and the Breg which joins it below the town forms the Danube. From 1723 Donaueschingen was the seat of the Princes Fürstenberg, whose territories passed to Baden and Württemberg in 1806.

Schloss

On the east side of the town stands the Schloss (originally Baroque; rebuilt in 1772 and again in 1893), with sumptuously furnished state apartments (tapestries; Renaissance,

"Source of the Danube"

Baroque and Rococo furniture). The Schloss is open to the public from Easter to September; in October a festival of contemporary music is held here.

South-east of the Schloss, in the beautiful Schlosspark, can be seen the so-called **Donauquelle** (Source of the Danube; "To the sea, 2840km/1765 miles"), in an enclosure designed by A. Weinbrenner, with an allegorical representation of the Baar (the upland region between the southern Black Forest and the Swabian Alb) and the young Danube (by A. Heer, 1896).

Above the Schloss, to the north, is the Karlsbau, with the **Fürstenberg Collections** (notable in particular for the fine paintings of the Swabian and Franconian schools of the 15th and 16th centuries, including works by Lucas Cranach, Hans Holbein the Elder, Matthias Grünewald and Bartholomäus Zeitblom; also natural history and folk collections).

To the west of the Schloss stands the **Stadtkirche** (St John's; 1727–47), in Bohemian Baroque style, designed by the Prague architect M. Kanka.

Town Centre

To the west of the church, at Haldenstrasse 5, is the **Hofbibliothek** (Court Library), with a scholarly collection of books, a music collection and many old German manuscripts, including Codex C of the "Nibelungenlied" (13th c.).

Donauwörth   K 6

Land: Bavaria
Altitude: 403m/1322ft
Population: 17,000

Dortmund

Dortmund

Situation and characteristics	The former free imperial city of Donauwörth lies on a ridge of hills above the confluence of the Wörnitz and the Danube. It has preserved its old town walls.

The Town

Tanzhaus Fuggerhaus	The town's main street is the wide Reichsstrasse, with its handsome gabled houses one of the finest streets in Bayerisch-Schwaben. In the "Tanzhaus" at No. 34 is the Archaeological Museum and at the west end of the street the Fuggerhaus, a Renaissance mansion of 1539.
Heiligkreuz Abbey	A little way west is the former Benedictine abbey of Heiligkreuz, now occupied by a school. The Heilig-Kreuz-Kirche (Holy Cross Church; 1717–22) is a handsome Baroque building by Josef Schmuzer, with rich stucco ornament and frescoes.
Parish church Town Hall	On the south side of Reichsstrasse is the large Gothic parish church (1444–67) and at the east end of the street the Late Gothic Town Hall (Rathaus; 1309; restored in neo-Gothic style in the 19th century).
Riedertor Hintermeierhaus	On the banks of the Görnitz stands the Riedertor, now housing a museum on the history of the town. A bridge leads on to the island of Ried, on which is the Hintermeierhaus (Heimatmuseum).

Harburg

Schloss	10km/6 miles up the Wörnitz valley is the charmingly situated little free imperial city of Harburg, over which looms Schloss Harburg (13th–18th c.), with the art collection of the Princes Oettingen-Wallerstein.

Neuburg an der Donau

30km/19 miles downstream we come to Neuburg an der Donau (pop. 26,000). In the walled upper town is the massive Schloss (1530–50; fine inner courtyards). In Karlsplatz are handsome buildings of the 16th–19th centuries.

Dortmund   F 3

Land: North Rhine-Westphalia
Altitude: 86m/282ft
Population: 573,000

Situation and characteristics	Dortmund, the largest city in Westphalia, lies on the eastern edge of the Ruhr (see entry) in the fertile Hellweg area watered by the upper Escher. The foundations of its economy are the iron and steel industry and engineering, but in addition it has huge breweries whose annual output exceeds even that of Munich.

Old Town

The central feature of the old town is the Alter Markt, with the Municipal and Provincial Library (1957).

St Reinold's Church	North-east of the Alter Markt stands the Reinoldikirche (St Reinold's Church; 13th c.), with a Late Gothic choir (15th c.). Its 104m/341ft high tower, with the heaviest peal of bells in Westphalia, is the landmark and emblem of the city.
St Mary's Church *Marienaltar	Opposite St Reinold's Church is the Marienkirche (St Mary's; 12th and 14th c.; Protestant), whose principal treasure is the Marienaltar, by the Dortmund master Konrad of Soest.

The Westenhellweg and Ostenhellweg pedestrian zones, which begin here, are the city's principal shopping streets.

The Petrikirche (St Peter's Church (14th–15th c.)), on the north side of Westenhellweg, has a large and beautiful altar from Antwerp (c. 1521), with 633 gilded figures. To the south of Westenhellweg is the 14th century Propsteikirche (R.C.), with a 15th century high altar.

*St Peter's Church

Nearby, at Hansastrasse 3, can be found the Museum of Art and Culture (Museum für Kunst- und Kulturgeschichte; history of the town; church history, old furniture, gold coins, medieval and 19th century pictures, 17th and 18th century culture, folk art).

Museum of Art and Culture

Near the east end of Ostenhellweg is the Museum am Ostwall (20th century art, painting, objets d'art, sculpture, graphic art; works of the Expressionist group "Die Brücke").

Museum am Ostwall

At Münsterstrasse 271, to the north of the city centre, some distance beyond the railway station (Hauptbahnhof), we come to the Natural History Museum (Naturkundemuseum; fossils from the Messel shale-mine at Darmstadt, minerals, reconstructions of dinosaurs; aquarium; children's museum).

Natural History Museum

Harbour

North-west of the city are the harbour installations on the Dortmund-Ems Canal (272km/169 miles long). Adjoining is the Fredenbaum leisure park.

Southern Districts

To the south of the city centre lies a large park in which are the Westfalenhalle (Trade Fair Centre, with seating for 23,000; several subsidiary halls), the Ice Stadium (Eisstadion;

*Westfalenhalle

Alter Markt, with St Reinold's Church

ice-skating and roller-skating), the Westfalenstadion (seating for 54,000) and the "Rote Erde" athletics stadium.

Westfalenpark   Immediately east is the Westfalenpark (area 70 hectares /175 acres), where the Federal Garden Show was held in 1959 and 1969. Here too are the 212m/696ft high Television Tower (Fernsehturm) known as Florian, with a revolving restaurant at 138m/453ft, and the German Rosarium.

Rombergpark   Farther south is the Rombergpark, with the Botanic Garden (tropical houses, arboretum) and the Zoo (Tiergarten).

Hohensyburg

12km/7½ miles south, on a wooded crag above the Ruhr valley, stands the ruined Hohensyburg, which was destroyed in the 13th century; it now houses Dortmund's Casino. Just to the west are the Vinceturm (panoramic views) and the Emperor William Memorial (1902). Below the crag lies the Hengsteysee, an artificial lake formed by the construction of a dam in 1928.

Cappenberg

Schloss   18km/11 miles north of Dortmund is Cappenberg, with a Schloss occupied by the 19th century statesman Freiherr vom Stein in his last years; it now houses the Freiherr vom Stein Archives.

*Stiftskirche   The Stiftskirche, a former collegiate church (12th and 14th c.), has richly carved 16th century choir-stalls. The church treasury contains a famous reliquary (c. 1165) in the form of a head of the Emperor Frederick Barbarossa, presented by the Emperor to his godfather Otto von Cappenberg.

Dresden   F–G 9

Capital of the *Land* of Saxony
Altitude: 120m/394ft
Population: 520,000

Situation   Dresden lies in a wide basin in the upper Elbe valley, which extends for a distance of 40km/25 miles from Meissen to Pirna between the foothills of the Eastern Erzgebirge, the steep scarp of the Lusatian granite plateau and the Elbsandsteingebirge (Elbe Sandstone Hills). Dresden has been favoured over the centuries by its beautiful setting, its agreeable climate and its situation on important trade routes.

Sights

**Zwinger

Dresden's most celebrated tourist attraction is the Zwinger, a gem of courtly Baroque architecture in which overflowing creative power and clarity of form are most happily combined.

The best approach to the Zwinger is over the old moat (the Zwingergraben) to the rear of the Theatre (Schauspielhaus; 1912–13) and through the Kronentor. On the front of this gateway, which is topped by the royal crown of Poland, can be seen the emblems of the Saxon/Polish dynasty of Augustus the Strong, who had the Zwinger built (by M. D. Pöppelmann, 1710–32) as a celebration of his power.

The Zwinger shows an extraordinary variety and magnificence of form: the majestic 32-bayed Long Gallery on the south side, the four symmetrically arranged pavilions on

Wallpavillon, in the Zwinger

the east and west sides, the Wallpavillon in the centre of the semicircular arched gallery at the west end – with its musical lightness the particular jewel of the Zwinger – and the Nymphenbad (Bath of the Nymphs) with its graceful fountains and mythological female figures (from the workshop of Balthasar Permoser, who collaborated with Pöppelmann on the construction of the Zwinger).

In the Long Gallery, to the right of the Kronentor, is the entrance to the Porcelain Collection (Porzellansammlung), the second largest in the world, with early Chinese pottery and Chinese porcelain of the finest period, the famous "Dragoon vases", Böttger stoneware and a unique display of Meissen porcelain.

*Porcelain collection

On the inner side of the Glockenspielpavillon, adjoining the Porcelain Collection, is a carillon of 40 porcelain bells, also from the Meissen manufactory.

In the Mathematisch-Physikalischer Salon in the south-west pavilion can be seen a collection of scientific instruments of the 13th to 19th centuries, including geodetic apparatus and a collection of clocks.

*Collection of scientific instruments

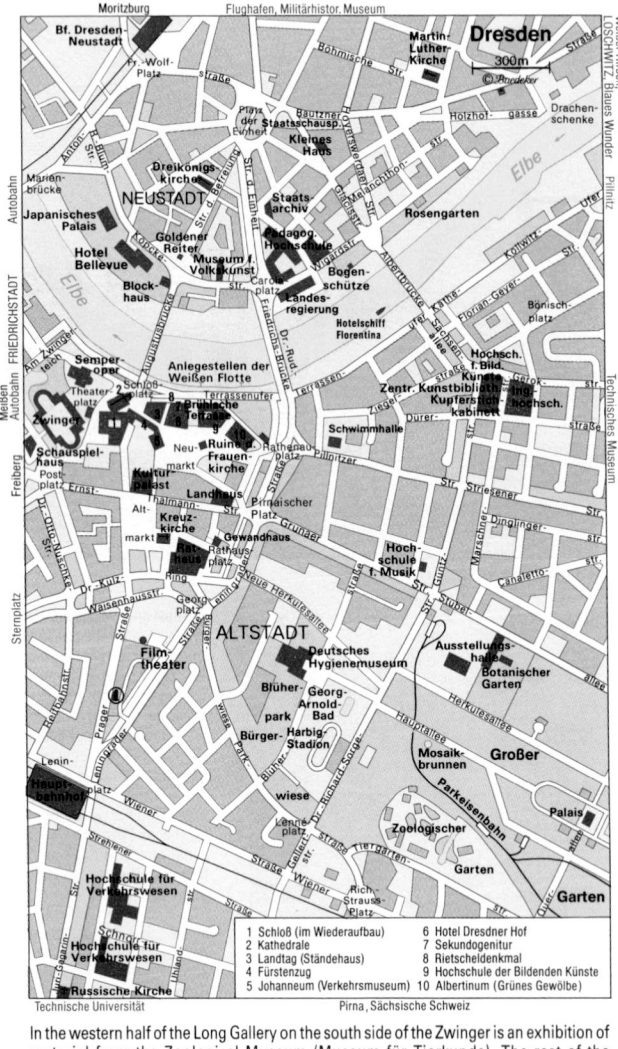

Dresden

300m

© Baedeker

1 Schloß (im Wiederaufbau)
2 Kathedrale
3 Landtag (Ständehaus)
4 Fürstenzug
5 Johanneum (Verkehrsmuseum)
6 Hotel Dresdner Hof
7 Sekundogenitur
8 Rietscheldenkmal
9 Hochschule der Bildenden Künste
10 Albertinum (Grünes Gewölbe)

Zoological
Museum

In the western half of the Long Gallery on the south side of the Zwinger is an exhibition of material from the Zoological Museum (Museum für Tierkunde). The rest of the museum's collection is in the Fasanenschlösschen at Schloss Moritzburg (see page 173). Also in the Long Gallery is a permanent exhibition on "Animals in the History of Art".

** Gallery of
Old Masters

On the north side of the Zwinger, which was originally open, is a linking wing built in 1847–54 by Gottfried Semper, who played a leading part in the architectural development of Dresden in the 19th century. At the west end of this wing is the Picture Gallery of Old Masters (Gemäldegalerie Alte Meister), one of the world's great art galleries, whose treasures include works by Flemish and Dutch painters of the 15th and

Semper's Opera House, Theaterplatz

17th centuries (van Eyck, Rubens, Frans Hals, Rembrandt, Vermeer, etc.), German paint-ing of the 16th–18th centuries (Dürer, Holbein, Cranach, Graff, Tischbein, etc.), Spanish and French painting of the 17th and 18th centuries (Velázquez, Murillo; Poussin, etc.) and – the high point of the collection – Italian painting of the 15th–18th centuries, particularly Renaissance works (Raphael, "Sistine Madonna"; Giorgione, "Sleeping Venus"; Titian, "The Tribute Money"; Botticelli, Correggio, the Carracci, Guido Reni, Tintoretto, etc.). The Museum is at present closed; selected works are temporarily displayed in the Albertinum (see below).

At the east end of the north wing is the Historical Museum (Historisches Museum), with long-range weapons of the 16th–18th centuries, weapons of cold steel of the 15th–18th centuries, hunting arms and equipment of the 16th and 18th centuries, armour (in-cluding the magnificent parade armour of Elector Christian II, 1562–64), helmets and shields of the 16th and 17th centuries and the regalia worn by Augustus the Strong at his coronation as king of Poland in 1697.
The Historical Museum is also temporarily closed for renovation.

*Historical Museum

*Theaterplatz

Beyond the portico of the Picture Gallery lies the Theaterplatz, one of Germany's finest squares. In the centre stands an equestrian statue (by Schilling, 1883) of King John, who made a name for himself as a student and translator of Dante.

The west side of the square is dominated by the Opera House (the Semperoper), the second opera house built by Gottfried Semper on this site (the first one having been burned down in 1869). Like the Picture Gallery, it is in the style of the Italian High Renaissance. From 1878 until the end of the Second World War it was Dresden's most magnificent theatre; after wartime destruction it was restored between 1977 and 1985 very much in its original form.

**Opera House

At the south-east corner of the square is the Altstädter Wache (Old Town Guard-House; 1830–31), designed by Karl Friedrich Schinkel on the model of the Guard-House in Berlin.

Altstädter Wache

Panoramic view of the Old Town from the New Town

Taschenbergpalais

Farther south-east stands the Taschenbergpalais, a Baroque palace (by Pöppelmann, 1707–11; side wings 1756 and 1763), also rebuilt after wartime destruction. In front of the palace is the neo-Gothic Cholera Fountain (by Semper, 1843), which was brought here in 1925.

*Cathedral (Hofkirche)

The Hofkirche (Court Church) of Dresden, built between 1738 and 1755, was raised to cathedral status in 1980.

The site of the church, at the end of the bridge over the Elbe, was chosen by the Elector as a position commanding the Elbe area. The church, in Italian High Baroque style, was designed by the Roman architect Gaetano Chiaveri. After his departure in 1743 the work was continued by Sebastian Wetzel and others. The church was consecrated in 1751 and finally completed in 1755.

During the devastating Allied bombardment of 1945 the interior was burned out and most of the vaulting collapsed, leaving only the tower unscathed. The church was restored after the war.

The exterior of the church is striking, with its 85.5m/280ft high tower and its 78 statues in niches and on the balustrades. Notable features of the interior are the processional ambulatories, Balthasar Permoser's magnificently carved pulpit (1722), the altarpiece of the Ascension (by Mengs, 1750–51) and the Silbermann organ (1750–53), Silbermann's last and finest work. In four burial vaults are the remains of kings and princes of Saxony. An urn contains the heart of Augustus the Strong; his body was buried in Krakow.

Nepomuk Chapel

The Nepomuk Chapel, with a Pietà and an altar of Meissen porcelain by Friedrich Press, was consecrated in 1973 as a "memorial chapel for the victims of February 13th 1945 and of all unrighteous violence".

Schloss

*Georgentor

Opposite the entrance to the Cathedral, at the end of Augustusstrasse, stands the Georgentor, the first part of the Schloss to be restored after the war (1964–69). On the west side is a Renaissance doorway from the original building. The sculptural decoration, including the equestrian statue of Duke George, was the work of Christian Behrens.

In Augustusstrasse, on the outside wall of the Langer Gang (below), can be seen the famous Fürstenzug (Procession of Princes), a 101m/330ft long parade of Margraves, Dukes, Electors and Kings of the house of Wettin, together with leading figures in the arts and sciences, commissioned to mark the centenary of the Wettin dynasty. This great mural in sgraffito technique (by Wilhelm Walter, 1870–76), was later (1907) transferred in the Meissen manufactory on to 24,000 porcelain tiles, covering a total area of 957 sq.m/10,300 sq.ft. *Fürstenzug

The Langer Gang (by P. Buchner, 1586–91), well restored after the last war, is a long wing linking the Georgenbau of the palace with the Johanneum (see below). Along its inner side is a long Tuscan-style arcade with 22 round-headed arches which leads to the Stallhof (Court Stables), the tilt-yard, the horse-trough and horse-pond. Langer Gang

The old Stallgebäude (Stable Building) in the Neumarkt, now the Johanneum, also dates from the late 16th century, with alterations in the 18th and 19th centuries; the external staircase was added in 1729. From 1722 to 1856 it was a picture gallery, and since 1956 it has housed the Transport Museum (Verkehrsmuseum; railways, urban transport, motor vehicles, shipping, air travel; special section on the history of the bicycle). Stallgebäude (Johanneum)
To the left of the main front is the Schöne Pforte ("Beautiful Doorway"; not restored), a jewel of Renaissance architecture (before 1555) which was originally the entrance to the palace chapel.
In front of the Johanneum stands the Peace Fountain (Friedensbrunnen), originally the Turks' Fountain (Türkenbrunnen).

Frauenkirche

Until February 1945 the Neumarkt was perhaps the most picturesque square in the Baroque city. It is now occupied only by the ruins of the Frauenkirche (Church of Our Lady; 1726–43), which with its famous 95m/312ft high stone dome was once Germany's largest Protestant church and the great landmark and emblem of Dresden. There are now plans to rebuild it. Neumarkt

*Brühlsche Terrasse

The Brühlsche Terrasse (Brühl Terrace), famed as the "balcony of Europe", is best approached from the Schlossplatz by a broad flight of steps. This area on the site of the

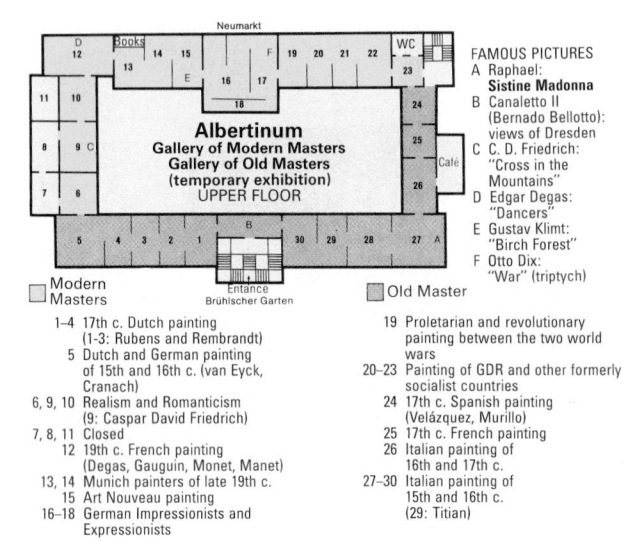

FAMOUS PICTURES

A Raphael:
Sistine Madonna

B Canaletto II
(Bernado Bellotto):
views of Dresden

C C. D. Friedrich:
"Cross in the
Mountains"

D Edgar Degas:
"Dancers"

E Gustav Klimt:
"Birch Forest"

F Otto Dix:
"War" (triptych)

Albertinum
Gallery of Modern Masters
Gallery of Old Masters
(temporary exhibition)
UPPER FLOOR

☐ Modern
Masters   ▨ Old Master

1–4 17th c. Dutch painting
(1–3: Rubens and Rembrandt)
5 Dutch and German painting
of 15th and 16th c. (van Eyck,
Cranach)
6, 9, 10 Realism and Romanticism
(9: Caspar David Friedrich)
7, 8, 11 Closed
12 19th c. French painting
(Degas, Gauguin, Monet, Manet)
13, 14 Munich painters of late 19th c.
15 Art Nouveau painting
16–18 German Impressionists and
Expressionists

19 Proletarian and revolutionary
painting between the two world
wars
20–23 Painting of GDR and other formerly
socialist countries
24 17th c. Spanish painting
(Velázquez, Murillo)
25 17th c. French painting
26 Italian painting of
16th and 17th c.
27–30 Italian painting of
15th and 16th c.
(29: Titian)

old ramparts was granted to Count Heinrich von Brühl (1700–63), an intimate of Frederick Augustus II (Augustus III) and from 1733 Director of the royal Art Collection, who in 1738 had it laid out as a pleasure garden, with a number of buildings which have not survived. In 1814 the terrace was opened to the public and the flight of steps at the west end was built. The sculptured groups on the staircase representing Morning, Noon, Evening and Night (by J. Schilling, 1863–68) were replaced in 1908 by bronze casts.

Dolphin Fountain

Of the original layout of the terrace there survive only the Dolphin Fountain (by Pierre Coudray, 1747–49) in the gardens at the east end and the wrought-iron railings surrounding it (c. 1745).

College of Art

Half way along the Brühlsche Terrasse is the College of Art (Hochschule für Bildende Künste), originally built (1891–94) to house the Royal Saxon Academy of Art and the Saxon Society of Arts.

Moritz Monument

At the north-east corner of the terrace wall is the Moritz Monument (restored 1956), Dresden's oldest surviving monument, erected by Elector Augustus in memory of his brother Moritz, killed in the battle of Sievershausen in 1553.

Below the Brühlsche Terrasse, on the banks of the Elbe (Terrassenufer), is the main landing-stage for the boats of the White Fleet (Weisse Flotte) which ply on the river.

**Albertinum

The Albertinum, an art gallery with a collection of international standing, was built by Carl Adolf Canzler in 1884–87, incorporating part of the old Arsenal (Zeughaus) of 1559–63. It was named after the then king of Saxony, Albert.

**Gallery of
Modern Masters

On the upper floor of the Albertinum (entrance from Brühlsche Terrasse) is the Gallery of Modern Masters (Gemäldegalerie Neue Meister), which was separated from the Gallery of Old Masters in 1931. It has a rich collection of works of the Romantic, Biedermeier and Realist periods; French, Polish, Romanian, Hungarian and Belgian painting of the 19th century; and German Impressionists and Expressionists. Pictures by the Expressionists, Cubists and other modern schools were withdrawn from the gallery as "degenerate art" by the Nazis, many of them being sold abroad, and many other works of art were destroyed in February 1945. It has been possible to fill some of the gaps by new acquisitions.

Some 200 important works from the Gallery of Old Masters (see page 164) are at present displayed in this gallery.

On the intermediate floor of the Albertinum (entrance in Georg-Treu-Platz) are the treasures of the Grünes Gewölbe (Green Vault), so named after the original home of the collection founded by Augustus the Strong in the Grünes Gewölbe of the Electoral palace. The collection includes gold, silver, jewellery and ivories of the 14th–18th centuries from the Electoral Treasury.

**Grünes Gewölbe

The sculpture collection, on the lower floor of the Albertinum (entrance in Georg-Treu-Platz), includes examples from Egypt and western Asia as well as Greek, Roman and Etruscan work. During the 20th century much contemporary sculpture has also been acquired.

Sculpture

Also in the Albertinum (entrance in Georg-Treu-Platz) is the Coin Cabinet (Münzkabinett), with over 200,000 coins (only a small proportion of which can be displayed), medals, dies, seals and seal impressions, including all the coins and medals minted in Saxony.

Coin Cabinet

In front of the main entrance to the Albertinum is the old Hofgärtnerei (Court Gardener's Office), a plain Baroque building (c. 1750) part of which is now occupied by the Protestant church.

Hofgärtnerei

The Print Cabinet (Kupferstichkabinett) of Dresden's State Art Collections, at Güntzstrasse 34 (east of the Albertinum), contains some 180,000 sheets and series of graphic art and 25,000 drawings (including watercolours and pastels) by European artists from the 15th century onwards.

*Print Cabinet

Ernst-Thälmann-Strasse and Altmarkt

From the busy Pirnaischer Platz Ernst-Thälmann-Strasse (1954–57), Dresden's main east–west artery, runs west to Postplatz. This is the beginning of the new city centre developed since the Second World War.

Pirnaischer Platz

On the right-hand side of Ernst-Thälmann-Strasse is the old Landhaus (by F. A. Krubsacius; restored), a building in early neo-classical style with a double Rococo staircase. It is now occupied by the Museum on the History of Dresden (Museum für Geschichte der Stadt Dresden).

*Landhaus
(Museum)

On the left of Ernst-Thälmann-Strasse lies the Altmarkt, the city's central square since the 13th century (destroyed in 1945). It owes its present handsome and imposing aspect to the use of typical Dresden Baroque architectural forms in the rebuilding which began in 1953.

Altmarkt

Another historic building is the Kreuzkirche (Church of the Holy Cross; early 13th c.), the oldest church within the town walls. It was completely destroyed in 1760 during the Seven Years' War, after which it was rebuilt in its present Baroque form (by Schmidt and Exner, 1764–92). The famous Kreuzchor (choir) dates from the original church.

*Kreuzkirche

The new district north of the Town Hall has preserved something of the atmosphere of old Dresden with its little lanes, passages and courtyards. In this area is the restored Baroque and neo-classical Gewandhaus (Cloth Hall; by J. F. Knöbel, 1768–70), now a hotel. To the rear of the building can be found the Baroque Dinglingerbrunnen. In Weisse Gasse is the 19th century Gänsediebbrunnen (Goose-Stealer Fountain).

Gewandhaus

Friedrichstadt

To the west of the old town, in the district of Friedrichstadt, a planned development initiated by Augustus the Strong in 1730, stands the Baroque Palais Marcolini, which

Palais Marcolini

dates from around that time. Much altered in the 19th and 20th centuries, it is now the District Hospital (not open to the public), but preserves some of the original interior decoration. Napoleon and Metternich met and negotiated in the Chinese Room in 1809. The east wing was occupied by Richard Wagner in 1847–49.

St Matthew's
Church

Near the cemetery stands the Matthäuskirche (St Matthew's Church; 1728–30), with a burial vault containing the tomb of its architect, Matthäus Daniel Pöppelmann (1662–1736); there is a commemorative tablet on the church.

Eastern Districts

*Public Health
Museum

To the south-east of the old town is Lingnerplatz, in which (No. 2) is the monumental building (1928–30) occupied by the German Public Health Museum (Deutsches Hygiene-Museum), an institution established to promote health education and healthy living. Among the exhibits is the famous "Glass Woman", first displayed in 1930.

*Grosser Garten

From the front of the Museum the main avenue (Hauptallee) of the Grosser Garten (Great Garden) runs south-east. In these gardens, laid out in the French style from 1676 onwards, is the Palais (by J. G. Starcke, 1678–83), the earliest and one of the most imposing Baroque palaces in the Electorate of Saxony. Around it are a number of Kavaliershäuschen (lodgings for members of the court) and groups of Baroque sculpture.

*Church of Christ

In the Strehlen district, to the south of the Grosser Garten, can be seen the twin-towered Christuskirche (Church of Christ; 1903–05), the purest example of Art Nouveau architecture in Dresden.

Museum of
Technology

In the Blasewitz district, some distance away from the Grosser Garten near the bridge over the Elbe (the "Blaues Wunder": see below), at Renhold-Becker-Strasse 5, is the Museum of Technology (Technisches Museum). Its most important collections are in the fields of electronics and micro-electronics, computer technology and electronic data-processing, precision engineering and photography. Other interesting exhibits include musical boxes, gramophones and the early forms of "peep-show", ancestors of the cinema.

University of Technology

To the south of the old town is the University of Technology (Technische Universität), originally an Institute of Technical Education established in 1828 which from 1900 onwards expanded to occupy a whole district of the town.

*Russian Orthodox
Church

In Juri-Gagarin-Strasse is the Russian Orthodox Church (Russische Kirche; 1872–74), with onion-domed towers. It contains Russian icons over 200 years old.

Neustadt (New Town)

The "new town" on the right bank of the Elbe also suffered heavy damage in 1945.

*"Golden
Horseman"

In the Neustädter Markt can be seen the statue of Augustus the Strong (1736) known as the Golden Horseman (Goldener Reiter). He is depicted in the pose of a Caesar, wearing Roman scale armour and seated on a curvetting horse.

Neustädter Wache

To the left is the Blockhaus (by Z. Longuelune; rebuilt), originally the Neustädter Wache (Guard-House; 1755).

Museum of
Folk Art

To the right, now half concealed by recent buildings is the Jägerhof (1568–1613), a Renaissance building which now houses the Folk Museum (Staatliches Museum für Volkskunst). Most of the material comes from Lusatia, the Erzgebirge and Vogtland.

Japanisches Palais

In Karl-Marx-Platz can be found the Japanisches Palais (Japanese Palace; enlarged in Baroque and neo-classical style in 1727–37 under the direction of M. D. Pöppelmann), richly decked with chinoiserie. Originally built to house Augustus the Strong's collection of porcelain, it now contains the study collections of the Provincial Museum of Prehistory and the Museum of Ethnography.

Strasse der Befreiung

The Strasse der Befreiung (Liberation Street) runs north from the Neustädter Markt.

At No. 13, once the home of the 19th century painter Wilhelm von Kügelgen, is the Museum of the Early Romantic Period (Museum der Frühromantik).

Museum of Early Romantic Period

Farther north stands the Dreikönigskirche (Church of the Three Kings; by Pöppelmann and Bähr, 1732–39), completely destroyed in 1945 and now in course of rebuilding. The only surviving quarter of Baroque burghers' houses in Dresden is to be found in this area, particularly in Rähnitzgasse.

Dreikönigskirche

At Dr-Kurt-Fischer-Platz 3 is the Museum of Military History (Militärhistorisches Museum; German military history to 1945 and the military history of the German Democratic Republic; collection of tin soldiers).

Museum of Military History

The Provincial Museum (Landesmuseum), at Marienallee 12, has some 2 million volumes. Attached to the Library is a Museum of the Book, which displays fine examples of printing since the 16th century and illustrates the development of printing down to the present day. Among its treasures is one of the only three surviving Maya manuscripts.

Provincial Library

Loschwitz and Weisser Hirsch

Between the outer districts of Blasewitz and Loschwitz the Elbe is spanned by the Loschwitzer Brücke, popularly known as the "Blaues Wunder" ("Blue Wonder"). This is a steel suspension bridge with a span of 141.50m/464ft which at the time of its construction (1891–93) caused some sensation.

*Loschwitzer Brücke ("Blaues Wunder")

From Körnerplatz a cableway (1895: one of the oldest in Europe) runs up to the residential district of Weisser Hirsch. At the upper station is the Luisenhof restaurant (fine views).

Cableway (at present out of action)

Dresden has three Schlösser on the Elbe: Albrechtsberg (late neo-classical), the Ligner-Schloss (after 1850; late neo-classical) and Schloss Eckberg (1859–61; neo-Gothic).

Schlösser

At Schillerstrasse 19 can be found the Schillerhaus, which belonged to the Körner family (commemorative tablet on Körnerweg 6). Schiller lived here in 1785–87 while writing his play "Don Carlos".

Schillerhaus

Wachwitz

Farther upstream, in Wachwitz, rises the 252m/827ft high Television Tower (Fernsehturm; café and viewing platform), from which there are far-ranging views of Meissen, the Elbe Sandstone Hills, the Eastern Erzgebirge and the Lusatian Uplands.

Television Tower *View

Hosterwitz

In Hosterwitz are the fishermen's church of Maria am Wasser (St Mary by the Water; originally Late Romanesque, remodelled in Baroque style in 1774) and the Carl Maria von Weber Memorial Museum (Dresdner Strasse 44), in a little house once occupied by the composer.

Fishermen's Church Maria am Wasser

*Pillnitz

The palaces and palace park of Pillnitz (which can be reached by boat: Weisse Flotte, departing from the Terrassenufer) are one of the finest palace complexes created during

Palaces

the reign of Augustus the Strong. On the banks of the Elbe stands the Wasserpalais (Water Palace), and on the opposite side of the pleasure garden (Lustgarten) is its exact counterpart, the Bergpalais (Hill Palace; by M. D. Pöppelmann and Z. Longuelune, 1722–24). Both palaces are in the clearly articulated style of Late Baroque, with a profusion of chinoiserie. The side wings (by C. T. Weinlig and Exner, 1788–91) and the New Palace (Neues Palais; by C. F. Schuricht, 1818–26) are still in Baroque style; in the Fliederhof and the Schlosswache (Guard-House) the neo-classical style takes over.

Craft Museum

In the Bergpalais is the Craft Museum (Museum für Kunsthandwerk), which is a section of Dresden's State Art Collections. Its collections include fine furniture, musical instruments, glass, pewter, Dutch and French faience and stoneware and textiles. Also of interest are the Weinling Room (c. 1800) and an exhibition on "Industrial Design in the 19th and 20th Centuries".

Schlosspark

To north and west of the palaces extends the Schlosspark, laid out in English style. Within the park are an Orangery (c. 1730), an English Pavilion (1789), a Chinese Pavilion (1804) and a famous Japanese camellia over 200 years old (in the camellia house).

Weinbergkirche

North-east of the park is the Weinbergkirche (by M. D. Pöppelmann, 1723–27). It has a relief of the Last Supper by J. G. Kretzschmar (1648), originally in the chapel (now demolished) of the Schloss in Dresden.

Dresdner Heide

The Dresdner Heide (Dresden Heath) is a popular recreation area to the north-east of the city, an expanse of wooded country traversed by small streams, 50 sq.km/19 sq. miles in extent. In the centre of the heath is the Saugarten (footpaths).

Gross-sedlitz

*Baroque garden

On a hill above the Elbe at Gross-sedlitz (16km/10 miles south-east) lies one of the most perfect Baroque gardens in Saxony. It was laid out in the French style between 1719 and

Schloss Moritzburg

1726 for Count Wackerbarth as a pleasure garden attached to one of his palaces. After the estate was acquired by Augustus the Strong in 1723 it was given its present Baroque form by the best Dresden architects of the day (M. D. Pöppelmann, Z. Longuelune and J. C. Knöffel).

Of particular beauty is the Baroque staircase with curving balustrades and groups of putti known as the "Stille Musik" ("Quiet Music"). It is now established that this was designed by Pöppelmann.

Stille Musik

During the summer months there are frequent festivals and dance displays in this beautiful natural setting.

*Schloss Moritzburg

14km/9 miles north-west of Dresden, in a landscape reserve, is Schloss Moritzburg, an Electoral hunting lodge and pleasure palace in the ochre and white of Saxon Baroque. Here, on a low granite hill in a marshy depression in the Friedewald, Duke (later Elector) Moritz built in 1542–44 a modest hunting-box which developed into a large hunting lodge. Then, during the reign of Augustus the Strong, in 1723–36) Z. Longueline, M. D. Pöppelmann and J. C. Knöffel built the palace as we see it today. The old hunting lodge and its chapel (1661–71) were incorporated in the new structure. Celebrated sculptors including Balthasar Permoser, J. C. Kirchner and Benjamin Thomae carved the gay Baroque statues on the balustrades of the carriage ramp and the terrace. The decoration and furnishing of the interior (wallpaper, furniture, painting, etc.), still preserved almost complete and unaltered, were the work of the court painter Louis de Silvestre, the interior decorator Raymond Leplat and the wallpaper designer Pierre Mercier. Outstanding among the pictures are works by Lucas Cranach the Younger and A. Thiele and the "Man of Sorrows" by Permoser in the chapel (at present in course of restoration).

The Baroque Museum in the Schloss has a select collection of applied and decorative art of the 16th–18th centuries – sedan chairs, coaches, porcelain, furniture, wallpaper, etc. There is also a large collection of hunting trophies.

*Baroque Museum

In the lower rooms of the Schloss is a memorial museum in honour of the painter and sculptress Käthe Kollwitz, who died in Dresden in 1945, with a small collection of her works. In Käthe-Kollwitz-Platz is a memorial stone.

Käthe Kollwitz Memorial Museum

On the east side of the Schlosspark stands the Fasanenschlösschen ("Pheasants' Palace"), an elegant little Rococo palace (chinoiserie) built and decorated by J. D. Schade and J. G. Hauptmann between 1769 and 1782 for Frederick Augustus III, who used it occasionally as a summer residence. The Dresden Zoological Museum now uses the rooms of the palace, with stucco ceilings and Rococo wallpaper, to display a collection of native birds.

Fasanen-schlösschen

The game park, with an area of 40 hectares/100 acres, also dates from the time of Augustus the Strong. Here in large open enclosures live moufflon, red deer, fallow deer and wild pigs. There are smaller enclosures for martens, foxes, pheasants and falcons.

Game park

A stud farm was established in Moritzburg in 1828 with the object of breeding crossbreeds and heavy (draught) horses. The stud now breeds mainly crossbreeds for riding. The parades of stallions attract up to 50,000 visitors annually.

Stud farm

Radebeul

The main feature of interest in Radebeul, lying just north-west of Dresden in a beautiful setting (Lössnitz landscape reserve, with vineyards on the slopes of the hills), is the Karl May Museum at Karl-May-Strasse 5, which has an exhibition commemorating the popular 19th century writer of adventure stories and Europe's largest collection of material on the life and culture of the North American Indians.

Karl May Museum

The Hoflössnitz Heimatmuseum (Lössnitzgrundstrasse 16) is housed in a Renaissance building of 1650.

Tharandter Wald

Situation
The Tharandter Wald (area 6000 hectares/15,000 acres), now a landscape reserve, lies south-west of Dresden on the northern edge of the Eastern Erzgebirge, between the Wilde Weisseritz to the east and the Colmnitzbach to the south-west. It is the largest expanse of woodland within easy reach of Dresden after the Dresdner Heide, and is a very popular recreation area with the population of the city.

Duderstadt   F 5

Land: Lower Saxony
Altitude: 175m/575ft
Population: 23,000

Situation and
characteristics
The medieval town of Duderstadt, in the Eichsfeld to the south-west of the Harz, is huddled within the 3km/2 mile long circuit of its walls. It has something like 500 half-timbered houses.

*Townscape

Town Hall
The central feature of the town is the Obermarkt, with the Town Hall (Rathaus; 13th–16th c.). This is an imposing half-timbered building with three small towers and sandstone arcades on the ground and first floors (historical exhibition; carillon).

St Cyriakus
Heimatmuseum
A short way east of the Town Hall is the church of St Cyriakus or Oberkirche (14th–16th c.; R.C.). Beyond it, in a Baroque house of 1767, is the Eichsfeld Heimatmuseum.

Marktstrasse
St Servatius
In Marktstrasse, which runs west from the Town Hall, are a number of handsome half-timbered houses. In the Untermarkt is the Protestant parish church of St Servatius (or Unterkirche; 15th–16th c.), with an interior partly decorated in Art Nouveau style.

Westerturm
To the north of the Untermarkt stands the Westerturm (1424), with a twisted spire, the only surviving town gate.

Town walls
There is an attractive walk round the medieval walls (about 1 hour).

Duisburg   F 2

Land: North Rhine-Westphalia
Altitude: 33m/108ft
Population: 525,000

Situation and
characteristics
The industrial and commercial city of Duisburg (pronounced Düsburg), on the western edge of the Ruhr (see entry), at the confluence of the river Ruhr with the Lower Rhine, can claim two superlatives to its credit: it takes first place in Germany in the production of steel, and its harbour on the river Ruhr is the largest inland port in the world.

Central Area

Town Hall
In the Burgplatz stands the Town Hall (Rathaus; 1897–1902; Mercator Room). In the Salvatorkirche, to the north of the Town Hall, is the epitaph of the famous cartographer Gerhard Mercator (d. 1594).

Königstrasse
In Königstrasse (pedestrian zone), the main street in the city centre, is König-Heinrich-Platz, with the Municipal Theatre (Stadttheater) and the Mercator Hall (1962), a multi-purpose hall for concerts, congresses, sporting events, performances of various kinds and exhibitions.

Port installations, Duisburg-Ruhrort

In Düsseldorfer Strasse, which branches off the south side of Königstrasse, is the Wilhelm Lehmbruck Museum (entrance in Friedrich-Wilhelm-Strasse), with 20th century sculpture and painting. The collection includes numerous works by the sculptor Wilhelm Lehmbruck (1881–1919), who was born in Duisburg-Meiderich.

*Wilhelm Lehmbruck Museum

Farther east along Friedrich-Wilhelm-Strasse can be found the Museum of the Lower Rhineland (Niederrheinisches Museum; history of the town, cartographic collection).

Lower Rhineland Museum

On the Kaiserberg, to the east of the town, is the Zoo, with a spacious open enclosure, a large monkey house, an aquarium, a dolphinarium and a "whalarium".

*Zoo

Ruhrort

The Schwanentorbrücke, a bascule bridge north-west of the Town Hall, links the city centre with the northern district of Ruhrort, which has grown in size and importance through ironworking and the shipment of Ruhr coal. Its extensive port installations (area 918.6 hectares/2269 acres; 20 docks; freeport under construction), handle some 60 million tons annually.
At the "harbour mouth" is the Museum of Inland Shipping (Museum der Deutschen Binnenschiffahrt), with the museum ship "Oscar Huber".

Port installations

There are regular cruises (about 2 hours) round the port installations from March to October; departures from the Schifferbörse in Duisburg-Ruhrort and the Rheingarten in Duisburg-Homberg.

Harbour tours

Düsseldorf

F 2

Capital of the *Land* of North Rhine-Westphalia
Altitude: 38m/125ft
Population: 580,000

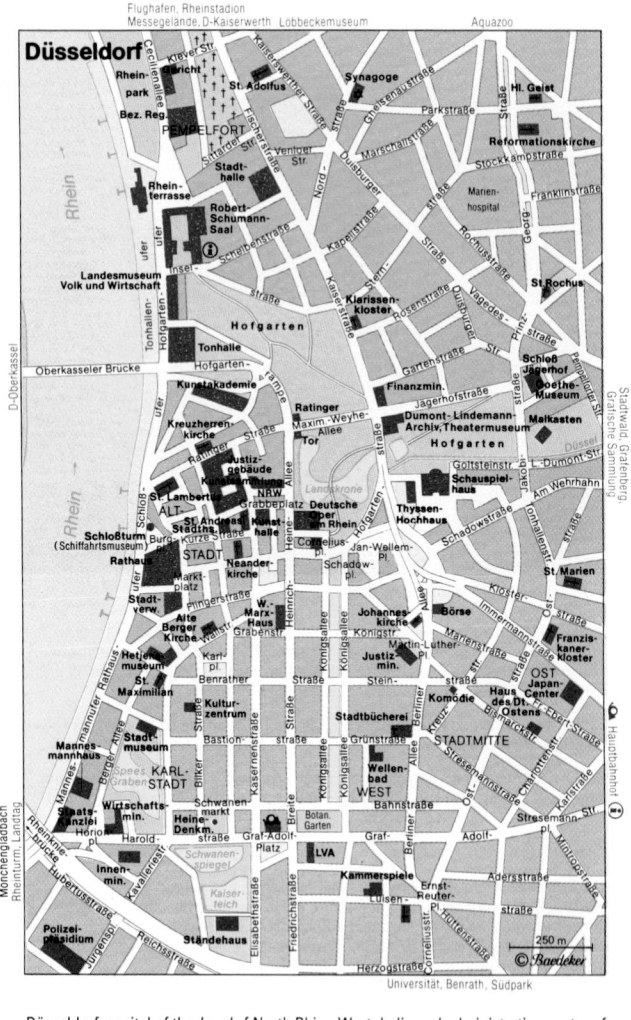

Flughafen, Rheinstadion
Messegelände, D-Kaiserwerth Löbbeckemuseum   Aquazoo

Düsseldorf

Oberkasseler Brücke

Universität, Benrath, Südpark

Situation and characteristics	Düsseldorf, capital of the *Land* of North Rhine-Westphalia and administrative centre of the industrial area of North Rhineland-Westphalia, lies on the Lower Rhine, here some 310m/340yds wide. It is a university town, a centre of art and fashion, a city of congresses and trade fairs. This old Electoral capital is a town of wide streets crowded with traffic and lined by elegant shops, with a ring of parks and gardens encircling the city centre.

*Königsallee

Düsseldorf's elegant shopping street and promenade is the Königsallee (familiarly known as the "Kö"), lined by exclusive shops, galleries, restaurants and cafés. It extends

Triton Fountain, Königsallee

Landtag and Rheinturm

on both sides of the old town moat from Graf-Adolf-Platz in the south to the Hofgarten in the north. There are two new shopping arcades, the Kö-Galerie and the Kö-Karree, opened in 1985. At the north end of the Kö is the Triton Fountain.

*Art Collection

In Grabbeplatz, on the left of the Heinrich-Heine-Allee, which runs parallel to the Kö, can be found a new building (1986) with a façade of polished dark-coloured stone which houses the North Rhine-Westphalia Art Collection (Kunstsammlung Nordrhein-West-falen), with a notable collection of works by Paul Klee, numerous works of modern art and the Julius Bissier Collection. Opposite it, on the south side of the street, is the Kunsthalle (periodic exhibitions), with a piece of sculpture by Max Ernst, "Habakkuk".

St Andrew's Church

Adjoining the Kunsthalle is the Baroque Andreaskirche (St Andrew's Church), with the mausoleum of the princely house of Pfalz-Neuburg.

Old Town (Altstadt)

Town Hall

The old town lies to the west of the Heinrich-Heine-Allee and south of the Andreaskirche. In the Marktplatz stands the imposing Town Hall (Rathaus), with a large equestrian statue of Elector John William II (by Gabriel Grupello, 1711) in front of it.

Schlossturm

In Burgplatz, north of the Town Hall, stands the Schlossturm (Castle Tower), all that remains of the old Schloss. It now houses the Shipping Museum (Schiffahrt-Museum; ship models).

Hetjens Museum
Municipal Museum

To the south of the Marktplatz, in the Palais Nesselrode, is the Hetjens Museum (ceramics of eight millennia). The Municipal Museum (Stadtmuseum) is housed in the Spee'sches Palais, situated on the edge of a park.

Mannesmann
Building

South-west of the Municipal Museum, on the edge of the old town, are the high-rise Mannesmann Building (1956–58) and the old Mannesmann offices (1911–12). In front of the Mannesmann Building are a fountain and a piece of sculpture, both in high-grade stainless steel.

Rheinpark Bilk

*Rheinturm
*Landtag

On the banks of the Rhine lies the recently laid out Rheinpark Bilk. In the park are the 234m/768ft high Rheinturm, with a restaurant (views), and the new Landtag (the Parliament of North Rhine-Westphalia), on a ground-plan of intersecting circles. Here too the Rhine is spanned by the Rheinkniebrücke, opened to traffic in 1969.

*Hofgarten

The city centre is bounded on the north by the large Hofgarten, a park originally laid out about 1770. On its south side are the Academy of Art (Kunstakademie), the Opera Haus (Deutsche Oper am Rhein), the Theatre (Schauspielhaus; 1968–70) and the high-rise Thyssen Building (Thyssen-Hochhaus).

Dumont-Lindemann
Archives
Goethe Museum

A litle way north, on Jägerhofstrasse, are the Dumont-Lindemann Archives (Municipal Museum of the Theatre). At the east end of Jägerhofstrasse is the Baroque Schloss Jägerhof, with the Goethe Museum (Kippenberg Foundation) and a collection of porcelain.

*Ehrenhof

Tonhalle

On the north-west side of the Hofgarten is the Ehrenhof (1925–26), a group of buildings designed to house exhibitions, museums, concerts and other events. The first of these is the domed rotunda of the Tonhalle, a concert hall, which also contains in the Grünes Gewölbe (Green Vault) the Museum of Art's collection of glass.

Adjoining is the Landesmuseum Volk und Wirtschaft ("People and the Economy"), with a variety of displays, dioramas, working models, etc. In the basement can be seen a reproduction of a coal-mine.

The most northerly museum in the complex is the Museum of Art (Kunstmuseum): European art from the Middle Ages to the present day, with special emphasis on German art of the 19th and 20th centuries; drawings and graphic art; fine collection of glass.

*Nordpark

The Nordpark was laid out for an exhibition in 1937. At the north entrance (with two figures of Horse-Tamers) is the Löbbecke Museum of Natural History, with an Aqua-Zoo.

At the west end of the Nordpark is the Japanese Garden, presented to Düsseldorf by the city's Japanese community. Within a relatively small area it presents an astonishing variety of landscapes.

City Centre

In Immermannstrasse is the Japanese Centre (Japan-Center), built in 1977–79, with a massive entrance front of polished stone (Japanese shops, restaurants, hotel, offices).

The Railway Station (Hauptbahnhof) was reopened in 1985 after complete rebuilding at a cost of some 600 million DM. It is a junction for the Federal Railways, the S-Bahn and the U-Bahn. There is a broad shopping mall.
South-east of the station is Bertha-Süttner-Platz (new layout), with steel sculpture by Horst Antes and a pool. The buildings facing the square are examples of Post-Modern architecture.

Southern Districts

The Südpark was considerably enlarged for the Federal Garden Show of 1987, and is now the largest continuous open space within the city.

A bridge links the Südpark with the campus of Düsseldorf University (founded 1965). The University Botanic Garden (open to the public) has a domed hothouse and an Alpine garden.

Surroundings of Düsseldorf

10km/6 miles south-east, in the district of Benrath (incorporated in the city in 1929), is Schloss Benrath, a Rococo palace built by Nicolas de Pigage in 1756 (sumptuous interior; park; museum of local natural history).

Kaiserswerth was also incorporated in Düsseldorf in 1929. In the 13th century church of St Suitbertus can be seen the beautiful reliquary of the saint (13th–14th c.). Nearby are the ruins of an imperial stronghold (Kaiserpfalz) of the Emperor Frederick I (Barbarossa).

10km/6 miles east of Düsseldorf is the Neander valley, in which the skull of Neanderthal Man was discovered. In the valley are a prehistoric museum and a game park.

At the Breitscheid motorway junction, 16km/10 miles north-east of Düsseldorf, is Minidomm, a miniature city with models of both historic and modern buildings.

See entry

Eberswalde-Finow   D 9

Land: Brandenburg
Altitude: 30m/100ft
Population: 55,000

Eberswalde-Finow

Situation and characteristics | The town of Eberswalde-Finow lies 30km/20 miles north-east of Berlin in the Eberswalde *urstromtal* (ice-margin trench).

Sights

Parish church St Maria Magdalena
The parish church of St Maria Magdalena, a brick-built Early Gothic church (beginning of 14th c.) with fine groined vaulting (rebuilt 1874–76), has three doorways with figural decoration, a bronze font (13th c.) and a polyptych of 1606 on the altar.

The Little Concert Hall (originally the chapel of the hospice of St George, a 13th century brick building which was restored in 1973) is used for concerts and recitals.

At Kirchstrasse 8 is the Heimatmuseum (exhibitions on the history of the town and on metalworking).

The Adler-Apotheke (Eagle Pharmacy) at Steinstrasse 3 occupies the old Ritterhaus (Knights' House), a medieval half-timbered building.

In Goethestrasse, just inside the town walls, can be seen the Barbaraglocke, a bell cast in 1518 by H. van Kampen which cracked in 1888 and again in 1909.

The Arboretum (Forstbotanischer Garten) in Schwappachweg, laid out more than 100 years ago, contains within its 27 hectares/67 acres over 1000 species of trees both native and foreign and a number of specialised botanic gardens.

*Zoo
Near here, fitting beautifully into the landscape, is the Zoo (Tierpark), founded in 1958.

**Chorin Monastery

Location: 9km/6miles N
The little town of Chorin (B 2) with its ruined monastery lies in the Chorin landscape reserve (terminal moraines). In 1258 Cistercian monks established the monastery of Mariensee on a little island in the Parsteiner See, and then in 1273 moved to Chorin. The monastery was dissolved in 1542, and thereafter the building was occupied by the Electoral authorities. During the Thirty Years' War it was several times plundered and set on fire, and later in the 17th century it was used as a quarry of building stone. In the early 19th century K. F. Schinkel took the first steps towards conserving the monastery, and in the 20th century it was extensively restored from 1954 onwards. Since then the building has been used for various cultural events; particularly popular are the symphony concerts during Chorin's "Musical Summer". Even in a state of partial ruin, the monastery is still the finest example of North German brick-built Gothic in Brandenburg.

Bad Freienwalde

Location: 17km/11miles E
On the slopes falling down from the Barnim plateau to the Oderbruch, on B 167, is the spa of Bad Freienwalde. Its mineral springs have been used for treatment since 1684, its mud baths since 1840, and Freienwalde (officially recognised as a spa in 1924) is now widely reputed as a health resort for the treatment of rheumatism. The old spa buildings and guesthouses were designed by such well-known Berlin architects as Schlüter, Langhans and Schinkel.

*Oderland Museum
At Uchtenhagenstrasse 2, in a house of 1560 with a Baroque façade, is the interesting Oderland Museum.

The Schloss is a neo-classical building (1798–99) by David Gilly, altered in 1837 and 1909. In the landscaped park (laid out by Lenné, 1820) is a little tea-house (Langhans, 1795). The parish church of St Nicholas, an Early Gothic building in granite, rebuilt in brick in 1453, has a Late Gothic font, a fine altarpiece and a pulpit of 1623. The half-timbered Baroque church of St George (17th c.; restored 1973) has a notable altar of 1698, a work of the Schlüter school.

*Niederfinow Ship-Lift

Location: 11km/7miles E
At Niederfinow, on B 167, is a famous ship-lift. Efforts were made at an early stage to overcome the difference in level between the rivers Havel and Oder by the construction

Chorin Monastery, Eberswalde-Finow ▶

Ship-Lift, Niederfinow

of locks. The Finow Canal (1746) had a chain of seventeen locks, while the Oder-Havel Canal (1906–14) had a series of four "steps", each of 9m/30ft. The present ship-lift was built alongside this canal between 1927 and 1934, overcoming the 36m/120ft difference in level in a single step. Because of the poor subsoil the lift could not be built directly on the slope, but is connected with the Oder-Havel Canal by a 157m/172yd long bridge.

Eckartsberga

See Naumburg, Surroundings

Eichstätt   K 6

Land: Bavaria
Altitude: 388m/1273ft
Population: 13,000

Situation and characteristics

The picturesque old town of Eichstätt at the foot of the Franconian Alb in the Altmühltal nature park, with the massive Willibaldsburg looming over it, has the stamp of an ecclesiastical city; it is the see of a bishop and the seat of a Catholic University. It is a town of fine Baroque buildings, often with something of an Italian air. It is still surrounded by remains of its medieval walls.

Old Town

Cathedral

In the Domplatz stands the Romanesque/Gothic Cathedral (Dom; 11th–14th c.), with a Baroque west front. In the west choir are the canopied altar, which contains the remains of St Willibald (first bishop of Eichstätt, d. 787), and a seated figure of the saint, the finest

work of the local sculptor Loy Hering (1484–c. 1554). In the north transept is the stone
Pappenheim Altar (by Veit Wirsberger, c. 1495).
On the south-east side of the Cathedral is a two-storey cloister (1420–30), with the fine
two-aisled hall of the Mortuarium (15th c.; "Beautiful Column", 1489).

To the south of the Cathedral, in the Baroque Residenzplatz, can be found the former   *Residenzplatz
Electoral Palace (17th–18th c.; by Angelini and Gabrieli), lodgings for members of the
court, a 19m/62ft high Mariensäule (column in honour of the Virgin) of 1777 and the
Diocesan Museum (Treasury).

South-east of the Cathedral, in Leonrodplatz, are the Schutzengelkirche (Church of the   Leonrodplatz
Guardian Angel; 17th c.), with a very fine Baroque interior, the Bishop's Palace (c. 1730)
and the Dompropstei (Deanery; 1672).
From here Ostenstrasse leads to the summer palace of the Prince-Bishops (by Gabrieli,
1735), beyond which is the Hofgarten.

In the nearby Kapuzinerkirche (Capuchin Church; 17th c.) is a copy (1189) of the Holy   Capuchin Church
Sepulchre in Jerusalem.

North of Domplatz lies the Marktplatz, with the Town Hall (Rathaus; 15th and 19th c.), the   Marktplatz
Stadtpropstei (18th c.) and the Willibald Fountain (1695).
North-west of the Marktplatz, reached by way of Westenstrasse, is the Baroque abbey
church of St Walburga (17th c.), with the burial chapel of the saint (d. 779).

The Bergér Museum, to the west of the town in the outlying district of Blumenberg, has   Bergér Museum
fine examples of fossils from the local limestone, minerals and shells. Fossils can be
collected in the nearby quarry.

Willibaldsburg

Above the town (750m/850yd drive) stands the Willibaldsburg (by Elias Holl, 1609–19),
which was the residence of the Prince-Bishops until 1725.

In the castle are the Jurassic Museum (Juramuseum), with fossils from the Jurassic   *Jurassic Museum
limestones of the surrounding area (including the skeleton of an archaeopteryx), and the
Museum of Prehistory and the Early Historical Period (Ur- und Frühgeschichtliches
Museum).

At the foot of the hill, beyond the Altmühl, is Rebdorf Monastery, a house of Augustinian   Rebdorf
canons dating from the 12th century.

From Eichstätt through the Altmühl Valley to Weissenburg

The road ascends the winding valley of the Altmühl, past Rebdorf. After passing through
Dollnstein (beautiful parish church; town walls) it comes to Solnhofen.

The beautiful little town of Solnhofen is noted for its quarries of Jurassic limestone, in   Solnhofen
which numerous fossils have been found. In the Town Hall is the Bürgermeister Müller
Museum (fossils, lithography). There are remains of the Sola basilica (seven building
phases from the 6th century onwards).

In a bend on the river lies the old-world little town of Pappenheim, with the 15th century   Pappenheim
Stadtkirche (Gothic), the Galluskirche, which dates from Carolingian times and two
Schlösser of 1608 and 1822. On the hill above the town stands the ancestral castle of the
Counts Pappenheim.
Shortly before Treuchtlingen the road leaves the Altmühl valley and turns north towards
Weissenburg.

Weissenburg (pop. 17,000), on the western slopes of the Franconian Alb, still preserves a   Weissenburg
number of buildings dating from the time when it was a free imperial city (1360–1802),

including the Late Gothic Town Hall (1476), the Carmelite church (15th c.; now a cultural centre), with an interesting image of the saint known in Germany as St Kümmernis (St Uncumber; a bearded woman on a cross), the Late Gothic Andreaskirche (St Andrew's Church; 14th–15th c.) and the imposing Ellinger Tor, a town gate of 1469–1510. There are remains of Roman baths, discovered here in 1977; the Roman Museum (Römermuseum) contains other ancient finds.

Eifel   H 2

Land: Rhineland-Palatinate

Situation and characteristics

The Eifel, an upland region some 70km/45 miles long and 30km/20 miles wide between the Rhine, the Mosel and the Rur, is a residual range of hills averaging 600m/2000ft in height and reaching its highest point in the Hohe Acht (746m/2448ft) which was disrupted by more than 200 volcanoes. The lava flows from these extinct volcanoes can still be clearly distinguished in the present landscape pattern, particularly around the Laacher See, the Nürburgring and the towns of Daun and Manderscheid.

*Landscape

Maare

Also of volcanic origin are the romantically beautiful *maare* so characteristic of the Eifel – old volcanic craters, mostly now filled by small lakes. A particularly fine example of a *maar* is the 52m/170ft deep Laacher See, surrounded by more than forty lava vents. Equally beautiful are the *maare* around Daun, particularly the Gemündener Maar and the melancholy Totenmaar.

Dams

In recent years a number of large dams have been constructed in the north-western Eifel, forming artificial lakes and producing attractive new landscape patterns, such as the dam in the Urft valley and the Schwammenauel reservoir in the river Rur. The rivers, the *maare* and the lakes have great attractions for anglers and water sports enthusiasts, and the abundant snow of the Hocheifel and Schnee-Eifel offers excellent skiing.

Through the Northern Eifel

The starting-point of this round trip is Andernach, in the Rhine valley (see entry).

* Maria Laach

The road runs west from Andernach via Nickenich to the famous abbey of Maria Laach, one of the great beauties of the Middle Rhine. The abbey, founded in 1093, has been occupied since 1892 by Benedictine monks from Beuron. The six-towered Romanesque church, consecrated in 1156, contains the Early Gothic tomb of its founder, Count Palatine Henry II.

The beautiful Laacher See, ringed by forest-covered hills, is the largest of the *maare* in the Eifel. To the north is the Veitskopf (427m/1401ft), to the west the Laacher Kopf (445m/1460ft), to the south Thelenberg (400m/1312ft, to the east the Krufter Ofen (463m/1519ft) – all extinct volcanoes.

The road now continues south via Mendig.

Mayen

At the mouth of the Nette valley we come to Mayen (pop. 20,000), in Roman times a staging-point on the military road from Trier to the Middle Rhine. In the vicinity of the town there are basalt and slate quarries. Above the old town with its gates, towers and remains of walls (13th–15th c.) looms the picturesque Genovevaburg (13th c., with later renovation and rebuilding); in the east wing is the Eifel Museum (Eifeler Landschaftsmuseum).

* Nürburgring

From Mayen the road runs west to the Nürburgring (constructed 1925–27), which ranks as the finest and most demanding car racing circuit in the world. The classic northern loop (20.8km/13 miles) encircles the Nürburg over the hills and valleys of the Eifel. It is a tremendous challenge to both cars and drivers – among them such famous names as

Rudolf Caracciola, Hans Stuck, Alberto Ascari, Juan Manuel Fangio, Stirling Moss and Count Berghe von Trips. In recent years, however, the original track has been found to be inadequate for modern racing cars, and a completely new Grand Prix course was opened in 1984. This 4.542km/2.8 mile long circuit is one of the most modern and safest in the world; it can be combined with the northern loop. On certain days visitors can drive their own cars on the Nürburgring (charge). Car-Racing Museum.

Near the northern loop is the little town of Adenau (pop. 3000). Attractive half-timbered houses in Markt; 11th century parish church; Eifel Farmhouse Museum in Kirchplatz.

Adenau

North-west of Adenau lies Blankenhein, in the German-Belgian Nature Park. Above the town is the 12th century castle of the Counts of Manderscheid-Blankenstein, now a youth hostel. Near the parish church, enclosed by a wall, is the source of the river Ahr.

Blankenheim

Schleiden has two old churches and a castle which was once the seat of the Counts of Schleiden.

Schleiden

The little town of Monschau lies in the narrow Rur valley, close to the Belgian frontier. Above the town are an old watch-tower and a ruined castle.

Monschau

North of Schleiden and north-east of Monschau is the Schwammenauel artificial lake, a reservoir with a capacity of 205 million cu.m/45 billion gallons formed by a dam on the Rur (1934–38); it is now a popular recreation area. To the south of this, in a closed military area, is the Urftstausee, formed by a dam on the river Urft.

Artificial lakes

From here B 266 leads east by way of Gemünd to Kommern (in the commune of Mechernich), with the Rhineland Open-Air Museum (Rheinisches Freilichtmuseum; farmhouses, domestic equipment).

Kommern

From Mechernich the route continues to Münstereifel (a spa offering the Kneipp cure), surrounded by old walls and towers. Beautiful parish church (11th c.); Town Hall (14th and 16th c.); ruined castle.

Bad Münstereifel

Altenahr, in the middle Ahr valley, has a Romanesque parish church (Gothic choir) and the extensive ruins of Burg Are (magnificent view of Ahr valley).

Altenahr

In the lower Ahr valley, the largest red wine area in Germany, is Bad Neuenahr-Ahrweiler, with medieval walls and gate towers. St Lawrence's Church (13th and 14th c.). Wine Museum in the Altes Backhaus (Old Bakehouse).

Bad Neuenahr-Ahrweiler

The road reaches the Rhine valley at Sinzig, from which it is a short distance south to Andernach.

Through the Southern Eifel

The starting-point of this trip is Trier, in the Mosel valley (see entries).

From Trier the road runs north to Bitburg (pop. 12,000). In Bedaplatz is the Haus Beda cultural centre, with the Eifel-Ardennes Museum (pictures, fossils, Roman mosaics). In the eastern part of the centre, on Denkmalstrasse, is the local Heimatmuseum (domestic interiors, folk traditions). Bitburg is famed for its brewery (open to visitors).
At Otrang, 6km/4 miles north, are the remains of a Roman villa (1st century A.D.).

Bitburg

In Gondorf, 10km/6 miles east, is a leisure park, the Eifelpark.

Eifelpark

North-east of Bitburg lies the picturesque little town of Kyllburg. On the Stiftsberg stands an old 13th century keep (views). The Stiftskirche has beautiful stained glass (16th c.).

Kyllburg

North of Bitburg (either direct on B 51 or via Kyllburg) is Prüm, with a former Benedictine abbey (partly by Balthasar Neumann). The most notable features of the church are the beautiful high altar and the tomb of Emperor Lothair I (d. 855).

Prüm

Gerolstein	Farther east lies Gerolstein, in the volcanic Eifel (mineral springs). In a 16th century building is the local Heimatmuseum (art, domestic interiors, iron-casting). On the Schlossberg can be seen the ruins of the 13th century Löwenburg (destroyed in 1691). Around the little town are steep dolomitic crags.
Daun	In the centre of the volcanic Eifel is Daun (mineral springs). South-east of the town is the Gemündener Maar (bathing lido, boat hire), at the foot of the Mäuseberg (561m/1841ft). Nearby is the Totenmaar.
Ulmen	From Daun an interesting detour can be made to Ulmen (15km/9 miles east), with the Bergkirche, a ruined castle and the Ulmener Maar. From Daun the route turns south.
Manderscheid	Manderscheid is charmingly situated 90m/300ft above the valley of the Lieser, with two castles once held by the Counts of Manderscheid (whose line died out in 1780). To the west is the Meerfelder Maar. The road continues south to Wittlich and returns to the Mosel valley, which is followed back to Trier.

Eisenach   G 5

Land: Thuringia
Altitude: 215m/705ft
Population: 50,000

Situation and characteristics	Eisenach, the old capital of the Landgraves of Thuringia, lies on the north-western edge of the Thuringian Forest (see entry), at the foot of the Wartberg with its legendary stronghold of the same name. Many great names are associated with the town and the castle, including the medieval poets Walther von der Vogelweide and Wolfram von Eschenbach, Martin Luther, Johann Sebastian Bach, Richard Wagner, Franz Liszt and the 19th century Low German writer Fritz Reuter. At the Eisenach Congress of 1869 August Bebel and Wilhelm Liebknecht founded the German Social Democratic Workers' Party.

Old Town

Markt	In the centre of the old town is the Markt (known in the Middle Ages as the Mittwoch-markt, the Wednesday Market), surrounded by handsome old buildings.
Schloss Thuringian Museum	At the north end of the Markt stands the Schloss (1742–51), in relatively plain Baroque style. In the left-hand wing is the Thuringian Museum, with Thuringian faience and porcelain of the 18th and 19th centuries, Thuringian glass of several centuries and a picture gallery (mainly old German masters). There are tablets commemorating Goethe's friend Charlotte von Stein and Luise von Göchhausen (who copied the original version of Goethe's "Faust" and thus preserved it for posterity), both of whom were born in Eisenach.
Town Hall	The Town Hall (Rathaus), carefully restored after the Second World War, is basically a Late Gothic building with Renaissance features and a leaning tower. On the lower floor can be seen reliefs and ornament by the Renaissance sculptor H. Leonhardt.
Parish church	Also in the Markt is the parish church of St George, a hall-church with a richly furnished interior (tombs of Landgraves of Thuringia). Luther preached in this church on May 2nd 1521, in spite of the fact that he had been outlawed by the imperial authorities. Johann Sebastian Bach was baptised here on March 23rd 1685; there are frequent performances of his works in the church.
Fountain	Outside the west door of the church can be found an old market fountain with a figure of St George, the town's patron saint (by H. Leonhardt, 1549).
* Luther House	At Lutherplatz 8 is the Luther House (formerly belonging to the Cotta family), restored after suffering bomb damage in 1944. The house is now a memorial museum, with the historic Luther Room and rare Bibles and religious works of Luther's time.

In Predigerplatz is the Predigerkirche (Preachers' Church; Dominican), with a collection of religious sculpture (works of the Thuringian school of woodcarvers, 12th–16th c.).

Predigerkirche

In Georgenstrasse stands the Hospital Church of St Anne, with an inscription recording its foundation by St Elizabeth of Hungary in 1226.

At the corner of Georgenstrasse and Schiffsplatz is the Hellgrevenhof, thought to be the oldest building in the town. According to legend the sorcerer Klingsor and Heinrich von Ofterdingen lodged here after flying from Hungary to Eisenach on Klingsor's cloak.

Hellgrevenhof

At Frauenplan 21 is the modest Bach House, with an interesting collection of material on the life and work of the Bach family, particularly Johann Sebastian, and a collection of historic musical instruments.
In the square can be seen a statue of Bach (by Donndorf).

*Bach House

North-east of the Town Hall stands the Nikolaikirche (St Nicholas's Church), a fine example of Romanesque architecture (basilican type, with a flat roof; 12th c., extensively restored 1867–69).

St Nicholas's Church

On the south side of the church is a stretch of the old town walls, with the Nikolaitor (St Nicholas's Gate; c. 1200), the oldest surviving town gate in Germany.

Nikolaitor

Southern Districts

At Reuterweg 2, outside the old town, is the Fritz Reuter and Richard Wagner Museum, in which the Low German writer Fritz Reuter (1810–74) lived and died. In addition to memorial and exhibition rooms there is a Wagner Library, the largest and finest after the one in Bayreuth (see entry).

Fritz Reuter and Richard Wagner Museum

In Wartburgallee is the exhibition room of the Wartburg car manufacturing firm, with a collection of veteran and vintage cars.

*Wartburg Car Exhibition

Bach House, garden front

187

Eisenach

Burschenschaft
Monument

On the Göpelskuppe can be seen the Burschenschaft Monument (Burschenschaftsdenkmal; by W. Kreis), erected in 1902 to commemorate the Wartburgfest of 1817, a meeting of some 500 representatives of student fraternities (*burschenschaften*) in German universities to protest against the restoration of the old regime and the fragmentation of Germany into petty princely states.

** Wartburg

Legend and
history

One of the most historically interesting castles in Germany crowns the Wartberg above Eisenach. According to the legend the Wartburg was founded by Ludwig the Jumper in 1067. With the growing strength and importance of the Landgraves the military stronghold soon became also a centre of government and culture. This was the scene of the famous Sängerkrieg ("Singers' War"), a contest between the minnesingers of the High Middle Ages, including Wolfram von Eschenbach, Heinrich von Ofterdingen, Heinrich von Veldecke and Walther von der Vogelweide, which provided the theme of Wagner's "Tannhäuser".

In 1235 the Landgravine Elizabeth, a Hungarian princess who cared for the sick and the poor in the Wartburg, was canonised as St Elizabeth of Hungary. Martin Luther, under the name of "Junker Jörg", lived in the Wartburg in 1521–22 under the protection of the Elector. While staying here he translated the New Testament from the original Greek, making a major contribution to the development of modern German.

The castle

The only means of access to the Wartburg is by the drawbridge (Zugbrücke) and gatehouse (Torhaus) near the north end. After passing through several arched gateways (some of them with fragments of Romanesque and Gothic pillars), we come into the outer ward (Erster Burghof), with half-timbered buildings of the 15th and 16th centuries (restored) – wall-walks, the Ritterhaus (Knights' House), the Vogtei (Governor's Residence), with a fine oriel window. Between the outer and inner wards is an imposing complex, consisting of the Torhalle (gatehouse), the Dirnitz (winter residence), the Neue Kemenate (the Landgravine's quarters) and the Berchfrit (keep), all in neo-Romanesque and neo-Gothic style.

Wartburg

The inner ward (Zweiter Burghof), with the Gaden (Hall), the castle cistern (Zisterne), the south tower (Südturm; 13th c.) and the Late Romanesque Palace (Palas), is the oldest and finest part of the whole castle. Other buildings which formerly stood in this area have disappeared.

In the Palace are the Romanesque Knights' Hall (Rittersaal; groined vaulting), the southern Kemenate and the dining hall (columns with fine eagle capitals). In similar style is the Elisabeth-Kemenate (mosaics with scenes from the life of St Elizabeth, 1902–06). The simple chapel was built about 1320. On the first floor are the Elisabeth-Galerie (frescoes by Moritz von Schwindt), the Sängersaal (in which the contest between minnesingers is said to have taken place) and the Landgrave's Room. The whole of the third floor is occupied by the Festsaal, with rich 19th century decoration.

Palace

From the Romanesque part of the Palace we pass into the museum in the Neue Kemenate and the Dirnitz. Among the most notable items to be seen here are a number of fine works of art in the Wartburg collection – Late Gothic tapestries, paintings by Lucas Cranach the Elder, sculpture from the workshop of Tilman Riemenschneider and a carved press designed by Albrecht Dürer. There is also an exhibition on the history of the Wartburg. Also of interest are the 15th century Pirckheimerstübchen and the 17th century Schweizerzimmer.

Neue Kemenate
Dirnitz

The wall-walk on the west side of the castle leads past the Eseltreiberstübchen (Donkey-Driver's Room) to the Lutherstube (Luther's Room), almost unchanged since Luther's time, with pictures by Lucas Cranach the Elder.

Lutherstube

Surroundings of Eisenach

To the east of the town rise the white limestone crags of the Hörselberge (rare flora). The Grosser Hörselberg (484m/1588ft) was, according to legend, the home of Wotan, Tannhäuser and Frau Venus. From the Hörselberg plateau there are extensive views. Nearby are the Venus and Tannhäuser Cave and the Jesusbrünnlein (fountain).

Hörselberge

Below the Wartburg lies the 200m/220yd long Drachenschlucht (Dragon's Gorge), with bizarrely shaped rock walls up to 10m/33ft high. From the Hohe Sonne guest-house on the Rennsteig there is a good view of the Wartburg.

Drachenschlucht

To the south, in an attractive setting of woodland and meadows, stands Schloss Wilhelmsthal (1712–19; altered by G. H. Krohne in 1741). The gardens, originally laid out in Baroque style, were converted into a landscaped park around 1800.

Wilhelmsthal

15km/9 miles south-west on B 84 is Marksuhl, which has a Renaissance Schloss with a richly decorated gateway. The parish church is an aisleless Baroque building.

Marksuhl

13km/8 miles north we reach Mihla. Its main features of interest are the Rotes Schloss (Red Castle; Renaissance), with a massive stone ground floor and two half-timbered upper floors, a richly decorated doorway, three oriels and a Knights' Hall (1631) with stucco decoration; the Graues Schloss (Grey Castle), a two-storey Renaissance building with three gables and a tower on each side; and the village church, an aisleless Baroque building of 1711, with an aumbry and a winged altar of the 15th century.

Mihla

Eisenberg

G 7

Land: Thuringia
Altitude: 292m/958ft
Population: 13,400

Eisenberg, chief town of a district, lies 20km/12½ miles north-west of Gera between the Saale and the Weisse Elster. It is an industrial town (manufacture of pianos) and also an attractive holiday resort on the northern edge of a tract of wooded country; the Mühltal in particular attracts many visitors.

Situation and
characteristics

Sights

Town Hall

In the charming old town centre stands the Town Hall (Rathaus; 1579, enlarged 1593), a three-storey Renaissance building with two towers and two richly decorated round-arched doorways.

St Peter's Church

Also in the rectangular Marktplatz are the aisleless Late Gothic church of St Peter (1494; altered 1880; extensively restored 1990), the Superintendentur (1580), a three-storey Renaissance building, the Mohrenbrunnen (Moor Fountain; 1727) and burghers' houses of the 16th–18th centuries.

Schloss
Christianenburg

Schloss Christianenburg (now occupied by local government offices) is a three-storey Baroque building (1678–92) with an imposing doorway in the main block. The Schloss-kirche (1680–92) has galleries round three sides, rich stucco decoration and wall and ceiling paintings by Italian artists; it is now used as a concert hall. The beautiful Schloss-garten was laid out in 1683 (rose-garden).

Surroundings of Eisenberg

Bürgel

12km/7½ miles south-west on B 7 lies Bürgel. At Töpfergasse 14 is the Ceramic Museum, which illustrates the development of this potters' town with a tradition going back more than 300 years; old potter's kiln.

Thalbürgel

Thalbürgel has a Benedictine church, a Romanesque basilica founded in 1133. After the dissolution of the monastery in 1526 the buildings fell into a state of dilapidation; they were restored in "historicising" style between 1863 and 1890.

*Teufelstal

The Teufelstal (Devil's Valley) lies near the Hermsdorf motorway junction (Hermsdorfer Kreuz), in an area which preserves some stands of old beeches. The Eisenach-Dresden motorway is carried over the valley on Europe's largest single-span prestressed concrete bridge (1936; 138m/453ft wide, 253m/276yds long, 61m/200ft high).

Eisenhüttenstadt   E 9

Land: Brandenburg
Altitude: 40m/130ft
Population: 48,000

Situation and
characteristics

Eisenhüttenstadt lies 20km/12½ miles south of Frankfurt an der Oder, at the junction of the Oder-Spree Canal with the Oder. It takes its name from an ironworks (*eisenhütte*) established here in 1951.

Old Town

Church

In the Fürstenberg district, on the high west bank of the Oder, stands a Gothic hall-church (c. 1400), the exterior of which has been restored after suffering war damage.

Municipal Museum

Near the church, at Löwenstrasse 4, is the Municipal Museum (Stadtmuseum; history of the town, crafts, development of ironworking, contemporary art).

Fire Service
Museum

In Fellertstrasse is the Fire Service Museum (Feuerwehrmuseum), with over 500 exhibits.

Surroundings of Eisenhüttenstadt

Neuzelle
*Baroque church

In Neuzelle, 9km/6 miles south on B 112, can be found the Baroque church (richly furnished interior) belonging to a former Cistercian monastery, with extensive conventual buildings.

The main features of interest in Beeskow (30km/20 miles west) are the old town, with its walls and Dicker Turm ("Fat Tower"), and the Biological Heimatmuseum in the Burg.

Beeskow

Eisleben

F 7

Land: Saxony-Anhalt
Altitude: 128m/420ft
Population: 27,100

Eisleben, lying some 35km/22 miles west of Halle in the south of the eastern Harz foreland, is an old-established copper-mining town best known as the place where Martin Luther (1483–1546) was born and died.

Situation and characteristics

Sights

On the west side of the Markt, which is notable for the uniformity of its architecture, stands the Late Gothic Town Hall (Rathaus; 1509–30), on the north side of which is a double external staircase. In front of the Town Hall can be seen a Luther Monument (by R. Siemering, 1882).

Town Hall

The Marktkirche (Market Church; dedicated to St Andrew) is a 15th century hall-church with a richly furnished interior (sarcophagi of Counts of Mansfeld, Luther's pulpit). The tower, built on to the church, houses the fine church library (manuscripts and printed editions of Luther's Bible; Eike von Repgow's "Sachsenspiegel", etc.).

*Marktkirche

The old town houses of the Counts of Mansfeld (15th–17th c.), in the Markt are now partly occupied by local government offices.

Stadtschlösser

A few paces from the Markt, at Andreaskirchplatz 7, is the house in which Luther died, now a memorial museum.

Sterbehaus Luthers

Luther's birthplace . . .

. . . and the room in which he died

Museums	In Vikariatsgasse is the Heimatmuseum (history of the town and of mining) and adjoining the Natural History Museum (Naturkundemuseum; geology, economy, flora and fauna of the Eisleben area).
*Luther's birthplace	Luther's birthplace (Lutherstrasse 16) has a display of documents illustrating his life and work.
Churches	Other interesting churches in Eisleben are the Nikolaikirche (St Nicholas's; 15th c.), the Annenkirche (St Anne's; 16th–17th c.) and the parish church of SS. Peter and Paul (15th–16th c.), in which Luther was baptised, with the Late Gothic St Anne's Altar (c. 1500).

Surroundings of Eisleben

Wiederstedt	In Oberwiederstedt (15km/9 miles north) can be seen the house in which the poet and novelist Novalis (Friedrich von Hardenberg, 1772–1801) was born. This Renaissance Schloss with a staircase tower (c. 1551) has recently been restored and is now a cultural centre, with a Novalis Museum.
Mansfeld	The Schloss in Mansfeld (15km/9 miles north-west), the ancestral seat of the Counts of Mansfeld, is now a church home. The complex includes two Renaissance mansions, a 15th century church with a winged altarpiece from the Cranach workshop (1520) and extensive fortifications.

Elbe Valley G 10 – B 4

Länder: Saxony, Saxony-Anhalt, Brandenburg, Mecklenburg-West Pomerania, Lower Saxony, Hamburg, Schleswig-Holstein

The Elbe, with a total length of 1165km/724 miles, is a major waterway of great importance both for national and international shipping.

Weisse Flotte	The ships of the Weisse Flotte ("White Fleet") offer visitors attractive opportunities of seeing the scenic beauties of the Elbe valley from the river itself.
Ecology	As a result of the numerous industrial plants on both banks of the Elbe harmful substances of all kinds – salts, heavy metals, hydrocarbons – find their way into the river, endangering its biological system. This applies particularly to the upper part of the valley, around Pirna, Dresden and Riesa. Measures to reduce this pollution (e.g. extension of existing sewage and purification plants, improvement of purification installations within factories) are in preparation.
The Elbe within Czechoslovakia	The Elbe rises at an altitude of 1400m/4600ft in the Riesengebirge, flows in a wide arc through the Bohemian Basin (where it is known as the Labe), makes its way through the Bohemian Hills and enters German territory in the Elbsandsteingebirge (Elbe Sandstone Hills). In its course through Germany its most important tributaries are the Schwarze Elster, the Mulde, the Saale, the Havel and the Elde. Downstream from Hamburg it forms a funnel-shaped estuary and finally reaches the North Sea at Cuxhaven.
Tourist centres	The towns in the Elbe valley which are of most interest to visitors include Pirna, Dresden, Meissen, Torgau, Wittenberg, Dessau, Magdeburg, Tangermünde, Lauenburg, Hamburg and Cuxhaven (see entries).

*Landscape

The Elbe traverses a variety of landscapes in its passage through Germany – a canyonlike valley in the Elbsandsteingebirge (see Saxon Switzerland), an open valley round Dresden, the depression between Riesa, Schnackenburg and Boizenburg and finally the Vierlande, the Marschlande (fenlands) and the Altes Land near Hamburg.

The open stretch of valley on the upper Elbe, 40km/25 miles long and 4–7km/2½–4½ miles wide, extends northward from Pirna by way of the dense industrial concentration around Dresden to beyond Meissen. In the north it is sharply bounded by the Lusatian granite plateau, and in the south rises gently into the Erzgebirge (see entry). The favoured climate of this area permits intensive market gardening, fruit- and vine-growing.

Upper Elbe

The Elbe depression downstream from Riesa consists mostly of level meadowland of alluvial soil which is used for grazing livestock, with some areas of sandy soil and dunes. The low-lying land is protected from river spates by dykes, to the rear of which there are frequently dead channels or oxbow lakes. Along the edges of the depression there are expanses of dunes covered with pines and occasionally mixed forest.
A masterpiece of European landscape gardening is the Wörlitz Park (see Wörlitz), on the left bank of the Elbe above Dessau (see entry).

Elbe depression

Below Wittenberge extend the Elbe fenlands, which lie partly below sea level and are in danger of flooding when the river is full. From here down to Lauenburg extends the Elbufer-Drawehn Nature Park. At Cuxhaven the river cuts between the two Wattenmeer National Parks, one in Schleswig-Holstein and the other in Lower Saxony (see North Sea).

Fenlands

Elster Valley

G 7 – F 7

Länder: Saxony-Anhalt, Saxony, Thuringia

The 247km/153 mile long Weisse (White) Elster, a right-bank tributary of the Saale, rises on the western edge of the Elstergebirge, in the frontier area between Germany and Czechoslovakia. In its upper course, at heights above 450m/1475ft, it receives numerous tributaries from the upper Vogtland. At Wünschendorf, the "gateway of the Vogtland", the river emerges from the hills at a height of 200m/650ft. It then flows through the foreland area between Gera and Zeitz and continues through the Leipzig lowlands to join the Saale above Halle. Around Leipzig open-cast lignite mining has made some diversions of the river necessary.

On the upper Elster, depending on geological conditions, narrow stretches of valley alternate with wider ones. Between Bad Elster and Oelsnitz, centre of the Vogtland carpet-making industry, there is room for the road and the railway to run together down the valley, but below the Pirk Dam, at the bend in the river near Weischlitz, the valley narrows sharply. Here the river is flanked on both sides by sheer walls of diabase rock.

Pirk Dam

The best known and most beautiful gorge in the Elster valley is the Steinicht landscape reserve between Plauen and Elsterberg, where the diabase crags on either side of the river rise to heights of 60–70m/200–230ft.

Steinicht landscape reserve

Below the junction of the Trieb, which here opens out into a large lake (4.5 sq.km/1¾ sq. miles) formed by the Pöhl Dam, with the Weisse Elster the two-level Elstertal Bridge (1846–51; 283m/309yds long, 69m/226ft high) carries the Dresden-Plauen railway line over the Elster valley.

Elstertal Bridge

The dimensions of the Elstertal Bridge, however, are far exceeded by those of the famous Göltzschtal Bridge (1846–51), which spans the Göltzsch at Netzschkau (5km/3 miles before its junction with the Weisse Elster above Greiz). The Göltzschtal Bridge is one of the largest brick-built arched bridges in the world, 574m/628yds long and 78m/256ft high, with 81 arches on four levels.

** Göltzschtal Bridge
(Pic. pages 194/5)*

Emden

C 3

Land: Lower Saxony
Altitude: 4m/13ft
Population: 51,000

Göltzschtal Bridge

Situation and characteristics

The old Frisian town of Emden, situated near the point where the river Ems flows into the Dollert inlet, is the most westerly German port on the North Sea and the largest after Hamburg and Bremen. Lying at the end of the Dortmund-Ems Canal, the port mainly serves the Ruhr (coal, ore and grain; oil terminal). The Ems-Jade Canal also provides a link with Wilhelmshaven (see entry). Other important industries are shipbuilding, car manufacture and the handling of North Sea gas. From the outer harbour there is a ferry service to the island of Borkum (see North Sea Coast, East Frisian Islands).
The layout of the town is characterised by its numerous canals (*delfte*).

The Town

Town Hall

In the centre of the town, on the Ratsdelft (boat moorings), stands the New Town Hall (Rathaus), built in 1959–62 on the foundations of the old Renaissance Town Hall which was destroyed in 1944 (fine view of the town from the tower). In addition to municipal offices the Town Hall also houses the East Frisian Museum and the Municipal Armoury (Rüstkammer; equipment of the old town militia, 16th–18th c.).

Ratsdelft
Otto-Huus

On the Ratsdelft can be seen the historic lightship "Deutsche Bucht" (1917). Here too is the Hafentor (Harbour Gate; 1635). Nearby, at Grosse Strasse 1, is the Otto-Huus, with a collection of curios assembled by the Emden-born comedian Otto Waalkes.
South-west of the Town Hall are the ruins of the Late Gothic Grosse Kirche (Great Church); the tower was restored in 1965–66.
In the east of the old town is the Neue Kirche (New Church; 1643–48; restored).

*Kunsthalle

The Kunsthalle, in the north-west of the old town at Hinter dem Rahmen 13, was presented to the town by Henri Nannen (contemporary art; special exhibitions).

Port

3km/2 miles south-west of the old town lies the port (motor launch services from the Ratsdelft; harbour cruises), at the end of the Dortmund-Ems and Ems-Jade Canals.

Emsland   D 2–3

Land: Lower Saxony

The Emsland, an expanse of flat country with tracts of moorland, lies on both sides of the middle Ems, which here flows broadly parallel to the Dutch frontier. The river rises in the Senne Heath, is joined at Meppen by the Dortmund-Ems Canal and flows into the Dollart near Leer.

With its poor moorland and heath soil and its marginal situation, the Emsland was for centuries one of the least developed areas in Germany. Unsuccessful attempts at cultivating the land were made during the 18th and 19th centuries, but it was only after the First World War that the population began to increase. Under the Nazis inmates from concentration camps in the area were used as forced labour for work on the land.

Situation and characteristics

Erfurt   G 6

Capital of the *Land* of Thuringia
Altitude: 243m/797ft
Population: 216,000

Erfurt, formerly a powerful trading and university town with a history going back 1200 years, lies in a wide stretch of the Gera valley, in the south of the fertile Thuringian Basin. It belonged to the Electorate of Mainz until 1802, when it passed to Prussia. Erfurt was the meeting-place of church Synods and Imperial Diets and the scene of the Congress of Erfurt (Napoleon's meeting with the Tsar of Russia and the German princes) in 1808. The first German Garden Show was held here in 1838.

Situation and characteristics

Domberg and Petersberg

In spite of some bomb damage during the Second World War Erfurt's charming old town centre has largely been preserved intact. Since the war much restoration of old buildings has been done. The dominant features of the town are its two medieval churches, the Cathedral and St Severus, on the Domberg (Cathedral Hill) in the heart of the city.

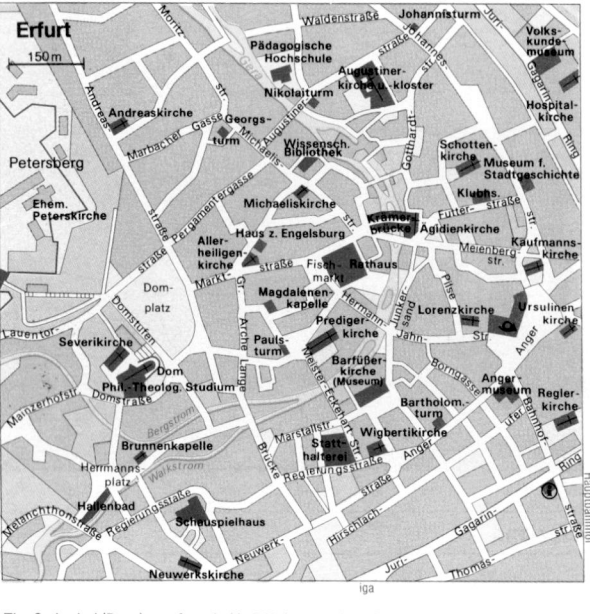

| *Cathedral | The Cathedral (Dom) was founded in 742. In 1154 the original church was replaced by a Romanesque basilica, to which the High Gothic choir was added in 1349–70. In 1455–65 it was rebuilt as a hall-church, with a huge hipped roof spanning the nave and aisles. The Cathedral has three towers, which in medieval times had tall steeples like those of St Severus (the present spires are 19th century). In the central tower is one of the largest bells in the world, the "Maria Gloriosa", which is famed for the beauty of its tone. The fifteen tall windows in the choir are masterpieces of medieval stained glass, unique in Germany in their size and unity of theme. Among the Cathedral's other treasures are the sumptuous Baroque high altar, the finely carved 14th century choir-stalls, the stucco figure of the Virgin and a figure of Wolfram (both *c.* 1160), and the tomb of Count von Gleichen and his two wives (mid 13th c.). |

* St Severus — The Severikirche (St Severus; first recorded in 1121) is an Early Gothic hall-church with double lateral aisles and a richly furnished interior (sarcophagus of St Severus and 15m/49ft high font, two masterpieces by local sculptors).

* Domplatz — In the Domplatz are two handsome old houses which survived the bombardment of the town by the French in 1813 – the 18th century Grüne Apotheke (Green Pharmacy) and the house "Zur Hohen Lilie", one of the finest Renaissance buildings in Erfurt (restored 1964–69).

St Peter's Church — Opposite the Domberg rises the Petersberg (St Peter's Hill), once crowned by St Peter's Monastery (founded 1060; rebuilt 1103–47; burned down during the French bombardment of the citadel in 1813). The Peterskirche (St Peter's Church), a Romanesque aisled basilica, is one of the earliest buildings of the Hirsau school in Thuringia. There are also extensive remains of the old citadel on the Petersberg (1664–1707). From the top of the hill there is a fine view of Erfurt.

Town Centre

Fischmarkt — Marktstrasse leads into the Fischmarkt, where the east–west and north–south trade routes intersected. In the centre of the square is a figure of Roland (1591), the symbol of

Erfurt: Kaufmannskirche, Cathedral and St Severus's Church

municipal authority. On the west side of the square is the house "Zum Roten Ochsen" (1562), on the north side the house "Zum Breiten Herd" – two richly decorated Renaissance buildings.

North-east of the Fischmarkt is the famous Krämerbrücke, on the old east–west trade route. First recorded in 1117, it spans the Gera at the old ford (now again visible). The bridge, with houses along both sides (originally there were 62), is one of the most interesting features of Erfurt (shops selling arts and crafts and antiques). *Krämerbrücke

On the near side of the Krämerbrücke is the Michaelisstrasse, lined with old burghers' houses. No. 39 was the old Erfurt University (1392–1816). The building is now occupied by the Wissenschaftliche Bibliothek (Library), with the world-famous Amploniana Collection (535 volumes containing 4000 works in 15th century and earlier manuscripts). Michaelisstrasse

In Allerheiligenstrasse is the Engelsburg, which around 1511 was the meeting-place of a group of humanists led by Crotus Rubeanus and Ulrich von Hutten. Engelsburg

Farther along Michaelisstrasse is Augustinerstrasse, with a well-known Augustinian monastery (founded 1277) and Augustinian church (1290–1350). The young Martin Luther became a monk here in 1505; his cell is shown to visitors. Among the surviving conventual buildings is the beautiful Comthureihof (1570–93). Augustinian Monastery

Augustinerstrasse leads into Johannesstrasse, in the eastern part of which are numerous handsome old houses, including the richly decorated house "Zum Stockfisch" (Late Renaissance, 1607), now occupied by the Museum of Municipal History; the house "Zum Mohrenkopf" (1607), with fine half-timbering; the house "Zur Mühlhaue", with traces of Gothic work; and the high-gabled house "Zum Grünen Sittich und Gekrönten Hecht" (before 1600), also with fine half-timbering. Museum of Municipal History

Farther south along Johannesstrasse is the Kaufmannskirche (Merchants' Church), with a richly decorated interior by local Renaissance masters. The parents of Johann Sebastian Bach were married in this church. Kaufmannskirche

* Anger

Johannesstrasse joins the Anger ("Meadow"), one of the town's oldest streets, now completely restored and lined with shops and restaurants. At the corner of the Anger and Trommsdorfstrasse is the Ursuline Convent, with a richly furnished interior (not open to the public).

Packhof
(Anger Museum)

At the corner of the Anger and Bahnhofstrasse can be found the old Packhof (formerly a custom-house of the Electorate of Mainz), a richly decorated Baroque building which is now occupied by the Anger Museum (fine art collection).

Bartholomäusturm

Farther along the Anger is the Bartholomäusturm (St Bartholomew's Tower), the stump of a tower (12th c.) belonging to the family chapel of the influential Counts von Gleichen, whose town house was here. The tower has a carillon (1979) of 60 bells cast in the Apolda bell foundry (see entry).

On the opposite side of the street (Nos. 28–29) can be seen the house called "Zum Grossen Schwantreiber und Paradies". Farther along the street is the Dacherödensches Haus (Nos. 37–38), with the finest Renaissance doorway in the town (16th c.), which was frequented by some of the leading intellectual figures of the Goethe period, including Goethe himself, Schiller and Wilhelm von Humboldt, who became engaged to Carolina von Dacheröden.

Statthalterei

Farther along the street, past a monumental fountain of 1889–90 and the Wigbertikirche (1210), the court church of the Electoral governors of the town, is the Statthalterei, the old governor's residence, the town's most monumental secular building. Formed in 1711–20 from two older patrician houses, it has magnificent Renaissance decoration and a handsome Baroque façade. The Great Hall (area 200 sq.m/2150 sq.ft) was the scene of a memorable meeting between Napoleon and Goethe in 1808. Goethe frequently stayed in a nearby house belonging to the Dukes of Saxony-Weimar at Regierungsstrasse 72.

Churches

Erfurt once had some 36 parish churches and chapels and 15 religious houses, earning it the style of the "many-towered city".

Barfüsserkirche

The Barfüsserkirche (Church of the Discalced Friars) in Barfüsserstrasse has the oldest stained glass in Erfurt (13th c.) and some fine monuments. It is now occupied by the Museum of Medieval Art. Organ recitals are given in the choir.

Predigerkirche

The Predigerkirche (Preachers' Church; Dominican) in Predigerstrasse is second only to the Cathedral and the town's museums in its treasures of art.

Also in Predigerstrasse is the house "Zum Güldenen Heer" (No. 7), one of Erfurt's few Rococo buildings.

Brunnenkapelle

The Brunnenkapelle (Fountain Chapel) on Fischersand is now the seminary chapel and oratory of the Faculty of Theology and Philosophy.

Neuwerkskirche

The Neuwerkskirche in Neuwerkstrasse has an unusually rich Baroque interior, with the Neuwerk Madonna.

St Lawrence's Church

Near Hermann-Jahn-Strasse is the Lorenzkirche (St Lawrence's Church), with the earliest tombstones in Erfurt bearing inscriptions in German rather than Latin.

Reglerkirche

The Reglerkirche in Bahnhofstrasse has the largest carved altar in Erfurt (1450–60).

Schottenkirche

In Schottenstrasse stands the Schottenkirche (originally founded by Iro-Scottish monks), one of Erfurt's few surviving Romanesque buildings and perhaps its oldest church (before 1150).

Folk Museum

The Folk Museum (Museum für Volkskunde), housed in the Directors' House of the old Hospital, has an interesting collection of material on the history of the town.

*International Garden Show

Also worth seeing is the International Garden Show (Internationale Gartenbauausstellung), an area of 100 hectares/250 acres on the site of the Cyriaksburg, a medieval stronghold on the south side of Erfurt. There is a Gardening Museum, which also commemorates the first Garden Show in 1838.

Within the Garden Show grounds are an observatory (frequent special exhibitions) and an outlook tower, both housed in towers belonging to the old Cyriaksburg. Between the towers can be seen an old woad mill, a relic of the days when the production of dye from woad was an important element in the town's economy.

Zoo

To the north of Erfurt, on the Roter Berg, is the Thuringian Zoo (Thüringer Zoopark), with some 1100 animals, including rare species of monkeys (black-and-white colobuses, John's langurs, Entellus langurs, Douc langurs).

Surroundings of Erfurt

South-west of Erfurt stands Schloss Molsdorf, one of the finest Rococo buildings in Thuringia, built by Count von Gotter between 1736 and 1745. Thoroughly restored, it is now a museum. It is set in a beautiful park laid out in 1826.

*Schloss Molsdorf

Erlangen

I 6

Land: Bavaria
Altitude: 285m/935ft
Population: 100,000

Erlangen lies a few kilometres north of Nürnberg at the junction of the Schwabach with the Regnitz. Long famous as a university town, it has preserved its Baroque aspect.

Situation and characteristics

The Town

In the Marktplatz (Schlossplatz) are two handsome Baroque buildings: the Stutternheim Palace (1728–30), now housing the Municipal Museum and Art Gallery, and the Schloss, the old Margravial Palace.

Marktplatz
(Schlossplatz)

The Schloss (1700–04) has been occupied since 1825 by the Frederick Alexander University, which was originally founded in Bayreuth and was transferred to Erlangen in 1743. It was amalgamated in 1961 with the Nürnberg College of Economic and Social Sciences. To the rear of the building extends the Schlossgarten, partly in French and partly in English style, with the curious Huguenot Fountain and the beautiful Orangery (both 1706). On the north side of the gardens are the Botanic Garden and the Margravial Theatre (1715; restored 1959). On the north side is the University Library, which possesses valuable manuscripts and works of graphic art (including self-portraits of Dürer and Grünewald).

Schloss
University

In the old town are the three principal Protestant churches – the Hugenottenkirche (Huguenot Church; 1686–93), the Neustädterkirche (New Town Church; 1723–37) and the Dreifaltigkeitskirche or Altstädterkirche (Trinity Church, Old Town Church; 1709–21). The Old Town Hall (Altes Rathaus; 1731–36), adjoining Trinity Church, now houses the Municipal Museum (history of the town since the Middle Ages).

Old town

Surroundings of Erlangen

In the south-eastern district of Tennenlohe is the Forest Museum (Waldmuseum), opened in 1975 (forestry equipment; exhibitions on ecological themes). Attached to the museum is an exhibition area.

Forest Museum

Erzgebirge (Ore Mountains)   G 9 – H 8

Land: Saxony

Situation and topography	The Erzgebirge range lies on the German-Czech border, extending for some 130km/80 miles from south-west to north-east between the Elstergebirge and the Elbsandsteinge-birge (Elbe Sandstone Hills), with a breadth of 40km/25 miles. The hills, mainly built up from granites, gneisses, mica schists and porphyries, rise out of the Middle Saxon Uplands, gradually increasing in height towards the south-east from 350–450m/1150–1475ft to 800–900m/2600–2950ft and beyond the crest – which marks the frontier be-tween Germany and Czechoslovakia and the centuries-old boundary between Saxony and Bohemia – falling steeply down to the Ohre (Eger) rift valley.
*Fichtelberg *Auersberg	The highest peak in the Erzgebirge, Klínovec or Keilberg (1244m/4082ft) lies within Czechoslovakia; the highest peak on German territory is its neighbour, the Fichtelberg (1214m/3983ft). The second highest peak in the Saxon Erzgebirge is the Auersberg (1019m/3343ft), near Johanngeorgenstadt. Among other prominent peaks are a number of isolated table-like hills in the central Erzgebirge, like the Bärenstein (898m/2946ft), the Pöhlberg (832m/2730ft) and the Schei-benberg (805m/2641ft), in which the gneiss amd mica schist have been protected from erosion by covering layers of basalt.

Places of Interest in the Western Erzgebirge

The western Erzgebirge offers a wide range of features of interest, recreation areas and holiday centres. Among them are the Augustusburg, a 16th century hunting lodge of the Electors of Saxony situated on the edge of the Zschopau valley, within easy reach of Chemnitz; the Sachsenring motor-racing circuit (8.7km/5½ miles long) at Hohenstein-Ernstthal; Schneeberg (see entry); the outlook tower on the forest-covered Auersberg; the regularly planned little town of Annaberg (see Annaberg-Buchholz), with its monu-mental Late Gothic church of St Anne and the Frohnauer, an old ironworks; and the health resort of Seiffen (see entry), centre of the Saxon toy-making industry, with the Erzgebirge Toy Museum.

Artificial lakes	Among popular recreation areas, particularly in summer, are the numerous artificial lakes (reservoirs) formed by the building of dams (e.g. on the Flöhe, the Rauschenbach and the Sosa).

Places of Interest in the Eastern Erzgebirge

Like the western part of the range, the eastern Erzgebirge is a popular recreation area at all times of year. In the Gottleuba valley are Berggiesshübel (Kneipp cure), which has been operating as a spa since 1722 and Bad Gottleuba, a spa since 1861 (chalybeate springs; mud baths). At Frauenstein, on the edge of the Obere Freiberger Mulde land-scape reserve, can be seen the ruins of one of the largest castles in Saxony. There are other castles at Dohna, Weesenstein, Bärenstein and Lauenstein in the Müglitz valley.

The principal attractions at the higher levels in the eastern Erzgebirge are the hill towns of Altenberg (see entry) and Geising with their demonstration mines; the Geisingberg, a round-topped basalt hill (824m/2704ft) on which the mining of tin (still continuing) began around 1440; the scattered village of Zinnwald-Georgenfeld, on the crest ridge of the Erzgebirge; the Kahleberg (905m/2969ft), the highest peak in the eastern Erzgebirge, with the Blockmeer nature reserve; and the Georgenfeld moors, also a nature reserve.

Oberwiesenthal

Situation and characteristics	At the foot of the Fichtelberg (1214m/3983ft), the highest peak in the Saxon Erzgebirge, is Oberwiesenthal, once a little hill town and now a popular holiday resort and crossing-

point into Czechoslovakia. Its development as a resort began at the end of the 19th century, when visitors were attracted to the area for winter sports.

The ascent of the Fichtelberg (1214m/3983ft) is a rewarding experience. On the summit stands the Fichtelberghaus (rebuilt 1965–67), with a 42m/138ft high outlook tower, from which in clear weather there are magnificent views extending for up to 100km/60 miles. The easiest way to the summit is by the cableway (built 1924; 1175m/1285yds long, height difference 305m/1000ft; cabins for 45 persons).

Fichtelberghaus
**Views

In the town centre are numbers of attractive old houses, most of them built after the fire of 1863, with later alterations. In the Markt is a milestone of 1730 (originally used for measuring posting stages).

Markt

Below the Markt can be found the Martin Luther Church (consecrated 1866). In winter a large Weihnachtskrippe (Nativity scene) is set up in the church.

Martin Luther Church

In the Altes Forsthaus (Old Forester's House) at Karlsbader Strasse 3 is an interesting exhibition on the development of winter sports in the Fichtelberg area.

Altes Forsthaus

The Erzgebirgsbahn, a narrow-gauge railway with steam engines which runs to Cranzahl, 17.3km/10¾ miles away, is a great tourist attraction.

*Erzgebirgsbahn

Near the town are ski slopes in varying grades of difficulty, with chair-lifts and ski-tows, a large ski-jump (1972–74) and three smaller jumps (both winter and summer skiing). At Oberwiesenthal is a bob racing run (1100m/1200yds long, 18 bends, drop of 134m/440ft; starting-point on Fichtelberg plateau). There are also a biathlon course and langlauf trails. The Ski Stadium is on the road up the Fichtelberg.

*Sports facilities

Essen

F 2

Land: North Rhine-Westphalia
Altitude: 116m/381ft
Population: 620,000

Essen, lying between the rivers Emscher and Ruhr, is the largest city in the Ruhr. It owes its importance as the metropolis of the Ruhr and the headquarters of many large industrial organisations (including Ruhrkohle AG, the largest German mining company, and Rheinisch-Westfälische Elektrizitäts AG) to its situation in the middle of the Rhineland-Westphalia industrial area. In addition to its heavy industry (associated particularly with the name of Krupp) it has a variety of other industries (electrical engineering, chemicals, etc.).

Situation and characteristics

Many industrial plants in Essen can be visited on conducted tours. For details consult the local tourist information office (see Practical Information).

Factory tours

Central Area

In the Burgplatz stands the Minster (R.C.), one of Germany's oldest churches (9th–14th c.). The most notable features of the interior are a seven-branched bronze candelabrum (*c.* 1000) and the "Golden Madonna" (*c.* 1000; the oldest figure of the Virgin in the round in western Europe). The rich church treasury can be seen in the Bishop's Palace (1955–56).

*Minster

The city's principal shopping streets (pedestrian zone) are Kettwiger Strasse and Limbecker Strasse, which run north-west from the Markt. In the square is the little Marktkirche (Market Church; Protestant), which is thought to date from the 11th century (renovated 1952).

Pedestrian zone

To the east of the Markt lies the City-Center, a modern shopping complex, the new Town Hall (Rathaus; 106m/348ft high) and the Old Synagogue (Alte Synagoge; exhibition on Jewish resistance and persecution).

*Town Hall
Old Synagogue

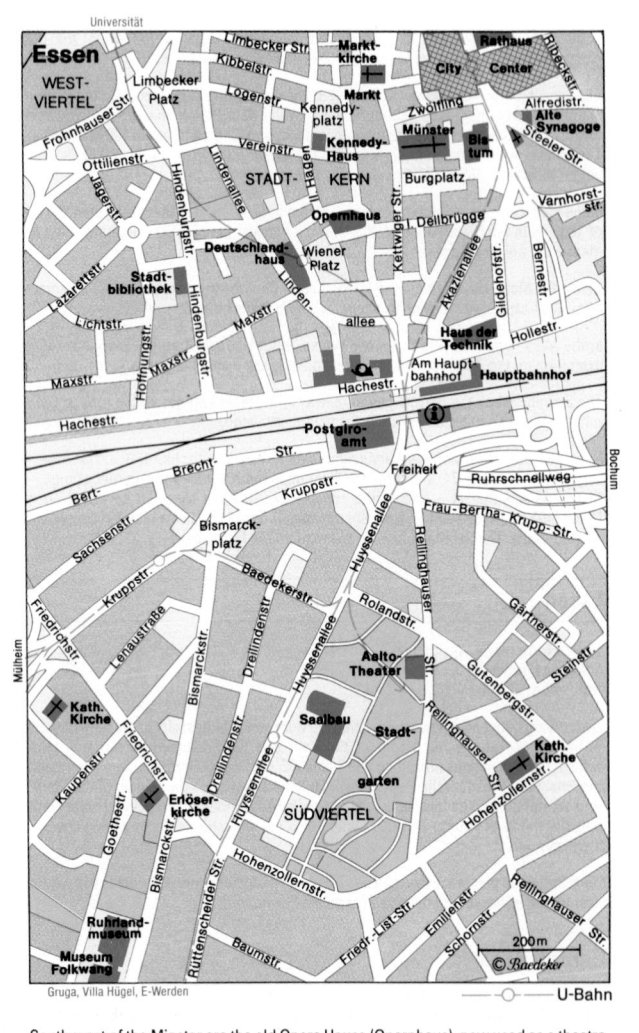

Gruga, Villa Hügel, E-Werden

——○—— U-Bahn

Opera House	South-west of the Minster are the old Opera House (Opernhaus), now used as a theatre, and the German Poster Museum (Plakatmuseum).

South of the City Centre (Südviertel)

Stadtgarten ** Aalto Theatre	To the south of the railway station (Hauptbahnhof) is the busy square known as the Freiheit, from which Huyssenallee leads south-west to the beautiful Stadtgarten (Municipal Park), with the Saalbau (1949–54) and the new Theatre (opened 1988) which was designed by the Finnish architect Alvar Aalto (1898–1976).
* Folkwang Museum	South-west of the Stadtgarten, in Bismarckstrasse, can be found the Museum Centre (1983), with the Folkwang Museum and the Ruhrlandmuseum.

Aalto Theatre

The Folkwang Museum, perhaps the most important art gallery in the Ruhr, mainly displays painting from around 1800, European sculpture since the 13th century and art and applied art from outside Europe.

The Ruhrland Museum has collections on the natural history, art and culture of the Ruhr, and is one of the most important museums in this field in North Rhine-Westphalia. Outstations of the museum are two 16th century ironworks, the Halbach-Hammer (see below) and the Deilbach-Hammer in the Kupferdreh district, and the Isenburg, a ruined castle of 1288.

Ruhrland Museum

Farther south-west lies the beautiful Grugapark (70 hectares/175 acres), laid out in 1929 for the *Great Ruhrland Garden* Show and enlarged in 1952 and 1965, with the Grugahalle (1958), an outlook tower, exhibition halls, a botanic garden, animal enclosures, an aquarium, an amusement park, fountains and several restaurants. A narrow-gauge railway, the Grugabahn (3.5km/2 miles), runs through the park.

*Grugapark

West of the park, in the Nachtigallental (Nightingale Valley), is the Halbach-Hammer, a 16th century ironworks.

Halbach-Hammer

South of Essen are the Stadtwald (Municipal Forest), with the Vogelpark (Bird Park; about 1000 birds), and the Heissiwald, with an animal enclosure.

Stadtwald

Baldeneysee

South of the Stadtwald lies the Baldeneysee, an artificial lake 8km/5 miles long formed by the construction of a dam in 1933. The open country around the lake is a popular recreation area. On its north side is the little Schloss Baldeney (13th, 17th and 19th c.).

Also on the north side of the lake, set in a large park, is the Villa Hügel, a grandiose mansion built by the Krupp family. There is a historical collection in the Kleines Haus, and periodic special exhibitions are held in the villa.

*Villa Hügel

Werden

°Abbey church

Werden abbey church (13th c.), to the south of the Baldeneysee, which belonged to a Benedictine abbey founded by St Ludger, is one of the finest Late Romanesque churches in the Rhineland (Late Baroque interior; treasury, with a bronze crucifix of 1060 and St Ludger's Chalice, c. 900).

Esslingen   K 4

Land: Baden-Württemberg
Altitude: 241m/791ft
Population: 88,000

Situation and characteristics

The industrial town of Esslingen lies in the middle Neckar valley (see entry) with its extensive vineyards, a short distance upstream from Stuttgart. It preserves a number of important historic buildings dating from the time when it was a free imperial city.

Town Centre

Stadtkirche

In the Marktplatz stands the twin-towered Stadtkirche (Town Church, dedicated to St Dionysius; Protestant), built on 8th century foundations in the transitional style of the 13th–14th centuries, with a High Gothic choir. It has a fine interior, excavations in which in 1960–63 brought to light remains of earlier churches, a crypt and a hut of the Urnfield culture of the 13th–11th centuries B.C.; the remains can be seen by visitors.
Opposite the choir of the church is the old Speyerer Pfleghof, a former hospice now occupied by the Sektkellerei Kessler, the oldest Sekt firm in Germany, founded in 1826.

St Paul's Minster

On the west side of the Marktplatz is the Early Gothic St Paul's Minster (built by Dominicans 1233–68; R.C.), one of the oldest surviving churches of a mendicant order in Germany.

°Frauenkirche

To the north of St Paul's, beyond the ring of streets marking the line of the old fortifications (footbridge), can be found the High Gothic Frauenkirche (Church of Our Lady; 1321–1516), with a magnificent tower designed by Ulrich von Ensingen, architect of Ulm Minster. The tower contains a museum (at present closed).

Neckarhalde

Behind the Frauenkirche is a footpath which leads through an old town gate into the vineyards on the Neckarhalde (the slopes of the Neckar valley).

New Town Hall °Old Town Hall

In Rathausplatz is the New Town Hall (Neues Rathaus), occupying the Palmsches Palais (1746). Opposite it is the Old Town Hall (Altes Rathaus), a half-timbered building of 1430 by H. Schickhart, rebuilt in 1586–89 with a Renaissance façade (clock with mechanical figures, carillon). The Municipal Museum at present housed here is being moved to the Gelbes Haus in the Hafenmarkt (see below).

Burg

To the north the Burgberg (Castle Hill) rises above the old town, with a covered flight of steps and the Burgsteige leading up to the top. The Burg dates from the time of the Hohenstaufens. From the Dicker Turm (Stout Tower; restaurant) and the remains of the old town walls (wall-walk) there are fine views.

Old Town

The old town (now mostly a pedestrian zone) lies to the south of the Marktplatz and Rathausplatz. The Innere Brücke (Inner Bridge), with a small chapel dedicated to St Nicholas, spans the two arms of the Neckar Canal, which are separated by the island known as the Maille (park).

Municipal Museum

In the Hafenmarkt is the Gelbes Haus (Yellow House), which consists of two Baroque houses and an old tower house. The Municipal Museum is now being installed here.

Esslingen: Marktplatz and Burg

On the south edge of the town centre, between the railway and the Neckar, stands the Villa Merkel, now occupied by the Municipal Art Gallery.

Villa Merkel

Ettal

M 6

Land: Bavaria
Altitude: 878m/2881ft
Population: 1000

The altitude and winter sports resort of Ettal, situated in a high valley in the Ammergebirge, at the foot of the Ettaler Mandl (1634m/5361ft), is famed for its Benedictine abbey. The monks produce a fragrant herb liqueur (Ettaler Klosterlikör), made according to an ancient recipe.

Situation and characteristics

* Ettal Abbey

The Benedictine abbey of Ettal was founded in 1330 by Emperor Ludwig the Bavarian. The church, originally a Gothic structure on a centralised plan, was converted into a domed Baroque church by Enrico Zuccali between 1710 and 1726 and restored after a fire by Josef Schmuzer in 1744–52.

Features of the sumptuous interior are the fine fresco in the dome (1752), the masterpiece of J. J. Zeiller of Reutte (Tirol); six beautiful side altars by J. B. Straub (1757–62); and a famous 14th century image of the Virgin by Pisano in the tabernacle on the high altar.

In front of the church are the abbey's boarding school (until 1744 the Knights' Academy) and a grammar school.

205

Ettal Abbey

Surroundings of Ettal

Ettaler Mandl — 3km/2 miles north rises the Ettaler Mandl (1634m/5361ft; 2½–3 hours' climb from Ettal, or by cableway from Oberammergau to the Laberjoch, then 15 minutes on foot).

*Linderhof — 11km/7 miles west of Ettal in magnificent mountain scenery, is Schloss Linderhof, built by G. Dollmann for King Ludwig II of Bavaria, following Rococo models (1874–78; conducted tours of interior). Park, with fountains.

Fichtelgebirge   H 7

Land: Bavaria

Situation and characteristics — This range of hills, mostly covered with fir forests, lies in the north-eastern corner of Bavaria, forming a link between the Erzgebirge and the Franconian Forest (see entries) and between the Upper Palatinate Forest and Bohemian Forest. The main elements in the economy of the area are agriculture, woodworking, textiles and ceramics; there is a considerable porcelain industry in and around Selb.

Landscape

In this upland region of granites and slates are the sources of the Main, the Saale, the Eger and the Naab, whose courses take them to all points of the compass. It consists of three ranges of hills surrounding the Wunsiedel basin in horseshoe formation: the Waldsteingebirge (878m/2881ft) to the north-west, the highest peaks (Ochsenkopf, 1024m/3360ft; Schneeberg, 1053m/3455ft) to the south-west and the ridge formed by Kösseine (940m/3084ft) and the Steinwald (966m/3169ft) to the south-east.

The charm of the Fichtelgebirge lies in the magnificent expanses of forest and the extraordinary rock formations and tumbles of rock produced by weathering, the most striking of which is the Luisenburg. Then there are the deeply indented valleys, particularly those of the Weisser Main, the Ölschnitz, the Steinach and the Eger.

From Bad Berneck to Selb

The best known and most attractive route through the Fichtelgebirge from west to east is the Fichtelgebirgsstrasse from Bad Berneck to Marktredwitz (40km/25 miles). | Fichtelgebirgsstrasse

The pleasant little town of Bad Berneck (Kneipp cure) lies in the narrow valley of the Ölschnitz at its junction with the Weisser Main. Above the pretty Marktplatz is the Colonnade, from which there is a path up to Burg Wallenrode (fine views) and the ruined Hohenberneck (14th c.). | Bad Berneck

Bischofsgrün, in the centre of the Fichtelgebirge, is a good base from which to explore the surrounding country and a winter sports centre. In the 15th–18th centuries it was famed for the production of stained glass. | Bischofsgrün

Above Bishofsgrün, to the south, rises the Ochsenkopf (1024m/3360ft; radio transmitter; panoramic views). A cableway goes up to the summit. A scenic road runs round the west and south sides of the hill to join the Glasstrasse, coming from Bayreuth (see entry). | Ochsenkopf

To the west of the junction with the Glasstrasse is the altitude and winter sports resort of Warmensteinach, with a parish church of 1705. | Warmensteinach

Fichtelberg owes its origin to the mining of micaceous iron ore (until 1862). To the north-east lies the beautiful forest-ringed Fichtelsee. 3km/2 miles east of the town the Glasstrasse joins the Fichtelgebirgsstrasse, which continues east. | Fichtelberg

Wunsiedel, the chief place in the Fichtelgebirge, was the birthplace of the novelist Jean Paul (Richter; 1763–1825). Old silver-mine. | Wunsiedel

3km/2 miles south is the Luisenburg, a magnificent rock labyrinth named after Queen Luise of Prussia, with an open-air theatre in which the Luisenburg Festival is held annually in summer. | Luisenburg

Bad Alexandersbad (mineral springs, mud baths) is prettily situated on the eastern slopes of the Luisenburg. The Schloss was built in 1783 as a spa establishment. Queen Luise of Prussia took the cure here in 1805. | Bad Alexandersbad

The Fichtelgebirgsstrasse ends in Marktredwitz, an old-world little town with the tower of a 14th century castle. In the Town Hall is a Goethe Room. The Theresienkirche was founded by the Empress Maria Theresa in 1774 for troops from the Egerland. The route continues north on the Porzellanstrasse. | Marktredwitz

The industrial town of Selb, on the northern fringes of the Fichtelgebirge, is famed for its porcelain and ceramic manufactories (Hutschenreuther, Rosenthal, etc.; technical college). | Selb

The return from Selb to Bad Berneck can be by way of Marktleuthen and Weissenstadt, in the Waldsteingebirge. From the Grosser Waldstein (880m/2887ft) there are fine panoramic views. | Grosser Waldstein

Fläming

E 7–8

Länder: Brandenburg, Saxony, Saxony-Anhalt

The Fläming Hills (named after Flemish settlers who came here in the 12th century) are the middle section of the ridge of hills which extends for over 100km/60 miles, ranging in width between 30km/20 miles and 50km/30 miles, from the Altmark in the north-west to | Situation and topography the Lusatian Hills in the south-east. It is bounded on the north by the Baruth *urstromtal* (ice-margin trench), on the west and south by the valleys of the Elbe and Schwarze Elster, on the east by the Dahme valley.

The western part of the Fläming range, the Hoher Fläming, reaches a height of 201m/659ft in the Hagelberg; the highest point in the eastern part, the Niederer Fläming, is the Golmberg (178m/584ft). In the Fläming hilly country formed by terminal moraines alternates with rolling ground moraines and level expanses of outwash sand. Much of the area is covered with pine forests; only in the central part of the range is there mixed forest (beeches). There are numerous dry valleys, formed in different climatic conditions and now seldom carrying any water.

Hoher Fläming

Features of interest in the Hoher Fläming are the Hagelberg, with a monument commemorating a victory over Napoleon's forces in 1813, and the little towns of Belzig and Wiesenburg. In Belzig is Burg Eisenhardt, with a 33m/108ft high keep (13th c.) from which there are extensive views. The Schlosspark in Wiesenburg is notable for its many different species of trees. Nearby is Burg Rabenstein, now a youth hostel.

Niederer Fläming

The main tourist attraction of the Niederer Fläming is the old Cistercian monastery (founded 1170) of Zinna, near Jüterbog. The frescoes brought to light here during restoration work are among the finest Gothic wall paintings in Germany.

Flensburg   A 5

Land: Schleswig-Holstein
Altitude: 20m/65ft
Population: 87,000

Situation and characteristics

Flensburg, Germany's most northerly port and the most important town in Schleswig, is attractively situated between wooded ranges of hills at the head of the fjord-like Flensburger Förde, the northern shore of which is in Denmark.

Sights

Südermarkt
St Nicholas's Church

The main shopping street in the old town runs from south to north under the names of the Holm, Grosse Strasse and Norderstrasse, in which there are a number of well restored patrician and merchants' houses (18th and 19th c.). At the south end is the beautiful Südermarkt, surrounded by gabled houses, with the large Stadtkirche (Town Church) of St Nicholas (14th and 16th c.; Rococo high altar, Renaissance organ).

Natural History Museum

To the east of St Nicholas's Church, on the Süderhofenden, is the Natural History Museum (Heimatmuseum; native flora and fauna, geological history). The same building houses the Municipal Library.

St John's Church

Farther east, near Angelburger Strasse, is St John's Church, the oldest in the town (12th c.; wall paintings, etc.).

Nordermarkt

In the Nordermarkt, the old market-place, are the Neptune Fountain (1758) and the Schrangen (1595), in which the bakers and butchers once sold their wares.

* Municipal Museum

South-west of the Nordermarkt can be found the little Gothic church of the Holy Ghost (Heiliggeistkirche, 1386; from 1588 a Danish church). In Lutherplatz is the Municipal Museum (Städtisches Museum; culture, art, folk art; Emil Nolde Collection; changing exhibitions).

To the north of the Nordermarkt is the little brick-built church of St Mary (13th and 15th c.; Renaissance altar).

To the east, on the harbour, is the Kompagnietor (1583) and at Norderstrasse 8 the Alt-Flensburger Haus (1780), family home of the airship pioneer Hugo Eckener (1868–1954).

On the Schiffsbrücke is the interesting Shipping Museum (Schiffahrtsmuseum; pictures and models of ships, nautical apparatus and equipment); museum harbour (Museumshafen).

Shipping Museum

At the north end of the old town rises the massive Nordertor (1595).

* Nordertor

Glücksburg

Glücksburg, 9km/6 miles north-east of Flensburg, has a Schloss built in 1582–87, with a museum displaying pictures, tapestries and leather wall coverings.

* Schloss

Franconian Forest (Frankenwald)   H 6–7

Land: Bavaria

The Franconian Forest (Frankenwald), which extends south-east between the Thuringian Forest and the Fichtelgebirge (see entries), is a range of hills of medium height, an undulating plateau at an average height of 600m/2000ft with only a few isolated peaks rising out of it. The highest point is the Döbraberg (795m/2608ft; panoramic views) near Schwarzenbach am Wald.

Situation and characteristics

Landscape

The towns and villages mostly lie on the plateau, the greater part of which has been cleared of forest. The unspoiled scenic beauties of the Franconian Forest are to be found particularly in the deeply indented river valleys (Höllental, valley of the Wilde Rodach, Rodach valley).

Franconian Switzerland (Fränkische Schweiz)   H 6

Land: Bavaria

The name of Franconian Switzerland has been applied since the 16th century to the northernmost part of the Franconian Alb (Fränkische Alb), between Bayreuth, Bamberg and Nürnberg (see entries), with its impressive rock formations. It is a gently rolling plateau, between 500m/1650ft and 600m/2000ft in height, slashed by winding steep-sided valleys 100–200m/330–660ft deep. The valleys offer a varied landscape pattern with their green meadowland, attractive villages, high-perched old castles and curiously shaped dolomitic crags. The plateau, once used only for grazing sheep, is now cultivated arable land.

Situation and characteristics

* Landscape

The principal beauty spots are the Wiesent valley, the Ailsbach valley which joins it below the little hill town of Gössweinstein and the Püttlach valley, with the extraordinary rock village of Tüchersfeld.
Other attractive places include Streitberg, Muggendorf and Pollenstein, near which are interesting stalactitic caves (notably the Binghöhle at Streitberg and the Teufelshöhle at Pottenstein).

There are also numbers of little resorts offering a variety of attractions – curious rock formations, viewpoints, caves, castles and wooded valleys – for walkers and holidaymakers. The principal centre of the area is Behringersmühle (with Gössweinstein).

Tour of the Franconian Switzerland

The starting-point of the tour is the old city of Nürnberg (see entry), leaving on the motorway or on B 4, signposted to Erlangen.

Forchheim

North of Erlangen we reach Forchheim, where the Wiesent valley opens into the Regnitz basin, the western gateway of the Franconian Switzerland. Forchheim was originally a Carolingian imperial stronghold, and later became the strongest fortified town in the bishopric of Bamberg. The old town preserves a number of trim old half-timbered buildings (Old Town Hall, 14th–16th c.) and the Gothic parish church of St Martin (14th–15th c.). Nearby is the Pfalz, built between 1353 and 1383 as the residence of the Prince-Bishops, with the Pfalzmuseum (material of the prehistoric and early historical periods).

Gössweinstein

From Forchheim B 470 runs north-east. Gössweinstein, commandingly situated on a steep crag above the Wiesent valley, has a beautiful pilgrimage church by Balthasar Neumann (1730–39). Conspicuous above the town is the Burg.

Pottenstein

The little town of Pottenstein stands charmingly situated in a basin framed in high dolomitic crags. The Late Gothic parish church has a beautiful high altar of 1730. Museum of Franconian Switzerland (geology, folk traditions). Above the town is the Burg, with a collection of weapons. Nearby is the Teufelshöhle (Devil's Cave; open to visitors).

From Pottenstein the route continues south-east to join the motorway to Bayreuth at Pegnitz. Then west on B 22 to Bamberg. From Hollfeld there are possible detours into the beautiful Kleinziegenfeld valley and to Waischenfeld.

From Bamberg we return to Nürnberg on the motorway via Forchheim.

Bad Frankenhausen

See Kyffhäuser Hills

Frankfurt am Main   H 4

Land: Hesse
Altitude: 212m/696ft
Population: 616,000

In this guide the description of Frankfurt has been deliberately kept short, since fuller information is provided in the "Frankfurt" volume in the same series.

Situation and characteristics

This old imperial city on the Main, by virtue of its central situation an intermediary between North and South Germany, is one of the most important commercial and economic centres in the country, with the headquarters of the Bundesbank, the leading German stock exchange and numerous major banks. Numerous international trade fairs are held in Frankfurt every year.

High-rise buildings

Since the Second World War and the period of postwar reconstruction the central area of Frankfurt has taken on a new aspect. The city's skyline is now dominated by the great cluster of high-rise buildings in the banking quarter.
The offices of the Dresdner Bank, at 166m/545ft, are one of the tallest buildings in the city.
The Cooperative Bank (Bank für Gemeinwirtschaft) occupies a 156m/512ft high tower

Skyline of "Mainhattan"

block (by R. Heil, 1977) in Theaterplatz, clad with natural-coloured aluminium and reflective insulating glass. One of the more recent additions to the skyline is the 117m/384ft high Torhaus (by O. M. Ungers), a tower block within a tower block which has become the new Trade Fair emblem. The 155m/509ft high glass-fronted twin towers of the Deutsche Bank in the Taunus Gardens were designed by the ABB group (Hanig, Scheid and Schmidt). Other high-rise buildings are under construction or at the planning stage.

All this has earned Frankfurt the names of "Mainhattan" and "Chicago on the Main".

Central Area

In the centre of the city lies the square called An der Hauptwache (large shopping area in underpass; S-Bahn and U-Bahn station), with the Baroque Hauptwache (Guard-House; renovated 1981–82). From this square Frankfurt's main shopping and commercial streets radiate: the Zeil (pedestrian zone), going east, and Kaiserstrasse (with many places of entertainment in side streets), which runs south-west by way of the Rossmarkt (Gutenberg memorial) and Kaiserplatz to the city's main station (Hauptbahnhof; 1883–88, with later renovation), one of the largest stations in Europe.

Hauptwache

South-west of Kaiserplatz, in Theaterplatz, is the Municipal Theatre (Städtische Bühnen), with three houses (opera, theatre, chamber theatre).
On the north side of the Theatre towers the BfG-Hochhaus, the offices of the Cooperative Bank.

Theaterplatz

To the north of the Rossmarkt stands the Stock Exchange (Börse; built 1879, rebuilt 1957), the largest stock exchange in Germany, with an annual turnover of more than 40 billion DM.

Stock Exchange

A little way north of the Stock Exchange is the Eschenheimer Turm (1400–28), the finest relic of the old town walls, which are now replaced by the ring of gardens enclosing the old town.

Eschenheimer Turm

211

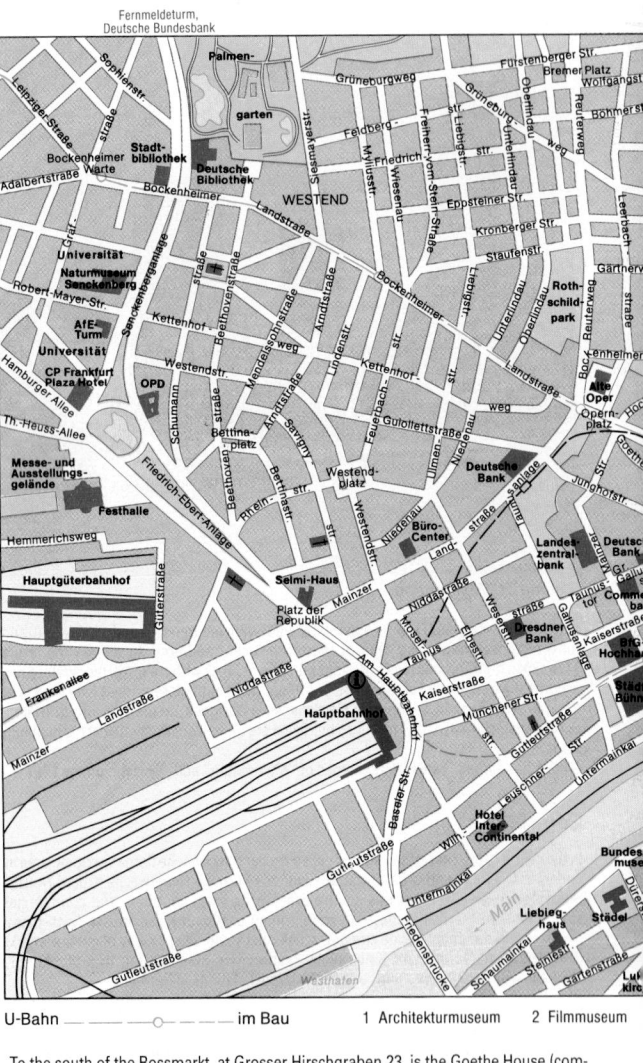

Fernmeldeturm,
Deutsche Bundesbank

U-Bahn ———— ——○—— —— im Bau   1 Architekturmuseum   2 Filmmuseum

*Goethe House

To the south of the Rossmarkt, at Grosser Hirschgraben 23, is the Goethe House (completely rebuilt on the basis of old plans in 1946–51), in which the great German writer was born on August 28th 1749 and lived until 1765. The interior (now a museum) has been restored to its original condition.
Adjoining is the Haus des Deutschen Buchhandels (Book Trade House), headquarters of the central organisation of publishers and booksellers.

St Paul's Church

To the south of the Hauptwache, in Paulsplatz, stands the Paulskirche (St Paul's Church; built 1790–1833, restored 1948), a plain neo-classical building on a centralised plan in

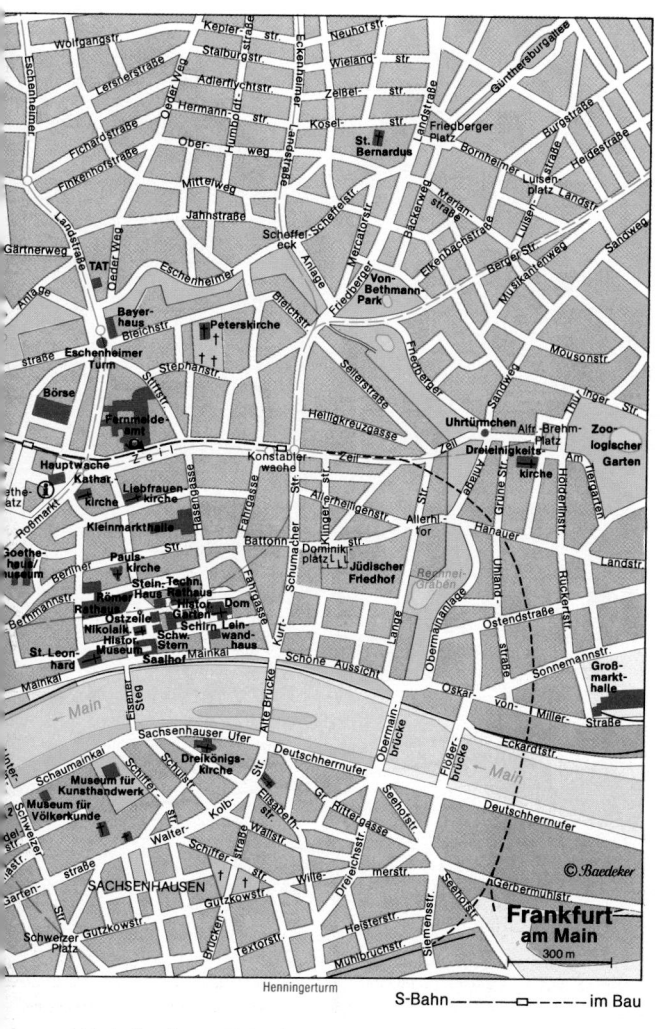

Henningerturm

S-Bahn———□————im Bau

which the first German National Assembly met in 1848–49. The presentation of the Frankfurt Goethe Prize and the annual Peace Prize of the German Book Trade takes place here.

Römerberg

South-east of the Paulskirche is the Römerberg, an irregularly shaped square with the Justice Fountain (Gerechtigkeitsbrunnen) in the centre. Reconstruction of the square,

which suffered severe destruction during the Second World War, was completed in 1986, with a new "Kulturschirn" (leisure and cultural zone – *schirn* being an old Frankfurt word for the open-fronted shops which were once a common feature of the old town).

On the west side of the Römerberg is the Römer, a complex of eleven formerly separate buildings of the 15th–18th centuries, including the Old Town Hall (Altes Rathaus), with an Imperial Hall (Kaisersaal) which was once the scene of splendid banquets. To the west stands the New Town Hall (Neues Rathaus; 1900–08). To the south of the New Town Hall, on the banks of the Main, is the Gothic church of St Leonhard (14th c.; R.C.), with Romanesque doorways. `* Römer`

On the south side of the Römerberg we come to the Nikolaikirche (St Nicholas's Church; carillon). Beyond this, reaching down to the Mainkai, can be found the Historical Museum (Historisches Museum), completed in 1972 (history of Frankfurt, children's museum, communications centre). Incorporated in the building are the Rententurm (1455) and the Saalhof (originally dating in part from 9th c.; altered in 18th and 19th c.). `St Nicholas's Church` `Historical Museum`

On the east side of the Römerberg is the Ostzeile, with six buildings in traditional style erected in the early eighties, to the south of which is the house known as the Schwarzer Stern (Black Star) and to the north the Steinernes Haus (Stone House; restored 1957–60), headquarters of the Kunstverein (Art Society). `* Ostzeile`
From here the Alter Markt, on which are the Technical Town Hall (Technisches Rathaus), the new Schirn-Kunsthalle (periodic exhibitions) and the Historical Garden (remains from the Roman and Carolingian periods), leads to the Cathedral.

The Gothic Cathedral (Dom; R.C.), in red sandstone, was built in the 13th–15th centuries (restored after suffering heavy damage in 1944). Its 95m/312ft high tower is a city landmark. From 1562 onwards the coronation of the Emperor took place under the crossing (Election Chapel on south side of choir). Beneath the tower is a magnificent "Crucifixion" by Hans Backoffen (1509). In the Marienkapelle can be seen the Maria-Schlaf-Altar (Dormition of the Virgin Altar, 1434). In the choir is the grave-slab of King Günter von Schwarzburg, who died in Frankfurt in 1349. In the south transept is a large organ (80 stops). There are also a number of carved side altars (15th–16th c.). `* Cathedral`

East of City Centre

The Zoo, south-east of the old Friedberger Tor has a fine collection of animals of many different species (Exotarium, with rooms for different climatic conditions; Crocodile Hall; Insectarium; Nocturnal Animals House; Bird Hall). There is an outstation for hoofed and steppe animals at Ginnheim in the Nidda valley, north-western outskirts of the city. `* Zoo`

North-West and West of City Centre

At the old Bockenheimer Tor can be found the Old Opera House (Alte Oper; originally built 1880), which was reopened in 1981, after rebuilding, as a congress and concert hall. `Old Opera House`

1.5km/1 mile north-west on the Bockenheimer Landstrasse is the beautiful Palmengarten (Palm Garden; native, subtropical and tropical flora). On its south side is the Deutsche Bibliothek (German Library; 1957–59), which collects all German-language books published in Germany or abroad. Facing it, on the Bockenheimer Landstrasse, stands the Municipal and University Library (Stadt- und Universitätsbibliothek). `Palmengarten` `Deutsche Bibliothek`

North-east of the Palmengarten is the Grüneburgpark (29 hectares/72 acres), with the Botanic Garden. `Grüneburgpark`

North-west of the Grüneburgpark, on the outskirts of the city, lies the Volkspark Niddatal (Nidda Valley People's Park), remodelled in 1989 for the Federal Garden Show. `Volkspark Niddatal`

1km/¾ mile north of the Palmengarten rises the 331m/1086ft high Telecommunications Tower (Fernmeldeturm; 1977), with a viewing platform and a restaurant. `* Telecommunications Tower`

◀ *Römer, with Justice Fountain*

Heinrich Hoffmann
Museum

To the south of the Palmengarten, at Schubertstrasse 20, is the Heinrich Hoffmann Museum, devoted to the author of "Struwwelpeter" (also material on the history of medicine).
There is a Struwwelpeter Collection, with original drafts and rare editions of the book, at Hochstrasse 45–47, near the Old Opera House.

University
*Senckenberg
Museum

In the Senckenberg Gardens is the extensive range of buildings occupied by the Johann Wolfgang Goethe University (founded 1914) and the Senckenberg Natural History Museum, one of the most modern museums of natural history in Europe (fossils, minerals, large mammals, development of man; research collection). The Senckenberg Society has an institute of marine research (established 1928) in Wilhelmshaven (see entry).

Trade Fair Grounds (Messegelände)

Some 500m/550yds south of the University are the Trade Fair Grounds, with the Festhalle (built 1907–09; renovated 1986). With a total area of 40 hectares/100 acres, ten exhibition halls and the Torhaus (1985), the Trade Fair Grounds offer facilities for numerous trade fairs and exhibitions, including the International Book Fair, the Frankfurt International Trade Fair, the International Motor Show, the Frankfurt Art Fair and the International Computer Fair. The Messeturm (by Helmut Jahn, 1990) is 256m/840ft high.

**Museumsufer

Along the Schaumainkai in the district of Sachsenhausen, on the left bank of the Main, there has developed in recent years an extraordinary concentration of museums, some of them of international standing.

*Städel Institute

In the centre of this area, the Museumsufer, is the Städel Art Institute (Städelsches Kunstinstitut), with the Municipal Gallery, an excellent collection of painting from the 14th century to the present day (Rembrandt, Cranach, Dürer, Goya; Italian, Dutch and Flemish masters).

Museum of
Applied Art

The Museum of Applied Art (Museum für Kunsthandwerk), housed in the neo-classical Villa Metzler and a new building opened in 1985, has some 30,000 items of European and Asian applied art – furniture, tapestries, glass, ceramics, books and manuscripts.

Museum of
Ethnography

The Museum of Ethnography (Völkerkundemuseum) is one of the finest museums of its kind in Germany.

Postal Museum

The German Postal Museum (Deutsches Postmuseum), the predecessor of which was opened in Berlin in 1878, has been housed in Frankfurt since 1958. The exhibits illustrate the history of the postal service and telecommunications.

Liebieghaus

In the Liebieghaus is the Museum of Ancient Sculpture (Asian and Egyptian, Greek and Roman, medieval, Renaissance and Baroque).

Architectural
Museum

The German Architectural Museum (Deutsches Architekturmuseum) illustrates the interaction between social and ecological objectives, the technical capacity available and ideas of architectural design.

Film Museum

The Film Museum has five sections: from the camera obscura to the Lumière brothers; the work of the Lumière brothers; history of the cinema; the language of film; and sound in film.

Sachsenhausen

"Ebbelwei"

Sachsenhausen is the place to enjoy a Frankfurt speciality, the cider (*ebbelwei*) which is sold in many cider bars here, particularly in Grosse and Kleine Rittergasse, Rauschergasse, Textorgasse and Klappergasse. Visitors may take some time to get used to the sharp taste and alcoholic effect of *ebbelwei*. Favourite dishes to accompany it are Rippchen mit Kraut (pickled ribs of pork with sauerkraut) and Schwartenmagen mit Musik (onions with vinaigrette dressing).

*Rhine-Main Airport (Rhein-Main-Flughafen)

The Rhine-Main Airport, the largest airport in Germany, lies 10km/6 miles south-west of the city centre, at the intersection of the Cologne-Munich and Hamburg-Basle motorways (the Frankfurter Kreuz). In terms of flights handled it is exceeded only by London Heathrow, and it is planned to increase the airport's capacity to 30 million passengers a year. The southern part of the airport is occupied by the US Air Force's base, with a monument commemorating the Berlin air-lift, the counterpart of the one in Berlin.

Surroundings of Frankfurt am Main

20km/12½ miles north-west, in the Taunus (see entry), is the picturesque little town of Königstein, with Burg Königstein looming over it (first recorded 1225; blown up by French troops 1796; panoramic views).
| Königstein

10km/6 miles beyond this is the Grosser Feldberg (881m/2891ft), the highest peak in the Taunus (radio transmitter; fine views).
| Grosser Feldberg

See entry
| Offenbach

Frankfurt an der Oder   E 9

Land: Brandenburg
Altitude: 22m/72ft
Population: 87,000

Frankfurt an der Oder, situated on the frontier with Poland, is the third largest town in the *Land* of Brandenburg. There are few remains of the old trading centre and university town of the past, but Frankfurt has a number of interesting modern buildings erected since the last war, which caused heavy destruction.
| Situation and characteristics

Sights

The Town Hall (Rathaus) in the old Marktplatz with its imposing decorated gables, built after 1253 in North German brick-built Gothic style, attests the wealth of the old Hanseatic town.
| *Town Hall

Other attractions in the Town Hall are the Galerie Junge Kunst ("Young Art" Gallery; over 8000 works of painting, graphic art and sculpture) in the Rathaushalle, the old court room (Gerichtshalle) and the historic Ratskeller.
| Galerie Junge Kunst

The Kleist Museum at Faberstrasse 7 (between the Town Hall and the Oder) is devoted to the life and work of the dramatist Heinrich von Kleist (1777–1811), a native of Frankfurt.
| *Kleist Museum

In the old Junkerhaus at C.-P.-E.-Bach-Strasse 11, one of Frankfurt's few surviving historic buildings, is the Viadrina District Museum (after the Latin name of the Oder). The doorway is a copy of the old entrance to the University. The museum illustrates the history of the town and district down to 1933.
| District Museum

From the museum the Oderpromenade (recently replanned) leads past the old Crane and the Friedensbrücke (Peace Bridge; frontier crossing to Slubice in Poland) to the
| Peace Church

Town Hall

Concert Hall

Friedenskirche (Peace Church; formerly St Nicholas's), the oldest building in the town (13th c.). Notable features of the church are the groined vaulting and the choir, which preserves some Romanesque features. The neo-Gothic towers date from 1881–93.

*Concert Hall

The C. P. E. Bach Concert Hall (formerly the church of a Franciscan friary), opened in 1967, is noted for its excellent acoustics. The interior of this Early Gothic hall-church has fine reticulated and stellar vaulting. The west gable has rich Gothic tracery; on the east gable are blind pointed arches. There is a fine organ by the Frankfurt firm of Sauer. In a modern annex can be seen an exhibition on the life and work of C. P. E. Bach, who was a student in Frankfurt from 1734 to 1738 and became choirmaster of St Mary's Church.

In the adjoining Late Baroque Collegienhaus are the Municipal Archives (with the oldest surviving record, a document of 1287). Demonstrations of historic musical instruments are given in the second part of the building.

Parks and gardens

There are pleasant walks to be enjoyed in the town's parks and gardens, which extend in a belt of green from the Linaupark in the north (open-air theatre) by way of the Lenné-Park on the line of the old fortifications (modern sculpture) to the gardens on the Oderallee (Gertraudenplatz, Anger).

Surroundings of Frankfurt an der Oder

Boat trips

A boat trip on the Oder – departures from the Oderpromenade and Friedensglocke (Peace Bell) – is an excellent way of seeing some of the places of interest in the surrounding area, such as Eisenhüttenstadt (see entry), Ratzdorf, Lebus and Eberswalde-Finow (see entry).

Freiberg

G 8

Land: Saxony
Altitude: 416m/1365ft
Population: 50,400

Freiberg, the first free mining town in Germany, lies 30km/20 miles east of Chemnitz at the foot of the Eastern Erzgebirge, on a plateau above the Freiberger Mulde. Once the most populous town in the Margraviate of Meissen, Freiberg with its silver-mines was a great source of wealth for the rulers of Saxony.

Situation and characteristics

Sights

The whole of Freiberg's old town with its well preserved houses is protected as a national monument. In the pedestrian zones visitors will find many interesting old architectural details (buildings, keystones, doorways, reliefs) as well as modern features, including fountains and emblems of craft guilds.

Town centre

The town's great attraction, however, is the Cathedral (Dom), a Late Gothic hall-church (1485–1501), with remains of its Romanesque predecessor and the famous "Golden Gate" (Goldene Pforte; *c.* 1230). The interior is richly furnished, with the "Tulip Pulpit" (by Hans Witten, 1508–10), the "Miners' Pulpit" (1638) and a Silbermann organ (1711–14), the oldest and largest of the surviving Silbermann organs in Saxony.

**Cathedral

In the Untermarkt is the Domherrenhof (Canons' Lodging; 1484), a Late Gothic patrician house now occupied by the Municipal and Mining Museum (Bergbaumuseum).

Domherrenhof (Mining Museum)

Also of interest is the Mineral Collection of the Bergakademie (Mining Academy) at Brennhausgasse 14.

Mineral Collection

Near the Kreuzteich stands Schloss Freudenstein, a 16th century Renaissance building.

Schloss Freudenstein

In the Obermarkt are the Late Gothic Town Hall (Rathaus; 1470–74, with later rebuilding), with the Lorenzkapelle (St Lawrence's Chapel); the Kaufhaus at Obermarkt 16 (Renaissance; 1545–46); the Schönlebehaus at Obermarkt 1, a large three-storey patrician house of the early 16th century; and a house at Obermarkt 17 with the finest Early Renaissance doorway in Freiberg (1530).

*Obermarkt

The Petrikirche (St Peter's Church; 1404–40), a Late Gothic hall-church, has a Silbermann organ (1716–17), as has the neo-Gothic Jakobikirche (St James's Church; 1890–92).

Churches

Another fine church is the Nikolaikirche (St Nicholas's; 14th–15th c.), a Late Gothic hall-church with a richly furnished interior.

St Nicholas's Church

At Waisenhausstrasse 10, near St Peter's Church, is the Natural History Museum (Naturkundemuseum), which, among much else, illustrates the effect of mining on the landscape.

Natural History Museum

The history of mining in the town is recalled by a demonstration mine ("Alte Elisabeth"; *c.* 1850), the old Abraham pit (*c.* 1840) and the Freiberger Hammerwerk, an ironworks of around 1600.

Surroundings of Freiberg

7km/4½ miles south of Freiberg on B 101 is Brand-Erbisdorf, with the Huthaus zum Reussen (1837). In the Late Gothic parish church is a life-size figure of a miner (by S. Lorentz, 1585). South-east of the town lies the Erzenglerteich, an artificial pond created to provide a water supply for the mines.

Brand-Erbisdorf

20km/12½ miles south-east is Frauenstein, with remains of a castle which was burned down in 1728, including the north tower (known as Dicker Merten, "Fat Martin"), the south tower and the ruins of the "palace" (residential quarters).

Frauenstein

Below the castle is the Renaissance Schloss (by H. Irmisch, 1585–88), now housing a museum. There is also a Heimatmuseum, with a collection on the life and work of the celebrated organ-builder Gottfried Silbermann (b. 1683 in Kleinbobritzsch, near Frauenstein; d. 1753 in Dresden).

Freiburg im Breisgau   L 3

Land: Baden-Württemberg
Altitude: 278m/912ft. Population: 176,000

Situation and characteristics

Freiburg, a commercial and administrative centre as well as an episcopal and university city, lies between the Kaiserstuhl and the Black Forest (see entry) at the point where the river Dreisam enters the Upper Rhine plain. It is the gateway to the southern Black Forest. The 1284m/4213ft high Schauinsland, Freiburg's own domestic mountain, lies within the city boundaries, and only a few kilometres away is the wild and romantic Höllental ("Hell Valley"). The little streams (*bächle*) which provided water supply and drainage in the medieval town still flow through the streets of the old town, and in the paving of many streets there are decorative mosaics of river pebbles.

Sights

The main axis of the town, rebuilt after heavy destruction in the Second World War, is Kaiser-Joseph-Strasse (pedestrian zone), which divides the old town into an eastern half, with the Minster, and a western half with the Town Hall and the University. On the south side stands the old Martinstor (St Martin's Gate).

**Minster

The Minster (13th–16th c.) is one of the great masterpieces of Gothic architecture in Germany. It has a beautiful interior, with many works of art: 14th century stained glass in the aisles; on the high altar a famous altarpiece (1512–16) by Hans Baldung Grien, his finest work; an altarpiece in the University Chapel by Hans Holbein the Younger (*c.* 1521).

1 Ursulinenkirche	5 Archbishop's Palace	9 Sickingen Palace
2 Old University	6 Kaufhaus	10 Museum of Modern Art
3 University Church	7 Wenzingerhaus	11 Natural History Museum,
4 St Martin's Church	8 Seminary Church	Museum of Enthography
		12 Adelhauser Kirche

Frieburg Minster ▶

From the platform of the delicately articulated tower (c. 1320–30; 116m/381ft high) there are magnificent views.

Münsterplatz
In the Münsterplatz a number of fine old buildings have been preserved. On the south side (No. 10) is the red Merchants' Hall (Kaufhaus; 1532), with arcading and stepped gables, flanked by oriel windows with pointed roofs; at No. 30 is the Wenzingerhaus (rebuilt 1761); and on the north side is the 15th century Kornhaus, rebuilt in 1969–71.

*Augustinian Museum
In Salzstrasse, occupying an old house of Augustinian Hermits, is the Augustinian Museum (Augustinermuseum), with the artistic and historical collections of the city and the Upper Rhine region (including Matthias Grünewald's "Miracle of the Snow", stained glass and sculpture from the Minster, pictures by Baden painters and glassware).

Schwabentor
At the end of Salzstrasse rises the 13th century Schwabentor (Swabian Gate; wall paintings; dioramas with tin figure).

West of the Schwabentor, in the Gerberau, is the Adelshauser Kloster, an old convent now occupied by the Natural History Museum (Museum für Naturkunde), with departments of geology (precious stones, with demonstrations of fluorescence), botany and zoology (native fauna, beekeeping). Here too is the Museum of Ethnography (Museum für Völkerkunde; East Asia, Egypt, Black Africa, North American Indians, Australia, South Seas).

Rathausplatz
In the western part of the old town lies Rathausplatz, with a statue of Berthold Schwarz, a Franciscan friar who is said to have invented gunpowder in 1359.

On the west side of the square can be seen the New Town Hall (Neues Rathaus; carillon at noon) and the Old Town Hall (Altes Rathaus; 16th c.). On the north side is the Gothic St Martin's Church, with a beautifully restored interior and cloister.

Haus zum Walfisch
In neighbouring Franziskanerstrasse is the Haus zum Walfisch (House of the Whale), a Late Gothic burgher's house with a beautiful oriel window, said to have been built in 1516 as a residence for Emperor Maximilian in his old age.

University
In Bertholdstrasse are the Old University (Alte Universität) and the University Church (17th c.; restored). Farther west, on the Ring, are the Municipal Theatre (Stadttheater; 1910; exterior rebuilt 1963), the new University Library and the University, with buildings of various periods ranged round a courtyard. To the south, on an old bastion, is the Mensa (students' refectory; 1963).

Colombi-Schlösschen
To the north of the Theatre, set in a park, is the Colombi-Schlösschen (1859), with the Museum of Prehistory and the Early Historical Period (Museum für Ur- und Frühgeschichte).

*Schlossberg
On the Schlossberg (460m/1510ft; cableway and lift), once crowned by the stronghold of the Dukes of Zähringen, are the remains of three old castles and a column in honour of Bismarck. From the Kanonenplatz (on an old bastion) there is a fine view of the city and the Minster.

Surroundings of Freiburg

Schauinsland
21km/13 miles south rises Freiburg's own mountain, Schauinsland (1284m/4213ft). There is a cableway to the summit at Horben. The road up the hill was formerly a well-known car-racing track.

*Kaiserstuhl
North-west of Freiburg, rising directly out of the Rhine plain, is the Kaiserstuhl (557m/1828ft), a hill of volcanic origin. It is worth a visit for the sake of the scenery, the rich flora and fauna and – not least – the famous wines produced here (Achkarren, Bickensohl, Ihringen, Oberrotweil).

Breisach
South-west of the Kaiserstuhl, on a steep-sided crag above the Rhine, lies the little town of Breisach. The 14th century Minster (St Stephan) has an imposing high altar of 1526 and a magnificent wall painting by Martin Schongauer, who died in Breisach in 1491.

Freising

Land: Bavaria
Altitude: 471m/1545ft
Population: 36,000

The old Bavarian town of Freising, the see of a bishop from the 8th to the 18th century, lies on the high left bank of the Isar, here flowing along the north side of the Erlinger Moos.

Situation and characteristics

The Town

On the Domberg stands the twin-towered Cathedral (Dom), a brick-built Romanesque basilica (1160 onwards), with a Baroque interior (by the Asam brothers, 1723–24) and fine choir-stalls of 1488. In the crypt (12th c.) is the reliquary of St Corbinian. Also on the Domberg is the Diocesan Museum.

Cathedral

In the north-eastern district of Neustift is the church of a former Premonstratensian monastery, rebuilt in 1751 by J. B. Zimmermann and Ignaz Günther.

Neustift

On a hill to the south-west can be found the Benedictine abbey of Weihenstephan. The monastic buildings (1671–1705) are now occupied by the oldest working brewery in the world (with beer-garden) and institutes belonging to the Munich University of Technology.

Weihenstephan

South-east of Freising, beyond the Isar, is the great level expanse of the Erdinger Moos, on which Munich's new airport, due to replace the existing airport of München-Riem, is under construction. Since it may be necessary to lower the water table in order to reduce the possibility of fog this may lead to changes in the ecology of this moorland area.

Munich Airport

Freising Cathedral

Freudenstadt

Land: Baden-Württemberg
Altitude: 700m/2300ft
Population: 20,000

Situation and
characteristics

The climatic resort of Freudenstadt in the northern Black Forest is one of the most frequented holiday places in the region and is also a popular winter sports resort.

The Town

* Marktplatz

The central feature of the town is the spacious Marktplatz, surrounded by arcaded houses. With an area of 4.5 hectares/11 acres, it is one of the largest market squares in Germany.
In the centre of the square are the Stadthaus (Town House), with the Heimatmuseum, and the Head Post Office.

Stadtkirche

At the south corner of the Marktplatz stands the Stadtkirche (Town Church), built in 1601–08 and restored in 1951. It consists of two naves at right angles to one another, one for men and the other for women; lectern of 1140, borne by figures of the four Evangelists, and 11th–12th century font.

Kurviertel

On the south side of the town, which here merges into the park-like natural fir forest (the "Palm Forest"), is the Kurviertel (spa quarter), with the Kurhaus (enlarged 1989) and the Kurgarten. At the foot of the Kienberg is the Kurmittelhaus (treatment facilities).

Surroundings of Freudenstadt

Baiersbronn

7km/4½ miles north-west of Freudenstadt is Baiersbronn, a popular summer and winter resort. In the outlying district of Klosterreichenbach is a Romanesque church which belonged to a Benedictine abbey.

Altensteig

20km/12½ miles north-east of Freudenstadt, in the Nagold valley, is Altensteig, with an old castle looming over it. 3km/2 miles away, on a narrow ridge of hills, we come to the little town of Berneck, with the Schloss (1846) of the Freiherren (Barons) von Gültlingen.

Alpirsbach

17km/10½ miles south of Freudenstadt, in the Kinzig valley, lies the little town of Alpirsbach, which has a fine Romanesque church, originally belonging to a Benedictine house founded in 1095, with a Romanesque and Gothic cloister. Other features of interest are a museum on the history of the town and the Alpirsbacher Glasbläserei (glass-blowing works).

Friedrichshafen

Land: Baden-Württemberg
Altitude: 402m/1319ft
Population: 53,000

Situation and
characteristics

Friedrichshafen, famed as the birthplace of the zeppelin, is the largest town on Lake Constance (see entry) after Konstanz, a considerable industrial town and an important port on the lake.

Sights

Harbour Station

On the busy harbour is the Harbour Station (Hafenbahnhof; 1933). The town centre lies to the west.

Graf-Zeppelin-Haus and Schloss

In the town centre (rebuilt after wartime destruction) are the Late Gothic parish church of St Nicholas (R.C.) and the five-storey Town Hall (Rathaus; 1953–56), which also houses the Lake Constance Museum (Bodenseemuseum; prehistory and early historical period, art since the Gothic period) and a collection of models and parts of zeppelins.

Parish church
Museum
*Zeppelin collection

From the commercial harbour Seestrasse and its continuation on the lakeside road run west, passing the beautiful Stadtgarten (Zeppelin Memorial), to the boating harbour; fine views of the lake and the Alps.

Seestrasse

At the boating harbour can be found Graf-Zeppelin-Haus, a cultural and congress centre opened in 1985.

Graf-Zeppelin-Haus

A little way north, in Friedrichstrasse, is the Upper Swabian School Museum (Oberschwäbisches Schulmuseum), with typical classrooms of 1850, 1900 and 1930.

School Museum

To the west of Graf-Zeppelin-Haus, set in a park, is the Schloss (1654–1701), with its conspicuous church. Now the residence of Duke Karl von Württemberg, it is not open to the public.

Schloss

225

Fulda   G 5

Land: Hesse
Altitude: 332m/189ft
Population: 60,000

Situation and characteristics

The old episcopal city of Fulda is beautifully situated in the valley of the river Fulda, between the foothills of the Rhön (see entry) and the Vogelsberg. The 18th century Prince-Bishops gave the town its Baroque stamp.

The Town

Stadtschloss

The Stadtschloss, formerly the residence of the Prince-Abbots, was completed in 1730 to the design of Johann Dientzenhofer. It is now occupied by the municipal authorities. Visitors are shown the historical apartments (Princes' Hall, Imperial Hall, Hall of Mirrors) with their magnificent stucco decoration. Here too can be seen a collection of Fulda porcelain.
On the north side of the Schlossgarten (with theatre, indoor swimming pool and sports facilities) is the Baroque Orangery (by Maximilian von Welsch), now a conference and congress centre. In front of the Orangery can be seen the massive Flora Vase (1728).

Cathedral
*Cathedral Museum

In the Domplatz, to the west of the Schloss, stands the Cathedral (Dom; by Johann Dientzenhofer, 1704–12). In the crypt are the remains of St Boniface (d. 754). Cathedral Museum (religious art; cathedral treasury).

*St Michael's Church

North of the Cathedral is the Michaelskirche (St Michael's Church), one of the oldest churches in Germany (rotunda and crypt of 822). Behind it is the Bishop's Palace (Bischöfliches Palais).

Frauenberg

Ten minutes' walk north of the Schlossgarten is the Frauenberg monastery (founded *c.* 800; present buildings 1780; Baroque church), from which there is a fine view.

Provincial Library

In Heinrich-von-Bibra-Platz, between the Schloss and the railway station (Bahnhof), can be found the Provincial Library (Landesbibliothek), with valuable codices and Gospel books from the old Fulda monastery school and a 14-line Gutenberg Bible.

Old Town Hall
Vonderau Museum

In the old town (mostly now a pedestrian zone), to the south of the Schloss, stands the Old Town Hall (Altes Rathaus; originally 16th c.; restored). Nearby, in a former Jesuit seminary in Universitätsstrasse, is the Vonderau Museum (prehistory, folk traditions, natural history).

Fire Service Museum

Beyond the river Fulda, in the Neuenberg district (St-Laurentius-Strasse), is the German Fire Service Museum (Feuerwehrmuseum), with fire engines from 1808 to 1937 and a collection of documents.

St Andrew's Church

Also in Neuenberg is the Andreaskirche (St Andrew's Church), which belonged to the Benedictine monastery of Andreasberg. In the crypt are fine 11th century wall paintings.

St Peter's Church

In the north-eastern district of Petersberg is St Peter's Church, which preserves the remains of St Lioba (d. *c.* 780). In the upper church can be seen relief slabs of the 12th century. In the crypt are what are believed to be the oldest wall paintings in Germany (836–847). Good view of the town.

Surroundings of Fulda

Fasanerie

The Baroque Schloss Fasanerie (Adolphseck; 1730–56) 6km/4 miles south of Fulda, once the summer residence of the Prince-Abbots of Fulda, now houses a museum (tapestries, furniture, porcelain, glass, ancient sculpture).

Fürstenberg

See Neustrelitz, Surroundings

Fürth   I 6

Land: Bavaria
Altitude: 294m/965ft
Population: 98,000

Fürth, situated at the junction of the rivers Pegnitz and Rednitz, which here form the   Situation and
Regnitz, is now almost continuous with Nürnberg (see entry). The first railway line in   characteristics
Germany, opened in 1835, was between Fürth and Nürnberg.

The Town

Although it has some well preserved stone and half-timbered houses of the 17th and
18th centuries, Fürth is predominantly a modern town.
In the busy Königsstrasse stands the Town Hall (Rathaus; 1844–50), modelled on Flo-
rence's Palazzo Vecchio, with a tower which is a landmark of the town.
At the south end of the street is the Municipal Theatre (Stadttheater; 1900). Opposite it, to
the south-east, lies the Stadtpark, which extends to the Pegnitz, with the neo-classical
Auferstehungskirche (Church of the Resurrection).
On the nearby Hornschuch-Promenade are a number of well restored houses of the
Gründerzeit (the early 1870s, the period of prosperity after the foundation of the German
Empire).
To the west of the old-world Marktplatz is the 14th century Michaelskirche (St Michael's
Church), with a fine Late Gothic tabernacle.

Surroundings of Fürth

In the north-western district of Burgfarmbach (5km/3 miles away) can be found the old   Burgfarmbach
Schloss of the Counts of Pückler-Limburg, now housing the Municipal Archives, Library
and Museum (German and Dutch art of the 16th–19th c.; history of the town).

12km/7½ miles west is the picturesque little town of Cadolzburg, above which are its   Cadolzburg
massive old castle (15th–16th c.) and an outlook tower.

Füssen   M 6

Land: Bavaria
Altitude: 800m/2625ft
Population: 15,000

This old town on the Lech, between the Ammergau and Allgäu Alps, is a popular altitude   Situation and
resort and winter sports centre. It has also a spa in the outlying district of Bad Faulen-   characteristics
bach. It lies at the end of the Romantische Strasse (see entry), and is a good base for visits
to the famous royal castles of Neuschwanstein and Hohenschwangau.

The Town

Above the town stands the Hohes Schloss, formerly the summer residence of the   Hohes Schloss
Prince-Bishops of Augsburg. Originally built in 1291, it has been little changed since

Schloss Neuschwanstein

around 1500. It is now occupied by local government offices (Knights' Hall, chapel and Staatsgalerie, with Gothic pictures and sculpture).

St Mang Abbey

At the foot of the castle hill is the Benedictine abbey of St Mang (founded 728), with a Baroque church (by J. J. Herkomer, 1701–17). There are an old tower and a crypt, with wall paintings of the Reichenau school (*c.* 980), both dating from the 10th–11th centuries. The conventual buildings are now occupied by municipal offices and the Municipal Museum (history of the monastery; lute- and violin-making in Füssen). Fine state apartments (Banqueting Hall, Library, Papal Apartments). In the adjoining St Anne's Chapel can be seen a Danse Macabre by Jakob Hiebeler (1602).

Spitalkirche

Near the bridge over the Lech is the Heilig-Geist-Spitalkirche, the church of the Hospital of the Holy Ghost, with a lively and colourful Rococo façade (1748–49).

Bad Faulenbach

To the west of the town centre lies the outlying district of Bad Faulenbach (spring of sulphurous water, mud baths, natural baths). Beyond this, in the Faulenbach valley, are the Mittersee and Obersee (bathing stations).

Surroundings of Füssen

Forggensee

1km/¾ mile north is the 11.5km/7 mile long Forggensee, an artificial lake formed by the damming of the Lech (boat rental; excursions on lake).

Hopfensee
Weissensee

North-west and west of Füssen are the Hopfensee and Weissensee, both with bathing stations, boat rental and facilities for water sports.

5km/3 miles south-east of Füssen we come to Schloss Neuschwanstein, one of the "fairytale castles" of King Ludwig II of Bavaria. This towered and battlemented fantasy was built by E. Riedel in 1869–86 to the design of the stage painter Chr. Jank. Conducted tours of the sumptuous interior (Throne Room, Singers' Hall; views). *Neuschwanstein

Lower down is Schloss Hohenschwangau, a neo-Gothic castle built for King Maximilian II in 1832–36 to the design of the stage painter D. Quaglio (frescoes by Moritz von Schwindt). Hohenschwangau

From Schwangau there is a cableway up the Tegelberg (views; skiing area). Tegelberg

See Ettal, Surroundings Linderhof

To the Wieskirche

Steingaden, 20km/12½ miles north-east of Füssen, has a twin-towered Romanesque church which belonged to a Premonstratensian monastery founded in 1147 and secularised in 1802. The exterior is still Romanesque, but the choir was remodelled in Baroque style in 1740–45 and decorated with stuccowork by craftsmen from Wessobrunn. Renaissance choir-stalls (1534); remains of a Late Romanesque cloister (early 13th c.). In the churchyard is the little Romanesque St John's Chapel. *Steingaden

5km/3 miles south-east of Steingaden, set against the backdrop of the Ammergau Hills in the Alpine foreland, is the widely famed Wieskirche or Kirche in der Wies ("Church in the Meadow"). This pilgrimage church, built 1746–54, is the finest achievement of the great Baroque architect Dominikus Zimmermann and one of the maturest creations of German Rococo architecture. *Wieskirche
The interior, with its consummate assimilation of architecture and decoration, creates a magnificent effect of light and space. A porch leads into the oval nave with its shallow-vaulted roof, in which eight columns form a kind of ambulatory. The choir, with the much

Wieskirche

revered image of the Scourging of Christ on the altar, is narrow and elongated, and is also surrounded by an ambulatory. The sumptuous stucco ornament and ceiling paintings were the work of Johann Baptist Zimmermann, the architect's brother. Dominikus Zimmermann himself spent the last years of his life in the nearby inn run by his son.

Bad Gandersheim   E 5

Land: Lower Saxony
Altitude: 125m/410ft
Population: 12,000

Situation and characteristics

Bad Gandersheim is a well known brine spa (recommended for rheumatism, gynaecological disorders, children's diseases and ailments of the respiratory organs) in the Leinebergland (see entry), between the Harz and the Solling plateau. It is famed as the home of Roswitha of Gandersheim, Germany's first woman writer.

The Town

*Stiftskirche

The town is dominated by the 11th century Romanesque Stiftskirche, now a Cathedral, with a richly furnished interior. Immediately east of the church are the abbey buildings (*c.* 1600), with a beautiful Renaissance gable and the Imperial Hall (1753). In front of it is the Roswitha Fountain (1978).

Town Hall

Nearby is the Markt, surrounded by half-timbered houses, with the Town Hall (Rathaus), a charming Renaissance building which incorporates the Moritzkirche (St Maurice's Church). In the Town Hall is the Heimatmuseum.

Bracken

Also in the Markt is the Bracken, the town's oldest burgher's house (1473).

St George's Church

The Georgskirche (St George's Church; 1550) on the west side of the town has a Romanesque tower and a flat timber roof decorated with carving.

Spa installations

1km/¾ mile north of the town centre are the modern spa installations, with the Kurhaus and a forest swimming pool (brine bath).

Einbeck

15km/9 miles south-west is the little town of Einbeck, once a Hanseatic city, with remains of its old fortifications and many 16th century half-timbered houses. The establishment of a brewery here in 1378 brought the town great prosperity.

Old town

In the Markt stands the Town Hall (Rathaus; 1550–56), with a half-timbered upper floor and three slate-roofed towers. Opposite it is the Marktkirche or Jacobikirche (Market Church, St James's Church; 13th c.; west end altered in Late Baroque style). Farther north is the Münsterkirche or Alexanderstiftskirche (14th–15th c.).
At the corner of Marktstrasse and Knochenhauerstrasse can be seen the Eickesches Haus (*c.* 1600), one of the town's finest half-timbered buildings. At the end of Marktstrasse is the Neustädtische Kirche or Marienkirche (New Town Church, St Mary's Church; 15th–16th c.).

To the east of the town is the Gothic St Bartholomew's Chapel, with the tomb of Friedrich Sertümer (1783–1841), discoverer of morphine, who was a chemist in Einbeck from 1806 to 1820.

Garmisch-Partenkirchen   M 6

Land: Bavaria
Altitude: 720m/2360ft
Population: 27,000

Garmisch-Partenkirchen, on the Deutsche Alpenstrasse (see entry), is one of the busiest tourist and holiday places in the Bavarian Alps (see entry), a well known climatic resort and the leading German winter sports resort. The Winter Olympics of 1936 and the International Alpine Skiing Championships of 1978 were staged here.

The wide valley of the Loisach is enclosed by mighty mountain massifs – to the north Kramer and the Wank, to the south the towering Wetterstein group, with the Kreuzeck, the jagged Alpspitze and the Dreitorspitze, and, rearing up behind the Grosser Waxenstein, the Zugspitze, Germany's highest mountain (2963m/9722ft).

Situation and characteristics

Garmisch

Garmisch, with its picturesque old houses (particularly in Frühlingstrasse), lies on the banks of the Loisach, beyond the railway. In Richard-Strauss-Platz is the Kongresshaus, set in the Kurpark.

The New Parish Church (Neue Pfarrkirche; St Martin's), built by Josef Schmuzer (1730–33), has a rich Baroque interior (Wessobrunn stucco-work). The Old Parish Church (Alte Pfarrkirche; 15th–16th c.) has remains of Gothic wall painting.

Parish church

Near the Zugspitze station (Zugspitzbahnhof) is the Olympic Ice Stadium (Olympia-Eisstadion) and at Zöppritzstrasse 42, beyond the Loisach, the Richard Strauss Villa, home of the composer who died in Garmisch in 1949.

Ice Stadium

Partenkirchen

In Partenkirchen, the eastern part of the town, lying between the river Partnach and the Wank, are the handsome Town Hall (Rathaus; 1935) and the Werdenfelser Heimatmuseum (Ludwigstrasse 47).

From Florianplatz there is a superb view of the Zugspitze massif to the south.

*View

A 15-minute walk above the town brings the visitor to the St Anton gardens (fine views), with the pilgrimage church of St Anton (1704; ceiling painting by J. E. Holzer, stucco ornament).

St Anton

South of Partenkirchen, on the Gudiberg, is the Olympic Ski Stadium (Olympia-Skistadion),with two Olympic ski-jumps. Nearby is the lower station of the Eckbauerbahn (see below).

Ski Stadium

*Cableways

From the Olympic Ski Stadium in Partenkirchen up the Eckbauerhöhe (1236m/4055ft; fine panoramic views).

Eckbauerbahn

From the entrance to the Partnachklamm (see below) to the Alpenhotel Forsthaus Graseck (903m/2963ft).

Graseckbahn

Cableway (large cabins) from Garmisch up the Hausberghöhe (1347m/4420ft), from which the Kreuzwanklbahn continues to the Kreuzwankln (1550m/5086ft).

Hausbergbahn

Cableway (large cabins) from Garmisch up the Kreuzeck (1650m/5415ft); fine views, particularly of the nearby Alpspitze.

Kreuzeckbahn

Osterfelderbahn	Cableway (large cabins) from Garmisch up the Osterfelderkopf (2050m/6725ft). From there cableway (large cabins) to the Hochalm (1700m/5600ft).
Wankbahn	Cableway (small cabins) from Partenkirchen, 3000m/3300yds long, to an upper station on the Wank at 1755m/5760ft. From the summit (1780m/5840ft) there is a magnificent view of the Garmisch basin.

**Zugspitze

Cableways	There are three routes to the summit of the Zugspitze: The Bayerische Zugspitzbahn, built 1928–30, is a masterpiece of railway engineering. As far as Grainau it runs on ordinary rails; from there a rack railway goes up to the Schneefernerhaus (2650m/8695ft); and the final stage is a cableway (large cabins) to the summit station at 2950m/9680ft. From the Eibsee a cableway (large cabins) runs direct to the summit station. In Austria, the Tiroler Zugspitzbahn, a cableway, takes its passengers up to the summit ridge from Obermoos, near Ehrwald (23km/14 miles by road from Garmisch; frontier crossing).
The summit	The upper station of the Bayerische Zugspitzbahn is on the eastern summit; the platform on the top of its tower is the highest point in Germany (2966m/9731ft). On the nearby western summit (2963m/9722ft) are the Münchner Haus (1897) and a weather station. On the eastern summit is a gilded iron cross (2962m/9718ft; only for those with a good head for heights). The Zugspitze is known to have been climbed by surveyors in 1820, but was probably climbed earlier by local people. From the summit there are magnificent views in all directions – to the south the Central Alps, from the Hohe Tauern to Silvretta, with Furchetta (Dolomites to the rear, and Ortler and Bernina; to the west the Lechtal and Allgäu Alps, with Tödi and Säntis in the distance; to the north the Alpine foreland with its lakes; to the east Karwendel, the Tegernsee and the Kitzbühel Alps, the Watzmann and Dachstein.
Zugspitzplatt	The Schneefernerhaus (see above) stands on the northern edge of the Zugspitzplatt, the highest skiing area in Germany (7.2 sq.km/2¾ sq. miles), with the best snow. There are several ski-lifts.

Surroundings of Garmisch-Partenkirchen

*Partnachklamm	3km/2 miles south-east is the wild and romantic Partnachklamm, a rocky gorge on the river Partnach, with tunnels and galleries.
*Höllentalklamm	6km/4 miles south-west of Garmisch-Partenkirchen is the Höllentalklammhütte (1045m/3429ft), from which there is a track (1km/¾ mile), with numerous tunnels and bridges, to the end of the gorge.
Grainau Eibsee	South-west of Garmisch-Partenkirchen the village of Grainau lies in rolling park-like country at the foot of the Waxensteine, which are separated from the Loisach valley by the Höhenrain (extensive views). Higher up is the Eibsee, from which there is a good view of the Waxenstein and the Riffelwand on the Zugspitze. (Cableway to summit of Zugspitze: see above.)

Gelsenkirchen   F 2

Land: North Rhine-Westphalia
Altitude: 28m/92ft
Population: 283,000

The industrial metropolis of Gelsenkirchen, on the Rhine-Herne Canal, is the centre of the Emscher Lippe region. In the past the dominant elements in the economy were coal-mining and heavy industry, but there is now also a considerable textile industry. Increased efforts are being made to promote the establishment of small and medium-sized firms.

Situation and characteristics

City Centre

Notable buildings in the central area are the Hans-Sachs-Haus (Town Hall), built of clinker brick, and the Music Theatre with its great areas of glass wall.

Theatre

In the northern district of Bismarck, on the Rhine-Herne Canal, is the Ruhr Zoo, with more than 1000 animals, African and South American steppes, etc.

Ruhr Zoo

Buer

The city is well supplied with parks and gardens. In the northern district of Buer is a green belt, with the Berger See, a moated house (Haus Berge) and the Parkstadion, a stadium with seating for 70,000 spectators.

Parkstadion

In Horster Strasse can be found the Municipal Museum (Städtisches Museum; modern art, from Realism to the present day).

Museum

Horst

In the western district of Horst lies Nienhausen Park (30 hectares/75 acres), a recreation area with a "Leisure House" (Freizeithaus), a swimming pool (artificial waves), sports facilities and play areas. To the north-west is the Gelsentrab trotting track (1203m/1316yds long).

Nienhausen Park

Gelsentrab

Gera

G 7

Land: Thuringia
Altitude: 204m/669ft
Population: 131,000

The Thuringian town of Gera, 50km/30 miles south of Leipzig, lies on the middle course of the Weisse Elster, at the intersection of important traffic routes.

Situation and characteristics

Sights

The Markt, surrounded by buildings homogeneous in style, is one of the finest market squares in Thuringia. The most striking building in the square is the Town Hall (Rathaus; 16th c., rebuilt 1573–76 after destruction), with a Baroque mansard roof, a tall and elegant tower over the main entrance and three subsidiary entrances.
Another notable old building in the square, the 16th century Municipal Pharmacy (Stadtapotheke), has a richly decorated Renaissance oriel window.
In the centre of the square is the Samson Fountain (Simsonbrunnen; by C. Junghans, 1685–86).

*Markt
*Town Hall

A few paces from the Town Hall can be seen the old Regierungsgebäude (Government Building), a three-storey Baroque building originally erected in 1720–22 and rebuilt after a fire in 1780, incorporating some 16th c. work (north wing). The central range is four-storeyed, articulated by pilasters and a triangular pediment.

Regierungsgebäude

Near the old Regierungsgebäude, at Strasse der Republik 2, is a three-storey Baroque building of 1732–38 (much restored), originally a prison and orphanage, which is now occupied by the History Museum (Museum für Geschichte).

History Museum

Giessen

St Salvator's Church	Near the Town Hall stands the Salvatorkirche (St Salvator's Church; Baroque, 1717–20), with a flat painted ceiling. In the aisles are double galleries, with interesting decoration and furnishings (c. 1900).
Natural History Museum	Adjoining the church is the Schreibersches Haus, a three-storey Baroque building (1687–88) with a richly decorated Baroque hall. It now houses the Natural History Museum (Museum für Naturkunde), with collections on the life and work of five Thuringian ornithologists (Brehm father and son, Liebe, Hennicke and Engelmann).
Trinity Church, St Mary's Church	Two notable Gothic buildings are the Trinity Church (Trinitatiskirche), an aisleless, basically Gothic, church with a three-storey closed choir (flat painted ceiling), and the parish church of St Mary, also aisleless (Late Gothic, c. 1400).
Burghers' houses	Among the finest burghers' houses in the town are the Ferbersches Haus at Greizer Strasse 37–39, now occupied by the Museum of Applied Art (Museum für Kunsthandwerk); the Haus J. Buttermann (18th c.), with sculptural decoration on the doorway; a Baroque house at Steinweg 15; and the Schreibersches Haus (see above).
Orangery *Otto Dix Exhibition	The Orangery, a semicircular Baroque building (1729–32) north-west of the city centre, now houses the Gera Art Gallery and a permanent exhibition of works by the Gera-born painter Otto Dix (1891–1969).

Surroundings of Gera

Wünschendorf	10km/6 miles south of Gera is Wünschendorf, with the Veitskirche (St Vitus's Church), which is basically Early Romanesque, and a covered wooden bridge of 1786. In the Mildenfurth district is a former monastic church (1193) which was converted into a hunting lodge after 1617; there are still some remains of the original basilica.
Weida	Schloss Osterburg (basically Romanesque), 13km/8 miles south on B 92 in Weida, has a massive keep, a guard-room and a Heimatmuseum. Other features of interest in the town are the Renaissance Town Hall, the "plague pulpit" (1608) in the old churchyard (1564), a Renaissance doorway (1580) and a number of 17th and 18th century tombs.

Giessen

Land: Hesse
Altitude: 157m/515ft
Population: 75,000

Situation and characteristics	This old university town on the Lahn, in the wide Giessen basin, is the largest town in central Hesse, with a number of important industrial plants. The great chemist Justus von Liebig, the originator of nitrogenous fertilisers and inventor of meat extract, lived and taught here from 1824 to 1852.

The Town

Altes Schloss	In Brandplatz stands the Altes Schloss (14th c.; destroyed 1944, rebuilt 1980), now housing the picture gallery and department of applied art of the Upper Hesse Museum (furniture, sculpture, ceramics, painting from the Gothic period to the 20th century). There are other sections of the Museum in the Burgmannenhaus and Wallenfels'sche Haus (see below).
Botanic Garden	Adjoining the Altes Schloss is the Botanic Garden (1609), the oldest of its kind in Germany.
Neues Schloss	To the north-east can be found the Neues Schloss, a handsome 16th century half-timbered building. Beside it is the Zeughaus (Arsenal; 1590, renovated 1958–62).

In Georg-Schlosser-Strasse, on the west side of the city centre, are two other sections of the Upper Hesse Museum: in the Burgmannshaus the department of local history and folk traditions (arts and crafts, costumes, furniture), and in the neighbouring Wallenfels'sches Haus the department of prehistory, the early historical period and ethnography (Stone and Bronze Ages, Roman colonisation, the great migrations; Far East, Africa, America, Australia, Oceania).

Burgmannshaus
Wallenfels'sches
Haus

Farther south, at Liebigstrasse 12, is the former Chemical Institute, now occupied by the Liebig Museum, with the great chemist's original laboratories and a collection of documents.

Liebig Museum

Gifhorn   D 6

Land: Lower Saxony
Altitude: 54m/177ft
Population: 36,000

Gifhorn is situated in the low-lying valley of the river Aller, which is joined here by the Ise. First mentioned in the records as a town in 1370, it prospered as a result of its situation on the "salt road" from Lüneburg to Braunschweig and the "grain road" from Magdeburg to Celle.

Situation and
characteristics

The Town

In and around the Marktplatz are a number of 16th and 17th century half-timbered buildings, including the Old Town Hall (Ratskeller and Municipal Archives) of 1562.

Marktplatz

North-east of the Marktplatz stands the old Guelph Schloss, built for Duke Franz in the mid 16th century, with a beautiful chapel. It is now occupied by the District Heimatmuseum.

Schloss

South of the Schloss is St Nicholas's Church (1734–44), with a Baroque altar.

St Nicholas's
Church

North-east of the Schloss are the Schloss-see and the Mühlensee. In this area is the International Mill Museum (Mühlenmuseum), with six historic old windmills and watermills and an exhibition hall (models of windmills).

*Mill Museum

Hankensbüttel

30km/20 miles north of Gifhorn, in a park-like area of woodland and heath, we come to Hankensbüttel. Features of interest in this little town are the Wulff Hunting Museum in the Oerrel district, the 14th century Isenhagen Convent (now a Protestant house of retreat for women) and the Otter Centre (otters, martens, etc.) on the Isenhagener See.

The Preussenzug, a nostalgic old steam train, runs between Hankensbüttel and Brome during the summer.

Steam train

Göppingen   K 5

Land: Baden-Württemberg
Altitude: 318m/1043ft
Population: 52,000

Göppingen lies in the beautiful foreland of the Swabian Alb (see entry). The town was held by the Hohenstaufens from the 12th century until 1319. It was ravaged by great fires in 1425 and 1782, and thereafter was almost completely rebuilt. It is now a considerable industrial town (metalworking, chemicals, textiles, toys).

Situation and
characteristics

The Town

Schloss	Opposite the Stadtkirche (Town Church; by H. Schickhardt, 1618–19; interior remodelled in Baroque style) is the Schloss (1559–69), with the richly ornamented Rebenstiege.
Municipal Museum	To the south of the Hauptstrasse is the Storchen, a little 16th century half-timbered mansion, now housing the Municipal Museum (Städtisches Museum; finds from the Hohenstaufen period).
Märklin Museum	South-east of the town centre, near the open-air swimming pool, can be found the Märklin Museum, with old and modern model railways.
Faurndau Stiftskirche	In the western district of Faurndau is a Romanesque Stiftskirche (early 13th c. frescoes).
Natural History Museum	In the south-western district of Jebenhausen, in the old Badhaus of 1610, stands the Natural History Museum (Naturkundliches Museum; fossils from the Swabian Jura).

Surroundings of Göppingen

Kaiserberge	North-east of the town rise the three "Kaiserberge" (imperial hills) of Hohenstaufen (684m/2244ft), Rechberg (707m/2320ft) and Stuifen (757m/2484ft). This was the territory of the Hohenstaufens, in their day one of Europe's most powerful ruling families. On the Hohenstaufen can be seen remains of their ancestral castle, destroyed during the 16th century Peasant War. There is also a ruined castle on the Rechberg.
Lorch	North of Göppingen by way of Wäschenbeuren (near which is the attractive little Wäscherschlössle) is Lorch, with a Late Gothic church built on the site of a fort on the Limes (the Roman frontier defence line). Above the town is the old Lorch monastery, with a Romanesque church (tombs of members of the Hohenstaufen dynasty).
Welzheim	There are other remains of the Limes in the little town of Welzheim, north-west of Lorch: the partly reconstructed East Fort (Ostkastell) and the Rötelsee fort. An open-air Limes Museum is in course of development.

Görlitz · F 10

Land: Saxony
Altitude: 221m/725ft
Population: 79,200

Situation and characteristics	Görlitz (Sorbian Zhorjelc) lies on the river Neisse, exactly on the 15th degree of eastern longitude. It owes its present importance to the two important frontier crossings into Poland over the Neisse and to its industries (manufacture of goods wagons, engineering, electronic and optical apparatus).

Postplatz and Demianiplatz

	The streets and buildings around the Postplatz, in the modern town centre, date mainly from the late 19th century. The only medieval building is the Late Gothic Frauenkirche (Church of Our Lady; 1459–86).
Dicker Turm	Near the Warenhaus (department store) stands the Dicker Turm (Stout Tower; before 1305), with the town coat of arms carved in sandstone (1477). To the left is the Annenkapelle (St Anne's Chapel; 1508–12), with a series of Late Gothic statues.
* Kaisertrutz	To the north, in Demianiplatz, are the Kaisertrutz, a massive round tower (1490), now housing a section of the Municipal Museum on the history of the town, and the handsome Reichenbacher Turm (before 1376; upper part 1485, Baroque roof 1782), with the

arms of the Lusatian League of Six Cities, of which Görlitz was a member; in this tower is another section of the Museum.

Obermarkt

To the east of the two towers lies the old Obermarkt (Upper Market). On the north side of the square (No. 29) is a Baroque house of 1718 with a riot of sculptural decoration on its colossal pilasters.

On the south side of the Obermarkt stands the Trinity Church (Dreifaltigkeitskirche; choir 1371–81, nave 15th c.). Notable among its Late Gothic furnishings are the monks' stalls (1484), an "Entombment" (1492), a figure of Christ resting (*c.* 1500), an altar with the "Golden Virgin" (*c.* 1511) and a High Baroque reredos.
Brüderstrasse, which leaves the west corner of the Obermarkt, is lined with handsome Renaissance and Baroque buildings.

Trinity Church

On the right-hand side of Brüderstrasse (No. 8), projecting slightly into the street, is the Schönhof, with a corner oriel richly articulated by pilasters, which is believed to be the oldest burgher's house in Germany (by W. Roskopf the Elder, 1526).

Schönhof

*Untermarkt

The Untermarkt (Lower Market), which was the heart of medieval Görlitz, is also surrounded by Late Gothic, Renaissance and Baroque buildings. Several of the houses (Nos. 2, 3, 4, 5, 22) preserve interiors characteristic of great merchants' houses during the town's economic heyday between 1480 and 1547. On the east side of the square are the Late Gothic Lange Lauben (Long Arcades), once the shops of cloth merchants, and a Baroque house, the Brauner Hirsch. On the north side is the old Ratsapotheke (Municipal Pharmacy; 1550), with a double sundial, a house at No. 22 with a Late Gothic doorway known as the "Whispering Arch" (Flüsterbogen) and a Renaissance house of 1536 at No. 23.

On the west side of the square is the Town Hall (Rathaus), built in several phases. The most recent extension is the New Town Hall (1902–03). The oldest part is at the south end (before 1378), with W. Roskopf's famous external staircase (Justice Column, 1591; coat of arms, 1488, of King Matthias Corvinus, who for a time held Lusatia) and the tower, with two historic old clocks (1584). The Untermarkt is divided into a northern and a southern half by a range of Renaissance and Baroque buildings known as the Zeile occupying the site of the original 13th century town hall.

*Town Hall

There are a number of notable buildings in the old streets to the east of the Untermarkt. At Neiss-strasse 30 is a building with a magnificent Baroque doorway (1726–29) which now houses the Municipal Art Collections (Städtische Kunstsammlungen). At Neiss-strasse 29 is the "Biblical House" (1570), with reliefs of Old and New Testament scenes, one of the finest examples of German Renaissance architecture.

Municipal
Art Collections

The most interesting Early Renaissance house in Görlitz is at Peterstrasse 8 (by W. Roskopf the Elder, 1528).

Parish Church of SS Peter and Paul

In the north-east of the old town can be found the most imposing medieval building in Görlitz, the parish church of SS Peter and Paul (1423–97), the Late Gothic successor to a Late Romanesque basilica of around 1230. It has Renaissance porches on the side doorways and two neo-Gothic towers (1889–91). St George's Crypt ranks as the finest Late Gothic interior in Upper Lusatia.

Nearby are the fortress-like Waidhaus or Renthaus, the town's oldest secular building, and the compact Vogtshof (now occupied by a boarding school) on the steep slope down to the river Neisse, built in the early 19th century on the site of an old castle.

Waidhaus

237

Nikolaivorstadt

St Nicholas's Church

To the north of the old town, beyond the Nikolaiturm (St Nicholas's Tower; before 1348) is the Nikolaivorstadt, the site of the earliest settlement, with the Nikolaikirche (St Nicholas's Church; present building 1452–1520) and its churchyard, the Nikolaifriedhof (many Baroque monuments, including the tomb of the philosopher Jacob Böhme).

Holy Sepulchre

In the west of the Nikolaivorstadt is the Heiliges Grab (Holy Sepulchre; 1481–1504), a copy of the Holy Sepulchre in Jerusalem, with representations of the scenes of Christ's Passion.

Surroundings of Görlitz

*Landskrone

To the south-west of the town is the Landskrone (420m/1378ft), with an outlook tower, a restaurant and a monument commemorating the early 19th century writer Theodor Körner.

Goslar   E 5

Land: Lower Saxony
Altitude: 320m/1050ft
Population: 50,000

Situation and characteristics

This old imperial city on the northern fringes of the Harz (see entry) owed its origin in the 10th century to the discovery of a rich vein of silver on the Rammelsberg, and as a free imperial city it reached its peak of power and prosperity in the early 16th century. It still preserves most of the old town walls built at that time, with their massive gates and towers, its medieval churches, the Kaiserpfalz (imperial palace) and many handsome half-timbered buildings – an attractive townscape which survived the Second World War unscathed.

*Old Town

Markt

In the old-world Markt is the Marktbecken, a fountain with two bronze basins and a gilded imperial eagle added in the 13th century as a symbol of Goslar's status as a free imperial city.

Town Hall

On the west side of the square stands the Town Hall (Rathaus), the main part of which dates from the 15th century. On the upper floor is the magnificent 16th century Huldigungssaal (Hall of Homage), with Late Gothic wall and ceiling paintings and carved woodwork (Gospel book of 1320, silver ewer of 1477).

Kaiserworth

On the south side of the square is the Kaiserworth (1494), the old guild-house of the tailors' guild, with eight 17th century statues of emperors. At the left-hand corner is the figure of the "Dukatenmännchen" ("Ducat Man").

Goslar Museum

From here Worthstrasse leads to the Goslar Museum (history of the town, geology and fauna of the Harz; mining; works of art from the old cathedral).

Marktkirche
Brusttuch

To the west of the Town Hall stands the Late Romanesque Marktkirche (Market Church). Opposite it is the west front of the Brusttuch, a burgher's house of 1526 with rich carved decoration.
Near here is the Bäckergildenhaus (Bakers' Guild-House; 1501–57). Farther west is the Siemenshaus (1693), ancestral home of the Siemens family of industrialists.

Tin Figure Museum

In Münzstrasse, which runs north from the Marktkirche, can be found the Tin Figure Museum (Zinnfigurenmuseum; dioramas, etc.).

*Kaiserpfalz

Towards the south of the old town, in the large square called Kaiserbleek, is the Kaiserpfalz, the oldest surviving Romanesque palace in Germany, built in the reign of Emperor Henry III (1017–56). The 47m/154ft long Reichssaal (Imperial Hall) has wall paintings

Goslar

Kaiserpfalz, Goslar

(1879–97) by Hermann Wislicenus. In St Ulrich's Chapel is Henry's tomb, with his heart in a casket in the base.

To the east of the Kaiserpfalz is the Domkapelle (Cathedral Chapel; *c.* 1150), originally the porch of Goslar Cathedral, which was demolished in 1820–22. It contains the imperial throne with its surrounding stone screens (11th c.). — Domkapelle

A little way north, on the Hoher Weg, are the Doll and Musical Instrument Museum (Puppen- und Musikinstrumente-Museum) and the Grosses Heiliges Kreuz, an old religious house (founded as the Hospital of St John in 1254), with an exhibition of arts and crafts. — Grosses Heiliges Kreuz

To the north of the Markt is the Jakobikirche (St James's Church; 11th–16th c.; R.C.), with a fine Pietà (*c.* 1525). To the west of this are the Mönchehaus (Monks' House), a half-timbered building of 1528 now occupied by the Museum of Modern Art (Museum für moderne Kunst), and the Neuwerkkirche, a monastic church founded in 1186 (fine wall paintings in choir). Opposite this is the Achtermannsturm, all that remains of one of the old town gates, the Rosentor. — St James's Church / Museum of Modern Art

Other relics of the past on the line of the old fortifications are the Breites Tor (1505) on the east side of the town; the Zwinger, a round tower built in 1517 (medieval armoury and torture chamber), to the south-east; and the Romanesque Frankenberg Church (12th c.; wall paintings) to the west. — Town walls

Above the town to the south-east rises the Rammelsberg (636m/2087ft), with the Roeder mine-shaft (conducted visit). — Rammelsberg

Surroundings of Goslar

3km/2 miles north-west is Riechenberg Monastery, a former house of Augustinian canons, with the ruins of the monastic church of St Mary (12th c.; crypt with ornamented columns and capitals). — Riechenberg

239

Grauhof

In Grauhof, 4km/2½ miles north, is an 18th century Baroque church with a richly decorated interior.

°Oker valley

6km/4 miles south-east lies the Okertal, a wild and romantic valley with magnificent rock scenery and the Romkerhall Falls.

Gotha   G 6

Land: Thuringia
Altitude: 270m/885ft
Population: 57,800

Situation and characteristics

The former princely capital of Gotha lies in the northern foreland of the Thuringian Forest between Eisenach and Erfurt. One of the oldest towns in Thuringia, it rose to prosperity in the Middle Ages with its trade in woad and corn and became the home of leading humanists and teachers and of Conrad Ekhof (1720–78), the "father of acting in Germany".

*Schloss Friedenstein

The town is dominated by the imposing Schloss Friedenstein (1643–54), a huge Early Baroque palace (100m/110yds by 140m/155yds) of three wings laid out round a central courtyard, with a handsome interior (Baroque, Rococo, neo-classical). Built on the site of the earlier castle of Grimmenstein, it provided a model for other palaces in Thuringia and beyond. It has been extensively restored in recent years.

Within the palace complex are a church, with a burial vault containing the magnificent sarcophagi of the rulers of Gotha, and a theatre (Ekhoftheater), one of the oldest surviving Baroque theatres in Germany.

The Schlossmuseum posesses rich art treasures (including "The Lovers of Gotha", the earliest German double portrait, and works by Dutch masters), a collection of 100,000 coins and collections of antiquities and Chinese art.

Library
Folk Museum

Also in Schloss Friedenstein are a research library, with over half a million volumes as well as 5500 European and 3300 Oriental manuscripts, and the Museum of Regional History and Folk Art (Museum für Regionalgeschichte und Volkskunst), with collections of textiles, musical instruments and weapons.

*Cartographic Museum

In the old Pagenhaus (Pages' House) is the Cartographic Museum (established 1985), the only one of its kind in Europe, which illustrates Gotha's famed mapmaking traditions.

Museum of Nature

To the south of the Schloss is the Museum of Nature (Museum der Natur), in French neo-Renaissance style.

Park

Round the Schloss lies a landscaped park laid out in 1770. From in front of the palace there is a fine view of the town. To the right is a massive monument in honour of Landgrave Ernest I, and to the left of this the Wasserkunst, a neo-Baroque decorative channel (1892) for the Leina Canal (constructed in the 14th c.).

The Town

*Town Hall

At the foot of the Hauptmarkt stands the Town Hall (Rathaus; 1567–77; recently restored), a handsome Renaissance building which was originally a Merchants' Hall, later a princely residence and from 1665 the Town Hall. It has a charming Baroque fountain. On either side of the square are handsome old burghers' houses.

Lucas Cranach House

On the east side of the square can be seen the Lucas Cranach House (18th c., with an earlier doorway; commemorative plaque).

Hospital of Mary Magdalene

Nearby, on the Brühl, is the Hospital of Mary Magdalene, founded in the 18th century on the site of an earlier hospital probably built by St Elizabeth of Hungary, with a Baroque doorway crowned by figural sculpture.

Hauptmarkt and Town Hall

In Klosterplatz are the Augustinian church and convent (richly furnished interior, Baroque pulpit, Gothic relief carving). In the picturesque cloister are the grave-slabs of well known figures.
Augustinian Church

In the Neumarkt stands the Margaretenkirche (St Margaret's Church), a Late Gothic hall-church remodelled in Baroque style in the 17th and 18th centuries and rebuilt after suffering heavy damage in the Second World War. The tower is 65m/213ft high.
St Margaret's Church

Surroundings of Gotha

Within easy reach of Gotha is the Grosser Inselsberg (916m/3005ft), in the Thuringian Forest (nature reserve; superb views).
*Grosser Inselsberg

14km/8½ miles south-west we come to the old Thuringian doll-making town of Waltershausen, with Schloss Tenneberg (first mentioned in the records in 1176; present building 16th c.), which contains a Heimatmuseum (history of doll-making in Waltershausen). In the Markt stands the Gotteshilfkirche (1719–23), a large Baroque church on a central plan.
Waltershausen

Near Friedrichroda is the Marienglashöhle, a cave containing rare colourless crystals (guided visits).
*Marienglashöhle

15km/9 miles south is Ohrdruf, where St Boniface, the "Apostle of the Germans", began his mission in Thuringia with the foundation of a monastery. Schloss Ehrenstein (1550–90) is a Renaissance palace (restored 1976 onwards) with a richly decorated doorway and a massive tower, once the residence of the Counts von Gleichen. Heimatmuseum (palls, Gotha caps); fine Rococo hall.
Ohrdruf

The Tobiashammer is an example of early metalworking technology – a forge established in 1634 which in the 18th century became a copper rolling-mill, with three water-powered hammers.
Tobiashammer

Georgenthal
Georgenthal, 17km/10½ miles south has the remains of a Cistercian monastery founded in 1155. In the Late Gothic Kornhaus is a Heimatmuseum. North-west of the monastery is a Renaissance Schloss. The village church (Late Romanesque) has a richly decorated organ-case (18th c.).

Bad Langensalza
18km/11 miles north is Bad Langensalza, chief town of a district and a spa (sulphurous water) since 1812. It has a picturesque old town with restored burghers' houses (decorated façades, carved doorways). In Schloss-strasse is the Klopstock House, in which the 18th century poet Friedrich Gottlieb Klopstock, author of the "Messiah", stayed in 1748–50. In the Markt are the Baroque Town Hall (1742–52) and the Market Fountain (1582). There are two Late Gothic churches, St Boniface's (14th–15th c.) and St Stephen's (founded 1398; rich interior). In Thälmannplatz is a Heimatmuseum. A little Baroque palace, Friederikenschlösschen (1749–50), is now occupied by a club. Of the old fortifications (12th–14th c.) there survive seventeen towers and one town gate, the Klagetor ("Wailing Gate").

Göttingen   F 5

Land: Lower Saxony
Altitude: 150m/500ft
Population: 138,000

Situation and characteristics
Göttingen, in the Leine valley, is one of the German university towns with the richest heritage of tradition, and many Nobel Prize winners have studied or taught here. The old town, with many half-timbered buildings, is surrounded by a ring of gardens on the line of its old walls.

Sights

Old Town Hall "Gänseliesel"
In the centre of the old town, in the Markt, stands the Old Town Hall (Altes Rathaus; 1369–1443), now a cultural centre, with a fine Great Hall (wall paintings by Hermann Schaper, 1853–1911). In front of it is the graceful Gänseliesel-Brunnen ("Goose Lizzie" Fountain; 1901). The figure of the goose-girl on the fountain is "the most-kissed girl in Germany", since tradition requires that every new-fledged graduate must kiss her on the mouth.

St John's Church
The Johanniskirche (St John's Church; 14th c.), the town's oldest church, situated to the west of the Old Town Hall has a Romanesque north doorway. The two towers have different types of roof; from the north tower there are fine panoramic views.

University Library
To the north-west is the Municipal and University Library (Universitätsbibliothek), with some 3 million volumes and a collection of manuscripts.

St Mary's Church
South-west of the Library stands the Marienkirche (St Mary's Church), formerly the church of the Teutonic Order (begun c. 1300), with an altar of 1524.

St James's Church
In Weender Strasse, Göttingen's principal shopping street (partly pedestrianised), which bisects the town centre from north to south, is the Gothic Jacobikirche (St James's Church; 14th c.), with a 74m/243ft high west tower of 1426 and a beautiful carved altar of 1402.

Barfüsserstrasse
North-east of the Markt, in Barfüsserstrasse, are the old Ratsapotheke (Municipal Pharmacy), a handsome half-timbered building of 1553; the Junkernschänke (No. 5; rebuilt 1547–49, with a richly decorated façade); and the Bornemannsches Haus of 1536 (No. 12; Early Renaissance, with Gothic elements).

Aula
St Alban's Church
Farther east, in Wilhelmsplatz, is the neo-classical Aula (Great Hall) of the University (1835–37). In the pediment is sculpture by Ernst von Bandel (1800-76), who also created the Hermannsdenkmal (see Detmold, Surroundings). Just east of this are the Albanikirche (St Alban's Church; 15th c.), with a winged altar of 1499, and the Stadthalle (1964).

Beyond this again, on the Reinsgraben, can be found the department of urban archaeology of the Municipal Museum (see below).

To the north, on the line of the old town walls, lies Theaterplatz, with the Deutsches Theater (1890) and the University's Ethnographic Collection. Farther north is the Botanic Garden.

Theaterplatz

To the west of the Theatre, on the Ritterplan, is the Hardenberger Hof (1592), the town's only Renaissance palace, with the Municipal Museum (Städtisches Museum).

Municipal Museum

The Auditorium Maximum (1862–65) on the northern edge of the town centre houses the University's Art Collection.

Auditorium Maximum

On the south side of the town centre, in Turmstrasse, can be seen a stretch of the old 13th century town walls. In this area too are two old mills, the Odilienmühle and the Lohmühle, and the Bismarckhäuschen, an old bastion in which Otto von Bismarck lived as a student in 1832–33.

Town walls

Surroundings of Göttingen

17km/10½ miles east of Göttingen is Ebergötzen, where Wilhelm Busch lived during his childhood and, with his friend Erich Bachmann, played the pranks which later provided the material for his story about Max and Moritz. There are mementoes of Busch in the Wilhelm-Busch-Mühle.

Ebergötzen

Greifswald

B 8

Land: Mecklenburg-West Pomerania
Altitude: 6m/20ft
Population: 68,000

The old Hanseatic town of Greifswald lies 5km/3 miles west of the outflow of the river Ryck into the Greifswalder Bodden, an offshoot of the Baltic. For centuries the town played an important part in maritime trade. The patriotic poet Ernst Moritz Arndt and the painter Caspar David Friedrich lived and worked in Greifswald.

Situation and characteristics

Sights

In the centre of the town is the Markt, with the medieval Town Hall (Rathaus), originally built in brick in the 14th century in Gothic style, rebuilt after a fire in 1738–50 and altered in the 19th century and again in 1936, and handsome burghers' houses, also in brick-built Gothic style.

*Markt
Town Hall

A few minutes' walk away, in Theodor-Pyl-Strasse, can be found the residence of the head of a 14th century Franciscan friary. It is now a museum (mementoes of Ernst Moritz Arndt and Caspar David Friedrich).

Museum

Near the Platz der Freundschaft are three churches which feature prominently in the townscape. The oldest of the three, the St-Marien-Kirche (St Mary's; 14th c.), very typical of the churches of Mecklenburg and Pomerania with its brick walls and groined vaulting, is of impressive spatial effect. The chapel of St Anne on the south side of the church was built in the early 15th century. Notable features of the interior are the pulpit (1577; fine intarsia work) and a memorial stone (15th c.) commemorating Burgomaster Heinrich Rubenow, who was murdered in 1462.

St Mary's Church

The Cathedral of St Nicholas (originally 13th c.; east end extended and rebuilt in 14th c.; restored 1980–89), a brick-built Gothic church, dominates the skyline of the town centre with its curving Baroque steeple. It contains a Late Gothic painting of the Virgin with

*Cathedral

seven professors in prayer (presented by Heinrich Rubenow in 1460) and wall paintings of 1420–50.

The Jakobikirche (St James's Church; 13th c.) was rebuilt in the 14th century as a brick-built Gothic hall-church with groined vaulting.	St James's Church
In Rubenowplatz is the Baroque building of the Ernst Moritz Arndt University (1747–50). In front of it is a monument (by F. A. Stüler, 1856) to its founder, Heinrich Rubenow.	University
On the east side of the square stands the old Hospice of St Spiritus (the Holy Ghost), founded in the 13th century, soon after the town was granted its municipal charter, as a home for the old, poor and sick.	*St Spiritus
The town's fortifications, still preserved in part, were mostly built during the siege of Greifswald by Wallenstein in the Thirty Years' War (1627–31). The 17th century Fangelturm in Hafenstrasse was part of the fortifications.	Town walls

Greifswald-Eldena

In the Eldena district are the ruins of Hilda Monastery (founded 1199), a Cistercian house to whose colonising activity the foundation of the town and many other settlements in the surrounding area was due. Dissolved after the Reformation, in 1535, it became a residence of the Dukes of Pomerania; then in 1634 it was presented to the University. After being sacked by Swedish forces in 1637 it fell into decay, and finally was used by the Swedish military authorities as a quarry of building material. In the early 19th century, however, the paintings of Caspar David Friedrich and the artistic sensibility of the Romantic period led to the scheduling of the ruins as an ancient monument in 1828, and steps were then taken for its conservation.

*Hilda Monastery

Wieck

A wooden bascule bridge based on Dutch models (1887) in the neighbouring district of Wieck is a popular tourist attraction. Also of interest are the old fishermen's and sea-captains' houses (some of them thatched with reeds).

*Bascule bridge

Greiz

G 7

Land: Thuringia
Altitude: 250–476m/820–1562ft. Population: 34,000

The town of Greiz lies some 35km/22 miles south of Gera in a long basin in the narrow wooded valley of the Weisse Elster, enclosed by forest-covered ridges of hills. This one-time capital of the little principality of Reuss is known as the "pearl of the Vogtland".

Situation and characteristics

Sights

The town is dominated by the Schlossberg (Castle Hill) and the Oberes Schloss (Upper Castle) which crowns it. Originally medieval, the castle was rebuilt in 1540 after a fire and extended in the 18th century. It consists of a number of irregular ranges of buildings on an almost elliptical plan, with numerous ornamental gables on the east wing. There are some remains of Renaissance interior decoration and some rooms in Baroque and Rococo style. The Schloss is now an outstation of the Weimar State Archives.

*Oberes Schloss

On the right bank of the Elster lies the old town, with the Unteres Schloss (Lower Castle; originally 13th c.; remodelled in neo-classical style in 1802–09 after a fire). Some early 19th century furnishings have been preserved. The annexe, with tower (1885–86), is now occupied by the Heimatmuseum.

Unteres Schloss

◀ *Ruins of the church of Hilda Monastery, Greifswald-Eldena*

Güstrow

Hauptwache	The neo-classical Hauptwache (Guard-House; 1817–19) now houses the tourist information office.
°Summer Palace	In the park, originally laid out around 1650 as a small Baroque pleasure garden and converted about 1800 into a landscaped park in the English style, stands the Summer Palace (Sommerpalais; 1779–89), a three-storey building in early neo-classical style. The palace now houses the "Satiricum" (caricatures and satirical drawings from Hogarth to Daumier and the present day) and collections of books and prints (English mezzotints, prints and woodcuts). The library, originally belonging to the Princes of Reuss, contains some 24,000 volumes, mainly works of the French Enlightenment and the Goethe period.
°Stadtkirche	The Stadtkirche (Town Church) of St Mary, rebuilt in 1820 after a fire, has a neo-classical interior.

Güstrow   C 7

	Land: Mecklenburg-West Pomerania Altitude: 8m/26ft Population: 39,100
Situation and characteristics	Güstrow, once the seat of the Dukes of Mecklenburg-Güstrow, lies 40km/25 miles south of Rostock in the valley of the Nebel. Its great tourist attractions are the Cathedral, the Schloss and the Ernst Barlach Memorial Museum, but it has many other fine old buildings.

Sights

°Schloss	In Franz-Parr-Platz, in the south of the town, stands the Schloss (begun under the direction of Franz Parr in 1558–66; north wing by P. Brandin, 1587–89; east wing completed 1598), the finest Renaissance building in Northern Germany, with an elegantly articulated main front and a richly decorated interior (stucco ceiling ornament, ceiling paintings). Since its complete restoration in 1964–72 the Schloss has been the cultural centre of Güstrow, with the Schlossmuseum (painting, sculpture and applied art by 16th century German, Italian and Dutch masters; collection of antique vases), the Municipal and District Library, a concert hall and Renaissance gardens.
Heilig-Geist-Kapelle	North-east of the Schloss is the Gothic Heilig-Geist-Kapelle (Chapel of the Holy Ghost; 14th c.; much altered 1863), a plain brick building.
Theatre	North-west of the church can be found the neo-classical Ernst Barlach Theatre (1828–29), the oldest theatre in Mecklenburg.
Municipal Museum	In a 17th century Baroque building at Franz-Parr-Platz 7 is the Municipal Museum (Stadtmuseum; history of the region and the town, arts and crafts).
°Cathedral	In the south-west of the town stands the Cathedral of SS. Mary, John the Evangelist and Cecilia (1226–1335, with later additions). Among the most notable features in the interior are the Late Gothic high altar, with panel paintings of scenes from Christ's Passion (c. 1500), the "Güstrower Domapostel" of the Lübeck master C. Berg (c. 1530), a crucifix of around 1370, the epitaph of Duke Ulrich III and his wife and the genealogy of the house of Mecklenburg (by P. Brandin, 1585–99). In the north hall is a bronze sculpture by Barlach, "The Floating Man" (originally 1926–27; melted down 1944; re-cast 1952).
	In the Domplatz are a number of handsome Renaissance houses of the 16th and 17th centuries (Nos. 14, 15/16, 18).
Town Hall	Domstrasse leads to the Markt, which since the 1797–98 rebuilding of the 16th century Town Hall (Rathaus) in neo-classical style has had a unified neo-classical character.
Parish church	The parish church (Stadtpfarrkirche), originally built 1503–22, was altered in the 19th century. It has a Late Gothic winged altar (Bormann Altar, 1522).

Ernst Barlach Memorial Museum, Güstrow

The Gertrudenkapelle (St Gertrude's Chapel; *c.* 1430), north-east of the old town, is now an Ernst Barlach memorial (Gedenkstätte), with important examples of the sculptor's work, including the "Wanderer in the Wind", the "Apostle", the "Doubter", the "Chained Witch" and "Mother Earth".

* *St Gertrude's Chapel

Ernst Barlach's studio at Heidberg 15 is now a memorial museum containing most of the work he left behind him (over 100 works of sculpture, together with drawings, printed graphic art and books).

*Ernst Barlach Memorial Museum

Surroundings of Güstrow

Bützow, 12km/7½ miles north-west of Güstrow has a brick-built Early Gothic church (Late Gothic winged altar, Renaissance pulpit of 1617) and a neo-Gothic Town Hall (1846–48).

Bützow

Gütersloh

E 4

Land: North Rhine-Westphalia
Altitude: 78m/256ft
Population: 209,000

The industrial town of Gütersloh lies to the south of the Teutoburg Forest (see entry). The principal branches of industry are engineering, textiles and publishing.

Situation and characteristics

The Town

The heart of the old village which grew into the present town was the Alter Kirchplatz. Flanking the square are handsome old half-timbered houses, including the Veerhoff-haus, now occupied by the Kunstverein (Art Association). To the south is the striking new Municipal Library (Stadtbibliothek).

Alter Kirchplatz

Municipal Museum	To the north-east, at Kökerstrasse 7–9, can be found the Municipal Museum (Stadtmuseum; mainly medical and industrial history).
Railway Museum	To the north is the Mühlenstroth Narrow-Gauge Railway and Steam Engine Museum (Kleinbahn- und Dampflokmuseum). Trips on an old narrow-gauge railway (weekends only).

Hagen   F 3

Land: North Rhine-Westphalia
Altitude: 106m/348ft
Population: 209,000

Situation and characteristics

Hagen lies on the northern fringe of the Sauerland (see entry), extending its tentacles into the valleys, surrounded by wooded hills, of the rivers Ruhr, Ennepe, Lenne and Volme. The industries of this city, situated at the intersection of important traffic routes, include ironworking and iron products, the manufacture of accumulators, foodstuffs, textiles and papermaking.

Central Area

Model of solar system

In Friedrich-Ebert-Platz stands the Town Hall (Rathaus), which has on its tower a gilded sphere of special steel representing the sun, set up here in 1965. It has a diameter of 1.39m (just over 4½ft) – a billionth part of the sun's diameter – and the whole of the solar system is distributed about the town on the same scale, with bronze plates on the pavements marking the orbits of the planets.

Osthaus Museum

To the south of the Town Hall, at Hochstrasse 73, is the Karl Ernst Osthaus Museum (20th century art), in a monumental Art Nouveau building designed by Henry van de Velde. There are a number of other Art Nouveau houses elsewhere in the town.

Municipal Museum

Adjoining the Osthaus Museum is the Municipal Museum (Museum für Stadt- und Heimatgeschichte; development of the town, domestic interiors).

Selbecke

*Open-Air Museum

In the southern district of Selbecke can be found the interesting Westphalian Open-Air Museum (Westfälisches Freilichtmuseum), covering an area of 34 hectares/85 acres in the Mäckingerbach valley, with numerous industrial installations (including mills, smithies and a variety of workshops) from different parts of Westphalia.

Eppenhausen

The villa development of Hohenhagen in the Eppenhausen district reflects the town-planning ideas of the Werkbund (founded in 1907 to promote good industrial design). Its central feature is the Hohenhof, a house built by van de Velde for Karl Ernst Osthaus in 1906–08.

Hohenlimburg

Schloss

In the south-eastern district of Hohenlimburg stands Schloss Hohenlimburg (13th–14th c., with later alterations), now housing a museum (folk art and traditions, domestic interiors, history of region, prehistory and early historical period). Schlossfestspiele (Festival) held in the courtyard in summer (drama, ballet, concerts).

Surroundings of Hagen

Hengsteysee

10km/6 miles north of Hagen lies the Hengsteysee, the first artificial lake (reservoir) created in the Ruhr (1928): recreation area, water sports.

See Iserlohn

25km/15 miles south-east is Altena, with the ancestral castle (originally 13th c.) of the Counts von der Mark, beautifully situated above the Lenne valley. The youth hostel opened here in 1912 was the first in Germany.

Halberstadt   E 6

Land: Saxony-Anhalt
Altitude: 125m/410ft
Population: 47,000

Halberstadt, an old-established episcopal city famed for its architectural treasures and now the chief place in the northern Harz foreland, lies 40km/25 miles south-west of Magdeburg on the river Holtemme.

Situation and characteristics

Sights

The town's principal landmark is the Cathedral (Dom) of St Stephen, an aisled Gothic basilica with transept. Begun in 1239, it was finally consecrated in 1491. The west front, flanked by two tall towers, is one of the finest creations of Gothic architecture in Germany.

*Cathedral

The famous Cathedral Treasury in the upper cloister houses a rich collection of liturgical vestments and utensils, tapestries and sculpture.
The most notable features of the interior are the stained glass (some 450 panes in all), a Romanesque Triumphal Cross group and a number of fine monuments.

**Treasury

The Deanery (Dompropstei; now occupied by the municipal authorities), in Renaissance style, was built by the first Protestant bishop of Halberstadt (1592–1611).

Deanery

On the west side of the Domplatz is the Liebfrauenkirche (Church of Our Lady), a 12th century Romanesque basilica with transept (fine stucco relief on choir screen).

*Liebfrauenkirche

North of the church can be seen the Petershof, the former Bishop's Palace, with some remains of Renaissance work.

Petershof

Adjoining the Cathedral, at Domplatz 36, is the old Domkurie (Cathedral offices), a Baroque building of 1782 which is now occupied by the Municipal Museum (Städtisches Museum; prehistory and the early historical period, religious sculpture in wood, furniture, medieval pottery and pewterware).

Domkurie (Museum)

At Domplatz 37 is the Heineanum, an ornithological museum founded by Ferdinand Heine in the mid 19th century, with what was then one of the largest collections in Europe. The museum now has over 16,000 specimens of birds and 5000 eggs, as well as a large ornithological library.

Heineanum

The Gleimhaus (Domplatz 31) is now a museum devoted to the life and work of the poet Johann Wilhelm Ludwig Gleim, who died in Halberstadt in 1803, with a library of 20,000 volumes, 15,000 sheets of graphic art and 10,000 original manuscripts, together with portraits of Gleim's contemporaries.

*Gleimhaus

Other notable churches in addition to the Cathedral are the Marktkirche (Market Church) of St Martin, a 13th century Gothic hall-church with a figure of Roland (1433) on the west front; the parish church of St Catherine, another Gothic hall-church (after 1300) which originally belonged to a Dominican monastery; and the parish church of St Andrew, originally belonging to a Franciscan friary (after 1300; destroyed 1945; choir, with triangular apse, rebuilt).

Churches

Surroundings of Halberstadt

South of the town is the Baroque hunting lodge of Spiegelsberge (1769–82; now a restaurant). In the cellar is the "Great Tun" (capacity 132,760 litres/29,204 gallons) from

Spiegelsberge

Schloss Gröningen, made in 1594 by M. Werner, who was also responsible for the famous Great Tun of Heidelberg. In the park are the mausoleum of Freiherr (Baron) von Spiegel, numerous grottoes, two outlook towers and an animal enclosure.

Huy

From Halberstadt a road runs by way of Sargstedt to the Huy, a 20km/12½ mile long ridge of wooded limestone hills. Near Dingelstedt are the remains of the Huysburg, a Benedictine monastery. The church (consecrated c. 1121) is one of the finest Romanesque churches in the Harz region (with Gothic west front, roofs and gables). It has a fine Baroque interior, with a high altar of 1777–86 (altarpiece by Stratmann of Paderborn), two side altars of 1793 (by Hinse of Hildesheim), a pulpit of around 1730, a late 17th century font and monuments of the 14th and 18th centuries.

Osterwieck

27km/17 miles from Halberstadt, in the Harz foreland, is Osterwieck, a little town founded in the 8th century which has preserved its medieval aspect, with numerous 16th and 17th century half-timbered buildings. St Stephen's Church has a Romanesque west end and a Late Gothic nave and choir.

Wegeleben

Wegeleben, 12km/7½ miles east, has an Early Gothic aisled basilica with transept (c. 1300) and a fine Town Hall with an external staircase and a clock (Renaissance, 1592; altered 1711).

Gröningen

3km/2 miles north-east on B 81 is Gröningen, with scanty remains of its Schloss (1586). The church of St Veit (St Vitus), belonging to a Benedictine monastery founded in 936, was originally a flat-roofed aisled basilica (12th c.), with ceiling paintings and a Romanesque font.

Kroppenstedt

Kroppenstedt, 7km/4½ miles from Gröningen on B 81, has a Late Gothic Town Hall. Opposite it is a cross of 1651. The parish church of St Martin is a double-aisled hall-church with a timber ceiling (Late Gothic); on the north side are two Renaissance doorways (1611, 1616).

Dedeleben

At Dedeleben is the Westerburg, one of the best preserved moated castles in the northern Harz, with impressive ramparts and moats surrounding the original Gothic castle.

Hamersleben
*Stiftskirche

24km/15 miles north of Halberstadt we come to Hamersleben, with a notable Romanesque Stiftskirche, a flat-roofed aisled basilica (begun 1111–12) with fine cubiform capitals. The choir screen (c. 1200) has figural decoration. Over the altar is one of the oldest altar canopies in Germany (a baldachin-like structure borne on columns; early 13th c.). There are remains of Late Gothic frescoes; also fine Baroque furnishings. Part of the Late Gothic cloister (end of 15th c.) has been preserved. The conventual buildings were renovated in the mid 18th century.

Halle an der Saale   F 7

Land: Saxony-Anhalt
Altitude: 76–136m/247–446ft
Population: 330,000

Situation and
characteristics

Halle, a city with a history reaching back more than a thousand years, lies on the lower Saale, below its junction with the Weisse Elster, on the western edge of the fertile Leipzig basin (Saxon Lowland) with its rich seams of lignite. The town's early prosperity was based on the salt trade, as its very name indicates (*hall* = "salt"). An old and famous university town, it was the birthplace of Georg Friedrich Händel, the composer known in English-speaking countries as Handel.

Boat services

The landing-stage used by passenger boats on the Saale is below Burg Giebichstein. Boats ply down the Saale to Trotha, Wettin and Bernburg, upstream to the Rabeninsel (extension to Röpzig planned).

Old Town

From Thälmannplatz a pedestrian zone extends along Leipziger Strasse to the centre of the old town.

Costumes of the Halle salt-workers *Markt Church, Handel Monument, Red Tower*

At the intersection with the Hansering stands the Leipziger Turm (15th c.), a relic of the town's fortifications. Leipziger Turm

The Ulrichskirche (St Ulrich's Church; 1319–41), a two-aisled hall-church, has been used since 1976 as a concert hall.

At the end of Leipziger Strasse is the spacious Markt with its five towers. *Markt

On the north side of the square is the Roter Turm (Red Tower; 1418–1506), an 84m/276ft high clock-tower which was originally built as an expression of the townspeople's will to assert their rights. The new building of steel and glass (1976) which surrounds it is used for exhibitions. On the tower can be seen a stone copy (1719) of an earlier wooden figure of Roland (1250). *Roter Turm

The four-towered Marktkirche (Market Church) of St Mary, built in 1529 on the site of two Romanesque predecessors, is a Late Gothic hall-church without a choir. Luther preached in the church, and in the 18th century Handel played the organ. *Marktkirche

To the south of the Markt, at Grosse Märkerstrasse 10, is the Historical Museum (Geschichtsmuseum der Stadt), in a house once occupied by the philosopher Christian Wolff (1679–1754). Historical Museum

Just off the Alter Markt stands the Moritzkirche (St Maurice's Church; 1388–1511), a Late Gothic hall-church with sculpture by Konrad von Einbeck. St Maurice's Church

On Franckeplatz, south-east of the town centre, are the Francke Foundations (Franckesche Stiftungen), built from 1698 onwards on the initiative of the Pietist A. H. Francke as a poorhouse and orphan school; Francke Memorial by C. D. Rauch (1829). *Francke Foundations

North-west of the Markt, at Grosse Nikolaistrasse 5, can be found the Händelhaus (Handel House), in which the composer was born in 1685; it is now a museum. *Handel House

To the west of the Hallmarkt, in Mansfelder Strasse, is the Saltworks Museum (Halloren- und Salinenmuseum), which illustrates the method of extracting salt by boiling and the way of life of the old salt-workers (Halloren). Once a month, on a Sunday, there is a demonstration of salt-boiling. Saltworks Museum

The Cathedral (Dom), reached from the Markt by way of Grosse Klausstrasse, was originally an Early Gothic hall-church (1280–1330) but was much altered in later centuries; its most notable features are its round-headed gables. Cathedral

Immediately south of the Cathedral is the Residenz (1531–37).

Geiseltal
Museum

In the Domplatz is the Geiseltal Museum, with a collection of fossils from the lignite deposits in the nearby Geisel valley.

*Moritzburg

To the north of the Cathedral, reached by way of Mühlgasse and the Schlossberg, stands the Moritzburg (1484–1503), a stronghold of the Archbishops of Magdeburg designed to cow the citizens of Halle. Linked with the old town walls, it was protected on one side by an arm of the Saale and on the other three sides by a moat. It was burned down in 1637, during the Thirty Years' War.

Moritzburg
State Gallery

In the early 20th century the Burg became a museum. It now houses the State Art Gallery (Staatliche Galerie; mainly 19th and 20th century German painting).

Saaleaue (Saale Meadow)

On the west side of the town lies the Kulturpark Saaleaue, a leisure park on the island of Peissnitz, with exhibition halls, an open-air theatre, a miniature railway, a Space Planetarium and various sports facilities, including an ice-rink.

*Burg Giebichenstein

Museum of
Architecture

Farther downstream is Burg Giebichenstein, from 961 a residence of the Archbishops of Magdeburg. Part of the Oberburg (Upper Castle), which was destroyed during the Thirty Years' War, survives as a ruin (in which excavations were carried out in 1960–61); it now houses a Museum of Architecture. The Unterburg (Lower Castle) is now occupied by the College of Industrial Design.

Burg Giebichenstein, on the banks of the Saale

To the north of Burg Giebichenstein is the Zoo (entrance in Reilstrasse). From the outlook tower on the Reilsberg there are wide views of Halle and the surrounding area.

Zoo

South-east of the Burg, in Richard-Wagner-Strasse, can be found the Provincial Museum of Prehistory (Landesmuseum für Vorgeschichte), housed in an Art Nouveau building (by Wilhelm Kreis, 1913–14).

Museum of Prehistory

Dölauer Heide

North-west of the town is Halle's "municipal forest", the Dölauer Heide (Dölau Heath), an area of 765 hectares/1890 acres (mainly pine forest) designated as a landscape reserve, with two nature reserves. Among features of interest are a number of Neolithic burial mounds and remains of a fortified Stone Age settlement. On the Kolkberg is an outlook tower. The church in Dölau has a Late Gothic winged altar (c. 1500).

Surroundings of Halle

In the village of Petersberg (12km/7½ miles north), conspicuously situated on the hill of that name (250m/820ft) which dominates the surrounding plain, stands the church of an Augustinian house (founded 1128) which was closed in 1538. The church itself, an aisled cruciform basilica, was burned down in 1565, rebuilt almost in its original form in 1853 and renovated from 1958 onwards.

Petersberg

On a round-topped porphyry hill 20km/12½ miles north-east of Halle on B 100 is a completely preserved double chapel (c. 1170), all that is left of a castle belonging to the Margraves of Landsberg. The chapel was originally two-storeyed; a third storey was added in the 15th century to provide living accommodation (restored in 1860–61 and again in 1928–30).

Landsberg

Hamburg

C 5

Capital of the *Land* of Hamburg
Altitude: 6m/20ft
Population: 1.6 million

In this guide the description of Hamburg has been deliberately kept short, since fuller information is provided in the "Hamburg" volume in the same series.

The Free Hanseatic City of Hamburg, Germany's largest city after Berlin, is one of the sixteen *Länder* of the Federal Republic. Its favourable situation at the head of the long funnel-shaped estuary of the Elbe has made it one of the leading ports and commercial cities of Europe and a link between the sea and Germany's network of inland waterways. The *Land* of Hamburg also includes the islands of Neuwerk and Scharhörn, far to the north-west at the mouth of the Elbe estuary.

Situation and characteristics

Central Area

The townscape of Hamburg owes its particular charm to the large basin of the Binnen-alster (Inner Alster), in the centre of the city, round which run the elegant Jungfernstieg (with the Alsterpavillon café and the landing-stage used by the Alster boats) and the Ballindamm (with the offices of the Hapag-Lloyd shipping line, founded in 1847 as HAPAG). To the west of the Neuer Jungfernstieg, in Dammtorstrasse, is the State Opera House (Staatsoper; 1855).

* Binnenalster

West and south-west of the Binnenalster the creation of pedestrian zones in recent years has added a number of new *passagen* (shopping arcades and lanes) to those already

* Passagen

existing. Lined with shops, boutiques, restaurants, etc., they make this a pleasant area in which to stroll about.

*Aussenalster

The line of the old fortifications, with the Lombardsbrücke and Kennedybrücke, separates the Binnenalster from the Aussenalster (Outer Alster) to the north. This popular sailing area can also be reached from the Jungfernstieg on one of the Alster boats. Along its west side are beautiful parks and gardens.

Pöseldorf

Immediately west of the parks and gardens is the redeveloped Pöseldorf area (galleries, boutiques, cafés and bars, etc.; painted house-fronts).

Fleete

To the south of the Binnenalster are a number of canals (*fleete),* with locks, linking it with the Elbe (Herrengrabenfleet, Bleichenfleet, Alsterfleet and Nikolaifleet; sightseeing cruises). These canals mark the division between the old town (Altstadt) and the new town (Neustadt).

*Kunsthalle

To the east of the Ballindamm, on the Glockengiesserwall, stands the Kunsthalle, an art gallery (altarpieces by Meister Bertram of Minden and Meister Francke, works by Philipp Otto Runge and Caspar David Friedrich and minor Dutch masters; important special exhibitions).

*Town Hall

In the centre of the old town is the Rathausmarkt, with the Town Hall (Rathaus; 1886–97), a sumptuous neo-Renaissance building. Behind it is the Stock Exchange (Börse).

Eastern Central Area

Mönckebergstrasse

St Peter's Church

From the Rathausmarkt the wide Mönckebergstrasse, Hamburg's principal shopping and business street, lined with imposing offices and business houses, leads past St Peter's Church (St Petri; founded in 14th c.; rebuilt in neo-Gothic style 1844–49; 133m/436ft high tower) to the Central Station (Hauptbahnhof), north-east of which is the Schauspielhaus (Theatre).

* Museum of Art
and Industry

Facing the station, to the south-east, is the Museum of Art and Industry (Museum für Kunst und Gewerbe), which ranks after the Bavarian National Museum in Munich (see entry) as the most comprehensive display of German, European and Asian applied art in Germany (in particular china, furniture and silver from northern Germany and the Netherlands and applied art from East Asia) and a collection of works by Kokoschka.

Markthalle
Deichtorhallen

South of the station are the Markthalle (communications centre) and the Deichtorhallen (restored and reopened in 1989; art exhibitions).

St James's Church

To the south of Mönckebergstrasse, in Steinstrasse, can be found St James's Church (St Jacobi; 14th c., restored 1959 after severe damage in the Second World War), with medieval altars and an Arp Schnitger organ.

* Chilehaus

Farther south, in Burchardplatz, is the boldly conceived ten-storey Chilehaus (by Fritz Höger, 1922–24), perhaps the best-known building in the business quarter. Nearby is the Sprinkenhof (by Fritz Höger and H. and O. Gerson, 1927–31). Farther east stands the Cityhof (1956), a group of four 42m/138ft high office blocks.

Ost-West-Strasse
St Catherine's
Church

From the Messberg, a busy square on the south side of the Chilehaus (Messberghof, in clinker brick; by H. and O. Gerson, 1923–25), the wide Ost-West-Strasse leads west past St Catherine's Church (St Katharinen; 14th–17th c., rebuilt 1956) and the 147m/482ft high Nikolaikirchturm, the tower of St Nicholas's Church (completely destroyed during the Second World War) and over the Nikolaifleet, Alsterfleet and Herrengrabenfleet into the new town (Neustadt).

* St Michael's
Church

In the new town is Hamburg's traditional emblem and landmark, the Baroque St Michael's Church (St Michaelis; by E. G. Sonnin, 1750–62). From the 132m/433ft high tower, familiarly known as "Michel" (lift), there are fine views. In a courtyard to the east are the Krameramtswohnungen, dwellings originally built to house the widows of members of the Krameramt (Shopkeepers' Guild); in House C is a museum.

Planten in Blumen Park and Congress Centre ▶

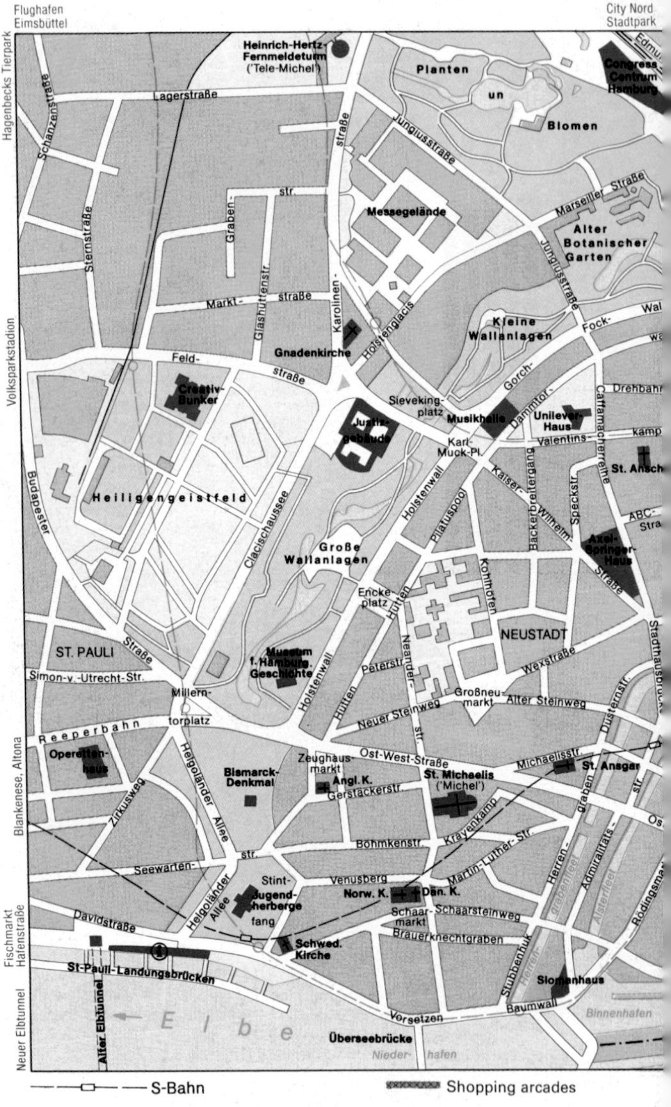

Flughafen
Eimsbüttel

City Nord
Stadtpark

— S-Bahn   Shopping arcades

The ** Port

The Port of Hamburg extends over an area of some 100sq.km/40sq. miles between the Norder- and the Süderelbe, from the two Elbe bridges in the east to the former fishermen's island of Finkenwerder in the west. It is a tidal harbour, accessible at all states of

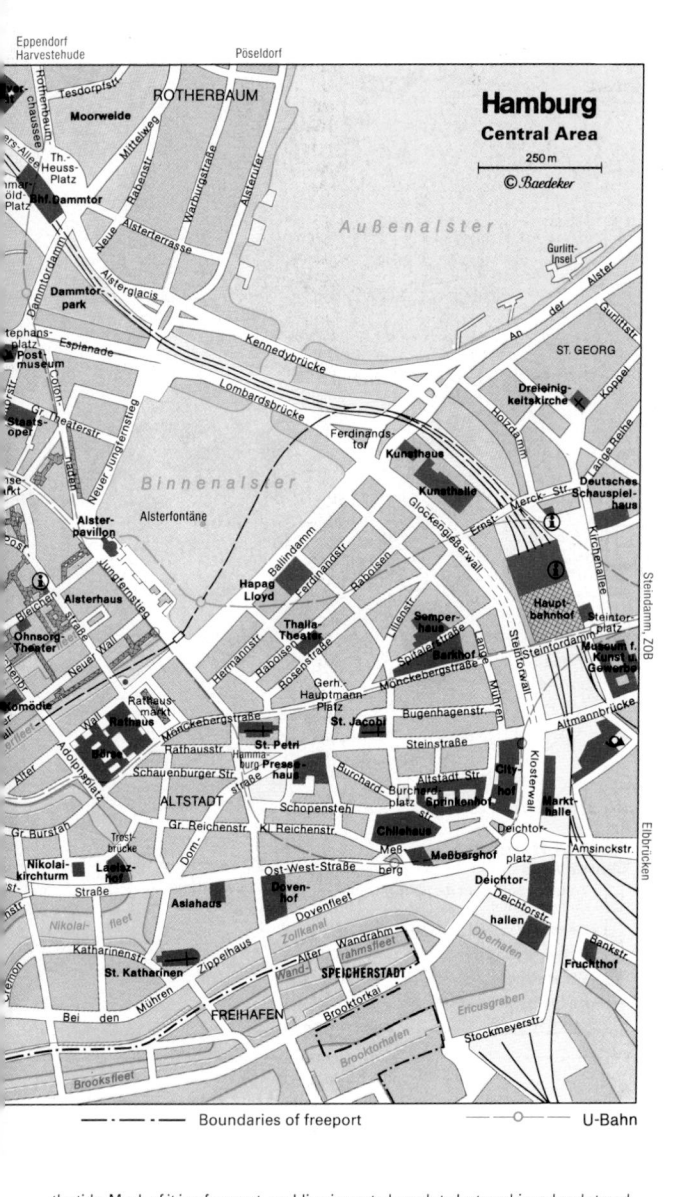

Eppendorf
Harvestehude   Pöseldorf

ROTHERBAUM

Moorweide

Hamburg

Central Area

250 m

© *Baedeker*

Außenalster

Boundaries of freeport   U-Bahn

the tide. Much of it is a free port, enabling imported goods to be transhipped and stored without payment of duty.

A tour round the port is a fascinating experience. The boats leave from the St Pauli   *Harbour tours
landing-stages (Landungsbrücken; museum ship "Rickmer Rickmers"), which are used

257

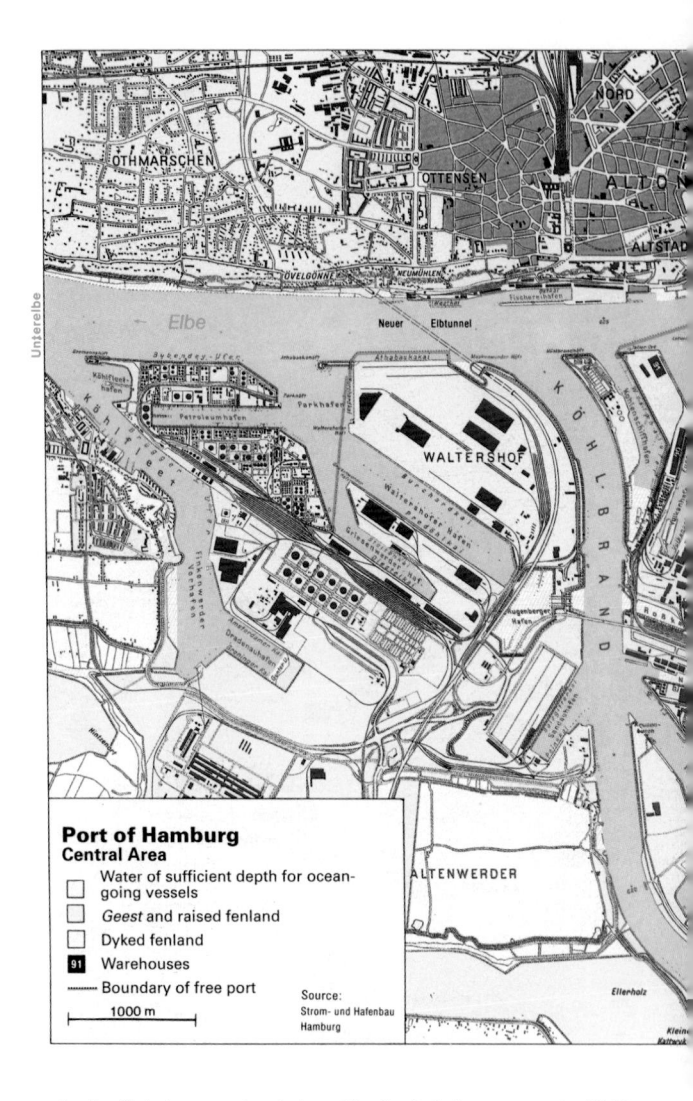

Port of Hamburg
Central Area

☐ Water of sufficient depth for ocean-
going vessels

☐ *Geest* and raised fenland

☐ Dyked fenland

91 Warehouses

········· Boundary of free port

|—— 1000 m ——|

Source:
Strom- und Hafenbau
Hamburg

by all traffic in the port and on the lower Elbe. Nearby is the entrance to the Old Elbe Tunnel (448m/490yds long) leading to the island of Steinwerder (shipyards).

Hafenrand-
promenade

The Hafenrandpromenade, a pedestrian route round the harbour, runs from the Messberg to the Fischmarkt. It is planned to extend it to Oevelgönne-Neumühlen (see below).

*Speicherstadt

On the Brookinsel, to the south of the Zollkanal, lies the Speicherstadt (Warehouse

258

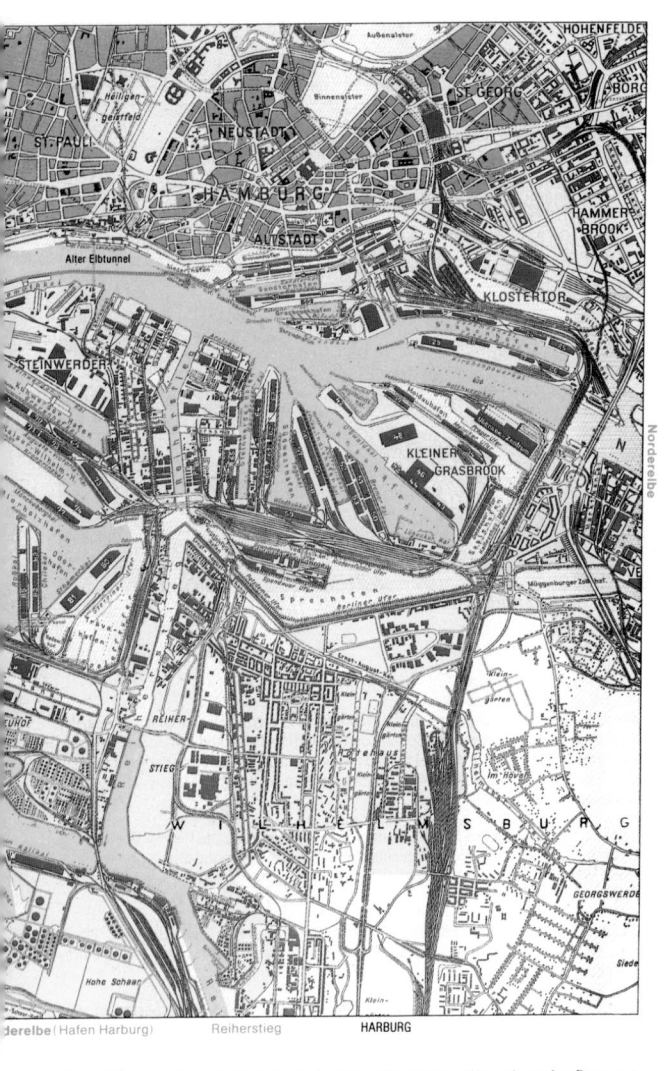

derelbe (Hafen Harburg)   Reiherstieg   HARBURG

District; freeport area), built at the end of the 19th century. Here, along the *fleete,* are continuous lines of brick-built warehouses up to seven storeys high, used for the storage of tobacco, coffee, rum, dried fruit and spices, as well as optical, mechanical and electronic apparatus, Oriental carpets, etc.

The harbour installations on the left bank of the Elbe are spanned by the Köhlbrand-brücke, a bridge 3.9km/2½ miles long and up to 54m/177ft high (opened 1974) which has become a new Hamburg landmark.

*Köhlbrandbrücke

Norderelbe, Binnenalster and Aussenalster

Wallringpark

At the St Pauli landing-stages begin the Wallringpark, a recreation area which takes in the Planten un Blomen park, the Old Botanic Garden and the Kleine and Grosse Wallanlagen, the gardens laid out on the line of the old fortifications. To the south is the Alter Elbpark (Old Elbe Park), with the Bismarck Memorial (on the model of the medieval figures of Roland), erected in 1906.

Museum on History of Hamburg

To the north, beyond the Millertordamm, is the Museum on the History of Hamburg (Museum für Hamburgische Geschichte; 1913–22), now protected as a national monument, with a rich collection of material, including dioramas of the port at various stages in its history, ship models, etc.

*Planten un Blomen

North of the Museum extends the popular park known as Planten un Blomen ("Plants and Flowers"). At its north end are the Congress Centre (1973) and the 32-storey Hamburg Plaza Hotel.

Trade Fair Grounds

At the west end of the Wallringpark are the Trade Fair Grounds (Messegelände), with twelve exhibition halls and a total area of some 60,000 sq.m/72,000 sq.yds.

*"Tele-Michel"

Opposite the north-west entrance to the park, in Rentzelstrasse, rises the 272m/892ft high Heinrich Hertz Telecommunications Tower (Fernmeldeturm; 1968), popularly known as "Tele-Michel", with a revolving restaurant at 132m/433ft.

Rotherbaum

Museum of Ethnography

To the north of the Wallringpark lies the district of Rotherbaum, with the extensive campus of Hamburg University. On Rothenbaumchaussee is the Museum of Ethnography (Völkerkundemuseum; Africa, America, South Seas).

St Pauli

Beyond the Grosse Wallanlagen and the Glacischaussee is the Heiligengeistfeld (30 hectares/75 acres), scene of the Domfest, a popular festival held in March-April and November/December.

The main axis of the St Pauli district is the Reeperbahn (originally the street of the rope-makers), famed for its bars and places of entertainment. In the past its attractions were its striptease joints and its shady hotels renting rooms by the hour, but with the risk of AIDS it has increasingly switched to amusement arcades, discotheques, etc. In David-strasse can be seen the legendary Davidswache police station. In the Grosse Freiheit is the Baroque façade of St Joseph's Church (R.C.), flanked by places of entertainment.

Reeperbahn
Grosse Freiheit

Altona

To the west, above the high bank of the Elbe, lies the district of Altona, with the once celebrated street of neo-classical houses (now protected as historical monuments) known as the Palmaille. In Museumstrasse, which runs north from the end of the Palmaille, is the Altona Museum (geology; landscape, settlement and economy of Schleswig-Holstein and the Lower Elbe; figureheads of galleons).

*Altona Museum

At the west end of the Palmaille is the Altonaer Balkon ("Altona Balcony"), with fine views of the river and the port. On the banks of the Elbe can be found the fishing harbour.

*Altonaer Balkon

To the north, in the Bahrenfeld district, lies the Volkspark (160 hectares/400 acres; laid out 1914–15 and 1918–20), with play areas and sports grounds, allotments and a swimming pool (open in summer). Here too is the Volkspark Stadium (1951–53; 60,000 seats), built up from rubble from demolished buildings.

Volkspark

Oevelgönne

In Oevelgönne, on the lower Elbe, is the Museum Harbour (Museumshafen; 1977), with historic ships still in working order. On the Elbuferweg are many trim pilots' houses. The Oevelgönner Seekiste (Sea-Chest) displays a variety of maritime curios.

*Museum Harbour
Elbuferweg

Also in Oevelgönne is the northern entrance to the New Elbe Tunnel (Neuer Elbtunnel; A 7 motorway), the south entrance to which is at the container terminal on the left bank of the Elbe. The tunnel, 3.3km/2 miles long, with three lanes in each direction, runs under the river at a depth of up to 27m/89ft.

New Elbe Tunnel

Farther west, in the Klein Flottbek district, lies the beautiful Jenischpark, rising to the north of the Elbchaussee. In the park are the neo-classical Jenisch-Haus, with rooms reflecting the taste of the prosperous middle classes, in styles ranging from Louis XVI to Art Nouveau, and the Ernst-Barlach-Haus (sculpture, drawings, printed graphic art).

Jenischpark

Blankenese

There is an attractive drive along the Elbchaussee to Blankenese (14km/8½ miles west of the city centre), a former fishing village with numbers of handsome villas on the Süllberg (86m/282ft; fine view).

*Elbchaussee

Stellingen

In the north-western suburb of Stellingen is Hagenbeck's Zoo (Tierpark), excellently laid out on modern lines, with its large stock of animals arranged according to the part of the world from which they come, most of them in free-range enclosures ("troparium", dolphinarium).

*Hagenbeck's Zoo

Winterhude

North of the Aussenalster, in the Winterhude district, can be found the Winterhude Municipal Park (Stadtpark), with a Planetarium housed in an old water-tower.

Planetarium

Vierlande and Marschlande

The Vierlande ("Four Lands") and Marschlande (Fenlands), south-east of the city, are fertile areas of low-lying land between the Elbe and the *geest* (sandy heathland), traversed by two old arms of the Elbe.

Billwerder

On the north-western edge of the Marschlande are the Boberg dunes and the Achtermoor (bird sanctuary). Billwerder has the church of St Nicholas (originally Baroque) and, on the Billdeich, the German Painters' and Lacquerworkers' Museum.

Bergedorf

Bergedorf has a 13th century Schloss, rebuilt in the early 19th century, which now houses the Museum of Bergedorf and the Vierlande. To the south-east is Hamburg Observatory.

Curslack

In Curslack, to the south of Bergedorf, is the Vierlande Open-Air Museum (old houses).

Harburg

Harburg, until 1937 an independent town (first recorded around 1140 as Horneburg), lies on the south bank of the Süderelbe, at a point where a ridge of sandy heathland, with the wooded Harburger Berge (Schwarze Berge), comes close to the river. Now incorporated in Hamburg, it is predominantly industrial (oil refineries) and has an important industrial harbour.

On the Lämmertwiete, to the north of the Marktplatz (known as the Sand), are a number of 17th and 18th century half-timbered houses (restored). In Museumsplatz, near the Rathausplatz, is the Helms Museum (prehistory and the early historical period).

Surroundings of Hamburg

Willkommhöft

6km/4 miles downstream from Blankenese (see above), at the Schulau ferry-house, can be found the Willkommhöft ship-greeting station, where ships arriving or departing during daylight are greeted by the playing of their national anthem and the hoisting of their national flag.

* Ahrensburg

23km/14 miles north-east of Hamburg is the Schleswig-Holstein town of Ahrensburg, with Schloss Ahrensburg, now a museum (splendid interiors reflecting the way of life of the country nobility).

Friedrichsruh

In the Sachsenwald, 30km/20 miles east of Hamburg, can be seen the Friedrichsruh hunting lodge, which was acquired by Bismarck in 1871 (Bismarck Museum and Mausoleum).
A special attraction is the Butterfly Garden (native and tropical butterflies in glasshouses).

Kiekeberg

At Ehestorf, south-west of Hamburg-Harburg, the Kiekeberg Open-Air Museum exhibits houses of the 17th–19th centuries from Lüneburg Heath.

Altes Land

See entry

Neuwerk

Neuwerk and Scharhörn: see Cuxhaven, Surroundings

Hameln   E 4

Land: Lower Saxony
Altitude: 68m/223ft
Population: 58,000

Situation and characteristics

Hameln (Browning's "Hamelin town in Brunswick"), delightfully situated in the broad Weser valley between two hills, the Klüt and the Schweineberg, is famed as the city of the

Ratcatcher's House *Leisthaus*

Pied Piper. The old town has many half-timbered houses and buildings in Weser Renaissance style.

The Town

In the Markt is the Early Gothic Marktkirche (Market Church of St Nicholas; rebuilt 1957–58), formerly the boatmen's church, as the golden ship on the spire indicates. Opposite it is the Dempterhaus (1607), with a beautiful oriel.

Markt

To the east of the Markt is Osterstrasse, at No. 2 of which is the imposing Hochzeitshaus ("Marriage House", once used by the townspeople for festive occasions), in Weser Renaissance style (1610–17), with a carillon and the Pied Piper clock, with mechanical figures (daily at 1.5, 3.35 and 5.35pm). The Pied Piper pageant play is performed in front of the Hochzeitshaus.

Hochzeitshaus

Beyond this are the Stiftsherrenhaus (No. 8; 1558), with fine carving, and the Leisthaus (No. 9; 1589), which together house the Municipal Museum (Städtisches Museum; prehistory and early historical period, domestic interiors, gold and silver, ceramics, pewterware, the Pied Piper legend).

Museum

On the east side of the old town are the former Garrison Church (1712) and the Stift zum Heiligen Geist (1713).

Here too is the Pied Piper's House (Rattenfängerhaus; 1603), a magnificent example of Weser Renaissance architecture, with an inscription referring to the Pied Piper legend on the side wall in Bungelosenstrasse.

*Pied Piper's House

To the south of the Markt lies Bäckerstrasse. At No. 16 is the Rattenkrug (built 1250, rebuilt in Renaissance style in 1568), with a beautiful voluted gable; at No. 12 is the Löwenapotheke (Lion Pharmacy), with a Gothic gable of 1300; and a few paces east is the Kurie Jerusalem (*c.* 1500), now a children's music and painting school.

Bäckerstrasse

Hamm

Minster	Near the Münsterbrücke stands the massive Minster of St Boniface (11th–14th c.), with a Romanesque tower over the crossing topped by a Baroque crown. Features of the interior are the crypt under the high choir, a 13th century tabernacle and the 14th century "Stifterstein" (Founders' Stone) on the pier at the crossing, with figures of the founders holding a model of the Minster.
Wallstrasse	The line of the old fortifications is marked by a ring of "Wallstrassen". On the north side are the Pulverturm (Powder Tower) and Haspelmathturm, the only surviving relics of the fortifications.

Tündern

5km/3 miles south of Hameln is the outlying district of Tündern, with a village museum (Dorfmuseum; prehistory, local crafts, farming). In Hof Zeddies visitors can see a permanent Country Life Exhibition run by the Hameln Museum; windmill (1893).

Surroundings of Hameln

Fischbeck *Stiftskirche	7km/4½ miles north-west is Fischbeck, with an interesting Stiftskirche: Triumphal Cross group (1250); wooden figure of the foundress, Helmburg (c. 1300); silk embroidery; eagle lectern (14th c.); 16th century tapestry with the legend of the church's foundation.
*Hämelschenburg	11km/7 miles south we come to Schloss Hämelschenburg, a magnificent building with three wings, begun in 1588, which is one of the great masterpieces of the Weser Renaissance. The Bridge Gate, with a figure of St George, dates from 1608. Some of the rooms are open to visitors.

Bodenwerder

20km/12½ miles south-east (higher up the Weser valley; boat services) is the little town of Bodenwerder (pop. 6000), with a medicinal spring (brine with iodine content), remains of the old town walls and some half-timbered houses.

The mansion once occupied by Baron Karl Friedrich Hieronymus von Münchhausen (1720–97), famed for his tall stories, is now the Town Hall (with a Münchhausen Room). In Münchhausenplatz is the baron's birthplace, with an unusual fountain depicting one of his adventures in front of it. At the west end of the town is the Lügengrotte ("Liar's Cave"), where he used to tell his tales.

A Münchhausen pageant play is performed in the Kurpark from May to October.

Hamm   F 3

Land: North Rhine-Westphalia
Altitude: 50m/165ft
Population: 180,000

Situation and characteristics	Hamm, in the north-east corner of the Ruhr (see entry), is now, following a local government reorganisation in 1975, one of the largest in area of German towns.

Sights

Old town	In the town centre are a number of old burghers' houses, restored after destruction in the Second World War, the oldest of them dating from the 17th century. In Antonistrasse can be seen the Stuniken-Haus, a Late Baroque merchant's house, and in Südstrasse is the

Münchhausen Fountain, Bodenwerder

Vorschulze-Haus, another Late Baroque house (1744), which now houses the municipal department of culture (exhibition rooms).

The Gustav Lübcke Museum displays the rich private collection of the art dealer of that name, which he made over to the city. The main strength of the collection lies in its furniture, ceramics, glass and book illumination from the Gothic period onwards; also prehistory and the early historical period, an Egyptian collection and Greek and Roman antiquities. New premises for the museum are at present under construction.

*Gustav Lübcke Museum

The Maximilianpark, a leisure park with a congress and conference centre, was laid out for the first Garden Show in North Rhine-Westphalia in 1984 on the site of the old Maximilian pit. The former coal-washing plant was converted by Horst Rellecke, a local artist, into a huge structure of glass and steel in the form of an elephant. Also in the park are a large collection of butterflies and a Railway Museum (with a simulation of a driver's cab).

Maximilianpark
*Glass Elephant

The Pauluskirche (St Paul's Church; Protestant) dates from the 13th century, when the town was founded. In subsequent centuries – most recently in 1945 – the church was damaged or destroyed, but was always rebuilt. The transept and choir are Romanesque; the nave and square tower date from about 1330.

St Paul's Church

The Romanesque Reginenkirche (St Regina's Church; Catholic parish church) is thought to have been founded about 1200. It has a Romanesque font, the reliquary of St Regina and a 16th century high altar from Antwerp.

St Regina's Church

The church of St Pankratius (Pancras), a Protestant parish church originally built about 1000, has preserved some Romanesque work in the west tower and the south wall; the pattern of the interior is set by the Gothic transept and choir. 13th century font; frescoes of *c.* 1330–40 in choir.

St Pankratius

Land: Hesse
Altitude: 108m/354ft
Population: 86,000

Situation and
characteristics

Hanau, situated in a fertile plain at the junction of the Kinzig with the Main, is an important road and rail junction and a considerable industrial town.

Old Town

Marktplatz

In the Marktplatz stands the New Town Hall (Neustädtisches Rathaus; built 1725–33, rebuilt 1962–65), with a carillon. In front of it can be seen a monument to Jacob and Wilhelm Grimm, founders of German philology, who were born in Hanau.

Goldsmiths' House

North of the Marktplatz is the Old Town Hall (rebuilt 1958), now the Goldschmiedehaus (Goldsmiths' House; exhibition of Hanau jewellery, reproduction of an old goldsmith's workshop, special exhibitions). In front of the house is the Justice Fountain (1611).

Wilhelmsbad

3km/2 miles north-west of the old town lies the district of Wilhelmsbad, once a summer residence of the Landgraves of Hesse and, until its mineral spring dried up, a fashionable spa. The old spa features (lakes, artificial ruins, hermitage) were renovated in the 1960s, and this is now an attractive and popular recreation area.

Puppet Museum

At Parkpromenade 4 is the Hessian Doll Museum (Puppenmuseum; dolls from ancient times to the present day; dolls' houses).

Philippsruhe

Schloss

South of Wilhelmsbad and west of the old town, on the Main, stands Schloss Philippsruhe (Baroque; much altered 1875–80), which now houses the Hanau Historical Museum (ceramics, silver, pictures; Brothers Grimm Collection). Part of the Schlossgarten is a sculpture garden (works by contemporary sculptors). The Brothers Grimm Fairytale Festival is held here every summer.

Büdingen

30km/20 miles north-east of Hanau, on the southern fringe of the Vogelsberg, is the little town of Büdingen (pop. 18,000).

*∗ Old town

There are still considerable stretches of the old town walls (15th–16th c.), with round towers, on the north and west sides of the town. In the Marktplatz is the Late Gothic Old Town Hall, with the Heuson Museum (history and folk traditions of the region); in this area too there are many old half-timbered buildings. To the south-east is the 15th century Marienkirche (St Mary's Church).
The formidable castle of the Princes of Isenburg and Büdingen, originally dating from the 13th century, was much altered in the 15th–17th centuries. It has handsome state apartments and contains a museum. The Gothic chapel has a Romanesque pediment over the doorway.
In the nearby village of Grossendorf is the Remigiuskirche, one of the oldest churches in Germany, dating back in part to Ottonian and Salian times.

Capital of the *Land* of Lower Saxony
Altitude: 55m/180ft
Population: 510,000

Hannover (in English usage Hanover), on the river Leine, is capital of the *Land* of Lower   Situation and
Saxony and an important industrial and commercial centre, with a university, a medical   characteristics
school, a veterinary college and academies of music and drama. Its trade fairs are of
international standing. With the Mittelland Canal and its motorway and rail connections
it is a major centre of communications. Its extensive parks – the Eilenriede, Maschpark
with its lake, Lönspark, the Zoo, the Herrenhausen Gardens – justify Hannover's claim to
be "the city in the country".

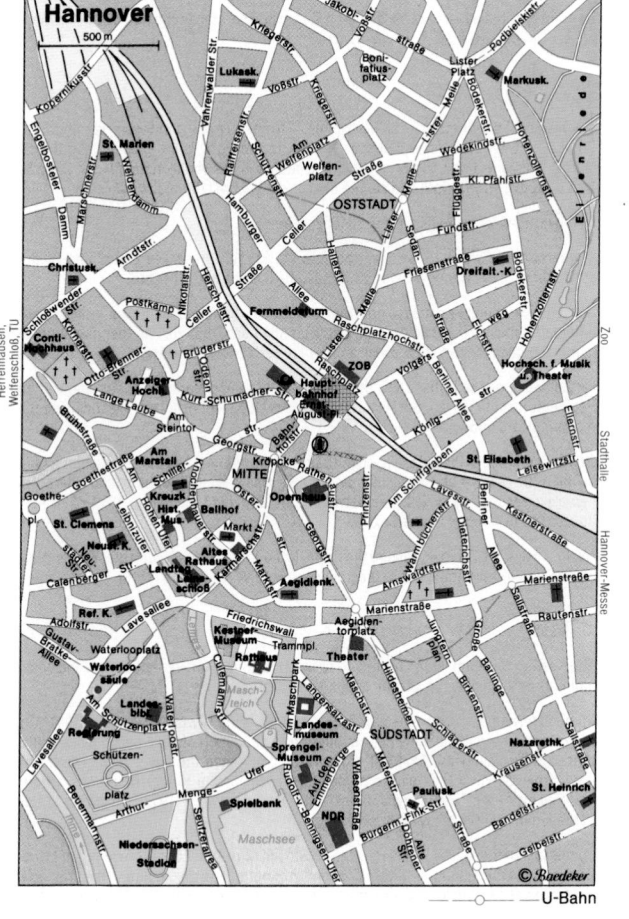

————○———— U-Bahn

Hannover (Hanover)

"Red Thread"
The "Red Thread" ("Roter Faden") is a red line in the paving which guides visitors to 47 points of interest in the central area (some of them accessible only on foot).

City Centre

Railway station
The main railway station (Hauptbahnhof) is at the north-eastern corner of the central area. In front of it can be seen an equestrian statue of King Ernest Augustus, a favourite meeting-point.

Telecommunications Tower
North of the station rises the 144m/472ft high Telecommunications Tower (Fernmeldeturm).

Kröpcke
Passerelle
The hub of the modern city's life is the square called the Kröpcke, with the Kröpcke-Center, an office block almost 60m/200ft high. The square is approached from the station by Bahnhofstrasse, with the sunken Passerelle, a shopping street 750m/820yds long and up to 20m/65ft wide.

*Opera House
South-east of the square, in the dignified Georgstrasse, stands the neo-classical Opera House (Opernhaus; by G. L. Laves, 1845–52).

Old Town

*Marktplatz
South-west of the Kröpcke is the Marktplatz, in the centre of the old town, with the Late Gothic Old Town Hall (Altes Rathaus; 15th c.). In front of it is the graceful neo-Gothic Market Fountain (1881). In the centre of the square is the Marktkirche (Market Church; 14th c.; 15th c. bronze font and carved altar), with a 97m/318ft high tower.

Leibnizhaus
To the north-west is the Leibnizhaus (1652; rebuilt).

Kramerstrasse
Kramerstrasse, which runs west from the Markt, still preserves something of the atmosphere of old Hannover with its handsome half-timbered houses.

Ballhof
Between Knochenhauerstrasse and Burgstrasse can be found Hannover's finest half-timbered building, the Ballhof, built between 1649 and 1665 for the then fashionable game of battledore and shuttlecock and for concerts; now a theatre.

Historical Museum
Farther west, on the Hohes Ufer, the scene of a large flea market on Saturday, are the Beginenturm (14th c.) and the Historical Museum (1963–66; history of the town and the region, folk traditions).

Leineschloss
On the south side of the old town, on the banks of the river, stands the Leineschloss, built in the 17th century as the residence of Duke Georg von Calenberg and altered in neo-classical style by G. L. Laves between 1817 and 1842. Rebuilt in 1958–62, it now houses the Landtag of Lower Saxony.

Neustädter Kirche
North-west of the Schloss, beyond the Leine, is the 17th century Neustädter Kirche (New Town Church), with the tomb of the philosopher G. W. Leibniz (d. 1716).

South of the Old Town

*Kestner Museum
The Kestner Museum, at the north end of the Maschpark, houses antiquities, including an important Egyptian collection, applied and decorative art.

Town Hall
Immediately adjoining the museum, in Trammplatz, is the Town Hall (Rathaus; 1901–13), in the style of the Wilhelmine period, built on a foundation of 6026 beech piles, with a domed tower almost 100m/330ft high which dominates the city's skyline (lift; fine panoramic view). In the hall are models of the town; the Hodler Room has a huge painting by the well-known Swiss artist, "The Oath of Loyalty" (1913). On the south side of the Town Hall lies the Maschteich.

*Landesmuseum
To the east of the Maschpark stands the Provincial Museum (Landesmuseum) of Lower Saxony, with prehistoric, natural history and ethnographic collections and the Provincial Art Gallery (Landesgalerie; European art from the Romantic period to the present day).

Town Hall, on the Maschteich

To the south of the Landesmuseum can be seen the Sprengel Museum (international 20th century art). In front of the museum is a "stabile" by Alexander Calder.

Sprengel Museum

The Maschsee, a lake 2.4km/1½ miles long and up to 530m/580yds across, was created in 1934–36. It is Hannover's largest sports and recreation area (motorboat services, bathing station, sailing school, footpaths round lake). On the west side of the lake is the Niedersachsen-Stadion (Stadium of Lower Saxony; seating for 60,000), built in 1952–54 on banks of rubble from demolished buildings. In the adjoining Sportpark can be found the Stadionbad (swimming pool). At the north-west corner of the lake can be found the Spielbank (Casino). On its east side are the offices of the North German Broadcasting Corporation (Norddeutscher Rundfunk, NDR).

Maschsee

Herrenhausen

From Königsworther Platz, on the east side of which is the Continental Building (Conti-Hochhaus), Nienburger Strasse runs north-west, parallel to the Herrenhäuser Allee (laid out in 1726), passing the University, which occupies the Welfenschloss (Guelph Palace; 1857–66), in the Welfengarten.

On both sides of the road are the magnificent Herrenhausen Gardens. To the left, in the Georgengarten, a beautiful English-style park, is the Wallmodenschlösschen, with the Wilhelm Busch Museum (drawings, paintings, letters and manuscripts; Heinrich Zille Collection). On the right is the Berggarten, a botanic garden with orchid and cactus houses. At the north end of the gardens stands the Mausoleum built by G. L. Laves in 1842–46 for King Ernest Augustus (d. 1851) and Queen Friederike (d. 1841), with marble figures by C. D. Rauch. The Mausoleum also contains the tombs of other Guelph princes, including George ! of Britain.

*Herrenhausen Gardens

To the south lies the geometrically designed Grosser Garten (Great Garden; 1666–1714), the best preserved example of an Early Baroque garden in Germany, with a cascade, fountains, an orangery and a garden theatre.

*Grosser Garten

Gallery Wing	The palace of Herrenhausen, at the end of the Herrenhäuser Allee, was destroyed during the Second World War. The only surviving part of the palace is the Gallery Wing (Galeriegebäude; 1698). In the middle section is the Baroque Hall, two storeys high, with a large cycle of frescoes on the story of Aeneas by the Italian painter Tommaso Giusti. It is now a concert hall used for the summer festival, "Music and Drama in Herrenhausen".
Museum	The Fürstenhaus, to the west of the Gallery Wing, contains the Herrenhausen Museum, with furniture and furnishings from the destroyed palace.

Eilenriede

On the east side of the city extends the beautiful municipal forest of Eilenriede (639 hectares/1578 acres), another large recreation area, with footpaths and bridle paths, playing areas and open spaces for relaxation and sunbathing.

Zoo	On the western edge of the Eilenriede park are the Zoo; the Congress Centre, with the Stadthalle and Stadtpark; the Niedersachsenhalle (Lower Saxony Hall); the Glashalle and Eilenriedehalle; and the Eilenriede Stadium.
Hermann Löns Park Tiergarten	At the east end of the Eilenriede park lies the Hermann Löns Park, a beautiful landscaped park with an old windmill. Adjoining is the Tiergarten, laid out by Duke John Frederick in 1679 as a hunting park, with old trees and some 200 red deer, wild horses and wild pigs.

Trade Fair Grounds

To the south-east of the city can be found the Trade Fair Grounds (Messegelände; 97 hectares/240 acres), where every year at the end of April is held the Hannover Fair, one of the world's most important industrial shows. Within the grounds rises the 83m/272ft high Hermesturm (views).

Hannoversch Münden

See Münden

The Harz   E–F 6–7

Länder: Lower Saxony, Saxony-Anhalt, Thuringia

Situation and characteristics	The Harz, covering an area some 95km/59 miles long and up to 30km/20 miles across, is the range of hills which extends farthest into the North-West German lowlands. The higher regions are still largely forest-covered, though in recent years there has been great concern over the dying of the trees. Until 1990 the Harz was cut in two by the boundary between West and East Germany, which approximately coincided with the topographical division between the Oberharz and Unterharz.

*Landscape

The landscape of the Oberharz (Upper Harz) to the west, a hilly region much indented by valleys, is markedly different from the rolling plateau of the Unterharz (Lower Harz) to the east. On the boundary between the two rises the Brocken, a bare round-topped eminence which in German legend was the meeting-place of the witches on Walpurgis Night. Rising to 1142m/3747ft, it is the highest point of North Germany.

Oberharz	The Oberharz is largely covered by forest, with an economy based on forestry, mining and stock-farming. Narrow rocky valleys such as the Okertal and Bodetal, particularly on the north side, cut deep into the hills, to which a series of old-world little towns give a particular charm. The heavy snowfall has promoted the development of important winter sports centres.

In contrast to the Oberharz, which drops steeply down to the lowlands, the Unterharz falls more gradually away. Its tracts of level ground are covered with beech forests or have been brought into cultivation. The eastern Harz foreland, particularly the Magdeburger Börde, is especially fertile thanks to its covering of loess.

Unterharz

The mining of silver, copper, lead, zinc and iron ore was formerly of predominant economic importance, particularly in the Oberharz. A rich vein of silver was discovered near Goslar in the 10th century, and by the 16th century mining had spread to more than thirty towns and villages. This period saw the development of the seven free mining towns of Grund, Wildemann, Lautenthal, Clausthal, Zellerfeld, St Andreasberg and Altenau and of other mining towns. After a period of decline during the Thirty Years War the mining industry revived in the early 18th century; then in 1775 a Mining Academy was founded in Clausthal – still in existence as a faculty of Clausthal University of Technology. In the 19th century the mines began to be worked out.

Mining

Round Trip through the Western Harz

The starting-point of the tour is Goslar (see entry), on the northern fringes of the Harz. Leave Goslar on the road which runs south-west up the Gose valley, passing the Bocksberg (726m/2382ft). At Hahnenklee (see Goslar, Surroundings) can be seen a wooden church in the style of a Norwegian *stavkirke*.

Clausthal-Zellerfeld, with a University of Technology which incorporates its 18th century Mining Academy, lies on the Oberharz plateau. In Zellerfeld, which was rebuilt on a regular grid after a great fire in 1672, stands the church of St Salvator (1674–83). Adjoining the church is the Calvörsche Bibliothek (Library; manuscripts of the Reformation period, etc.). On the north side of the square is the Oberharz Mining and Heimatmuseum.
Clausthal has the largest timber-built church in Germany, the Marktkirche (Market Church; 1639–42). Opposite it is the main building of the Mining Academy (Bergakademie; founded 1775), now housing the collections of the Institute of Mineralogy. In Hindenburgstrasse is the birthplace of the great bacteriologist Robert Koch (1843–1910).

Clausthal-Zellerfeld

6km/4 miles west a road branches off on the right to the holiday resort of Wildemann. 10km/6 miles farther north is the Innerste-Stausee (reservoir).

Wildemann
Innerste-Stausee

The main road continues to Bad Grund, the oldest of the seven mining towns of the Oberharz. It has also been frequented for over a century as a spa; the road from Clausthal-Zellerfeld passes the spa installations. The Markt is surrounded by attractive 17th century half-timbered houses; parish church of 1640.
From here the route continues to the junction with the road from Bad Gandersheim (see entry), which is followed to Osterode.

Bad Grund

The medieval town of Osterode lies at the point where the river Söse emerges from the Harz. A little to the west the river is dammed to form a reservoir. On the Kornmarkt, the town's main square, is the Englischer Hof, a Renaissance building of 1610. To the east of this is the parish church of St Ägidii (St Giles; rebuilt 1545). Behind the church is the Town Hall (1552), and near this is the richly decorated Ratswaage (Municipal Weigh-House; 1553). The historic old Ritterhaus houses the Heimatmuseum.

Osterode

The road continues to Herzberg, another little town with attractive half-timbered buildings. Above the town stands the Schloss (1510), birthplace in 1629 of Ernest Augustus, first Elector of Hannover and ancestor of the Hanoverian kings of Britain.

Herzberg

At the point where the Oder leaves the artificial lake created by the Oder Dam (see below) and enters the Harz foreland is Bad Lauterberg, originally a copper-mining town founded in the 15th century and now a popular spa (Kneipp cure). In the northern part of this long straggling town is the Kurpark (Wissmann Park).

Bad Lauterberg

A few kilometres south-east of Bad Lauterberg we reach Bad Sachsa, a summer resort and winter sports centre. 4km/2½ miles north is the Ravensberg, from which there are extensive views.

Bad Sachsa

St Andreasberg	From Bad Lauterberg the road turns north-east, following the Oder, and runs past the Oder Dam. Turning left at the Oderhaus forester's house, we come to St Andreasberg, one of the seven mining towns of the Oberharz. In the upper town is the parish church (1798). To the north of the town extends the beautiful Kurpark, on the west side of which is the Samson silver-mine (843m/2766ft deep; conducted visits).
Braunlage	From the Oderhaus forester's house the main road continues to Braunlage, in the high valley of the Warme Bode. On the south side of the town lies the attractive Kurgarten, and near this is the Heimatmuseum. To the north of the town is the Wurmberg (971m/3186ft; cableway; outlook tower).
Altenau	North-west of Braunlage the road forks. Straight ahead is Bad Harzburg (see below); the road to the left passes another dam on the Oder and comes to Altenau, another of the seven old mining towns. In the Markt is a 17th century wooden church with an altar of 1719.
Bad Harzburg	The main road now continues north, passing the beautiful Rádau Falls, to Bad Harzburg, on the northern fringes of the Harz. The spa installations are in Herzog-Wilhelm-Strasse, which leads through the whole length of the town; farther south is the beautiful Kurpark. Above the town rises the Grosser Burgberg (483m/1585ft; cableway), from the top of which there are magnificent views. From here the road follows the west side of the hill to return to Goslar.

Harz-Hochstrasse

The Harz-Hochstrasse (B 242) traverses the western Harz between Bad Grund and Braunlage (see above).

Eastern Harz

	The old roads ran past the Harz on the north and south. On the fringes of the hills there grew up many small and medium-sized towns whose inhabitants earned their subsistence from mining, industry and trade: places such as Ilsenburg, Wernigerode (see entry), Blankenburg (see Wernigerode, Surroundings), Thale and Ballenstedt (see entries), Nordhausen and Sangerhausen (see entries), Mansfeld and Eisleben (see entry), which now attract many visitors with their picturesque old buildings and beautiful setting or as centres for walks and climbs in the surrounding hills.
*Harzquerbahn	Only one old road crossed the Harz from north to south, between Wernigerode and Nordhausen, and this is now followed by the Harzquerbahn, a narrow-gauge railway opened in 1899.
*Brocken	The Brocken (1142m/3747ft) rises above the treeline into an expanse of stunted scrub and alpine meadows. It is the highest point in the granite mass which has thrust its way through the local slates and greywackes. After the upthrust of the Harz in the Tertiary era the granite summit of the Brocken, like that of the Ramsberg (582m/1910ft) was exposed by erosion. The best approach to the Brocken is from Wernigerode or the altitude and winter sports resort of Schierke; there is also a nostalgic old steam railway.
Hochharz National Park	The area around the Brocken was declared a National Park in 1990.
Harz foreland	The main tourist attractions in the northern Harz foreland are the old town of Quedlinburg (see entry), with its historic buildings and associations with German history, and the episcopal city of Halberstadt (see entry) with its rich cathedral treasury.
Bode valley	See Thale, Surroundings

Havelland   D 7–8

Land: Brandenburg

Situation and topography	The Havelland is the area north-west of Potsdam which is bounded on the east, south and west by the river Havel and on the north by its tributary the Rhin. It has a varied

landscape pattern: stretches of low-lying moorland including the Havelländisches Luch, expanses of sandy soil subject to flooding (e.g. above the town of Brandenburg), fields of inland dunes as in the Kremmener Forst, ground moraines such as the Nauener Platte and the Rhinower Ländchen and isolated hills formed by terminal moraines such as the Wietkiekenberg (126m/413ft) near Ferch.

Landscape

Particularly attractive is the middle course of the Havel, a 343km/213 mile long river (navigable for a distance of 228km/142 miles) which rises near Neustrelitz in the Mecklenburg lake district. In the central section of its course, between Potsdam and Plaue, the river widens into a series of long winding lakes, the best known of which are the Schwielowsee, Trebelsee, Beetzsee (see Brandenburg) and Plauer See (see entry).

Havel

The Havel lake district offers great variety of scenery within a relatively small area – flat low-lying country, river meadows, lakes, ground and terminal moraines. The beauties of this area are best seen from the water.

The lakes

The Havel itself is a busy waterway, with numerous canals (with locks) short-circuiting its windings. The system of canals also links the Havel with the Elbe and the Mittelland Canal to the west and the Oder to the east.

Canals

The flanks of the Havel valley and the hilly moraine country, with their excellent climate, have long been covered with great expanses of fruit orchards. The centre of the fruit-growing area is the island town of Werder, which attracts large numbers of visitors to its spring festival when the fruit-trees are in blossom.
In the flat country arable farming is predominant. In the depressions there is intensive growing of fodder crops to meet the needs of the large dairy farms. In the dune areas there are plantations of pines, on the terminal moraines mixed forest.

Agriculture

The most important towns on the Middle Havel are Potsdam (see entry), Werder and Brandenburg (see entry); on the lower Havel are Plaue, Premnitz, Rathenow and Havelberg. Most of them are considerable industrial towns and also have numerous tourist attractions. The Heimatmuseum in Rathenow illustrates the history of the town's optical industry.

Towns

Hechingen

L 4

Land: Baden-Württemberg
Altitude: 490m/1608ft
Population: 17,000

Hechingen, until 1850 capital of the principality of Hohenzollern-Hechingen, lies at the foot of the Hohenzollern, a hill to the south of the town. The Zollerngraben is still an active centre of seismic activity.

Situation and characteristics

The Town

In the Schlossplatz are the Neues Schloss (1819–20) and the Altes Schloss, which now houses the Heimatmuseum, the Hohenzollern Collection, the Bürgerwehr (Civic Militia) Museum and the Steuben Collection.

Neues Schloss
Altes Schloss

To the south stands the Stiftskirche of St Jakobus (St James; 1779–83), in the Zopfstil ("pigtail style") characteristic of the transition between Rococo and neo-classicism. To the left of the high altar is the bronze grave-slab (by Peter Vischer) of Count Eitel Friedrich II of Zollern (d. 1512) and his wife.

St James's Church

Near the station is the former Franciscan church of St Luzen (1589), with rich stucco decoration.

St Luzen

Burg Hohenzollern, Hechingen

Roman villa | 3km/2 miles north-west of the town centre can be seen the remains (partly recon-structed) of a Roman villa (1st–3rd c. A.D.) discovered in 1976.

*Burg Hohenzollern

Commandingly situated on the Hohenzollern, to the south of the town, is Burg Hohen-zollern, the ancestral seat of the house of Hohenzollern. The present buildings, apart from the 15th century St Michael's Chapel, were erected between 1850 and 1867 in a reproduction of earlier styles. Some rooms in the castle are open to the public; there is a valuable treasury.

Heidelberg   L 4

Land: Baden-Württemberg
Altitude: 110m/360ft
Population: 135,000

Situation and characteristics | Heidelberg, the old capital of the Palatinate and an ancient university town celebrated in song and poetry, lies at the point where the Neckar emerges from the hills of the Odenwald into the Rhine plain. Over the old town, caught between the river and the hills, looms its famous ruined castle. The best general views of the town in its beautiful setting are to be had from the Theodor Heuss Bridge and the Philosophenweg.

Old Town

From Bismarckplatz, at the south end of the Theodor Heuss Bridge, the 2km/1¼ mile long Hauptstrasse runs east to the Karlstor (1775).

Half way along the Hauptstrasse, in the Baroque Palais Morass, can be found the Palatinate Museum (Kurpfälzisches Museum), with a collection of great artistic and historical interest (Windsheim Apostles' Altar, by Tilman Riemenschneider; cast of the lower jaw of Heidelberg Man, c. 500,000 years old).

* Palatinate Museum

Farther east are the Heiliggeistkirche (Church of the Holy Ghost; 1400–41), formerly the burial-place of the Electors Palatine; the Town Hall (Rathaus, 1701–03; from the nearby Kornmarkt a view of the castle); and the Haus zum Ritter, a Renaissance building of 1592. Here too, in the old Palais Weimar, is the Museum of Ethnography (Völkerkundemuseum).

On the south side of the Hauptstrasse lies Universitätsplatz, with the Old University (Alte Universität; 1711). On its east side, in Augustinergasse, is the Pedellenhaus, with the student prison (Karzer) which was in use from 1778 to 1914 (open to visitors). The New University (Neue Universität) was built in 1928–31, with American aid. Behind it rises the Hexenturm (Witches' Tower), once part of the town's fortifications.

University

Opposite, in Grabengasse, are the richly stocked University Library (Universitätsbibliothek), whose principal treasure is the 14th century "Manessische Handschrift", an illuminated manuscript book of medieval songs, the Seminargebäude and the Mensa (students' refectory) in Universitätsplatz. The little Peterskirche (15th c.) is now mainly used as the university church.

Between the Hauptstrasse and the Neckar are the narrow streets and lanes of the old town. On the Neckarstaden (left bank of the river) is the old Marstall (Court Stables), now housing the University's art collection.

Neckarstaden

Farther downstream stands the Stadthalle (1903) used for congresses and other events. Here too is the landing-stage of the passenger boats on the Neckar (to Mannheim and Neckarsteinach). Upstream are the Karl Theodor Bridge, known as the Old Bridge (fine views), and the twin-towered Brückentor (Bridge Gate).

Stadthalle
* Karl Theodor Bridge

From the Philosophenweg ("Philosophers' Path"), which runs east from the north end of the Theodor Heuss Bridge along the right bank of the Neckar, on the slopes of the Heiligenberg (see below), there is a famous view of the town and the castle.

* Philosophenweg

Also on the north side of the Neckar are the Zoo (in Tiergartenstrasse), the Botanic Garden (in Hofmeisterweg) and a number of recently built University institutes.

**Heidelberg Castle

The Castle can be reached either by the funicular which runs up from the Kornmarkt (continuing to Molkenkur and Königstuhl), on foot by the Burgweg (15 minutes' walk) or by car on the winding Neue Schloss-strasse. Built of red Neckar sandstone on the terraced hillside (alt. 195m/640ft), the Castle is one of the noblest examples of German Renaissance architecture. This once splendid Electoral residence was built mainly in the reigns of Electors Otto Heinrich (1556–59), Friedrich IV (1583–1610) and Friedrich V (1610–20). After its destruction by the French, who devastated the Palatinate in 1689 and 1693, it has remained a ruin – in situation, size and picturesque beauty the most magnificent ruin in Germany.

On the east side of the picturesque courtyard (dramatic performances in summer) is the Ottheinrichsbau (Otto Heinrich Building; 1557–66), the finest achievement of the early Renaissance in Germany; on the lower floor can be found the German Pharmacy Museum (Deutsches Apothekenmuseum). On the north side of the courtyard are the Gläserner Saalbau (Glass Hall) and the Friedrichsbau, one of the outstanding monuments of the mature Renaissance style in Germany (by Johann Schoch, 1601–07), with statues of rulers of the Palatinate (originals inside the building). On the west side is the Frauenzimmerbau (Women's Apartments; c. 1540), with the Königssaal (Royal Hall). Set back a little are the Library (c. 1520) and the Gothic Ruprechtsbau (c. 1400). A passage leads under the Friedrichsbau to the terrace (magnificent view).

Heidelberg

Old Bridge and Heidelberg Castle

To the left of the Friedrichsbau, lower down, is the Cellar (Keller) with the famous Great Tun of 1751, which has a capacity of 220,000 litres/48,400 gallons. Opposite can be seen a wooden figure of the court fool Perkeo (c. 1728).
From the Great Terrace a superb view can be enjoyed.

Surroundings of Heidelberg

*Königstuhl

7km/4½ miles east of Heidelberg rises the Königstuhl (568m/1864ft; funicular), with an 82m/269ft high television tower; extensive views of the Rhine plain, Neckar valley and Odenwald.

Mauer

South-east of Heidelberg we come to Mauer (reached by way of Neckargemünd), where Heidelberg Man was discovered; here is a Prehistoric Museum.

*Schwetzingen

12km/7½ miles west of Heidelberg, in the Rhine plain, is Schwetzingen, famed as a centre of asparagus-growing. It has an 18th century palace, Schloss Schwetzingen, which was a summer residence of the Electors of the Palatinate (concerts in summer). The Schloss-garten (73 hectares/180 acres), laid out partly in the French and partly in the English style, contains a number of 18th century buildings (including a Rococo theatre by Nicolas de Pigage, 1746–52; festival performances) and works of sculpture.
A more modern feature of Schwetzingen is the Bellamar bathing centre (whirlpool, flume, sauna, solarium, games rooms, etc.).

Hockenheim

Hockenheim, a few kilometres south of Schwetzingen, is famed for its Grand Prix racing circuit (Motodrom). Motor Sport Museum, with many motorcycles and racing cars, a multi-media show and a collection of documents. At Obere Hauptstrasse 8, in the town centre, is a Tobacco Museum. Aquadrom swimming pool.

Weinheim

The town of Weinheim an der Weinstrasse, 17km/10½ miles north of Heidelberg, has preserved part of its medieval walls. In the old town are the Old Town Hall (1554) and historic old half-timbered houses. Higher up is Schloss Berckheim, set in a beautiful park.

Above the town are the ruins of Burg Windeck (12th–13th c.; view); still higher up is the Wachenburg (1913).

Heilbronn

Land: Baden-Württemberg
Altitude: 159m/522ft
Population: 110,000

The former free imperial city of Heilbronn, the largest and most important industrial and commercial town in Lower Swabia, lies on both banks of the Neckar (here canalised), with a harbour of some size. The old town on the right bank of the river was almost completely destroyed during the Second World War, and only a few of its historic buildings survived. Heilbronn is the centre of an important wine-producing region.
The town has a literary memorial in Heinrich von Kleist's play "Käthchen von Heilbronn".

Situation and characteristics

Sights

In the Marktplatz of the reconstructed old town stands the Town Hall (Rathaus), restored on the basis of Renaissance models, with a fine astronomical clock (1580). The tall house at the south-west corner of the square is known as "Käthchen's House", although Kleist's play has no historical basis.

Town Hall

The nearby Kilianskirche (St Kilian's Church) dates from the 13th and 15th centuries; the 62m/203ft high tower was built in 1513–29. It has a very fine high altar (1498) by Hans Seyfer.
Outside the church, on the south wall, can be seen a fountain with seven spouts, recalling the sacred spring of the ancient Alemanni which gave the town its name ("healing spring").

*St Kilian's Church

South of the Markt are the rebuilt church of SS. Peter and Paul (13th and 18th c.; R.C.), originally the church of the Teutonic Order, and the Deutschhof (rebuilt 1950), which now houses the Municipal Museum.

Deutschhof

Nearby is the Fleisch- und Gerichtshaus (Meat Hall and Courthouse; 1598), with the Natural History Museum. In front of it, in a small square, is the Käthchen Fountain (1965). On the bank of the river is the landing-stage used by the Neckar passenger boats.

Fleisch- and Gerichtshaus

In the south-west of the old town, on the banks of the Neckar, stands the Götzenturm (Götz's Tower; 1392), in which Goethe sets the death of Götz von Berlichingen in his play of that name (although in fact Götz died in Burg Hornberg, on the Neckar, in 1562: see Neckar Valley).

Götzenturm

To the east of the Markt extends the wide avenue called the Allee, running north-south. On the far side of this lies the Stadtgarten (Municipal Park), with the Festhalle ("Harmonie").

Festhalle

At the north end of the Allee is the Theatre (1982. South-west of this is the Early Gothic St Nicholas's Church (restored).

Theatre
St Nicholas's Church

From St Nicholas's Church Turmstrasse leads to the Bollwerksturm, the only relic, apart from the Götzenturm, of the town's 13th century walls.

To the west, outside the town centre, can be found the Schiesshaus, an elegant Rococo building which survived the Second World War unscathed; now used as a concert hall.

Schiesshaus

Surroundings of Heilbronn

6km/4 miles north of Heilbronn, on the right bank of the Neckar, is Neckarsulm. In the old castle of the Teutonic Order is the German Two-Wheels Museum (Deutsches Zweirad-museum; pedal cycles and motorcycles).

Neckarsulm

Bad Wimpfen

The ancient little town of Bad Wimpfen (pop. 6000), 15km/9 miles north of Heilbronn, is also a spa (brine baths).

Wimpfen im Tal

The lower town, Wimpfen im Tal, is still completely surrounded by a low wall. Its most notable feature is the magnificent Knights' Church of St George (13th–15th c.; west front 10th c.), one of the earliest examples of Gothic architecture in Germany, with a beautiful cloister. The old knights' houses are now occupied by Benedictine monks from Grüssau Abbey in Silesia.

*Wimpfen am Berg

Higher up the steep flank of the valley is the upper town, Wimpfen am Berg. It grew up around a Hohenstaufen stronghold of the 13th century, and with its gates and towers still preserves a medieval aspect. In the west of the town are the Saalbau, with fine dwarf arcades (view of Neckar valley) and the handsome Steinhaus, once an imperial residence (museum). The chapel contains a collection of material on the history of the church.

The most prominent features on the town's skyline are the massive square Red Tower (Roter Turm; 13th c.), to the east of the Saalbau, and the 55m/180ft high Blue Tower (Blauer Turm; view).

In the Markt stands the Stadtkirche (Town Church; choir c. 1300, nave 1468–1516), with fine furnishings, including a Crucifixion group by Hans Backoffen (early 16th c.). To the west of the Markt is the Dominican Church (13th and 18th c.), with a Late Gothic cloister. Near the Town Hall is the Wormser Hof, with the Doll Museum (Puppenmuseum; dolls since 1860).

The Konventshaus, at Langgasse 2, houses the Ödenburg Heimatmuseum (historical development of the Ödenburg region, now Sopron in Hungary).

At Kronengässchen 2 can be found the unusual Glücksschwein Museum ("Good Luck Museum"), with some 2500 exhibits.

In the Kurpark, north-west of Wimpfen am Berg, is the spa establishment, with the Kursaal and the Pump Room.

Heiligenstadt   F 5

Land: Thuringia
Altitude: 250–300m/820–985ft
Population: 16,000

Situation and characteristics

Heiligenstadt, a town with a history reaching back more than a thousand years, lies some 90km/56 miles north-west of Erfurt on the north-western edge of the Thuringian Basin, at the foot of the hills of Iberg and Dün in the Leine valley.

For centuries the chief town of the Eichsfeld area, which was held by the Archbishops of Mainz, Heiligenstadt has preserved a number of historic buildings. It was the birthplace of the famous woodcarver Tilman Riemenschneider, and the 19th century writer Theodor Storm lived and worked in the town for some years.

Sights

*St Martin's Church

Large stretches of the old town walls have been preserved. The oldest building in Heiligenstadt is the former monastic church of St Martin, around which the town grew up, an aisled Gothic basilica (1304–1487) with a bronze Gothic font. In the tympanum of the north doorway can be seen a figure of St Martin on horseback (c. 1350). Heinrich Heine was baptised in this church in 1825.

Schloss

The Schloss, at Friedensplatz 8, is Baroque (by C. Heinemann, 1736–38).

*St Mary's Church

The Propsteikirche of St Mary (also known as the Altstädter Kirche or Liebfrauenkirche) is a Gothic hall-church (second half of 14th c.) with two octagonal towers. It has a beautiful figure of the Virgin (1414), a bronze font of 1492 and wall paintings of 1507.

Opposite the north doorway is the cemetery chapel of St Anne, an Early Gothic building (after 1300) on an octagonal plan, with an eight-sided stone pyramid and lantern.

Nearby, at Kollegiengasse 10, can be found the former Jesuit College, a Baroque building with a richly decorated main doorway (by C. Heinemann, 1739–40). It is now occupied by the Eichsfeld Heimatmuseum (history of town and region; collection of birds).

Eichsfeld Heimatmuseum

In the new town stands the parish church of St Ägidien (St Giles; after 1333), with a richly furnished interior (reredos, 1638; bronze Gothic font and beautiful winged altar, 15th c.; 17th c. choir-stalls).
Adjoining the church is the Maria-Hilf-Kapelle (1405).

St Giles Church

From here it is only a few paces to the New Town Hall (Neues Rathaus; 1739; Baroque, with later alterations). In front of the Town Hall, in the Markt, is the Neptune Fountain (c. 1736).

New Town Hall

In the Leine valley, below the town walls, lies the Heinrich Heine Park, with the Kneipp Baths and the oldest memorial (1815) commemorating the German war of liberation in 1813.

Heinrich Heine Park

Heligoland   B 3

Land: Schleswig-Holstein
Area: 2.1 sq.km/520 acres
Population: 2000

The island of Heligoland (Helgoland in German) lies in the Deutsche Bucht (Heligoland Bay) some 70km/45 miles from the Elbe estuary and 50km/30 miles west of the Eiderstedt peninsula (see Husum, Surroundings). It is a rocky island of red sandstone with fringes of white dunes and a rich vegetation cover.
Heligoland is now a popular holiday resort, attracting visitors with its mild climate, pure sea air and modern spa installations, as well as its duty-free facilities.
The local fishermen enjoy the long-established privilege of bringing visitors ashore; incoming vessels must therefore discharge their passengers into the fishermen's boats.

Situation and characteristics

There are daily boat services from Cuxhaven (see entry), and during the season also from Wilhelmshaven and Bremerhaven (see entries) and many mainland seaside resorts. The crossing from Bremerhaven takes three hours; a day trip allows about six hours on the island.
There are flights from Hamburg (see entry) to Heligoland; in summer several times daily. The flight takes between 40 minutes and an hour.

Access

Since Heligoland is a customs-free area it attracts many visitors with the prospect of buying spirits, tobacco goods, sweets, cameras, textiles, cosmetics, perfume, etc., at bargain prices. It should be borne in mind, however, that visitors who exceed the permitted allowances of duty-free goods (which are less generous than the allowances for persons travelling between European Community countries) will be charged duty when returning to the mainland. For details see a leaflet which can be obtained from the customs authorities.

Customs regulations

Heligoland has belonged to Germany since 1890, when it was exchanged by Britain for the protectorate of Zanzibar. It was then developed as a naval base, and was of strategic importance during the Second World War. In April 1945 it suffered heavy damage in Allied air attacks. After the war the remaining inhabitants were evacuated, and in 1947 the fortifications were blown up. Thereafter it was used by the RAF as a bombing target. After its restoration to Germany in 1952 the reconstruction of the shattered island began.

History

*The Island

Heligoland consists of three parts – Unterland, Mittelland and Oberland – together with the little neighbouring island of Düne.

"Lange Anna"

Unterland

Unterland, on the south-east side of the main island, has been completely redeveloped since 1952, with the Kurhaus, the Town Hall (1961) and numerous hotels and guest-houses. To the north are the Biological Research Station, with a seawater aquarium, and the spa installations, with a heated open-air seawater swimming pool.

Mittelland

South-west of Unterland is the rather higher Mittelland, formed when the fortifications were blown up in 1947. To the south is the artificially constructed harbour (trips round the island from the landing-stage).

Oberland

Oberland, linked with Unterland by a lift and a flight of 181 steps, is a triangle of rock some 1500m/1650yds long and up to 500m/550yds across, largely flat and grass-covered, rising to a height of 58m/190ft above the sea. On the east side lies the village (rebuilt), with St Nicholas's Church (1959; tower 33m/108ft high) and the bird-watching station. The former anti-aircraft tower to the west of the village is now a lighthouse. At the northern tip of the island are an isolated stack known as the Hengst (Stallion) or "Lange Anna" ("Big Anna") and the Lummenfelsen (Guillemots' Rock), the highest point on the island.
There is an attractive walk round the island on the cliff-top path.

Düne

About 1.5km/1 mile east of Unterland, separated from it by an arm of the sea some 10m/35ft deep (ferry), is the little island of Düne. There is good bathing on the beaches on the north and south sides of the island (Nordstrand, Südstrand), with a camping site and an area for nude bathing (FKK). At the east end is the airstrip used by the local air service.

Helmstedt E 6

Land: Lower Saxony
Altitude: 140m/460ft
Population: 28,000

Helmstedt, situated in a depression between the Lappwald and the Elm range, preserves some attractive 16th century half-timbered houses and remains of its 15th century walls. In 1576 Duke Julius of Brunswick established a Protestant university here, the Academia Julia, which for a time was the most frequented university in Germany but which was abolished in 1810. In the surrounding area are large deposits of lignite.

Situation and characteristics

The Town

In the Marktplatz stand the handsome neo-Gothic Town Hall (1906) and the Herzogliches Hoflager (Ducal Warehouse), a richly decorated half-timbered building of 1567. At the end of the street called Papenberg is the parish church of St Stephen (13th and 15th c.), which has a high altar of 1644, the "Moses Pulpit" (1590) and a brass font (also 1590).

Marktplatz

On the east side of the town is the Benedictine monastery of St Ludger, founded in the 9th century and dissolved in 1803 (Imperial Hall, with fine Baroque stucco decoration). It is entered by the handsome Türkentor (1716). In the courtyard is the double chapel of SS. Peter and John (c. 1050). Beneath the church (Romanesque; much altered in 1556 and in 1890) is a Romanesque crypt (11th c.).

St Ludger's Monastery

In Juliusplatz stands the Juleum (1592–97), the palatial main building of the old University. Notable features of the interior are the Auditorium Maximum, the Library (c. 30,000 titles) and, in the cellar, the District Heimatmuseum.

Juleum

On a low hill to the west of the town is the Augustinian nunnery of Marienberg, founded in 1176, with a Romanesque church (13th c. wall paintings) and a collection of vestments and tapestries.

Marienberg

Herford

E 4

Land: North Rhine-Westphalia
Altitude: 68m/223ft
Population: 62,000

The old Hanseatic town of Herford lies in the fertile hilly region between the Wiehengebirge and the Teutoburg Forest (see entry), at the junction of the Aa with the Werre. It has a variety of industry, in particular furniture manufacture and textiles. The Baroque architect Matthäus Daniel Pöppelmann was born in Herford in 1662.

Situation and characteristics

The Town

The old town lies around the Minster of the former convent (13th c.; 16th c. Late Gothic font), the oldest of the larger hall-churches of Westphalia. Opposite the church is the Town Hall (1917).

Minster

Farther west is the 14th century Jakobikirche (St James's Church).

On the Deichtorwall (on the west side of the old town) can be found the Municipal Museum (history, culture and art of the town and the former abbey).

Museum

To the north-east, in the Neuer Markt, stands the Johanniskirche (St John's Church; mid 14th c.), with beautiful 14th and 15th century stained glass.

St John's Church

In Höckerstrasse (pedestrian zone), which runs south-west from the Neuer Markt, is the Bürgermeisterhaus (Burgomaster's House; 1538), with a handsome Late Gothic stepped gable. This is said to have been the birthplace of Matthäus Daniel Pöppelmann.

Bürgermeisterhaus

Another notable building is the Remensnider-Haus in nearby Brüderstrasse, a half-timbered house of 1521 with rich figural decoration.

Remensnider-Haus

To the east of the town centre, on the Lutterberg, is the 14th century Stiftberg Church (St Mary's; west tower 1904), one of the finest Gothic hall-churches in Westphalia, with a Late Gothic tabernacle.

Stiftberg Church

Surroundings of Herford

Enger	In Enger (9km/6 miles north-west) the former monastic church of St Dionysius (12th and 14th c.) contains the sarcophagus of Duke Wittekind of Saxony, whose date of death is given as 807, with a magnificent relief grave-slab (c. 1100).
Bünde	Bünde (13km/8 miles north-west) is the centre of the Westphalian tobacco industry. It has an interesting Tobacco Museum (tobacco pipes of varying origin, tobacco jars, a cigar 1.60m/5¼ft long).

Bad Hersfeld   G 5

Land: Hesse
Altitude: 278m/912ft
Population: 30,000

Situation and characteristics	Bad Hersfeld, a spa and festival city, lies amid wooded hills in a wide basin in the lower Fulda valley, which is joined here by the Haune, between the Rhön (see entry) and the Knüll range. Its mineral waters (containing sulphates of sodium and magnesium) are recommended in the treatment of liver, gall bladder, intestinal and gastric conditions and disorders of the metabolism. The old town, still partly encircled by its walls, has numbers of fine old burghers' houses. The town's traditional industry is cloth-making.

The Town

Marktplatz Stadtkirche	The spacious Marktplatz is surrounded by handsome old burghers' houses. To the east stands the 14th century Stadtkirche (Town Church), with a massive tower and a Late Gothic interior (organ of 1974; recitals). Opposite it, to the south, is the Town Hall (originally 14th c.; enlarged in Renaissance style c. 1600). In the Neumarkt, in the southern part of the old town, is the Heimatmuseum.
*Stiftskirche	To the west of the town can be seen the imposing ruins of the Stiftskirche (11th and 12th c.), which was destroyed by the French in 1761. The church, over 100m/330ft long, with a separate bell-tower, is the setting of an annual festival. The adjoining buildings, to the south, are now occupied by the Heimatmuseum (history of local crafts).
Spa district	In the south-west of the town lies the spa district, with the Kurhaus and three mineral springs.

Hessian Uplands (Hessisches Bergland)   G–H 4–5

Land: Hesse

Situation and characteristics	The Hessian Uplands – once the territory of a Germanic tribe, the Chatti – have the most varied topography in the whole of the German Central Uplands. They extend from the river Werra in the east to the Rhine between Mainz and Koblenz in the west and from Karlshafen on the Weser in the north to the Neckar at Heidelberg in the south. They are broken up into numerous valley areas and small ranges of hills, which reach their greatest height in the Rhön (see entry), with the Gross Wasserkuppe (950m/3120ft). To the west are the Westerwald and the Taunus (see entries), in the Rhenish Uplands. Between the Main, the Rhine plain and the Neckar is the Odenwald (see entry), the southern part of which lies in Baden-Württemberg. To the east are the Hessian depression, which extends from the Main between Frankfurt and Hanau by way of the fertile Wetterau (between the Taunus and the Vogelsberg) and the Lahn valley between Giessen and Marburg to the rivers Schwalm and Fulda (continuing in the Weser valley), and the Hessian Uplands proper.

Landscape

Vogelsberg	North-east of the Taunus, and separated from it by the Wetterau, rises the Vogelsberg, a flat-topped cone some 50km/30 miles in diameter which was originally a much higher

volcano. The old lava flows, the line of which can still be traced in the valleys radiating from the hill, form the largest mass of basalt in Germany. The summit area consists of the unpopulated Oberwald, a tract of forest (mainly beech and oak) at a height of over 600m/2000ft, rising to 772m/2533ft in the Taufstein.

From the Vogelsberg the ridge of hills runs east to the Rhön, the northern part of which is in Thuringia and the southern part in Bavaria.

To the north of the Rhön lies the Seulingswald, a wooded upland region of sandstone extending to the Hönebach pass between the rivers Werra and Fulda, which here come within 16km/10 miles of one another.

Seulingswald

Beyond this, extending between the Werra and the Fulda to their junction at Münden (see entry), is the Meissnerland, a region of varied topography within which are the Ringgau to the east, the Hoher Meissner (750m/2460ft) in the middle and the Kaufunger Wald to the north, reaching its highest point in the Bilstein (640m/2100ft).

Meissnerland

To the west of the Fulda and north of the Vogelsberg is the little Knüllgebirge, a grass-covered basaltic plateau reaching its highest point in the Eisenberg (636m/2087ft) and falling steeply down on the south.

Knüllgebirge

Farther north-west we come to the Hainagebirge, an outlier of the Rhenish Uplands which reaches a height of 675m/2215ft in the Kellerwald. It is a densely forested area with deeply indented valleys, in one of which is the great Eder Dam.

Hainagebirge

To the west of Kassel-Wilhelmshöhe extends the Habichtswald, a basalt plateau some 4km/2½ miles long and broad, reaching its highest point in the Hohes Gras (615m/2018ft) and falling away steeply on all sides.

Habichtswald

The most northerly part of the Hessian Uplands is the Reinhardswald (see Weserbergland).

Hiddensee

See Rügen

Hildesheim

E 5

Land: Lower Saxony
Altitude: 70m/230ft
Population: 100,000

The old episcopal city of Hildesheim lies in the north-western Harz foreland, in the fertile valley of the Innerste. The churches built by Bishop Bernward (993–1022) and his successors made Hildesheim a treasure-house of Early Romanesque architecture, and the town's many half-timbered buildings contributed to its unique charm and interest. Then in March 1945, shortly before the end of the war in Europe, Hildesheim suffered heavy damage in an air attack which destroyed 70% of the town's buildings. Accordingly the town now has a predominantly modern aspect, with a few islands of tradition here and there in the form of rebuilt and restored historic buildings.

Situation and characteristics

The Rosen-Route is a "tourist trail" round the town, marked by signs in the street paving, which takes in 21 of the principal sights.

Rosen-Route

Sights

In the central area of the town, which is still surrounded by the old moat, is the Markt, completely restored to its original form from 1983 onwards.

Markt

Hildesheim

Knochenhauer-Amtshaus

The most notable building in the Markt is the Knochenhauer-Amtshaus (Butchers' Guild-House). The original building of 1529 was completely destroyed in 1945, but has been rebuilt in its original form, using the same materials (oak beams, sometimes with clay cladding) and the original building techniques (beams joined by oak dowels). Adjoining is the Bäckeramtshaus (Bakers' Guild-House; originally 1800, completely destroyed in 1945), the rebuilding of which was completed in 1988.

On the east side of the square stands the Late Gothic Town Hall (Rathaus; rebuilt). Facing it, to the south, is the Tempelhaus (Templar House; 14th and 15th c.), with a Renaissance oriel of 1592. In the centre of the square is a fountain (a modern copy of the original fountain of 1540).

St Andrew's Church "Huckup"

South-west of the Markt, beyond the busy Hoher Weg (pedestrian zone), is Andreasplatz, with the Andreaskirche (St Andrew's Church; Romanesque, with Gothic choir; restored). Nearby, at the corner of Hoher Weg and Schuhstrasse, can be seen a statue (1905) of the "Huckup", a legendary Hildesheim figure who is the incarnation of a bad conscience.

Magdalenenkirche

The Magdalenenkirche (13th c.; R.C.), to the west of the old town, contains the beautiful Elffen Altar (1520) and the silver reliquary of St Bernward (1751).

St Michael's Church

To the north, on a commanding eminence, stands the Michaeliskirche (St Michael's Church; Protestant), one of the finest Romanesque basilican churches in Germany. The church was begun in the 11th century, in the time of Bishop Bernward, and altered in the 12th century; restored after the last war. The most notable features of the interior are the painted wooden ceiling of the nave (genealogy of Christ, 12th c.) and the Angel Choir. In the crypt can be seen the stone sarcophagus of St Bernward.

Cathedral

In the south-west of the old town is the Romanesque Cathedral (Dom). Built between 1054 and 1079 on the remains of an earlier 9th century Romanesque basilica, it was badly damaged in 1945 and was re-consecrated in 1960 after the completion of restoration work. It contains numerous treasures of art, among them the brazen doors of Bishop Bernward (1015), a column carved with scenes from the life of Christ (1020) and a bronze font of about 1240. Over the altar is a large wheel chandelier presented by Bishop Hezilo (11th c.), with a representation of the Heavenly Jerusalem. On the outer wall of the east choir is the famous "thousand-year-old rose-bush" (grown since the war from cuttings taken from the original rootstock). In the cloister garth is St Anne's Chapel (1322).

In the adjoining Diocesan Museum is the Cathedral Treasury (including the silver Cross of St Bernward).

Roemer-Pelizaeus Museum

To the west of the Cathedral, in the square called Am Steine, can be found the Roemer-Pelizaeus Museum, with the most important Egyptological collection in Germany after the Egyptian Museum in Berlin (see entry), as well as outstanding collections of natural history and ethnography. Periodic special exhibitions.

Heiligkreuzkirche

On a terrace to the east of the Cathedral stands the Heiligkreuzkirche (Church of the Holy Cross; R.C.). Originally Romanesque, it was remodelled in Baroque style in the 18th century.

St Godehard's Church

On the south side of the old town is the Godehardikirche (St Godehard's Church; 1133–72), one of the best preserved Romanesque churches in Germany, with a beautiful interior (Late Gothic altar of St Benedict, 1518).

Lappenberg Memorial

On the Lappenberg, on the site of the Synagogue which was destroyed in 1938, can be seen a cube-shaped marble memorial with bronze reliefs depicting the history of the Jews. Near here is the Kehrwiederturm ("Return Again" Tower; 1465), the only surviving tower from the old fortifications.

St Maurice's Church

On the Moritzberg, to the west of the town, is St Maurice's Church (St Mauritius; 11th c.), with a well preserved cloister and the tomb of Bishop Hezilo (1054–79).

Hildesheim-Sorsum

Afrika Manyatta

In the western district of Sorsum is the Afrika Manyatta Museum (African folk art; sale of Kenyan craft products).

Hildesheim Cathedral

See Wolfenbüttel, Surroundings

Synagogue Memorial

Salzgitter

Hof

H 7

Land: Bavaria
Altitude: 495m/1625ft
Population: 52,000

Hof, situated on the upper Saale, between the Fichtelgebirge and the Franconian Forest, is the most important industrial town in northern Bavaria (textiles, metalworking, brewing).

Situation and characteristics

The Town

In Klosterstrasse, on the west bank of the Salle, stands the Town Hall. Facing it, to the east, is the parish church of St Michael (1380–86; restored in neo-Gothic style 1834).

Town Hall

The street called Altstadt and Lorenzstrasse lead south to the Lorenzkirche (St Lawrence's Church; 1292, with much later alteration), with the Hertnid Altar, a Late Gothic winged altar of 1480.

St Lawrence's Church

To the north of the Town Hall, in the street called Am Unteren Tor, can be found the Hospitalkirche (Gothic, with a Baroque coffered ceiling of 1688–89 and a carved altar of 1511). Nearby is the Vogtland Museum (regional history, crafts and house interiors; natural history).

Hospitalkirche Museum

To the north-east of the town lies the Theresienstein Park (70 hectares/175 acres), with a Botanic Garden, a small Zoo and an outlook tower on the Labyrinth-Berg.

Municipal Park

Hohenlohe

See Swabian Castle Country

Holsteinische Schweiz ("Switzerland of Holstein")   **B 5–6**

Land: Schleswig-Holstein

Situation and characteristics

The "Switzerland of Holstein" is a region of hills and lakes – the remains of an Ice Age ground and terminal moraine – on the Wagrien peninsula in eastern Holstein, between Lübeck Bay and Kiel Bay. With its beautiful beech forests and its shimmering sheets of water it is one of the most attractive stretches of country in Germany. At its east end is the Bungsberg (164m/538ft), the highest point in the whole of Schleswig-Holstein. The area was given its name in the 19th century, with the idea of exploiting the current fashion for holidaying in Switzerland.

*Landscape

Malente-Gremsmühlen

The centre of the Holsteinische Schweiz is the friendly little climatic and health resort (Kneipp cure) of Malente-Gremsmühlen, delightfully situated between the Dieksee and the Kellersee, which is the starting-point of the popular "Five Lakes" trip.

Eutin

The nearby town of Eutin was once a favourite resort of writers and painters. Its summer festival, with opera performances in the Schlosspark, is widely famed.

Plön

Plön has a Late Renaissance castle. Set in an attractive lake district, it is a popular water sports centre. The largest and most beautiful of the lakes is the Grosser Plöner See, which has an area of 30 sq.km/11½ sq. miles.

Plöner See in the "Switzerland of Holstein"

Bad Homburg vor der Höhe

Land: Hesse
Altitude: 192m/630ft
Population: 51,000

Bad Homburg vor der Höhe, at the foot of the Taunus, is one of the most famous of German spas, and has also developed into an important congress and conference centre. In its beautiful Kurpark are hot chalybeate saline springs which are used in the treatment of gastric, intestinal and gall-bladder diseases and metabolic disorders.

Situation and characteristics

The Town

The principal shopping street is Louisenstrasse (pedestrian zone), with the Kurhaus (Festival Hall).

On the north side of the Kaiser-Friedrich-Promenade, which runs parallel to Louisenstrasse, is the Kurpark (44 hectares/110 acres), an English-style landscaped park laid out by P. J. Lenné in 1854, with the Kaiser-Wilhelm-Bad, the Casino, several carbonic mineral springs, the Siamese Temple and beautiful gardens and clumps of trees.

*Kurpark

The Taunus Baths (Taunus-Therme), in a style showing Far Eastern influence, were opened in 1984. They occupy the site of an earlier spa establishment which was burned down in 1983.

*Taunus Baths

On the west side of the town, dominated by the 13th century White Tower (Weisser Turm), is the Schloss (17th–19th c.; Banqueting Hall, Hall of Mirrors).

Schloss

Surroundings of Bad Homburg

The Saalburg (7km/4½ miles north-west) is a reconstruction of a fort on the Limes, the defensive zone on the Roman frontier, built between 1898 and 1907 on the foundations of a fort which stood on this site. The fort measures 221m/242yds by 147m/161yds. Finds from the site are displayed in the Saalburg Museum.

*Saalburg

In Neu-Anspach, north-west of the Saalburg, can be found the Hessenpark open-air museum, with typical old Hessian peasants' and craftsmen's houses. Some of the workshops are occupied by working craftsmen. There are a variety of exhibitions and other events.

Hessenpark

24km/15 miles north-west of Bad Homburg is the Grosser Feldberg (880m/2887ft), the highest peak in the Taunus (see entry). On top of the hills rises a 70m/230ft high telecommunications tower. On the Kleiner Feldberg (827m/2713ft) is an outlook tower (views extending over the Spessart and the Odenwald).

*Grosser Feldberg

Höxter

Land: North Rhine-Westphalia
Altitude: 91m/299ft
Population: 35,000

Höxter lies on the left bank of the Weser in an attractive setting of wooded hills, those on the right bank forming part of the Solling range (see Weserbergland). Nearby is Corvey Abbey, once a leading centre of western culture.

Situation and characteristics

The Town

In the old town are numerous Renaissance half-timbered buildings dating from the 16th century. Among the finest are the Dechanei (Deanery) of 1561 in Markstrasse, once the

Half-timbered houses

town house of the noble Amelunxen family, with an oriel window and fine rosette-patterned half-timbering; Haus Hütte (1565), at Nikolaistrasse 10; in Westerbachstrasse, a relatively wide street along which the old trade route known as the Hellweg entered the town, the Tillyhaus of 1598 (No. 33), where the imperial general Count Tilly is said to have stayed several times during the Thirty Years War, Haus Hottensen (1537) at No. 34, and a charming group of houses (restored) at Nos. 2–10. Opposite the west front of St Kilian's Church is the Küsterhaus (Verger's House), a fine half-timbered building of 1595.

Town Hall	The Town Hall, with a richly carved oriel and an octagonal staircase tower, dates from 1610–13. In the entrance hall is a Late Romanesque stone relief (c. 1260) depicting the master of the municipal weigh-house. The tower houses a carillon of 35 bronze bells (daily at 8.55 and 11.55am and 2.55, 5.55 and 8.55pm).
St Kilian's Church	North-east of the Town Hall stands the Romanesque Kilianikirche (St Kilian's Church; 12th and 13th c.; Protestant), with two prominent west towers of unequal height. Notable features of the interior are a Crucifixion group of 1520 on the high altar, the pulpit (1597) and the font (1631). To the north is the Early Gothic Marienkirche (St Mary's Church; 13th c.).

Corvey

**Abbey	2km/1¼ miles north-west of Höxter is Corvey Abbey, in its day the most distinguished Benedictine house in northern Germany. Founded in 822 by Ludwig the Pious, it was secularised in 1803; it now belongs to the Duke of Ratibor. Of the old abbey church there survives the magnificent west work (873–85), the oldest building of the early medieval period in Westphalia. In the interior can be seen the two-storey Imperial Chapel, with remains of wall paintings (9th c.). The present abbey church has a magnificent Baroque interior. On the south side is the tomb of A. H. Hoffmann von Fallersleben, author of the German national anthem, "Deutschland über Alles", who was librarian in Schloss Corvey.
Schloss	Of the Baroque period, too, are the plain undecorated buildings of the former abbey, now the Schloss. Its most notable features are the Abbot's Gallery, the Imperial Hall, the Library and the Museum (history of the abbey; Hoffmann von Fallersleben; local history and folk traditions).

Surroundings of Höxter

*Köterberg	17km/10½ miles north-west is the Köterberg (497m/1631ft), with a television tower and the Köterberghaus; fine panoramic views of the Solling and Vogler hills, the Lippe Uplands and the Eggegebirge.
Holzminden	10km/6 miles north-east, on the right bank of the Weser, lies Holzminden, with handsome 17th century half-timbered houses. 37km/23 miles farther down the Weser valley is Baron Münchhausen's town of Bodenwerder (see Hameln, Surroundings).
Neuhaus im Solling	16km/10 miles east of Höxter is the altitude resort and winter sports centre of Neuhaus im Solling, with a former hunting lodge of the Kings of Hanover (1768–91).
Fürstenberg	6km/4 miles south of Höxter, beyond the Weser, stands Schloss Fürstenberg (concerts), now part of the Fürstenberg porcelain manufactory (established 1747). Adjoining is the present manufactory, with a museum.

Hoyerswerda   F 9

Land: Saxony
Altitude: 116m/381ft
Population: 69,700

The Lusatian town of Hoyerswerda (Sorbian Wojerecy) lies 50km/30 miles south of Cottbus in the valley of the Schwarze (Black) Elster. Before 1949 an unimportant small town, Hoyerswerda has multiplied its population tenfold as a result of the development of mining and electricity production in this area.

Situation and characteristics

Hoyerswerda lies in the Sorbian language area, and in 1912 the Domowina, an organisation designed to resist the increasing oppression of Sorbs by Germans, was founded in the town. (Domowina is a poetical name for "home" in the Sorbian language).

Sights

The Town Hall (Rathaus) was built in 1429 and rebuilt in Renaissance style in 1680. Over the round-arched doorway are colourful coats of arms.

Town Hall

The three-storey Schloss, which first appears in the records in the 13th century, was much altered in later centuries; in its present form it dates mainly from the Renaissance. It is now occupied by a museum. In front of the building can be seen a Saxon posting milestone of 1732.

Schloss

The Amtshaus is a two-storey Baroque building of 1702. The 18th century dramatist Lessing was frequently a guest here as a young man.

Amtshaus

The Late Gothic parish church (16th c.) suffered heavy destruction in 1945 (restored 1985). The aisleless Baroque Kreuzkirche dates from the 18th century.

Churches

Surroundings of Hoyerswerda

Farther down the valley of the Schwarze Elster is the old mining town of Senftenberg (Sorbian Zly Komorow). It has a fine Schloss (15th–16th c.), now housing the District Museum, with a collection of Lusatian art. There are fine old trees in the Schlosspark. In the castle courtyard is a sculpture by Ernst Barlach, "The Beggar".
The Senftenberg Lakes are a holidaymaker's paradise, with a nature reserve of 300 hectares/750 acres and seventeen beaches.

Senftenberg

Hunsrück
H 2–3

Land: Rhineland-Palatinate

The Hunsrück, the most southerly part of the Rhenish Uplands on the left bank of the Rhine, facing the Taunus (see entry) on the right bank, lies between the Rhine, the Mosel, the lower Saar and the Nahe.

Situation and characteristics

Landscape

The Hunsrück is an upland region between 400m/1300ft and 500m/1650ft high out of which rises a long ridge of quartzite hills reaching their highest point in the Erbeskopf (816m/2677ft), the highest peak in the left-bank Rhenish Uplands. While the gently rolling plateau has lost much of its forest cover and is dotted with little towns and villages, the hills are covered with one of the largest areas of forest in Germany (mainly conifers) – the Bingerwald and Soonwald to the east, the Idarwald and Hochwald to the west.

Hunsrück-Höhenstrasse (Ridgeway)

The Hunsrück-Höhenstrasse runs through the finest stretches of the Hunsrück. On the road are the little altitude resort of Kastellaun (ruined castle) and the resorts of Morbach,

Thalfang and Hermeskeil (chief place in the Hochwald). The road from Bingen (see Rhine Valley) to the Hunsrück passes through the ancient little towns of Stromberg, Simmern (chief town of the Hunsrück) and Kirchberg.

Edelsteinstrasse   See Idar-Oberstein

Husum
B 4

Land: Schleswig-Holstein
Altitude: 5m/16ft
Population: 24,000

Situation and characteristics
Husum, situated on the west coast of Schleswig-Holstein, in the Husumer Au, which serves as a natural harbour, is the cultural centre of northern Friesland. After a storm tide in the 14th century which brought about a change in the conformation of the land, Husum began to develop its own shipping trade. As the birthplace of the poet and novelist Theodor Storm (1817–88) this "grey city by the sea" features in many of his stories.

The Town

Marktplatz
In the Marktplatz stands the Town Hall (Rathaus), originally built in 1601, with much later alteration. On the east side of the square is the neo-classical Marienkirche (St Mary's Church; 1829–33), with a bronze font of 1643. At No. 8 is the birthplace of Theodor Storm and at No. 31 in the Wasserreihe the Theodor Storm House (museum).

Schloss
The Schloss (1577–82) has been restored and is open to the public. Beautiful gardens.

Ostenfelder Bauernhaus
Beyond the Neustädter Friedhof (New Town Cemetery) can be seen the Ostenfelder Bauernhaus (Farmhouse; c. 1630), which has been in the Ostenfelder Bauernhaus Open-Air Museum since 1899.

Nissenhaus
To the south of the Markt is the Nissenhaus (1937–39), built of clinker brick, with the North Frisian Museum (natural history, local history and folk traditions).

Harbour
The harbour, on the west side of the town, is the starting-point for trips to the North Frisian Islands (see North Sea Coast).

Eiderstedt Peninsula

South-west of Husum the Eiderstedt peninsula extends into the Wattenmeer. Characteristic of this area are the large and handsome farmhouses (*haubarge*).

Roter Hauberg
10km/6 miles south-west of Husum, at Simonsberg, is the Roter Hauberg, a fine old farmhouse which now belongs to the Eiderstedt Heimatmuseum at St Peter-Ording (see below).

Tönning
On the Eider estuary, which bounds the south-east side of the peninsula, is the little port of Tönning with its charming old gabled houses and the Romanesque and Gothic Laurentiuskirche (St Lawrence's Church; c. 1220), with a Baroque tower.

On the harbour stands the Packhaus (1783), with an exhibition on the history of the town.

Garding
Farther west is the little town of Garding. In the Markt are the Late Romanesque parish church and the birthplace (No. 6) of the great classical scholar Theodor Mommsen (1817–1903).

St Peter-Ording
At the western tip of the peninsula lies the popular health resort of St Peter-Ording.

Harbour, Tönning

In St Peter-Süd are the Romanesque and Gothic parish church, standing on higher ground, and the Eiderstedt Heimatmuseum.

The North Frisian Islands, off the coast, form part of the Wattenmeer National Park (see North Sea Coast and Sylt).

North Frisian Islands

Idar-Oberstein

H 2

Land: Rhineland-Palatinate
Altitude: 260m/850ft
Population: 36,000

Attractively situated at the junction of the Idar with the Nahe, with crags of melaphyre (basaltic rock) towering 125m/410ft above it, Idar-Oberstein is one of Germany's leading centres of the trade in precious stones and the jewellery industry, with well-known gem-cutting establishments.

Situation and characteristics

Oberstein

In Oberstein is the Idar-Oberstein Museum (precious stones, fossils, fluorescence cabinet; history of the town).

Museum

Above the town lies the Rock Church (Felsenkirche), built into a cave on the hillside; the porch dates from the 11th century (enlarged in 1482). Higher up on the steep-sided crag are two ruined castles (11th and 12th c.).

Rock Church

Idar

Idar extends up the Idar valley, with the 22-storey Diamond and Precious Stone Exchange (Diamant- und Edelsteinbörse), in which is the fascinating Museum of Precious Stones (Edelsteinmuseum).

Diamond Exchange
** Museum

291

Gem-Cutting Centre

On the outskirts of Idar, in Tiefensteiner Strasse, can be found the Wieherschleifferei, an old gem-cutting centre where visitors can see the stones being cut and polished.

Steinkaulenberg

In the Algenroth district is the entrance to the precious stone mines in the Steinkaulenberg (conducted visits).

Deutsche Edelsteinstrasse (German Precious Stones Route)

The Deutsche Edelsteinstrasse (marked by a stylised diamond) runs through the Hunsrück (see entry) to the north of Idar-Oberstein in a circuit of 58km/36 miles, taking in over a dozen places with gem-cutting establishments.

Ilmenau   G 6

Land: Thuringia
Altitude: 540m/1772ft
Population: 32,500

Situation and characteristics

Ilmenau lies 20km/12½ miles from Suhl on the north-eastern fringes of the Thuringian Forest, surrounded by wooded hills. In recent years it has developed into a considerable industrial town and educational centre. It has many associations with Goethe, who often visited Ilmenau as a minister of the Duchy of Weimar.

Sights

*Goethe Memorial Museum

In the Amtshaus in the Markt, a plain Baroque building of 1756, stands the Goethe-Gedenkstätte (Memorial Museum; rooms occupied by Goethe, with period furniture). The same building houses the Heimatmuseum (porcelain; history of silver- and copper-mining).

Town Hall

The two-storey Town Hall (Rathaus) has a Renaissance doorway and the magnificent coat of arms of the Counts Henneberg on the façade. In the Marktplatz is the Hennebrunnen, a fountain of about 1752.

Stadtkirche

The nearby Stadtkirche (Town Church), an aisleless Renaissance building (1603), was rebuilt in the 18th century after a fire.

Zechenhaus

The oldest house in the town is the Zechenhaus on the Sturmheide, seat of the Ilmenau mining authority from 1691.

Associations with Goethe

"Goethe Trail"

There is a well marked "Goethe Trail" ("Auf Goethes Spuren"), which runs from Ilmenau via Gabelbach to Stützerbach, a distance of 18km/11 miles. The route is waymarked with the letter "G", and there are explanatory tablets at the various sites.

*Gabelbach

Goethe frequently stayed in the Gabelbach hunting lodge. Visitors can see the rooms which he occupied when he came here with the Duke of Weimar to hunt, with documents, drawings and other mementoes. In the rooms occupied by the Duke is a small museum on Goethe's natural history studies in the Thuringian Forest.

*Kichelhahn

North of Gabelbach is the little house on the Kichelhahn where Goethe wrote his well-known poem "Über allen Gipfeln ist Ruh'". On the summit of the Kichelhahn (861m/2825ft) stands an outlook tower from which there are panoramic views.

Grosser Hermannstein

A short distance from the Kichelhahn tower is the Grosser Hermannstein, with a cave which Goethe liked to visit.

On the Schwalbenstein, a crag (fine view) near the Schöffenhaus, Goethe wrote the fourth act of his play "Iphigenie" on a single day in 1779.

Schwalbenstein

Surroundings of Ilmenau

In Stützerbach, now a holiday resort and spa (Kneipp cure), where Conrad Röntgen carried out his first experiments in developing the X-ray tube, is the Goethehaus (Kneippstrasse 18), with mementoes of Goethe's visits. The house also contains an interesting exhibition on the history of glass manufacture (with demonstrations). Stützerbach has an 18th century Baroque church (aisleless) with a vaulted timber ceiling and a west tower topped by a curving roof.

Stützerbach

Oehrenstock has a small Mining Museum, illustrating the history of mining in the Ilmenau area.

Oehrenstock

Farther east are the impressive remains of the Benedictine house of Paulinzella, founded in 1112 (restored 1965–69). This is a fine example of the work of the Hirsau school of church builders, which began to spread from southern Germany at the end of the 11th century.

*Paulinzella

Ingolstadt

K 6

Land: Bavaria
Altitude: 365m/1198ft
Population: 93,000

This former residence and stronghold of the Dukes of Bavaria lies on the southern fringes of the Franconian Alb in a wide plain in the Danube valley. The old town (pedestrian zone) with its many historic buildings is still surrounded by considerable remains of its medieval fortifications.

Situation and
characteristics

The Town

In the centre of the old town is the Rathausplatz, with the Old Town Hall (Altes Rathaus; formed by the combination of four Gothic houses in 1882), the New Town Hall (Neues Rathaus; 1959) and the 15th century Spitalkirche, which has 16th century wall paintings. To the north of the Old Town Hall stands the St-Moritz-Kirche (St Maurice's Church), and beyond this the Obere Franziskanerkirche (Upper Franciscan Church), both dating from the 14th century.

Rathausplatz

From the Moritzkirche Ludwigstrasse runs east to the massive old Herzogsschloss (Ducal Castle; 15th c.), which has one of the finest Gothic secular interiors in Germany. Since 1972 it has housed the Bavarian Army Museum (Armeemuseum; military technology from the Middle Ages to the First World War).

Schloss
Army Museum

South-west of the Schloss are the Municipal Theatre (Stadttheater) and the old Herzogskasten (a relic of a 13th century castle), now the Municipal Library. In nearby Tränktorstrasse is the Museum of Concrete Art (Museum für Konkrete Kunst; painting, sculpture).

From the Moritzkirche Theresienstrasse leads west to the Liebfrauenmünster (Minster of Our Lady; 15th–16th c.), the largest Late Gothic hall-church in Bavaria. The most notable features of the light interior are the largest and finest Renaissance stained glass window in Bavaria (1527), behind the high altar, and the brass marking the tomb of Dr Johann Eck, leader of the Counter-Reformation in Bavaria and opponent of Luther.

Minster

Farther west, on the edge of the old town, rises the massive Kreuztor with its seven towers and turrets (1385).

*Kreuztor

293

Kreuztor, Ingolstadt

Museum on History of Medicine	In Anatomiestrasse, which bounds the old town on the south-west, is the Alte Anatomie, now housing the Museum on the History of Medicine (Medizinhistorisches Museum; history of medical research and practice since ancient times).
Municipal Museum	To the north-west of the town centre, in the Cavalier Hepp building (1838–43; restored), part of the town's neo-classical fortifications, is the Municipal Museum (Stadtmuseum; geology, archaeology, history of the town since the Stone Age).
Asamkirche	North of the Minster, in Neubaustrasse, stands the Rococo Asamkirche (church of Maria de Victoria), built by the Asam brothers in 1732–36, with a large ceiling painting. In the sacristy can be seen the famous Lepanto Monstrance (1708), with a representation of the naval battle of Lepanto (1571).

Iserlohn

F 3

Land: North Rhine-Westphalia
Altitude: 247m/810ft. Population: 90,000

Iserlohn, situated on a plateau in northern Sauerland (see entry), surrounded by forest-covered hills, is one of the most important industrial and commercial towns in Westphalia.

Situation and characteristics

The Town

The town has preserved some remains of its old walls. A little way south of the Markt is St Mary's Church (St Marien), with a Romanesque west tower. It has a Flemish carved altar (c. 1400) and Gothic choir-stalls (c. 1500).

St Mary's Church

Lower down can be seen the Bauernkirche (Countryfolk's Church) of St Pankratius (Pancras), originally Romanesque but later rebuilt in Gothic style.

Bauernkirche

To the south-east, in the Haus der Heimat, is the Municipal Museum (geology, history of the town and of local industry).

Museum

4km/2½ miles west, on the road to Letmathe, can be found the entrance to the Dechenhöhle (on right of road), a stalactitic cave discovered in 1868, with an interesting museum.

Dechenhöhle

Hemer

At Hemer, 7km/4½ miles east, is the Heinrichshöhle (discovered 1812), which is accessible for a distance of 350m/385yds.

Heinrichshöhle

Nearby is the "Felsenmeer" ("Sea of Rock"), a series of rocky gorges below tall beech trees.

Balve

15km/9 miles south-east of Hemer lies Balve. The parish church of St Blasius (Blaise) is a hall-church of the late 12th c., with 13th century wall paintings. Adjoining the church is the Museum of Prehistory (minerals, fossils, finds from the Balver Höhle).

At the north end of the town is the Balver Höhle (Balve Cave; 80m/260ft long by 20m/65ft wide), which was occupied by man in the Ice Age. It is now used as a hall for concerts and other events.

Balver Höhle

At Wocklum, near the Balver Höhle, is the Luisenhütte, a charcoal-fired smelting works of 1732 which operated until 1865 (open to visitors).

Luisenhütte

Jena

G 7

Land: Thuringia
Altitude: 160m/525ft
Population: 103,000

The university town of Jena, long renowned as a centre of learning, lies in the valley of the Saale beneath the steep limestone cliffs bordering a wooded plateau. During the 19th and 20th centuries Jena established an international reputation as a centre of precision engineering and the optical industry.

Situation and characteristics

Central Area

The Markt, the only part of the old town which escaped destruction by bombing during the Second World War, is now protected as a historic monument. On its south-west side

*Markt
Town Hall

stands the Late Gothic Town Hall (Rathaus), a double building with two hipped roofs. On the tower is a clock with mechanical figures.

Alte Göhre (Municipal Museum)

Another Gothic building in the Markt (restored) is the Alte Göhre, with a striking gable on the north front. It now houses the richly stocked Municipal Museum (Stadtmuseum; history of the town and university, medieval religious art, folk art and traditions). Also in the Markt is the Gothic-arched entrance to the 15th century inn Zur Sonne (at the sign of the Sun).

Stadtkirche

To the north of the Markt stands the Stadtkirche (Town Church) of St Michael, which was Jena's most prominent landmark until the building of the University's high-rise block. Restored after suffering war damage, it shows influences from Bohemia, Upper Silesia and South Germany in its architecture. Notable features of the interior are the figure of St Michael (one of the oldest pieces of sculpture in wood in Thuringia) and the bronze relief of Luther, originally destined for his tomb in Wittenberg.

*Collegium Jenense

South-west of the Markt can be found the Collegium Jenense, originally a Dominican monastery, which housed the "First University" of Jena for some three hundred years until its move to the Goetheallee. An interesting feature is the students' prison (Karzer), with inscriptions and drawings by the students confined there. Among those who taught here were the philosophers Hegel, Fichte and Schelling.

University and Botanic Garden

University Tower

Jena's most prominent landmark is the University Tower (Universitäts-Hochhaus; 1972), 120m/395ft high. On the 26th floor is a café; from the top there is a magnificent panoramic view of the town.

Town walls

There are a number of remains of the town's old fortifications, notably the Pulverturm (Powder Tower), the Johannistor (St John's Gate) and the Anatomieturm (Anatomy Tower).

Friedrich Schiller University

The main building of the Friedrich Schiller University, situated at Goetheallee 1, on the site of the old ducal castle, is protected as a historic monument. Built between 1905 and 1908, it has a richly decorated interior. In the Aula (Great Hall) can be seen a well-known picture by Ferdinand Hodler depicting the students of Jena setting out for war in 1813. In the lobbies are portraits of scholars who taught at the University.

Goetheallee

At Goetheallee 23 is the imposing Baroque building of the "Second University", which until 1908 was the main University building. At No. 18 is the house of the Frommann family, which in Goethe's time was frequented by the leading intellectual figures of the day, including Goethe himself.

The site of the old ducal pleasure garden is now occupied by the Botanic Garden, with 12,000 plants from all over the world, an alpine garden with 2000 species of plant and an arboretum with some 800 species of deciduous and coniferous trees.

The house once occupied by the Inspector of the Botanic Garden (Goetheallee 26), where Goethe frequently stayed, now houses a Goethe Memorial Museum (Goethe-Gedenkstätte).

*Zeiss Planetarium

A little way north of the Goethe-Gedenkstätte is the famous Zeiss Planetarium (a domed building of 1926, now scheduled as a historic monument). Renovated and modernised in 1983–85, the Planetarium is equipped with the latest technology, including a computer-controlled projection system.

Southern Districts

*Optical Museum

In Carl-Zeiss-Platz, in the south-west of the town, is the Optical Museum (1965), with some 12,000 exhibits, including high precision optical apparatus. A particular attraction is the multi-spectral camera MKF 6, which has made a valuable contribution to space research.

Beside the Red Tower (Ernst-Thälmann-Ring 10) stands the Romantiker-Haus, once the home of the philosopher J. G. Fichte and now a museum of the early Romantic period in Germany (centred particularly on the Jena group of Romantics, including the young Schelling, the Schlegel brothers, Tieck and Novalis). On the upper floors of the building are the art collections of the Municipal Museum (art of the 15th–20th c.).

*Romantiker-Haus

At Schillergässchen 2 is the Schiller-Gedenkstätte (Memorial Museum), a house occupied by Schiller while teaching at the University. Here he worked on his plays "Wallensteins Lager" ("Wallenstein's Camp") and "Maria Stuart" and completed the "Jungfrau von Orleans" ("Maid of Orleans").

Schiller
Memorial Museum

At Berggasse 7 can be found the Ernst Haeckel House (museum) and at the Neutor (No. 1) the Phyletic Museum (Museum of Races). At Kahlaische Strasse 1 is the Hilprecht Collection (cuneiform tablets; the world's oldest town plan).

Museums

Schiller Church

In Charlottenstrasse in Jena-Ost, beyond the Saale, stands the Schillerkirche (Schiller Church), originally the church of the village of Wenigenjena, in which Schiller married Charlotte von Lengefeld in 1790.

Viewpoints

The best view of Jena and the Saale valley is to be had from a hill outside the town, the Landgrafen (outlook tower).

Landgrafen

On a hill above the Ziegenhain district is the Fuchsturm, a relic of one of the three castles which once stood on the hill.

Fuchsturm

There are also fine views from the Jenzig, the "Rigi of Jena".

Jenzig

Surroundings of Jena

Kahla (16km/10 miles south on B 88) has preserved its old fortifications. On the south-west side of the town is a double ring of walls.

Kahla

Conspicuously situated above the town the Leuchtenburg houses a Heimatmuseum (history of hunting, etc.) and a youth hostel.

*Leuchtenburg

Hummelshain, 7km/4½ miles south-east of Kahla, was once a hunting preserve of the Dukes of Altenburg. The Rieseneck hunting and stalking ground (17th–18th c.) is one of the largest surviving establishments of its kind.

Hummelshain

At Cospeda, 4km/2½ miles north-west, can be found a museum commemorating the battle of Jena and Auerstedt (1806), with a diorama of the battle, weapons and uniforms.

Cospeda

At Dornburg (12km/7½ miles north-east on B 88) are three castles (the Dornburger Schlösser) perched on steep-sided limestone crags and set in beautiful parks. Dornburg, originally founded in the 10th century as a stronghold on the frontier with Sorb territory, passed in 1691 to the Duchy of Saxony-Weimar. The castles are best known for their associations with Goethe. The Altes Schloss (1521), to the north, preserves some Romanesque work. To the south is the so-called "Goetheschloss" (1539), in which Goethe stayed for some time in 1828; there is a Goethe Room, opened in 1960. Between these two is the little Rokokoschlösschen (1736–47), with a terraced garden, where Goethe also liked to stay.

*Dornburg Castles

Kaiserslautern

Land: Rhineland-Palatinate
Altitude: 233m/764ft
Population: 100,000

Situation and characteristics

The old "Barbarossa town" of Kaiserslautern, situated at the intersection of important traffic routes, is the cultural and economic centre of the Palatinate Forest (Pfälzerwald: see entry), with a University (1970) and the Palatinate Theatre (Pfalztheater).

Sights

Stiftsplatz

In the centre of the town lies the Stiftsplatz, with the three-towered Early Gothic Stiftskirche (13th–14th c.; Protestant). In the porch is a memorial, with figures of Luther and Calvin, commemorating the union of the two Protestant denominations (1818). In front of the church can be seen the "Schöner Brunnen" ("Beautiful Fountain").

To the north-east is St Martin's Church (14th c.; R.C.). West of this is the neo-Renaissance Fruchthalle (1843-46), originally the fruit and vegetable market, now a public hall.

Of the old Barbarossa castle (originally founded by Charlemagne and enlarged by the Emperor Frederick Barbarossa in 1153–58) only fragments survive. The Burg built by Count Palatine John Casimir about 1570 was much altered in 1935; it contains the fine Casimir Hall.

Museumsplatz

In Museumsplatz, in the north of the town, is the Landesgewerbeanstalt (Craft Institute), with the Pfalzgalerie (19th and 20th c. art).

Heimatmuseum

To the north-east, near the Mainzer Tor (Mainz Gate; Kaiserbrunnen, by Gernot Rumpf), is the Theodor Zink Museum (Heimatmuseum; periodic special exhibitions).

Kamenz

Land: Saxony
Altitude: 198m/650ft
Population: 18,600

Situation and characteristics

Kamenz (Sorbian Kamjénc), chief town of a district, lies in western Upper Lusatia on the Schwarze Elster, below the Hutberg. Here in 1729 was born Gotthold Ephraim Lessing, the great German writer of the Enlightenment.
In about a third of the communes in Kamenz district the population is predominantly Sorb. Many women and girls still wear the characteristic local costume on Sundays and holidays.

Sights

Town Hall

In the old Markt stands the Town Hall (Rathaus), rebuilt in Italian Renaissance style after a fire which devastated the town in 1842.

The Andreasbrunnen (St Andrew's Fountain; 1570), an elaborate sandstone structure with a figure of Justitia, is one of the few surviving Renaissance works in Kamenz.

Malzhaus

In Zwingerstrasse, which runs north-west from the Markt, is another Renaissance building, the Malzhaus (Malthouse; No. 7). Beside it is the 16th century Basteiturm, a relic of the town's fortifications, which were demolished in 1835.

The Easter Riding, a Sorbian Festival in Panschwitz-Kuckau ▶

Museum of Western Lusatia	In Pulsnitzer Strasse, which cuts across Zwingerstrasse, is the Ponickau-Haus (No. 16), an old burgher's house with a Baroque façade added in 1745 which now houses the Museum of Western Lusatia (Museum der Westlausitz; prehistory and the early historical period, etc.).
St Mary's Church	On a 35m/115ft high greywacke crag stands the town's principal church, St Mary's (Late Gothic, c. 1400–80), built of the local granite, with graceful sandstone tracery in the windows. The most notable features of the interior are the Marienaltar (rich woodcarving, 15th c.), the Michaelisaltar (1598) and a Crucifixion group of around 1500.
Katechismus-kirche	Close by is the Katechismuskirche (1358), thought to be the oldest building in the town. It was originally incorporated in the town's fortifications (embrasures on upper floor).
*Lessing Museum	A handsome modern building at Lessingplatz 1-3 houses the Lessing Museum, with mementoes of Lessing's life and work and a Lessing library.
St Anne's Church	Opposite the Lessing Museum, in the Platz der Jugend, stands the Late Gothic church (1493–99) of the former Franciscan friary of St Anne, with altars dedicated to St Anne, St Francis, the Saviour and the Virgin (carved wood, 1510–20). During the rebuilding of the monastery after the 1842 fire the roof turrets (by Gottfried Semper) were added. The Mönchsmauer (Monks' Wall) along the north and east sides was part of the old fortifications of the monastery, which lay outside the town walls.
St-Just-Kirche	The Gothic church of St Justus (St-Just-Kirche; 1377) has a cycle of Gothic wall paintings (c. 1380) and a Late Gothic winged altar.

Hutberg

*View	From the outlook tower on the Hutberg (294m/965ft) there are fine views of the town and the countryside of Western Lusatia.

Surroundings of Kamenz

Pulsnitz	12km/7½ miles south-west lies Pulsnitz, a town famed for its gingerbread and as the birthplace of the sculptor Ernst Rietschel (1804–61). Among features of interest are the parish church of St Nicholas (originally Late Gothic; rebuilt in 1745 after a fire; Rietschel Memorial Chapel in sacristy); the Renaissance Town Hall (1555), with a monument to Rietschel in front of it; and the Observatory, with a large collection of meteorites. Scheduled as historic monuments are the old dyeworks in Bachstrasse, the 18th century pottery kiln at Ernst-Thälmann-Strasse 4 and the Perfert, a fortified granary dating from the time of the Hussite raids (c. 1420).
Königsbrück	16km/10 miles west is Königsbrück, with a Baroque Schloss (now a sanatorium) and a Baroque parish church (begun 1682).
Panschwitz-Kuckau	In Panschwitz-Kuckau (8km/5 miles south-east) can be found Marienstern Convent (founded 1248), with a 14th century hall-church (Baroque west front). The church has a richly furnished interior (partly the work of artists from Prague; 13th century Pietà). Also of interest are the nuns' cells, the Abbess's Lodging, the Neuer Konvent and several Baroque buildings.
Rosenthal	Rosenthal, 10km/6 miles east, has a Baroque pilgrimage church (1778), with an octagonal Baroque chapel of 1766 and the Administratur of 1755.

Karlsruhe   K 3–4

Land: Baden-Württemberg
Altitude: 116m/381ft
Population: 270,000

This former Grand-Ducal capital lies close to the Rhine in the north-western foothills of the Black Forest (see entry). The town centre is laid out in a fan-shaped pattern with the Schloss as its focal point.

Situation and characteristics

Schloss

In the centre of the town is the spacious Schlossplatz, with the Schloss (Grand-Ducal Palace), built by Friedrich von Kesslau between 1752 and 1785, partly on the basis of plans by Balthasar Neumann. It now contains the richly stocked Landesmuseum (prehistory and early historical period, antiquities, applied art, folk art and traditions, Art Nouveau collection). Behind the palace lie the extensive gardens (Schlossgarten), with the Orangery (part of the Landesmuseum: see below) and the Botanic Garden. To the north of the Schlossgarten can be found the State Majolica Manufactory (Staatliche Majolika-Manufaktur; guided visits).

Landesmuseum

On the south-west side of the Schlossplatz, at Hans-Thoma-Strasse 2–6, is the Staatliche Kunsthalle (State Art Gallery), with an important collection (German masters, including Cranach, Grünewald, Holbein and Strigel; Dutch and French painting of the 17th and 18th centuries; major works of the modern Baden school). There is a "children's museum", with pictures hung at the right level for children. In an annexe is the Hans Thoma Museum, with works by the landscape painter Hans Thoma (1839–1924). In the Orangery can be seen a permanent display of German painting from 1890 to the present day.
To the north of the Kunsthalle is the Federal Constitutional Court (Bundesverfassungsgericht; 1968).

*Art Gallery

South-west of the Kunsthalle, at Karlstrasse 10, is the Prinz-Max-Palais (history of the town; Municipal Gallery; periodic special exhibitions).

Prinz-Max-Palais

Stadtgarten and Schwarzwaldhalle

Karlsruhe

Central Area

Marktplatz Pyramid	South of the palace, on its axis of symmetry, is the Marktplatz (pedestrian zone, shopping arcades), with the 6.50m/20ft high red sandstone pyramid which has become the emblem of Karlsruhe. It contains the burial vault of the town's founder. On either side of the square, which divides the long Kaiserstrasse into two parts, are the Stadtkirche (Town Church; Protestant) and the Town Hall (Rathaus), both designed by Friedrich Weinbrenner.
Kaiserstrasse	Along Kaiserstrasse (pedestrian zone) to the west, past the handsome Head Post Office, is the Mühlberger Tor. Farther west, at Röntgenstrasse 6, we come to the Upper Rhineland Writers' Museum (Oberrheinisches Dichtermuseum; manuscripts, first editions, letters, etc.).
Museum am Friedrichsplatz	South-west of the Marktplatz lies the Friedrichsplatz, with the Museum am Friedrichsplatz (Landessammlungen für Naturkunde; natural history, with vivarium). Beyond this, in the Nymphengarten, is the Baden Library (Landesbibliothek; 1964).
Rondellplatz	From the Markt Karl-Friedrich-Strasse runs south to Rondellplatz, with the Constitution Column (Verfassungssäule) and the old Margravial Palace, one of Weinbrenner's finest buildings (restored), and the overpass at the Ettlinger Tor. To the south-east is the Baden State Theatre (Badisches Staatstheater; 1970–75; opera and drama), in front of which is an unusual sculpture, the "Musengaul" (the "Muses' Nag").

Festplatz

Congress Centre	Ettlinger Strasse continues south to the Festplatz (on right), round which is the Congress and Exhibition Centre, with the new Stadthalle (1985), the Konzerthaus, the Nancy-Halle, the Schwarzwaldhalle (Black Forest Hall) and the Gartenhalle.
Stadtgarten	From here the beautiful Stadtgarten extends south to the railway station (Hauptbahnhof), with the Japanese Garden, the Vierordt Baths, the Tulla Baths and the Zoo. To the east of the Vierordt Baths, at Werderstrasse 63, is the Transport Museum (Verkehrsmuseum).

Karlsruhe-Durlach

Turmberg	Durlach, once the seat of the Margraves of the Zähringen line and now part of Karlsruhe, has preserved an attractive old quarter. The Schloss now houses the Pfinzgau Museum (regional history) and the Heimatmuseum of the Carpathian Germans. Within easy reach is the Turmberg (225m/738ft), with the Durlacher Warte (fine views of the town and the Upper Rhine plain).

Surroundings of Karlsruhe

Ettlingen	8km/5 miles south lies the town of Ettlingen, with a former Margravial palace (1728–33); beautiful chapel with frescoes by C. D. Asam; museum. Schlossfestspiele (Festival) in June/August.
	At weekends in summer there are trips in an old steam train through the Alb valley to Bad Herrenalb.
Bruchsal	See entry
Rastatt	See entry

Kassel

Land: Hesse
Altitude: 163m/535ft
Population: 191,000

Kassel, the cultural, economic and administrative centre of northern Hesse, is delightfully situated at the foot of the Habichtswald in a basin in the Fulda valley. Numerous
cultural establishments (including a Gesamthochschule or comprehensive higher educational establishment) and official agencies (Federal Labour Court, Federal Social
Court) are based here. In the artistic field Kassel is noted for its avantgarde "documenta"
exhibitions. Within the city limits is Wilhelmshöhe, a popular health resort (Kneipp cure).

Situation and
characteristics

Central Area

The main shopping and business street of Kassel is the Obere Königsstrasse (pedestrian
zone), which runs south-west from Königsplatz, past Friedrichsplatz, to Brüder-Grimm-
Platz. Near the south-west end of the street is the Town Hall (Rathaus; 1905–09).

On the north-east side of Friedrichsplatz is the Museum Fridericianum, a neo-classical
building (by Simon Louis du Ry, 1769–79) which since 1955 has housed the "documenta" exhibition of modern art, held every few years.
On the south-east side of the square stands the Staatstheater (1958–59; opera, ballet,
drama).

Museum
Fridericianum

To the north of the Theatre, in the Ottoneum (16th c.), the oldest permanent theatre in
Germany, is the Natural History Museum (Naturkundemuseum).

Natural History
Museum

To the south of the Theatre, on the banks of the Fulda, lies the Karlsaue, a beautiful
wooded park (area 160 hectares/400 acres) in which are the Orangery (1701–11; used for
part of the "documenta" exhibitions), the Marble Baths, a sumptuous structure built in
1720 to the design of the sculptor Pierre Etienne Monot, and the flower-covered island of
Siebenbergen. To the east extends Fulda-Aue, a popular recreation area (bathing and
wind-surfing; regatta course).

*Karlsaue

In Brüder-Grimm-Platz, at the end of the Obere Königsstrasse, is the Torwache (now
used for exhibitions), the home from 1814 to 1822 of Jacob and Wilhelm Grimm,
world-famed for their collection of folk tales and fairytales and for their great German
dictionary (completed only in 1971).

Torwache

On the south side of the square are the Hessian Provincial Museum (Landesmuseum;
medieval tapestries, applied and decorative art, etc.) and the German Wallpaper
Museum (Tapetenmuseum).

Landesmuseum
*Wallpaper Museum

Behind the Landesmuseum, to the south-east, can be found the Hessian Provincial
Library (Landesbibliothek), which counts among its treasures a manuscript of the medieval "Hildebrandslied", written in Fulda monastery about 800.

*Provincial
Library

A little way east, at Schöne Aussicht 2, stands the Palais Bellevue, with a museum
devoted to the Grimm brothers (working copies of the fairytales, scholarly works, letters,
translations of the tales into many languages). Facing it, to the south-west, is the Neue
Galerie (painting and sculpture since 1750).

Brüder-Grimm-
Museum

From the Town Hall Friedrichstrasse (pedestrian zone) runs north-west to the long
narrow Ständeplatz, with the Municipal Museum (Stadtmuseum) and a number of
modern high-rise blocks.

Ständeplatz

Kassel

Wilhelmshöhe

From Brüder-Grimm-Platz the Wilhelmshöher Allee leads in a dead straight line for 5km/3 miles to the outlying district of Wilhelmshöhe, a health resort and spa (Kneipp cure).

Schloss

The neo-classical Schloss Wilhelmshöhe was built for Landgrave William IX (later Elector William I) by Simon Louis du Ry and Heinrich Christoph Jussow (1786–1801). From 1807 to 1813 it was the residence of Jérôme Bonaparte, appointed king of Westphalia by Napoleon. Napoleon III of France was lodged here in 1871 after his capture at Sedan, and it later became a summer residence of the Emperor William II.

**State Art Collections Schlossmuseum

The palace, with a sumptuously appointed interior, now houses the State Art Collections and the Schlossmuseum. The State Art Collections include the fine Gallery of Old Masters, the nucleus of which was a collection assembled by Landgrave William VIII (many works by Dutch painters, including 17 Rembrandts and 11 van Dycks; Italian and Spanish paintings), a Print Cabinet, and collections of classical and prehistoric antiquities. The Schlossmuseum displays furniture, glass and ceramics.

*Bergpark

On the eastern slopes of the Habichtswald lies the Bergpark, described by the great art historian Georg Dehio as "perhaps the most magnificent achievement of the Baroque style in the blending of architecture and landscape".

*Kurhessen-Therme

At the entrance to the park are the Kurhessen-Therme (Baths), designed for sport and recreation (brine baths; indoor and outdoor swimming pools; water-chute; entertainment facilities, etc.).

Löwenburg

South-west of the Schloss can be seen the Löwenburg, an artificial ruin built in 1793–97 (pictures and old furniture in interior).

Fountains and cascades

On the west side of the park are the Grosse Fontäne (Great Fountain; 53m/174ft), artificial waterfalls and cascades. On the highest point on the hill (525m/1723ft) stands the Octagon, with a 32m/105ft high column topped by an 8m/26ft high figure of Hercules with his club (which can accommodate eight people). The park is particularly impressive on summer evenings when the fountain, the cascades and the figure of Hercules are illuminated.

Surroundings of Kassel

*Wilhelmsthal

11km/7 miles north-west is Schloss Wilhelmsthal, built by François de Cuvilliés in 1753–67 as a summer residence for the Elector. It is one of the most charming Rococo palaces in Germany, with a sumptuous interior (including a Gallery of Beauty, with paintings by Johann Heinrich Tischbein).

Oberkaufungen

In Oberkaufungen, 11km/7 miles east, can be seen a church which belonged to a Benedictine convent founded in 1017 by the Empress Kunigunde, wife of Henry II.

Fritzlar

25km/15 miles south-west of Kassel lies the town of Fritzlar (pop. 15,000), situated above the left bank of the Eder.

With some 450 half-timbered buildings, Fritzlar has preserved much of its medieval aspect. In the Hochzeitshaus (Marriage House; c. 1580) is a Regional Museum (prehistoric antiquities, history of the town, collection of stoves).

Cathedral

On the highest point in the town stands the twin-towered Cathedral of St Peter (12th–14th c.). In the crypt is the Late Gothic tomb of St Wigbert, first abbot of Fritzlar. Also of interest are the 14th century cloister, the rich Treasury, the Cathedral Museum and the Cathedral Library (manuscripts of the 8th–17th centuries, incunabula).

Hofgeismar

23km/14 miles north of Kassel on the Deutsche Märchenstrasse (German Fairytale Route) is Hofgeismar (pop. 15,000).

The old town with its handsome half-timbered houses is still largely surrounded by its ring of walls. The Romanesque and Gothic Altstädter Kirche (Old Town Church) has a beautiful Passion Altar (c. 1335). In the Town Hall is the Municipal Museum (prehistory and the early historical period, history of the town and garrison, treasury of silver, ceramics). Nearby, in Apothekenstrasse, is the Pharmacy Museum (Apothekenmuseum).

In the former Kurpark, north-east of the town, are the Gesundbrunnen, a chalybeate mineral spring housed in a classical temple, and the little neo-classical Schloss Schönburg.

Gesundbrunnen

The Fairytale Route continues north-east through the Reinhardswald to the outlying district of Sababurg. On a basalt cone can be seen the ruins of a hunting lodge built in the late 15th century which is famed as the setting of one of the Grimm brothers' fairytales. Below it is a game park, with a Museum of Forestry and Hunting.

Sababurg

Kempten

L 5

Land: Bavaria
Altitude: 689m/2261ft
Population: 58,000

Kempten, chief town of the Allgäu, lies on the river Iller, on a site once occupied by a Celtic settlement and later by the Roman Cambodunum (1st c. A.D.), remains of which have been excavated since 1982. Lower down, on the banks of the Iller, is the crowded old town of Kempten, above which is the new town built in the 17th century by the Prince-Abbots.

Situation and characteristics

New Town

In Residenzplatz is the extensive range of buildings of the Residenz (1651–74), the Baroque palace of the Prince-Abbots (serenade concerts in summer). Adjoining the west wing is the former Stiftskirche, a domed Baroque church (St Lorenz; by M. Beer and J. Serro, 1652–66) which was the first large church in South Germany to be built after the Thirty Years' War.

Residenz

A short distance west we come to the Kornhaus (c. 1700; hall and Heimatmuseum). To the north is the Hofgarten, with the Orangery (1780).

South-west of the Residenz is the neo-classical Zumsteinhaus (1802), with the Cambodunum Roman Collection and Natural History Collections (geology and biology of the Allgäu).

Zumsteinhaus

At Westendstrasse 21, to the west of the Residence, can be found the Allgäuer Burgenverein (Allgäu Castles Association), with a permanent exhibition of models of castles.

Allgäuer Burgenverein

In the old Marstall (Court Stables) in Landwehrstrasse is the Alpine Gallery (Alpenländische Galerie), an outstation of the Bavarian National Museum in Munich.

Alpine Gallery

Cambodunum Archaeological Park

Old Town

Rathausplatz

The Town Hall (Rathaus), originally built in 1474, was rebuilt in Renaissance style in the 16th century (façade decorated with coats of arms). South-east of the Town Hall stands the St-Mang-Kirche, a Late Gothic church (Baroque interior) dedicated to St Magnus, the town's patron saint. Near the church can be seen the St Mang Fountain.

Above the bridge over the Iller (St-Mang-Brücke) rises the beautiful Burghalde (open-air theatre; fine view of the chain of the Alps).

Cambodunum Archaeological Park

On the right (east) bank of the Iller is the excavated site of the Roman settlement of Cambodunum, which has been laid out as an archaeological park. Visitors can see the foundations of the temple precinct (some buildings restored). Further excavations are in progress. Finds from the site are displayed in the Zumsteinhaus (see above).

Immenstadt

South of Kempten, 24km/15 miles up the Iller valley, lies Immenstadt (pop. 14,000), situated at the foot of the Immenstädter Horn on the German Alpine Highway (Deutsche Alpenstrasse: see entry).

In the Marienplatz, in the historic old town, is the Schloss (1620) of the Counts Königsegg-Rothenfels. The Baroque parish church of St Nicholas has fine frescoes and Gothic sculpture.

Grosser Alpsee

To the west of Immenstadt extends the 3km/2 mile long Grosser Alpsee (water sports), under the Gschwendner Horn (1450m/4757ft). Part of the lake is a nature reserve.

Kiel

Capital of the *Land* of Schleswig-Holstein
Altitude: 5m/16ft
Population: 245,000

Kiel, capital of the *Land* of Schleswig-Holstein and a university town, is attractively situated at the south end of the Kieler Förde, an arm of the sea which extends some 17km/10½ miles inland. It is an important shipbuilding town and port (ferry to Scandinavia) with a considerable range of industry.

Situation and characteristics

Central Area

In the centre of the old town, on the Alter Markt, is the Nikolaikirche (St Nicholas's Church; Late Gothic, altered in the 19th century; restored), with a beautiful altar of 1460, a font of 1344 and a pulpit of 1705. In front of the church can be seen a sculpture by Ernst Barlach, "The Intellectual Fighter" (1928).

St Nicholas's Church

Farther south, opposite the railway station (Hauptbahnhof), is the Sophienhof "cultural quarter", inaugurated in 1988. This two-storey building houses the Stadtgalerie (Municipal Gallery; periodic special exhibitions), the "Stadtbildnerei" (Municipal Picture Library; loan of contemporary pictures), conference and function rooms, shops, restaurants, etc.
At the Bahnhofsbrücke (Station Bridge) is the landing-stage used by ships plying in the Kieler Förde and the boats doing harbour cruises.

Sophienhof

To the west of the Markt lies the Kleiner Kiel, all that is left of an arm of the firth which once encircled the old town. To the south-west are the Opera House (Oper; 1952–53, extension 1973) and the New Town Hall (Neues Rathaus; 1907–11), with a 106m/348ft tower (lift; views of town and Förde).

Kleiner Kiel

Near the Seegartenbrücke landing-stage, to the east of the Markt, can be found the old Fischhalle (Fish Market; 1909–10), which now houses the Shipping Museum (Schiffahrtsmuseum; development of the harbour, shipbuilding and seafaring). In the Museumshafen (Museum Harbour) are a number of historic old ships.

Shipping Museum

North of the Markt is the former refectory (rebuilt in 1950 as a student residence) of a Franciscan friary, founded in 1241, which was the original site of the University. East of the Markt, on the shores of the firth, we come to the town's Cultural Centre (Kulturzentrum), built on the foundations of the Schloss which was destroyed during the Second World War, with the Provincial Library, a concert hall, the Pomeranian Foundation (art gallery) and other amenities. Adjoining is the beautiful Schlossgarten. To the west, in the 17th century Warleberger Hof, is the Municipal Museum (Stadtmuseum; history of the town, satirical graphic art, applied art, photography).

Cultural Centre

Farther north, at Düsternbrooker Weg 1, is the Kunsthalle (Art Gallery; German painting of the 17th–20th centuries, Rohlfs and Nolde Collection, graphic art, antiquities).

Kunsthalle

To the west, at Hegewischstrasse 3, are two important University museums. The Museum of Ethnography (Völkerkundemuseum) displays artifacts from Africa, East Asia and Oceania. The Zoological Museum has specimens of Ice Age animals, fauna of the North Sea and Baltic coasts and skeletons of whales.

Museum of Ethnography
Zoological Museum

The Institute of Marine Biology (Institut für Meereskunde), to the north of the Seeburg boating harbour, has an interesting Aquarium (freshwater and seawater), which includes a seals' pool. Opposite it, to the west, is the Old Botanic Garden, with an arboretum.

Institute of Marine Biology

Düsternbrook

A very beautiful part of the town is Düsternbrook, enclosed by an undulating strip of woodland. On the shores of the firth stands the Landeshaus, seat of the Landtag and the

Harbour, Kiel-Schilksee

government of the *Land*. At the Blücher Bridge is moored the "Gorch Fock", a sailing ship used by the German navy for training. On the Hindenburg-Ufer is the Düsternbrook boating harbour.

University

To the west of the town lies the extensive campus of the Christian Albrecht University. At Olshausenstrasse 40 is an interesting Mineralogical and Petrographic Museum (minerals, meteorites, fossils).

Botanic Garden

North-west of the campus is the University Botanic Garden, with some 9000 species of plants from all over the world.

Kiel-Molfsee

*Open-Air Museum

In the southern district of Molfsee can be found the Schleswig-Holstein Open-Air Museum (Freilichtmuseum), with old peasant houses and craftsmen's workshops.

Laboe

*Naval Memorial

Opposite the district of Friedrichsdorf (ferry service), on the east shore of the firth, lies the seaside resort of Laboe, with the 72m/236ft high Naval Memorial (Marine-Ehrenmal; 1927–36). Built in the form of a ship's prow, it now commemorates the naval dead of both world wars. There is a lift to the viewing platform.

In front of the Memorial can be seen a German submarine, U 995 (museum).

Kirchheim unter Teck   K 4

Land: Baden-Württemberg
Altitude: 311m/1020ft
Population: 33,000

Kirchheim unter Teck, in the foreland of the central Swabian Alb (see entry), is an important industrial town (metalworking, furniture manufacture, electrical products).

Situation and characteristics

The Town

The main street of the picturesque old town is Marktstrasse (pedestrian zone). At the north end of which stands the Town Hall (Rathaus), a magnificent half-timbered building of 1724.

Town Hall

Behind the Town Hall is the Martinskirche (St Martin's Church), the origins of which are believed to date back to the 7th century. It was given its present form in the 14th and 15th centuries. It has the remains of frescoes (1463) and a Renaissance monument.

St Martin's Church

The Kornhaus (c. 1550), in front of the church in Max-Eyth-Strasse, now houses the Municipal Museum (geology, prehistory and the early historical period, folk art and traditions) and a picture gallery.

Kornhaus Museum

In the south-west of the old town is the 16th century Schloss (guided tour of state apartments).

Schloss

To the south of Kirchheim rises the 775m/2543ft high Teck (outlook tower).

Teck

Holzmaden

5km/3 miles east of Kirchheim is Holzmaden, famed for the numerous Jurassic fossils found in the area. The Hauff Museum has a rich collection, including particularly fossils, some 150 million years old, from the Jurassic Sea (saurians and a large slab containing water-lilies of the Lower Jurassic; also fossils from the Dogger and Malm formations of the Upper Jurassic).

**Hauff Museum

Bad Kissingen

H 5

Land: Bavaria
Altitude: 201m/659ft
Population: 23,000

Bad Kissingen, in the beautiful valley of the Franconian Saale, is one of the most frequented spas in Bavaria. Its hot brine springs, containing carbonic acid and usually iron, are used in both drinking and bathing cures for affections of the digestive organs, metabolism and cardio-vascular system and gynaecological conditions.

Situation and characteristics

The Spa

The activity of the spa centres on the Kurgastzentrum (resort administration, swimming pool, etc.). On the west side of the Kurgarten is the Regentenbau (1911–13), with a main hall and function rooms, on the south side is the large Wandelhalle (indoor promenade; 1910–11) and on Prinzregentenstrasse the Kurhausbad (1927), all designed by Max Littmann.

Kurgarten

In the cross wing of the Wandelhalle are the two main drinking fountains, the Rakoczy (11.1°C/52°F) and the Pandur. On the north side of the Kurgarten is the Maxbrunnen (10.4°C/50.7°F).

Opposite the Wandelhalle, on the right bank of the Saale, lies the Luitpoldpark, with the Luitpold Baths (therapeutic exercise bath, steam bath, fitness studio, etc.) and the Luitpold Casino.

Luitpoldpark

South-east of the Luitpoldpark can be found the Ballinghain, with a beautiful open-air swimming pool on the terrace (water-chute, diving tower). Nearby are the remains of the

Ballinghain

Kurgarten and Arkadenbau

castle of Bodenlauben, home of the minnesinger Otto von Botenlauben (d. 1245); fine panoramic views.

Gradierhaus

2.5km/1½ miles north of the Kurgarten, on the left bank of the Saale (15 minutes by motorboat), are the Gradierhaus ("graduation house" for the evaporation of brine) and the Heinz Kalk Clinic, with a 94m/308ft deep artesian well (19.1°C/66.4°F; 2% salt content), with a variation in level of up to 3m/10ft.

Coach Trips

Bad Bocklet

Visitors can travel in an old mail coach to Bad Bocklet (acidic chalybeate spring; mud baths), 10km/6 miles north in the romantic Saale valley.

Aschach

There are also coach trips from Bad Kissingen to Schloss Aschach (art collection; conducted visits).

Kleinwalsertal

M 5

A German customs enclave in the Austrian province of Vorarlberg
Altitude: 1100–1250m/3600–4100ft

Situation and characteristics

Although the Kleinwalsertal, south-west of Oberstdorf (see entry), is part of the Austrian province of Vorarlberg it is cut off from Austria by the mountains, and accordingly is included within the German customs area and uses German currency. The population came here from the Swiss canton of Valais around 1300 and have preserved distinctive characteristics of their own.

*Landscape

The undulating valley bottom, caught between precipitous limestone peaks with a sparse covering of forest and traversed by the river Breitach, is one of the most attractive

Mail-coach service from Bad Kissingen to Bad Bocklet

Summer in the Kleinwalsertal

and best known of the mountain valleys, with widely scattered villages whose alpine climate has made them popular altitude resorts and whose abundance of snow attracts skiing enthusiasts.

From Oberstdorf to the Kleinwalsertal

From Oberstdorf the road crosses the Stillach and runs south past the hamlet of Reute (alt. 887m/2910ft) and the lower station of the chair-lift up Söllereck (1706m/5597ft; upper station 1350m/4430ft) to the Walser Schanz frontier crossing. It then continues along the slopes of the Schlappolt and Fellhorn. To the right are the Gottesackerwände and Hoher Ifen (2232m/7323ft; chair-lift to Ifenhütte), with the Widderstein to the rear.

Riezlern

The chief place in the valley is Riezlern (alt. 1098m/3603ft; pop. 2000; Casino). There is a cableway up the Kanzelwand (1980m/6496ft; superb views), which along with the Fellhorn (see Oberstdorf) is an excellent skiing area. There are rewarding climbs from Riezlern – to the Schwarzwasserhütte (1651m/5417ft; c. 3½ hours), and from there to the Hoher Ifen (c. 2 hours).

Hirschegg

In the central stretch of the valley is Hirschegg (alt. 1124m/3688ft; pop. 1500), with a church above the village and many hotels. Chair-lift to the Heubergmulde.

Mittelberg

Mittelberg (alt. 1218m/3996ft; pop. 1500) lies below the north side of the pyramidal Zwölferkopf and the Widderstein. The parish church has 14th century frescoes. Cableway up the Walmendinger Horn (1993m/6539ft).

Baad

At the head of the valley, in magnificent scenery, is the hamlet of Baad (alt. 1251m/4105ft).

Kleve

E 1

Land: North Rhine-Westphalia
Altitude: 17m/56ft
Population: 46,000

Situation and characteristics

The town of Kleve in the Lower Rhineland was once capital of the duchy of Kleve, known in English as Cleves (Henry VIII's fourth wife, Anne of Cleves, was a daughter of the Duke of Cleves). It is linked with the Rhine, 6km/4 miles north, by the Spoy Canal (the continuation of an old arm of the Rhine), which was first constructed in the 11th century.

The Town

Schloss

In the centre of the town, on higher ground, stands the old castle of the Dukes of Kleve (15th–17th c.), the "Schwanburg" of the Lohengrin legend. The tower now houses a geological museum and an art gallery; the rest of the building is occupied by local government offices and is not open to the public.

Stiftskirche

In the Kleiner Markt is the Stiftskirche (Church of the Assumption; 1341–1426), with tombs of the Dukes of Kleve and a Marienaltar (Altar of the Virgin).

Minorite Church
Museum

To the north of the town centre, in Kavarinerstrasse, can be found the former Minorite Church (15th c.), with carved choir-stalls of 1474. At Kavarinerstrasse 33 is Haus Koekkoek, with the Municipal Museum (Stadtmuseum; regional art since Roman times; changing exhibitions).

Tiergarten
(Zoo)

On the hills to the west of the town lies the beautiful Tiergarten, originally laid out in 1653–57 (red deer, wild pigs, reindeer, wolves, bears, etc.).

Emmerich

13km/8 miles north-east, across the Rhine, is the old free imperial and Hanseatic city of Emmerich (pop. 32,000), the last German town on the river.

The old town was rebuilt after the Second World War on its original plan. The Gothic Aldegundiskirche (St Aldegund's Church; 15th c.) has a notable interior. Downstream is the Minster of St Martin (11th–15th and 17th c.), which preserves the reliquary of St Willibrord (10th c.), the earliest surviiving example of goldsmith's work from the Lower Rhineland. At Martinikirchgang 2 is the Museum of the Rhine, with models of old Rhine ships, technical apparatus, etc.

Klingenthal   H 7

Land: Saxony
Altitude: 530–935m/1740–3065ft
Population: 13,400

Klingenthal lies directly on the frontier with Czechoslovakia in the wooded upper Vogt-land, at the foot of the Aschberg (936m/3071ft). It has been noted since the 19th century for the manufacture of musical instruments, and is also a popular holiday and winter sports resort.

Situation and characteristics

Sights

In the centre of the long straggling town is the parish church (1736–37; dedicated to the Prince of Peace), a Baroque building on an octagonal ground-plan with three-storey galleries amd a three-stage dome-like curving roof topped by a lantern. Since the destruction of the Frauenkirche in Dresden it is the largest church of the kind in Saxony. In front of the former District House of Culture is a sculpture, the "Accordion Player", which has become the emblem of Klingenthal.

Parish church

Markneukirchen

Markneukirchen, 20km/12½ miles west of Klingenthal, also makes musical instruments.

The town's principal attraction is the Paulusschlössel (1784), a Late Baroque palace with two semicircular tower-like projections on the façade. On the courtyard front and the west wing are arcades and galleries. Bronze figure of a violinist (1970).

Paulusschlössel

The Paulusschlössel now houses the Museum of Musical Instruments (Musikinstrumentenmuseum), with some 2300 instruments from Europe, the Islamic countries, the Far East, Africa and America. The collection includes viola da gambas from Nürnberg and Augsburg, a viola da gamba made by Johann Christian Hoffmann, a friend of Johann Sebastian Bach, accordions, musical boxes, barrel organs, phonographs and a valuable Swiss domestic organ of 1838. Examples of all the instruments now made in Markneukirchen, Klingenthal and Schöneck are displayed in the east wing.

Museum of Musical Instruments

Koblenz   H 3

Land: Rhineland-Palatinate
Altitude: 60m/200ft
Population: 110,000

This former residence of the Electors of Trier, beautifully situated at the junction of the Mosel (see Mosel Valley) with the Rhine, is an important traffic junction and one of the

Situation and characteristics

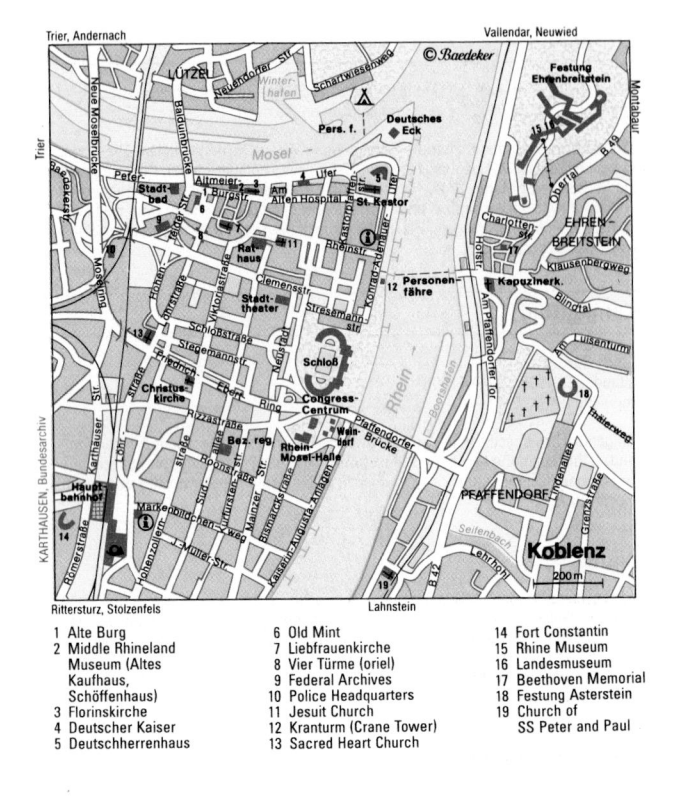

1 Alte Burg
2 Middle Rhineland
  Museum (Altes
  Kaufhaus,
  Schöffenhaus)
3 Florinskirche
4 Deutscher Kaiser
5 Deutschherrenhaus

6 Old Mint
7 Liebfrauenkirche
8 Vier Türme (oriel)
9 Federal Archives
10 Police Headquarters
11 Jesuit Church
12 Kranturm (Crane Tower)
13 Sacred Heart Church

14 Fort Constantin
15 Rhine Museum
16 Landesmuseum
17 Beethoven Memorial
18 Festung Asterstein
19 Church of
   SS Peter and Paul

leading centres of the wine trade on the Rhine. The town is dominated by the fortress of Ehrenbreitstein on the right bank of the Rhine.

Sights

Schloss	Below the Pfaffendorf Bridge, close to the banks of the Rhine, is the neo-classical Schloss, built in 1777–86 by the last Elector of Trier, Clemens Wenzeslaus (now occupied by government offices; art exhibitions).
* St Castor's Church	Downstream we come to St Castor's Church, founded in 836 on a site which was then outside the town. In its present form it dates mostly from the 12th century. The treaty of Verdun, which divided up the Carolingian empire, was signed here in 843.
Deutsches Eck	Beyond this is Deutsches Eck ("German Corner"), the tongue of land between the Rhine and the Mosel. Here stood until the Second World War the Emperor William Monument, the base of which now bears the Monument to German Unity (fine views, particularly downstream).
	Nearby can be found the Deutschherrenhaus, the remains of a castle of the Teutonic Order (evening serenade concerts in the Blumenhof in summer).
Liebfrauenkirche	On the highest point in the old town is the Romanesque Liebfrauenkirche (Church of Our Lady; 12th–15th c.), with a Gothic choir and Baroque towers. To the east of this is the

314

Town Hall (Rathaus; 1695–1700), in front of which can be seen the Schängelbrunnen, a monument to the young scalliwags of Koblenz. A little way north is the Florinsmarkt, with the Romanesque and Gothic Florinskirche (12th–14th c.; Protestant) and, housed in the Altes Kaufhaus (Old Merchants' Hall), the Middle Rhineland Museum (Mittelrhein-Museum; history of the town, Middle Rhineland sculpture of the 13th–16th c., pictures of the Baroque and Romantic periods and the 20th century).

On the banks of the Mosel stands the Alte Burg (1276–80), the old castle of the Electors of Trier, now housing the Municipal Archives and Library. Here the Balduinbrücke (1343–1420) crosses the Mosel to the district of Lützel. Upstream is the New Mosel Bridge (Neue Moselbrücke; 1954), near which are the Langemarck Barracks, with the Military Study Collection (weapons, cannon, vehicles, uniforms). | Alte Burg

The beautiful Rheinanlagen (Rhine Gardens) extend upstream from the Schloss for some 4km/2½ miles to the island of Oberwerth (swimming pool, with water-chute; stadium). Above the Pfaffendorf Bridge is the Weindorf ("Wine Village"), built in 1925 and rebuilt in 1951. Nearby is the Rhein-Mosel-Halle. | Rhine Gardens Weindorf

*Ehrenbreitstein

The Pfaffendorf Bridge (rebuilt 1952) leads to the district of Ehrenbreitstein, on the right bank of the Rhine, which is dominated by the Fortress of Ehrenbreitstein (alt. 118m/387ft; reached either by chair-lift or on a road branching off B 42). Built in 1816–32 on the site of an earlier stronghold of the Electors of Trier, the fortress now houses the Landes-museum (State Museum of Technology) and the Rhine Museum (hydrography, hydraulic engineering, shipping, fishing). From the terraces there are fine views of the town, the Rhine and the mouth of the Mosel.

Surroundings of Koblenz

4.5km/3 miles south of Koblenz is the Rittersturz (166m/545ft), a viewpoint on an outlier of the Hunsrück (see entry) which rises sheer from the Rhine. | Rittersturz

Farther south, above the Rhine, stands Schloss Stolzenfels (154m/505ft; 15 minutes' climb). The neo-Gothic castle, now a museum, was built by K. F. Schinkel (1836–42). | Stolzenfels

See Rhine Valley | Lahnstein

Königstein (Saxony)

See Saxon Switzerland

Konstanz   M 4

Land: Baden-Württemberg
Altitude: 407m/1335ft
Population: 70,000

Konstanz, beautifully situated close to the Swiss frontier on the stretch of the Rhine between the Obersee and the Untersee, is the largest town on Lake Constance (see entry), an important cultural centre with a University and a College of Engineering and an active theatrical and musical life. It is also a favourite congress and conference centre, and has two limnological institutes, a weather station and the headquarters of Radio Bodensee. | Situation and characteristics

Old Town

South-east of the old town is the Harbour (built 1839–42), the base of the German Railways fleet of ships on Lake Constance and of a number of private shipping companies. At its north-western corner is the Kaufhaus (1388), a warehouse for the trade with | Harbour Council Building

Italy, also known as the Council Building (Konzilsgebäude), having been the meeting-place of the conclave of cardinals which elected Pope Martin V in 1417; it is now used for concerts and congresses.

Dominican monastery

To the north of the Stadtgarten (Municipal Park), on an island in Lake Constance, is a former Dominican monastery (dissolved 1785), with a beautiful cloister; it is now a hotel. Count Zeppelin, inventor of the rigid airship (see Ludwigshafen), was born here in 1838.

*Minster

In Münsterplatz with its handsome old canons' houses stands the Minster (11th, 15th and 17th c.; R.C.), with a beautiful main doorway (relief decoration of 1470) and a fine interior (choir-stalls of 1460; gold discs of 11th–13th c.). In St Maurice's Chapel is a 13th century Holy Sepulchre. From the tower (1850–57) there are fine views.

Nature Museum
Picture Gallery

To the west, in Katzgasse, are the Lake Constance Nature Museum (Bodensee-Naturmuseum; prehistory and early historical period, ecology) and the Wessenberg Picture Gallery (German, Dutch and Italian painting of the 15th–18th centuries).

Hohenzollernhaus

To the south, in the Obermarkt, can be found the Hohenzollernhaus, in front of which Burgrave Friedrich of Nürnberg was invested with the fief of Mark Brandenburg in 1417. Nearby is the Town Hall (Rathaus; 1593), with frescoes of 1864 on the outside walls.

Rosgarten Museum

South-east of the Town Hall, in Rosgartenstrasse, is the "Haus zum Rosgarten", the medieval butchers' guild-house, now occupied by the Rosgarten Museum. This has a rich collection of local and regional interest, covering geology, palaeontology, the history of the town and the art and culture of the whole Lake Constance area. Of particular interest are the exhibits on the pile-dwelling culture (see Meersburg, Unteruhldingen) and the collection of pictures.
South of this stands the Trinity Church (Dreifaltigkeitskirche), which has fine frescoes of 1407.

Hushaus
Schnetztor

To the west of the Trinity Church is the Hushaus (Huss House), wrongly thought to have been the house of the Bohemian Reformer John Huss, and the 14th century Schnetztor, a relic of the medieval fortifications.

Niederburg

Between the Minster and the Rhine is the Niederburg, the oldest part of the town, originally inhabited by craftsmen and fishermen – a maze of narrow streets and lanes with many burghers' houses of the 13th–16th centuries. In Brückengasse are the Haus zur Inful (or Haus am Tümpfel; 15th–16th c.; cellars of an old hospice) and the Zoffingen monastery (founded 1257; 14th c. church, with frescoes). Between Rheingasse and Konzilstrasse stands the Regierungsgebäude (government offices, formerly the Cathedral Deanery; 1609).

Rheintorturm
Pulverturm

A little way north rises the massive Rheintorturm (Rhine Gate-Tower; 14th–15th c.). West of this, on the wall flanking the Rhine, are statues (19th c.) of Bishops Conrad I (d. 975) and Gebhard II (d. 995) and Dukes Berthold of Zähringen (d. 1077) and Leopold of Baden (d. 1852). Beyond these is the Pulverturm (Powder Tower; 14th c.).

Petershausen

From the Rheintorturm the Rheinbrücke leads over the river to Petershausen, the main part of the new town, with large residential districts and most of the town's recreation facilities.

Klosterkaserne

Immediately left of the bridge is the Klosterkaserne (Abbey Barracks), originally a Benedictine abbey. The buildings, excellently restored, now house a cultural and communications centre (Municipal Archives).

Seestrasse

From the end of the bridge Seestrasse runs east (with fine views of the old town), passing the Casino, to the boating harbour. In Villa Prym (1908; Art Nouveau frescoes) are the Haus des Gastes ("Visitors' House") and an art school.

1.5km/1 mile farther east is a thermal spring drilled in 1975 (30°C/86°F; therapeutic exercise bath).

Thermal baths

Wollmatinger Ried

To the west of Konstanz extends the Wollmatinger Ried (435 hectares/1074 acres), a marshy area overgrown with reeds which is now a nature reserve (nesting area for birds).

**Mainau

The "flower island" of Mainau (area 45 hectares/110 acres) lies 7km/4½ miles north of Konstanz off the southern shore of the Überlinger See. It attracts many visitors with its beautiful parks and gardens, luxuriant with semitropical and sometimes tropical vegetation. It is now owned by a foundation headed by the Swedish Count Lennart Bernadotte. On the island is a Schloss (1739–46) built for the Grand Duke of Baden, with a large coat of arms of the Teutonic Order on the gable; a notable feature of the interior is the White Hall. To the west are an old defensive tower (one of the original sixteen) and the gatehouse.

*Reichenau

6km/4 miles west of Konstanz, in the Untersee, lies the island of Reichenau, connected with the mainland by a causeway. With an area of 428 hectares/1057 acres, it is the largest island in Lake Constance; cultivation of early vegetables (37 hectares/91 acres under glass).

The three churches belonging to the once world-famed monastery of Reichenau, founded in 724 by Charles Martel, Charlemagne's grandfather, are among the finest

*Churches

Mainau *Reichenau*

examples of Early Romanesque art in Germany, both for their architecture and for their magnificent frescoes. They are St George's Church in Oberzell (fine wall paintings of the Ottonian period), the Minster of St Mary and St Mark (rich treasury in sacristy) and the church of SS Peter and Paul in Niederzell.
At the north-western tip of the island is Schloss Windegg (14th–15th c.).

Köthen F 7

Land: Saxony-Anhalt
Altitude: 75m/246ft
Population: 34,500

Situation and characteristics

Köthen, once capital of the principality of Anhalt-Köthen, lies in a gently undulating plain 30km/20 miles north of Halle.

Sights

Marktkirche

The oldest building in the town, which still preserves part of its medieval ring of walls (c. 1560), is the Late Gothic Marktkirche (Market Church) of St James (founded 1400, completed at end of 16th c.). The towers were rebuilt about 1897.

Schloss
(Museum)

The Schloss is in Renaissance style (1547–1608). In the north wing, the Ferdinandsbau (added in 1823 by Gottfried Bandhauer), is the Naumann Museum, named after the zoologist Johann Friedrich Naumann (1780–1857), founder of scientific ornithology in Germany. It is the only ornithological museum of the Biedermeier period to have survived in its original condition. In addition to Naumann's collections of birds the museum also displays his watercolours.

Bach
associations

In the Ludwigsbau wing of the Schloss (1823) can be seen a room in which Johann Sebastian Bach lived and worked. There is also a Bach memorial room in the Historical Museum in Museumsgasse.

St Agnus

The church of St Agnus (1694–98), in Dutch Baroque style, has paintings from the studio of Lucas Cranach and by Antoine Pesne.

Zoo

The Zoo (with some 150 species of animals), established in 1884, occupies the site of the old Fasanerie (Pheasantry).

Surroundings of Köthen

Aken

13km/8 miles north of Köthen on B 187A is Aken. The Town Hall (Rathaus; 1490, enlarged in 1609) is an interesting building, with a brick-built ornamental gable (15th c.). St Nicholas's Church, an aisled basilica, dates from the 12th century.

Gröbzig

The Synagogue in Gröbzig (14km/8½ miles south-west), built in 1796, is one of the few to have escaped destruction in 1938. It is now a museum, with a rich collection of liturgical utensils and other evidences of Jewish life and culture.

Krakow am See C 7

Land: Mecklenburg-West Pomerania
Altitude: 60m/200ft
Population: 3600

Situation

The little spa of Krakow lies on the shores of the Krakower See, an irregularly shaped lake, dotted with islands, in a well-wooded region with many lakes.

Sights

The Stadtkirche (Town Church) is a long rectangular brick building originally founded in 1230; the present structure dates from 1762. The most notable features of the interior are the reredos and pulpit (both 1705) and the north gallery (1744) decorated with coats of arms.

Stadtkirche

Surroundings of Krakow

There are charming views from the hills around the town of the beautiful landscape of forest and lakes.

＊View

The Krakower See (Lake Krakow) has an area of 15.9 sq.km/6 sq. miles. One of the most beautiful nature reserves in the region is the Krakower Obersee (bird nesting area; pleasure craft prohibited).
The Untersee is a landscape reserve.

Lake Krakow

In the surrounding area are numerous "Huns' graves" (megalithic chamber tombs; Serrahn, Marienhof, etc.), burial mounds (Kuchelmiss, Serrahn, Charlottenthal, Gross Tessin, Klein Tessin) and ring-shaped stone-settings (at Bellin and on the island of Lindwerder).

Tombs and stone-settings

Krefeld

F 2

Land: North Rhine-Westphalia
Altitude: 40m/130ft
Population: 230,000

The industrial city of Krefeld, with its eastern district of Uerdingen extending to the left bank of the Rhine, is the main centre of the German velvet and silk industry, which has been established here since the early 18th century. Other important industries are the manufacture of plush, steel and metal products and pharmaceuticals.

Situation and characteristics

The Town

The old town with its regularly planned 18th century extensions forms a large rectangle bounded by the Ostwall, Südwall, Westwall and Nordwall.

On Theaterplatz, in the town centre, is the Seidenweberhaus ("Silk-Weavers' House"), a new public hall opened in 1975. Adjoining it is the Theatre.

Seidenweberhaus

Farther west stands the Town Hall (Rathaus), housed in the neo-classical Schloss (1791–94), which was enlarged for the purpose in 1860.

Town Hall

On the Westwall (Karlsplatz 35), in an imposing building erected in 1897 and extended in 1912, is the richly stocked Kaiser-Wilhelm-Museum (applied and decorative art, modern painting, Italian Renaissance sculpture).
To the north can be seen the church of St Dionysius (1754–68; R.C.).

Kaiser-Wilhelm-Museum

To the north-east of the centre, at Wilhelmshofallee 91–97, are Haus Lange and Haus Esters, two notable buildings (1928–30) by Mies van der Rohe, now used for exhibitions of modern art.

Haus Lange
Haus Esters

The old Heeder wallpaper factory, in Virchowstrasse to the south of the railway station, has been converted into a cultural centre (music, drama, cabaret).

Heeder factory

North-east of the city centre, reached by way of Uerdinger Strasse, is the Zoo, with over 1000 animals of 280 different species (Tropical Monkey House, Large Mammal House,

Zoo
Botanic Garden

319

Bird Hall). To the south is the Schönwasserpark, with the Botanic Garden (native and exotic plants).

"Schluff"

In summer the historic old steam train "Schluff" runs trips from the Hülser Berg (north-west of the city) to St Tönis, a distance of 13.6km/8½ miles.

Linn

Burg

To the east, between the motorway and the Rhine, is the district of Linn, with a 14th century moated castle which belonged to the Elector of Cologne. In the outer ward can be found a small hunting lodge built about 1740 which now contains a collection of old furniture and musical instruments.

In the vicinity of the Burg are the Museum of the Lower Rhineland (Niederrheinisches Museum; prehistory and the early historical period, history of the *Land* and the town, folk art and traditions) and the German Textile Museum (textiles and costumes from all over the world).

Kyffhäuser Hills   F 6

Land: Thuringia

Situation and topography

The Kyffhäuser range, 19km/12 miles long by 7km/4½ miles wide, rises like a miniature version of the Harz above the Goldene Aue ("Golden Meadow") below the southern edge of the Harz, a fertile and densely populated depression watered by the river Helme, and the Frankenhausen valley (the Diamantene Aue, "Diamond Meadow"), both of which merge into the Unstrut depression.

*Barbarossa Cave

In the southern part of the range, near Rottleben, can be found the Barbarossahöhle, a gypsum cave with huge underground chambers and lakes which is associated with the Emperor Frederick I Barbarossa ("Redbeard"). Legend has it that the Emperor lies asleep here in an underground palace and that some day he will return and bring better times.

Monument

On the site of the old imperial stronghold of Burg Kyffhausen, situated on the Kyff-häuserburgberg at an altitude of 457m/1499ft, stands a huge monument in honour of Barbarossa, 81m/266ft high, erected between 1890 and 1896. The architect was Bruno Schmitz, who was also responsible for the "Battle of the Nations" monument at Leipzig. From the monument there are extensive views over the Kyffhäuser range and the Goldene Aue, extending northward to the Harz and southward to the Thuringian basin. Visitors can also see the excavated remains of Burg Kyffhausen, with the castle well (176m/577ft deep), and a museum.

Bad Frankenhausen

Situation and characteristics

At the foot of the Kyffhäuser Hills, in the wide valley of the Kleine Wipper, some 60km/40 miles south-west of Halle, lies Bad Frankenhausen, a spa (saline springs) whose mild climate and wooded surroundings attract many visitors.

Sights

*Schloss (Museum

The Baroque Schloss (built 1689 onwards; restored 1973–75) houses the District Heimat-museum, with a rich store of material on the history of the town and the region and displays on the 16th century Peasant War and the battle of Frankenhausen in 1525.

Other features of interest are the Altstädter Kirche (Old Town Church; 12th c., Roma-nesque); the Oberkirche (partly Romanesque), with a leaning tower; and the Baroque Unterkirche (1691–1704), with a richly furnished interior (fine gravestones, large Strobel organ). About half the circuit of the old town walls has been preserved.

There are a number of handsome burghers' houses dating from the heyday of the salt trade, including the Angerapotheke, the Schwanendrogerie and a house at Klosterstrasse 14.

Burghers' houses

Above the town, near the Schlachtberg (Battle Hill), where the battle of 1525 began, can be found a circular building (1975) housing a monumental panorama of the Peasant War (1987).

Panorama

Surroundings of Bad Frankenhausen

At Heldrungen is an old moated castle, enlarged and strengthened in the early 16th century, in which the peasant leader Thomas Müntzer was confined after being taken prisoner in the battle of Frankenhausen. After being destroyed in 1645 the castle was rebuilt in 1664–68 with fortifications in the Italian-French style (restored from 1974 onwards).

Heldrungen

Kyritz

D 7

Land: Brandenburg
Altitude: 34m/112ft
Population: 10,200

Kyritz, chief town of a district, lies 70km/45 miles north of Potsdam on the river Jäglitz, to the west of a chain of lakes.

Situation

Sights

The parish church of St Mary, brick-built on a high stone base, dates from the second half of the 15th century (remodelled in Baroque style in 1708–14). It has a 16th century font and a pulpit of 1714.

Parish church

In spite of numerous fires the town has preserved a number of 17th century half-timbered houses with fine carving and inscriptions on the beams, for example at Johann-Sebastian-Bach-Strasse 36 and Bahnhofstrasse 44 (1699), as well as a number of 18th century houses with overhanging eaves.
There are some remains of the medieval town walls on the east side of the town.

*Half-timbered
houses

Surroundings of Kyritz

South-east of Kyritz lies the village of Kampehl. In the burial chapel of the village church is the mummified body of the Ritter von Kahlbutz (d. 1703), whose life and death were the subject of many legends.

Kampehl

In Wusterhausen (8km/5 miles south-east on B 5) is the church of SS Peter and Paul, with fine frescoes and a Gothic arched gateway between the pastors' houses. At Karl-Liebknecht-Strasse 4 and 6 are two old half-timbered houses with carved beams and Rococo doorways.

Wusterhausen

Neustadt an der Dosse (12km/7½ miles south) has a Baroque parish church (1673–96) and the Late Baroque buildings and offices of the old State Stud Farm.

Neustadt

Lahn Valley

G–H 3

Länder: Hesse, North Rhine-Westphalia

The Lahn rises at an altitude of 600m/2000ft in the southern Rothaargebirge and flows into the Rhine at Lahnstein after a course of 218km/135 miles (though the distance as the crow flies from its source to its junction with the Rhine is only 80km/50 miles).

Down the Lahn Valley

Lahn Holiday Route	The starting-point of this route is Siegen (see entry). The Lahn-Ferienstrasse (Lahn Holiday Route), which is specially signposted, runs close to the river for most of the way, avoiding main roads.
	From Siegen the route at first follows B 42 to Netphen and then turns south-east by way of Deuz and Hainchen to reach the source of the Lahn, at the foot of the Stiegelburg (683m/2241ft). Here the Lahn Holiday Route starts.
Bad Laasphe	The first place of any size is Bad Laasphe (pop. 16,000; Kneipp cure), with handsome half-timbered houses in the town centre. On a steep-sided hill north-west of the town can be seen the 18th century Schloss of the Princes zu Sayn-Wittgenstein-Hohenstein (not open to the public). Beyond Bad Laasphe the road crosses the boundary between the *Länder* of North Rhine-Westphalia and Hesse.
Biedenkopf	Biedenkopf (pop. 14,000) lies in well-wooded country in the "Hinterland" of Hesse. On the Schlossberg is a 14th century castle of the Landgraves of Hesse which now houses the Hinterland Museum (geology, furniture, weapons, costumes).
Marburg	See entry
Giessen	See entry
Wetzlar	See entry
Braunfels	South-west of Wetzlar, at some distance from the Lahn, is Braunfels, still partly surrounded by its old walls (Heimatmuseum, Forest Museum). Above the town is a handsome Schloss (13th, 17th and 19th c.) of the Princes of Solms-Braunfels, now containing a museum (pictures and sculpture of the 14th–18th centuries, regional history).
Weilburg	Weilburg lies on a rocky ridge above the Lahn. Above the old town is a large Schloss (16th and 18th c.), with a picturesque inner courtyard and beautiful gardens. At Weilburg the Lahn flows through a tunnel.
Runkel	Runkel has a number of handsome old half-timbered houses. Above the town is the ancestral castle of the Princes of Wied (12th and 17th–18th c.). On the other side of the Lahn is Burg Schadeck (15th c.).
Dietkirchen	At Dietkirchen is the Romanesque church of St Lubentius (12th c.), finely situated above the Lahn. Below the high altar lies the stone sarcophagus of St Lubentius (d. 400), the evangeliser of the Lahn valley.
Limburg	See entry
Diez	Diez has an Early Gothic parish church (13th c.; handsome monuments) and a castle (11th and 17th c.) which belonged to the Princes of Nassau-Orange. 1.5km/1 mile north, on the Lahn, is Schloss Oranienstein (1662–1709) and to the south Schloss Schaumburg (18th c.; enlarged in 19th c.), with a 42m/138ft high tower, and Balduinstein.
Arnstein	On an isolated conical hill at Obernhof can be seen the Premonstratensian monastery of Arnstein, with a Romanesque church (Baroque interior).
Nassau	In the lower Lahn valley is the little town of Nassau, with a handsome half-timbered Town Hall (1607) and a Schloss of 1621. This was the birthplace of the Prussian statesman and reformer Freiherr vom Stein (1757–1831). Above the left bank of the river are two ruined castles, Burg Stein and Burg Nassau.
Bad Ems	Beyond Nassau lies the old-established spa of Bad Ems (thermal springs, 27–57°C/81–135°F; recommended for the treatment of respiratory diseases, cardiac conditions and disorders of the metabolism).
	At Lahnstein the Lahn flows into the Rhine.

Dietz an der Lahn

Landsberg am Lech L 6

Land: Bavaria
Altitude: 630m/2067ft
Population: 20,000

The old town of Landsberg with its medieval town walls, gates, towers, churches and gabled houses is picturesquely situated above the right bank of the Lech at the south end of the Lechfeld, which extends north to Augsburg. It lies on the Romantische Strasse (see entry). | Situation and characteristics

Old Town

In the handsome triangular Hauptplatz stands the Town Hall (Rathaus; 1699), with a sumptuous stucco façade (1719) by Dominikus Zimmermann. The interior is at present in course of restoration; it contains a large painting by the German-English artist Hubert Herkomer (1849–1914). | Town Hall

Nearby is the Late Gothic parish church of the Assumption (1458–88), with a Baroque interior (1702): stucco decoration of the Wessobrunn school, fine stained glass (15th–16th c.) in choir, Gothic figure of the Virgin (by Hans Multscher, 1437) on high altar. | Parish church

Farther north is the Rococo Johanniskirche (St John's Church; by Dominikus Zimmermann, 1750–52). | St John's Church

From the square it is a short distance through the Schöner Turm ("Schmalztor"), up the steep Alte Bergstrasse and then left to the Heilig-Kreuz-Kirche (Holy Cross Church; 1752–54), a former Jesuit church with a richly appointed Baroque interior, beautiful ceiling paintings and an arcaded courtyard. Here too is the Municipal Museum (Stadt-museum; pictures, medieval sculpture, history of the region, local craft products). | Heilig-Kreuz-Kirche Municipal Museum

Bayertor	At the upper end of Bergstrasse rises the 36m/118ft high Bayertor (Bavarian Gate; 1425), an imposing and completely preserved Gothic town gate.
Mutterturm	On the far side of the river is the neo-Romanesque Mutterturm, Hubert Herkomer's studio (collection of graphic art). To the south, in the Lechauen (Lech water meadows), lies the Landsberg game park.

Bad Wörishofen

25km/15 miles west of Landsberg, on the Swabian Spa Route (Schwäbische Bäderstrasse), we come to the little spa of Bad Wörishofen, where Sebastian Kneipp developed the famous Kneipp water-cure. There is a Kneipp Museum in the Klosterhof.

Schongau

30km/20 miles south of Landsberg, in the Lech valley, lies the picturesque little town of Schongau (pop. 11,000), still partly surrounded by its old walls. On the long Marienplatz in the upper town is the Ballenhaus, an old warehouse of 1515. The parish church (17th–18th c.) has stucco decoration of the Wessobrunn school and ceiling paintings by Matthäus Günther.

Altenstadt	3km/2 miles north-west of Schongau is the village of Altenstadt, with the Romanesque church of St Michael (1210–30), which contains a fine Romanesque crucifix.
Hohenpeissenberg	East of Schongau, at Hohenpeissenberg, rises an isolated hill, the Hoher Peissenberg (998m/3274ft), on the summit of which are a church of 1619 and a radio transmitter; magnificent view of the chain of the Alps.
Wessobrunn	To the north of Hohenpeissenberg is Wessobrunn, with a Benedictine monastery founded in 753 and dissolved in 1803. The upper floor has stucco decoration of the Wessobrunn school, the prevailing style in Upper Bavaria and Upper Swabia until 1720.
Ammersee	See entry
Starnberger See	See entry

Landshut   K 7

Land: Bavaria
Altitude: 393m/1289ft
Population: 57,000

Situation and characteristics	The old ducal town of Landshut, now the chief town of Lower Bavaria, is picturesquely situated on the river Isar, here divided into two arms. The pattern of the town centre is set by two wide streets, Altstadt and Neustadt, with 15th and 16th century gabled houses. Above the town to the south is the imposing bulk of Burg Trausnitz.

Sights

Town Hall	In the town's main street, Altstadt, lined with handsome Late Gothic gabled houses, is the Town Hall (Rathaus; 14th–15th c.). During renovation in 1861 the Great Hall was decorated in neo-Gothic style, with large historical paintings (depicting the marriage of the last Duke of Landshut with a Polish princess in 1475, which was celebrated by a banquet in this hall).
Stadtresidenz Museums	Opposite the Town Hall stands old Stadtresidenz (town palace of the Dukes), with the German Wing (Deutscher Bau; 16th and 18th c.) and the Italian Wing (Italienischer Bau;

1537–43), the first Italian Renaissance palace in Germany. Sumptuous state and residential apartments, with the State Picture Gallery (German masters, 18th and 19th century painting) and the Municipal Museum.

Farther along Altstadt to the south can be found the Late Gothic church of St Martin (14th–15th c.), the finest achievement of Hans Stethaimer, the leading architect of the Late Gothic period in Bavaria (whose tomb, with a bust, is between the two south doorways). A striking feature of the church is its slender tower (c. 1500), the tallest in Bavaria (133m/436ft). The church contains a fine carved figure of the Virgin by Hans Leinberger (c. 1520).

* St Martin's

At the north end of Altstadt is the Heiliggeist-Kirche (Church of the Holy Ghost; 1407–61), which was partly the work of Hans Stethaimer.

Heiliggeist-Kirche

On a steep hill above the town (464m/1522ft; by road 2km/1¼ miles, on foot from Dreifaltigkeitsplatz 15 minutes) is Burg Trausnitz, founded by Duke Ludwig I in 1204, at the same time as the town, and until 1503 the seat of the Wittelsbach Dukes of Lower Bavaria. Between 1568 and 1578 it was rebuilt by Prince William as an imposing palace in the Italian style (Fürstenbau, with state apartments and the Narrentreppe or Fools' Staircase, decorated with wall paintings; Late Romanesque chapel).

* Burg Trausnitz

In the northern suburb of St Nikola, on the left bank of the Isar, can be found the Cistercian nunnery of Seligenthal, with a sumptuous Rococo church (1732–34; stucco ornament and ceiling paintings by Johann Baptist Zimmermann).

Seligenthal

Bad Lauchstädt

F 7

Land: Saxony-Anhalt
Altitude: 117m/384ft
Population: 4200

The little spa of Bad Lauchstädt lies on the river Laucha, to the west of Merseburg. A settlement on this site first appears in the records in the 9th century, and it is named as Lochstete in a document of 1341. Its heyday came after the discovery of its mineral springs around 1700. In the late 18th and early 19th centuries the Weimar Theatre, under Goethe's direction, put on performances here in summer.

Situation and characteristics

Sights

The Goethe Theatre (built by H. Gentz in 1802; restored 1966–68) is the only neo-classical theatre in Central Europe which has preserved wooden stage machinery of the Late Baroque period in working order. During the summer there are performances of operas, operettas and plays.

* Goethe Theatre

In the Kurgarten are the old mill-pond, the Herzogspavillon (Duke's Pavilion; 1735, probably by J. M. Hoppenhaupt), the Quellpavillon (Spring Pavilion) and Badepavillon (Bathing Pavilion), both 1776, the Kursaal (with murals by G. A. Pellicia to the design of K. F. Schinkel, 1823) and the Colonnades (a timber-built promenade of 1775–87 with architectural painting and shopkeepers' stalls; concerts in winter).

Kurgarten

The Schloss still preserves a beautiful Early Renaissance oriel. Nearby are the Town Church (17th c.) and the 17th century Amtshaus.
The little Town Hall in the Markt, a plain Baroque building of 1678, has the town's coat of arms over the doorway.

Lauenburg Lakes

C 6

Land: Schleswig-Holstein

To the east of the Elbe-Lübeck Canal, between Gross-Grönau in the north and Büchen in the south, extends the Lauenburg Lakes Nature Park, a region of forests and lakes covering some 400 sq.km/155 sq. miles.

Situation and characteristics

*Landscape

With more than 40 lakes, the area is a paradise for water sports enthusiasts, offering endless scope for bathing, sailing and rowing.

Lauenburg

Lauenburg, the most southerly town in Schleswig-Holstein, lies on the high north bank of the Elbe. In Elbstrasse, in the old lower town, are a number of handsome 16th and 17th century half-timbered houses; at No. 59 is the Elbe Shipping Museum. The church of Mary Magdalene was built in 1227 but was much altered in later centuries; the south doorway dates from 1598. On the Schlossberg (fine views) is the Schlossturm, a relic of the old castle of the Dukes of Saxony-Lauenburg.

Schamebeck   See Lüneburg, Surroundings

Ratzeburg

From Lübeck (see entry) there are motor-launch services up the river Wakenitz to the long Ratzeburger See. On an island in the lake is Ratzeburg, once the seat of the Dukes of Lauenburg.

Cathedral   At the north end of the old town, which is linked with the mainland by three causeways, stands the magnificent Cathedral (Dom; 12th–13th c.), which ranks after Lübeck Cathedral as one of the oldest Romanesque buildings in brick. Adjoining is the Stiftsgebäude (13th c.), with wall paintings in the cloister.

Museums   In the Domhof are the District Museum (local history, uniforms and weapons) and the Andreas-Paul-Weber-Haus, with lithographs by the artist of that name (1893–1980). In Barlachplatz is the Ernst Barlach Museum (sculpture, drawings, woodcuts).

Ratzeburg Cathedral

Mölln

South-west of Ratzeburg is Mölln, the town of Till Eulenspiegel, the legendary jester who is supposed to have died here in 1350 and is commemorated by his gravestone, a monument and an Eulenspiegel Museum.

Leer (East Friesland)   C 3

Land: Lower Saxony
Altitude: 6m/20ft
Population: 30,000

This old town on the river Leda, near its junction with the Ems, styles itself the "gateway to East Friesland". Its red-brick buildings show the influence of the Early Baroque architecture of the Netherlands.

Situation and characteristics

The Town

By the harbour are the neo-Renaissance Town Hall (Rathaus; 1892) and the Alte Waage (Old Weigh-House; 1714).
Nearby are Haus Samson (1643; now a wine-shop), with an old-style East Frisian interior, and the Heimatmuseum (East Frisian domestic interiors, history of shipping).

Harbour

In the west of the old town can be found the Haneburg, a 17th century Renaissance building which is now occupied by the Volkshochschule (adult education centre).

Haneburg

To the north of the town, in the Protestant cemetery, is a 12th century crypt, all that remains of the church of St Ludger.

Crypt

Weigh-House and Town Hall, Leer

Evenburg	To the east of the town centre stands the Evenburg, a 17th century moated castle (altered in the 19th century) in a beautiful park.
Waldzoo-Park	In the eastern district of Logabirum lies the Waldzoo-Park, a leisure park with an animal enclosure.

Leinebergland E 5

Land: Lower Saxony

Situation and characteristics	The river Leine (281km/175 miles long, navigable for 112km/70 miles), rises in the Eichsfeld in Thuringia and flows into the Aller at Schwarmstedt. The Leinebergland, a region of varied scenery, extends between the Weserbergland (Weser Uplands) and the Harz.

Landscape

West of the Leine are a series of hills – Külf (260m/853ft), the Thüsterberg (433m/1421ft), the Duinger Berg (330m/1083ft), the Duinger Wald (221m/725ft) and Selter (396m/1299ft). To the rear are the long ridge of Ith (439m/1440ft), with its picturesque limestone crags, and Hils (477m/1565ft; sandstone), which form a transition to the Weserbergland (see entry).

To the east of the river are Heber (305m/1001ft), the Sackwald (330m/1083ft) and the limestone plateau of the Sieben Berge (Seven Hills; 398m/1306ft), said to be the scene of the fairytale "Snow-White and the Seven Dwarfs". To the north extends the Hildesheimer Wald (281m/922ft).

Alfeld	See entry
Bad Gandersheim	See entry
Einbeck	See Bad Gandersheim, Surroundings

Leipzig F 7

Land: Saxony
Altitude: 118m/387ft
Population: 556,000

Situation and characteristics	The city of Leipzig, long famed for its trade fairs, lies in the Saxon Lowland at the junction of the Weisse Elster and the Pleisse. Situated as it was on important trade routes, the town developed, after being granted the privilege of holding fairs, into a considerable commercial town, the leading city in Saxony after Dresden. It also became a centre of art, culture and learning. Its importance as a centre of the book trade is shown by its old-established publishing houses, its major libraries, including the German Library (Deutsche Bücherei) and the German Central Library for the Blind, its International Book Fairs and annual exhibitions of the finest books of the year, its College of Graphic and Book Art and its large printing and publishing houses.

The City
*The Markt and Round About

*Old Town Hall	The Markt, for many centuries the hub of the city's life, is dominated by the Old Town Hall (Altes Rathaus), a Renaissance building erected by Burgomaster Hieronymus Lotter in

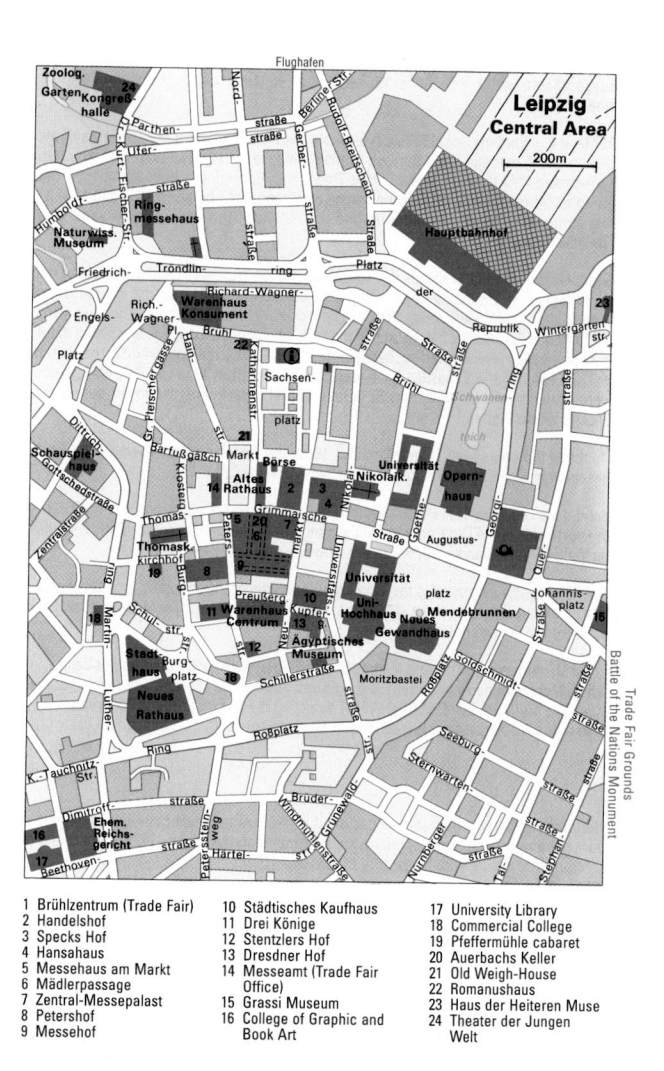

Leipzig
Central Area
200m

1 Brühlzentrum (Trade Fair)
2 Handelshof
3 Specks Hof
4 Hansahaus
5 Messehaus am Markt
6 Mädlerpassage
7 Zentral-Messepalast
8 Petershof
9 Messehof
10 Städtisches Kaufhaus
11 Drei Könige
12 Stentzlers Hof
13 Dresdner Hof
14 Messeamt (Trade Fair Office)
15 Grassi Museum
16 College of Graphic and Book Art
17 University Library
18 Commercial College
19 Pfeffermühle cabaret
20 Auerbachs Keller
21 Old Weigh-House
22 Romanushaus
23 Haus der Heiteren Muse
24 Theater der Jungen Welt

1556 but much altered in later centuries. The tower, with a Baroque crown, is placed asymmetrically over the main entrance. Above the entrance is a roofed balcony for public announcements and proclamations, where the town trumpeters, in traditional costume, emerge at weekends. The colonnades along the front were built in 1907, replacing the wooden shops and booths which formerly stood here.

In the Old Town Hall can be found the Museum on the History of Leipzig, with a collection of pictures and views of the town and a permanent exhibition, "Leipzig Yesterday, Today and Tomorrow" (Ratsstube and Festsaal).

Leipzig

*Weigh-House	On the north side of the Markt is the Old Weigh-House (Alte Waage) built in 1555 by Burgomaster Lotter, rebuilt in 1963–64 after wartime destruction and recently renovated.
Barthels Hof	At Markt 8 is Barthels Hof (1523), a typical old warehouse built for the purposes of the Leipzig fair. A passage leads through to the Kleine Fleischergasse, with the Haus zum Kaffeebaum ("At the sign of the Coffee-Tree"; No. 4), originally built about 1500 and occupied from 1694 by a historic inn, which was frequented between 1833 and 1844 by the composer Robert Schumann and his friends and fellow musicians (the "Davidsbündler").
*St Thomas's Church	South-west of the Markt stands the Thomaskirche (St Thomas's Church), home of the world-famed St Thomas's Choir. Originally built around 1212 as the church of an Augustinian house, it was much altered in later centuries. In the 15th century it was given the form of a Late Gothic hall-church in the style of Upper Saxony. The west front dates from renovation work carried out between 1872 and 1889. Luther preached in the church in 1539, and Johann Sebastian Bach was choirmaster from 1723 to 1750; his remains were brought here in 1950 from St John's Church which was destroyed during the Second World War.
Bach Archives	Opposite the church, at Thomaskirchhof 16, is the Bosehaus, occupied by the Bach Research Institute and Memorial and the Bach Archives.
*Naschmarkt *Old Exchange	Behind the Old Town Hall lies a quiet little square, the Naschmarkt, laid out in 1556. On the north side is the Old Commercial Exchange (Alte Handelsbörse), an Early Baroque building by J. G. Starcke (1678–87). It is now used for social events.
*Mädlerpassage	Opposite the Naschmarket is the Mädlerpassage, one of the shopping arcades characteristic of Leipzig. All of them (Mädlerpassage, Königshofpassage, Messehofpassage) are linked with one another.
*Auerbachs Keller	In the Mädlerpassage are steps leading down to Auerbachs Keller (Auerbach's Cellar), in which Mephistopheles practises his magic arts in Goethe's "Faust". At the head of the steps is a sculpture by M. Molitor (1913) depicting the figures in the cellar scene. Also in the Mädlerpassage is a carillon in Meissen porcelain.

Sachsenplatz

	North of the Markt is Sachsenplatz, laid out in 1969 on the site of buildings destroyed during the war. In the centre of the square are ornamental fountains (1972) and a ceramic column with scenes from the history of the town (1972).
*Romanushaus	On the west side of the square, in Katharinenstrasse, are a series of Baroque burghers' houses. The finest of them is the Romanushaus, at the corner of the Brühl. Built by J. G. Fuchs in 1701–04 for Burgomaster F. C. Romanus, this is a four-storey house with a finely articulated façade. The Fregehaus was also rebuilt by Fuchs in 1706–07 (reconstructed 1986).
St Nicholas's Church	South-east of Sachsenplatz, between Nikolaistrasse and Ritterstrasse, stands the Nikolaikirche (St Nicholas's Church), with a striking tower (75m/245ft high). Originally built in the 12th century, it was considerably altered in various styles in later centuries. The neo-classical interior is of impressive effect, with galleries and altarpieces by A. F. Oeser.

Augustusplatz

	Augustusplatz originally lay outside the town walls, and until 1831 one of the old town gates, the Grimma Gate, stood here.
University	The dominant feature in the square is now the 34-storey high-rise block (1973; 142.50m/468ft high) occupied by the University, with a panoramic café at 110m/360ft.

Sachsenplatz

The University church which formerly stood here was demolished after suffering heavy destruction during the war.
Incorporated in the lecture theatre block is the Schinkeltor (by K. F. Schinkel and Ernst Rietschel, 1836), the entrance to the old University, the Augusteum.

Adjoining the University is the old Moritzbastei (Bastion; 1515), the only relic of the town's old fortifications.

Moritzbastei

At Schillerstrasse 6 can be found the interesting Egyptian Museum.

Egyptian Museum

Immediately east of the University is the new Gewandhaus (Neues Gewandhaus; by R. Skoda, 1981), a magnificent new home for the world-famed Gewandhaus Orchestra. The three-storey hall, with the amphitheatre-like Grosser Saal (Schuke organ) and Kleiner Saal, is decorated with numerous paintings by modern artists.

*Gewandhaus

From Augustusplatz Goethestrasse and the Georgiring lead north to the monumental railway station (Hauptbahnhof; 1902–15), the largest railway terminus in Europe.

*Railway station

East of Augustusplatz, in Johannisplatz, is the Grassi Museum (1925–27), built of red Rochlitz porphyry (ethnography, applied and decorative art, musical instruments).

*Grassi Museum

South-Western Districts

At the south-west corner of the old town stands the New Town Hall (Neues Rathaus), a monumental building in the style of the German Late Renaissance (by H. Licht, 1899–1905). It occupies the site of the 13th century Pleissenburg, which was pulled down in 1897–98. The stump of a tower from the old castle is incorporated in the central tower (115m/377ft high) of the new building.

*New Town Hall

South-west of the New Town Hall is the domed building once occupied by the old

Museum of Art

Supreme Court (Reichsgericht; 1888–95), now the Museum of Art (Museum der Bilden-den Künste), with pictures by German, Italian and Dutch masters from the 15th century onwards. Of particular interest are the collections of historical material and sculpture of the 19th and 20th centuries.

Trade Fair Grounds and Battle of the Nations Monument

In Strasse des 18 Oktober (Deutscher Platz) can be found the German Library (Deutsche Bücherei; by O. Pusch, 1914–16), set up with the object of collecting all books and publications in German. It also houses the German Museum of Books and Writing. *German Library

In Philipp-Rosenthal-Strasse is the Russian Church (the Memorial Church of St Alexius; by W. A. Pokrowski, 1912–13), with a gilded onion dome. It was built to commemorate the 22,000 Russians who fell in the Battle of the Nations at Leipzig in 1813. *Russian Church

Between the Deutscher Platz and the Wilhelm Külz Park are the extensive Trade Fair Grounds (Messegelände), on which the Technology Fair was held for the first time in 1920. Trade Fair Grounds

The Battle of the Nations Monument (Völkerschlachtdenkmal; by B. Schmitz and C. Thieme, 1898–1913) is an imposing structure in the monumental style favoured at the turn of the century, built on the occasion of the hundredth anniversary of the Battle of the Nations. There is a viewing platform at a height of 91m/299ft. *Battle of the Nations Monument

Gohlis

In the northern district of Gohlis, in Menckestrasse, is the Gohliser Schlösschen, a mansion built by F. Seltendorff in 1755–56 for C. Richter, a Leipzig councillor. In the Great Hall is a ceiling painting, "The Life of Psyche", by A. F. Oeser (1779). *Gohliser Schlösschen

A little way north, at Menckestrasse 42, can be seen the last surviving cottage from the old village of Gohlis. Schiller lived in this little house in 1785 and composed his "Ode to Joy" here.

Surroundings of Leipzig

Delitzsch (22km/13½ miles north of Leipzig) has some well preserved remains of its old fortifications (Hallischer Turm, 16th c.; Breiter Turm, c. 1400; moat). The Town Church of SS. Peter and Paul is a 15th century hall-church. The Schloss (16th–17th c.) is now a museum. Delitzsch

At Eilenburg (22km/13½ miles north-east) is a castle founded by Henry I in the 10th century at a crossing of the river Mulde. From the Sorbenturm (12th c.) there are good views of the town and the Mulde valley. The Town Hall, a Renaissance building of 1545, was destroyed in 1945 but was rebuilt after the war. Museum on the Mansberg. Observatory. Eilenburg

The main features of interest in Grimma (30km/20 miles south-east) are the Frauenkirche (Early Gothic, 1230–40), the Augustinian monastery (c. 1290), later used as a school, the Schloss (c. 1200), and the Renaissance Town Hall (1538–85), in the Marktplatz. Grimma

Lemgo E 4

Land: North Rhine-Westphalia
Altitude: 101m/331ft
Population: 41,000

◀ *University tower block, with the Mägdebrunnen (Maids' Fountain)*

| Situation and characteristics | Lemgo lies in the valley of the Bega, in the forest-covered Lippe uplands. The oldest town in the territory of Lippe, it has preserved many Renaissance features. |

The *Town

Town Hall	In the Markt, lined with handsome gabled houses, stands the Town Hall (14th–17th c.), with a Gothic stepped gable, an arcade and a fine Renaissance oriel (1612). Opposite it is the Ballhaus (1609).
St Nicholas's Church	To the east is St Nicholas's Church (13th c., with a Gothic extension): Romanesque reredos, Early Baroque high altar, Renaissance monuments, beautiful font (1597).
	Around St-Nikolai-Kirchhof are a number of charming old half-timbered houses.
Mittelstrasse	Mittelstrasse (pedestrian zone) is lined with old stone and half-timbered houses. At No. 17 is the Alt-Lemgo inn (1587), at No. 24 Haus Sonnenuhr (1546), at No. 27 Haus Sauerländer (1569), at No. 36 the Planetenhaus (1612). On either side of the street are two old defensive towers, the Johannisturm (St John's Tower) and the Pulverturm (Powder Tower).
*Hexenbürgermeisterhaus	In the Breite Strasse, which runs south from the Markt, stands the Hexenbürgermeister-haus ("Witch-Burgomaster's House"), a magnificent Renaissance building of 1571, now occupied by the Heimatmuseum; Engelbert Kämpfer Room, with mementoes of Kämpfer, a native of Lemgo who travelled to Japan in the 17th century.
St Mary's Church	Close by, in Stiftstrasse, is St Mary's Church, a Gothic hall-church (1320). It has a Scherer organ of 1600 (annual organ festival).
Junkerhaus	In Hamelner Strasse, which runs east from the town, can be seen the Junkerhaus, covered externally and internally with grotesque carvings by its eccentric owner, Karl Junker.
Schloss Brake	South-east of the old town is Schloss Brake, a 13th century moated castle; the tower and north wing (16th c.) were Renaissance additions. It contains a Museum of the Weser Renaissance.

Surroundings of Lemgo

| Sternberg | 13km/8 miles north-east of Lemgo is Burg Sternberg, the seat of a noble family of that name. It now houses a collection of old musical instruments. Concerts with historic instruments. |

Limburg an der Lahn   H 3

Land: Hesse
Altitude: 130m/427ft
Population: 30,000

| Situation and characteristics | Limburg lies in the fertile Limburg Basin between the hills of the Taunus and the Westerwald. It is a town of picturesque half-timbered houses dominated by the Cathedral. |

Sights

| *Old town | In the centre of the old town, particularly around the Fischmarkt, are numbers of old half-timbered buildings (Town Hall, 14th c.; Hallenhaus, 15th c.). Here too, at No. 22, is the Municipal Art Gallery. |

Limburg Cathedral ▶

Excursions on the Lahn to Balduinstein.

*Cathedral

Towering over the old town, high above the Lahn, stands the seven-towered Cathedral (Dom; 13th c.; R.C.), one of Germany's finest Late Romanesque churches, with frescoes of the 13th–16th centuries. In the south transept is the monument of Konrad Kurzbold (d. 948), founder of the Cathedral.

Schloss

Behind the Cathedral is the old castle of the Counts of Lahn, dating in part from the 13th century.
At the foot of the castle is the Town Church (14th c.) and adjoining it the Bishop's Palace, with the Cathedral treasury (Cross reliquary of 959).

Surroundings of Limburg

Burg Runkel

7km/4½ miles east of Limburg can be found Burg Runkel (12th c., partly rebuilt in 17th and 18th c.; open to visitors), the ancestral seat of the Princes of Wied.

Lindau   M 5

Land: Bavaria
Altitude: 402m/1319ft
Population: 25,000

Situation and characteristics

Lindau, the largest town on the Bavarian shores of Lake Constance (see entry), consists of the picturesque old town on an island in the lake (its area recently increased to 68.8 hectares/170 acres by land reclamation to provide car parking in the north-west of the town), with the harbour used by the Lake Constance "White Fleet", and the garden city of Lindau (residential districts, recreational facilities, industry), spaciously laid out amid orchards on the morainic slopes of the mainland. The two parts of the town are linked by a bridge (the Neue Seebrücke) and a causeway carrying the railway.

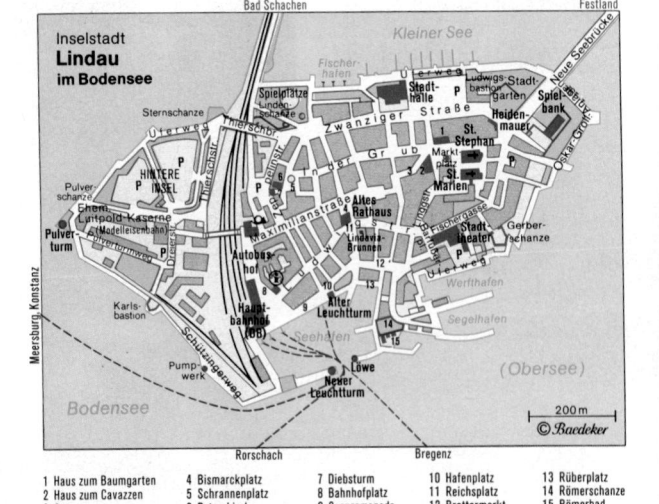

1 Haus zum Baumgarten	6 Peterskirche	11 Reichsplatz
2 Haus zum Cavazzen	7 Diebsturm	12 Brettermarkt
3 Cramergasse	8 Bahnhofplatz	13 Rüberplatz
4 Bismarckplatz	9 Seepromenade	14 Römerschanze
5 Schrannenplatz	10 Hafenplatz	15 Römerbad

The Island Town

On the south side of the island lies the Harbour, with the old lighthouse (Alter Leucht-turm), the 13th century Mangturm, between the Hafenplatz and the Seepromenade. At the ends of the outer harbour walls are Lindau's best-known landmarks, the 6m/20ft high Bavarian lion (Löwe; 1853–56) and the 33m/108ft high new lighthouse (Neuer Leucht-turm; 1856), from which there are magnificent views of the town and the Alps. — *Harbour

The old town, much of which is now for pedestrians only, has preserved beautiful old streets of Gothic, Renaissance and Baroque houses. Particularly attractive is Maximilian-strasse, the main street of the town, with its trim patrician houses, arcades, fountains and pavement cafés. — *Old town

In Reichsplatz, to the south, stands the Old Town Hall (Altes Rathaus; built 1422–36, rebuilt in Renaissance style 1578), with a colourful façade, in which are the Municipal Archives and the old Municipal Library. — Old Town Hall

To the north-west, in Schrannenplatz, is the Peterskirche (St Peter's Church; founded about 1000), which became a war memorial chapel in 1928; it has the only surviving frescoes by Hans Holbein the Elder (c. 1480). Close by is the Diebsturm (Thief's Tower) of 1420 (view). — St Peter's Church

In the Marktplatz, near the east end of the town, are the Neptune Fountain and the Haus zum Cavazzen, with the Heimatmuseum and the municipal art collection.
Diagonally opposite the Haus zum Cavazzen is the handsome Baroque Haus zum Baumgarten. — Haus zum Cavazzen

On the east side of the Marktplatz are the Protestant parish church of St Stephen (1180; remodelled in Baroque style 1782) and the Catholic parish church of St Mary (Rococo interior, damaged by the collapse of the roof in 1987). St Mary's, originally belonging to a women's house of retreat which was dissolved in 1802, was built in 1748–52 on the site of a minster destroyed in a great fire in 1729–30. — St Stephen's St Mary's Church

There is a pleasant walk round the island on the Uferweg, with fine views from two old bastions, the Gerberschanze and the Sternschanze, and from the Pulverturm (Powder Tower) and Pulverschanze. — *Uferweg

In the old Luitpold-Kaserne (Barracks), at the west end of the island, a large model railway layout can be visited. — Model railway

Lippstadt   F 3

Land: North Rhine-Westphalia
Altitude: 77m/253ft
Population: 62,000

The old Hanseatic town of Lippstadt, on the Lippe, lies between Paderborn and Soest and between the Münsterland and the Sauerland. — Situation

The Town

In the Marktplatz stands St Mary's Church (13th–16th c.; Protestant), with Late Gothic and Renaissance wall and ceiling paintings, a tabernacle of 1523 and a Baroque high altar (17th c.). — St Mary's Church

A handsome old house of 1656 in Rathausstrasse houses the Heimatmuseum (religious art, domestic life, documents). The house has fine stucco ceilings. — Heimatmuseum

In the west of the old town is the ruined Early Gothic church of St Maria de Lippia – one of the most important of its kind in Germany – which belonged to an Augustinian nunnery dissolved about 1550. — St Maria de Lippia

Löbau

St Nicholas's Church   To the south of St Maria, in Klosterstrasse, is the Nikolaikirche (St Nicholas's Church). The massive west tower (12th c.) is the oldest surviving structure in the town; the church itself was mostly rebuilt in the late 19th century.

Cappel   North-west of the old town, in the district of Cappel, can be found the 12th century Romanesque church of a former Premonstratensian nunnery (now a secular retreat for women and boarding school). Cappel also has a Zoo, with some 500 animals.

Overhagen Herringhausen   To the south-west are the districts of Overhagen (with a moated castle of 1619) and Herringhausen (moated castle of 1730).

Schwarzenraben   Outside the town, to the south-east, stands the Baroque moated castle of Schwarzenraben (1765–68).

Löbau   F 10

Land: Saxony
Altitude: 267m/876ft
Population: 18,600

Situation and characteristics   Löbau (Sorbian Lubij), the chief town of a district, lies to the west of the Löbauer Berg (449m/1473ft), some 20km/12½ miles south-west of Görlitz. A cloth-making town, it was also the largest market for yarn in Upper Lusatia and the second largest market for corn in Saxony, though always overshadowed by its more powerful sister towns in the Lusatian League of Six Cities, Bautzen and Görlitz.

Sights

Town Hall   The Baroque Town Hall (1711) has preserved a Late Gothic tower and vaulted cellar. The handsomest burghers' houses in the Markt are Nos. 16 and 17 on the north side (Baroque), No. 14 on the west side (Late Renaissance) and No. 3 on the east side (neo-classical).

St John's Church   To the east of the Town Hall is the Johanniskirche (St John's Church), an aisleless Early Gothic church with 17th and 18th century alterations. Until the Reformation it belonged to a Franciscan friary, in the refectory of which the meetings of the League of Six Cities were held in the 14th and 15th centuries.

Old Cemetery   There are a number of notable Baroque gravestones and monuments in the Old Cemetery (Alter Friedhof), to the south of the old town. Particularly fine can be seen the burial vault of a great merchant prince, M. Lücke (1733).

Municipal Museum   At Johannisstrasse 5 is the Municipal Museum (Stadtmuseum; history of the town, culture and crafts of Upper Lusatia).

Lübben   E 9

Land: Brandenburg
Altitude: 53m/174ft
Population: 14,300

Situation   The old town of Lübben (Sorbian Lubin), lies some 50km/30 miles south-east of Berlin at the narrowest point in the Spree valley.

Sights

Town walls   The town still preserves some remains of its old walls – the round Hexenturm (Witches' Tower), the square Trotzer and a *wiekhaus* (a house built into the wall), with Gothic blind arches and tracery.

The Schloss is in Late Renaissance style. Particularly fine are the east gable and the sandstone doorway on the north side with the arms of the Electorate of Saxony. The Heraldic Hall (Wappensaal) in the tower containing the residential apartments has been restored.

Schloss

The old Baroque Ständehaus (House of the Estates; now the Municipal Archives) also has the arms of the Electorate of Saxony on the doorways.

The Paul-Gerhardt-Kirche (originally St Nicholas's Church) is a brick-built Late Gothic hall-church with a richly furnished interior. It was the last charge of the famous 17th century Protestant pastor and hymn-writer Paul Gerhardt, who is buried in the church. There is a monument to him outside the church.

*Paul-Gerhardt-Kirche

Boat trips through the beautiful Spreewald (see entry) are a popular attraction (departures from the Strandcafé).

*Boat trips

Lübbenau

E 9

Land: Brandenburg
Altitude: 50–52m/164–171ft
Population: 21,800

The little Lusatian town of Lübbenau (Sorbian Lubnjow) lies on the southern fringes of the beautiful Oberspreewald (Upper Spree Forest). It is the gateway to the Spreewald (see entry), a landscape reserve of 287 sq.km/111 sq. miles.

Situation and characteristics

Sights

In the Markt is the Town Church of St Nicholas, a plain Baroque building of 1738–41. It has a notable interior, including a fine monument of 1765.

St Nicholas's Church

In the oldest part of the town stands the neo-classical Schloss, built between 1817 and 1839 on the site of an earlier moated castle. Much altered, it is now a training centre. The Orangery (1820) now houses a museum.

Schloss

The fine old Courthouse (1745–48) is now occupied by the Spreewald Museum (history of the region, local costumes).

*Spreewald Museum

The oldest building in the town is a two-storey half-timbered building at the entrance to the Schloss.

An exhibition hall opposite the half-timbered house contains an old locomotive and rolling-stock of the Spreewaldbahn, a narrow-gauge railway which ran between Cottbus and Lübben, as well as some traditional Sorb costumes.

Spreewaldbahn

Lehde

Near Lübbenau is the romantically situated little village of Lehde, with the Spreewald Open-Air Museum (Freilandmuseum). Here numerous old farmhouses with their original furnishings illustrate the life of Sorb peasants in the 19th century.

*Spreewald Open-Air Museum

*A Walk in the Spreewald

The most famous walk in the Spreewald is from the Spreeschlösschen restaurant to the Wotschowska restaurant, on a footpath (laid out in 1911) which crosses 15 bridges, under which glide the Spreewald boats. The walk takes about an hour.

Spreewald Open-air Museum, Lehde

Lübeck   B 6

Land: Schleswig-Holstein
Altitude: 11m/36ft
Population: 207,000

Situation and characteristics	The former free imperial city and Hanseatic town of Lübeck is now a busy port and industrial centre. The oval old town, ringed by water, preserves much of its medieval aspect. The Trave, which flows into the Baltic 20km/12½ miles north of the town, enables vessels of up to 6m/20ft draught to reach the town's harbour, while the Elbe-Lübeck Canal, opened in 1900, gives river shipping access to the Baltic.
Boat trips	Cruises round the town, the canals and the harbour; excursion ships to Travemünde, to the Lauenburg Lakes (see entry) and on the Elbe-Lübeck Canal.

Old Town

**Holstentor	At the west entrance to the old town can be found the very emblem of Lübeck, the massive twin-towered Holstentor (1477), now housing the Museum on the History of the Town (large model of Lübeck as it was about 1650; shipping).
Museum ship	Near the Holstenbrücke, on the Trave, is the museum ship "Mississippi".
*Town Hall	In the Markt, in the centre of the old town, stands the Town Hall (Rathaus), one of the most magnificent in Germany, built in the 13th–15th centuries in dark glazed brick, with a Renaissance addition of 1570 fronting the building.
*St Mary's Church	At the north end of the Markt is the Marienkirche (St Mary's Church; 13th–14th c., restored), the model for many other brick-built churches in the Baltic area. It contains a

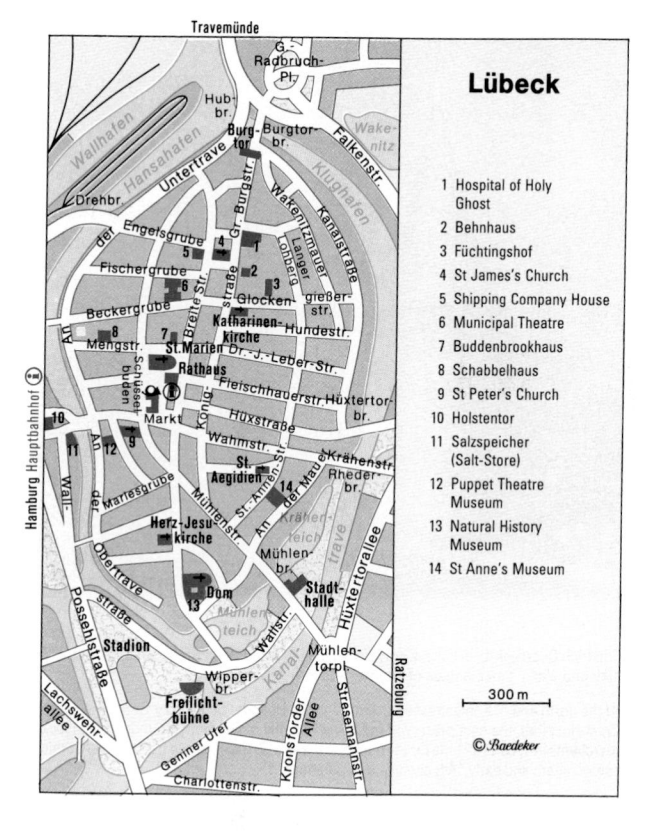

Travemünde

Lübeck

1 Hospital of Holy
   Ghost
2 Behnhaus
3 Füchtingshof
4 St James's Church
5 Shipping Company House
6 Municipal Theatre
7 Buddenbrookhaus
8 Schabbelhaus
9 St Peter's Church
10 Holstentor
11 Salzspeicher
   (Salt-Store)
12 Puppet Theatre
   Museum
13 Natural History
   Museum
14 St Anne's Museum

300 m

© Baedeker

tabernacle of 1476–79. In the south tower is a memorial chapel, containing the bells
which crashed to the ground during a bombing raid in 1942.

To the north of the Marienkirche, at Mengstrasse 4, is the Buddenbrookhaus, famed as
the setting of Thomas Mann's novel "Buddenbrooks"; the house (1758; restored)
belonged to the novelist's family from 1841 to 1891. At Nos. 48–50 is the Schabbelhaus
(rebuilt after destruction during the Second World War; now a restaurant, with a traditional Lübeck interior).

Buddenbrookhaus
Schabbelhaus

In the Breite Strasse (partly pedestrians-only), at No. 2, is the Haus der Schiffergesellschaft (Shipping Company House; 1535), now a restaurant, which with its old furniture
and furnishings gives a vivid impression of one of the old business houses of Lübeck.
Opposite it is the Gothic Jakobikirche (St James's Church; 14th c.), with two historic
organs.

St James's Church

In Königstrasse, which runs parallel to the Breite Strasse on the east, stands the Katharinenkirche (St Catherine's Church; 14th c.), a noble example of High Gothic, now a
museum (on the façade nine figures by Ernst Barlach and Gerhard Marcks).

St Catherine's
Church

Farther along Königstrasse is the neo-classical Behnhaus (1783), with a collection of 19th
and 20th century art; works of the Romantic school, including in particular pictures by

Behnhaus
Drägerhaus

341

Holstentor, Lübeck

Friedrich Overbeck (b. in Lübeck in 1789). Adjoining is the Drägerhaus (art and culture of 19th and 20th c.; mementoes of Thomas and Heinrich Mann).

*Hospital of Holy Ghost

At the north end of Königstrasse can be found the Hospital of the Holy Ghost (Heiligen-Geist-Hospital), the best preserved medieval hospital in Germany, founded by Lübeck merchants in 1280 as a home for the poor and the sick. In the entrance hall are Late Gothic carved altars and early 14th century wall paintings.

Burgtor

At the end of the Grosse Burgstrasse, the continuation of Königstrasse to the north, stands the Burgtor (13th and 15th c.), with remains of an old circuit of walls.

Füchtingshof

In Glockengiesserstrasse, which runs east from Königstrasse, is the snug and attractive Füchtingshof (No. 25), built in 1639 to house merchants' and sea-captains' widows.

St Peter's Church *View

South-west of the Markt, in Schmiedestrasse, stands the Gothic Petrikirche (St Peter's Church; 13th–14th c., restored). Fine views from the tower.

Cathedral

At the south end of the old town is the twin-towered Cathedral (Dom; Protestant), founded in 1173 by Henry the Lion and enlarged in Gothic style in the 13th and 14th century (rebuilt after heavy war damage). In the nave are a font of 1455 and a fine Triumphal Cross group (1477) by the Lübeck master Bernt Notke. An adjoining building houses the Natural History Museum (special exhibitions only).

*St Anne's Museum

North of the Cathedral is St Anne's Museum, housed in a former convent dedicated to St Anne, which presents an excellent survey of Lübeck art from the early medieval period to the 18th century. Of particular interest are the sculpture and painting, together with works of art salvaged from Lübeck churches in 1942.

Travemünde

Travemünde, now part of Lübeck, is the most fashionable and liveliest German resort on the Baltic, with its Kurhaus, Kursaal, Casino, swimming pool (seawater, with artificial waves), Kurpark and wide seafront promenade, all dominated by the Hotel Maritim (158m/518ft; viewing platform). The old town huddles around the 16th century parish church of St Lawrence.

In the Passat Harbour on the Priwall peninsula is moored the four-masted barque "Passat", once a merchant navy training ship and now used by the German-French Youth Welfare Organisation (Jugendwerk) as a hostel and training school (open to visitors during the season).

"Passat"

Ludwigsburg

K 7

Land: Baden-Württemberg
Altitude: 292m/958ft
Population: 76,000

With its palaces and parks and the central area of the town around the Marktplatz, Ludwigsburg, situated on a plateau above the Neckar a few kilometres north of Stuttgart, preserves the aspect and atmosphere of a princely capital of the Baroque period.

Situation and characteristics

**Ludwigsburg Palace

The Palace (Residenzschloss), built by various architects between 1704 and 1733 on the model of Versailles, is the largest surviving Baroque palace in Germany. The interior (452 rooms) is richly appointed in Baroque, Rococo and Empire style (conducted tours; Palace Festival in summer). In the New Wing is a section of the Württemberg Provincial Museum devoted to the courtly art of the Baroque period.

In the beautiful park ("Blühendes Barock" garden show in summer) are an aviary and a Fairytale Garden. On the east side of the park Mömpelgardstrasse boasts a terrace of Baroque houses.

Park

Ludwigsburg Palace

Ludwigshafen

Porcelain Manufactory	To the east of the palace, in Schorndorfer Strasse, can be found the old Porcelain Manufactory, recently restored. During the restoration the original kilns were rediscovered.
Forum am Schlosspark	To the south of the palace, beyond the Bärenwiese gardens, is the Forum am Schlosspark, a concert hall and theatre opened in 1988. Part of the Palace Festival is staged here.
Favoritepark	North of the palace (pedestrian bridge over the main road) lies the Favoritepark (game park, nature reserve), with the little Baroque palace of Favorite (1718–23).
Monrepos	The avenue through Favoritepark runs in a straight line to the little palace of Monrepos (1760–64), on the lake.

Central Area

The Baroque town centre lies to the west of the palace and the main road. Here, in Marstallstrasse, is the Graevenitz Palace (restored), built by Duke Eberhard Ludwig for his mistress Countess Graevenitz (1686–1744).

Town Church Trinity Church	In the Marktplatz (Market Fountain, with a statue of Duke Eberhard Ludwig, founder of the town) are the twin-towered Town Church (Stadtkirche; 1718–26; Protestant) and the plain Trinity Church (Dreieinigkeitskirche; 1721–27; R.C.). Also in the square is the birthplace of the 19th century writer Justinus Kerner. In the vicinity are the birthplaces of the poet Eduard Mörike (1804–75; Kirchstrasse 2), the writer on aesthetics F. T. Vischer (1807–87; Stadtkirchenplatz 1) and the theologian David Friedrich Strauss (1808–74; Marstallstrasse 1). To the north of the Marktplatz lies the Holzmarkt, in which can be seen an obelisk bearing copper plaques with the portraits of these four famous sons of Ludwigsburg.

Surroundings of Ludwigsburg

Asperg	5km/3 miles west of Ludwigsburg is the little town of Asperg (Fire Brigade Museum). High above the town, topping a conical hill, rises the fortress of Hohenasperg, now a penal establishment (conversion into a cultural centre planned). Among those confined in the old fortress were the poet Christian Daniel Schubart (1777–87) and the economist Friedrich List (1824–25). There is an attractive walk round the fortress (views).
Markgröningen	A few kilometres west of Asperg, on the rim of the Glems valley, we come to Markgröningen. The central area of the little town, which has recently been restored, has many half-timbered buildings of the 15th–17th centuries; particularly fine is the imposing Town Hall. The church (14th and 15th c.) has the oldest choir-stalls in South Germany. A popular annual event is the Schäferlauf ("Shepherds' Race") in August.

Marbach

8km/5 miles north-east of Ludwigsburg, high above the right bank of the Neckar, lies Marbach, birthplace of the great German dramatist Friedrich Schiller (1759–1805). The house in which he was born, a modest half-timbered building at Nicklastorstrasse 31, is now a memorial museum.

** Schiller Museum	The National Schiller Museum has a large collection of Schiller's works and mementoes of him. Associated with the Museum are the German Literary Archives, with extensive holdings of autograph manuscripts, books and documents representing all phases of German literature since the 18th century.

Ludwigshafen 〡 3

Land: Rhineland-Palatinate
Altitude: 94m/308ft
Population: 162,000

The modern city of Ludwigshafen lies on the left bank of the Rhine, immediately opposite the town of Mannheim in Baden. It is internationally known as the headquarters of BASF, the Badische Anilin- und Soda-Fabrik.

The Town

In the city centre, at Berliner Strasse 23, is the Wilhelm Hack Museum, with a colourful façade by Joan Miró, which contains the municipal art collection (20th century European painting; Late Roman, Frankish and medieval art).

Ludwigslust

Land: Mecklenburg-West Pomerania
Altitude: 36m/118ft
Population: 13,600

Ludwigslust, chief town of a district, lies on the Ludwigslust Canal, 35km/22 miles south of Schwerin. With its Baroque and neo-classical buildings this former princely capital, seat of the Grand Dukes of Mecklenburg-Schwerin, is one of the best preserved town layouts of the 18th–19th century.

The Town

The layout of the town is centred on a main axis running from the Schloss to the Town Church (by J. J. Busch). The Late Baroque Schloss (1772–76) is built in brick with a facing of Elbe sandstone. It has a striking main front, with 40 over-life-size statues and 14 vases along the roof. The principal feature of the interior is the Golden Hall, two storeys in height, with rich decoration (partly in papier-mâché).

Schloss Ludwigslust

Below the main front is a richly decorated cascade (1780), fed by a specially constructed canal (1757–61).

Town Church

Directly south of the Schloss, forming a striking contrast to the low half-timbered buildings on either side of it, stands the Town Church (Stadtkirche; 1765–70), preceded by a portico with six monumental columns. It contains a colossal painting of the "Adoration of the Shepherds" (1772–1803). Facing the altar is the ducal box, with luxuriant decoration (partly in papier-mâché). 200m/220yds east of the church are two pylon-like bell-towers (1791–92).

*Schlosspark

North and west of the Schloss extends the Schlosspark. It was originally laid out in Baroque style, but in the early 19th century part of it was converted into a landscaped park by P. J. Lenné. Among surviving Baroque features are the Grand Canal and stone bridge (both c. 1760) and, farther north, the artificial ruin and the Swiss cottage (Schweizerhaus).

Lüneburg   C 5

Land: Lower Saxony
Altitude: 17m/56ft
Population: 60,000

Situation and characteristics

The old salt-working and Hanseatic town of Lüneburg lies on the navigable river Ilmenau at the north-east corner of Lüneburg Heath (see entry), on the edge of the Elbe lowlands. It is one of the principal centres of North German brick-built architecture, with numerous buildings of the Late Gothic and Renaissance periods. A new inland port on the Elbe Lateral Canal began to operate in 1976.

Boat trips

Excursion boats ply on the Ilmenau, the canals and the Elbe.

Central Area

*Am Sande

In the centre of the town is the charming square called Am Sande ("On the Sand"), which is surrounded by old brick-built houses, some of them with fine stepped gables. At the west end of the square can be seen the old Brewhouse (1548), now occupied by the Chamber of Industry and Commerce.

Museum of East Prussia

To the south, at Ritterstrasse 10, is the Museum of East Prussia (Ostpreussisches Landesmuseum; land and culture of East Prussia).

Brewing Museum

In Heiliggeiststrasse is the Brewing Museum (Brauereimuseum; brewing technology, goblets, etc.).

St John's Church

The Johanniskirche (St John's Church; 14th c.), dominating the east end of the square, has a 108m/354ft high tower. Notable features of the interior (with double aisles flanking the nave) are the imposing high altar (1485), the beautiful choir-stalls (1589) and a number of monuments.

Lüneburg Museum

To the south-east is the Museum of the Principality of Lüneburg (archaeology, history of the region, religious art, town guilds, peasant furniture; specialised library).

*Town Hall

From Am Sande the Kleine and Grosse Bäckerstrasse (pedestrian zone) run north to the Markt, with the Diana Fountain (Luna Fountain) of 1530. On the west side of the square stands the Town Hall (Rathaus), a group of buildings dating from the 13th–18th centuries with a Baroque façade of 1720 richly decorated with figures. Of the many well preserved rooms in the interior the most notable are the arcaded Court Room (c. 1330) with its stained glass windows and painted timber ceiling (c. 1530); the Cloth Hall (c. 1450), with reproductions of the famous Lüneburg municipal silver plate; the Old Chancery (1433); the Great Council Chamber (1466–84) with its fine carving; and the Princes' Hall (15th c.). In the Town Hall tower is a carillon of 42 bells of Meissen porcelain.

Am Sande, Lüneburg

On the western edge of the old town is the Michaeliskirche (St Michael's Church; 14th–15th c.). | St Michael's Church

From the Kalkberg (57m/187ft; nature reserve) there are fine views. At the foot of the hill is a geologically interesting subsidence area over the Lüneburg salt deposits. | Kalkberg

North of the Markt stands the Nikolaikirche (St Nicholas's Church; consecrated 1409). To the east of this, on the banks of the Ilmenau, are the Altes Kaufhaus, an old warehouse of 1745 with a Baroque façade, the Old Crane (Alter Kran; mentioned in the records as early as 1336) and the Abbot's Mill (Abtsmühle). | St Nicholas's Church *Old Crane

On the outskirts of the town, to the north-east, is the former nunnery of Lüne (14th–15th c.), now a women's house of retreat, with a rich collection of embroidery (on show only during one week in August). | *Lüne Convent

Spa District

The spa district lies south-east of the old town. The old saline springs near Lambertiplatz were in use from 956 to 1980; they now form the German Salt Museum. | Salt Museum

Surroundings of Lüneburg

6km/4 miles north is Bardowick, which has a Cathedral (SS. Peter and Paul) with Late Romanesque west work and an aisled Gothic nave; carved winged altar of 1525, fine Late Gothic choir-stalls. | Bardowick

10km/6 miles north-east of Lüneburg and 8km/5 miles east of Bardowick, on the Elbe Lateral Canal, is the Scharnebeck ship-lift, which raises and lowers ships 38m/125ft in water-filled "troughs" 100m/120yds long, 12m/40ft wide and 3.50m/11½ft deep. | Scharnebeck

Lüneburg Heath

Land: Lower Saxony

The beautiful Lüneburg Heath (Lüneburger Heide), a ridge of sandy heathland formed from Ice Age deposits of sand, extending between the Aller and lower Weser in the south-west and the Elbe in the north-east, is the largest expanse of heathland in Germany, reaching a height of 169m/554ft in the Wilseder Berg. The principal rivers draining into the Elbe are the Ilmenau, Luhe, Aue, Seeve, Este and Oste.

Old-time railways	The "Ameisenbär" ("Ant-Bear"), from Soltau to the Lüneburg Heath Nature Reserve.

The "Celler-Land-Express", from Celle (see entry) to the Südheide Nature Park and to Hankensbüttel (see Gifhorn, Surroundings).

The "Heide-Express", from Lüneburg (see entry) or Winsen an der Luhe to Soltau.

The "Preussenzug" through the district of Gifhorn (see entry).

Coach trips

There are many opportunities for trips on the Lüneburg Heath in old mail coaches or horse-drawn carriages.

*Landscape

The dry and infertile stretches of higher ground, between which lie tracts of bog, are covered for much of their extent by heather, which during the flowering season in August brings a touch of life and colour to the rather melancholy landscape. Variety is given by the curiously misshapen juniper bushes, the sandy tracks caught between clumps of birches and the red brick farmhouses nestling amid groups of oak-trees. Numerous "Hunengräber" ("Huns' graves"; megalithic tombs) are a reminder that men lived here in prehistoric times.

The expanse of real heath country has been steadily reduced in recent years. The traditional bee-keeping and the rearing of moorland sheep, which destroyed so many trees, have declined sharply, replaced by forestry, arable farming and industry (mining of diatomite, extraction of oil). The areas on the fringes of the Heath, such as the Aller and Elbe fenlands, are horse-breeding country.

*Lüneburg Heath Nature Reserve

The finest heath scenery is to be found in the central part of the Heath. Here in 1921 an area of some 20,000 hectares/50,000 acres around the village of Wilsede was designated as the first German nature reserve.

*Wilseder Berg
Totengrund

In the centre of the nature reserve rises the Wilseder Berg (169m/554ft), the highest point in the North German lowlands, from which there are extensive views of the Heath. South-east of the hill is the Totengrund ("Dead Men's Ground"), a low-lying area covered with heather and juniper through which the dead were borne from Wilsede to Bispingen for burial.

Game Park

On the north-eastern border of the nature reserve, near Hanstedt-Nindorf, lies the Lüneburg Heath Game Park, with over 1000 animals, including bear, elk and many birds.

Soltau

In the centre of Lüneburg Heath is Soltau, a popular base from which to explore the Heath. Many handsome old half-timbered houses.

Heide-Park

The great tourist attraction in the Soltau area is the Heide-Park (Heath Park), a leisure and amusement park with a cableway, a Wild West railway, a water-chute, a Mississippi steamer and a variety of other entertainments and sideshows.

Fallingbostel

South of Soltau, in the Böhme valley, is the spa (Kneipp cure) of Fallingbostel. 2km/1¼ miles, in beautiful heath country (nature reserve), can be seen the grave of Hermann Löns (1866–1914), a popular local writer.

South-east of Fallingbostel, in a large military training area (access permitted only on the first and third weekends in the month), are the "Seven Stone Houses" (Sieben Steinhäuser), a group of megalithic chamber tombs (now only five in number), the largest of which has a capstone measuring 5m/16ft by 4.20m/14ft supported on seven uprights.

"Seven Stone Houses"

See Celle, Surroundings

Bergen

5km/3 miles west of Fallingbostel is Walsrode, on the northern outskirts of which is a large Bird Park (Vogelpark; 22 hectares/54 acres), with 6000 birds from every continent and climatic zone and a Birdcage Museum.

*Walsrode Bird Park

Uelzen

On the east side of Lüneburg Heath lies the old Hanseatic town of Uelzen (pop. 36,000), which has preserved a number of handsome medieval stone and half-timbered houses. In St Mary's Church (1270) is the "Golden Ship", the emblem of the town.

To the south of the town is Schloss Holdenstedt, with a very fine collection of glasses.

Holdenstedt

South-west of Holdenstedt can be found Hösseringen Museum Village (Lüneburg Heath Farming Museum), with old Heath peasant houses arranged in the form of a village.

Hösseringen Museum Village

See Gifhorn, Surroundings

Hankensbüttel

Lusatia (Lausitz)

F 9 – G 10

Länder: Brandenburg, Saxony

The name Lusatia (German Lausitz, Sorbian Lusica, meaning "moorland") is given to an old historical region between the middle Oder and middle Elbe valleys, watered by the upper Spree and the Neisse. Originally the name referred only to the Slav-occupied territory of Lower Lusatia, which in the 12th century passed to the Margraves of Meissen of the Wettin line, but later the name of Upper Lusatia was applied to the area occupied by another Slav tribe around Bautzen (Budyšin) and Görlitz (Zhorjelc), in which the powerful League of Six Cities was formed in the 14th century.

Situation and characteristics

Lusatia is an area of mixed ethnic composition, with over 500,000 Germans and some 100,000 Sorbs living side by side along the Spree, between the Spreewald and the Lusatian Uplands. The Sorbs are a residue of the old Southern Slavs who from the 6th century onwards, during the great migrations, settled in the area bounded on the east by the Oder, the Queiss and the Bober, on the south by the Erzgebirge and Fichtelgebirge, on the west by the Saale and on the north by a line running from Frankfurt an der Oder by way of Jüterbog to Zerbst. From the 8th century onwards the Frankish rulers sought to incorporate the Sorbs in the German state, for example by the systematic settlement of German peasants, craftsmen and miners. Only in Lower Lusatia did the Slav population retain a greater degree of independence, which was further fostered by the Reformation; and in this area the Sorbian language and Sorbian literature began to develop. Finally in 1912 the Domowina, an organisation for the promotion of Sorbian culture, was founded. After the repression of Sorbian and Slav aspirations during the Nazi period the Landtag of Saxony passed a law in 1948 granting cultural autonomy to the Sorb population. The Sorbs are now free to celebrate their own festivals, practise their own customs and wear their own traditional dress.

The Sorbs

The landscape of Lower Lusatia (Niederlausitz) is dominated by the Lusatian Hills with their extensive moraines, tracts of sand and gravel soil, often covered with pine forests,

Lower Lusatia

and *urstromtäler* (ice-margin trenches). The highest hills, to the west of Senftenberg, rise to almost 180m/590ft.

Lower Lusatia is a great lignite-mining area, and a major contribution is made to the economy by the production of electricity in large lignite-fired power stations and by gas production. The old open-cast lignite workings when flooded by ground-water form attractive recreation areas (Knappensee, Senftenberg lakes).

Upper Lusatia	Upper Lusatia (Oberlausitz) is a region of intensively cultivated loess farming land, long hill ridges on the granite of the Lusatian Plateau, tracts of forest at the higher levels, flat-bottomed valleys and long straggling industrial villages. The highest point in the Lusatian Uplands is the Valtenberg (589m/1933ft).
	In the past the economy of Upper Lusatia depended mainly on its cottage industry of linen-weaving. This has left its mark in the traditional type of weavers' houses, the *umgebindehäuser:* two-storey half-timbered houses with external beams supporting the upper storey.
Görlitz	See entry
Löbau	See entry
Bautzen	See entry
Zittau	See entry
Kamenz	See entry

Magdeburg   E 7

Capital of the *Land* of Saxony-Anhalt
Altitude: 50m/165ft
Population: 289,000

Situation and characteristics	Magdeburg, an important inland port at the intersection of the Mittelland Canal and the Elbe-Havel Canal, lies on the Elbe at the eastern edge of the fertile Magdeburger Börde. It was the home of the great scientist Otto von Guericke, who was also a diplomat and burgomaster of the town, and the birthplace of the composer Georg Philipp Telemann.

Domplatz (Cathedral Square)

*Cathedral	In the Domplatz, towards the south end of the old town, stands the Cathedral (Dom), an aisled basilica built between 1209 and 1520. Among the many treasures of art in the interior, particularly in the ambulatory, are the alabaster figures of St Maurice and the Risen Christ (both 1467), the Gothic choir-stalls (c. 1340), the seated figures of the Emperor Otto I and his wife Editha (1230–40), a number of fine grave-slabs (including that of Archbishop Wichmann, late 12th c.) and Ernst Barlach's memorial for the dead of the First World War (1929). On the Paradise Doorway can be seen figures of the Wise and Foolish Virgins (c. 1245–50). Below the choir are the excavated remains of the earlier Ottonian church (begun 955, burned down 1207).
	In the Domplatz are a number of Baroque house-fronts (rebuilt) and the town's oldest house, a half-timbered building of around 1600.
*Convent of Our Lady	Just north of the Domplatz is the Convent of Our Lady (Kloster Unser Lieben Frauen). The church (c. 1064–1230) is now the Georg Philipp Telemann Concert Hall. The conventual buildings (1135–50), including the cloister, the fountain-house, the chapel and the refectory, are now occupied by exhibitions (small sculpture in the refectory, older sculpture in wood in the barrel-vaulted central range). In the gardens are large modern works of sculpture.

Alter Markt (Old Market Square)

Town Hall	On the east side of the Alter Markt is the most handsome secular building in the old town, the Town Hall (Rathaus), a two-storey Baroque building of 1691–98. In the north part of the building, for example in the Ratskeller, is 12th–13th century vaulting.

Magdeburg Cathedral ▶

Main Valley

* "Wine-cellar in the Buttergasse" | At the north-west corner of the Alter Markt can be found the Romanesque "wine-cellar in the Buttergasse", which is believed to have been the basement of the old Tanners' Guild-House.

* Magdeburg Horseman | The "Magdeburg Horseman" (Magdeburger Reiter) in the Alter Markt is believed to be the oldest post-antique free-standing equestrian statue in Germany. In 1966 the original statue was replaced by a copy (under a canopy) and can now be seen in the Municipal Museum (Otto-von-Guericke-Strasse 68–73).

Monuments | Near the Town Hall are the Dr Eisenbart Monument (commemorating a notorious 17th century physician), the Otto von Guericke Monument and a monument to Luther. Nearby, too, is the ruined Late Gothic church of St John (Johanniskirche), with exhibitions on the history of the town in the room under the tower and the crypt.

Elbuferpromenade (Riverside Promenade)

Lukasturm | Visitors can get a general impression of the town by walking along the Elbuferpromenade, which follows the left bank of the Elbe from the Lukasturm (mid 15th c.), which stood at the north-east corner of the town's fortifications.

St Peter's Church Magdalene Chapel | Near the north end of the promenade can be seen two interesting buildings: St Peter's Church (Petrikirche; c. 1380 to end 15th c.) and the early 14th century Magdalene Chapel.

*Rotehorn Park (Kulturpark Rotehorn)

On the east bank of the Elbe, between the Stromelbe and the Alte Elbe, lies the Rotehorn Park (established 1871), with a variety of facilities for recreation and relaxation.

Stadthalle Outlook tower | On the west side of the park is the Stadthalle (1927), flanked by the Pferdetor (Horse Gate; sculpture by M. Rossdeutscher) and an outlook tower (Aussichtsturm).

Surroundings of Magdeburg

* Rothensee ship-lift | 14km/8½ miles north of Magdeburg is the Rothensee ship-lift (1938), linking the Elbe and the Mittelland Canal. Here ships are raised and lowered 16m/52ft in a "trough" 85m/93yds long and 12m/39ft wide.

Leitzkau | Leitzkau (28km/18 miles south) has a Renaissance Schloss (begun 1564) which belonged to a branch of the Münchhausen family and remains of a Romanesque monastic church.

Schönebeck | Schönebeck (18km/11 miles south-east) has an Early Gothic church with two Baroque towers and numbers of Baroque houses. In the Salzelmen district are a Late Gothic hall-church with a richly furnished interior and a number of handsome half-timbered burghers' houses. District Museum (salt-working in Schönebeck, shipping on the Elbe). Of the old brine spa (1802; the first in Germany) there survive the "evaporation hall" in the Kurpark and the Solturm (Brine Tower).

Hadmersleben | The convent church in Hadmersleben (27km/17 miles south-west) is mainly Early Gothic. Below the Nuns' Gallery is the Romanesque Lower Church (11th c.), with groined vaulting borne on stocky columns with finely carved capitals. Of the conventual buildings there survive the 12th century chapterhouse and part of the Late Gothic cloister (under Baroque upper storeys).

Main Valley   H 7 – H 4

Länder: Bavaria, Hesse

The river Main, with a total length of 524km/326 miles, is formed by the junction of the Weisser Main (White Main), which rises on the Ochsenkopf in the Fichtelgebirge (see entry), and the Roter Main (Red Main), coming from the Franconian Jura, which meet below Kulmbach (see Bayreuth, Surroundings).

Landscape

The Main breaks through the Franconian Jura at Lichtenfels, cuts through the hills between the Hassberge and the Steigerwald in its westward course between Bamberg and Hassfurt, describes a wide bend at Kitzungen through the vine-growing limestone region of the Franconian Plateau and flows round the Spessart sandstone plateau between Gemünden and Aschaffenburg – with the red rock walls of the Spessart to the north and the Odenwald to the south coming close to the river at certain points – to reach the Middle Rhine plain just before Aschaffenburg. It then flows through the Rhine-Main industrial region to join the Rhine opposite Mainz.

Viniculture

The production of Franconian wine was promoted at an early stage by Charlemagne and later by the monasteries and bishops in the region. The main vine-growing area lies in the Main triangle around Würzburg, but much wine is also produced on the western slopes of the Steigerwald and on the Frankenhöhe; in the side valleys of the Main and the Saale and Tauber valleys, however, it has lost much of its former importance.

The wines of Franconia, which are noted for their strength and vigour, are among the most characteristic of German wines. Apart from the small red wine area around Klingenberg, producing an excellent Spätburgunder, this is predominantly a region of white wines. Particularly good are the wines produced in and around Würzburg (Stein and Leisten), around Randersacker (Pfülben, Sonnenstuhl, Spielberg and Teufelskeller), in Escherndorf (Lump, Fürstenberg, Hengstberg), at Iphofen (Julius-Echter-Berg, Kronsberg), in Rödelsee (Küchenmeister) and Volkach (Ratsherr).

From Frankfurt through the Main Valley to Kulmbach (Bayreuth)

From Frankfurt am Main (see entry) the route follows B 8 or the motorway to Aschaffenburg (see entry) and then runs up the left bank of the Main. At Grosswallstadt is a dam; on the opposite bank is Kleinwallstadt, which has a fine Rococo church (1752).

The little town of Obernburg occupies the site of a Roman fort (museum in the Römerhaus). It preserves its old town gates and towers.	Obernburg
Opposite Trennfurt is the little town of Klingenberg, which is famed for its red wine. Above the town stands a ruined castle.	Klingenberg
In Kleinheubach is the Baroque Schloss of the Princes Löwenstein. Opposite it are Grossheubach (half-timbered Town Hall, 1612) and, higher up, the Franciscan friary of Engelsberg with its Baroque pilgrimage church (view).	Kleinheubach
See entry	Miltenberg
At Mondfeld a ferry crosses the river to the little town of Stadtprozelten, above which rises a massive ruined castle, the Henneburg (12th–15th c.).	Stadtprozelten
At the junction of the Tauber with the Main lies the pretty little town of Wertheim. In the Marktplatz are a number of handsome half-timbered houses, and nearby is the plain Gothic parish church, with tombs of the Counts of Wertheim (15th–18th c.) in the choir. Glass Museum. Above the town is Burg Wertheim (enlarged in 16th c.).	Wertheim

Beyond Wertheim it is possible to short-circuit the long northward loop in the Main and make direct for Würzburg (see below). The road following the Main valley turns north, still on the left bank of the river.

Main Valley

Marktheidenfeld	At Marktheidenfeld a bridge links the Main wine-producing area with the Spessart (see entry). Large Maradies swimming pool.
Lohr	The road continues north, passing Rothenfels (Town Hall of 1599, Renaissance parish church, large castle), to Lohr, an old-world little town of half-timbered houses. In the Marktplatz stands the large Renaissance Town Hall (1599–1602) and to the north-west the old 16th century Schloss of the Electors of Mainz, with the Spessart Museum.
Gemünden	Gemünden lies at the junction of the Franconian Saale with the Main. Above the town is a ruined castle, the Scherenburg (13th–14th c.). The Huttenschlösschen houses a Transport Museum.
Karlstadt	The old-world little town of Karlstadt, still surrounded by its old walls, was the home of the fanatical Reformer Andreas Bodenstein (known as Karlstadt; 1480–1541). In the Markt is the Town Hall (1422). In St Andrew's Church (14th–15th c.) can be seen a statue of St Nicholas by Tilman Riemenschneider.
Würzburg	See entry
	From here it is possible, if you are pressed for time, to head direct for Bamberg by way of Dettelbach (see below) and Ebrach (Cistercian abbey, 1688–1740). The main route passes through the little wine towns of Randersacker and Eibelstadt and then Sommerhausen, still surrounded by its old walls and towers, with the smallest theatre in Germany, the Torturm-Theater.
Ochsenfurt	The little town of Ochsenfurt has a handsome Town Hall (the "New Town Hall" of 1488–99) and many half-timbered buildings. In the Gothic parish church are a tabernacle from the workshop of Adam Kraft and a statue of St Nicholas by Tilman Riemenschneider. Heimatmuseum (local costumes, etc.).
Marktbreit	This old-world little place was once a prosperous town thanks to its coffee trade and the shipping trade on the Main. On the banks of the river is the Old Crane (1784). Large Town Hall (1579) and Baroque burghers' houses; Renaissance Schloss (1580) of the Counts of Seinsheim.
Kitzingen	Kitzingen, which ranks after Würzburg as a centre of the wine trade, lies in a fertile basin in the Main valley. The town's principal landmark is the Falterturm (15th–16th c.), which now houses the German Shrovetide (Carnival) Museum. In the Marktplatz stand the fine Renaissance Town Hall (1561–63), the massive Marktturm (c. 1360) and the Protestant parish church (17th c.), with a Baroque façade. In the Etwashausen district is the Heiligkreuzkirche (Holy Cross Church; 1741–45) by Balthasar Neumann.
Iphofen	From Kitzingen a detour can be made to the charming little wine town of Iphofen, with well preserved town walls, three fortified gates and other old buildings (Late Gothic parish church, Amtshaus of 1693, Town Hall of 1717).
Dettelbach	Farther up the Main valley is Dettelbach (which can also be reached direct from Würzburg), an old-world little town still surrounded by its 15th century walls, with 36 towers and two gates. Handsome Late Gothic Town Hall (1492–1512). At the far end of the town is the pilgrimage church of Maria im Sand (16th–17th c.), with a sumptuous main doorway and an altar with a much venerated image of the Virgin (1779).
Volkach	The route continues by way of Münsterschwarzach (Benedictine monastery with church of 1935–38; Mission Museum) to the little town of Volkach, famed for its wine. Old town gates; handsome gabled houses (16th–18th c.); Renaissance Town Hall (1544); Late Gothic parish church (15th c.).
	North-west of the town, on the vine-clad slopes of the Kirchberg, stands the Gothic pilgrimage church of St Maria im Weingarten (Mary in the Vineyard), with a famous "Madonna with Rosary" (1521) by Tilman Riemenschneider.
Schweinfurt	See entry

Vineyards near Volkach

Hassfurt, in the upper Main valley, has remains of its old town walls and gates. In the Markt are the Gothic Town Hall (15th c.) and the twin-towered parish church (15th c.), with a figure of St John the Baptist by Tilman Riemenschneider in the choir. At the east end of the town is the Late Gothic Ritterkapelle (Knights' Chapel; 1390–1455), with 226 coats of arms on the outside of the choir and on the reticulated vaulting of the interior.

Hassfurt

See entry

Bamberg

The route continues north by way of Staffelstein, Vierzehnheiligen and Banz (see Coburg, Surroundings), followed by Lichtenfels and Burgkunstadt.

See Bayreuth, Surroundings

Kulmbach

See entry

Bayreuth

Mainz

H 3

Capital of the *Land* of Rhineland-Palatinate
Altitude: 88m/289ft
Population: 190,000

Mainz, capital of the *Land* of Rhineland-Palatinate and a university town, a former Electoral and Archiepiscopal capital with a great past, is situated on the left bank of the Rhine opposite the mouth of the Main. It lies in the fertile Mainz Basin, the most northerly part of the Upper Rhine plain, and is the western focal point of the Rhine-Main economic region. It is the city of Gutenberg, with important publishing houses, but it is also the centre of the Rhine wine trade (Sekt cellars), a major traffic junction and commercial and industrial city, with the headquarters of two broadcasting corporations, ZDF (Second Television Channel) and SWF (South-Western Broadcasting); and it is one of the great centres of the Carnival.

Situation and characteristics

Sights

In the centre of the city stands the six-towered Cathedral (Dom) of St Martin and St Stephen, which ranks along with the cathedrals of Speyer and Worms as one of the supreme achievements of Romanesque religious architecture on the Upper Rhine. The Cathedral was begun in 975, but most of the building dates from the 11th–13th centuries.

*Cathedral

The Cathedral contains numerous fine bishops' tombs. In the cloister is the Diocesan Museum.

*Monuments

On the north side of the Cathedral are the Domplätze (Cathedral Squares), which were replanned in 1975. At the north-east corner of the squares can be found the Gutenberg Museum, a museum of world printing, with the 42-line Gutenberg Bible (1452–55) and a reproduction of Gutenberg's printing-house.

*Domplätze
*Gutenberg Museum

On the banks of the Rhine are the Town Hall (Rathaus; 1970–73) and the Rheingoldhalle (1968). In Rheingoldstrasse are two towers which formed part of the town's fortifications, the Eisenturm (Iron Tower; *c.* 1240) and the Holzturm (Wooden Tower; 14th c.).

*Town Hall

In the old town with its narrow streets and half-timbered houses, to the south of the Cathedral, are two fine Baroque churches, the Seminary Church and St Ignatius's (St Ignaz).

Old town

In Gutenbergplatz (in which the 50th degree of latitude north is marked in the paving) is the Theatre. Opposite stands a statue of Johann Gutenberg (1398–1468), a native of Mainz, who invented the art of printing with movable type about 1440.

Theatre

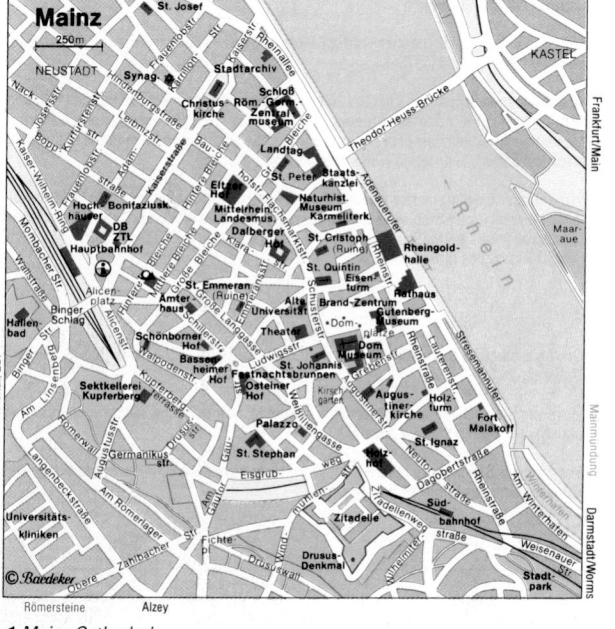

◀ *Mainz Cathedral*

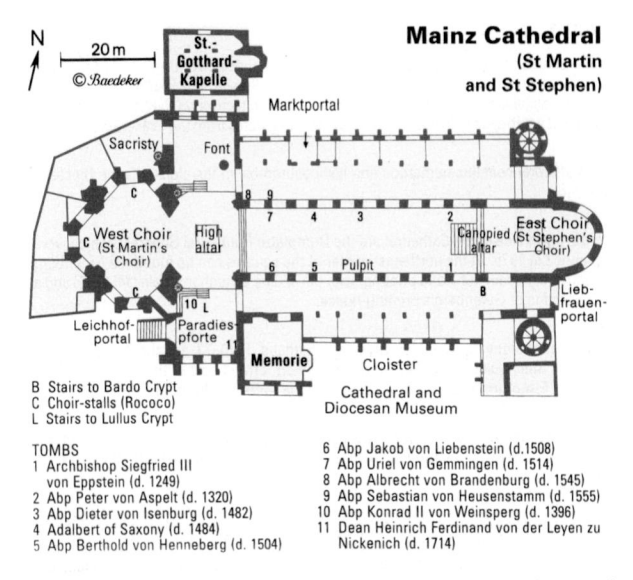

Mainz Cathedral
(St Martin
and St Stephen)

N
20 m
© Baedeker

St.-
Gotthard-
Kapelle

Marktportal

Sacristy
Font

West Choir
(St Martin's
Choir)

High
altar

East Choir
(St Stephen's
Choir)

Canopied
altar

Pulpit

Lieb-
frauen-
portal

Leichhof-
portal

Paradies-
pforte

Memorie

Cloister

Cathedral and
Diocesan Museum

B Stairs to Bardo Crypt
C Choir-stalls (Rococo)
L Stairs to Lullus Crypt

TOMBS
1 Archbishop Siegfried III
  von Eppstein (d. 1249)
2 Abp Peter von Aspelt (d. 1320)
3 Abp Dieter von Isenburg (d. 1482)
4 Adalbert of Saxony (d. 1484)
5 Abp Berthold von Henneberg (d. 1504)

6 Abp Jakob von Liebenstein (d.1508)
7 Abp Uriel von Gemmingen (d. 1514)
8 Abp Albrecht von Brandenburg (d. 1545)
9 Abp Sebastian von Heusenstamm (d. 1555)
10 Abp Konrad II von Weinsperg (d. 1396)
11 Dean Heinrich Ferdinand von der Leyen zu
   Nickenich (d. 1714)

To the west, in Schillerplatz, are a number of handsome noble mansions and an unusual
Carnival Fountain (1966).

St Stephen's Church * Stained glass	The Gothic church of St Stephen (14th c.), higher up to the south, has magnificent stained glass by Marc Chagall (1973–84).
Schloss * Roman-Germanic Museum	Just downstream from the Theodor Heuss Bridge is the old Electoral Palace (17th and 18th c.), with fine state apartments. It now houses the Roman-Germanic Central Museum, with collections of prehistoric and Roman antiquities and material of the early historical period, restoration workshops and laboratories.
Landesmuseum	In the Grosse Bleiche stands the twin-towered Peterskirche (St Peter's Church; 1752–56). In the Marstall (Court Stables) is the Museum of the Middle Rhineland (Mittelrheinisches Landesmuseum; antiquities, pictures) and a little way east the Natural History Museum (Naturhistorisches Museum).

University

On the plateau to the west of the town lies the campus of the Johannes Gutenberg
University.

* Roman aqueduct	To the south-east are the Römersteine ("Roman Stones"), the remains of a Roman aqueduct of the 1st century A.D.
* Mainzer Sand	The Mainzer Sand nature reserve, between the two western suburbs of Mombach and Gonsenheim, has interesting steppe flora.

Surroundings of Mainz

Ingelheim	15km/9 miles west of Mainz, on the left bank of the Rhine, is the old wine town of Ingelheim, with the remains of a Carolingian imperial stronghold and the palace chapel (much altered).

20km/12½ miles south of Mainz we come to Oppenheim, with the Katharinenkirche (St Catherine's Church; 13th–15th c.), one of the finest Gothic churches on the Rhine. Also of interest is the German Wine Museum.

Mannheim

Land: Baden-Württemberg
Altitude: 97m/318ft
Population: 300,000

Thanks to its favourable situation on the right bank of the Rhine at its junction with the canalised Neckar this former capital of the Electors of the Palatinate has developed into an important commercial and industrial centre, with one of the largest inland harbours in Europe.

Situation and characteristics

The town was laid out in the 17th and 18th centuries on a regular grid of 136 rectangles (now 144), in which each block is designated by a letter and a number.

Central Area

The main shopping and business streets (mostly pedestrianised) in the regularly laid out central area are the Planken and the Kurpfalzstrasse, which intersect in Paradeplatz.

In the Marktplatz are the Old Town Hall (Altes Rathaus) and the Lower Parish Church (Untere Pfarrkirche; R.C.), a double building erected in 1701–23. A short distance away can be found the Jewish Centre (Jüdisches Zentrum), with the Synagogue (built 1987).

Marktplatz
*Synagogue

The Planken and Heidelberger Strasse lead south-east to Friedrichsplatz (fountains), in which are the Water Tower (Wasserturm; 1888), Mannheim's emblem and landmark, and the Rosengarten Hall and Congress Centre.

Water Tower

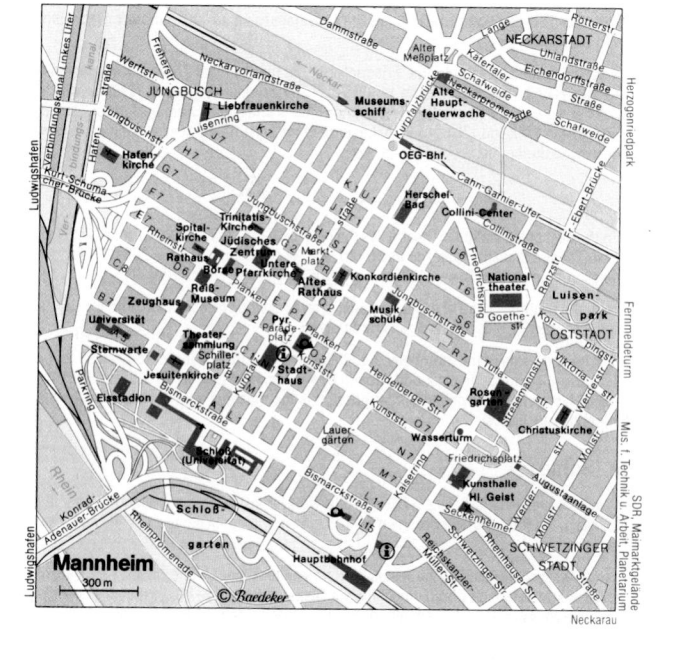

Water-Tower, Mannheim

Kunsthalle

To the south of the Water Tower stands the Kunsthalle (painting and sculpture of the 19th and 20th centuries).

National Theatre

North of Friedrichsplatz, on the Friedrichsring, is the National Theatre (Grosses and Kleines Haus), built on this site in 1955–57. The original theatre of 1779, in which Schiller's plays "Die Räuber", "Fiesco" and "Kabale und Liebe" were performed for the first time in 1782 and 1784, stood to the north of the Electoral Palace (see below); it was destroyed during the Second World War.

Luisenpark

To the east of the National Theatre lies the Luisenpark (41 hectares/101 acres), with the Lake Theatre, a plant house, an aquarium, animal enclosures and the 205m/673ft high Telecommunications Tower (1975; revolving restaurant at 125m/410ft).

Planetarium

Near the south-east end of the Luisenpark, in an oval area enclosed by the motorway, is the Planetarium, a domed hall (air-conditioned).

Museum of
Technology
and Labour

On the north side of the motorway oval stands the Museum of Technology and Labour (Landesmuseum für Technik und Arbeit), opened in 1990 (history of industrialisation, social history). An outstation of the museum is the museum ship "Mannheim" in the harbour (see below).

Electoral Palace (Schloss)

The Baroque Electoral Palace (1720–60), one of the largest in Germany, standing near the banks of the Rhine, is now occupied by the University (conducted tours of the historical apartments).

Jesuit Church
Theatre Museum

North-west of the palace is the Jesuit Church (Jesuitenkirche), a fine Baroque building of 1733–60 (restored), and adjoining it the old Observatory (1772–74). To the north are the Theatre Museum (Theatersammlung) and the Arsenal (Zeughaus; 1777–78).

In the old Arsenal, and since 1988 mainly in the new building to the north, can be found the Reiss Museum (archaeology and ethnography), named after two honorary citizens of Mannheim, Carl and Anna Reiss.

Reiss Museum

Port (Hafen)

The Port of Mannheim consists of the Commercial Harbour (on the 3km/2 mile long tongue of land between the Rhine and the Neckar), the Industrial Harbour (on the north side of the Neckar), the Rheinau Harbour (11km/7 miles upstream in Rheinau) and the Old Rhine Harbour and Oil Harbour (on the Friesenheimer Insel). Altogether there are 20 harbour basins (docks). Harbour cruises from the Kurpfalzbrücke.

By the Kurpfalzbrücke lies the museum ship "Mannheim" (part of the Museum of Technology and Labour: see above), an old paddle-steamer (ship models, collection of documents).

Museum ship

Surroundings of Mannheim

See entry

Ludwigshafen

See Heidelberg, Surroundings

Schwetzingen

Marburg

G 4

Land: Hesse
Altitude: 180m/590ft
Population: 75,000

The Hessian university town of Marburg is attractively situated on the Lahn. The picturesque old town with its narrow winding streets and stepped lanes extends in a semicircle up the steep slopes of the Schlossberg. A modern note is added by the various institutes and clinics of the University.

Situation and characteristics

Old Town

Marburg's finest building is the famous St Elizabeth's Church (1235–83; towers *c.* 1340), after the Liebfrauenkirche in Trier (see entry) the earliest church in Germany in purely Gothic style.
The original furnishings are almost completely preserved, including (in the sacristy) the golden shrine (*c.* 1250) which until 1539 contained the relics of St Elizabeth of Thuringia. In the choir are a carved wooden figure of St Elizabeth (15th c.) and 13th and 15th century stained glass. In the south transept are the tombs of Hessian princes (13th–15th c.). In the chapel under the north tower can be seen the tomb of President Hindenburg (1847–1934).

*St Elizabeth's

On Deutschhausplatz, in an old granary, is the Mineralogical Museum.

Mineralogical Museum

To the south of St Elizabeth's Church is a group of University clinics, adjoining which is the Old Botanic Garden. Farther south-east, in the Ernst-von-Hülsen-Haus in Biegenstrasse, beyond the Mühlgraben, is the University Museum of Art.

University

A short distance away, at the foot of the Schlossberg, charmingly situated above the Lahn, is the neo-Gothic building (1874–91) occupied by the University (founded 1527), with the 14th century University Church.

A little higher up lies the Markt, with the Town Hall (1525; on the staircase tower a clock with mechanical figures). To the north of the Town Hall, half way up the Schlossberg, is the Lutheran Church (1297); from the Kirchhof there is a fine view of the old town.

Town Hall

Marburg, dominated by its Schloss

A little way west, at Kugelgasse 10, can be found an ethnographic museum.

*Schloss

High above the old town rears the Schloss (287m/942ft), in the 15th and 16th centuries a seat of the Margraves of Hesse and in 1529 the scene of the Colloquy of Marburg between Luther and Zwingli. In the Schloss is the University Museum of Cultural History. Magnificent Knights' Hall (*c.* 1300); chapel (13th c.). Interesting conducted tour of the casemates (Saturdays only).

Nearby, at Landgraf-Philipp-Strasse 4, is the University Museum of Religion.

Frankenberg

30km/20 miles north of Marburg, on a hill on the right bank of the river Eder, is the little town of Frankenberg, with remains of its medieval fortifications and many handsome half-timbered houses.

On the highest point in the town stands the Gothic Liebfrauenkirche (Church of Our Lady; 1286–1360), which was modelled on St Elizabeth's Church in Marburg. Between the Upper and Lower Markets is the Town Hall (1509), a half-timbered building with a slate-clad upper part and eight oriels with pointed helm roofs. To the south-east is the former Cistercian convent of St Georgenberg (13th–16th c.; Heimatmuseum).

Eder Dam

North-east of Frankenberg can be found the Eder Dam (Edertalsperre), which has formed a 27km/17 mile long lake, now a popular recreation area and water sports centre. Boat trips on the lake.

Märkische Schweiz ("Brandenburg Switzerland") D 9

Land: Brandenburg

The Märkische Schweiz, the "Switzerland of Brandenburg" (the Mark or March of Brandenburg), is a wooded region of hills and valleys lying between the Barnim plateau in the west and the Lebus plateau in the east. The chief place in the area is the charming little town of Buckow, with a history going back more than 700 years.

Situation and topography

*Landscape

The charm of the area round Buckow lies in its hills and steep-sided valleys and in the deep basins created by the melting of the hard masses of ice after the last ice age.

This is a popular recreation area within easy reach of Berlin (by rail via Müncheberg or S-Bahn via Strausberg and then bus). There is plenty of good walking in the carefully tended parks and on the numerous waymarked footpaths. One of these leads to the Bollersdorfer Höhe (130m/427ft), from which there is a fine view of the Schermützelsee. Boat trips on the lake.

In Buckow can be seen the Brecht-Weigel House, where Bertolt Brecht wrote two of his plays and a cycle of "Buckow Elegies"; it is now a museum.

*Brecht-Weigel House

Mecklenburg Lake District C 6–8

Land: Mecklenburg-West Pomerania

The Mecklenburg lakes – well over a thousand in number, large and small – lie in an upland region in the Northern Morainic Ridge, partly forest-covered, partly arable land and pasture. This is an increasingly popular holiday region. Many of the lakes are linked by rivers (the Elde, the Havel, the Warnow, the Nebel, the Peene, the Ücker) or canals, with endless scope for boating and camping holidays.

Situation and topography

*Landscape

The lakes are particularly numerous in the western part of the Mecklenburg lake district (Mecklenburgische Seenplatte), around the Schweriner See (alt. 37m/121ft, area 65.5 sq.km/25 sq. miles: see Schwerin, Surroundings). There is another concentration in the area between Sternberg and Krakow (Krakower See, alt. 48m/157ft, area 15.7 sq.km/6 sq. miles: see Krakow am See).
To the east, between Plau and Waren, are the "Grosse Seen" ("Great Lakes"), drained by the Elde, which flows into the Elbe: the Plauer See (38.7 sq.km/15 sq. miles: see entry), the Fleesensee (11 sq.km/4¼ sq. miles), the Kölpinsee (20.5 sq.km/8 sq. miles) and the largest of the Mecklenburg lakes, Müritz (116.8 sq.km/45 sq. miles), all lying at a height of 62m/203ft.

To the south-east are the "Kleinseen" ("Little Lakes") round the town of Neustrelitz (see entry) and to the south of Lychen and Templin.

Kleinseen

There are also a number of lakes of some size to the north of the inner terminal moraine: in the Güstrow basin the Inselsee, in the "Mecklenburg Switzerland" (see below) the Malchiner See (14.3 sq.km/5½ sq. miles) and the Teterower See, to the south of Neubrandenburg the Tollensesee (17.4 sq.km/6¾ sq. miles, alt. 15m/49ft), the Feldberger Seen and theÜckerseen.

Malchiner See
Kummerower See
Tollensesee

Mecklenburg Switzerland

The "Mecklenburg Switzerland" (Mecklenburgische Schweiz), between Teterow and Malchin in central Mecklenburg, is a region of terminal moraines marked by wide

Situation and *landscape

Mecklenburg lake district: the Tollensee

variations in height and covered by great expanses of beech forest. Here the rounded hills of the terminal moraines (e.g. Hardtberg, 123m/404ft; Röthelberg, 97m/318ft) are juxtaposed with lakes lying only just above sea level (Kummerower See, 32.6 sq.km/12½ sq. miles; Malchiner See, 14.3 sq.km/5½ sq. miles). The Teterower See, on the western fringe of the Mecklenburg Switzerland, is only 2.3m/7½ft above sea level, although it is almost 100km/60 miles from the mouth of the Peene, which drains all these lakes into the Baltic.

*Viewpoints

There are magnificent views of the Mecklenburg Switzerland from the Röthelberg and from the Heidberg (93m/305ft), near Teterow.

Meersburg

L–M 4

Land: Baden-Württemberg
Altitude: 410m/1345ft
Population: 5500

Situation and characteristics

The little town of Meersburg on Lake Constance, noted for its wine, is picturesquely situated on the steeply sloping shores of the lake at the point where the Überlinger See merges into the Obersee. The pattern of the town was set mainly during the period when it was the seat of the Bishops of Konstanz (1526–1803). There is a ferry service between Meersburg and Konstanz (see entry) on the other side of the lake; the crossing takes 20 minutes.

*Upper Town

Altes Schloss

In the upper town stands the oldest inhabited castle in Germany, the Altes Schloss or Meersburg, which has a history going back to the 7th century; its four round towers date

from 1508. From 1526 until the completion of the Neues Schloss in 1750 it was the residence of the Bishops of Konstanz. In 1838 it became the property of Freiherr Joseph von Lassberg, brother-in-law of the poetess Annette von Droste-Hülshoff, who lived here from 1841 until her death in 1848. Fine state apartments; collection of weapons; Droste Room.

To the east, in Schlossplatz, is the Neues Schloss, built by Balthasar Neumann in 1741–50 as the new residence of the Bishops of Konstanz (Dornier Museum; Municipal Art Collections; Mesmer Memorial Room, commemorating the inventor of mesmerism). Sumptuous staircase hall; ceiling paintings by Joseph Ignaz Appiami, stucco decoration by Carlo Pozzi. The chapel, two storeys in height, was decorated by Joseph Anton Feuchtmayr and Gottfried Bernhard Goez.

Neues Schloss

To the north of Schlossplatz lies the Marktplatz, with handsome half-timbered buildings and the Obertor (Upper Gate; 1300–30).

Marktplatz

Farther north-west, near the Town Church, is a former Dominican convent (15th c.; remodelled in Baroque style), now occupied by the Bible Gallery, the Municipal Library and the Municipal Museum.

Bible Gallery
Municipal Museum

East of the Obertor, beyond the busy Stettener Strasse, is the Fürstenhäusle or Fugger-häusle, surrounded by vineyards, which was acquired by Annette von Droste-Hülshoff in 1843 (Droste Museum).

Fürstenhäusle

The most attractive link between the upper and lower towns is Steigstrasse, lined with handsome half-timbered houses.

Steigstrasse

Lower Town

The lower town, on the shores of the lake, is traversed by Unterstadtstrasse and the Seepromenade, which runs parallel to it along the lake.

At the east end of the Seepromenade is the Gredhaus, an old granary of 1505 (ticket office for the Federal Railways ships on Lake Constance).

Unteruhldingen

6km/4 miles north-west of Meersburg, off the main road, we come to the holiday resort of Unteruhldingen, with a boating harbour and an interesting Reptile House.

*Open-Air Museum of Prehistory
The principal attraction of Unteruhldingen is the Open-Air Museum of German Prehistory (Freilichtmuseum Deutscher Vorzeit), founded in 1922 by the archaeologist Hans Reinerth, with two reconstructed settlements of pile dwellings and a museum displaying material recovered by excavation.

Birnau
See Überlingen, Surroundings

Meiningen   G 5

Land: Thuringia
Altitude: 286m/938ft
Population: 25,900

Situation and characteristics
Meiningen, noted in the past for its theatre and its associations with Schiller and still a well-known Thuringian cultural centre, lies between the Rhön and the Thuringian Forest.

Sights

*Schloss Elisabethenburg
Schloss Elisabethenburg, a Baroque palace built in 1682–92 on the site of an earlier Late Gothic castle as the residence of the Dukes of Saxony-Meiningen, now houses the State Museums. It has a sumptuously appointed interior; particularly notable are the staircase hall, the Tower Room, the Garden Room and the Brahms Hall in the south wing, formerly the palace church.

State Museums
The State Museums comprise a valuable art collection (pictures by European masters of the 15th–19th centuries), a Theatre Museum (development of the Meiningen reform of the theatre), a section on the history of music, a department of cultural history (in the Baumbachhaus at Burggasse 22; literary museum; costumes of southern Thuringia) and a department of natural history.

Goethe Park
The beautiful Goethe Park was originally laid out in 1782 as the English Garden. In an artificial lake in the park is the tomb of Duke Charles, modelled on Rousseau's tomb at Ermenonville, near Paris.

Burghers' houses
Meiningen has preserved many burghers' houses of the 16th–18th centuries, including the Büchnersches Hinterhaus at Georgenstrasse 20, the Alte Posthalterei at Ernestiner Strasse 14, the Rautenkranz at Ernestiner Strasse 40 and the Steinernes Haus (Stone House) at Anton-Ulrich-Strasse 43.

Wasungen

12km/7½ miles north-west of Meiningen is Wasungen, a little town noted for its centuries-old Carnival, with many half-timbered buildings, including the Town Hall, the Amtshaus and numerous burghers' houses and aristocratic mansions. The Town Church in its present form is an aisleless Renaissance building of 1584–96 incorporating earlier work, with a tower which is basically Late Gothic; fine 17th century carving in the interior. The tower known as the Pfaffenburg (1387) is a relic of the town's medieval fortifications.

Meissen   F 8

Land: Saxony
Altitude: 109m/358ft
Population: 35,000

Meissen lies 15km/9 miles north-west of Dresden at the junction of the Triebisch and the Meisa with the Elbe. With a history going back more than a thousand years, it has many fine old buildings but is chiefly famed for its porcelain manufactory, the first to be established in Europe.

**Burgberg (Castle Hill)

Commandingly situated above the town on the Burgberg are the Albrechtsburg, the Cathedral and the former Bishop's Palace.

The Albrechtsburg, founded in 929 and built in its present form by Arnold of Westphalia, is one of the finest secular buildings of the Late Gothic period. It was the seat of Electors Ernst and Albrecht of the Wettin dynasty.
On the courtyard side of the castle is a large spiral staircase. The rooms in the interior have richly decorated vaulting and ceilings. The paintings in many of the rooms date from the renovation of the castle about 1870. On the ground floor can be seen an exhibition on the history of the Albrechtsburg.

*Albrechtsburg

The Early Gothic Cathedral (Dom), was begun about 1260 but was much altered and extended (nave, west doorway, Fürstenkapelle, Georgenkapelle) in later centuries. The figures of the founders (c. 1260) were the work of sculptors from Naumburg. The interior is richly furnished (religious pictures, many monuments). The two west towers, destroyed by lightning in 1547, were rebuilt in 1903–08.

*Cathedral

In the Domplatz are canons' houses and the Kornhaus.

Domplatz

The Town

In the Afranische Freiheit, which is reached by way of the Mitteltor, the Vordertor and the Schlossbrücke, are St Afra's Church (c. 1300), the old conventual buildings and the presbytery of St Afra's, with a Renaissance corner oriel (1535).

*St Afra's Church

Meissen Cathedral and Albrechtsburg *Vincenz Richter Restaurant*

Memmingen

Frauenkirche	The Frauenstufen (Steps) lead to the Frauenkirche (15th c.). In the tower is a porcelain carillon (1929).
Brauhaus	Nearby are the old Brauhaus (Brew-House; 1569), with a Renaissance gable, and the Tuchmachertor (Clothmakers' Gate), a magnificent example of Renaissance architecture. Here too is the historic old Vincenz Richter wine-bar and restaurant.
Town Hall	In the Markt stands the Late Gothic Town Hall (c. 1472), with fine decorative gables.
Municipal Museum	The old Franciscan church (founded c. 1258) is now the Municipal Museum (at present closed). In the cloister are grave-slabs and works of sculpture (including some by J. J. Kändler).
Theatre	The old Cloth Hall (16th c.) in Theaterplatz, at one time used as a warehouse, was converted in 1851 into the Municipal Theatre.
St Martin's Chapel	The Romanesque St Martin's Chapel (c. 1200), on the Plossen, has a beautiful Late Gothic altar.
St Nicholas's Church	In the Neumarkt is the Nikolaikirche (St Nicholas's Church; c. 1100, altered in 13th c.), with remains of Early Gothic wall paintings. It is now a memorial to the dead of the First World War, with large works of porcelain sculpture (by E. P. Börner, 1921–29).
**Porcelain Manufactory	To the south of St Nicholas's is the State Porcelain Manufactory. Visitors can see the showroom and demonstration workshops (showing the various processes involved in the manufacture of porcelain).

Memmingen L 5

Land: Bavaria
Altitude: 595m/1952ft
Population: 38,000

Situation and characteristics	The old free imperial city of Memmingen, still partly surrounded by its old walls with their imposing gates and preserving much of its Gothic and Renaissance aspect, lies in the foreland of the Allgäu Alps. The main elements in its economy are industry, cheese manufacture and its trade in agricultural produce.

Old Town

The picturesque old town, traversed in a wide arc by the Stadtbach, is still partly surrounded by medieval walls.

Markt	The central feature of the old town is the Markt, with the Renaissance Town Hall (1589; Rococo stucco decoration of 1765), the Steuerhaus (arcades of 1495; façade rebuilt 1909) and the Grosszunft (1453; remodelled in Baroque style 1718), the town's patrician club.

In Ulmer Strasse, north of the Markt, are the Parishaus (1736), now housing the Municipal Gallery, and the Grimmelhaus (18th century stucco decoration). At the Ulmer Tor (Ulm Gate; 1495) Ulmer Strasse leaves the old town.

St Martin's Church	To the west of the Markt stands the Gothic St Martin's Church, with its 66m/217ft high tower the town's principal landmark. Fine Gothic choir-stalls (1501–07) by the Memmingen school of wood-carvers.
Museum	On the north side of St Martin's Church is the Hermannsbau, a Late Baroque mansion (1766) now occupied by the Municipal Museum (prehistory and the early historical period, pictures, furniture, faience, etc.).
Kinderlehrkirche	South-west of St Martin's Church can be found the Kinderlehrkirche (originally an Antonian monastic church; 14th–15th c.), with frescoes.

Farther south is the Fuggerbau (1589), the Memmingen agency of the Fuggers, the great merchant dynasty of Augsburg. During the Thirty Years' War Wallenstein stayed here in 1630 and Gustavus Adolphus in 1632.

To the east of the Fuggerbau, beyond the Stadtbach, lies the Weinmarkt, with the guild-houses of the weavers and the shopkeepers. Here in 1525, during the Peasant War, the rebellious peasants drew up their "Twelve Articles".

On the southern edge of the old town is the Gothic Frauenkirche (Church of Our Lady), which is first mentioned in the records in 1258; fine cycle of frescoes (school of Bernhard Strigel) in the nave and choir.

Surroundings of Memmingen

4km/2½ miles west of Memmingen is Buxheim, with the old Carthusian monastery of Maria Saal (founded 1402; conventual buildings and church remodelled in Baroque style in 17th–18th c.). The Baroque choir-stalls by Ignaz Weibel are among the finest examples of woodcarving in South Germany.

At Illerbeuern, 10km/6 miles south of Memmingen, is the Swabian Farmhouse Museum, the oldest open-air museum in Bavaria.

See Landsberg, Surroundings

Ottobeuren

South-west of Memmingen, in the valley of the Westliche Günz, lies the spa of Otto-beuren (Kneipp cure).

Ottobeuren is mainly famed for the great Benedictine monastery with its magnificent Baroque church. The church was built from 1737 onwards to the design of Johann Michael Fischer, with stucco decoration by Johann Michael Feuchtmayr and frescoes by Johann Jakob and Franz Anton Zeiller. The famous organs in the choir (1766) were built by Karl Joseph Riepp.

Bad Mergentheim   I 5

Land: Baden-Württemberg
Altitude: 210m/689ft
Population: 20,000

Bad Mergentheim lies in the valley of the Tauber, ringed by hills covered with forest and vineyards. It has three mineral springs containing carbonic acid, with a high salt content (the Karls-, Wilhelms- and Albertquelle) and one saline spring (the Paulsquelle), which are used in both drinking and bathing cures for the treatment of affections of the gall bladder, liver, stomach and intestines. The historic old town forms a charming contrast to the modern spa installations.

Bad Mergentheim lies on the Romantische Strasse (see entry).

The Town

In the Marktplatz with its handsome half-timbered houses stands the Town Hall (1564). To the north is the Late Gothic Minster of St John (13th c.; vaulting 1584; wall paintings). To the south of the Markt is the Marienkirche (St Mary's Church; 14th c.; restored in neo-Gothic style), which contains the bronze monument of Walter von Cromberg, Grand Master of the Teutonic Order.

Bad Mergentheim

Schloss

On the eastern edge of the old town is the large Castle of the Teutonic Order (16th c.), once the residence of the Grand Master of the Order. The Baroque church was built in 1730–35 to the design of Balthasar Neumann and François Cuvilliés; ceiling paintings (1734–35) by Nikolaus Stuber. In the castle are the Museum of the Teutonic Order (history of the town and of the Order; mementoes of the 19th century poet Eduard Mörike; religious art; domestic life) and a collection of old dolls' houses.

Spa district

On the right bank of the Tauber, reached by way of the Schlosspark, lies the spa district, with the Kursaal, pump room, indoor promenade, treatment and bathing facilities and the beautiful Kurpark.

Solymar

To the east of the Kurpark, near the Albertquelle, are the Solymar Baths, with a swimming pool (artificial waves), water-chute, saline baths, sauna, play areas, etc.

Game Park

South-east of the town centre can be found the Game Park (Wildpark; bison, bears, wolves, vultures, cormorants), with a museum of native German animals (dioramas).

Stuppach

*Stuppach Virgin

In the church of Stuppach, a district of Mergentheim 6km/4 miles south of the town centre, can be seen the famous Stuppach Virgin, a panel painting by Matthias Grünewald (1517–19).

Weikersheim

10km/6 miles east, on the left bank of the Tauber, is the picturesque little town of Weikersheim, the very pattern of a small princely capital of the 16th–18th centuries. In the Baroque Markt are the Late Gothic Town Church and the Tauberland Village Museum.

Schlossgarten and Orangery, Weikersheim

The Renaissance Schloss occupies the site of a medieval moated castle. The interior is almost completely preserved (fine Knights' Hall). The Hohenlohe Museum has a notable collection of porcelain and ceramics.

Behind the Schloss is the Schlossgarten (1708–10), with statuary and an Orangery (in course of restoration).

Creglingen

See Rothenburg, Surroundings

Tauberbischofsheim

16km/10 miles north of Bad Mergentheim, in the vine-clad middle Tauber valley, is the little town of Tauberbischofsheim, with handsome 18th century half-timbered buildings. In the old Schloss of the Electors of Mainz is the Tauber-Franconian Museum.

Merseburg

F 7

Land: Saxony-Anhalt
Altitude: 98m/322ft
Population: 48,400

The old episcopal city and ducal capital of Merseburg lies 10km/6 miles south of Halle on the western edge of the Querfurt plateau, where the Geisel flows into the Saale.

Situation

*Cathedral (Dom)

Above the town, on the high west bank of the Saale, are the Cathedral and the Schloss.

The palace church of Henry I (consecrated 931) was raised to cathedral status when the bishopric of Merseburg was established 968. The present building, originally Romanesque, was begun in 1015 and much altered in later centuries. A hall-church with four towers, it has a sumptuously furnished interior. In the west porch is a Late Gothic doorway with sculptured figures (including a bust of the Emperor Henry II with a model of the Cathedral). Notable features of the interior are the Baroque high altar (1668), the richly decorated Late Gothic pulpit and choir-stalls, a Romanesque font (c. 1150) and numerous monuments (11th–18th c.). Of particular quality are the bronze grave-slab of Rudolf of Swabia (d. 1180) and the sarcophagus of Bishop Thilo of Trotha (by Hermann Vischer the Elder).

On the south side of the Cathedral lies the cloister, with an Early Gothic west wing and the Romanesque chapel of St John.

The Cathedral Archives have a large collection of medieval manuscripts, including the famous Merseburg Spells (10th c.), one of the earliest documents in the German language, and a richly illuminated manuscript of the Vulgate (c. 1200).

Cathedral Archives
**Merseburg Spells

*Schloss

The Schloss, now occupied by local government offices and the District Museum, is a three-winged building of the Late Gothic and Late Renaissance periods which in spite of much later alteration has preserved a remarkable architectural unity. Its most striking features are the staircase towers, oriels, doorways and dormers in Late Renaissance style. The west wing was rebuilt after suffering heavy war damage.

On the north side of the Schloss extends the Schlossgarten (1661), with the Garden Saloon (by J. M. Hoppenhaupt, 1727–38). In the park are a portrait bust of Field-Marshal

Schlossgarten

Kleist von Nollendorf (by C. D. Rauch, 1825) and a monument (1816) commemorating the Battle of the Nations at Leipzig in 1813.

To the west of the Schlossgarten are the Renaissance-style Zechsches Palais (1782) and the Ständehaus (1892–95), both once occupied by the provincial parliament of Saxony.

Burgberg
Altenburg

To the north of the Schloss rises the Burgberg Altenburg (Altenburg Castle Hill), the original nucleus of the town (8th c.), on which there was already a settlement in prehistoric times. On the hill are the remains of St Peter's Monastery (conventual buildings, 13th c.) and St Vitus's Church (12th–17th c.).

Water-Tower

Between the Altenburg and the Schloss stands the Upper Water-Tower (Obere Wasserkunst; by J. M. Hoppenhaupt, 1738).

Old Town

Old Town Hall

The central feature of the old town is the Old Town Hall (15th–16th c.), mainly in Renaissance style.
In the Markt can be seen the Staupen Fountain. Nearby is the Town Church of St Maximus (much altered and rebuilt).

Neumarktkirche

On the east bank of the Saale is the Neumarktkirche (begun 1173).

Miltenberg

Land: Bavaria
Altitude: 127m/417ft
Population: 9500

Situation and
characteristics

The picturesque little Lower Franconian town of Miltenberg, its streets of handsome half-timbered houses still enclosed within its old walls and gates, is attractively situated in the Main valley (see entry), between the Odenwald and the Spessart. The oldest part of the town lies on the narrow left bank of the Main, under a steep wooded hill crowned by the Mildenburg.

The Town

*Markt

The charming old-world Markt, with the Market Fountain of 1583, is lined with half-timbered houses. On the north side of the square stands the parish church (14th c.; towers 1830). The former Amtskellerei (Markt 171), a fine 16th century half-timbered building, houses the Municipal Museum.

The Schnatterloch, a gate-tower, gives access to the Mildenburg (see below).

Hauptstrasse

East of the Markt, in the main street (Hauptstrasse), is the half-timbered Haus zum Riesen (1590), an old inn which is still a hotel. Past guests have included King Gustavus Adolphus of Sweden, Wallenstein and Prince Eugene of Savoy.

Farther along the street, in Engelsplatz, is the Baroque Franciscan Church (1667–87).

Town gates

At the east end of the Hauptstrasse rises the Würzburger Tor (1405), with a six-storey tower. On the west side of the town, at the station, is the Mainzer Tor. Close by is St Lawrence's Chapel (15th–16th c.).

Mildenburg

Above the town, set amid trees, is the Mildenburg (13th–16th c.), with a 27m/89ft high keep (panoramic views).

Amorbach

8km/5 miles south of Miltenberg lies the little town of Amorbach, which attracts many visitors.

Markplatz, Miltenburg ▶

Minden

Parish church
On the north side of the town is the twin-towered parish church (R.C.), a sandstone building erected in 1752–54 with a beautiful Rococo interior (ceiling paintings by Johann Zick, 1753). Opposite, to the west, is the Schloss of the Princes of Leiningen (18th–19th c.).

*Abbey church
To the south of the Markt is the fine Baroque church (also with two towers) of the old Benedictine abbey which stood here. Originally Romanesque, it was remodelled in Baroque style in 1742–47 by the Mainz court architect Maximilian von Welsch. The light interior, sumptuously decorated, is one of the finest Rococo creations in Germany. There is a famous Baroque organ (recitals in summer).

Michelstadt

See Odenwald

Minden   E 4

Land: North Rhine-Westphalia
Altitude: 46m/151ft
Population: 78,000

Situation and characteristics
The cathedral city of Minden lies in the Weser lowlands to the north of the Porta Westfalica, where the Weser breaks through the hills. It is an important centre of inland shipping traffic thanks to its situation at the point where the Mittelland Canal crosses the Weser.

Passenger ships
At the Schachtschleuse (the lock which provides a link between the Mittelland Canal and the Weser) is the landing-stage used by passenger ships on the Weser and the Canal (river and canal cruises; service between Minden and Vlotho in summer).

Mittelland Canal crossing the Weser

Lower Town

In the Domhof stands the Cathedral (Dom; 11th–13th c.; R.C.), rebuilt after its destruction during the Second World War. It is the finest Early Gothic hall-church in Westphalia, with an Early Romanesque west work and Late Romanesque choir and transept. In the rich cathedral treasury, among much else, is the Minden Cross (1070).

*Cathedral

In the nearby Marktplatz is the Town Hall, with a vaulted arcade (13th c.; restored). In the adjoining Scharn, Minden's main business and shopping street, is Haus Hagemeyer (1592), in Weser Renaissance style.

Town Hall

Upper Town

To the north-west, on the highest point in the upper town, is the Marienkirche (St Mary's Church; 11th c., rebuilt in 14th c.), with a tower 57m/187ft high.

St Mary's Church

To the south can be found the Martinikirche (St Martin's Church; originally Romanesque, rebuilt in Gothic style), with Late Gothic choir-stalls, a Renaissance font and a Baroque organ. Beyond it is the "Windloch", a picturesque and very narrow house – the oldest in the town.

St Martin's Church

Ritterstrasse leads south to the Minden Museum (folk art and traditions, peasant culture, crafts, costumes, shipping on the Weser, militaria), the Late Gothic St Simeon's Church and the 15th century St Maurice's Church.

Museum

To the north of the town is the intersection of Minden's two waterways, where the Mittelland Canal crosses the Weser at a height of 13m/43ft on an aqueduct 375m/410yds long. In the exhibition hall are working models of locks, etc.

Intersection of Weser and Mittelland Canal

*Porta Westfalica

At the Porta Westfalica ("Westphalian Gate"), 6km/4 miles south of Minden, the Weser breaks through the Wesergebirge and Wiehengebirge in a breach 800m/½ mile wide. On the Wittekindsberg to the west can be seen the Emperor William Monument (Kaiser-Wilhelm-Denkmal; 1896), from which there is a magnificent view of the Weser valley. On the Jakobsberg to the east is a telecommunications tower.

At Kleinbremen is an old iron-mine, now a show mine for visitors. It is reached on a nostalgic rail-car from Minden.

Iron-mine

Potts Park

In Dützen, 5km/3 miles west, lies Potts Park, a leisure and amusement park which is a children's paradise, with a model railway, an aerodrome, an aircraft, a submarine and a variety of other entertainments.

Westphalian Windmill and Watermill Route (Westfälische Mühlenstrasse)

The Westphalian Windmill and Watermill Route, of which there are three variants, all starting from Minden, takes in some 40 historic old windmills and watermills and a dozen other features of interest. On certain days some of the mills are set in motion and biscuits and cakes are sold.

Bückeburg

10km/6 miles south-east of Minden is Bückeburg, the old seat of the Counts of Schaumburg-Lippe.

Schloss

The most notable features of the Schloss (16th–19th c.) are the Golden Hall, with a painted coffered ceiling, and the chapel, with gilded Early Baroque wood-carving. To the west of the Schloss is the domed Mausoleum of the Schaumburg-Lippe family (interior decorated with a mosaic on a gold ground).

Helicopter Museum

In Sabléplatz, to the north of the Lange Strasse, is an interesting Helicopter Museum (Hubschraubermuseum; models and originals).

Mittenwald   M 6

Land: Bavaria
Altitude: 920m/3020ft
Population: 8300

Situation and characteristics

The health resort and winter sports centre of Mittenwald lies in the beautiful and sheltered valley of the Isar immediately below the towering Karwendel chain, framed on the south and west by forest-covered hills, above which rears the peak of the Wetterstein. Mittenwald is famed as a town of violin-makers (also manufacture of guitars, zithers, etc.; training school).

The Town

Characteristic of the little town, one of the most charming in the Bavarian Alps, are the old houses with frescoed exteriors (in the technique known as *lüftlmalerei),* which are to be found particularly in the Untermarkt and Obermarkt.

Parish church

The Baroque parish church with its painted tower was built by Josef Schmuzer in 1738–45. In front of it can be seen a statue of Mathias Klotz (1653–1743), founder of the town's violin-making industry.

Mittenwald violin-maker

Beside the church is the Violin-Making Museum (Heimatmuseum; domestic furnishings; stringed instruments, including a number of Klotz violins). — Violin-Making Museum

To the west and south-west of the town lie the spa installations and the Kurpark on the Burgberg. — Kurpark

Surroundings of Mittenwald

On the east side of the town a cabin cableway goes up to the Hohe Karwendelgrube (2244m/7363ft), below the western peak of the Karwendel range (2385m/7825ft). Panoramic views; footpath round the Karwendelgrube; mountain walks and climbs. — *Western Karwendel

To the west of Mittenwald rises the Hoher Kranzberg (1391m/4564ft), which can be climbed by way of St Anton (cableway from Mittenwald); from there on foot. — Hoher Kranzberg

Walchensee and Kochelsee

15km/9 miles north of Mittenwald, in a magnificent setting on the north-west side of the Karwendelgebirge, is the Walchensee (alt. 802m/2631ft), Germany's largest and deepest mountain lake (area 16.4 sq.km/6½ sq. miles; max. depth 192m/630ft). It supplies the water which powers the Walchensee hydroelectric station (1918–24), one of the largest in Germany, which takes advantage of the 200m/650ft drop to the Kochelsee. — Walchensee

From Urfeld, at the north end of the lake, the Kesselbergstrasse goes up the Kesselberg (rewarding climb to the Herzogstand) and then down through the forest (36 bends). 1.5km/1 mile off the road is the Walchensee hydroelectric station. — Kesselberg

The road continues along the east side of the Kochelsee (alt. 600m/1970ft; area 6.8 sq.km/2½ sq. miles; max. depth 66m/217ft) to the popular holiday resort of Kochel. In the centre of the village is a monument to Balthes, the blacksmith of Kochel, who led a party of peasants to free Munich from the Austrians and was killed in the battle of Sendlingen in 1705. — Kochelsee

To the west of Kochel lies the village of Grossweil, with an open-air museum on the Glentleiten (old peasant houses with original furnishings, workshops, etc.). Farther west again are Murnau and the Staffelsee (see Oberammergau, Surroundings). — Glentleiten Open-Air Museum

Mönchengladbach   F 2

Land: North Rhine-Westphalia
Altitude: 50m/165ft
Population: 260,000

Mönchengladbach, 20km/12½ miles west of the Rhine, is a busy industrial city, the chief centre of the Rhineland cotton industry, with textile mills, engineering and electrical engineering plants. The town's name ("Monks' Gladbach") comes from a Benedictine abbey founded here in 972 (dissolved 1802). — Situation and characteristics

The Town

In the Markt is the parish church of the Assumption (1469–1533; restored in its original form). — Parish church

Lower down, to the south, stands the Town Hall, in the former abbey, a Baroque brick building of 1663. Adjoining is the Late Romanesque Minster, the old abbey church of St Vitus (11th and 13th c.), with a beautiful choir (1275; 13th c. stained glass) and an early 12th century crypt; treasury. — Minster

| Abteiberg Museum | At Abteistrasse 27 is the municipal Abteiberg Museum, opened in 1982 (art since Expressionism, including works by Joseph Beuys, Andy Warhol, Robert Rauschenberg and Yves Klein; changing exhibitions). |

Rheydt

| Schloss | In the southern district of Rheydt is a Renaissance Schloss (15th and 16th c.), now housing the Municipal Museum of Art and Culture and the Museum of Weaving. |

Mosel Valley   I 1 – H 3

Land: Rhineland-Palatinate

The beautiful river Mosel (French spelling Moselle) is one of the longest of the Rhine's tributaries (545km/339 miles). It owes its name to the Romans (Mosella, the "Little Meuse"). It rises at the Col de Bussang in the southern Vosges (France), and between Perl and the junction with the Sauer at Oberbillig forms the natural frontier between Germany and the Grand Duchy of Luxembourg. The section of the river between Perl and Trier is known as the Upper Mosel (Obermosel), the section from Trier to Bullay as the Middle Mosel (Mittelmosel) and the section from Bullay to Koblenz as the Lower Mosel (Untermosel). Since 1964 the Mosel has been canalised, its gradient being regulated by ten dams (at Trier, Detzem, Wintrich, Zeltingen, Enkirch, St Aldegund, Fankel, Müden, Lehmen and Koblenz).

*Landscape

The most beautiful stretch of the Mosel valley, which is described below, is between Trier and the junction with the Rhine at Koblenz. After passing through the wide Trier basin it makes its way in innumerable bends through the Rhenish Uplands between the Hunsrück and the Eifel to enter the Rhine valley (see entry) at Koblenz. The ever-changing landscape is marked, particularly between Bernkastel and Cochem, by a succession of old castles on the slopes of the valley and in side valleys and by a string of old-world little towns and wine villages. The winding course of the river and the narrowness of its valley have prevented the development of any large towns, but by the same token have preserved the peace and charm of the Mosel.

| Mosel wines | The white wines of the Mosel, made from grapes grown on the slaty soil of the steep slopes above the river, are light, slightly acid wines with a flowery bouquet. In a poor year the lesser wines may prove to be slightly sour and to require the addition of sugar. The highest rated wines are Brauneberger and Oligsberger (produced around Brauneberg), Bernkasteler Doctor and the wines of Zeltingen ("Himmelreich") and Graach, which together with Piesporter and the wines of Winningen, Dhron, Erden, Zell ("Schwarze Katz") and Wehlen ("Sonnenuhr") are the best middle-grade wines. In addition there are Traben-Trarbach, Wintrich, Minheim, Ürzig, Bernkastel-Kues, Lieser and many others. |

| Boat trips | A pleasant way of seeing the Mosel valley is by boat (e.g. between Koblenz and Beilstein and between Bernkastel and Trier). |

*From Koblenz to Trier

| Mosel Wine Route | The route described below mainly follows the specially signposted Moselweinstrasse (Mosel Wine Route). From Koblenz to Treis-Karden there are alternative routes, one on the left bank and the other on the right bank. |

Left Bank

| Winningen | Winningen has the largest continuous vine-growing area on the Mosel and the best terraced vineyards. |

Burg Eltz

Kobern has two ruined castles; in the Oberburg is the beautiful Early Gothic chapel of St Matthias (c. 1235). Gondorf has two 13th century castles.

Kobern-Gondorf

The wine village of Hatzenport has a beautifully situated Late Gothic parish church with good 15th century stained glass. A detour can be made to Münstermaifeld (5km/3 miles north-west), with a fine Stiftskirche (SS. Martin and Severus; 10th–14th c.).

Hatzenport

At the junction of the Eltzbach with the Mosel lies the old-world little wine village of Moselkern. In the Eltz valley, picturesquely situated on a steep-sided crag, is Burg Eltz, which with its tall gables, towers and oriels is one of the finest of German castles. Built round a narrow courtyard, the castle dates from the 13th–16th centuries and contains original furnishings and works of art. On a hill facing Burg Eltz is Burg Trutzeltz.

Moselkern
* Burg Eltz

At Treis-Karden (with Karden on the left bank) the route on the left joins the one on the right.

Right Bank

In the village of Alken, which once had a municipal charter, are a number of old houses and remains of medieval walls. Above the village is Burg Thurant (built c. 1200, with much later alteration).

Alken

The attractive village of Brodenbach has a Rococo church with a beautiful high altar. To the south, in a side valley, is the Ehrenburg, one of the finest ruined castles in the Mosel area.

Brodenbach

At Treis-Karden (with Treis on the right bank) the two routes join.

Main Route

The little town of Treis-Karden, with its bridge over the Mosel, forms a link between the Hunsrück and the Eifel. Treis has a Late Gothic church, Karden a former Stiftskirche, the

Treis-Karden

three-towered church of St Castor (12th–13th c.), which preserves part of a Romanesque cloister and chapterhouse (Stiftsmuseum).

From here the route continues on the left bank of the Mosel.

Cochem

Cochem, with its old castle perched high above the town, is one of the most attractive places in the Mosel valley. In the old part of the town is St Martin's Church (15th c., rebuilt 1736). Town Hall (1739) in the Marktplatz. Above the town rises Burg Cochem (built *c.* 1020; destroyed by the French in 1689; restored in 19th c.).

**Ellenz
Beilstein**

At Ellenz there is a picturesque view of Beilstein, on the opposite bank (ferry), with the ruins of a castle destroyed in 1688.

**Alf an der Mosel
Bullay**

Alf on the left bank and Bullay on the right bank (bridge and ferry) are the gateway to the famed wine-producing region in the middle Mosel valley. 5km/3 miles south is the Marienburg, with the ruins of a Premonstratensian monastery destroyed in 1806. From here there is a fine view of the 12km/7½ mile long loop in the Mosel known as the Zeller Hamm.

Zell

At the south end of the Zeller Hamm the road crosses to the right bank. Just before this point lies the well-known wine town of Zell, with considerable remains of its old walls, St Peter's Church (1792) and a Schloss (1542) of the Electors of Trier.

Enkirch

On the east side of the long straggling town of Enkirch stands a Late Gothic monastic church (14th–15th c.).
The road continues south, passing below the scanty remains of the Starkenburg.

Traben-Trarbach

Beyond this, straddling the river, is the little town of Traben-Trarbach, the chief centre of the Mosel wine trade, with half-timbered buildings, handsome patrician houses and the Museum of the Middle Mosel. On Mont Royal, within a loop in the river, are the excavated remains of a French fortress.
The road now returns to the left bank.

**Kröv
Ürzig**

Kröv, once the capital of a self-governing territory within the Empire, and Ürzig, a few kilometres farther on, are typical old wine villages. 2.5km/1½ miles beyond Ürzig can be found the old Cistercian convent of Machern.

Bernkastel-Kues

The road continues to Wehlen and Bernkastel-Kues, famed for its wines and as a centre of the wine trade. On the right bank of the river, below Burg Landshut (view), is Bernkastel, with its pretty Marktplatz, its Town Hall of 1608 and its pillory. On the banks of the Mosel stands the Early Gothic St Michael's Church. A bridge leads over the Mosel to Kues, with the Cusanusstift (St Nicholas's Hospital; Late Gothic cloister), founded by the cardinal and philosopher Nicolaus Cusanus (Nikolaus Krebs, 1401–64), whose heart is buried in the Gothic chapel. In the library are his astronomical instruments and apparatus, including the oldest celestial sphere.
The road continues along the right bank.

Piesport

Across the river (bridge) is Piesport, famed for wines with a full bouquet.

Neumagen

Neumagen occupies the site of the Roman Noviomagus. Material recovered by excavation, including the famous carving of a wine-ship (copy in the town), is in the Landesmuseum in Trier.
The road now crosses to the left bank.

Trittenheim

Trittenheim has a handsome church of 1790–93. Above the town, in the vineyards, stands St Lawrence's Chapel (16th c.).

The road continues by way of Klüsserath and Mehring to Trier (see entry), Germany's oldest town.

Mühlhausen F 5–6

Land: Thuringia
Altitude: 230m/755ft
Population: 43,500

The old free imperial city and Hanseatic town of Mühlhausen lies on the river Unstrut between the Hainich plateau and the Oberes Eichsfeld. It has associations with Thomas Müntzer, the theologian who became a leader in the Peasant War of 1524–25.

Situation and characteristics

Old Town

The old town of Mühlhausen (protected as a historic monument) is in course of restoration. In the Untermarkt is the parish church of St Blaise (Blasius). Originally Romanesque, it was rebuilt in 1260 as a basilica with a vaulted roof and then (1270 onwards) continued as a Gothic hall-church with groined vaulting and round piers. The west end, with its octagonal towers (1260), is Early Gothic. The church was completed in the mid 14th century.

*Parish church

Close by are the 13th century St Anne's Chapel, which originally belonged to the Teutonic Order, and a number of handsome old burghers' houses, among them the Late Gothic Bürenhof (1607) and the Altes Backhaus (Old Bakehouse; 1631).

St Anne's Chapel

Mühlhausen has preserved considerable remains of its old town walls (Stadtmauer), which were begun in the 13th century. The best stretches are to the north of the Inneres Frauentor (rebuilt 1654), on the street called Hinter der Mauer and on the Lindenbühl. Along the top of the walls runs a wall-walk, beginning at the Marientor, with three medieval towers, the largest of which is the Rabenturm. The wall-walk and the Rabenturm are open to the public.

*Town Walls

In the Kornmarkt stands the Franciscan Church, an aisleless Gothic church of the 13th–14th centuries. Restored in 1973–75, it is now a memorial to the German Peasant War of 1524–25.

*Franciscan Church

In Ratsstrasse is the Town Hall (Rathaus), a building of some architectural interest incorporating work of different periods, partly stone-built and partly half-timbered. In the Gothic main building are the Councillors' Room of 1571 and the large Council Chamber. In the south wing are the Municipal Archives, with a permanent exhibition of archives and period furniture. In the courtyard can be seen a fountain of 1747.

Town Hall

The 14th century parish church of St Mary (Marienkirche), in which Thomas Müntzer once preached, is the largest church in Thuringia after Erfurt Cathedral, a Gothic hall-church with double aisles flanking the nave and an 86m/282ft high tower. It has rich sculptural decoration (on the south front four lifelike figures, including Emperor Charles IV and his wife), Late Gothic winged altars (15th and 16th c.) and a large Triumphal Cross group. Here Thomas Müntzer proclaimed his programme to the townspeople and the peasants of the surrounding area.

*St Mary's Church

Historic Buildings

Adjoining St Mary's Church, on the site of a medieval warehouse, is the three-storey Brotlaube, which dates in its present form from 1722.

Brotlaube

Mühlhausen has preserved a number of notable burghers' houses. In the vicinity of St Mary's Church, for example, there are Herrenstrasse 1 (Thomas Müntzer's house), Holzstrasse 1 (the old Thurn und Taxis post-office), Marienkirche 6 (after 1820; neo-classical interior) and the "Goldener Stern" inn (1542) at Obermarkt 8; and there are others around All Saints Church, including the Handwerkerhaus (1795) and the two old brewhouses at Steinweg 65 and 75.

Burghers' houses

Mülheim

F 2

Land: North Rhine-Westphalia
Altitude: 130m/412ft
Population: 172,000

Münden

Situation and characteristics

Mülheim lies in beautiful and varied country at the point where the Rhenish Uplands merge into the Lower Rhine plain, with the river Ruhr flowing through the city centre. Coal was mined here from the medieval period onwards, but the mines are now closed and the town's economy is centred on heavy industry and wholesale trade.

The Town

Old town

In the narrow streets of the old town are groups of old half-timbered houses now protected as historical monuments – houses typical of the Berg region with their stone bases and partial slate cladding. The most striking building in the old town is the Tersteegenhaus (Heimatmuseum).

St Peter's Church

In the centre of the old town stands St Peter's Church (Protestant), which preserves some Romanesque work of about 1200; a massive west tower was added in the 13th century. The church was extensively restored in 1870–72, and was rebuilt in 1949–58 after suffering war damage. The tower is 70m/230ft high.

Town Hall

North-west of St Peter's, near the Ruhr, is the Town Hall, whose 57m/187ft high tower is a landmark of the town. On the top floor is the Office Museum (Büromuseum); from the gallery there is a fine view of the town. The older part of the building dates from 1913–15, the newer part from 1965–69.

Museum of Art

At the east end of the Schlossbrücke, which spans the Ruhr near the Town Hall, is the Museum of Art (20th c. German art).

Schloss Broich

Schloss Broich (pronounced as if it were spelt Brooch), at the west end of the bridge, has origins going back to 883–884. Excavations carried out here in 1965–69 brought to light the best preserved secular building of the late Carolingian period in Europe.

River Station

South of the Schlossbrücke, on the lateral canal, is the River Station (Wasserbahnhof), departure point of the passenger ships of the "White Fleet".

Bismarck Tower

To the south of the town, on the Kahlenberg (near the Ruhr), stands the 27m/89ft high Bismarck Tower (far-ranging views).

Raffelberg Brine Baths

In the western district of Raffelberg, in a large park of almost 80 hectares/200 acres, are the Raffelberg Brine Baths. The natural brine comes from an 854m/2802ft deep shaft in the Concordia pit (now closed down).

Münden (Hannoversch Münden)   F 5

Land: Lower Saxony
Altitude: 130m/425ft
Population: 29,000

Situation and characteristics

The old-world little town of Münden, better known under its old name of Hannoversch Münden, is attractively situated on a tongue of land between the rivers Werra and Fulda (which here join to form the Weser) in a basin surrounded by the hills of the Reinhardswald, Bramwald and Kaufunger Wald. Alexander von Humboldt considered that it was one of the world's most beautifully situated towns. It is indeed picturesque with numbers of 16th and 17th century half-timbered houses, old churches and towers surviving from its medieval fortifications.

Sights

Town Hall

In the Marktplatz, which is lined with half-timbered houses, is the Town Hall (Rathaus), a Gothic building to which Georg Crossmann gave an imposing Renaissance façade in 1603–13.

St Blaise's Church

Facing the Town Hall, on the south side of the square, stands St Blaise's Church (St Blasii; 13th–16th c.), which has a bronze font of 1392, a sandstone pulpit of 1493 and the epitaph (by Loy Hering) of the Guelph Duke Erich I of Brunswick-Lüneburg, who made Münden his capital in the 16th century.

On the south side of the old town, adjoining the gardens which mark the line of the old fortifications, can be found the 17th century St Giles' Church (St Ägidien). On the north outside wall can be seen the tomb of the notorious 17th century physician Dr Johann Eisenbart.

St Giles' Church

To the north-east of the old town, close to the Werra, stands the Schloss (16th and 18th c.), now the municipal Cultural Centre. A little to the west are the Ochsenkopf craftsmen's workshops and the stone Werrabrücke (1397–1402).

Schloss

To the east of the old town lies the Forest Garden (Forstbotanischer Garten), established over 100 years ago by the Academy of Forestry, with a thousand different species of tree.

Forest Garden

On the Rabanerkopf, to the west of the town beyond the Fulda, is a 25m/80ft high outlook tower. In 1626, during the Thirty Years War, the imperial general Count Tilly constructed a redoubt at the foot of the hill.

Tilly Redoubt

Munich (München)   L 7

Capital of the *Land* of Bavaria
Altitude: 530m/1740ft
Population: 1.3 million

In this guide the description of Munich has been deliberately kept short, since a fuller account is provided in the "Munich" guide in the same series.

Munich, capital of the *Land* of Bavaria, lies on a gravel plain deposited by the Isar, 40–60km/25–40 miles from the fringes of the Alps. It is famed as a centre of art and learning, with its University and other higher educational establishments, its scientific institutes, its museums and theatres; and it is the seat of the European Patent Office, the Bundesfinanzhof (Supreme Financial Court) and the administrative offices of the Max Planck Society based in Göttingen, and the residence of a Catholic archbishop (diocese of Munich and Freising) and a Protestant bishop (diocese of Bavaria). It is an attractive city, with fine examples of Gothic, Renaissance, Baroque and neo-classical architecture. Its development in the 19th century was largely the work of King Ludwig I (1825–48).

Situation and characteristics

Central Area

The central point of old Munich is the busy Marienplatz, with the Mariensäule (Virgin's Column; 1638) and the neo-Gothic Town Hall (Rathaus; 1867–1908). On the tower of the Town Hall can be seen a clock with mechanical figures (11am, noon and 5pm; in summer also 9pm); from the gallery there are fine panoramic views, with the Alps in the distance (best when the föhn, a warm dry wind from the Alps, is blowing). On the east side of the square stands the Old Town Hall (Altes Rathaus; 15th c.); the tower was rebuilt after 1945.

Town Hall

To the south is St Peter's Church, the town's oldest parish church, probably founded in 1050, with a tower known as "Alter Peter" ("Old Peter"; fine views from the top).

St Peter's Church

To the south of the church lies the busy and colourful Viktualienmarkt, with its generous displays of fruit and vegetables, meat, fish, dairy produce and flowers, which in recent years have included increasing quantities of Southern European and exotic wares. The figures on the fountains represent well-known Munich characters.

Viktualienmarkt

South-west of St Peter's Church, in St-Jakobs-Platz, can be found the Munich Municipal Museum (Münchner Stadtmuseum), with a rich collection on the history and culture of

Municipal Museum

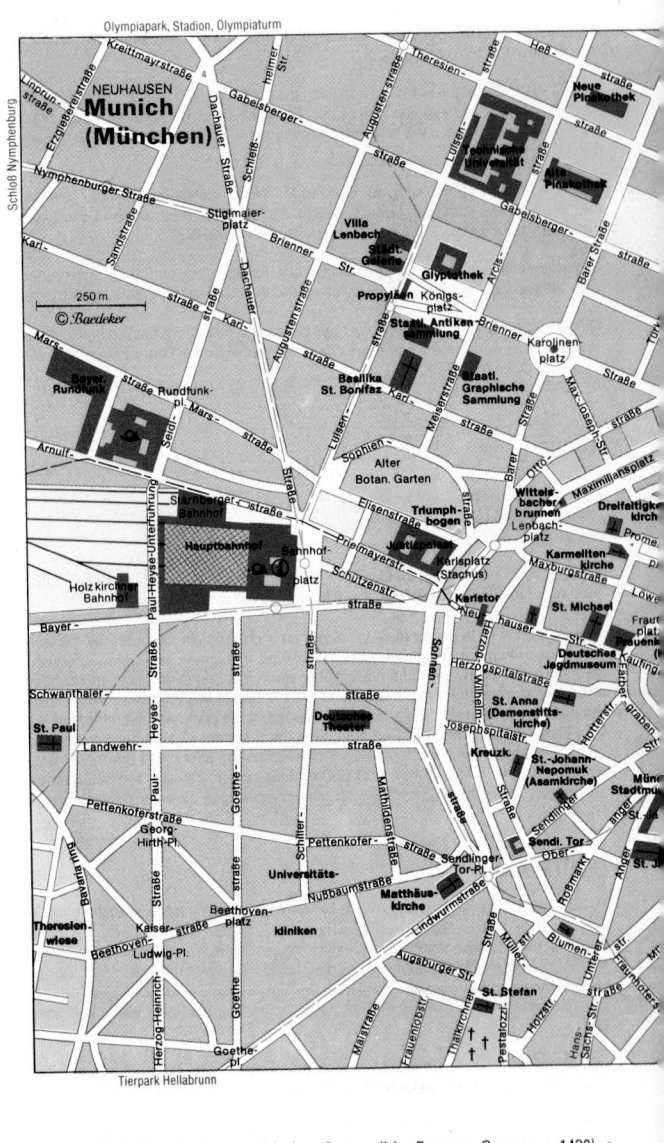

Olympiapark, Stadion, Olympiaturm

NEUHAUSEN
**Munich
(München)**

© Baedeker

250 m

Tierpark Hellabrunn

the town (including the famous "Morisco Dancers" by Erasmus Grasser, *c.* 1480), a museum of photography and film and collections of toys, puppet theatres and musical instruments.

°Asam Church

West of St-Jakobs-Platz, in Sendlinger Strasse (at the south end of which is the 14th century Sendlinger Tor), is the church of St John of Nepomuk, known as the Asam

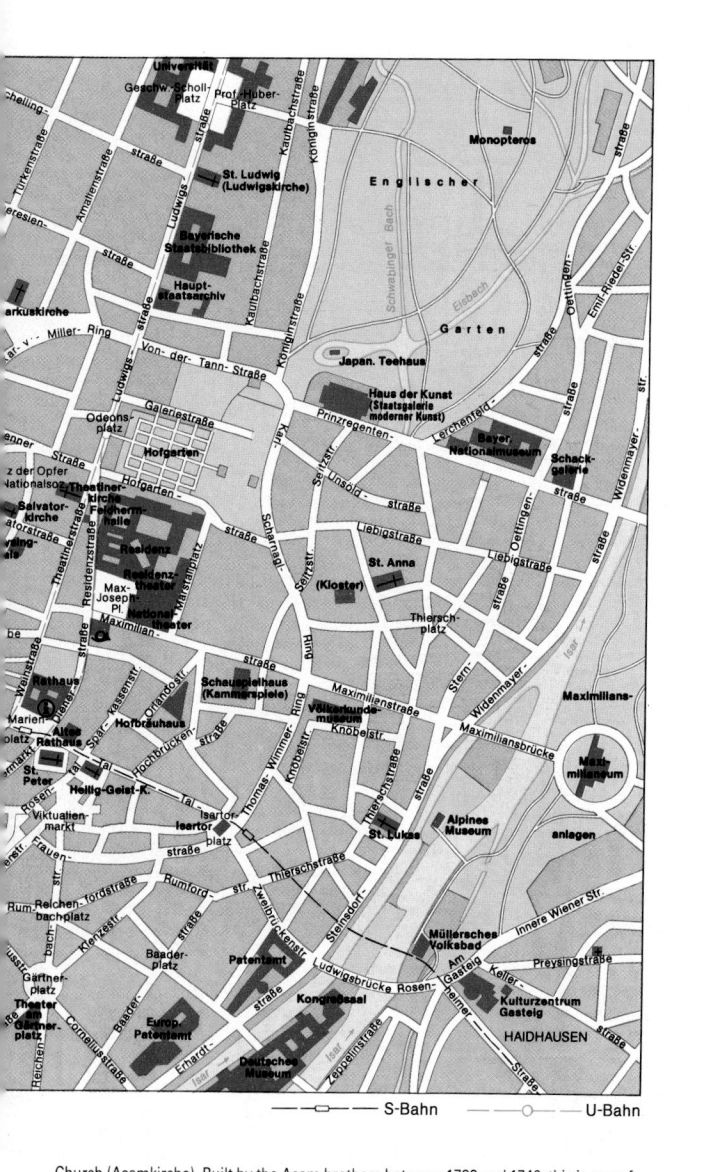

Church (Asamkirche). Built by the Asam brothers between 1733 and 1746, this is one of the most fanciful creations of South German Rococo.

To the east of Marienplatz is the street called the Tal ("Valley"), leading to the Isartor (see below). At the near end of the street, on the right, stands the Gothic Heilig-Geist-Kirche

Tal

(Church of the Holy Ghost; 13th–14th c.). A little way north of this is the Alter Hof, the oldest residence of the Dukes of Bavaria, founded in 1252.

Nearby, in the little square known as the Platzl, is the Hofbräuhaus, the famous and popular beer-hall.

Hofbräuhaus

The Isartor (14th c.; restored 1972) houses the unusual Valentin-Musäum, with a collection of pictures, curios and jokey exhibits (e.g. a fur-covered "winter toothpick", a dish of water labelled as "melted snow sculpture") commemorating a well-known local character, the actor and left-winger Karl Valentin (1882–1948).

Isartor
Valentin-Musäum

North-west from Marienplatz run Kaufinger Strasse and Neuhauser Strasse (pedestrian zone). Just north of Kaufinger Strasse is the Frauenkirche, the Cathedral of Our Lady, an imposing Late Gothic brick-built church (by Jörg von Halspach, 1468–88), whose twin domed towers are a characteristic Munich landmark. The most notable features of the interior are the beautiful 15th and 16th century stained glass, the tomb (1622) of Emperor Ludwig the Bavarian (1282–1347) under the south tower and the episcopal and ducal burial vault in the lower church (restored 1950).

* Frauenkirche

Farther west, in Neuhauser Strasse, are the German Hunting and Fishing Museum (Deutsches Jagd- und Fischereimuseum), housed in the former Augustinian Church, and St Michael's Church (a Jesuit church, formerly the court church), a Renaissance building (by G. Sustris, 1583–97) with an interior of impressive spatial effect which marked an epoch in the church architecture of Catholic South Germany. In the burial vault are the remains of more than thirty members of the Wittelsbach family, including King Ludwig II.

* St Michael's Church

At the end of Neuhauser Strasse stands the 14th century Karlstor, which leads into the busy Karlsplatz, popularly known as the Stachus, with fountains, a large underground shopping centre and a U-Bahn junction. On the north-west side of the square are the old Law Courts (Justizpalast) and the Old Botanic Garden.

Stachus

* Königsplatz

To the north of the Stachus lies the Königsplatz, a neo-classical square laid out by Leo von Klenze between 1816 and 1848, altered in 1935–37 by stone paving and new building and again altered in the 1980s.

On the north side of the square is the Glyptothek (by Klenze, 1816–30), with a collection of Greek and Roman sculpture, including the famous figures from the Aegina temple. Opposite it is the building (1834–48; restored 1967) housing the State Collection of Antiquities (Staatliche Antikensammlung; vases, Greek, Roman and Etruscan small sculpture, glass, gold jewellery).
On the west side of the Königsplatz are the Propyläen, a monumental gateway modelled on the Propylaia on the Acropolis in Athens.

Glyptothek
* *Antiquities*

North-west of the Königsplatz can be found the Villa Lembach, the former residence and studio of the famous 19th century painter Franz Lenbach, which now houses the Municipal Art Gallery (Städtische Galerie; Munich painting since the Gothic period, Lenbach collection). A short distance north-east is the University of Technology (Technische Universität).

Villa Lembach

To the east of the University of Technology are the Alte Pinakothek (by Klenze, 1826–36), reopened in 1957 after its destruction during the war, with a magnificent collection of old masters, and the Neue Pinakothek (new building, opened 1981).
From the Königsplatz the Brienner Strasse leads south-east by way of Karolinenplatz (obelisk commemorating the 30,000 Bavarians who fell in Russia in 1812) to the Odeonsplatz, one of Munich's finest squares, at the south end of Ludwigstrasse.

* * Alte Pinakothek
* Neue Pinakothek

Ludwigstrasse, the grandest of Ludwig I's monumental creations, runs in a dead straight line for a kilometre (¾ mile), passing the State Library (Staatsbibliothek), the Ludwigskirche and the University, to the Siegestor (Victory Gate; 1843–52), crowned by a bronze

Ludwigstrasse

◀ *Marienplatz, with the Town Hall and Frauenkirche*

figure of Bavaria in a chariot drawn by lions. It has a new inscription (1958): "Dedicated to victory, destroyed by war, calling for peace".

To the north of the Siegestor lies the district of Schwabing, which developed around the turn of the century into an artistic and bohemian quarter, a character it is now increasingly losing.

*Theatinerkirche

At the south-west corner of the Odeonsplatz is the Baroque Theatinerkirche (17th–18th c.), with a 71m/233ft high dome. The interior has rich stucco decoration; under the high altar is the burial vault of the Wittelsbachs.

To the south-west, at Prannerstrasse 10, can be found the Siemens Museum.

Feldherrnhalle

Immediately east of the Theatinerkirche is the Feldherrnhalle, built by Friedrich Gärtner in 1841–44) on the model of the Loggia dei Lanzi in Florence, as the counterpart to the Siegestor at the south end of Ludwigstrasse; statues (by Schwanthaler) of General Count Tilly and Prince Wrede.

*Residenz

To the east of the Feldherrnhalle is the Residenz, the old ducal palace built between the 16th and the 19th century, which was badly damaged during the Second World War but has since been restored.

Museum

In Residenzstrasse stands the Alte Residenz (Old Palace; 1611–19), with the State Coin Collection. In Max-Joseph-Platz is the Königsbau (by Klenze, 1826–42), with the Residenzmuseum (rooms in period style, porcelain, silver, etc.) and, in the east wing, the Treasury. On the Hofgarten front are the Festsaalbau (also by Klenze) and the State Collection of Egyptian Art (Ägyptische Sammlung). In the Apotheken-Pavillon is the rebuilt Altes Residenztheater (Cuvilliés Theatre; sumptuous Rococo interior), which formerly stood on the site now occupied by the Neues Residenztheater.

Hofgarten

To the north of the Residenz lies the Hofgarten, laid out in 1613–15 and bounded on the north and west by arcades. At the east end of the gardens the new State Chancellery (Staatskanzlei) and House of Bavarian History (Haus der Bayerischen Geschichte) are at present under construction, centred on the rump of the old Bavarian Army Museum (now in Ingolstadt: see entry).

*English Garden (Englischer Garten)

North-east of the Hofgarten, extending along the banks of the Isar, lies the English Garden, a large park (350 hectares/865 acres) laid out between 1789 and 1832, with clumps of fine old trees, expanses of grass, a lake, the Monopteros temple and the Chinese Tower. On the south side of the park is Prinzregentenstrasse, at the near end of which can be seen the neo-classical Prinz-Carl-Palais (1803–11).

*Haus der Kunst

On the left-hand side of Prinzregentenstrasse, on the edge of the English Garden, is the Haus der Kunst (House of Art; 1937), now housing the State Gallery of Modern Art (periodic special exhibitions).

Beyond this, in Lerchenfeldstrasse, is the State Prehistoric Collection.

**Bavarian National Museum

Farther along Prinzregentenstrasse we come to the Bavarian National Museum (Bayerisches Nationalmuseum), one of the leading collections of German art and applied art (including sculpture, tapestries and Nativity groups).

*Schack Gallery

Just beyond the National Museum is the Schack Gallery (19th century German painting).

Max-Joseph-Platz and Maximilianstrasse

Max-Joseph-Platz

Max-Joseph-Platz, on the south side of the Residenz, is surrounded by monumental buildings. On the east side stands the National Theatre (Opera House; built 1811–18, restored 1959–63), flanked by the new Residenztheater, built in 1948–51 on the site of the old Residenztheater which was burned down in 1944. On the north side of the square is the Königsbau of the Residenz, on the south side the old Head Post Office (now Post Office No. 1).

From Max-Joseph-Platz Maximilianstrasse, laid out between 1852 and 1859, in the reign of King Maximilian II, runs east to the Isar. At the near end, on the right, is the Mint (Münze; beautiful inner courtyard of 1565). Farther along are the Regierung (local government offices) of Upper Bavaria (on the left) and the State Museum of Ethnography (Völkerkundemuseum; on the right). At the far end of the street, on higher ground beyond the Isar, stands the Maximilianeum (1857–74), originally a training college for government officials and now the seat of the Bavarian parliament, the Landtag.

Maximilianstrasse

South-Eastern and Southern Districts

Upstream from the end of Maximilianstrasse are the Museum Island (Museumsinsel) and, on the left bank of the Isar the German Patent Office (Patentamt) and the European Patent Office.

On the island is the Deutsches Museum (German Museum), the largest museum of technology in the world, founded by Oskar von Miller in 1903. Here science, technology and industry are displayed and explained with a great range of exhibits and demonstration and working models.

**German Museum

In the southern district of Harlaching can be found Hellabrunn Zoo (Tierpark), with some 4000 animals from all over the world (Aquarium, Elephant House, Aviary, Polarium, etc.).

*Hellabrunn Zoo

Geiselgasteig

South of Harlaching, in Geiselgasteig, are the studios of the Bavaria Film Corporation. The great attraction here is the Bavaria Film Tour, which takes visitors round the studios and shows how various effects and stunts are produced.

*Bavaria Film Tour

Western Districts

In the south-west of the city, 1.5km/1 mile from the Stachus (see above), lies the Theresienwiese (popularly known simply as the Wiesn), where the Oktoberfest, Munich's great annual beer festival (actually beginning in mid September), is held. On the west side of the park a gigantic figure of "Bavaria" (by Schwanthaler, 1850) stands 30m/100ft high including the base (fine views). Beyond it is the Ruhmeshalle (Hall of Fame; by Klenze, 1843–53).

Theresienwiese

Nymphenburg

In the north-west of the city is Nymphenburg, a magnificent Baroque palace (1664–1728) set in a beautiful landscaped park with fountains and lakes. In the main palace are sumptuously appointed apartments; particularly notable is King Ludwig I's "Gallery of Beauty", with 24 portraits of women by the court painter Josef Stieler. In the south wing is the Marstallmuseum (Court Stables Museum; state carriages, sleighs, Nymphenburg porcelain).
The most notable of the buildings in the park is the Amalienburg, a little hunting lodge by François de Cuvilliés (1734–38).
In the north-eastern roundel to the rear of the palace is the Nymphenburg Porcelain Manufactory, founded in 1747 (showrooms).

*Palace

At the north end of the park can be found the Botanic Garden (hothouses, alpine garden, State Botanic Collection).

Botanic Garden

*Olympic Park (Olympiapark)

Some 5km/3 miles north-west of the city centre we come to the Olympic Park (formerly known as the Oberwiesenfeld), which was laid out for the 1972 Summer Olympics. Its

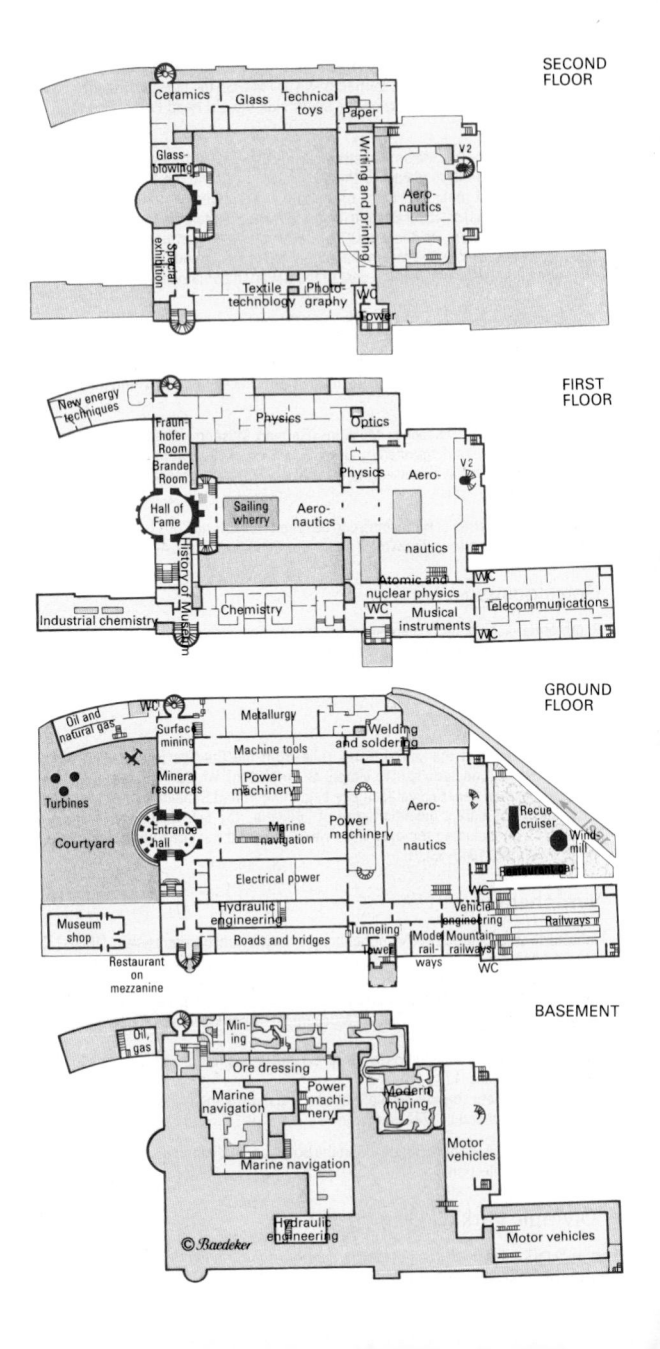

Munich

Deutsches Museum

SECOND FLOOR

Ceramics | Glass | Technical toys | Paper
Glass-blowing
Writing and printing
V 2
Aeronautics
Special exhibition
Textile technology | Photography | WC
Power

FIRST FLOOR

New energy techniques
Fraunhofer Room
Physics | Optics
Brander Room
Physics
Hall of Fame
Sailing wherry
Aeronautics
V 2
Aeronautics
History of Museum
Industrial chemistry
Chemistry
Atomic and nuclear physics
WC
Musical instruments
WC
Telecommunications
WC

GROUND FLOOR

Oil and natural gas
WC
Metallurgy
Surface mining
Welding and soldering
Machine tools
Mineral resources
Power machinery
Turbines
Aeronautics
Courtyard
Entrance hall
Marine navigation
Power machinery
Recue cruiser
Wind-mill
Electrical power
Restaurant car
Museum shop
Hydraulic engineering
Vehicle engineering
WC
Railways
Roads and bridges
Tunneling Tower
Model railways
Mountain railways
WC
Restaurant on mezzanine

BASEMENT

Oil, gas
Mining
Ore dressing
Marine navigation
Power machinery
Modern mining
Motor vehicles
Marine navigation
© Baedeker
Hydraulic engineering
Motor vehicles

Nymphenburg Palace and Park

Olympic Park

*Tent roof	main features are the 290m/950ft high Olympic Tower (revolving restaurant, viewing platforms), the Olympic Stadium, the Swimming Hall and the Sports Hall, all covered by a huge tent roof (76,000 sq.m/91,000 sq.yds) of acrylic glass supported on steel cables. To the north is the former Olympic Village.
BMW Museum	To the east are the BMW car-manufacturing works, with the striking "four-cylinder" high-rise office block and the BMW Museum.

Dachau

	17km/10½ miles north-west of Munich, on the Dachauer Moos, lies the town of Dachau, with an 18th century Schloss built in one wing of an earlier Renaissance building.
Concentration camp	The notorious Dachau concentration camp, in which some 32,000 people died during the Nazi period, is now a memorial site (Gedenkstätte; museum, collection of documents).

Schleissheim

*Palaces	At the east end of the Dachauer Moos lies Schleissheim, famed for its three palaces. The Schlosspark (1250m/1365yds long by 350m/380yds across), surrounded by canals, is laid out on a strictly symmetrical plan along its central axis. To the west is the Altes Schloss, a modest building of 1597–1616 which now contains an exhibition on "The Gospel in the Houses of the Peoples". The Neues Schloss (1701–04) is a long, regularly planned palace with a sumptuous interior (state apartments, collection of Baroque pictures). In front of it is a large garden, with flowerbeds, lawns and fountains, extending to Schloss Lustheim, a little pleasure palace of 1684–88.
**Porcelain collection	In Schloss Lustheim can be seen a famous collection of Meissen porcelain (some 1800 pieces, dating between 1710 and 1760).

Münster   E 3

	Land: North Rhine-Westphalia Altitude: 63m/207ft Population: 269,000
Situation and characteristics	Münster, situated on the river Aa and on the Dortmund-Ems Canal, is the geographical and economic centre of the Münsterland (see entry), the see of a Roman Catholic archbishop and a university town. It is a city of churches, of aristocratic mansions and handsome old burghers' houses. The old town is now surrounded by a ring of gardens on the line of the old fortifications.

Sights

Town Hall	In the Prinzipalmarkt, surrounded by arcades and gabled houses, is the Gothic Town Hall (Rathaus; 14th c., rebuilt), with the fine Peace Chamber (Friedessaal), in which the peace treaty between Spain and the Netherlands at the end of the Thirty Years War was signed in 1648 (see Osnabrück). Next to it is the Stadtweinhaus (Municipal Wine-House), a gabled building of the Late Renaissance.
*St Lambert's Church	At the north end of the Prinzipalmarkt stands the magnificent St Lambert's Church (Lambertikirche; 14th–15th c.). On the west tower are the three iron cages in which the bodies of the Anabaptists Johann von Leyden, Knipperdollinck and Krechting were displayed in 1536. To the north-east is the Krameramtshaus of 1588, now the Municipal Library.
Erbdrostenhof	At Salzstrasse 38 can be found the Erbdrostenhof, an aristocratic mansion built by the great Westphalian architect Johann Conrad Schlaun in 1754 (restored 1953–70. Beyond it is the Baroque St Clement's Church, also by Schlaun (restored).

To the west of the Prinzipalmarkt, in the spacious Domplatz, is the Cathedral (Dom) of St Paul, the largest church in Westphalia. Built between 1225 and 1265, it is in a style transitional between Romanesque and Gothic. On the south side, in the porch ("Paradies") of the west transept, are 13th century figures of apostles and saints. Notable features of the interior, which is of impressive spatial effect, are the numerous tombs of bishops and canons (including Cardinal von Galen, d. 1946) and an astronomical clock (1540) on the wall of the choir. The chapterhouse has fine panelling. In the Domkammer are displayed a variety of objects from the diocese's thousand years of history.

*Cathedral

On the south side of the Domplatz stands the Westphalian Landesmuseum of Art and Culture (medieval sculpture, pictures by German Impressionists, superb collection of stained glass). Adjoining this on the south, in the street called Rothenburg, is the Landesmuseum of Archaeology. On the west side of the Domplatz is the Bishop's Palace (Bischöfliches Palais).

*Landesmuseum

North-west of the Domplatz is the Gothic Liebfrauenkirche (Church of Our Lady) or Überwasserkirche (1340–46), with a richly articulated tower.

On the west side of the old town is the Schloss, the palace of the Prince-Bishops (by J. C. Schlaun, 1767–73; restored after destruction during the Second World War), which now houses the University of Westphalia. Beyond it lies the Schlossgarten, with the Botanic Garden.

Schloss

To the south-west of the old town lies the Aasee (40 hectares/100 acres), Münster's water sports paradise (water-bus, sailing school, boat hire).

Aasee

West of the Aasee, on the Sentruper Höhe, are the Mühlenhof Open-Air Museum and the All-Weather Zoo, opened in 1974 (over 2000 animals of 470 different species; dolphin show). Adjoining is the Westphalian Natural History Museum (Planetarium).

Mühlenhof
*All-Weather Zoo

Münster Cathedral

Surroundings of Münster

Rüschhaus

7km/4½ miles north-west of Münster can be found the Rüschhaus, a mansion built by J. C. Schlaun in 1745–49 as a summer residence, later occupied by the Westphalian poetess Annette von Droste-Hülshoff (museum).

Haus Hülshoff

3km/2 miles south-west of the Rüschhaus is Haus Hülshoff, a charming 16th century moated castle in which Annette von Droste-Hülshoff was born in 1797 (museum).

Burg Vischering
*Schloss
Nordkirchen

At Lüdinghausen, 28km/17 miles south-west of Münster, we come to the 16th century moated castle of Vischering. South-east of this is another moated house, Schloss Nordkirchen, a large Baroque building (early 18th c.) which is styled the "Westphalian Versailles".

Münsterland

E 2–3

Land: North Rhine-Westphalia

Situation and
characteristics

The Münsterland, which occupies the north-western half of Westphalia, is bounded on the north-east by the Teutoburg Forest and on the south by the river Lippe, while in the west it merges into the Lower Rhine plain. For the most part it is a flat or gently undulating region, out of which rise some ranges of flat-topped sandstone hills like the Beckumer Berge (173m/568ft) in the east, the Baumberge (186m/610ft) in the north-west and the Haard range (157m/515ft) in the south.

Landscape

The charm of the Münsterland lies principally in the contrast between the wide expanses of agricultural land with their substantial farmhouses and grazing cattle and the nearby

Burg Vischering

industrial zone. Its chief tourist attractions are its old towns, such as the Westphalian capital of Münster (see entry), and its numerous moated castles.

Lake Müritz   C 7–8

Land: Mecklenburg-West Pomerania

Lake Müritz (area 115.3 sq.km/44½ sq. miles) is the largest lake in the Mecklenburg lake district (see entry). The name is Slav, meaning "sea"; and indeed this great sheet of water, surrounded by woodland and fields, has the aspect of a sea, which can be whipped up in a storm into threateningly high waves.

Situation and characteristics

Landscape

The lake has an average depth of about 6.50m/21ft, with a maximum depth of 31m/102ft. It lies at an altitude of 62m/203ft above sea level, considerably higher than the second largest of the Mecklenburg lakes, the Schweriner See (37.40m/123ft). Thus, like the other "Great Lakes" drained by the river Elde to the Elbe, it is one of the Obere Seen (Upper Lakes) in the Mecklenburg lake district. It is linked by the Müritz-Havel Canal with the upper Havel and the numerous lakes in that area.

At the north end of Lake Müritz, around Waren, are a number of smaller lakes (the Binnenmüritz, the Tiefwarensee, the Feisnecksee), separated from it, either wholly or partially, by narrow strips of land, and round its north-east and east sides are other lakes (the Rederangsee, the Specker See, etc.). All of these are now included within the Müritz National Park (area 310 sq.km/120 sq. miles), established in 1990, notable for the large numbers of rare birds (cranes, white-tailed eagles, ospreys) which nest here.

Müritz National Park

Waren

Waren, chief town of a district, lies on the northern shore of Lake Müritz. In its setting of lakes and woodland it is an attractive holiday place.

Situation and characteristics

The parish church of St George (*c.* 1225), a brick-built Early Gothic basilica with a neo-Gothic choir (mid 19th c.) and a Late Gothic west tower (early 15th c.), has a notable Triumphal Cross group (14th c.).

St George's Church

The parish church of St Mary (13th c.) was originally an aisled Early Gothic church with a choir in Transitional style (late 13th c.). After being burned down in 1637 and 1671 it was rebuilt in 1792 as an aisleless church. The tower has a Baroque crown.

St Mary's Church

The oldest secular building in the town is the Old Town Hall, now occupied by the church verger and the organist.

Old Town Hall

In the Neuer Markt is the Löwenapotheke (Lion Pharmacy), a handsome half-timbered building with an 18th century façade.

Lion Pharmacy

The Müritz Museum at Friedensstrasse 5, founded in 1866 as a natural history museum, is now devoted to the culture of the region and the protection of nature and the environment (prehistoric finds from Mecklenburg, flora and fauna of the Müritz area).

Müritz Museum

Nahe Valley   I 2 – H 3

Land: Rhineland-Palatinate

The Nahe rises near Selbach in the southern Hunsrück (see entry) and follows a winding course amid forests and pastureland, sunny vineyards and steep rock faces before flowing into the Rhine at Bingen. Its total length is 116km/72 miles.

Landscape

Along the banks of the Nahe are a series of picturesque little towns – Idar-Oberstein (see entry), the town of jewellery and precious stones; Kirn, with the ruined Kyrburg looming over it; Bad Münster am Stein, at the foot of the porphyry wall of the Rheingrafenstein; and, opposite Bad Münster, the Ebernburg, birthplace of the celebrated knight Franz von Sickingen (1481–1523) and refuge of the humanist Ulrich von Hutten.

Bad Nauheim   H 4

Land: Hesse
Altitude: 144m/472ft
Population: 28,000

Situation and characteristics

The spa of Bad Nauheim, situated in the Wetterau, on the western slopes of the Taunus (see entry), is a town of regular streets, well preserved Art Nouveau buildings and beautiful parks and gardens. Its hot brine springs, rich in carbonic acid, are recommended for the treatment of cardio-vascular disease, rheumatism, psoriasis and nervous complaints.

The Town

Sprudelhof

In the Sprudelhof (Fountain Court), surrounded by Art Nouveau bathing establishments, are the Friedrich-Wilhelm-Sprudel (34°C/93°F), the Grosser Sprudel (30°C/86°F) and the Ernst-Ludwig-Sprudel (32°C/90°F), with a total flow of around 1.7 million litres/374,000 gallons a day.

Kurpark

To the west, merging into the forests of the Taunus, is the Kurpark (800 hectares/2000 acres), with the Kurhaus (large terrace) and a covered thermal brine pool. North-east of this is the Grosser Teich (rowing boats); on its west side is the Teichhaus-Schlösschen (Salt Museum).

Pump Room

Farther south is the Pump Room (Trinkkuranlage), with numerous drinking fountains. On the south-eastern outskirts of the town, in the New Kurpark, are large halls for the evaporation of brine. On Friedberger Strasse are the Usa Baths (water temperature 28–32°C/82–90°F; artificial waves, water-chute).

Johannisberg

To the west rises the Johannisberg (269m/883ft; observatory). From the top of the hill there are good views of the Steinfurt rose-growing area.

Surroundings of Bad Nauheim

Friedberg

A few kilometres south of Bad Nauheim is Friedberg, once a free imperial city, with a 14th–15th century castle, a Baroque country house set in a beautiful garden and the Wetterau Museum (regional history since Roman times).

Naumburg   F 7

Land: Saxony-Anhalt
Altitude: 108m/354ft
Population: 31,000

Situation and characteristics

The famous cathedral city of Naumburg lies on the north-eastern edge of the Thuringian Basin, just above the junction of the Unstrut with the Saale. Vines are grown on the slopes above the valley.

**Cathedral

The Late Romanesque and Early Gothic Cathedral (Dom) of SS. Peter and Paul, one of Europe's finest cathedrals, stands in the episcopal quarter of the town. It is an aisled cruciform basilica with a vaulted roof, two choirs, four towers and a cloister. Begun at some time before 1213, it underwent much alteration in later periods, down to the 19th century. The oldest part is the Romanesque crypt under the east choir (c. 1170), part of an earlier church on the site.

The twelve figures of founders in the west choir, masterpieces by some anonymous Naumburg master (after 1250), are world-famed. All the figures, carved in limestone, are life-size. The best known pairs are Uta and Ekkehard and Reglindis and Hermann.
Also of outstanding quality are the reliefs of the Passion on the west choir screen (the Last Supper, the Arrest of Christ, Christ before Pilate, the Scourging, the Bearing of the Cross, etc.; on the doorway the Crucifixion). Other notable features are the medieval stained glass in some of the windows, several altars and sculptures and a number of fine monuments.

*Founder Figures

On the south side of the Cathedral, incorporated in the cloister, is the parish church of St Mary (Marienkirche). A little way west is St Giles' Church (Ägidienkirche), with a two-storey Late Romanesque chapel (early 13th c.).

Town Centre

From the Cathedral Steinweg (crossing the Lindenring) and Herrenstrasse lead to the large and regularly laid out Markt. On the west side of the square stands the Late Gothic Town Hall (1527–38), with dormers on the gables. It has a richly decorated interior (spiral staircase, Council Chamber with stucco ceiling).

*Town Hall

On the south side of the Markt are the Schlösschen (No. 6) and a mansion which belonged to Duke Moritz of Saxony-Zeitz (No. 7).

Just off the square is St Wenceslas's Church (St Wenzel), a Late Gothic hall-church (1218–1523) with rich sculptural decoration which was the town's principal church outside the episcopal quarter. It has an organ by Z. Hildebrand on which Johann Sebastian Bach played and a painting by Lucas Cranach the Elder, "Christ the Friend of Children". The 67m/220ft high tower can be climbed during the summer months; fine views of the town from the top.

St Wenceslas's Church

Marienstrasse leads to the Marientor, an excellently preserved 15th century town gate, with an outer gateway, wall-walk, inner gatehouse, portcullis and watch-tower. On the outer gateway are a Virgin and Child and the town's coat of arms. Performances by the Naumburg Puppet Theatre are given in the inner gatehouse. There are some remains of the old town walls.

Marientor

Naumburg Cathedral

WT West towers
ET East towers

FIGURES OF FOUNDERS
(in West Choir)
  1 Dietrich
  2 Gepa
  3 Uta and Ekkehard
  4 Thimo
  5 Wilhelm
  6 Syzzo
  7 Dietmar
  8 Regelindis and Hermann
  9 Konrad
 10 Gerburg

To the west of the Cathedral, on the site of an old monastery dedicated to St Maurice, can be found the Late Gothic St Maurice's Church (St Moritz) and to the south of the Cathedral St Othmar's Church (Baroque).

St Maurice's Church

At Grochlitzer Strasse 49–51 is the Museum on the History of Naumburg.

Museum

Neckar Valley

L 4 – I 4

Land: Baden-Württemberg

The Neckar, with a total length of 371km/231 miles, rises at a height of 706m/2316ft on the Baar plateau, near Villingen-Schwenningen (see entry). At Rottweil (see entry) it cuts its way through the Muschelkalk limestone in a steep-sided valley. Just before the university town of Tübingen (see entry) the valley opens out and then narrows again as the river makes its way through the Upper Triassic rocks. At Plochingen it takes a sharp turn to the north-west; from this point it is canalised and is navigable by commercial shipping. After passing the old imperial city of Esslingen (see entry) it enters the Stuttgart basin and passes through the old ducal capital of Ludwigsburg (see entry) and the little town of Marbach, which has associations with Schiller. In the slopes above the river are vineyards. Beyond Heilbronn (see entry) the Neckar enters the upland country of the Odenwald.

From Heilbronn to Heidelberg

Leave Heilbronn on B 27, which runs north along the right bank of the Neckar to Neckarsulm (see Heilbronn, Surroundings). Beyond this, at Bad Friedrichshall-Kochendorf, is a rock-salt mine.

North of Bad Friedrichshall, on the other side of the river (bridge), lies the picturesque little town of Bad Wimpfen (see Heilbronn, Surroundings).

Beyond Wimpfen, on the left bank of the Neckar, are the ruined castle of Ehrenberg and, rather farther from the river, Schloss Guttenberg (12th–18th c.), with a museum (tin figures, dioramas, "library of wood") and a tower commanding wide views.
Below the castle nestles the village of Neckarmühlbach, with the German Small Car Museum.

Guttenberg

Above the little town of Gundelsheim (picturesque town centre), situated at a dam on the Neckar, is Schloss Horneck, a castle of the Teutonic Order, now occupied by a Heimatmuseum, the Heimathaus Siebenbürgen and an old people's home.

Gundelsheim

Above Neckarzimmern stands the ruined castle of Hornberg (small museum), which was destroyed in 1688. This was the seat of the knight made famous by Goethe's play, Götz von Berlichingen, who wrote his memoirs here and died in the castle in 1562. From the keep there are extensive views of the Neckar valley.
From Neckarelz the route continues on B 37.

Neckarzimmern

Beyond Neckarelz the Obrigheim nuclear power station comes into sight on the west bank. The valley now becomes narrower as the road runs through Neckargerach and below Burg Zwingenberg (festival in August and September).

Obrigheim

Eberbach, once a free imperial city, has preserved some of the towers in its old ring of fortifications. The old town centre has been well rehabilitated and "traffic-calmed". Museum in the Alter Markt. Medicinal springs, with spa facilities. To the north-east, above the town, are the remains of an old Hohenstaufen stronghold.

Eberbach

The little town of Hirschhorn lies at one of the most charming spots in the Neckar valley. Above the town are the Late Gothic Carmelite Church and the old castle (13th–16th c.) of the lords of Hirschhorn.

*Hirschhorn

◀ *Naumburg Cathedral*

View from Burg Neckarzimmern

Neckarsteinach

A few kilometres farther on is the picturesquely situated little town of Neckarsteinach, with a Gothic church. Above the town are four castles which belonged to the Ritter von Steinach.

Neckargemünd

Beyond Neckarsteinach a bridge crosses the river to Neckargemünd, where the Elsenz flows into the Neckar. At the east end of the town stands a triumphal arch erected in 1788 in honour of Elector Karl Theodor.

*Dilsberg

4km/2½ miles east, on a wooded conical hill, is the charming little town of Dilsberg, with the ruins of an old castle (open to visitors); magnificent view from castle walls.

From here the road continues to Heidelberg and Mannheim (see entries), where the Neckar flows into the Rhine.

Neubrandenburg   C 8

Land: Mecklenburg-West Pomerania
Altitude: 19m/62ft
Population: 90,000

Situation and characteristics

Neubrandenburg, the "town of the four gates", lies in Mecklenburg, on the north side of the Tollensesee.

Sights

*Town walls

The old town (pedestrian zone) is surrounded by an almost completely preserved circuit of fortifications (probably late 13th c.), consisting of a ring wall 2300m/2515yds long and 7.50m/25ft high, three moats and numerous towers, *wiekhäuser* (houses built into the walls) and gates.

Wiekhäuser   *Treptower Tor*

The town gates (restoration completed 1984) are particularly impressive – the Neues Tor (second half of 15th c.), the Friedländer Tor (24th–15th c.; now an art centre), the Stargarder Tor (14th–15th c.) and the Treptower Tor (*c.* 1400; now a museum of prehistory and the early historical period). | Town gates

St Mary's Church (Marienkirche; brick-built Gothic), in Ernst-Thälmann-Strasse, dates from the 13th–14th century. Burned down in 1945, it has been rebuilt as a concert hall and art gallery. | St Mary's Church

The monastic church of St John (13th and 14th c.), also in Ernst-Thälmann-Strasse, has a fine pulpit of 1588 and an 18th century reredos. | St John's Church

Of the old Franciscan friary (1260) in the north part of the old town there survives only the north wing (rebuilt in the Late Gothic period), which is now occupied by the registry office, with the cloister (*c.* 1300; interior altered in 16th c.; restored). | Franciscan friary

In Rostocker Strasse is the little hospital chapel of St George (brick-built; first half of 15th c.), with a wooden Baroque roof tower. | St George's Chapel

At Ernst-Thälmann-Strasse 35 can be seen a house once occupied by Fritz Reuter, the leading Low German dialect writer, who lived in Neubrandenburg from 1856 to 1863. It is now a memorial museum. | Fritz Reuter House

At Friedrich-Engels-Ring 7 is an exhibition on the history of the town. The art gallery in the Pferdemarkt displays contemporary art. | Museums

Neuruppin   D 8

Land: Brandenburg
Altitude: 40m/130ft
Population: 26,700

Neuss

<table>
<tr><td>Situation and characteristics</td><td>Neuruppin, birthplace of the novelist Theodor Fontane and the architect Karl Friedrich Schinkel, lies on the Ruppiner See, 90km/55 miles north-west of Berlin.</td></tr>
</table>

Sights

<table>
<tr><td>*Monastic church</td><td>The oldest building in the town is a former monastic church, all that survives of a Dominican monastery founded in 1246 (restored by Schinkel in 1836–41 and again in the 1970s; towers 1906–07). The church has fine late medieval furnishings.</td></tr>
<tr><td>*Heimatmuseum</td><td>In a neo-classical burgher's house (1790) at August-Bebel-Strasse 14–15 is the Heimatmuseum, with rooms commemorating Theodor Fontane and K. F. Schinkel. It also possesses the largest collection in existence of the illustrated broadsheets produced in Neuruppin between 1825 and 1900.</td></tr>
<tr><td>St Lazarus Chapel</td><td>In Siechenstrasse is the Late Gothic hospital chapel of St Lazarus (1491). In the Spitalhof is the "Uphus", the oldest half-timbered building in Neuruppin.</td></tr>
<tr><td>Tempelgarten</td><td>In the Tempelgarten (Temple Garden), laid out by A. Gentz in the 19th century, can be found a circular temple built by G. W. von Knobelsdorff in 1735 for Crown Prince Frederick of Prussia. Fine Baroque sculpture; rare species of trees.</td></tr>
<tr><td>St Mary's Church</td><td>The parish church of St Mary is an aisleless neo-classical church (by Berson and Engel, 1801–04) with a porch, a dome and a plain interior.</td></tr>
<tr><td>St George's Chapel</td><td>The hospital chapel of St George (brick-built Gothic, aisleless) has a Baroque stucco ceiling and a fine Late Gothic winged altar.</td></tr>
<tr><td>Burghers' houses</td><td>In the town centre, which is uniformly neo-classical in style, are numbers of handsome 18th century burghers' houses. On a house at Fischbänkenstrasse 8 is a plaque commemorating Karl Friedrich Schinkel.</td></tr>
</table>

Neuss   F 2

Land: North Rhine-Westphalia
Altitude: 40m/130ft
Population: 144,000

<table>
<tr><td>Situation and characteristics</td><td>The industrial town of Neuss with extensive port installations lies opposite Düsseldorf on the left bank of the Rhine. The name of the town, which was once a member of the Hanseatic League, comes from the Roman fort of Novaesium which was established here in A.D. 40.</td></tr>
</table>

Central Area

<table>
<tr><td>**Cathedral</td><td>The dominant feature of the city centre is the Minster (Cathedral) of St Quirinus. There was a monastery on this site in the 11th century, to which in 1050 the Pope presented the relics of St Quirinus. Thereafter the saint's cult spread widely in the Lower Rhineland. The church, which dates in its present form from the 13th century, is one of the most splendid creations of the Late Romanesque period on the Lower Rhine. The mighty dome was rebuilt in 1747 after a fire. Behind the high altar, in the central apse of the choir, can be seen the magnificent shrine of St Quirinus (1900). In the crypt under the choir (11th–12th c.) are remains of a red and white floor covering of the Carolingian period and two re-used Roman columns.</td></tr>
<tr><td>Arsenal</td><td>South-east of the Cathedral, in the Freithof, is the former Arsenal (Zeughaus; 1737–39), which until 1802 served as a church of the Observantine order.</td></tr>
<tr><td>Clemens Sels Museum</td><td>From the long Markt (below the Freithof) the Oberstrasse, the main axis of the central area, runs south-east to the massive Obertor, beside which is the Clemens Sels Museum.</td></tr>
</table>

Cathedral of St Quirinus

On the ground floor are large numbers of finds from the Roman fort, on the first floor applied and decorative art of the 14th–18th centuries and painting and sculpture of the 19th and 20th centuries, and on the second floor a rich collection of naive painting and sculpture from France, Germany and Eastern Europe.

Neuss-Gnadenthal

While the Roman civilian settlement was situated in the centre of present-day Neuss the military fort lay south-east of the town centre in the district of Gnadenthal. In the area now occupied by the Telecommunications School its position is marked by copies of Roman funerary stelae and a large sketch plan of the site.

Roman fort

In Gepa-Platz, a square in a residential district south-west of the Roman fort, a cult-site of Cybele – a masonry basin in which the priests performed bloody animal sacrifices – was excavated in 1956. It is now protected by a massive concrete structure.

Cult-site of Cybele

In the south-western district of Holzheim lies the "island" of Hombroich (pronounced as if it were spelt Hombrooch), an expanse of water meadows which has been made into an open-air museum. In five buildings which resemble sculpture are housed works of art from the early historical period to the present day (including watercolours by Cézanne); the main building (the "Labyrinth") is devoted to Oriental, African and Oceanian art and to Dadaist and Surrealist art.

*Insel Hombroich

Zons

Zons (now part of Dormagen), 15km/9 miles south-east of Neuss on the left bank of the Rhine, is a picturesque little town with well preserved old town walls. The 14th century fortress now houses the Heimatmuseum, with a fine collection of pewter (including many good Art Nouveau pieces). In the outer ward of the fortress is an open-air theatre.

Neustrelitz

Land: Mecklenburg-West Pomerania
Altitude: 83m/272ft
Population: 27,300

Situation and characteristics

Neustrelitz, once the seat of the Dukes of Mecklenburg-Strelitz, lies on the Zierker See. It is the gateway to the Neustrelitz lake district (Kleinseenplatte) with its 300 lakes.

Sights

Markt

The Late Baroque town centre is laid out in a star shape radiating from the Markt. The Markt, originally square, was given a circular form in 1866 and surrounded by two-storey houses, of which the Savings Bank, the pharmacy, the Café am Markt and the "Goldene Kugel" ("Golden Ball") have been preserved. The Town Hall (by Buttel, 1841) is in neo-classical style. There is a plaque commemorating Engelbert Humperdinck, composer of the fairytale opera "Hansel and Gretel", who died in Neustrelitz in 1921. A more recent monument is the memorial to the Soviet dead of the Second World War.

Town Church

The Town Church (1768–78) is in Late Baroque style with neo-classical features. The 45m/148ft high tower was added in 1831.

* Stadtpark

A particular attraction of Neustrelitz is the Stadtpark (Municipal Park), originally the Schlosspark. The Schloss itself, an 18th century half-timbered building by J. Löwe, was destroyed in 1945. The Baroque-style park, also laid out by Löwe, was much altered and extended after 1790; at one stage P. J. Lenné was involved in its replanning. Of the original Baroque layout there survives the main axis directed towards the Schloss; the rest of the area has been transformed into a landscaped park. At the end of the main avenue is the Temple of Hebe (1840). In the north-eastern part of the park is the "Avenue

Stadtpark, Neustrelitz

of the Gods" (Götterallee), with nine sandstone figures of the gods of antiquity and the Seasons (second half of 18th c.). Here too is the Orangery, originally Baroque (1755) but remodelled in neo-classical style by Schinkel and Buttel in 1840 (fine interior; restored 1986). To the west of the main avenue can be seen a bust of Field-Marshal Blücher (after a model by C. D. Rauch, 1816). In the north-western part of the park, on a low hill, stands a classical-style temple with four columns (by the Berlin architect Seelig, 1891) in memory of Queen Luise, with a marble statue of the queen (by A. Wolff, after an original by C. D. Rauch).

South-east of the site of the Schloss lies the Tierpark, originally established in 1721 as a ducal hunting preserve, with fine old trees and numerous enclosures for animals. The stock of animals was built up again in the years following the Second World War. The fine entrance gateway, with two figures of stags, was built by Buttel and Rauch to the design of K. F. Schinkel (1822).

Tierpark

There are a number of handsome mansions north-east and south-west of the Schloss and in the town centre. Particularly notable is the Gymnasium Carolinum (by F. W. Dunkelberg, 1806), with a commemorative tablet recalling that Heinrich Schliemann, the discoverer of Troy, and the painter Wilhelm Riefstahl were pupils at this grammar school.

Gymnasium Carolinum

Neustrelitz Lake District

B 5–6

The Neustrelitz lake district lies between Lake Müritz in the north-west and the Lychen–Templin lakes in the south-east, extending south as far as Mirow and Rheinsberg. The area is drained by the Rhin and the upper Havel.

Most of the Neustrelitz lake district is rolling wooded country, ranging in height between 80m/260ft and 120m/390ft, with variously oriented valleys containing small lakes.

*Landscape

Müritz-Havel Canal in Neustrelitz lake district

Expanses of heathland and tracts of sandy soil with dunes and plantations of pines alternate with terminal moraines covered with deciduous woodland which bound the lake district on north and south. There are only small patches of agricultural land.

Havel

In many of the valleys there are strings of lakes separated by dry areas or damp water meadows. The Havel itself, which rises in the Neustrelitz lake district, is now a river and now a lake.

The Müritz-Havel Canal links the Neustrelitz lakes with the Mecklenburg lake district (Lake Müritz, Kölpinsee, Fleesensee and Plauer See).

Nordhausen   F 6

Land: Thuringia
Altitude: 247m/810ft
Population: 48,000

Situation and characteristics

The old free imperial city and Hanseatic town of Nordhausen lies on the river Zorge, in the north-west of the Goldene Aue. This "gateway to the Southern Harz" is now an important traffic junction and a considerable industrial town. Two well-known local products are Nordhausen Doppelkorn (a rye spirit) and Nordhausen chewing tobacco.

Sights

Town walls

Nordhausen has preserved considerable stretches of its old town walls, built from 1180 onwards and extended in the 14th and 15th centuries.

Cathedral

The Cathedral of the Holy Cross, founded by Queen Mathilde in 962 as the church of a nunnery which in 1220 was converted by the Emperor Frederick II into a house of secular canons, is a Gothic hall-church (14th c.) with reticulated vaulting (16th c.) and octagonal pillars. It has a finely furnished interior, with a Baroque high altar (1726), 14th and 15th century grave-slabs and a tabernacle of 1455

St Blaise's Church

The parish church of St Blaise (15th c.), a Late Gothic hall-church with groined vaulting, has a Late Romanesque west work with two octagonal towers; fine pulpit of 1592.

*Old Town Hall

In the Markt is the three-storey Old Town Hall (1360; rebuilt in Late Renaissance style 1610; restored after 1945), with an arcade on the ground floor and a staircase tower topped by a double lantern.

On the west side is a figure of Roland (1717), a symbol of municipal authority since at least 1411, on the east side a memorial (by J. von Woyski) to the victims of air raids on the town in 1945.

Burghers' houses

Of Nordhausen's few surviving burghers' houses the most interesting are a half-timbered house of 1500 at Barfüsserstrasse 6, one of the finest secular buildings in the town; the Finkenburg, a Gothic half-timbered building (c. 1550) on the Wassertreppe; and a half-timbered house of Lower Saxon type (c. 1550) at Domstrasse 12.

Meyenburg Museum

At Alexander-Puschkin-Strasse 31 is the Meyenburg Museum (local finds of the prehistoric and early historical periods, results of research on the old town, furniture, porcelain, tomb brasses and coins; small ethnographic collection).

Stolberg

Situation and characteristics

The old mining and trading town of Stolberg, birthplace of the 16th century peasant leader Thomas Müntzer and now a popular holiday resort, is beautifully situated in three narrow and deeply indented valleys in the Southern Harz. With its romantic winding lanes and colourful half-timbered houses richly decorated with carving, it is a town of thoroughly medieval aspect.

Over the town on a steep-sided crag looms the Schloss (1200; newer part 1539–47), once the seat of the Counts Stolberg. In the south, west and south-east wings are a number of interesting rooms with stucco decoration. The neo-classical Red Hall in the south-east wing was designed by K. F. Schinkel. In a 13th century tower and a round outside tower is the castle chapel. — Schloss

The medieval town with its numerous half-timbered houses is protected as a historical monument. The Town Hall (1482) is unusual in having no internal staircases: the upper floors are reached on the steps leading to the church, which run up beside the Town Hall. It is said to have as many windows as there are weeks in the year. On the façade can be seen a sundial with the Stolberg arms. — *Town Hall

At Thomas-Müntzer-Gasse 19 is a richly decorated half-timbered building of 1535 which formerly housed the Mint, Consistory and District Court. It is now occupied by the Heimatmuseum, with the old Mint workshop and a Thomas Müntzer memorial room. The burgher's house adjoining the Museum (c. 1450), at Rittergasse 14, is believed to be the oldest house in Stolberg. Its six small rooms give some impression of the living conditions of medieval craftsmen. — Old Mint

Between the Markt and the Schloss, on the slopes of the hill, stands St Martin's Church (1485–90, with some earlier work), a Late Gothic aisled basilica with a richly furnished interior. In April 1525 Luther preached here against the peasant rising led by Thomas Müntzer.
North-west of the church is the aisleless St Mary's Chapel (consecrated 1482). — St Martin's Church

The Saigerturm and the Rittertor or Eselstor are relics of the town's 13th century fortifications. — Saigerturm, Rittertor

Nördlingen

K 6

Land: Bavaria
Altitude: 430m/1410ft
Population: 19,000

Nördlingen, chief town of the fertile Ries depression (a crater 10–25km/6–15 miles across caused by the fall of a meteorite 15 million years ago), between the Swabian and the Franconian Alb, is one of the three charming old free imperial cities (the others being Dinkelsbühl and Rothenburg) on the Romantische Strasse (see entry) between Würzburg and Augsburg. In the centre of the town is St George's Church, surrounded by a circular core of old houses, two outer rings of 16th and 17th century houses and a completely preserved circuit of medieval town walls. — Situation and characteristics

The *Town

In the Markt, in the exact centre of the town, is St George's Church, a Late Gothic hall-church (1427–1501), which has a Baroque high altar with Late Gothic carved figures. From the 90m/295ft high tower ("Daniel") there are fine panoramic views. — St George's Church

To the north of the church is the Late Gothic Town Hall (renovated 1934), with a handsome Renaissance external staircase of 1618.
Opposite the Town Hall is the Tanzhaus (1442–44; altered in 19th c.), with a statue of the Emperor Maximilian I (1513). — Town Hall

From the Markt Eisengasse leads to the Hafermarkt, in which is the Klösterle, a church which originally belonged to a house of Discalced friars. — Klösterle

Farther north, in a former hospital, is the Municipal Museum (geology of the Ries, prehistory and the early historical period, history of the town). There is also a new Ries Crater Museum. — Municipal Museum

To the south, near the town walls, is St Salvator's Church, originally the church of a Carmelite house (consecrated 1422), with 18th century frescoes. — St Salvator's Church

Neresheim Abbey

Town walls

There is an attractive walk (¾ hour) round the town on the old walls (14th–16th c.) with their fifteen towers.

Neresheim

*Abbey

20km/12½ miles south-west of Nördlingen is the little town of Neresheim, which is dominated by its Benedictine abbey (1699–1714), with a magnificent Baroque church (by Balthasar Neumann, 1745–92; ceiling paintings by Martin Knoller).

North Sea Coast   A 4 – C 1

Länder: Schleswig-Holstein, Lower Saxony, Bremen

Situation and characteristics

The German North Sea coast, some 300km/185 miles long as the crow flies, is divided into two parts, the East Frisian and the North Frisian area, by the estuary of the Elbe. Off both stretches of coast lie a string of islands which have become popular holiday resorts. The coastal area is an expanse of flat fenland protected by dykes, outside which is the Watt, an area of mud-flats which are dry only at low tide. The estuaries of the East Frisian rivers are protected from the inflow of sea-water by *siele,* gate-like sluices which close automatically at high tide.

Off the North Frisian coast are the Halligen, islands which are relics of an expanse of fenland not protected by dykes. Some of them are connected to the mainland by causeways.

Ecology

The harmful substances with which the North Sea is polluted come from various sources. Many rivers carry down salts, heavy metals and chemical residues from industrial conurbations and discharge them into the sea. Further pollution is caused by the dumping of dilute acids, the disposal of incinerated refuse and the uncontrolled jettisoning of ships' waste. The mortality among seals and the explosive growth of algae in recent years have been the most visible results of this endangering of the environment. In many areas there have been joint efforts by local people and holidaymakers to control pollution of the sea; a first "Holidaymakers' Parliament" was held at Frankfurt am Main in 1988; and the Association for the Protection of the German North Sea Coast (Schutz-gemeinschaft Deutsche Nordseeküste) is active in working for a clean North Sea and an unspoiled coast.

National Parks

The whole of the North Sea coast from the Danish frontier to the Elbe estuary, together with the North Frisian Islands (see below), now form the Schleswig-Holstein Watten-meer National Park. South-west of this extends the Lower Saxon Wattenmeer National Park, which takes in the East Frisian Islands (see below). Thus the German North Sea coast is an almost continuous protected area, interrupted only by the main shipping lanes.

The Watt

"Watt" is the name given to a coastal strip of land which at low tide is dry and at high tide is covered by the Wattenmeer. Along the German North Sea coast the Watt is between 7 and 10km (4½ and 6½ miles) wide, most of it lying inshore of the North and East Frisian Islands.

At low tide the Watt may look a tempting area for a walk, but it can be dangerous. In some parts of this flat coastal area the tide comes in with incredible speed, and visitors can easily be caught by the advancing waves, moving faster than they can. Walking in the Watt should, therefore, only be undertaken with a knowledgable guide, or at least after consulting the local tide tables. *Warning*

The unusual natural conditions in the Watt have given rise to an abundance of highly specialised forms of life. The Watt bottom consists of recent marine deposits (sand, silt, clay) with a high proportion of organic substances, which form the first link in the food chain. The Watt has little in the way of plant life: near high-water mark there are glassworts (*Salicornia europea*), farther seaward eelworts (*Zostera*), and occasionally also algae and seaweed. Most forms of animal life, therefore, have adjusted to the movement of the tides, either burying themselves in the ground at low tide or living permanently there. Only a few shellfish manage to survive above ground by storing water in their shells. Most of the denizens of the Watt (worms, shellfish, crustaceans) feed on organic substances floating in the water or lying on the bottom which they absorb in the water they breathe in or take in on the surface of the Watt. Some shellfish, shrimps and bristle worms are predators or scavengers. *Flora and fauna*

North Frisian Islands

The North Frisian islands of Sylt, Föhr and Amrum, lying off the north-west coast of Schleswig-Holstein, are ridges of sandy heathland (*geest*) which have escaped erosion or drowning by the sea and on Sylt and Amrum have been partly overlaid by dunes. While Sylt and Amrum have only narrow strips of fenland along their east coasts Föhr has a considerable area of fens. *Situation and characteristics*

Numerous prehistoric tombs bear witness to early human settlement. The islanders maintained their independence against the kings of Denmark. Then in the 19th century seaside resorts began to develop on the islands, with their healthy oceanic climate and unrestricted sunshine.

Sylt

See entry

Föhr

Föhr, the second largest of the North Frisian Islands (12km/7½ miles long and up to 8km/5 miles wide), lies south of Sylt, some 11km/7 miles from the mainland. Sheltered from the open sea by Sylt, Amrum and the Halligen, Föhr is surrounded by mud-flats. The southern part of the island is *geest* country, with no dunes; the north is fertile fenland, drained by canals and protected from the sea by a stone wall built in 1890. The islanders live mainly from tourism and agriculture.

Wyk
In the south-east of the island is the little town of Wyk, whose mild climate makes it a popular holiday resort (ferry service from the mainland port of Dagebüll), with a sandy beach and a seafront promenade. Frisian Museum (prehistory and the early historical period, domestic life, natural history, shipping).

From Dunsum, on the west coast of the island, it is possible at low tide to cross to the northern tip of Amrum on a track over the mud-flats (2km/1¼ miles).

Amrum

Amrum, the most southerly of the three North Frisian Islands, is 10km/6 miles long and up to 3km/2 miles wide. The main bathing beach is the 1km/¾ mile wide Kniepsand on the west side of the island (heavy surf).

Wittdün
The chief place on the island is the health resort of Wittdün (ferry service from the mainland via Föhr: see above).

From Wittdün a road runs north, passing the 67m/220ft high lighthouse (view; off the road to the right, at Steenodde, Bronze Age tombs), to the old Frisian village of Nebel, with richly decorated 18th century tombstones in the churchyard. To the west is a 7th century Viking cemetery excavated in 1845. To the north of the village of Norddorf is the starting-point of the walk over the mud-flats to Föhr (see above).

Nordstrand

The island of Nordstrand, lying off Husum (see entry), is connected to the mainland by a 2.5km/1½ mile long causeway. A 24km/15 mile long dyke surrounds an area of fenland which until a devastating storm tide in 1634 was part of the mainland. Odenbüll has a 13th century church (pulpit of 1605).

Südfall
To the west of Nordstrand is the little island of Südfall, one of the Halligen, which is used for the grazing of sheep (bird sanctuary).

Pellworm

Still farther west lies Pellworm, an island of fertile fenland enclosed by dykes. In the centre of the island is the Baroque New Church (1622), on an artificial mound (*warft*) the Romanesque Old Church, with a ruined tower.

Halligen

The Halligen are the small islands lying between Föhr and Amrum in the north and the Eiderstedt peninsula in the south. In the narrower sense the group includes only the islands of Oland, Langeness, Hooge, Gröde-Appelland, Habel, Nordstrandischmoor,

Norderoog, Süderoog and Südfall; but in the wider sense it is taken as including also the Hamburger Hallig (now linked with the mainland) and the larger islands of Nordstrand and Pellworm (see above).

The Halligen are the remains of an area of fenland which in prehistoric times was part of the mainland. In a storm tide they are flooded by the sea, apart from the houses and farmsteads on the man-made *warften*. As a result the soil is too salty to permit arable farming, and the land is used for the grazing of livestock.

The largest of the Halligen are the two dyked islands of Langeness (causeway to Dagebüll on the mainland) and Hooge. On the large Hanswarft on Hooge is the Hansensches Haus (1766), with the Königspesel (parlour), the finest example of an old Frisian house.

Langeness
Hooge

East Frisian Islands

The seven East Frisian islands of Borkum, Juist, Norderney, Baltrum, Langeoog, Spiekeroog and Wangerooge, which extend in a chain between the Ems and Weser estuaries, are now popular seaside resorts. Cars are allowed only on Borkum and Norderney.

Situation and
characteristics

Borkum

Borkum, lying 12km/7½ miles off the coast (ferry service from Emden), is the most westerly and the largest of the East Frisian Islands (8km/5 miles by 4km/2½ miles). At the west end is the town of Borkum, a seaside resort with a Kurhalle, a seafront promenade, two beaches (Nordstrand and Südstrand, part of which is a bird sanctuary), sea-water baths (artificial waves) and a 63m/207ft high lighthouse. In the eastern half of the island is the village of Ostend. There is a light railway from the harbour to the town of Borkum.

To the east of Borkum is the Lütje Hörn sand bank (bird sanctuary).

Lütje Hörn

Juist

East of Borkum is Juist (ferry from Norden-Norddeich), a long narrow island (17km/10½ miles long by up to 500m/550yds across) which is a popular holiday resort (no cars). The beautiful sandy beach on the north coast (Nordstrand) has a fringe of dunes. Half way along the south coast the little town of Juist has a seafront promenade, a museum (shipping, fishing, natural history, prehistory and the early historical period) and an art gallery (temporary exhibitions).

Off the west end of Juist is the island of Memmert (bird sanctuary).

Memmert

Norderney

Norderney (ferry from Norden-Norddeich) is the largest of the East Frisian Islands after Borkum (14km/8½ miles long, up to 2km/1¼ miles wide). It is the only island in the group with any great area of woodland (deciduous and coniferous). At the west end of the island lies the town of Norderney, the oldest seaside resort in Germany (founded 1797), with a beautiful Kurpark, a sea-water pool (artificial waves) and a casino. In the Argonnerwäldchen ("Little Argonne Forest") is a museum in a typical Norderney fisherman's house. There is a golf-course on the dunes.

Baltrum

Baltrum (ferry from Nessmersiel) is the smallest of the East Frisian Islands (6km/4 miles long by up to 1.5km/1 mile wide). It is a quiet and relaxing resort with a sea-water swimming pool (artificial waves).

411

Langeoog

Langeoog (ferry from Bensersiel) is 14km/8½ miles long by up to 2.5km/1½ miles wide. From the landing-stage a light railway runs to the resort of Langeoog (sea-water pool with artificial waves) at the west end of the island. Near the town is the new observation post of the German Sea Rescue Association.

Spiekeroog

The main feature of Spiekeroog (ferry from Neuharlingersiel) is a great expanse of dunes, partly covered by trees. In the eastern half of the island is a sandy beach more than 5km/3 miles long and 2km/1¼ miles wide, most of which has been formed only in the second half of this century – an illustration of the slow but steady eastward movement of all the East Frisian islands. The church (1696) in the little town of Spiekeroog contains fragments salvaged from one of the ships of the Spanish Armada which was wrecked off the island in 1588. The carriages of the light railway which runs west from the town are once again drawn by horses as they were originally.

Wangerooge

Wangerooge (9km/6 miles long by up to 1.5km/1 mile wide; ferry from Harle) is the most easterly of the East Frisian Islands. The little town of Wangerooge, in the centre of the island, is the second oldest German North Sea resort, founded in 1804; the older town was destroyed by a storm tide in 1854. Features of interest are the Old Lighthouse (Heimatmuseum), the new lighthouse and the West Tower. To the west of the town, in the coastal dunes, is a heated open-air swimming pool (sea-water). At the west end of the island is a narrow-gauge railway. Several bird sanctuaries.

Nürnberg (Nuremberg)   I 6

Land: Bavaria
Altitude: 340m/1115ft
Population: 465,000

Situation and characteristics

The ancient and famous town of Nürnberg (traditionally in English Nuremberg), once a free imperial city, lies in the well-wooded plain of the Middle Franconian Basin, on the river Pegnitz and the Rhine-Main-Danube Canal (the "Europa-Kanal"), making it Germany's newest port. It is the second largest city in Bavaria and one of the leading industrial and commercial centres in South Germany.

Lorenzer Seite ("St Lawrence Side")

Bahnhofsplatz

The Lorenzer Seite (named after its principal church, St Lorenz) is the district on the south side of the Pegnitz. The hub of the city's traffic is the Bahnhofsplatz, to the south-east of the town, round which are the railway station (Hauptbahnhof), the Head Post Office, the Frauentorturm and the Handwerkerhof Alt Nürnberg (half-timbered houses with traditional craft workshops).

Königstrasse

From Bahnhofsplatz the busy Königstrasse runs north-west into the old town. On the right is the 14th century St Martha's Church (Marthakirche; fine stained glass), in which the mastersingers held their singing schools between 1578 and 1620. Farther along, on the left, can be seen the Mauthalle, an old corn and salt store (1498–1512). Beyond this is a pedestrian zone leading to Lorenzer Platz, with St Lawrence's Church.

** National Germanic Museum

On the south side of the old town, at Kornmarkt 1, is the National Germanic Museum (Germanisches Nationalmuseum), partly housed in a former monastery, with a rich collection covering all aspects of German art and culture and a large library. The same building houses the Industrial Museum (Gewerbemuseum), installed here in 1989.

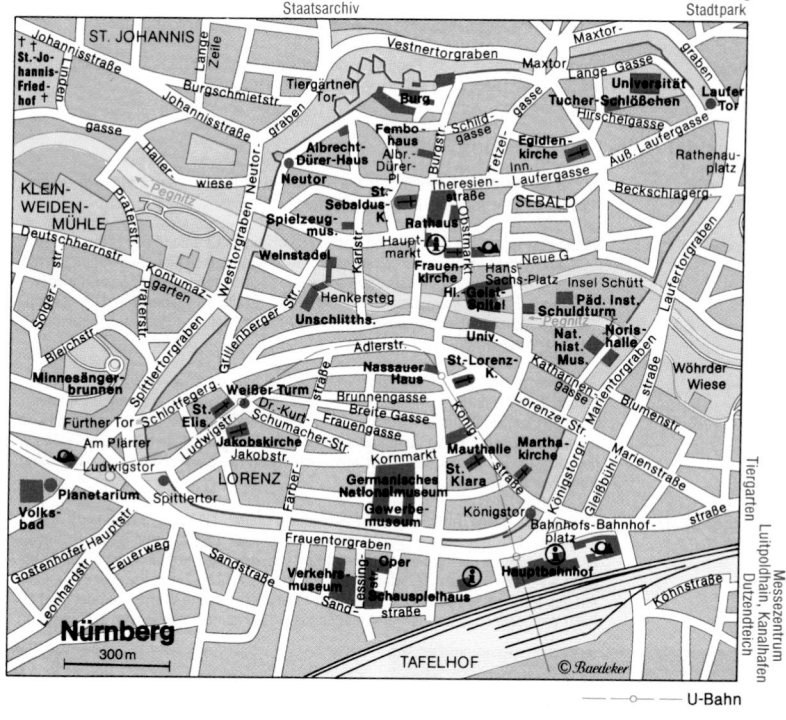

ST. JOHANNIS
Johannisstraße
St.-Jo-
hannis-
Fried-
hof
Burgschmietstr
Johannisstraße
gasse
Haller-
Vestnertorgraben
Maxtor-
Tiergärtner-
Tor
Burg
Fembo-
haus
Albrecht-
Dürer-Haus
Neutor
St.
Sebaldus-
K.
Spielzeug-
mus.
Weinstadel
Henkersteg
Unschlittb.
Minnesänger-
brunnen
Fürther Tor
Am Plärrer
Ludwigstor
Planetarium
Volks-
bad
Gostenhofer Hauptstr
Leonhardstr
Feuerweg

KLEIN-
WEIDEN-
MÜHLE
Deutschherrnstr
Sandel-
Pralerstr
Kontumaz-
garten
wiese
Pegnitz
Bleichstr
Spittlertorgraben
Weißer Turm
Dr.-Kurt-
Schumacher-Str
St.
Elis.
Jakobskirche
Jakobstr
LORENZ
Spittlertor
Sandstraße
Farber

Maxtor-
graben
Lange Gasse
Universität
Tucher-Schlößchen
Laufer
Tor
Hirschelgasse
Egidien-
kirche
Rathenau-
platz
Beckschlagerg
Theresien-
straße
SEBALD
Hans-
Sachs-Platz
Neue G
Insel Schütt
Nat.
hist.
Mus.
Päd. Inst.
Schuldturm
Noris-
halle
Wöhrder
Wiese
Kornmarkt
Mauthalle
St.
Klara
Martha-
kirche
Königstor
Bahnhofs-Bahnhof-
platz
Hauptbahnhof
Köhnstraße

Messezentrum
Luitpoldhain, Kanalhafen
Tiergarten
Dutzendteich

Nürnberg
300 m
TAFELHOF
© Baedeker

——o—— U-Bahn

Immediately south, outside the old town walls (entrance in Lessingstrasse), is the Transport Museum (Verkehrsmuseum; railways, postal services).

Transport Museum

The Frauentorgraben runs west, parallel to the southern section of the town walls (see below), to the Plärrer, a major traffic intersection. At No. 41 is the Nicolaus Copernicus Planetarium. From here the Spittlertor leads into the south-western part of the old town.

Plärrer

Near the Spittlertor, along Ludwigstrasse, is Jakobsplatz, with the 14th century St James's Church (Jakobskirche; Protestant). On the north side of the square is St Elizabeth's Church (R.C.), a domed church built between 1785 and 1806.

Jakobsplatz

From here Ludwigstrasse (now a pedestrian zone) and its continuation Karolinenstrasse lead to Lorenzer Platz (also reached direct from the station by way of Königstrasse: see above).

In Lorenzer Platz stands the twin-towered Gothic church of St Lawrence (St-Lorenz-kirche; 13th–15th c.; Protestant), the city's largest church. Above the beautiful west doorway (c. 1355) is a rose window 9m/30ft in diameter. Outstanding among the many works of art it contains are the "Annunciation" by Veit Stoss (1517–18) which hangs in the choir, the tabernacle by Adam Krafft (1493–96), the crucifix by Veit Stoss on the high altar, the Krell Altar (behind the high altar; c. 1480), with the oldest surviving representation of the town, and the superb stained glass (1477–93) in the choir.

St Lawrence's Church

North-west of the church is the Fountain of Virtue (1589), and opposite this is the tower-like Nassauer Haus (13th–15th c.).

From here the Museumsbrücke crosses the Pegnitz to the Sebalder Seite.

Bridges

From the bridges over the Pegnitz, particularly the Maxbrücke, the Weinstadel bridge and the Henkersteg, there are fine views of the old town.

Sebalder Seite ("St Sebaldus Side")

Hauptmarkt

On the north side of the Pegnitz is the Hauptmarkt, in which stands the 14th century "Beautiful Fountain", with numerous figures.

*Frauenkirche

On the east side of the square is the Gothic Frauenkirche (Church of Our Lady, 1352–61; R.C.). Above the porch with its rich sculptural decoration is the "Männleinlaufen", an old clock with mechanical figures (the seven Electors pacing round the Emperor Charles IV – a reference to the promulgation of the Golden Bull in 1356) which perform daily at noon. Notable features of the interior are the Tucher Altar (c. 1440) and two handsome monuments by Adam Krafft.

Town Hall

On the north side of the Hauptmarkt can be found the new Town Hall (Rathaus; 1954). Behind it, to the north, is the old building (by Jakob Wolff, 1616–22; magnificent doorways on west side); under it are the old dungeons and torture chamber (which can be visited). Between the two buildings is the famous Gänsemännchen fountain (c. 1555), depicting the figure of a Franconian peasant carrying two geese, with the water flowing from their beaks.

**St Sebaldus's Church

To the west of the Town Hall is St Sebaldus's Church (1225–73; Protestant), with a magnificent Gothic east choir (1379). On the outside of the choir is the Schreyer-Landauer tomb, a masterpiece by Adam Krafft (1492). Inside the church, on a pillar in the north aisle, can be seen the "Madonna in an Aureole" (1420–25). In the east choir is the famous tomb of St Sebaldus (1508–19), a masterpiece of the bronze-founder's art by Peter Vischer and his sons (silver sarcophagus of 1397 containing the saint's remains; on

"Beautiful Fountain"

Dürer House

414

the east end Peter Vischer with his leather apron and chisel). Behind the tomb is a moving Crucifixion group by Veit Stoss (1507 and 1520). Organ, with 6000 pipes.

To the west of the church, at Karlstrasse 13–15, we come to the Nürnberg Toy Museum (Spielzeugmuseum), with toys from many different countries and periods and a large model railway layout.

Toy Museum

At the north end of Albrecht-Dürer-Strasse, below the castle hill, is the 15th century Dürer House, in which Dürer lived from 1509 until his death in 1528. It displays copies of some of his works.
At the nearby Tiergärtner Tor is a perfectly preserved little medieval square.

Dürer House

In Burgstrasse, which leads up from the Town Hall to the Burg, is the late 16th century Fembohaus (No. 15, on left), the town's best preserved old patrician house, now occupied by the Heimatmuseum (domestic interiors, history of the town).

Fembohaus

To the north of the old town rises the Burg (alt. 351m/1152ft; 220m/240yds long, 50m/165ft across). All legitimate German kings and emperors from 1050 to 1571 resided in the castle, and many imperial diets were held here. At the lower end are the old imperial stables (Kaiserstallung), built in 1495 as a granary and now occupied by a youth hostel. Immediately west of this is the Pentagonal Tower, the oldest building in the town (c. 1040), a relic of an earlier castle on the site. Higher up is the Kaiserburg (Imperial Castle), built in the 11th century and much altered in later centuries, with the Sinwell Tower (panoramic views) and the "Deep Well". The castle (conducted visit) has a number of fine rooms, including the 12th century chapel, and contains some notable works of art.

*Burg

In Egidienplatz, near the east end of the Sebalder Seite, stands St Giles' Church (Egidienkirche; 1711–18), Nürnberg's only Baroque church. In the Gothic Tetzel Chapel is the Landauer tomb by Adam Krafft.
The Municipal Library, opposite the church to the north-west, incorporates the arcades of the Pellerhaus (1605) which stood on this site.

St Giles' Church

To the south, in Hans-Sachs-Platz, can be seen a monument to the cobbler and mastersinger Hans Sachs (1495–1576), whose workshop was near here. On the south side of the square, spanning an arm of the Pegnitz, is the Heilig-Geist-Spital (Hospital of the Holy Ghost), founded in 1331, in the courtyard of which is a Crucifixion group by Adam Krafft.

Hans-Sachs-Platz

From here the Spitalbrücke leads on to the island of Schütte, between two arms of the Pegnitz, with the 14th century Männerschuldturm ("Men's Fault" Tower). To the southeast are the Katharinenbau and the Natural History Museum.

*Town Walls

Nürnberg has preserved most of its circuit of walls (14th–15th c., strengthened in 16th–17th c.), with their numerous gates and towers.
The finest stretch of walls is on the west side of the town, between the massive Spittlertor (see above) and the former Maxtor. The best view of the walls, the old town and the Burg is from the Fürther Tor.

Eastern and South-Eastern Districts

On the east side of the town, at the Schmausenbuck, is the Tiergarten (Zoo), with a dolphinarium.

Tiergarten

To the south-east of the town is the Luitpoldhain, with the Meistersingerhalle (concert hall, congress centre). Farther south are the Dutzendteich park, with a number of small lakes, and the remains of the Reichsparteitaggelände, the arena built for Nazi party rallies.

Luitpoldhain
Dutzendteich

Near the Rhine-Main-Danube Canal, in the Schweinau district, rises the 282m/925ft high Telecommunications Tower (1980; viewing platform, revolving restaurant).

Telecommunications
Tower

Palm Beach   In Stein, on the west side of Nürnberg, lies the Palm Beach "Leisure Paradise" (indoor and outdoor swimming pools, water-chute, sauna, solarium, etc.).

North-Western Districts

St Johannis   In the north-western suburb of St Johannis can be found the St Johannis Cemetery, with
Cemetery   the graves of many notable citizens of Nürnberg, including Dürer, Veit Stoss, the humanist Willibald Pirkheimer and Hans Sachs.

Surroundings of Nürnberg

Schloss Neunhof   9km/6 miles north of Nürnberg is Schloss Neunhof, a moated castle first mentioned in the records in 1246, which is the best preserved of the mansions of Nürnberg patricians (of which there were originally about sixty around the town). In the castle is a Hunting Museum.

Schwabach   15km/9 miles south of Nürnberg we come to Schwabach. Handsome old half-timbered houses in the Markt; Late Gothic Town Church (15th c.), with a 13m/43ft high tabernacle of 1505 and a high altar of 1508 (altarpiece of the school of Michael Wolgemut, carving possibly by Veit Stoss).

Erlangen   See entry

Fürth   See entry

Oberammergau   M 6

Land: Bavaria
Altitude: 850m/2790ft
Population: 5000

Situation and   Oberammergau, situated in a wide basin in the Ammer valley, surrounded by the
characteristics   foothills of the Ammergau Alps, is a popular altitude and winter sports resort, famed for its woodcarving (with a state school of woodcarving) and still more widely known for its Passion Play.
The woodcarving tradition goes back to the 17th century, as does the Passion Play, which was first performed in 1634. The Passion Play was instituted in fulfilment of a vow made in 1633, when the town was stricken by plague. Since then it has been performed every ten years (next in the year 2000).

The Town

Many houses in the town are decorated externally with frescoes by Franz Zwirk (1748–92) in the technique known as *lüftlmalerei,* such as the Pilatushaus (1784; now a craft centre) and the Geroldhaus (1778).

Parish church   The sumptuous Rococo parish church (1736–42) is one of the finest creations of Josef Schmuzer; good ceiling paintings by Matthäus Günther.

Heimatmuseum   At No. 8 in the main street is the Heimatmuseum (local woodcarving, stained glass, Nativity groups).

Passion Play Theatre   At the north end of the village stands the Passion Play Theatre (1930), with seating for 4800 spectators and an open stage with the natural setting as a backdrop.

Laber   A cabin cableway ascends the Laber (1684m/5525ft; view), from which it is a 15 minutes' walk to the Ettaler Mandl (see Ettal, Surroundings).

Oberammergau wood-carver

On the west side of the town is a chair-lift to the Kolbensattel (1250m/4100ft).

Kolbensattel

Oberhof

G 6

Land: Thuringia
Altitude: 800–836m/2625–2740ft
Population: 3000

The holiday and health resort of Oberhof, 10km/6 miles north of Suhl, is attractively situated in the hills of the Thuringian Forest.

Situation and characteristics

*Winter Sports Centre

The name of Oberhof is inseparably associated with the development of winter sports. The first small ski-jump was constructed here in 1906, to be followed in 1925 by the large ski-jump on the Wadeberg; and in recent years Oberhof has established a great reputation as a winter sports centre. There are excellent training facilities for biathlon skiers, bobbers, bob racers and langlaufers. Among the facilities used for international competitions are the ski-jump complex on the Rennstein, the new biathlon stadium and the langlauf trail on the Grenzadler (World Cup contests). There is also a first-class training and competition bobsleigh run at the Obere Schweizerhütte.

Oberstdorf

M 5

Land: Bavaria
Altitude: 843m/2766ft
Population: 11,000

417

Bobsleigh run, Oberhof

Situation and characteristics	The substantial market town of Oberstdorf lies at the head of the Iller valley, which cuts deep into the Allgäu Alps. The three source streams of the Iller – the Trettach, the Stillach and the Breitach – converge just below the town. Its excellent climate and beautiful situation within a ring of towering mountains have made Oberstdorf the most popular altitude resort, climbing base and winter sports centre in the Allgäu (see entry).

The Town

	Behind the neo-Gothic parish church, with its conspicuous tower, is the old churchyard. To the south lies the Kurplatz, with a covered promenade. From here there is a magnificent view of the mountains.
Spa and Congress Centre	South-west of the church is the Spa and Congress Centre, with the Kurhaus and treatment centre. Nearby are the wave baths.
Heimatmuseum	To the east of the church can be found the interesting Heimatmuseum (among whose exhibits is the largest shoe in the world). Close by is the lower station of the Nebelhorn cableway (see below).
Ice Stadium	Beyond the Trettach is the large Ice Stadium. To the rear, higher up, are the two Schattenberg ski-jumps.

Surroundings of Oberstdorf

*Breitachklamm	2.5km/1½ miles north of Oberstdorf on B 19 a side road runs west to the Breitachklamm (gorge). From the parking place at the entrance to the gorge it is an hour's walk up the Klammweg to the Walser Schanz inn.
*Heini Klöpfer ski-jump *Fellhorn	From Oberstdorf a road ascends the Stillach valley. 5km/3 miles up the valley, off the road to the right, is the Heini Klöpfer ski-jump (maximum jump 170m/185yds), with a lift

Nebelhorn, near Oberstdorf

up to the starting-point (fine view of the Freibergsee). The road ends at the lower station of the cabin cableway up the Fellhorn (2037m/6683ft; extensive skiing area, with many ski-lifts; good hill walking; beautiful Alpine flora).

On the south-eastern outskirts of Oberstdorf is a cabin cableway running up to a station at 1932m/6339ft; ski-lifts), from which a chair-lift continues to the summit of the Nebelhorn (2224m/7297ft).

See entry

*Nebelhorn

Kleinwalsertal

Oberwiesenthal

See Erzgebirge

Odenwald

H 1–4

Länder: Baden-Württemberg, Hesse

The Odenwald is a beautiful upland region, some 40km/25 miles wide, extending along the east side of the Rhine plain between Darmstadt and Heidelberg and separated from the Spessart (see entry) to the north-east by the Main valley (see entry). The western part, the Vorderer Odenwald, in which the older rocks (granites) come to the surface and the forests are predominantly deciduous, is a region of rounded hills, much dissected by valleys, which along the western edge rise to 300–400m/900–1300ft above the Rhine plain. The Hinterer Odenwald, to the east, is a more uniform sandstone plateau covered with coniferous forest which merges in the south-east into the fertile limestone plain of the Bauland area. In the south the Neckar has cut its way through the hills in a beautiful winding valley, above which, at Eberbach, rises the Katzenbuckel (626m/2054ft), the highest peak in the Odenwald.

Situation and characteristics

Town Hall, Michelstadt

Through the Odenwald, from Frankfurt to Eberbach

Leave Frankfurt am Main by way of the southern district of Sachsenhausen.

Dieburg	Dieburg lies at a road junction where there was already a settlement in Roman times. Fine Baroque pilgrimage church (1701–20); museum, with finds from a Roman sanctuary of Mithras (2nd c. A.D.).
Gross-Umstadt	This little wine town lies on the Odenwald foothills sloping down to the Rhine plain. Historic old town centre, with Renaissance houses; Heimatmuseum in the Gruberhof.
Otzberg	3.5km/2 miles beyond Gross-Umstadt a side road branches off on the right to the Otzberg (368m/1207ft), crowned by an old castle.
Höchst	Höchst has a Gothic church of 1568. At Hummetroth, to the west, is the Haselburg, a relic of the Roman settlement which once stood here (2nd c. A.D.).
Breuberg	North-east of Höchst, off the main road, is Breuberg, over which looms the imposing Burg Breuberg (12th c.; fine interior).
Bad König	South of Höchst can be found the thermal resort of Bad König (drinking and bathing cures; recommended for rheumatism and disorders of the metabolism).
*Michelstadt	Michelstadt lies at the intersection with the Nibelungenstrasse, which runs from Worms to Wertheim. In the Markt stands the picturesque Town Hall (1484), one of the oldest oak-beamed buildings in Germany. Behind it is the Late Gothic church (1461–1537), with the tombs of the Counts of Erbach (14th–17th c.).

On the south-east side of the old town, in the Kellerei, a relic of the old castle, are the Odenwald Museum and the Toy Museum.

In Steinbach is Einhard's Basilica, built in the 9th century by Charlemagne's biographer Einhard. Nearby is Schloss Fürstenau (14th–16th c.).

*Einhard's Basilica

Erbach, the great centre of ivory-carving in Germany, has a training college and an Ivory Museum (ivory-carving from the Middle Ages to the present day). The Schloss (16th–17th c.), with a round tower of 1200, has fine collections of art and weapons; in the Einhard Chapel can be seen the stone sarcophagus of Einhard and his wife.

Erbach

On the plateau is Beerfelden, with the Mümlingquelle (the "Twelve-Spouted Fountain"). Some 600m/660yds from the town is a triple gallows.
From here the road crosses the watershed between the Main and the Neckar and descends to Eberbach, in the Neckar valley (see entry).

Beerfelden

Offenbach

H 4

Land: Hesse
Altitude: 100m/330ft
Population: 110,000

This busy industrial town, on the left bank of the Main above Frankfurt, is the main centre of the German leatherworking industry.
The Kaiser-Friedrich-Quelle, drilled in 1885, is a sodium spring with the highest alkaline content in Germany (table water).

Situation and characteristics

Sights

On the banks of the Main stands the Early Renaissance Schloss Isenburg (1564–78).

Schloss

Kirchgasse leads to the Büsing Park, with the Baroque Büsing-Palais (restored; cultural and congress centre) and the Park Baths. In a side wing added about 1900 is the Klingspor Museum (international printing and calligraphy since 1890).

Büsing-Palais
*Klingspor Museum

In Frankfurter Strasse, which leads west from the town centre, at No. 86, are the German Leather Museum and the German Shoe Museum.

*German
Leather Museum

In the west of the town is the Municipal Museum (history of the town; porcelain and faience; dolls' houses; section on Alois Senefelder, inventor of lithography).

Municipal
Museum

Surroundings of Offenbach

4.5km/3 miles south-west is Heusenstamm, with Schloss Schönborn (17th c.) and the parish church of SS Cecilia and Barbara (by Balthasar Neumann, 1739–44).

Heusenstamm

8km/5 miles south-east we come to Seligenstadt, named after a Benedictine abbey founded in 825 by Einhard, Charlemagne's biographer, with an Early Romanesque church ("Einhard's Basilica") which was altered in the 13th century. The remains of Einhard and his wife are preserved in a Baroque sarcophagus. There are remains of a Hohenstaufen stronghold and of the old town walls.

Seligenstadt

Offenburg

K 3

Land: Baden-Württemberg
Altitude: 161m/528ft
Population: 51,000

Oldenburg

Situation and characteristics	The busy town of Offenburg, situated at the point where the river Kinzig emerges from the foothills of the Black Forest into the fertile Upper Rhine plain, is an important road and rail junction and the chief town in the Ortenau wine-producing area.

The Town

Marktplatz	In the Marktplatz are the Town Hall (1741) and, south of this, the Königshof (1714–17), originally the residence of the imperial governor, now the police headquarters.
Ritterhaus Museum	To the east, in Ritterstrasse, stands the Ritterhaus (1784), with the Ritterhaus Museum (regional history, folk art and traditions, costumes, colonial history).
Fischmarkt	On the east side of the main street is the Fischmarkt, in which are the Lion Fountain (1599) and the Salt-House (1786). Nearby, at Glaserstrasse 8, can be seen the former mikve (Jewish ritual bath; 13th–14th c.).
Capuchin Convent	On the south side of the old town is a former Capuchin convent (1641–47), with a picturesque cloister.
Holy Cross Church	North-west of the Marktplatz stands the church of the Holy Cross (Heiligkreuzkirche; 17th–18th century. In front of it is a fine group of Christ on the Mount of Olives (1524).
Franciscan friary	In the northward continuation of the main street, on the left, is a Franciscan friary, with a Baroque church which has a Silbermann organ.

Oldenburg

Land: Lower Saxony
Altitude: 8m/26ft
Population: 138,000

Situation and characteristics	This former grand-ducal capital lies on the river Hunte and on the Hunte-Ems Canal. It is a university town, a marketing centre for the agricultural produce of the surrounding area and a town of varied industries.

The Town

Markt	In the centre of the old town, which is surrounded by gardens and watercourses on the line of its old fortifications, lies the Markt, with the Town Hall (1887) and St Lambert's Church (13th, 18th and 19th c.).
Haus Degode	West of the Markt is Haus Degode, a handsome half-timbered building of 1617.
Schloss	To the south of the Markt can be found the Grand-Ducal Palace (17th–18th c.), with the beautiful palace gardens behind it. It now houses the Landesmuseum of Art and Culture (art from the Gothic period to the present day, period furniture, folk art and traditions). A little way south of the museum is the Augusteum, a gallery of 20th century art.
Natural History Museum	Near the Augusteum, on the Damm (which runs south-east from the Schlossplatz), is the Museum of Natural History and Prehistory (geology and ecology of the region, archaeology).
Lappan	On the northern edge of the old town stands the Lappan, the tower of the old Chapel of the Holy Ghost (1468), the oldest building in the town and a prominent landmark; it is now occupied by the Verkehrsverein (tourist information office).
Municipal Museum	Farther north, in Raiffeisenstrasse, is the Municipal Museum (regional history and art), and to the north-east, beyond the railway station, the Weser-Ems-Halle (sporting events, concerts, congresses, etc.).

On the north-west side of the town centre is the Peter-Friedrich-Ludwigshospital, an elegant neo-classical building which now houses the town's Cultural Centre. Cultural Centre

Farther north-west, near the motorway, lies the Botanic Garden. Botanic Garden

Zwischenahner Meer

17km/10½ miles north-west of Oldenburg, in the Ammerland area, we come to the Zwischenahner Meer, a lake over 3km/2 miles long and up to 2.5km/1½ miles wide. On its southern shore is the spa (mud-baths, Kneipp cure) of Bad Zwischenahn, with an open-air museum of typical Ammerland houses.

Wildeshausen

40km/25 miles south-east of Oldenburg, on the river Hunte, lies the little town of Wildeshausen, with a 13th century church (14th c. wall paintings) and a Gothic Town Hall. To the south of the town are prehistoric burial areas (the Pestrup cemetery, the Kleinenkneter Steine).

West of Wildeshausen and north of Visbek, near the motorway, are the "Visbek Bride" and the "Visbek Bridegroom" – two Neolithic chamber tombs respectively 82m/269ft and 108m/354ft long. Visbek

Cloppenburg

42km/26 miles south-west of Oldenburg is Cloppenburg, with Germany's oldest museum village: 52 old buildings of the 16th–19th centuries, including a church, a village school, windmills and craftsmen's houses. * Museum village

Evening on the Zwischenahner Meer

Oranienburg   D 8

Land: Brandenburg
Altitude: 36m/118ft
Population: 28,600

Situation and characteristics
Oranienburg lies north of Berlin, to the west of the Lehnitzsee, which is traversed by the Oder-Havel Canal.

Sights

Schloss Oranienburg
Schloss Oranienburg was built in 1651–55 (by J. G. Memhardt and M. M. Smids) and altered and enlarged in 1688–95 (by J. A. Nering and M. Grünberg); on the town front can be seen an attic storey with figures of the Seasons. Restored in 1948–60 after wartime destruction, the interior is now entirely modern in style except for the Porcelain Cabinet (stucco ceiling; painting by Terwesten, restored 1965). The house is not open to the public.

Pleasure garden
The Baroque pleasure garden was converted into a landscaped park in the 19th century. Its most notable features are the gateway (by J. A. Nering, 1690) and the Orangery (by G. C. Berger, 1754; restored 1967).

Heimatmuseum
The Heimatmuseum occupies an Early Baroque house (1657) at Breite Strasse 1.

Old Orphanage
At Havelstrasse 29 is the Old Orphanage (1665–71), the right-hand half of which was destroyed during the Second World War.

* Sachsenhausen Concentration Camp (Memorial Site)

The first Nazi concentration camp was installed in an old brewery here in 1933; then in 1936 the Sachsenhausen mass extermination camp was built to the east of the town. Of the 200,000 inmates of the camp over 100,000 were murdered.
The Sachsenhausen Memorial Site, built between 1958 and 1961, was designed by a group of architects led by L. Deiters, with sculpture by R. Graetz and W. Grzimek.
A museum on the history of the camp is housed is the inmates' kitchen.

Osnabrück   E 3

Land: Lower Saxony
Altitude: 64m/210ft
Population: 150,000

Situation and characteristics
The old episcopal city and new university town of Osnabrück lies in the Hase valley, attractively framed by the hills of the Wiehengebirge and Teutoburg Forest. It is a busy commercial and industrial city, linked by a branch canal with the Mittelland Canal.

Sights

Cathedral
The historic centre of the city, in the heart of the old town, is the Cathedral (Dom) of St Peter (R.C.), founded by Charlemagne at the end of the 8th century and dating in its present form, with its massive south-west tower and the slenderer north-west tower, from the 13th century. Notable features of the interior are the fine bronze font (1225), the Triumphal Cross group (1250) and the 16th century statues of apostles on the pillars of the nave. The adjoining Diocesan Museum (entrance through the cloister) contains among much else the valuable cathedral treasury. In the Domhof can be seen the Löwenpudel ("Lion Poodle"), and in the Grosse Domsfreiheit are the Episcopal Chan-

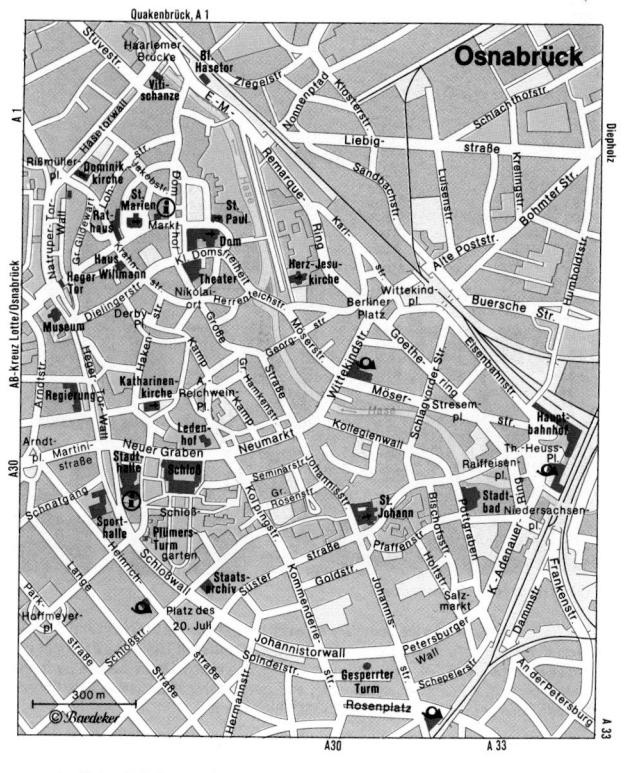

cery, the Bishop's Palace and a bronze statue of the statesman and historian Justus Möser (1720–94).

To the west of the Cathedral lies the Markt, surrounded by gabled houses (rebuilt in the original style). On the west side of the square stands the Town Hall (Rathaus; 1477–1512), with an interesting treasury and the Peace Chamber, in which the peace treaty between the Emperor, the Protestant Estates and the Swedes at the end of the Thirty Years' War was signed in 1648 (see also Münster). Immediately adjoining the Town Hall is the Municipal Weigh-House (1531).   *Town Hall*

St Mary's Church (13th–15th c.; Protestant), in the centre of the square, has a beautiful winged altar from Antwerp (1520), a 14th century Triumphal Cross group and the tomb of Justus Möser (under the ambulatory).   St Mary's Church

Between the Town Hall and the Heger Tor is a well restored quarter of the old town. In Krahnstrasse and Bierstrasse, to the west of the Markt, are a number of old half-timbered houses (Haus Willmann, 1586; Walhalla inn, 1690). Heger Strasse (old drinking-houses; antique shops) leads to the Heger Tor (rebuilt in neo-classical style in 1817 as the Waterloo Gate), part of the town's old fortifications. Other remains of the fortifications, along the "Wallstrassen" which now mark their line, are the Bucksturm (collection of medieval weapons and instruments of torture), the Bürgergehorsam, the Vitischanze, with the Bärenturm, and the Pernickelturm.   Heger Tor quarter

On the Heger-Tor-Wall is the Museum of Cultural History (folk traditions, history, art).   Museum

Old Town Hall, Osnabrück

Neuer Graben Schloss	The Neuer Graben marks the boundary between the old town to the north and the new town to the south. At its west end is the Stadthalle, and near this is the Palace of the Prince-Bishops (1668–90), now occupied by the University. On its north side is the Ledenhof, with a Renaissance bell-cote, and beyond this is St Catherine's Church (Katharinenkirche; 14th c.), with a 103m/338ft high tower.
St John's Church	In Johannisstrasse stands St John's Church (St Johann; 13th c.), the parish church of the new town, which grew up round it. It has a high altar (1525) of the school of the Master of Osnabrück.
Zoo	Farther south, on the Schölerberg, are the Zoo (with some 1800 animals) and the Museum am Schölerberg (planetarium; nature and the environment).

Surroundings of Osnabrück

Bad Iburg	16km/10 miles south of Osnabrück, in the Teutoburg Forest (see entry), lies the little spa (Kneipp cure) of Bad Iburg, with a castle of the Bishops of Osnabrück (17th and 18th c.). On the Dörenberg (331m/1086ft) is an outlook tower.
Tecklenburg	The little hill town of Tecklenburg lies 22km/13½ miles south-west of Osnabrück in the Teutoburg Forest. Commandingly situated above the town is a ruined castle (open-air theatre).
Bad Essen	24km/15 miles north-east of Osnabrück, at the foot of the Wiehengebirge, is the brine spa of Bad Essen, with handsome half-timbered houses and a 14th century church.

Oybin

See Zittau, Surroundings

Paderborn

Land: North Rhine-Westphalia
Altitude: 119m/390ft
Population: 122,000

The old Westphalian imperial, episcopal and Hanseatic city of Paderborn lies at the source of the Pader in the eastern part of the Münster lowlands, between the Teutoburg Forest and the Eggegebirge. The Pader emerges from the ground below the Cathedral at five different spots, with more than 200 springs.

Situation and characteristics

The Town

In the Domplatz, in the centre of the old town, stands the Cathedral of St Mary, St Liborius and St Kilian (11th–13th c.; R.C.), a long building (over 100m/330ft) with a 94m/308ft high west tower which is a distinctive landmark. The main south doorway (the Paradise Doorway) has interesting Romanesque figural decoration (1250–60). The most notable features of the interior are a number of fine monuments (including the tomb of Bishop Dietrich von Fürstenberg, d. 1618), the relics of St Liborius in the large crypt and the episcopal burial vault. In the cloister is an unusual stained glass window, the 16th century Hasenfenster ("Hare Window"), depicting three hares with only three ears between them.

*Cathedral

Entered from the cloister is the richly stocked Diocesan Museum (Shrine of St Liborius, 1627; Imad Madonna, *c.* 1050; sculpture, panel paintings, liturgical utensils, etc.).

*Diocesan Museum

Paderborn Cathedral

Pasewalk

	The foundations of a basilica dating from the time of Charlemagne were found under the Cathedral in 1979–80.
Kaiserpfalz	On the north side of the Cathedral are the remains of a Carolingian and a later Ottonian/Salian imperial stronghold (Kaiserpfalz) which were excavated and partly reconstructed from 1945 onwards (museum, function rooms). Here too is St Bartholomew's Chapel (1017), believed to be the oldest hall-church in Germany, with notably fine acoustics.
St Ulrich's Church	Opposite the Diocesan Museum, to the south, is St Ulrich's Church (12th c.; R.C.), Paderborn's oldest parish church, with an octagonal tower and a Baroque façade of 1746–49.
Town Hall	From the Domplatz a pedestrian street, the Schildern, runs south-west to Rathausplatz, which is dominated by the Town Hall, a magnificent three-gabled Late Renaissance building (1613–15). The Town Hall contains a natural history museum.
Heisingsches Haus	A little way west, in Marienplatz, can be seen the handsome Heisingsches Haus (c. 1600), with a richly decorated façade.
Sources of Pader	To the west of the Cathedral is the Abdinghofkirche (11th c.; Protestant), a twin-towered Romanesque church. Below the church, in a beautiful park, the sources of the Pader emerge.
Museum	To the north of the town centre is the Adam and Eve House, the town's oldest half-timbered building, with a richly carved façade. It is now occupied by the Museum on the History of the Town and the exhibition rooms of the Kunstverein (Art Association).
Busdorf Church	On the east side of the old town, entered through the remains of the Romanesque cloister, stands the Busdorf Church (11th, 12th and 17th c.), which has a crucifix of 1280, a Late Gothic tabernacle and monuments of the 15th–18th centuries.
	In the south of the old town are the Baroque Franciscan Church (1691) and the Jesuit Church (1682–84; formerly the University Church), which has a rich treasury.
Schloss Neuhaus	North-west of the town centre, in the Neuhaus district, is Schloss Neuhaus (13th–16th c.), once the residence of the Prince-Bishops, with four wings laid out round a central courtyard, massive corner towers and a moat. It is now occupied by a school and the Municipal Art Gallery.

Pasewalk

	Land: Mecklenburg-West Pomerania Altitude: 12m/39ft Population: 15,900
Situation and characteristics	Pasewalk, chief town of a district, lies on the river Uecker, in the rolling landscape of the northern Uckermark.

The Town

Town walls	Pasewalk has preserved some remains of its old town walls and a number of towers and gates – the Prenzlauer Tor (c. 1450) to the south, the Mühlentor (c. 1450) to the north-west and two towers, the "Kiek in de Mark" (1445) and the Pulverturm (Powder Tower; 15th c.).
St Mary's Church	The parish church of St Mary was built in the 14th century on granite foundations of the 13th century; it has a fine altar with a copy of Raphael's "Bearing of the Cross". The interior is at present in course of restoration. In front of the church stands the limestone Mordkreuz ("Murder Cross"; 1367).
St Nicholas's Church	St Nicholas's Church (13th–14th) was rebuilt in the Late Gothic period. The tower, badly damaged in 1945, was restored after the war.

The Hospital of St Spiritus in Ringstrasse is made up of three buildings, the oldest of which is a two-storey brick-built wing (c. 1500) with decorative blind arches on the gable. The Hospital is now an old people's home.

At Grosse Kirchstrasse 17 is the Elendshaus, a small brick building with a plaster cladding, formerly a poorhouse.

At the corner of Baustrasse and Kleine Kirchenstrasse can be seen the Jagdschlösschen, a small two-storey Renaissance hunting lodge.

Passau

Land: Bavaria
Altitude: 290m/950ft
Population: 52,000

The old episcopal city of Passau is magnificently situated on the Austrian frontier at the junction of the Danube, here only 240m/260yds wide, with the Inn (290m/315yds wide). With its houses in the Italian style characteristic of the towns in the Inn and Salzach valleys, dominated by the Oberhaus fortress and the Mariahilf church, it presents a townscape of arresting beauty. Alexander von Humboldt counted this "city of the three rivers" among the seven most beautifully situated towns in the world.

There are boat services from Passau down the Danube to the Black Sea.

The *Town

The old town lies on a narrow tongue of land between the Danube and the Inn, its houses huddling round a hill from which picturesque stepped lanes lead down to the two rivers. The flat-roofed houses in the German/Italian style characteristic of the towns in the Inn and Salzach valleys – often linked by flying buttresses across the street – mostly date from the period after the great fires of the 17th century which destroyed most of Passau's medieval buildings.

Central Area

The hub of the town's traffic is the Ludwigsplatz, near the railway station (Haupt-bahnhof). The Ludwigstrasse (mostly pedestrianised), running east from the square, with its continuation the Rindermarkt, is Passau's main business and shopping street. At the near end of the street stands the Votive Church (1613–19), and beyond this the Heiliggeist-Spital (Hospital of the Holy Ghost), founded in 1358, with a church of 1345 and 1422. South-west of the Hospital is the Nibelungenhalle, a hall used for congresses and a variety of other events.

Farther south, on the banks of the Inn, is the parish church of St Nicholas, with beautiful ceiling paintings of about 1720; Early Romanesque crypt.

On the Rindermarkt (Cattle Market) is the Baroque St Paul's Church (1678). South-west of this can be seen the so-called Römerwehr (a relic of the town's medieval fortifications).

In the Domplatz with its old canons' houses stands the Cathedral (Dom) of St Stephen. This consists of a Late Gothic east end 1407–1530, crowned by a dome, and a Baroque nave (by C. Lurago, 1668–78). The interior, with sumptuous stucco decoration (by G. B. Carlone, 1680–86), has a completely Italian stamp. The organ (1928) is one of the largest in the world, with 17,388 pipes and 231 stops.

To the east of the beautiful choir of the Cathedral lies the appealing little Residenzplatz, with old patrician houses and the New Bishop's Palace (Neue Residenz; 1712–72). In the palace are the Cathedral Treasury and the Diocesan Museum (entrance through Cathe-dral), which were installed here in 1989. Also in Residenzplatz is the Toy Museum (German and American toys), and in the Old Palace (Alte Residenz) the Municipal Theatre (originally the court theatre; 1783).

Passau

Passau, seen from the Inn

Town Hall

On the right bank of the Danube is Rathausplatz, with the Town Hall (Rathaus). Originally founded in 1398, this now incorporates a number of old patrician houses; tower (1893), 68m/223ft high. It contains a number of large historical paintings by Ferdinand Wagner.

Glass Museum

In the "Wilder Mann", an old patrician house, can be found the very interesting Glass Museum (Bavarian, Bohemian and Austrian glass from 1780 to 1935).

St Michael's Church

On the south side of the tongue of land between the two rivers stands the Jesuit church of St Michael (17th c.), with sumptuous stucco decoration.

Niedernburg

Farther along is the former Benedictine nunnery of Niedernburg, founded in the 8th century, which is now occupied by the order known as the Englische Fräulein. St Mary's Church dates from the 11th–17th centuries; in the Maria Parz Chapel can be seen the imposing monument of Abbess Gisela (d. about 1060).

Dreiflusseck

From the Dreiflusseck ("Three Rivers Corner"), near the landing-stages used by passenger boats on the Danube, there is an interesting view of the confluence of the yellowish-green Danube, the grey Inn and the brown Ilz.

Innstadt

On the right bank of the Inn, occupying the site of the old Celtic settlement of Bojodurum, is the Innstadt district, the "town on the Inn", at the west end of which is the church of St Severinus (8th, 12th and 15th–16th c.).

Roman Museum

To the east of St Severinus is the Roman Museum (Römermuseum). Here in 1974 were discovered the foundations of the Late Roman base of Bolotro (3rd century A.D.); after excavation the site was partly reconstructed. Material recovered by excavation is displayed in the Gruberhaus.

Mariahilf Church

Above the Innstadt stands the pilgrimage church of Mariahilf (1627). From still higher up there are fine views of the town of Passau, the confluence of the Danube and the Inn and the Veste Oberhaus.

*Veste Oberhaus

From the old town the Luitpoldbrücke crosses to the left bank of the Danube, from which a road cut through the rock in 1762 runs up the right bank of the Ilz. On the left, against the rock face, is St Salvator's Church (15th c.), now used as a concert hall. Beyond the bridge over the Ilz a road climbs up on the left to the former episcopal stronghold of Veste Oberhaus (13th–16th c.). This now houses the Municipal Museum on the History of Culture (Bohemian Forest Museum, Lower Bavarian Fire Service Museum, Art Gallery). From the outlook tower there are superb views.

Surroundings of Passau

Obernzell (14km/8½ miles east) has a charming Rococo parish church and an old castle of the Prince-Bishops (14th c.; Ceramic Museum).

Obernzell

On the Danube, 22km/13 miles east of Passau, is the Jochenstein power station (1956), in its day one of the largest hydroelectric stations in Europe.

*Jochenstein power station

Pfälzer Wald (Palatinate Forest)   I 3

Land: Rhineland-Palatinate

The Pfälzer Wald (Palatinate Forest) is an upland region of Bunter sandstone on the left bank of the Upper Rhine, immediately north of the Vosges. With an area of some 1350 sq.km/520 sq. miles, it is one of the largest expanses of forest in Germany: even the towns of Kaiserslautern and Pirmasens (see entries) are almost completely ringed by forest.

Situation and characteristics

Landscape

The hills rise very gradually from the Saar basin in the west and then fall steeply down to the Rhine plain in the east. At the east end, in the Haardtgebirge, are the highest peaks (Kalmit, 673m/2208ft). Here the hills are crowned by numerous ruined castles, while along the foot, on the Deutsche Weinstrasse (see entry), are vineyards.

Pforzheim   K 4

Land: Baden-Württemberg
Altitude: 274m/899ft
Population: 105,000

Pforzheim, famed as a centre of the goldsmithing and jewellery industry, lies on the northern fringe of the Black Forest (see entry) in a basin at the confluence of the rivers Enz, Nagold and Würm. As a base from which to explore the beautiful valleys of these rivers and the starting-point of three Black Forest ridgeway trails, Pforzheim (Porta Hercyniae) is the gateway to the northern Black Forest.

Situation and characteristics

Central Area

Of the old palace of the Margraves of Baden-Durlach there remain only the Archives Tower and the palace church (11th c., rebuilt). In the choir of the church are the Renaissance tombs of Landgraves of Baden.

Schlosskirche

At Westliche Karl-Friedrich-Strasse 243 can be found the Heimatmuseum (history of the town, domestic interiors, crafts). An interesting item is the first Oechsle scales, a device

Heimatmuseum

invented by a local goldsmith, Ferdinand Oechsle, for measuring the sugar content of wine.

Marktplatz

In the Marktplatz, in the south of the town, stands the Town Hall (1968–73; carillon). Close by is the Stadthalle. Farther south, in the angle between the Enz and the Nagold, is the Town Church (1964–68); from the detached tower, 76m/249ft high (lift), there are extensive views.

*Jewellery Museum

Still farther south is the Stadtgarten (Municipal Park), with the Reuchlinhaus (named after the humanist Johannes Reuchlin, 1455–1525, a native of Pforzheim). In the Reuchlinhaus is the Jewellery Museum (Schmuckmuseum), devoted to the local jewellery and clock-making industries, with periodic special exhibitions of art and applied art. Opposite the Reuchlinhaus can be seen the Schütt exhibition of precious stones.

*Museum of Technology

To the west of the Stadtgarten, at Bleichstrasse 81, is the Museum of Technology, run by the Federation of the Clock-Making and Jewellery Industry (manufacturing processes, old machinery and workshops).

St Martin's Church

In the east of the town stands the Romanesque church of St Martin (12th c.). In the choir are fine frescoes, long forgotten and then rediscovered during restoration work after the Second World War.

Roman villa

Near Kanzlerstrasse (in the direction of Mäuerach) are the remains of a Roman villa of the 2nd century A.D.

Game park

On Tiefenbronner Strasse lies a 15 hectare/37acre game park (native and exotic animals; breeding enclosure for eagle owls and snowy owls, etc.).

Eutingen

Country Museum

In the Eutingen district, down the Enz valley, is the Country Museum (opened 1983), in an old half-timbered house (arable farming, harvesting, stock-rearing, transport, etc.).

Maulbronn

**Abbey

18km/11 miles north-east of Pforzheim lies the little town of Maulbronn, charmingly situated in the vine-covered foothills of the Stromberg, with its famous Cistercian abbey (founded 1147), the most beautiful of all surviving German monasteries.

The large courtyard of the abbey is surrounded by handsome half-timbered buildings. The most notable of the conventual buildings, in a style transitional between Romanesque and Gothic, is the "Paradise", the porch of the church of St Mary (consecrated 1178), which has a stone crucifix of 1473 and 15th century choir-stalls. Adjoining is the magnificent cloister, with a fountain-house and the monks' and lay brothers' refectories.

Pirmasens   I 3

Land: Rhineland-Palatinate
Altitude: 368m/1207ft
Population: 52,000

Situation and characteristics

Pirmasens, a town with a history going back to the 8th century, lies some 35km/22 miles south of Kaiserslautern on the edge of the Pfälzer Wald Nature Park. The predominant element in its economy is the shoe industry. The heavy destruction suffered by the town during the Second World War has left it with few historic buildings.

The Town

Schlossplatz

The hub of the town's life is the spacious Schlossplatz. Together with the Hauptstrasse which cuts across it this now forms an unusually shaped pedestrian zone (Bismarck

Monument, in Art Nouveau style). A striking feature of the square is the Ramba-Treppe, a wide curving flight of steps with beautiful cascades. On the west side of the square stands the Old Town Hall (c. 1770), now occupied by the town's principal museums (Shoe Museum, Heimatmuseum, Bürkel Gallery). Facing it, on the east side of the square, is the Catholic parish church of St Pirminius, a brick-built neo-Gothic basilica (1897–1900).

Farther north is St John's Church (Protestant), built in 1750 and rebuilt in 1953.

In the southern part of the pedestrian zone is the Luther Church (originally Late Baroque), with a curving steeple. In front of the church can be seen the Shoemaker's Fountain, with a monument to a local master shoemaker, Joss, a pioneer of mechanical shoe manufacture.

Pirna

Land: Saxony
Altitude: 120m/395ft
Population: 47,600

Pirna, the "gateway to the Saxon Switzerland", lies at the point where the Elbe emerges from the Elbe Sandstone Hills into the Dresden basin. The old town has preserved numbers of handsome Late Gothic, Renaissance and Baroque buildings.

Situation and characteristics

Sights

The Late Gothic St Mary's Church (1466–79) is one of the largest hall-churches in Upper Saxony, with unusual vaulting and fine ceiling paintings (1544–46) in line with the new Protestant faith. The church also has fine Baroque furnishings.

**St Mary's Church

The Markt, with the Town Hall standing alone in the centre, reflects the styles of five centuries. The Town Hall itself – originally a merchants' warehouse and assembly hall – has 15th century work on the ground floor (much subsequent alteration), Gothic doorways, gables and windows, and a tower of 1718 with a mechanical clock (renovated 1612).

*Town Hall

In the Markt are several burghers' houses with handsome arched doorways, arcaded courtyards and oriels: e.g. No. 3 (c. 1500; doorway with ogee arch, five-fold canopy and bench recesses) and No. 7, the so-called Canalettohaus, a Renaissance building of 1520. The Marienhaus (No. 20), originally the Electoral Mint (1621–22), with a figure of the Virgin under the eaves on the second floor, is named after the Madonna (1514) at the corner of the building; Napoleon stayed in this house in 1813.

The church of the former Dominican monastery (originally Gothic, c. 1300; much altered subsequently) is a hall-church with groined vaulting. On the north side is the Late Gothic chapterhouse, now the Municipal Museum.

Monastic church

Other notable burghers' houses: Barbiergasse 10, Late Renaissance (1624), with a corner oriel; and Obere Burgstrasse 1, Late Renaissance (c. 1615), with a finely decorated oriel. Also of interest is a posting milestone of 1722.

Surroundings of Pirna

Dohna (8km/5 miles west) has the Late Gothic hall-church of St Mary, with a winged altar of 1518 and a richly decorated font.

Dohna

14km/8½ miles south-west is Weesenstein, with a large Schloss (14th–19th c.; now a museum) standing high above the river Müglitz; Schlosskapelle. Notable features of the interior are the Rococo wall paintings, Chinese-patterned wallpaper, banqueting hall with stucco ceiling (1619) and French leather wall-coverings. Baroque gardens (1781).

Weesenstein

Schloss Weesenstein

Plauen

Land: Saxony
Altitude: 300–525m/985–1725ft
Population: 74,000

Situation and characteristics

Plauen, the chief town of the Vogtland (see entry) and long famed for its lace, lies in the valleys of the Weisse Elster and its tributaries, reaching up the slopes of the surrounding hills. The beautiful forests which ring the town extend into its outskirts.

Sights

St John's Church

The town's principal church, St John's (consecrated 1122; rebuilt 1224 as a basilica, with later alterations; rebuilt after destruction in 1945), is a Late Gothic hall-church with Romanesque towers topped by Baroque crowns. The fine interior furnishings include a Late Gothic winged altar (16th c.), a pulpit of around 1700, a font of about 1520 and a crucifix (*c.* 1500) on the south side of the choir.

Malzhaus

The Baroque Malzhaus (Malthouse; 1727–30) incorporates remains of the medieval castle of the Counts Eberstein (*c.* 1100).

* Old Town Hall
New Town Hall

Near the Malzhaus is the Late Gothic Old Town Hall (1508), built on to which is the neo-Baroque New Town Hall (1912). The south front has a high Renaissance gable (after 1548) and a clock with mechanical figures. On the ground floor is a collection of Plauen lace.

Luther Church

The Luther Church (1693–1722) is one of the oldest Baroque churches on a centralised plan in Saxony. It has a Late Gothic winged altar (1490–95) by an Erfurt master.

Vogtland Museum

At Nobelstrasse 9–13 is the Vogtland Museum (local history, weaving and calico printing, folk art, Vogtland costumes).

Old and New Town Hall

The Elster Valley Bridge (Elstertalbrücke; pedestrians only) is protected as a historic monument. The overpass on Neustadtplatz, built of undressed stone, is one of the oldest of its kind in Europe. The first mention of a bridge here is in 1244.

*Elster Valley Bridge

Surroundings of Plauen

In the Syra valley are a beautiful park, an open-air theatre, the site of the town's Lace Festival and the Peace Bridge, built in 1903–05, with what was then the longest single span in Europe (90m/98yds).

Syra valley

At Syrau (7km/4½ miles north-west on B 92 and B 282) are the Drachenhöhle (a stalactitic cave) and the last surviving windmill in the Vogtland.

Syrau

Plauer See

C 7

Land: Mecklenburg-West Pomerania

The Plauer See (alt. 62m/203ft; 15km/9 miles long; area 38.7 sq.km/15 sq. miles) is the most westerly of the Upper Lakes (Great Lakes) in the Mecklenburg lake district. It lies on the western edge of the Müritz Lake Park landscape reserve.

Situation

On the west side of the Plauer See, at the point where the river Elde leaves the lake, is the little town of Plau (pop. 6500). Laid out on a regular plan in 1225–26, surrounded by walls and a moat in 1288 and protected by a fortress (of which there remains a 12m/40ft high tower with walls 3m/10ft thick), Plau long remained a typical Mecklenburg farming town, enjoying a brief period of prosperity as an industrial town (engineering, textiles) only in the 19th century.

Plau

The Plauer See is linked by the long narrow Petersdorfer See and the Malchower See with the Fleesensee (area 11 sq.km/4¼ sq. miles). On the Malchower See is the old island

Malchow

town of Malchow (pop. 8000; textiles, carpets, clothing manufacture), which received its municipal charter in 1235. This is a good base from which to explore the beautiful lake district of central Mecklenburg (see Mecklenburg Lakes), up the Elde valley. Downstream the Elde is linked by the river Stör with the Schweriner See (see Schwerin, Surroundings).

Alt Schwerin

In Alt Schwerin, near the northern shore of the Plauer See, can be found a Farming Museum, with a variety of old buildings and exhibits illustrating the history of farming in Mecklenburg from the Middle Ages to the present day.

Potsdam   E 8

Capital of the *Land* of Brandenburg
Altitude: 35m/115ft
Population: 143,000

Situation and characteristics

Potsdam lies south-west of Berlin in a beautiful setting of woodland and lakes. This former residence of the rulers of Prussia is a town of palaces and gardens in the style of Potsdam Rococo, but it is also the symbol of the military state built up by the Prussian kings. The planned development of Potsdam into a garrison town began in the reign of the "soldier king", Frederick William I (1713–40). Under his successor Frederick II, the Great (1740–86), the town and the army both grew in size, and by 1774 there were 139 barracks, military hospitals and other military buildings in Potsdam. To enhance the dignity of the capital the old palace was rebuilt, the new palace of Sanssouci was begun, and whole quarters of the town were pulled down and replaced by Baroque burghers' houses.

In 1991 the remains of Frederick William I and Frederick the Great were brought back to Potsdam.

Central Area

The Lange Brücke, the oldest bridge over the Havel, leads from the Teltower Vorstadt into the main part of the town, affording a fine view of the rebuilt town centre.

°Old Town Hall

In the Alter Markt stands the former Town Hall (now the House of Culture), a Baroque building (1753) with three-quarter-length Corinthian columns, a tower with a stepped dome and a gilded figure of Atlas with the world on his back, which is linked by an intervening wing with the Baroque Knobelsdorffhaus (1750).

°St Nicholas's Church

Diagonally opposite is the Nikolaikirche (St Nicholas's Church), a neo-classical church on a centralised plan built by Ludwig Persius in 1830–37, following a design by K. F. Schinkel. In front of the church can be seen an obelisk (1753) with the likenesses of the principal architects of Potsdam.

Freundschaftsinsel

Below the Lange Brücke is the Freundschaftsinsel (Friendship Island), with gardens laid out by Karl Foerster in 1953–54.

°Marstall (Film Museum)

Farther north, in Friedrich-Ebert-Strasse, can be found the Baroque Marstall (Court Stables; by J. A. Nering, 1675; G. W. von Knobelsdorff, 1746), now housing the Film Museum. Opposite the Marstall is the Karl Liebknecht Forum. In the Platz der Einheit (Unity Square) is the large General Library (1971–74).

French Church

On the south-east side of Bassinplatz is the French Church (Französische Kirche; 1751–52), a Baroque church on a centralised plan built by J. Boumann the Elder to the design of Knobelsdorff and remodelled in neo-classical style by Schinkel in 1832–33.

°Dutch Quarter

To the north of Bassinplatz lies the famous Dutch Quarter (Holländisches Viertel), with 134 brick houses in a uniform style built between 1737 and 1742 by J. Boumann the Elder and Dutch craftsmen.

Brandenburger Strasse

The Brandenburger Strasse pedestrian zone is a good example of the skilled restoration of historic buildings. The houses were built in 1733–39 in a uniform style – of two storeys, with overhanging eaves and rooms in the gable for the billeting of troops.

At the end of Brandenburger Strasse, in the Platz der Nationen, stands the Brandenburg Gate (Brandenburger Tor), a Baroque town gate modelled on a Roman triumphal arch built in 1770 by Karl von Gontard (inner side) and G. C. Unger (outer side).

*Brandenburg Gate

At the corner of Leninallee and Wilhelm-Külz-Strasse can be seen the Waterworks for the fountains in Sanssouci Park, built by Ludwig Persius in 1841–41 in the form of a Moorish-style mosque, with the chimney disguised as a minaret.

*Waterworks

In Wilhelm-Külz-Strasse is the Potsdam Museum and beside it the old Military Orphanage (1722).

Potsdam Museum

**Sanssouci Park

The park of Sanssouci is the creation of four generations. The oldest part of the park, to the east, was laid out between 1744 and 1756. These gardens, with their various buildings and works of art, are the most celebrated example of Potsdam Rococo, reflecting the personal influence of Frederick the Great.

The park is entered at the east end of the main avenue (Hauptallee), in Schopenhauer-strasse. Outside the entrance is an obelisk (by G. W. von Knobelsdorff, 1748). The main gate (also by Knobelsdorff, 1747) is modelled on a similar gate at Rheinsberg (see Neuruppin, Surroundings).

Along the avenues in the park are a series of "roundels". At the first one (with busts of four Moors) can be seen Neptune's Grotto (by Knobelsdorff, 1751–57).

Neptune's Grotto

At the Orange Roundel (by Dusart, 1650) is the Picture Gallery (Bildergalerie; by J. G. Büring, 1755–63). The pictures are mainly 17th century; they include works by Rubens, van Dyck, Tintoretto and Caravaggio.

Picture Gallery

At the foot of the vineyard is the Great Fountain, with representations of the four elements and mythological figures.

Great Fountain

**Sanssouci Palace

On the plateau stands the palace of Sanssouci (1745–47), built by Knobelsdorff on the basis of sketches by Frederick the Great. It is a single-storey Rococo building with an elliptical dome in the centre of the garden front and a circular room at each end. The garden front has rich plastic decoration (by F. C. Glume); on the rear front is the Grand Courtyard, enclosed by colonnades of Corinthian columns.

The most notable features of the interior are the oval Marble Hall, with double Corinthian columns; the Little Gallery, with decoration by Hoppenhaupt; the Concert Room, with murals by A. Pesne; the Bedroom and Study (by F. W. von Erdmannsdorff); the Library, with antique busts; and the Voltaire Room.

South-west of the palace are the Neue Kammern (New Rooms), originally built by Knobelsdorff in 1747 as an orangery and converted by G. C. Unger in 1771–74 into Frederick the Great's "gardener's house"; richly decorated interior (intarsia cabinets by the Spindler brothers). In front of the building is the "Fountain Roundel" and farther west the "Muses' Roundel" (by Glume, 1752, after a design by Knobelsdorff).

Neue Kammern

To the south of the Neue Kammern, in the Rehgarten (Deer Park), can be seen the Chinese Tea-House (Chinesisches Teehaus; by J. G. Büring, 1754–57), with a display of 18th century Chinese porcelain.

*Chinese Tea-House

The Orangery (now housing archives), in the style of an Italian Renaissance palazzo, was built by F. A. Stüler and L. Hesse (two pupils of K. F. Schinkel) to the design of Ludwig Persius between 1851 and 1862. The Raphael Room contains copies of 47 works by Raphael.

Orangery

South-east of the Orangery lies the Sicilian Garden (laid out by J. P. Lenné in 1857), composed mainly of Mediterranean plants, with numerous sculptures. Nearby (to the west of the Orangery) is the little Paradise Garden (by Persius, 1844).

Sicilian Garden

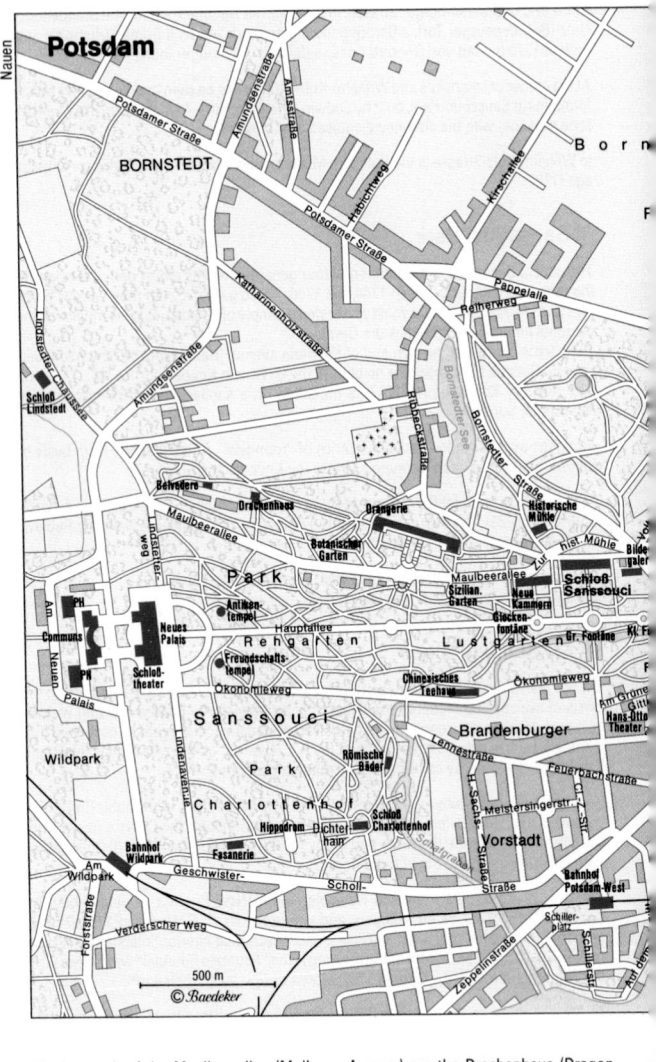

Drachenhaus

To the north of the Maulbeerallee (Mulberry Avenue) are the Drachenhaus (Dragon House; by Gontard, 1770), originally the vintner's house, and the Belvedere (by G. C. Unger, 1770–72).

*New Palace

At the west end of the Hauptallee stands the New Palace (Neues Palais; by Büring and Gontard, 1763–69), the last 18th century palace in Sanssouci Park, built in brick relieved by sandstone, with a copper dome. The interior is sumptuously decorated, particularly in the Marble Hall, the Upper and Lower State Apartments, the Marble Gallery and the Theatre.

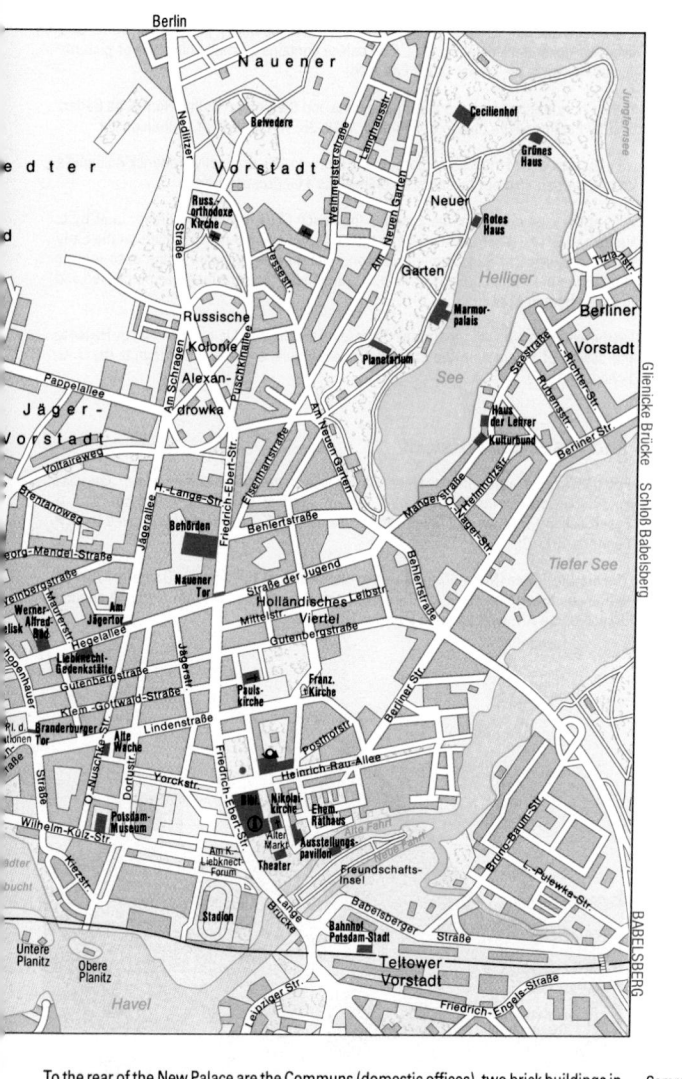

To the rear of the New Palace are the Communs (domestic offices), two brick buildings in Baroque style (by Gontard, 1765–69), with columned porticoes and curving external staircases; they are now occupied by a teachers' training college. Between the two buildings are Corinthian colonnades and a triumphal arch.

Communs

In front of the New Palace are the Ancient Temple (Antikentempel) and the Temple of Friendship (Freundschaftstempel), with a statue of Margravine Wilhelmine of Bayreuth. Both temples were built by Gontard on the basis of sketches by Frederick the Great.

In the southern part of Sanssouci Park can be found Charlottenhof Palace (designed by K. F. Schinkel, 1826–29). The most notable features of the palace are the staircase hall, with

*Charlottenhof Palace

a fountain, and the room (in the form of a tent) occupied by the great traveller and scientist Alexander von Humboldt. The palace contains a small collection of pictures (including works by Caspar David Friedrich).

Roman Baths

In the Charlottenhof park are the Hippodrome and the Roman Baths (Römische Bäder; built by Persius to the design of Schinkel, 1829–35), in the style of an Italian villa.

Marlygarten

Near the east end of the park we come to the Marlygarten, originally Frederick William I's kitchen garden, laid out by Lenné in 1845–46 as a landscaped park.

* Peace Church

Also at the east end of the park stands the Peace Church (Friedenskirche; built by L. Hesse and F. von Arnim in 1845–54 to the design of L. Persius), modelled on the Early Christian basilica of San Clemente in Rome. Its greatest treasure is the apse mosaic (1108) from the church of San Cipriano, Murano (near Venice) which was purchased and installed here in 1834.

On the avenue leading to the Grünes Gitter (exit) are the Villa Illaire (1844–46; by Hesse to the design of Persius), in the style of an Italian villa, and the Villa Liegnitz (by J. G. Schadow, 1841).

* Neuer Garten and Mauener Vorstadt

Potsdam's other large park, the Neuer Garten, lies on the shores of the Heiliger See. It is a landscaped park in the "sentimental" style of the late 18th century, laid out by J. A. Eyserbeck the Younger in 1789–91 on the model of Wörlitz Park and improved by J. P. Lenné in 1817–25.

Marble Palace
(Army Museum)

The Marble Palace (Marmorpalais), a neo-classical brick building (by Gontard, 1787–91) with a columned portico on the lake side, now houses the Potsdam Army Museum, a branch of the Army Museum in Dresden (founded 1971).

Cecilienhof: meeting-place of the Potsdam Conference, 1945

Among other buildings in the Neuer Garten (an obelisk, a Gothic temple, pyramids, the Red House, the Green House, the Dairy) is Schloss Cecilienhof (by P. Schultze-Naumburg, 1913–17), in the style of an English country house. This was the meeting-place of the Potsdam Conference of July–August 1945 (conference room, with its original furniture; rooms occupied by the heads of government).

* Cecilienhof

To the west of the Neuer Garten extends the Nauener Vorstadt. Here, on the Pfingstberg, is the Belvedere, built by Stüler and Hesse on the basis of sketches by Frederick William IV and Persius (1849–52, 1860–62).

Belvedere

On the road passing through the Russian colony of Alexandrowka are the Jewish cemetery (1743) and the Kapellenberg, on which is the Russian Orthodox church of Alexander Nevsky (1829; rich furnishings from St Petersburg).

Alexander Nevsky Church

The houses in the little settlement of Alexandrowka were built for the last twelve members of a 62-strong choir of Russian soldiers who found their way here during Napoleon's Russian campaign. The houses were based on Russian models, and the settlement was laid out by P. J. Lenné in the form of a St Andrew's cross.

* Alexandrowka

Babelsberg

The district of Babelsberg, famed in the early days of the cinema as the home of the Ufa film studios, originally grew up around Nowawes, an old colony of spinners and weavers, traces of which can still be detected near the church (Weberplatz). The church (by J. Boumann, 1752–53) is a modest aisleless building with galleries.

Nowawes

Babelsberg Park, Potsdam's third large park, was originally laid out by P. J. Lenné in 1832 and enlarged by Prince Pückler-Muskau from 1843 onwards.

* Babelsberg Park

Schloss Babelsberg, a neo-Gothic house on the English model (1834–35, Schinkel; 1845–49, J. H. Strack), is now occupied by the Museum of Prehistory and the Early Historical Period, with a rich collection of Bronze Age material of the Lusatian culture.

Schloss Babelsberg (Museum)

Einstein Tower on the Telegrafenberg

441

Telegrafenberg

*Einstein Tower

On the Telegrafenberg (94m/308ft) are a number of research establishments, including the Meteorological Observatory (1888–90), the Geodetic Institute (1889–92) and the Einstein Tower (by E. Mendelssohn, 1920–21), the most striking building on the hill, in a streamlined style influenced by Expressionism.

Surroundings of Potsdam

Caputh

Caputh (5km/3 miles south-west) has a Baroque Schloss (1662) with rich stucco decoration in the banqueting hall and a Summer Room in the basement faced with Delft tiles. At Waldstrasse 7 is the last house occupied by Albert Einstein before he left Germany in 1933.

Prenzlau   C 9

Land: Brandenburg
Altitude: 20m/65ft
Population: 23,800

Situation and characteristics

Prenzlau, once the chief town of the Uckermark, lies on the north side of the Unterueckersee some 80km/50 miles north of Berlin. The old town, situated on a terrace bordering the kilometre-wide Uecker depression, has preserved remains of its medieval fortifications and a number of fine churches.

Sights

*Fortifications

Prenzlau still has considerable stretches of its old town walls (13th–14th c.), with three gate-towers (Blindower Torturm, Mitteltorturm, Steintorturm), the Hexenturm (Witches'

St Mary's Church, Prenzlau

Markt, Quedlinburg

442

Tower), the Pulverturn (Powder Tower) and a number of *wiekhäuser* (houses built into the town walls).

In Ernst-Thälmann-Platz stands St Mary's Church (13th–14th c.), one of Germany's finest examples of brick-built Gothic architecture, with a magnificent east gable. The church was burned out in the closing days of the Second World War but has been rebuilt in its original form. It is planned to make it a Museum of Culture.
At the south-west corner of the church can be seen a bronze figure of Martin Luther (by Ernst Rietschel, 1903), a copy of the original in Worms.

St Mary's Church

Two other notable churches are the ruined St Nicholas's Church (mid 13th c.), the town's oldest parish church, and St James's Church (second half of 13th c.), a flat-roofed church built of undressed stone.

St Nicholas's Church
St James's Church

The monastic church of the Holy Cross (1275–1343) is brick-built in Early Gothic style. The refectory (now the Heimatmuseum) of the old Dominican monastery has wall paintings of 1516.

Holy Cross Church

This former Franciscan church (1235–70), known as Trinity Church since 1865, is a rectangular groin-vaulted church of undressed stone.

Trinity Church

The Sabinerkirche (Early Gothic, rebuilt 1816–17) has a fine altar of 1597.

Sabinerkirche

In the paving of Ernst-Thälmann-Platz can be seen the "Execution Stone" (Richtstein), the medieval place of execution.

Execution Stone

Quedlinburg

E–F 6

Land: Saxony-Anhalt
Altitude: 123m/371ft
Population: 29,000

Quedlinburg, lying on the river Bode in the northern Harz foreland, is an attractive town with many half-timbered houses and other fine old buildings, set in beautiful countryside.
Quedlinburg was the birthplace of the first German woman doctor, Dorothea Erxleben (1715), the educationalist Johann Christoph Guts Muths (1759) and Carl Ritter (1779), who ranks with Alexander von Humboldt as one of the founders of modern scientific geography.

Situation and characteristics

*Schlossberg

Above the town rises the Schlossberg, with the Renaissance Schloss (16th–17th c.); richly appointed state apartments (18th c.). In the conventual buildings of the old imperial abbey is the Schlossmuseum.

Schloss

The Romanesque church of St Servatius (12th c.) is an aisled basilica. In the crypt can be found the tomb of the Emperor Henry I and his wife Mathilde. The rich church treasury is displayed in the sacristy.

Stiftskirche

At the foot of the Schlossberg is a magnificent 16th century patrician house (now occupied by the Museum of Literature), in which the poet Friedrich Gottlieb Klopstock, the first of the German classical writers, was born in 1724.
Behind the Klopstock House (entrance from Finkenherd) is the Lyonel Feininger Gallery, with a large collection of watercolours and graphic art by the Expressionist painter of that name, an associate of Gropius at the Bauhaus.

*Klopstock House

South-west of the Schlossberg stands the monastic church of St Wigbert (Klosterkirche St Wiperti; 12th–13th c.), an aisled Romanesque basilica with a flat roof, a straight-ended choir and a Romanesque doorway. Under the choir is the aisled and barrel-vaulted St

*St Wigbert's Church

Quedlinburg Town Hall with its Renaissance doorway

Wigbert's Crypt (originally Carolingian, 9th c.; rebuilt after 961). During restoration work in 1956–57 a Romanesque doorway from a former monastery on the Münzenberg was built into the south side of the church.

Central Area

* Town Hall

In the Markt is the charming Town Hall (Rathaus), a two-storey Renaissance building with coats of arms on the doorway (1616–19) and a figure of Roland, probably dating from 1426.

St Blaise's and St Benedict's

Two other churches in the old town are the parish church of St Blaise (St Blasii; 1713–15, restored), an aisleless Baroque church on an octagonal plan, with galleries and a stucco ceiling, and the Market Church (Marktkirche) of St Benedict, a 15th century hall-church (14th c. choir; monuments) with barrel-vaulting and timber ceilings.

St Nicholas's Church

In the new town is the parish church of St Nicholas (Nikolaikirche), a 14th century Gothic hall-church with groined vaulting; richly decorated reredos, Early Gothic font.

* Museum of Half-Timbering

Quedlinburg has numbers of richly decorated half-timbered houses from a period of six centuries. The oldest is the Ständerbau (14th c.) at Wordgasse 3, now the Museum of Half-Timbering (Fachwerkmuseum).
The houses at Stieg 28 (Alter Klopstock) and Marktstrasse 2 represent the heyday of the Dutch style (c. 1560). Among the few old secular buildings in stone are the Hagensches Freihaus (Klink 11), a three-storey Renaissance building (1564), and the Grünhagenhaus (1701) in the Markt. In the new town, at Steinweg 22, is the Old Exchange (Alte Börse) of 1683.

Gernrode

Situation

7km/4½ miles south of Quedlinburg, at the foot of the Stubenberg, lies the old town of Gernrode, with a notable church.

A narrow-gauge steam railway, the Selketalbahn, runs 12km/7½ miles south to Herzgerode (see Selke Valley).

Selketalbahn

The former monastic church of St Cyriacus (probably begun about 959), now the parish church, is one of the finest churches of the Ottonian period in Germany. The present west end, main apse and crypt date from a rebuilding in the early 12th century. The church was thoroughly restored between 1858 and 1872.

* *Stiftskirche

Querfurt   F 7

Land: Saxony-Anhalt
Altitude: 172m/564ft
Population: 9700

Querfurt lies 25km/15 miles south-west of Halle in a fertile plain. Its castle, Burg Querfurt, is one of the oldest in Germany and also one of the largest (almost seven times the size of the Wartburg in Eisenach).

Situation and characteristics

*Burg Querfurt

The castle is surrounded by a double ring of walls; the inner ring dates from about 1200, the outer ring from about 1350. Outside the outer ring of walls is a moat, hewn from the rock, into which project three massive bastions. In the course of a conducted tour of the castle visitors are shown an underground passage between the castle and the south bastion.

Under Dicker Heinrich ("Fat Henry"), one of the castle's three towers, were found remains of a house of the Carolingian period – the oldest secular building in the Saale-Elbe region.

"Fat Henry"

Burg Querfurt

Church	In the centre of the castle courtyard stands the 12th century church, on a cruciform plan with three apses. In the burial chapel which was added in the 14th century is the tomb of Gebhard XIV of Querfurt (d. 1383).
	Round the castle courtyard are three Romanesque towers. One of them, the Pariser Turm, is open to the public as an outlook tower.
Museum	One of the two buildings within the castle, the Korn- and Rusthaus (granary and arsenal) houses the Castle and District Museum (history of the castle and the town of Querfurt; also periodic special exhibitions).

Old Town

Town Hall	In the Markt is the Town Hall, a Renaissance building with a Baroque tower (1699). In Otto-Dietrich-Strasse and the Freimarkt are a number of fine burghers' houses, some of them with beautiful doorways.
	The town has preserved some stretches of its old fortifications (an inner and an outer wall). The parish church of St Lambert is Late Gothic, with much subsequent alteration (most recently in the 17th century); it has a richly decorated reredos and pulpit by G. Müller.

Rastatt   K 3

	Land: Baden-Württemberg Altitude: 122m/400ft Population: 40,000
Situation and characteristics	Rastatt lies at the mouth of the Murg valley, where the river emerges into the Upper Rhine plain. After its destruction by French troops in 1689 the town was rebuilt on a uniform plan, and it still bears a distinct Baroque stamp.

*Rastatt Palace

	Rastatt Palace is an imposing Baroque building closely modelled on Versailles, with a garden front 230m/250yds long, which incorporates the adjoining town centre in its axis of symmetry. The interior decoration was the work of Italian artists. In the sumptuous palace church (by M. L. Rohrer, 1719–23) is the tomb of Margravine Sibylla Augusta (d. 1733).
Military Museum	The most important of the museums housed in the palace is the Military Museum, which illustrates German military history from the Middle Ages to the present day (uniforms, arms and armour, military decorations).
Freedom Museum	The Freedom Museum is devoted to the various freedom movements in the course of German history, with particular emphasis on the revolutions of 1789–90 and 1848–49.
Heimatmuseum	In a former Kavaliershaus (lodgings for members of the court) is the Heimatmuseum (history of the town and surrounding area since prehistoric times, revolutionary history, Gothic and Baroque sculpture, astronomical clock).

The Town

Kaiserstrasse	In Kaiserstrasse, a wide street running at right angles to the palace's axis of symmetry, stands the Baroque Town Hall (1750), with the Alexius Fountain in front of it. To the south-east are the Johannisbrunnen (St John's Fountain) and St Alexander's Church (1756–64), which has a sumptuous high altar.

Favorite

	South-east of the town, near Kuppenheim, can be found the little palace of Favorite (1710–12), built as a summer residence for Margravine Sibylla Augusta, widow of

Rastatt Palace

Ludwig Wilhelm I of Baden. The interior gives an excellent impression of aristocratic life
in the 18th century (collection of faience and glass).

Ravensburg

L 5

Land: Baden-Württemberg
Altitude: 477m/1565ft
Population: 43,000

The former free imperial city of Ravensburg, situated above the river Schussen on the
edge of the Ravensburg basin, is the economic and cultural centre of Upper Swabia (see
entry). It lies on the Upper Swabian Baroque Highway.

Situation and
characteristics

Old Town

The principal axis of the old town is the long-drawn-out Marienplatz. In its centre are the
square Blaserturm (16th c.) and the Weigh-House (1498). To the south is the Late Gothic
Town Hall (14th–16th c.), and beyond this the Kornhaus (14th–16th c.), now occupied by
the Municipal Library.

Marienplatz

Diagonally opposite the Kornhaus stands the large Town Church (Protestant), which
originally belonged to a Carmelite monastery founded about 1350 (14th and 15th c.
frescoes). In the adjoining chapel of the merchants' guild are patrician tombs of the
15th–18th centuries.

Town Church

From the Blaserturm Kirchstrasse runs north, parallel to Marienplatz, to the 14th century
Liebfrauenkirche (Church of Our Lady; R.C.), with a beautiful west doorway and fine
stained glass in the choir (1415). Immediately north of the church is the Frauentor, one of
the old town gates.

Liebfrauenkirche

447

Ravensburg, with the "Sack of Flour"

Town walls	From the Frauentor there is an attractive walk westward along the old town walls, which here are partly preserved, passing the Green Tower (14th–15th c.), the Painted Tower (14th–16th c.), the Untertor (Lower Gate; 14th and 16th c.) and the Spitalturm or Sauturm (14th c.).
St Judocus' Church	To the west of the northern section of Marienplatz stands the Gothic church of St Judocus (St Jodok; 1385), with a fresco of Christ which was brought to light in 1953.
Vogthaus Museum	To the north-west, at Charlottenstrasse 36, is the old Vogthaus, a handsome and well restored half-timbered building of 1380, which now houses the Municipal Museum (history of the town, domestic life in 15th–18th c., sculpture of 14th–18th c.).
Marktstrasse	From the Town Hall Marktstrasse runs south-east to the Obertor (1490). At the near end of the street, on the left, is the Brotlaube (1625), which was used as a theatre from 1698 until the 19th century; it is now an art gallery. In front of the Obertor is the guild-house of the Ravensburg Merchant Company (1446).
Mehlsack	Above the Obertor, to the south, rises the "Mehlsack" ("Sack of Flour" – so called because of the light colour of its masonry), a round tower 51m/167ft high which is a conspicuous Revensburg landmark.
Veitsburg	From the Obertor there is a pleasant walk through gardens to the Veitsburg, a little Baroque castle built in 1750 on the site of an earlier Guelph stronghold which was burned down in 1647; it is now a youth hostel.

Surroundings of Ravensburg

Weissenau	3km/2 miles south of the town centre can be found the former Premonstratensian monastery of Weissenau. The church (by Franz Beer, 1717–24) has stucco decoration by Franz Schmuzer and ceiling paintings by Karl Stauder.

Recklinghausen   F 2

Land: North Rhine-Westphalia
Altitude: 76m/249ft
Population: 119,000

The busy industrial town of Recklinghausen lies in the area known as the Neues Revier between the rivers Emscher and Lippe. Its economy is centred mainly on mining and manufacturing industry (metalworking, textiles, synthetic materials).

Situation and characteristics

The Town

In the centre of the old town with its narrow lanes stands St Peter's Church, Recklinghausen's oldest building. The original Gothic hall-church was considerably enlarged in 1520; its massive round pillars date from about 1700. Altarpiece by pupils of Rubens; Gothic tabernacle.

St Peter's Church

Opposite the church, to the west, is the Icon Museum, a collection unique in Western Europe which gives a comprehensive view of the icon-painting of the Eastern churches (some 600 icons of the 15th–19th centuries) and the development of the Coptic church in Egypt.

*Icon Museum

Farther west we come to the Engelsburg, a three-storey aristocratic mansion built about 1700 which later became the estate office of the Dukes of Arenberg; it is now a hotel. It has a richly appointed banqueting hall with a Baroque stucco ceiling.

Engelsburg

In Wickingplatz, on the north side of the old town, is the municipal Kunsthalle (modern art; special exhibitions during the Ruhr Festival).

Kunsthalle

In the Stadtgarten, in the north-west of the town, stands the Ruhrfestspielhaus (Ruhr Festival Hall); in front of it is Henry Moore's "Large Reclining Figure No. 5" (bronze). Also in the Stadtgarten are the Tierpark (Zoo) and Planetarium.

Festspielhaus

In the south of the town, at Hohenzollernstrasse 12, is the new Vestisches Museum, opened in 1987: geology (fossils), prehistory and the early historical period, history of the town, Christian art since the Romanesque period, domestic life, naïve art of the Ruhr.

Vestisches Museum

Regensburg   I–K 7

Land: Bavaria
Altitude: 333m/1093ft
Population: 128,000

The old free imperial city of Regensburg, the see of a bishop, lies at the most northerly point in the course of the Danube, which is joined here by the little river Regen and is navigable between Regensburg and the Black Sea.
Regensburg has the same significance for the art and culture of the early and high Middle Ages as have Nürnberg and Augsburg for later centuries.

Situation and characteristics

From Regensburg there are excursion ships to Walhalla (see below), Straubing and Passau; excursions into the Altmühl valley are also planned.

Boat trips

The medieval townscape is made up of numerous churches, the tower houses of great noble families and patrician houses of the 13th and 14th centuries such as are found nowhere else north of the Alps.

*Townscape

Old Town

The best view of Regensburg is to be had from the 310m/340yd long Stone Bridge (Steinerne Brücke; 12th c.) over the Danube, a masterpiece of medieval engineering.

Stone Bridge
*View

Regensburg

*Cathedral

Near the Stone Bridge lies the Domplatz (Cathedral Square), the hub of the city's life. The Cathedral (Dom) of St Peter (13th–16th c.), with its two tall spires (105m/345ft high) and magnificent west front (1395–1440), is the finest Gothic church in Bavaria. The interior is of great beauty and spatial effect; its most notable features are the superb stained glass (mostly 14th c.) and the figures of the Annunciation (c. 1280–90) on the two western piers of the crossing.

Adjoining the beautiful cloister (14th–16th c.) is the Romanesque All Saints Chapel (wall paintings). On the north side of the cloister is St Stephen's Chapel, which may date from Carolingian times.

The Cathedral is famed for its boys' choir, the "Domspatzen" ("Cathedral sparrows"). The Cathedral Treasury, displayed in the old Bishop's Palace, includes goldsmith's work and fine textiles of the 11th to the 20th century. On the north side of the Bischofshof are the arched gateway and east tower of the Porta Praetoria, the north gate of the Roman legionary camp, Castra Regina (2nd c. A.D.).

St Ulrich's
Church

On the south side of the Domgarten is the Early Gothic church of St Ulrich (c. 1025), with the Diocesan Museum (sacred art from the 11th century onwards).

Niedermünster

Adjoining the Bishop's Palace is the Niedermünster (12th and 17th–18th c.), with the tomb of St Erhard and 12th and 16th century frescoes. Under the church are the excavated remains of Roman, Merovingian, Carolingian and Ottonian buildings (conducted visit).

Shipping Museum

To the north of the Niedermünster the Danube is spanned by the Iron Bridge (Eiserne Brücke), near which is moored the museum ship "Ruthof/Ersekcsanad", an old paddle-steamer with an exhibition of material on the history of shipping in Bavaria.

Alter Kornmarkt

In the Alter Kornmarkt (Old Cornmarket), to the south of the Niedermünster, are the so-called Roman Tower (actually a relic of a Carolingian imperial stronghold) and the Herzogshof, a residence of the Dukes of Bavaria which is mentioned in the records as early as 988. On the south side of the square stands the Old Chapel (Alte Kapelle;

Regensburg Cathedral

originally built 1002; choir 1441–52), with a sumptuous Rococo interior. On the east side of the square is the Baroque Carmelite Church (1641–60; façade 1673).

In Dachauplatz (56m/60yd long stretch of Roman walls) is the Municipal Museum, housed in a former Minorite friary (prehistory, Roman times, history of the town, art of the 14th–19th centuries, folk art).

Municipal Museum

South-west of the Stone Bridge lies the old merchants' quarter, in which are a number of old tower-houses. The picturesque Old Town Hall (Altes Rathaus) dates from the 14th–18th centuries (historical apartments, medieval courtroom, collection of art and antiquities). The Imperial Hall (Reichssaal) was the meeting-place of the "Perpetual Imperial Diet", the first German parliament (1663–1806). The Baroque eastern wing, linked with the older part of the building by the tower, was added in 1661.

Old Town Hall

A little way north-west, at Keplerstrasse 5, is the house in which the astronomer Johannes Kepler died in 1630. It is now a museum (contemporary furniture, original instruments, working models, documents).

Kepler House

In Haidplatz, farther south-west, can be seen the 15th century New Weigh-House (Neue Waage), the scene of a famous disputation in 1541 between Melanchthon and Johann Eck.

Weigh-House

At the west end of the old town, in Jakobstrasse, is the Schottenkirche, built about 1150–80 by Irish ("Scottish") monks. The north doorway has enigmatic sculpture showing northern influence.

* Schottenkirche

South-east of Bismarckplatz is the Early Gothic Dominican Church (13th c.), in the ascetic style of the mendicant orders, with a finely proportioned interior.

* Dominican Church

On the south side of the old town lies Emmeramsplatz, with the Regierungsgebäude (government offices) and the Benedictine monastery of St Emmeram, one of the oldest in Germany, founded in the 7th century on the site of a Late Roman building (secularised 1803). It has a Romanesque porch (c. 1170), on the left of which is the entrance to St Rupert's Church (remodelled in Baroque style). Straight ahead is the doorway (with three 11th century limestone reliefs) of St Emmeram's Church (8th–12th c.). The church has a sumptuous Baroque interior by the Asam brothers (1731–33) and contains a number of magnificent tombs of the 12th–15th centuries (Hemma, wife of King Ludwig the German; Duke Henry the Quarrelsome; Duke Arnulf; St Emmeram). Under the church are three crypts (St Emmeram's, 8th–9th century; St Ramwold's, 10th c.; St Wolfgang's, 1052).

* St Emmeram's Church

The old conventual buildings became in 1812 the residence of the Princes Thurn und Taxis, German Postmasters-General until 1866. Parts of the palace, which was altered and enlarged in the 19th century, are open to the public, including the museum in the old court stables, the Marstall.

Schloss

To the west of the town, on the banks of the Danube, extends the Herzogspark, with the Herzogspalais (Ducal Palace), now occupied by the Natural History Museum of Eastern Bavaria (petrography, mineralogy, palaeontology, zoology, botany).

Natural History Museum

To the south, in the Stadtpark, is the East German Gallery.

Surroundings of Regensburg

At Donaustauf (11km/7 miles east of Regensburg), 96m/315ft above the Danube, is the Walhalla, a "German Temple of Fame" resembling the Parthenon; it was built by Leo von Klenze in 1830–42, during the reign of Ludwig I.

* Walhalla

At Kelheim (26km/16 miles south-west of Regensburg), commandingly situated above the Danube on the Michaelsberg, can be found the Hall of Liberation (Befreiungshalle; by Friedrich Gärtner and Leo von Klenze, 1842–63), a 59m/194ft high rotunda commemorating the wars of liberation of 1813–15. In the interior are 34 goddesses of victory by Ludwig Schwanthaler.

Kelheim
* Hall of Liberation

Bad Reichenhall

Land: Bavaria
Altitude: 470m/1542ft
Population: 19,000

Situation and characteristics

Bad Reichenhall lies in a sheltered situation in a wide basin in the Saalach valley, framed by hills, at the entrance to the Berchtesgadener Land (see Berchtesgaden), near the Austrian frontier. Within easy reach of the town are the Predigtstuhl (1613m/5292ft) and the Hochstaufen (1771m/5811ft).

The spa has strong brine springs which are used in the treatment of rheumatism and disorders of the respiratory passages.

The Town

Kurgarten

The activity of the spa centres on the Kurgarten, with the Old Kurhaus, the Evaporation Hall, the Pump Room, the treatment building and the brine springs. To the west, on Wittelsbacher Strasse, are the new Spa Centre, the Kur- und Verkehrsverein (tourist information office), the Casino and the Theatre.

Heimatmuseum

South-west of the Kurgarten, in the centre of the town (Getreidegasse 4), is the Heimatmuseum (Stone Age, Bronze Age, Celtic, Roman and later material; history of the town; salt-working).

Old Salt-Works

In the south of the town can be found the Old Salt-Works (Alte Saline; conducted tours; pumping station of 1839), with the springs (salt content up to 24%) which are used both for spa treatment and for the extraction of salt.

Above the salt-works is Burg Gruttenstein (13th c.; not open to the public).

Old Kurhaus, Bad Reichenhall

On the north-east side of the town is the former Augustinian monastery of St Zeno (founded 1136, dissolved 1803), with a Romanesque church (late 12th c.; altered in Late Gothic style 1512–20); beautiful west doorway, fine interior.

*St Zeno's Church

To the south of the town rises the Predigtstuhl (1613m/5292ft; cableway), which commands extensive views.

*Predigtstuhl

Remscheid

F 2

Land: North Rhine-Westphalia
Altitude: 360m/1180ft
Population: 123,000

Remscheid, situated in the wooded hills of the Bergisches Land (see entry), is the main centre of the German tool industry.

Situation and characteristics

The Town

In the Hasten district, at Cleffstrasse 2–6, is a handsome patrician house of 1779 containing two museums. The Heimatmuseum has a collection of furniture and furnishings, mainly Baroque, Empire and Biedermeier, and a Pewter Cabinet. The German Tool Museum illustrates the development of tools from the Stone Age to the present day, with old workshops, iron-smelting equipment, etc., and maintains a number of old ironworks on an "industrial trail" in the Gelpe valley.

Heimatmuseum
Tool Museum

The Röntgen Museum at Schwelmer Strasse 41, in the Lennep district, displays apparatus which belonged to the discoverer of X-rays, W. C. Röntgen, a native of Remscheid, as well as modern X-ray apparatus, and illustrates applications of X-rays in archaeology, materials technology, etc.

Röntgen Museum

Rendsburg

B 5

Land: Schleswig-Holstein
Altitude: 5m/16ft
Population: 30,000

The old town of Rendsburg, now a considerable industrial centre, is attractively situated between the river Eider, which here opens out into the semblance of a lake, and the Kiel Canal (Nord-Ostsee-Kanal). It is the most important inland port on the canal.

Situation and characteristics

The Town

The old town lies on an island in the Eider. In the Markt is the Old Town Hall, a half-timbered building of 1566.

Old town

A little way north is St Mary's Church (1287–93), with a richly furnished interior (fine Baroque altar of 1649, 14th century wall paintings).

St Mary's Church

To the east of the old town and the railway line, on Kieler Strasse, is the Elektromuseum (development of domestic electrical appliances since 1890).

Elektromuseum

South of the old town is the Neuwerk district, built between 1690 and 1695, with the spacious Paradeplatz. Just off the square is the Christkirche (1695–1700), an interesting Baroque church with a special seat for the king of Denmark.

Neuwerk

At the north-west corner of Paradeplatz is the Hohes Arsenal Cultural Centre (1989), with a Heimat- and Canal Museum and a Printing Museum.

Cultural Centre

Rendsburg Bridge

Jewish Museum	South-east of Paradeplatz, at Prinzessinstrasse 7–8, is the Jewish Museum.
Casting Museum	To the north of the Eider is the Casting Museum of the Ahlmann casting works, with fine examples of the delicate casting and wrought-iron work produced here.
*High-level bridge	To the south-east of the town is a high-level bridge (1910–13) carrying the railway over the Kiel Canal at a height of 42m/138ft. Underneath it is a transporter bridge for pedestrians and cars. Farther west are a road and a pedestrian tunnel under the canal.

Reutlingen
K 4

Land: Baden-Württemberg
Altitude: 376m/1234ft
Population: 97,000

Situation and characteristics	The old free imperial city of Reutlingen lies on the north-western slopes of the Swabian Alb (see entry). It is now an important centre of the textile, engineering and leatherworking industries.

Old Town

Listplatz	On the north-west side of the old town, beside the railway station, is Listplatz, with a monument to the economist Friedrich List (1789–1846), son of a Reutlingen tanner.
St Nicholas's Church	From Karlsplatz Wilhelmstrasse (pedestrian zone), the main axis of the old town, runs south-east, passing St Nicholas's Church (1358). In front of the church stands the Tanners' and Dyers' Fountain.

Marktplatz and Spital

Katharinenstrasse and Tübingen Gate

The spacious Marktplatz, farther along Wilhelmstrasse, and its surrounding buildings have recently been thoroughly renovated. On the Market Fountain can be seen a statue of the Emperor Maximilian II. On the north-east side of the square is the Neues Spital (New Hospital; 14th and 16th c.), now occupied by an adult education and cultural centre. The Town Hall has a picture by HAP Grieshaber, "The Battering Ram" (1966); it also houses the Municipal Archives and the Friedrich List Archives.

Marktplatz

Beyond this, still in Wilhelmstrasse, is St Mary's Church (1247–1343), one of the finest High Gothic churches in Swabia. The oldest part, to the rear, dates from the 12th century, the 73m/240ft high tower from 1494. The church has 14th century wall paintings, a Late Gothic Holy Sepulchre and a font of 1499.

*St Mary's Church

At the south-east end of Wilhelmstrasse is the Zwinger, a relic of the town's old fortifications.

South-west of St Mary's Church, near which can be found the Guild Fountain (1983), is an old monastic house, the Königsbronner Klosterhof (14th and 16th c.), which now houses the interesting Heimatmuseum (history of the town; the guilds; Friedrich List Room).

Heimatmuseum

To the west, in Lederstrasse, is the Spendhaus, a large half-timbered house (1518), originally a granary, now occupied by the Natural History Museum (fossils; dioramas; collection of insects).

Natural History Museum

On the western outskirts of the town lies Gmindersdorf, a workers' housing scheme built between 1903 and 1914 (recently restored).

Gmindersdorf

Rhine Valley

M 4 – E 1

States bordering the Rhine: Germany, Switzerland, Liechtenstein, Austria, France, Netherlands

Rhine Valley

N.B.
In this guide the description of the Rhine valley has been deliberately kept short, since a full account is provided in the "Rhine" guide in the same series.

General
The Rhine (German Rhein; Celtic Renos, Roman Rhenus; popularly "Vater Rhein", "Father Rhine") is Europe's most important waterway and scenically its most beautiful. With a total length of 1320km/820 miles, it originates in the eastern Swiss canton of Grisons, where the Vorderrhein and Hinterrhein unite to form the Alpenrhein (Alpine Rhine). It then flows through Lake Constance (see entry), goes over the Rhine Falls at Schaffhausen and continues on its way to Basle as the Hochrhein (High Rhine). There it turns north and, as the Oberrhein (Upper Rhine), flows through the Upper Rhine plain. Between Mainz and Bingen it turns west again and then bears north-west through the Rhenish Uplands as the Middle Rhine. Below Bonn it is known as the Lower Rhine. Within the Netherlands it divides into a number of arms which flow separately into the North Sea.

Width
The widest stretch of the Rhine is between Mainz and Bingen (between 400m/440yds and 800m/880yds). In its passage through the Rhenish Uplands it narrows to 250m/275yds at the Binger Loch (Bingen Hole) and 90–150m/100–165yds at the Loreley Rock. At Cologne it widens again to around 350m/380yds.
The river tends to wander a little and form islands (called "Aue" above Bingen and "Werthe" below) which add variety to the scenery.

Navigation
Navigation presents the greatest difficulty between Bingen and St Goar on account of the considerable gradient and the narrowness of the channel. The river authorities devote much effort to maintaining the navigability of the river by dredging and the blasting away of dangerous rock faces. The artificially created shipping channel is marked by buoys, beacons and floating booms, and at points where visibility is restricted the traffic upstream and downstream is regulated by warning signs (lights, flags, balls, revolving signs). Navigation on the Rhine, which within German territory is subject to the authority of the Federal Minister of Transport, was internationalised in 1831.

Roads
On both banks of the Middle Rhine there are railways and roads (on the left bank B 9, the Rheingoldstrasse; on the right bank B 42, the Loreley-Burgenstrasse), which carry heavy traffic.

*Landscape

The Upper Rhine plain, a rift valley some 30–40km/20–25 miles wide, is bounded on the east by the Black Forest (see entry), the Kraichgau and the Odenwald (see entry), on the west by the Vosges, the Haardt and the uplands of the northern Palatinate. Its loess soil makes it a fertile fruit- and vine-growing region (Markgräflerland, Kaiserstuhl, Ortenau, Deutsche Weinstrasse, Bergstrasse).

In its middle course the Rhine flows between the Rheingau (on right) and Rheinhessen (on left) for some 100km/60 miles. Both of these areas lie within the western Mainz basin, which forms the northern termination of the trough-like depression of the Upper Rhine plain and, like it, was the result of a rift in Tertiary times. The Rheingau and the Rhein-hessen uplands were at one stage submerged by water and were separated from one another only in geologically recent times. How far the water extended at one time is shown by the interesting fossil-rich deposits which can be seen in sand and marl pits at Gau-Algesheim, Sprendlingen, Messel and Weinheim.

At Bingen the river, which at Mainz had come up against the wall of the Taunus and made a sharp turn westward, changes its course again and flows through the Rhenish Uplands against the grain of the rock, cutting across the hard quartzites of the Hunsrück and the Taunus. In this resistant rock it is confined to a narrow gorge-like valley. The hills rose slowly from the Tertiary onwards, while the Rhine cut its way in stages into a pre-existing trough, creating a terraced landscape pattern; and as a result boulder clay deposited by the Rhine is found at varying altitudes.
The passage through the Rhenish Uplands, with its changes of gradient, also creates difficulties of navigation – at the Binger Loch (Bingen Hole), the legendary Loreley Rock

and St Goar. In the more open loess basins between these places there is room for prosperous settlements, for the growing of vines and fruit. These variations, together with the castles crowning the steep hills on either side and the islands in the river, produce an ever-changing pattern of scenery.

Below Koblenz, where the Mosel flows into the Rhine at Deutsches Eck, the valley opens out into the little Neuwied basin, where there has been a vigorous development of industry. Shortly before the river enters the Lower Rhine plain it passes on the right an outlier of the Westerwald, the distinctively shaped Siebengebirge (Seven Hills), forming a striking landmark at the lower end of the Middle Rhine.

The river then enters the Cologne or Lower Rhine lowlands, a gently undulating region. The Lower Rhine really begins at Duisburg. Then at Elten, below a hill crowned by a monastery, the Rhine crosses the frontier into the Netherlands.

From Mainz or Wiesbaden to Cologne

Left Bank

Leave Mainz (see entry) on the road going west along the left bank of the Rhine, skirting the uplands of Rheinhessen.

The little town of Ingelheim is famed for its red wine. Round the 12th century church in Niederingelheim can be seen the remains of an imperial stronghold of Charlemagne and Ludwig (Louis) the Pious. Oberingelheim has preserved its old walls and has a Romanesque and Gothic church. | Ingelheim

Bingen lies at the junction of the Nahe with the Rhine, above the "Bingen Hole" where the river breaks through the Rhenish Uplands. In the old town, above the Nahe, stands the Late Gothic parish church (15th–16th c.), with a Carolingian and Romanesque crypt. Above the town is Burg Klopp (13th c.; blown up by the French in 1711, rebuilt in the 19th century), which now houses a Heimatmuseum. | Bingen

Beyond Bingerbrück, in the middle of the Rhine, is the Mäuseturm ("Mouse Tower"), a 13th century toll-collecting post, where legend has it that Archbishop Hatto was eaten by mice. | Mäuseturm

From the old wine village of Trechtingshausen two castles, both open to the public, can be visited – Rheinstein (13th c.; extended 1825–29) and Reichenstein (11th c.; destroyed 1282, rebuilt about 1900). | Trechtingshausen

Looming over Niederheimbach is the massive tower of the Heimburg (private property), which was destroyed in 1639. In the Rhine lies the Lorcher Werth, a long narrow island. Above the town is the Märchenhain (Fairytale Grove), with groups of figures. | Niederheimbach

Bacharach, an old-established centre of the wine trade, is surrounded by its 16th century ring of walls and towers. Above the town is the ruined Burg Stahleck (youth hostel). In the Marktplatz are a number of 16th century half-timbered houses and the Late Romanesque St Peter's Church (13th c.). The Münzturm (Mint Tower) houses a Heimat- and Wine Museum. On the way up to Burg Stahleck are the ruins of the Werner Chapel (13th–15th c.). | Bacharach

The Frauenkirche (Church of Our Lady; 1308–31), in the old-world little walled town of Oberwesel, has a fine interior (Baroque organ). On the town walls on the lower side of the town is the Gothic Werner Chapel (c. 1300). Above the town is the Schönburg (restored from 1885 onwards; youth centre).
Beyond the town there is a fine view of the Loreley Rock. | Oberwesel

St Goar lies below the massive ruined castle of Rheinfels. The Stiftskirche (15th c.) has a Romanesque crypt of 1137, 15th century wall paintings and marble tombs of the 16th | St Goar and 17th centuries. The ruined castle is the largest of its kind on the Rhine (museum; view).

Boppard

Boppard, once a free imperial city, lies in the Bopparder Hamm, a large loop in the Rhine which is famed for its wine. On the Burggraben and in Karmeliterstrasse are considerable remains of a Roman fort. In the Markt stands the twin-towered church of St Severus (12th–13th c.), with Romanesque wall paintings. On the banks of the Rhine, in the tower of an old Electoral castle, is the Heimatmuseum. Within the commune of Boppard is the spa of Bad Salzig (hot springs containing Glauber's salt).
North of Boppard is the Vierseenblick viewpoint (chair-lift), from which there is a fine view of the Bopparder Hamm.

Rhens

Rhens, which appears in the records as early as the 9th century, still preserves stretches of its old walls and a number of 16th and 17th century half-timbered houses. 1km/¾ mile outside the little town is the Königsstuhl, a pulpit-like structure which until 1921 stood on the banks of the Rhine at the old meeting-place of the Electors of the Rhineland.
The road continues past the Rhens mineral spring and through the district of Stolzenfels to Koblenz.

Koblenz

See entry

The road now runs through the Neuwied basin.

Andernach

At Andernach the road returns to the Rhine. The town occupies the site of the Roman fort of Autunnacum. In later centuries it was a free imperial city, the possession of which was much disputed. The town walls and gates (14th–15th c.) are well preserved. Beside the Koblenz Gate, set in gardens, can be seen the ruins of a castle of the Electors of Cologne which was destroyed in 1689. In the Markt is the Late Gothic Town Hall (1572) and to the west of the square the beautiful Late Romanesque Liebfrauenkirche (13th c.).
Andernach is a good starting-point for a trip through the northern Eifel (see entry).

Bad Breisig

The popular spa of Bad Breisig has three springs at temperatures of between 26° and 34°C (79° and 93°F); Kurpark, two indoor thermal pools, outdoor pools. In Oberbreisig is the 13th century parish church of St Victor, with wall paintings; Niederbreisig has the Baroque parish church of the Assumption (1718) and some handsome burghers' houses (17th–18th c.).

Sinzig

Sinzig, the Roman Sentiacum, lies 2km/1¼ miles from the Rhine in the fertile "Golden Mile" near the mouth of the Ahr. An old stronghold of the Emperor Frederick Barbarossa now houses the Heimatmuseum. Remains of town walls. On higher ground is the Late Romanesque parish church of St Peter (13th c.).
At Sinzig a road branches off into the Ahr valley (see entry).

Remagen

Remagen, a town of Celtic origin, takes its name from the Roman fort of Ricomagus. At the lower end of the town is the neo-Romanesque parish church of SS Peter and Paul, with the nave of the original 11th century Romanesque church forming its porch. Below the terrace on which the church stands and near the Town Hall are remains of the Roman fort. The tower of the Remagen bridge, which collapsed in 1945, houses a Peace Museum.
The road continues through the districts of Rolandseck and Rolandswerth. In the Rhine are the islands of Nonnenwerth (Franciscan nunnery founded 1122) and Grafenwerth.

Rolandsbogen

The Rolandsbogen (Roland's Arch), 105m/345ft above the Rhine, is a remnant of the castle of Rolandseck, destroyed in 1475. Magnificent view of the Siebengebirge.

Then via Bonn to Cologne (see entries).

*Right Bank

The starting-point of this route is Wiesbaden (see entry).

Eltville

Eltville is picturequely situated amid vineyards and has large wine- and Sekt-making establishments. Of the old castle of the Archbishops of Mainz there remains only the

Rüdesheim

Niederwald Memorial

massive keep (1487; Gutenberg memorial). The 14th century Gothic parish church of SS Peter and Paul has a tabernacle of the late 14th century, a font of 1517 and a number of Renaissance tombs.

A detour can be made from Hattenheim to the Cistercian abbey of Eberbach, 3.5km/2 miles north, with a church of 1186; the conventual buildings (12th–14th c.) are now occupied by a state-owned wine estate.

The road continues to the little wine town of Oestrich-Winkel, passes under the prominently situated castle of Johannisberg (1757–59; wine-producing estate) and continues via Geisenheim to Rüdesheim.

Rüdesheim has developed since the late 19th century into one of the busiest tourist and holiday centres on the Middle Rhine, with a host of friendly restaurants and wine-taverns, particularly in the famous Drosselgasse. In the 10th century Brömserburg is the Rheingau Museum (history of wine-making). There are remains of two other castles, the Boosenburg (originally 10th c.) and the Vorderburg, and numerous old burghers' houses and aristocratic mansions (16th–18th c.). In the Brömserhof is a collection of mechanical musical instruments.

Rüdesheim

Conspicuously situated above Rüdesheim is the Niederwald Memorial, with a 10.50m/34ft high figure of Germania, commemorating the re-establishment of the German Empire in 1871 (magnificent views).

Niederwald Memorial

At the mouth of the Wisper valley (in which there are a number of old castles) is Lorch. The parish church of St Martin has a finely carved high altar (1483). There are a number of aristocratic mansions, notably the Hilchenhaus (16th c.). Above the little town stands Burg Nollig (private property).

Lorch

Kaub, once a customs collection point and pilot station, is now one of the leading wine towns on the Middle Rhine, with well preserved medieval walls. A statue of Field-Marshal Blücher commemorates the crossing of the Rhine by the Silesian army on New Year's night 1813/14; small Blücher Museum.

Kaub

Rhine Valley

*Pfalz

Above Kaub is Burg Gutenfels (13th c.). In the middle of the Rhine is the Pfalzgrafenstein (usually abbreviated to Pfalz), a fortress built in 1326 to enforce the collection of tolls on river traffic.

St Goarshausen

St Goarshausen, a long straggling place which has preserved much of its medieval core, lies at the foot of Burg Katz (14th c.; restored in 19th c.). At the upper end of the town are two 14th century watch-towers, relics of its medieval fortifications.

**Loreley Rock

The Loreley Rock is a massive slate crag rising to a height of 132m/433ft above the Rhine, here narrowed to only 113m/125yds. The fame of the Loreley Rock is due to a legend which became widely popular in the early 19th century – the story of the nymph who dwelt on the rock and lured boatmen to their destruction.

Kamp-Bornhofen

The double town of Kamp-Bornhofen lies under two castles, Burg Liebenstein and Burg Sterrenberg, the "Enemy Brothers". Bornhofen has a handsome Gothic church (1435) and a Franciscan friary (1680–84). Kamp has picturesque old half-timbered houses and a Late Gothic church which belonged to a convent of Franciscan nuns.

Braubach
*Marksburg

At the upper end of the ancient little town of Braubach are the ruins of the Philippsburg (1568). Romanesque cemetery chapel of St Martin (c. 1000); handsome half-timbered houses. Above the town stands the Marksburg, the only hilltop castle on the Rhine which has escaped destruction (museum).

Lahnstein

Lahnstein lies on both banks of the Lahn at its junction with the Rhine. On the left bank is Oberlahnstein, with remains of its old walls and the richly decorated Old Town Hall (Late Gothic, 15th c.). The Hexenturm (Witches' Tower) houses the Municipal Museum. To the east of the town are the Kurthermen Rhein-Lahn (baths, 30°C/86°F and 36°C/97°F). Niederlahnstein has preserved one or two old aristocratic mansions. At Lahnstrasse 8 is a famous old inn, a half-timbered building of 1697 on 14th century foundations. East of the town rises the Allerheiligenberg, on the summit of which are a monastery and a pilgrimage church.

The famous Loreley Rock

See entry

See entry   Koblenz

Neuwied, in the fertile Neuwied basin, was laid out on a regular plan from 1662 onwards. Set in a beautiful park is a palace modelled on Versailles (1706–56). Other features of interest are the meeting-house of the Moravian Brethren (1783–85) and the Mennonite church (1768).   Neuwied

Linz, situated on the fringes of the Westerwald opposite the mouth of the Ahr, has preserved a number of attractive and colourful half-timbered buildings, particularly on the Marktplatz (Late Gothic Town Hall of 1392) and Burgplatz. Burg Feith (14th c.) was a summer residence of the Archbishops of Cologne. The Late Romanesque parish church of St Martin, above the town, has 13th century wall paintings.   Linz

Bad Honnef is an attractive spa (Drachenquelle, "Dragon Spring") lying in a sheltered situation at the foot of the Siebengebirge. In the Markt is the parish church of St John the Baptist (12th and 16th–17th c.). In the Rhöndorf district is the house once occupied by Konrad Adenauer (1876–1967), first Chancellor of the German Federal Republic; it is now a memorial museum.   Bad Honnef

Königswinter is a popular resort at the foot of the Siebengebirge. A rack railway runs up to the summit of the Drachenfels, on which stand the ruins of a castle built in 1147 and destroyed in 1634; good views, extending as far as Cologne.   Königswinter

On the Petersberg is the former Petersberg Hotel, now a government guest-house.

The Siebengebirge, a range of hills at the north-western end of the Westerwald, extends along the right bank of the Rhine a short distance upstream from Bonn, offering one of the finest stretches of scenery in the whole length of the Rhine.   ◦Siebengebirge

Then via Bonn to Cologne (see entries).

Rhön   G–H 5

Länder: Bavaria, Hesse, Thuringia

The Rhön is an upland region lying between the upper courses of the Fulda and the Werra and between the river Sinn and the Franconian Saale. The southern and eastern parts of the area are in Bavaria, the north-western part in Hesse and the north-eastern tip in Thuringia.   Situation and characteristics

Landscape

The numerous isolated hills and larger ranges owe their origin to volcanic eruptions and lava flows of the Tertiary era which overlaid the older, less resistant limestones and sandstones and protected them from erosion. Depending on local conditions, the hills may be conical or may take the form of plateaux.
In many areas there are great expanses of meadowland, with isolated basalt hills rising above them. Pastoral farming, therefore, predominates. The harsh climate and heavy rainfall have led to the development of large areas of moorland.

The dissection of the hills by valleys has left only one continuous massif on the watershed, the Hohe Rhön (High Rhön), a plateau region between 700m/2300ft and 900m/2950ft covered with grass and high moorland.   Hohe Rhön

To the west of the Hohe Rhön is the Vorderrhön, with isolated hills, either conical in form (such as the Wachtküppel near Gersfeld) or hog-backed (Milseburg, near Poppenhausen).   Vorderrhön

The highest hill in the Rhön is the Wasserkuppe (950m/3117ft), the bare slopes of which are a favourite resort of gliding and hang-gliding enthusiasts (German Gliding Museum).   ◦Wasserkuppe

Rhön

<table>
<tr><td>Forested Rhön
* Kreuzberg</td><td>To the south of the Bischofsheim and Gersfeld basins lies the Forested Rhön (Waldreiche Rhön), with long ridges covered with mixed forest. The highest point is the Kreuzberg (932m/3058ft; Franciscan friary).</td></tr>
<tr><td>Kuppenrhön</td><td>The Northern Rhön or Kuppenrhön, in Thuringia, is a region of basalt hills between 600m/2000ft and 800m/2600ft in height, conical or round-topped in form.</td></tr>
<tr><td>Hohe Geba</td><td>One of the most striking parts of the Rhön is the Hohe Geba range to the west of Meiningen (now a landscape reserve), with the Gebaberg (751m/2464ft). There are other basalt hills between Vacha and Kaltennordheim reaching heights of between 650m/2130ft and 700m/2300ft.</td></tr>
</table>

Romantische Strasse (Romantic Highway)   H 5 – M 6

The Romantische Strasse is the oldest German tourist route. Extending from Würzburg in the north to Füssen in the south, a distance of some 350km/220 miles, it provides a link between Eastern Franconia and the Bavarian Alps.

From Würzburg (see entry) the route runs west and then turns south on B 27, cuts twice across the motorway and reaches Tauberbischofsheim (see Bad Mergentheim, Surroundings) in the beautiful Tauber valley. It then follows the valley, by way of Bad Mergentheim and Weikersheim (see Bad Mergentheim, Surroundings) to Creglingen (see Rothenburg, Surroundings) and the old free imperial city of Rothenburg.

From Rothenburg the route continues south, passing the Baroque princely capital of Schillingsfürst (8km/5 miles east, beyond the motorway), to Feuchtwangen (see Dinkelsbühl, Surroundings) and then descends to Dinkelsbühl in the Wörnitz valley. Beyond this are Wallerstein (Porcelain Museum in Neues Schloss) and Nördlingen (see entry). Then south-east via Harburg (see Donauwörth, Surroundings) and down the Wörnitz valley to Donauwörth in the Danube valley (see entry).

The route then ascends the wide Lech valley to Augsburg (see entry), Landsberg (see entry) and Schongau (see Landsberg, Surroundings).

Just before reaching Steingaden (see Füssen, Surroundings) the Romantische Strasse joins the Deutsche Alpenstrasse (see entry), and the two keep company to Füssen (see entry), near which, at Schwangau, are the celebrated royal castles of Hohenschwangau and Neuschwanstein.

Rosenheim   L 7

Land: Bavaria
Altitude: 451m/1480ft
Population: 51,000

<table>
<tr><td>Situation and characteristics</td><td>Rosenheim, situated at the junction of the Mangfall with the Inn, was from the earliest times an important trading town on the road from Italy to the north. The houses in the old town are in the German/Italian style characteristic of the towns in the Inn and Salzach valleys.</td></tr>
</table>

The Town

<table>
<tr><td>Max-Josefs-Platz</td><td>In the centre of the old town lies Max-Josefs-Platz, surrounded by arcades. It is linked by the Mittertor (Heimatmuseum) with Ludwigsplatz, in which stands the parish church of St Nicholas (originally Gothic; rebuilt 1881).</td></tr>
<tr><td>Art Gallery</td><td>To the south of the Town Hall, in Max-Bram-Platz, is the Municipal Art Gallery (works by Munich painters from Spitzweg onwards). To the west is another gallery, the Ausstellungsgalerie Lokschuppen, housed in an old railway engine-shed.</td></tr>
<tr><td>Stadthalle</td><td>On the site of the old salt-works is the Stadthalle (1982), with a sculpture garden.</td></tr>
</table>

Doberan Minster, near Rostock ▶

Rostock

Inn Museum   In Innstrasse, near the banks of the river, can be found the Inn Museum (hydraulic engineering, shipping).

Land: Mecklenburg-West Pomerania
Altitude: 13m/43ft
Population: 250,000

Situation and characteristics   Rostock, a famous and powerful Hanseatic and university town in the Middle Ages, is now an important port and industrial city (shipbuilding, fish-processing, building). At Warnemünde, Rostock's outer harbour, the river Warnow flows into the Baltic.

Sights

*Town Hall   In the Neuer Markt, in the centre of the rebuilt old town, is the 13th century Town Hall, with a Baroque façade (1727–29), built after the destruction of the old Ratslaube (arcade) in 1718.

*St Mary's Church   In the Markt are fine old gabled houses and the imposing Gothic Marienkirche (St Mary's Church); Baroque interior, with a bronze font of 1290, St Roch's Altar, an astronomical clock of 1472 (calendar extending to 2017) and a Baroque organ.

Old Mint   In the Ziegenmarkt, by the church, is the handsome façade of the Old Mint (Alte Münze: Rostock enjoyed the right to coin money from 1325 to 1864).

Lange Strasse   The rebuilding of Rostock after the Second World War began in the Lange Strasse, which runs west from St Mary's Church. It shows a successful mingling of traditional North German brick-built Gothic and modern features.
North of the Lange Strasse lies a rebuilt area of the old town, consisting of new buildings in traditional style and carefully restored old buildings (e.g. Wokrenter Strasse 40).

*Kröpeliner Strasse   South of the Lange Strasse, parallel with it, is Kröpeliner Strasse (pedestrian zone), with gabled houses of different periods.

University   In Universitätsplatz, to the south of Kröpeliner Strasse, are the main building of Rostock University (1867–70, neo-Renaissance), the old Palace (Baroque Hall), the neo-classical Hauptwache (Guard-House) and the "Fountain of the Joy of Life" (by J. Jastram and R. Dietrich). In front of the University can be seen a statue (by J. G. Schadow, 1819) of Field-Marshal Blücher, who was born in Rostock.

Monastery (Museum)   Immediately west of the University is the Monastery of the Holy Cross, now occupied by the Museum of Culture (Kulturhistorisches Museum).

Kröpeliner Tor (Museum)   At the end of Kröpeliner Strasse is the Kröpeliner Tor (13th–14th c., brick-built Gothic), now housing a museum.

Fischerbastion   To the north of the Kröpeliner Tor, reached by way of the Wallanlagen (the gardens on the line of the old fortifications), is the 17th century Fischerbastion.

Steintor   At the end of Steinstrasse, which runs south from the Neuer Markt, is the Steintor, rebuilt in Renaissance style, with the three historic coats of arms of Rostock.

Shipping Museum   In August-Bebel-Strasse can be found the Shipping Museum (Schiffahrtsmuseum). In the Schmarl district is moored an old ship of traditional type, the "Frieden" (shipbuilding museum).

Kunsthalle   On the Schwanenteich is the Kunsthalle (exhibitions).

*Warnemünde

Warnemünde, originally a small fishing village, was bought by the Town Council of Rostock from the Prince of Mecklenburg in 1323, and until the 20th century was administered by a governor appointed by the Council.

On the Alter Strom, Warnemünde

A typical 18th century fisherman's house in Theodor-Körner-Strasse houses the Heimat-museum, which illustrates the life and customs of the local seamen and fishermen. — Heimatmuseum

The picturesque street called the Alter Graben leads to the Warnemünde lighthouse (1897–98) and the West Pier. — Lighthouse / West Pier

Bad Doberan

B 7

Bad Doberan, formerly the summer residence of the Dukes of Mecklenburg, lies 15km/ 9 miles west of Rostock. It is famed for its Minster, which is unique in the Baltic area. The district of Heiligendamm was originally built as a seaside resort – the first in Germany. — Situation and characteristics

The town's great landmark is the Minster, a brick-built Gothic church (1294–1368; restored 1984) which originally belonged to a Cistercian monastery. One of the most beautiful churches in the Baltic area, it has a richly furnished interior, with a tabernacle 11.60m/38ft high, a huge Triumphal Cross group, fine altars, wood sculpture, grave-slabs and burial chapels. Of the old conventual buildings there survive the charnel-house (13th c.), the granary (c. 1270) and the brew-house (c. 1290). — *Minster

In the centre of the neo-classical town is the Kamp, a landscaped park in the English style, with the Saloon (Salongebäude; by T. Severin, 1801–02), now the seat of the District Council; the Grosses Palais (Severin, 1806–10), now occupied by offices; and the old Logierhaus (by Seydewitz, 1793), now a hotel. The two Chinese pavilions in the park are the only examples of chinoiserie in Mecklenburg (1808–09 and 1810–13; now a café and an exhibition hall). — Kamp

Rothenburg ob der Tauber   I 5

Land: Bavaria
Altitude: 425m/1395ft
Population: 12,000

Situation and
characteristics

The old Franconian imperial city of Rothenburg, one of the most attractive places on the
Romantische Strasse (see entry), is picturesquely situated on the steep bank of the
Tauber. With its walls and towers, almost untouched since the Thirty Years' War, it offers
unique charm and interest as a completely preserved little medieval town.

The **Town

*Town Hall

In the Marktplatz stands the imposing Town Hall (Rathaus), one of the finest in South
Germany. On Herrngasse is the Gothic part of the building (13th c.), with a 50m/165ft
high tower (16th c.; view); the market front is Renaissance (1572–78), with the fine
Imperial Hall (dramatic performances, concerts). On the north side of the square is the
former Ratstrinkstube (Council Tavern, 1466); clock with mechanical figures representing the "master draught" with which Burgomaster Nusch saved the town from
plundering by Imperial forces in 1621 (daily at 11am, noon and 1, 2, 3, 9 and 10pm).

Herrngasse

At the near end of Herrngasse (Gothic and Renaissance patrician houses), on the left, can
be seen the town's most beautiful fountain, the Herterich- or St-Georgs-Brunnen (1608).
Farther along the street is the Early Gothic Franciscan Church (fine grave-slabs). The
Herrngasse ends at the Burgtor, beside which is the Figurentheater.

Burggarten

At the Burgtor is the entrance to the Burggarten, laid out on the site of a Hohenstaufen
castle which was destroyed in an earthquake in 1356 (fine view).

*St James's
Church

North of the Town Hall is St James's Church (St Jakob; 1373–1436). In structure and
general effect the high altar (1466) is one of the finest in Germany. In the west choir is the
Altar of the Holy Blood (by Tilman Riemenschneider, 1501–04).

Town Hall, Rothenburg

North-west of the church, in a former Dominican nunnery, is the Imperial City Museum (Reichsstadtmuseum).

From the Marktplatz Schmiedgasse runs south. At the near end, on left (No. 3), is the Baumeisterhaus (1596) and next door (No. 5) the old Gasthaus zum Greifen (Griffin Inn), once the residence of Burgomaster Heinrich Toppler (d. 1408). Farther along, on right, is St John's Church (St Johannis; 1393–1403).

Nearby, at Burggasse 2, can be found the interesting Kriminalmuseum (torture-chamber).

At the end of the Untere Schmiedgasse, at a street intersection, is the Plönlein, one of the most picturesque spots in the town.

From here the passage under the Siebersturm leads into Spitalgasse, which runs past the Early Gothic Spitalkirche (on right) and the Spital (1574–78). In the picturesque Spitalhof is the Hegereiterhäuschen (1591) and at the end of the street the massive 16th century Spitaltor.

* Town Walls

There is an interesting and attractive walk (which takes about half an hour) round the town walls on the wall-walk, from the Spitaltor by way of the Rödertor (view) to the Klingentor and St Wolfgang's Church (1473–92).

Surroundings of Rothenburg

Below the Kobolzeller Tor is the little Kobolzell Church. On the far side of the Tauber (fine view of Rothenburg) stands the Topplerschlösschen, a tower-like house built in 1388 by Burgomaster Toppler.

The road (the Romantische Strasse) continues down the Tauber valley to Detwang, with a little church (Romanesque, altered in Gothic style) which has a fine Crucifixion group by Tilman Riemenschneider (c. 1512–13).

The Romantische Strasse continues to Creglingen. To the south of the town is the Herrgottskirche (1386–96), which has a magnificent carved altar dedicated to the Virgin by Tilman Riemenschneider (c. 1505–10).
The town has a Fire Service Museum (in the Schloss) and a Thimble Museum.

Rottweil

L 4

Land: Baden-Württemberg
Altitude: 600m/1970ft
Population: 23,000

The old free imperial city of Rottweil, picturesquely situated above the steep banks of the upper Neckar, has preserved many interesting old buildings. It is famed for its Carnival (Fasnet), with masks and costumes.

The Town

In the steep main street stands the Late Gothic Old Town Hall (1512) and opposite the Municipal Museum (Roman mosaic; history of the town; Carnival masks and costumes).

To the north is the Minster of the Holy Cross (13th–15th c.; R.C.), with numerous carved altars and an altar cross by Veit Stoss.

Rübeland

Hochbrückenstrasse

A finely decorated oriel

Parish church	The parish church, originally the church of a Dominican monastery, in Friedrichsplatz was begun in 1268 and remodelled in Baroque style from 1753 (ceiling paintings).
⚬St Lawrence's Chapel	Nearby, on the steep bank of the river, is St Lawrence's Chapel (*c.* 1580), with a collection of fine Gothic sculpture. A new building to house the collection is under construction beside the parish church.
Kapellenkirche	Near the intersection of the town's two main streets (Market Fountain of 1540) is the Kapellenkirche (originally Gothic, remodelled in Baroque style in 1717).
Roman baths	To the south-east of the old town the remains of Roman baths belonging to the settlement of Arae Flaviae, probably dating from the reign of Trajan, have been excavated. In nearby Königstrasse, which runs west from the town, are a number of works of modern sculpture, set up here in 1970.

Rübeland

See Wernigerode, Surroundings

Rudolstadt

See Saalfeld, Surroundings

Rügen

A–B 8

Land: Mecklenburg-West Pomerania
Area: 926 sq.km/358 sq. miles

The island of Rügen is the largest and scenically the most beautiful of the islands off the Baltic coast, separated from the mainland by the Strelasund, which is less than a kilometre (¾ mile) wide. It is linked with the mainland town of Stralsund (see entry) by a causeway constructed in 1936.

**Landscape

The much-lauded beauty of Rügen is created by the juxtaposition within a relatively small area of very different types of landscape. The south-western part of the island, which is predominantly flat agricultural country, contrasts with the forest-covered rounded hills to the north-east, which reach a height of 91m/299ft in Rugard (Ernst Moritz Arndt Tower, 27m/89ft high), near Bergen (see below), and are continued to the east in the Granitz hills (Tempelberg, 107m/351ft, with hunting lodge and 38m/125ft high outlook tower) between Binz and Sellin, which then slope steeply down to the sea. Between these ranges of hills and the peninsulas of Wittow (chief place Altenkirchen) and Jasmund (chief place Sassnitz) are the great sheets of water of the *bodden* (depressions drowned by the sea), including the Grosser and the Kleiner Jasmunder Bodden.

The Jasmund peninsula, consisting of massive layers of chalk with a thin morainic cover, reaches a height of 161m/528ft in the Piekberg.

Jasmund peninsula

The beautiful Stubnitz beech forests come to an abrupt end on the Königsstuhl, where a sheer chalk cliff with bands of flints plunges down to the sea from a height of 117m/384ft. The steep chalk cliffs of Stubbenkammer are a popular tourist attraction.

At the north-eastern tip of the Wittow peninsula are the lighthouse on Kap Arkona (46m/151ft) and remains of the ramparts of a fortified Slav settlement, the Jaromarsburg, which until its capture and destruction by the Danes in 1168 contained the principal sanctuary of the Western Slavs.

Wittow peninsula
Kap Arkona

In a sheltered inlet near Putgarten lies the old-world little fishing village of Vitt, once (like Vitte on the island of Hiddensee) a landing-place used by the herring fleets of the Hanseatic towns.

Vitt

In the south-east of the island is the little town of Putbus (pop. 5600), seat of the Princes of Putbus, with neo-classical buildings and a beautiful Schlosspark. Here too is Rügen's oldest seaside resort, established in the early 19th century on the Goor, near Lauterbach. The largest modern resorts (Binz, Sellin and Göhren) are also in this area.

Putbus

There are numerous prehistoric sites on Rügen, including remains of the Neolithic Lietzow culture, which supplied large areas of Central Europe with tools made from Rügen flint, and numerous megalithic chamber tombs and Bronze Age tumulus tombs.

Prehistoric sites

Sassnitz

Sassnitz lies on the Jasmund peninsula, to the south of the Stubbenkammer cliffs, surrounded on the north by the beautiful Stubnitz beech forests.

Situation and characteristics

From Sassnitz there are international ferry services to Trelleborg in Sweden and Klaipeda in Lithuania.

6km/4 miles north of Sassnitz are the chalk cliffs of Stubbenkammer, reaching a height of 119m/390ft in the Königsstuhl. Wide views from nearby crags.

*Stubbenkammer

25km/15 miles south-west on B 96 is Bergen, an important road junction. St Mary's Church, modelled on Lübeck Cathedral, is an outstanding example of North German brick-built Gothic architecture. Originally Romanesque (begun about 1180), it was rebuilt in the 14th century as a Gothic hall-church. It has a remarkable cycle of 13th century wall paintings of Old and New Testament scenes in the choir and transept. Also of interest is the grave-slab of Abbess Elizabeth (1473).

Bergen

Harbour, Sassnitz

Hiddensee

Situation and characteristics	The island of Hiddensee, lying off the west coast of Rügen like a protective breakwater, is 17km/10½ miles long from north to south but never much more than 1km/¾ mile wide and at its narrowest point only 125m/135yds across, with a total area of 18.6 sq.km/7 sq. miles. Exposed as it is to the north and west winds, Hiddensee is subject to the danger of violent storm tides. Hiddensee is accessible only by boat from Stralsund or Rügen, and no motor vehicles are permitted. As a holiday resort it offers broad sandy beaches and plenty of good walking.
*View	From the Dornbusch plateau in the north of the island there are fine panoramic views of the *bodden* and the hills of Rügen, the distant church towers of Stralsund and Barth, the Darss lighthouse and, in clear weather, the cliffs of the Danish island of Møn.
Kloster	The most northerly place on the island, Kloster, grew up around a monastery (*kloster*) founded here in 1297, when the island belonged to Denmark. A single arched doorway of the monastery survives. In the old churchyard of the monastery is the grave of the dramatist Gerhart Hauptmann (1862–1946), who spent holidays on Hiddensee.
Neuendorf	Neuendorf, founded about 1700, is the most southerly settlement on the island; with its whitewashed houses surrounded by green turf it is also the most charming.

Ruhr F 2–3

Land: North Rhine-Westphalia

N.B.	In German the Ruhr means the river Ruhr; the area known in English as the Ruhr is in German the Ruhrgebiet.

Hohenwartetalsperre ▶

Situation and
characteristics

The Ruhr, lying between the rivers Ruhr and Lippe, is one of Europe's largest industrial regions and a major element in the German economy. Founded originally on coal-mining, it has developed into a huge industrial complex centred particularly on iron and steel, engineering, chemicals and textiles. A dense network of roads, railways and waterways serves this heavily populated region, in which housing areas and industrial installations often merge imperceptibly into one another.

In spite of the predominance of industry the Ruhr also has excellent facilities for recreation, with many artificial lakes and parks.

See also Bochum, Dortmund, Duisburg and Essen.

Saale Valley   H 7 – E 7

Länder: Thuringia, Saxony-Anhalt

The Saale rises in the Fichtelgebirge and flows north-west down the slopes of the Franconian Forest amd the Thuringian Hills in a winding and deeply indented valley; then, emerging from the hills at Saalfeld, bears north-east. At Weissenfels it enters the Saxon Lowland and at Barby, after a course of 427km/265 miles, flows into the Elbe. From Naumburg it is navigable for small vessels, from Halle for larger ones.

The catchment area of the Saale takes in not only the Thuringian Hills and the northern part of the Thuringian Forest but also the whole of the Thuringian Basin, the Eastern Harz and its foreland, the Vogtland and part of the Saxon Lowland.

The Saale valley is divided into three very different sections: the upper valley as far as Saalfeld, the middle valley in the river's course through the fringes of the Thuringian Basin and the lower valley in the lowlands below Weissenfels.

*Upper Saale Valley

The upper Saale has carved a 150m/500ft deep valley through the Thuringian Hills, which lie at heights of between 500m/1650ft and 650m/2130ft. The windings of the river between the steep slopes of the valley create the contrasting scenic pattern which gives the upper Saale valley its particular charm.

Artificial lakes

The upper Saale between Blankenstein and Saalfeld now forms a chain of five artificial lakes (reservoirs). On this stretch of the river there are only a few kilometres which show it as it originally was when it was used for floating rafts of logs down from the hills, and on occasion threatened life and property with its spates.

*Bleilochtalsperre

The first of the five lakes, the Bleilochtalsperre, is also the largest: 28km/17 miles long by up to 2km/1¼ miles across, with a capacity of 215 million cubic metres (47 billion gallons). The dam, near Saalburg, is 65m/213ft high, 47m/154ft thick at the base and 7.2m/24ft thick and 205m/225yds long at the crown.

*Hohenwartetal-
sperre

Farther downstream is the Hohenwartetalsperre: 27km/17 miles long, with a capacity of 185 million cubic metres (41 billion gallons). The dam is 54.7m/179ft thick at the base and 6.7m/22ft thick and 412m/450yds long at the crown.

Middle Saale Valley

The middle valley of the Saale is also very beautiful. Its particular attraction lies in its numerous old castles, perhaps the most notable of which are Schloss Heidecksburg at Rudolstadt (see Saalfeld, Surroundings), the Leuchtenburg near Kahla (now a youth hostel), the well-known Domburger Schlösser (see Jena) and the ruined Burg Saaleck and Rudelsburg (see Naumburg).

Lower Saale Valley

Although industry and agriculture feature more prominently in the landscape of the lower Saale valley, there are also fine old castles and palaces to be seen in old towns such as Merseburg (see entry), Halle (see entry), Wettin and Bernburg (see entry), bearing witness to the eventful history of this region.

Saalfeld

G 6

Land: Thuringia
Altitude: 210m/689ft
Population: 33,600

Saalfeld, famed for its "Fairies' Caves", lies on the river Saale on the north-eastern fringes of the Thuringian Hills. A prosperous mining town in the Middle Ages and early modern times, it is now a considerable industrial town.

Situation and characteristics

Sights

The Markt is surrounded by a remarkably complete range of old buildings. The most notable of these is the old Hofapotheke (Court Pharmacy), originally built in 1180 as a tower-house for the governor of the town, acquired by the Town Council in 1468 for use as a warehouse and town hall, and rebuilt in its original style in 1882 after a fire.

Markt

The Town Hall, built after a great fire in 1517, is a handsome Late Gothic building with Renaissance additions.

*Town Hall

Near the Town Hall and the Hofapotheke is St John's Church (begun about 1380), one of the finest hall-churches in Thuringia. It has a richly furnished interior, with a Late Gothic Holy Sepulchre, a life-size figure of John the Baptist by H. Gottwalt (a pupil of Tilman Riemenschneider) and the middle panel of a triptych of 1480. On the outside are sandstone figures and reliefs which show the influence of the Parler school.

*St John's Church

Schloss Kitzerstein

473

Saalfeld

Town gates	Saalfeld preserves remains of its old walls and four gates, including the Oberes Tor and the Blankenburger Tor (both rebuilt in the 18th century).
Heimatmuseum	A few paces from the Markt, in Münzplatz, is a former Franciscan friary which now houses the Thuringian Heimatmuseum (medieval sculpture, coins minted in Saalfeld, folk traditions and country customs, history of the town and the mining industry).
Schloss	On the Petersberg stands the old castle of the Dukes of Saxe-Coburg-Saalfeld, now occupied by local government offices (fine stucco decoration and ceiling paintings in the staircase hall and the chapel).
St Gertrude's Church	Near the Schloss is St Gertrude's Church, with one of the finest carved altars produced by Saalfeld craftsmen. There are also fine carved altars in various village churches in the surrounding area.
*Hoher Schwarm Schloss Kitzerstein	The town's most striking landmark is the Hoher Schwarm, a relic of a four-towered castle modelled on Burg Thun in Switzerland. Close by, to the right, is Schloss Kitzerstein, now occupied by a music school.
St Nicholas's Church	Between the Hoher Schwarm and the Schloss is St Nicholas's Church, the town's oldest church (12th c.), which was converted into a dwelling-house in the 19th century.
Burghers' houses	Notable among the many fine burghers' houses in the town are the Stadtapotheke (Municipal Pharmacy) at Saalestrasse 11, a richly decorated Renaissance building, the Lieden, a row of medieval shops (12th–16th c., with later alterations), and old inns in the Markt.
*"Fairies' Caves"	The "Fairies' Caves", 1km/¾ mile south-west of the town, are a major tourist attraction, opened in 1914 in a disused alum shale mine. These colourful stalactitic caves display a fairytale world in a series of chambers with such names as Fairytale Cathedral, Castle of the Holy Grail, Venetian Grotto, etc.

Bad Blankenburg

	7km/4½ miles north-west of Saalfeld at the mouth of the beautiful Schwarza valley lies the popular spa of Bad Blankenburg, surrounded by high hills and dense forest.
Town Hall	In the Markt is the 15th century Town Hall, with the "Hungermännchen" (a figure with an inscription recording the high price of grain in the 14th century), the old Schwarzburg coat of arms and a tablet commemorating the educationalist Friedrich Fröbel (Froebel), who worked in the town in 1837–39.
Fröbel Memorial Museum	In Johannisgasse can be found the Fröbel Memorial Museum, opened in 1982 on the 200th anniversary of Fröbel's birth. There are many other Fröbel memorials and associations in the town.

Surroundings of Bad Blankenburg

Oberweissbach	In the village of Oberweissbach is the house in which Fröbel was born, now a museum.

Rudolstadt

Situation and characteristics	In the middle Saale valley, surrounded by wooded hills, is the former princely capital of Rudolstadt, with Schloss Heidecksburg looming over it. Wilhelm von Humboldt called this "one of the most beautiful spots in Germany".
*Heidecksburg	Above the river and the town rears Schloss Heidecksburg, a magnificent Baroque palace built by the Counts of Schwarzburg-Rudolstadt from 1737 onwards. It now houses a museum and art gallery.

In the Heinrich Heine Park is an open-air museum (peasant houses of the 17th–20th centuries). Open-air museum

In the old town stands Schloss Ludwigsburg (1734), a Baroque palace with a handsome banqueting hall. Old town

The Town Church is a hall-church rebuilt in Late Renaissance style in the 17th century, retaining many Late Gothic features. Town Church

---

Saarbrücken I 2

Capital of the *Land* of Saarland
Altitude: 230m/755ft
Population: 190,000

Saarbrücken, situated in the forest-fringed valley of the Saar, in the middle of the Saar coalfield, is the capital of the *Land* of Saarland and its economic and cultural centre. Situation and characteristics

St Johann

On the right bank of the Saar lies the lively St Johann district, with the town's principal business and shopping streets, the main railway station (south-west of which, on the banks of the river, is the Kongresshalle, built 1964–67), the Town Hall (Rathaus; 1897–1900) and the Geological Museum of the Saar Mining Company (Saarbergwerke) in Trierer Strasse.

St John's Church (St Johann; R.C.) was built by F. J. Stengel in 1754–58. The interior, largely destroyed during the French Revolution, was restored at various times during the 19th and 20th centuries. St John's Church

In Bismarckstrasse, which runs parallel to the river, are the State Theatre (Staatstheater) and, farther east, the Saarland Museum (Saarland Cultural Foundation), housed in two separate buildings, with the Old Collection and the Modern Gallery.
The Museum of Prehistory and the Early Historical Period (Museum für Vor- und Frühgeschichte), which also belongs to the Foundation, is on the left bank of the Saar, near the Ludwigskirche (see below). Saarland Museum

To the east of St Johann, on the southern slopes of the Eschberg, can be found the Zoo, with some 1000 animals of 220 different species (African House, Nocturnal Animals House). Zoo

Alt-Saarbrücken

On the left bank of the Saar is the old town of Saarbrücken. In Schlossplatz are the Old Town Hall (Altes Rathaus), in which is the Adventure Museum, and the Hereditary Prince's Palace, both designed by Stengel, and the 19th century Schloss, built on the site of an earlier palace by Stengel which was destroyed during the French Revolution. From the Schlossgarten there is a fine view of the town. Lower down stands the Late Gothic Schlosskirche (rebuilt 1956–58), with stained glass by G. Meistermann and tombs of the ruling family. Schlossplatz

North-west of the Schloss lies Ludwigsplatz, surrounded by Baroque houses. In the centre of the square is the Ludwigskirche (by Stengel, 1762–85; Protestant), restored after war damage, with a modern interior. *Ludwigskirche

On the north side of Ludwigsplatz is the Museum of Prehistory and the Early Historical Period (Museum für Vor- und Frühgeschichte), part of the Saarland Cultural Foundation.

St Arnual

The former Stiftskirche of St Arnual (13th–14th c.; Protestant), in the St Arnual district, 3km/2 miles south-west, has numerous tombs of members of the house of Nassau-Saarbrücken. *Stiftskirche

Schloss, Saarbrücken

German-French Gardens   On the south-west side of the town are the German-French Gardens (Deutsch-Französischer Garten; water organ; "Gulliver-Miniwelt").

Saar Valley   H–I 2

Länder: Saarland, Rhineland-Palatinate

The river Saar (French Sarre), known to the Romans as the Saravus, is formed by the junction of the Sarre Blanche and the Sarre Rouge, which both rise on Mt Donon in the Vosges (France), and flows into the Mosel at Konz. Between Sarreguemines (Saargemünd) and Saarbrücken it forms the frontier between Germany (Saarland) and France (Lorraine).

Landscape

In the wide upper valley of the Saar are a number of industrial towns – Saarbrücken (see entry), Völklingen, Saarlouis and Dillingen.
At Merzig, where the river is bordered by rich orchards, the valley narrows.

Mettlach
*Saar bend   At Mettlach (ceramic industry; Ceramic Museum in Schloss Ziegelberg; 18th c. Benedictine abbey) is a large bend in the Saar, surrounded by forest. The best views of the bend are to be had from the Cloef viewpoint and the ruined castle of Montclair.

Beyond Mettlach the river pursues a winding course through the hills.

Saarburg   Saarburg is the centre of the Saar wine trade. Above the town are the remains of an old castle of the Electors of Trier. In the centre of the town is a 20m/65ft high waterfall on the Leukbach, which flows into the Saar here.

Downstream from Saarburg are a series of picturesque little wine towns – Ockfen, Schoden, Wiltingen, Kanzem, Filzen, Könen. At Konz the Saar flows into the Mosel.

Saarland Trail

The Saarland Trail (Saarland-Rundwanderweg) is a continuous waymarked trail (273km/170 miles) with loops into the Moselgau to the north-west (41km/25 miles) and the Bliesgau in the south-east (60km/37 miles).

Bad Salzungen

G 5

Land: Thuringia
Altitude: 240m/150ft
Population: 21,500

Bad Salzungen lies in the wide Werra valley, between the Thuringian Forest and the Rhön.

Situation and characteristics

Sights

A number of carefully restored old buildings recall the town's long tradition as a spa, such as the large Gradierhäuser ("evaporation halls"; 1796 and 1905) and the Baths (1837).

The spa

The ruins of the Late Gothic Husenkirche, destroyed in 1945, have been left as a memorial.

Husenkirche

In the Marktplatz stands the Town Hall (1790). The Haunscher Hof, a Renaissance building of 1624, has a handsome half-timbered upper storey.

Town Hall

The Schnepfenburg (12th–14th c.; rebuilt after a fire) was the base of forces responsible for defending the brine springs against attack.

Schnepfenburg

The Town Church, originally neo-classical (1789–91), was later altered. St Wenceslas's Church (1481) is Late Gothic, with a 15th century pulpit.

Churches

Wilprechtroda has a 16th century mansion, a former moated castle, with a fine Renaissance doorway.

Wilprechtroda

Salzwedel

D 6

Land: Saxony-Anhalt
Altitude: 51m/167ft
Population: 23,200

Salzwedel, the second largest town in the Altmark (see entry), lies at the junction of the rivers Dumme and Jeetze. Its fine half-timbered buildings bear witness to the one-time prosperity of this old Hanseatic town situated at the intersection of important long-distance trade routes.

Situation and characteristics

Sights

Of the old castle there survive the keep, a massive round brick tower (probably 12th–13th c.) and remains of the chapel of St Anne.

Burg

There are considerable remains of the old town walls, particularly on the west and south (in the Peace Park), including the Karlsturm (14th–15th c.), a round brick tower, and

Town walls

	two square brick towers, the Neuperver Torturm (c. 1460–70) and the Steintorturm (c. 1520–30).
St Lawrence's Church	St Lawrence's Church, around which the old town grew up, was originally an aisled basilica (13th c.), which was used from 1692 to 1859 as a salt store and suffered considerable damage. The north aisle was restored in 1962.
St Catherine's Church	The newer part of the town is centred on St Catherine's Church (first mentioned in 1280; rebuilt in Late Gothic style c. 1450). The most notable features of the interior are the Corpus Christi Chapel (1490), the 15th century stained glass, the bronze font (1421), the baptistery screen (1567) and the pulpit (1592). Fine wall paintings showing part of the medieval town were discovered during restoration work in 1983.
Town Hall	Near St Lawrence's Church is the Town Hall of the old town (originally built 1509, and soon afterwards enlarged). In Late Gothic style, it has stepped gables, turrets and a chamber with stellar vaulting. It is now a lawcourt.
St Mary's Church	The parish church of St Mary (originally Late Romanesque, 12th c.; altered in Late Gothic style, 1450–68) is a brick-built basilica with double aisles, transept, choir with triangular end and groined vaulting. It has fine Late Gothic stained glass and wall paintings, a large Late Gothic winged altar (c. 1510), a pulpit of 1481, a Late Gothic Triumphal Cross group and a Late Romanesque lectern (c. 1200).
Friedrich Danneil Museum	The former Propstei (Deanery) is the Friedrich Danneil Museum, with a collection of material of the prehistoric and early historical periods in the Altmark; also the Salzwedel Madonna (13th c.) and a Late Gothic triptych by Lucas Cranach the Younger (1582).
Franciscan Church	To the east of the Burg is the church of a former Franciscan friary, a Late Gothic brick-built hall-church (15th c.). Most of the conventual buildings (probably 13th c.) have been preserved and are now occupied by municipal buildings.
Burghers' houses	Salzwedel has many richly decorated half-timbered burghers' houses. A notable example is the Hochständerhaus at Schmiedestrasse 30. Nearby, at Schmiedestrasse 17, is a 19th century building with a fine carved doorway of 1534, known as the Adam and Eve Doorway. One of the finest buildings in the town is the Ritterhaus at Badestrasse 9, with rich Renaissance carved decoration.

Sangerhausen F 6

	Land: Saxony-Anhalt Altitude: 158m/518ft Population: 33,500
Situation and characteristics	Sangerhausen, the eastern gateway to the Goldene Aue and an important road junction, lies in the southern Harz foreland. It was formerly a copper-mining town, but the last pits closed down in 1990.

Sights

Altes Schloss	In the south-east of the town can be seen the Altes Schloss (Old Castle; not open to the public), built about the mid 13th century along with the rest of the town's fortifications; it is now occupied by a music school. In the time of the Margraves of Meissen of the Wettin dynasty this was a frontier fortress on the border with Thuringia.
Town Hall	In the Marktplatz are a number of patrician houses of the 16th–18th centuries. The Town Hall was originally Late Gothic (1431–37) but was altered in the 16th century. It has an asymmetrical west gable; on the north front is a stone head.
Neues Schloss	On the south side of the Markt stands the Neues Schloss (New Castle; older part 1568), an imposing three-storey Late Renaissance building with the arms of the Elector of

Saxony over the entrance and oriels in the courtyard and at the east corner. It is now occupied by the District Court.

Dominating the Markt is the parish church of St James (14th–15th c.; altered 1711–17; restored 1974–75), a Gothic hall-church with a fine interior.

St James's Church

Also in the centre of the town is St Ulrich's Church (11th–12th c.), a Romanesque basilica with a vaulted roof which in the 13th century belonged to a Cistercian monastery.

St Ulrich's Church

At Strasse der Opfer des Faschismus 33 the Spengler Museum contains much material on the history of the town and on copper-mining, also a collection of prehistoric animal remains, including the almost completely preserved skeleton of a steppe elephant or mammoth, found in a gravel quarry at Edersleben in 1930 and recovered by an amateur geologist named G. A. Spengler.

Spengler Museum

A major attraction of Sangerhausen is the Rosarium, one of the largest rose-gardens in the world, with some 6500 different roses (altogether 55,000 plants), both cultivated and wild, in an area of some 13 hectares/32 acres.

Rosarium

Sassnitz

See Rügen

Sauerland

F 3

Land: North Rhine-Westphalia

The charming Sauerland ("South Land") is a beautifully wooded upland region, slashed by numerous winding river valleys, to the south of the Rhineland-Westphalia industrial zone. It rises to a height of 843m/2766ft in the Hegekopf, near Willingen, and to 841m/2759ft in the Kahler Asten on the Winterberg plateau.

Situation and characteristics

Landscape

The largest river in this densely populated region, which is bounded on the south by the Sieg, is the Ruhr, into which flows the Lenne at Hohensyburg. The varied beauties of the Sauerland lie in its old towns (Altena, Arnsberg, Attendorn, Brilon, Hohenlimburg, Iserlohn, Lüdenscheid, Niedermarsberg, etc.), in the deeply indented valleys of its rivers (Lenne, Möhne, Ruhr, Sorpe, Volme, etc.) with their large dams built to provide secure supplies of water and produce electric power and their many caves (Attahöhle, Dechenhöhle, etc.), and in the hills with their wide-ranging views.

To the south-west is the beautiful Bergisches Land (see entry), to the south the industrial Siegerland (see entry).

Through the Sauerland – a Circular Tour

The route suggested here starts and finishes at Hagen (see entry).

Leave Hagen on B 7, which leads east into the Lenne valley. After passing Hohenlimburg, which has a fine Schloss, and Letmathe it reaches a junction where a road goes off to the Dechenhöhle, a stalactitic cave discovered in 1888 (Cave Museum).

Dechenhöhle

The main road continues through the beautiful Lenne valley to the picturesquely situated town of Altena, with the ancestral castle of the Counts von der Mark (12th c.; youth hostel; Regional Museum). Then on to Balve (see Iserlohn, Surroundings), with the Balver Höhle (cave). To the east lies the beautiful artificial lake formed by the Sorpe dam.

Altena

Arnsberg	The old town of Arnsberg (remains of town walls; Sauerland Museum, Fire Service Museum) is magnificently situated on a ridge of hills encircled by the Ruhr; above the town is a ruined castle. A few kilometres north is the Möhne Dam (see Soest, Surroundings).
Meschede	Meschede lies at the junction of the Henne with the Ruhr. 1.5km/1 mile before the town is the moated castle of Laer (17th c.) – parish church of 1663, contains remains of a Carolingian crypt. To the north of the town can be seen a Germanic fortified settlement.
Brilon	The old Hanseatic town of Brilon, now a winter sports resort, has a 14th century Town Hall with a Baroque façade, a parish church of the 13th–14th century and a Municipal Museum (dinosaur remains, collection of stoves).
	The route now runs south-west by way of Olsberg.
Winterberg Kahler Asten	Winterberg, situated on a plateau commanding extensive views, has developed into the most popular winter sports resort in Sauerland. South-west of the town stands the Kahler Asten (841m/2759ft; outlook tower), on which are the sources of the Lenne and the Ruhr.
Schmallenberg	Schmallenberg has a Late Romanesque church (13th c.) and a number of handsome half-timbered buildings. 3.5km/2 miles east is the former Benedictine monastery of Grafschaft (conventual buildings 1727–49).
	Then west via Lennestadt.
Attendorn	See entry
Meinerzhagen	At the head of the Volme valley is Meinerzhagen, with a small Romanesque church (14th c.). 2.5km/1½ miles south-east is the moated castle of Badinhagen (17th c.).
	The return to Hagen is by way of Kierspe and Lüdenscheid (see Hagen, Surroundings).

Saxon Switzerland (Sächsische Schweiz)   G 9

Land: Saxony

Situation and characteristics	The name of "Saxon Switzerland" has been given since the Romantic period to an area of some 360 sq.km/140 sq. miles in the German part of the Elbe Sandstone Hills, the rest of which is in Czechoslovakia. It is an upland region lying at an average height of 400m/1300ft, much broken up and carved into bizarre rocky landscapes by the Elbe and its tributaries, between the Lusatian Fault in the north, the Eastern Erzgebirge (Gottleuba valley) in the west and the frontier with Czechoslovakia in the south.

**Landscape

In the course of time the present varied landscape forms have developed – the canyon-like Elbe valley and the narrow valleys of its tributaries; the tracts of relatively level ground lying 100–120m/330–390ft above the Elbe valley with their covering of gravel and silt, now under cultivation; the tabular hills with steep rock walls (Lilienstein, 415m/1361ft; Pfaffenstein, 429m/1408ft; Königstein, 361m/1184ft; Grosser Zschirnstein, 561m/1841ft), remnants of a once continuous sandstone plateau; rocky areas such as the Bastei (305m/1001ft) and the Schrammsteine (386–417m/1266–1368ft) – labyrinths of stone, with rock buttresses, battlements and pinnacles, gorges and defiles. Tertiary basalts are found only at a few places, for example on the Grosser Winterberg (552m/1811ft).

For many centuries this area was mainly a source of sandstone, used as building material in towns lower down the Elbe. Although Bad Schandau (see below) was frequented as a spa from around 1730, it was only in the early 19th century with its romantic quest for the beauty of nature that the area was "discovered" and given the name of the Saxon Switzerland. There is now an excellent network of waymarked paths and trails leading to the principal sights and natural beauties; and this is also a popular area with climbers.

Much of the Saxon Switzerland has recently been designated as a National Park.

Königstein

The popular holiday resort of Königstein, famed for what was once the mightiest fortress in Germany, lies below the 361m/1184ft high hill of that name in the Elbe Sandstone Hills.

Situation and characteristics

High above the town, prominently situated on its hill, stands the fortress of Königstein, covering an area of 9.5 hectares/23½ acres. A walk round the ramparts offers fine views of the Elbe Sandstone Hills and takes in almost all the important structures in the fortress itself.

*Festung Königstein
*View

The principal features of interest are the main entrance (after 1590); the well-house (1735), with the 152.50m/500ft deep well; the Old Arsenal (1594), on the ground floor of which is a large room with groined vaulting borne on massive columns; the Guard-house (Old Barracks, 1598); the Christiansburg, later called the Friedrichsburg (1589; altered 1721); the Georgenburg; the Magdalenenburg (1622–23); the New Arsenal (1631), with the aisled, groin-vaulted Johannessaal; and the Garrison Church, which preserves some 13th century work.

Museums in the fortress: a collection which includes Saxon guns of the 15th–18th centuries in the Old Arsenal; modern arms in the New Arsenal; temporary exhibitions in the Treasury.

Museums

The little town of Königstein has a fine parish church (originally Baroque, 1720–24; rebuilt 1810–23 after a fire), with a neo-classical interior. On the way up to the church can be seen marks showing high water levels.

Parish church

Bend in the Elbe at the Basteifelsen

Festung Königstein

Lilienstein	The Lilienstein (415m/1362ft), on the far side of the Elbe (ferry), must be climbed on foot. Fine views; remains of medieval castle; restaurant.
*Pfaffenstein	East of the Königstein rises the Pfaffenstein (427m/1401ft), with curious rock formations. Restaurant; Bronze Age site.

Bad Schandau

Situation and characteristics	Bad Schandau lies at the junction of the Kirnitsch with the Elbe, on the railway and road between Dresden and Prague (frontier crossing in Schmilka district). It is the largest holiday resort and spa in the Saxon Switzerland.
Brauhof	In the Marktplatz (No. 12) is the Brauhof, a Renaissance building with a beautiful doorway of 1680 and an octagonal stair tower on the courtyard side.
St John's Church	St John's Church, originally Late Gothic, was much altered in the 17th and 18th centuries; the interior was remodelled in 1876. Pulpit hewn from a single block of sandstone; altar of 1572 by H. Walter.
Heimatmuseum	The Heimatmuseum is at Badallee 10 (geology of the region, development of shipping on the Elbe and the tourist trade).
Half-timbered houses	In the districts of Ostrau (reached by 50m/165ft lift) and Postelwitz are old half-timbered houses and houses of the Saxon *umgebinde* type (with external beams supporting the upper storey and roof).

Schleiz   G 7

Land: Thuringia
Altitude: 440m/1445ft
Population: 8000

The former princely capital of Schleiz lies 35km/22 miles south of Gera in a basin in the Wisenta valley, in the wooded landscape of the Thuringian Hills. It is the gateway to the Schleiz lake district (some 1000 small lakes round Plothen).

Situation and characteristics

Sights

A dominant feature of the town is the parish church of St George (mainly 15th–16th c.; rebuilt after its destruction in 1945), with reticulated vaulting in the choir and a fine west tower; richly decorated reredos (by J. S. Nahl, 1721).

St George's Church

The Bergkirche, outside the town, is an aisleless Late Gothic church famed for its richly furnished interior (mainly 17th c.). Reredos of 1635; Late Gothic pulpit (15th c.; remodelled in Baroque style in 1670); early 16th century monument.

*Bergkirche

In the Neumarkt is the 16th century Old Mint (restored), the town's oldest secular building. The Schloss (16th and 19th c.) was destroyed during the Second World War.

Old Mint

Schleswig

B 5

Land: Schleswig-Holstein
Altitude: 56m/184ft
Population: 28,000

Schleswig, the old princely capital of the Dukes of Gottorp, is attractively situated at the head of the Schlei, a fjord-like inlet on the Baltic. The harbour is suitable only for pleasure craft.

Situation and characteristics

Old Town

In the heart of the old town stands the Gothic Cathedral (Dom) of St Peter, which dates mainly from the 12th–15th centuries, with a 110.50m/363ft high tower built in 1889–94. The most magnificent feature of the richly furnished interior is the Bordesholm Altar by Hans Brüggemann, the great masterpiece of medieval Low German carving, originally made for a house of Augustinian canons at Bordesholm in 1514–21 and installed in the Cathedral in 1666. Carved from oak, it stands almost 16m/52ft high and has no fewer than 392 figures. Other notable features are the massive marble tomb of King Frederick I of Denmark (d. 1533), the wrought-iron choir screen (Late Gothic), a beautiful font of 1418 and 12th and 13th century wall paintings. On the north side of the church is the cloister, with 14th century wall paintings.

Cathedral
*Bordesholm Altar

In the Markt is the neo-classical Town Hall (Rathaus; 1794) and adjoining it the Graukloster, a former Franciscan friary founded in 1234.

Markt

Farther north, in Stadtweg, is the Präsidentenkloster, founded in 1656 as a poorhouse.

Präsidentenkloster

Schleswig-Holm

South-east of the Markt, in the old fishermen's quarter of Holm on the shores of the Schlei, we come to St John's Convent (St-Johannis-Kloster), a house of Benedictine nuns founded in the 12th century. Late Baroque church; fine 13th century stalls in the chapterhouse.
In the centre of Holm is the fishermen's cemetery, surrounded by lime-trees.

St John's Convent

Friedrichsberg · Schloss Gottorp

In the Friedrichsberg district, situated on an island at the tip of the Schlei (which is now cut off from the rest of the inlet), stands Schloss Gottorp (originally 13th c.; in its present form 16th–18th c.), the largest princely palace in Schleswig-Holstein. From the mid 19th century it was used as a barracks; it now contains two museums.

*Museum of Art and Culture

The Landesmuseum of Art and Culture displays art treasures from all over Schleswig-Holstein from the 12th century to the present day (medieval sculpture, furniture and furnishings from noble mansions and ordinary houses, weapons; the medieval guilds; art of the 19th and 20th c., folk art).

**Archaeological Museum

The Landesmuseum of Archaeology, which belongs to Kiel University, has one of the finest collections of prehistoric material in Germany. Among items of outstanding interest are the famous Nydam Boat (23m/75ft long) of about A.D. 350, bodies recovered from bogs and runic stones from Haithabu (see below).

Municipal Museum

To the south of the Schloss, at Friedrichstrasse 7–11, can be found the Günderoth'scher Hof, a mansion built in 1834–36 for a Persian embassy which now houses the Municipal Museum (Städtisches Museum; history and archaeology of the town, faience, toys, works by local artists, history of printing).

*Haithabu

2km/1¼ miles south of Schleswig lies Haithabu, a Viking port and trading settlement on the Haddebyer Noor with a semicircular rampart which was destroyed in the 11th century.

Museum

Most of the material recovered from the site in excavations from 1900 onwards is displayed in the site museum, opened in 1985. Reconstructions and models illustrate the layout, the buildings and the fortifications of the Viking settlement and the way of life of its inhabitants. In the ship hall can be seen a reconstruction of a Viking longship.

Danewerk

To the west extends the Danewerk, a 15km/9 mile long earthwork constructed in the 9th century and maintained and strengthened until the 13th century, designed to protect the southern frontier of the Danish kingdom. In the 12th century the central section was reinforced by the Waldemarsmauer, a brick wall 3.5km/2 miles long, 7m/23ft high and 2m/6½ft thick.

Schmalkalden   G 5

Land: Thuringia
Altitude: 296m/971ft
Population: 17,000

Situation and characteristics

Schmalkalden, chief town of a district and a health resort, is charmingly situated in the valley of the same name, on the south-western slopes of the Thuringian Forest.

*Schloss Wilhelmsburg

Prominently situated above the town is Schloss Wilhelmsburg, a Renaissance castle built in 1585–89. After falling into a state of disrepair during the 19th century it was rebuilt in modified form and then, from 1964 onwards, comprehensively restored. The chapel, a handsome Protestant preaching church, has a Renaissance organ (1587–89). The banqueting hall has a coffered ceiling, the White Hall rich stucco decoration. Other rooms also have stucco decoration and wall paintings.

Regional Museum

The Regional Museum, housed in the castle, has a large collection of material on the history of the town (particularly of the 16th century) and the local iron and steel industry. From the castle there are magnificent views of the town and surrounding country.

Altmarkt

Town Hall

The whole of the old town is protected as a historical monument. In the Altmarkt stands the Town Hall (mainly Late Gothic, much altered at the beginning of the 20th century).

Above the Ratskeller is the room in which the 16th century League of Schmalkalden used to meet. In the lobby are murals (after Merian's plan) depicting the medieval town.

Also in the Altmarkt is the Late Gothic church of St George (1437–1509), one of the finest hall-churches in Thuringia. Stellar and reticulated vaulting; delicate window tracery; Late Gothic wall paintings (1503).
Above the sacristy is the Luther Room, now a museum displaying some of the church's treasures.

St George's
Church

At Altmarkt 5 the Todenwarthsche Kemenate can be seen, early 16th c., with Gothic stepped gables and windows. At Steingasse 11 is the Rosenapotheke (Rose Pharmacy), which is also a *kemenate* (a stone-built house which could be heated).

Todenwarthsche
Kemenate

Neumarkt

In the Neumarkt is the Hessenhof, an imposing half-timbered building. In the Trinkstube in the basement are some of the oldest surviving medieval secular wall paintings in Germany (c. 1220–50) – remains of a Late Romanesque cycle of scenes from Hartmann von Aue's Arthurian epic poem "Iwein, the Knight of the Lion".

*Hessenhof

The old town has many other fine burghers' houses, including the Grosse Kemenate and the Lutherhaus in Lutherplatz, in which the Reformer stayed in 1537.

Burghers' houses

Schmalkalden-Weidebrunn

In the Weidebrunn district to the north of the town centre can be seen the Neue Hütte, an old ironworks (restored) with a blast furnace of 1835.

Neue Hütte

Bad Schmiedeberg   F 8

Land: Saxony-Anhalt
Altitude: 90m/295ft
Population: 4500

The spa of Bad Schmiedeberg (mud baths) lies in a wide valley on the east side of the hilly and wooded Dübener Heide (Düben Heath).

Situation and
characteristics

Sights

The pattern of the town is set by the crooked main street with its 16th–18th century houses. Among them are a number of Renaissance buildings with bench recesses in the doorways.

In the Markt is the Town Hall (1570). Originally a Renaissance building, it was rebuilt in Baroque style (1661–63) after its destruction during the Thirty Years' War and restored in 1981. It has two fine doorways, sited asymmetrically.

Town Hall

The Kurhaus (c. 1900) is in neo-Renaissance style. On the ground floor are Art Nouveau tiles with masks.

Kurhaus

The Town Church (15th c.) was originally a Gothic hall-church but after the collapse of the vaulting was remodelled in Baroque style. The Ratsherrenloge (town councillors' box) was added in 1731. Fine interior, with a richly carved reredos (1680) and stalls of the Leipzig school.
Of the town's old fortifications there survives only one town gate, the Aue-Tor (15th c.).

Town Church

Schneeberg   G 8

Land: Saxony
Altitude: 475m/1558ft
Population: 21,000

Schwäbisch Gmünd

Situation and characteristics

Schneeberg, once an important silver-mining town, lies in the western Erzgebirge on the hill (470m/1542ft) from which it takes its name. The hills around the town rise to almost 600m/2000ft (Gleesberg, 593m/1946ft; Griesbacher Höhe, 578m/1896ft). The silver-mines of Schneeberg brought wealth to the Dukes of Saxony. It is now a considerable industrial town and a centre of Erzgebirge folk traditions, as well as a popular winter sports resort.

Folk art

Schneeberg has a long tradition of folk art. The House of Erzgebirge Folk Art was established in 1953, and wood and textile designers are trained in the School of Applied Art.

Sights

* St Wolfgang's Church

The town is dominated by Late Gothic St Wolfgang's Church (1515–40), one of the largest hall-churches in Saxony, now in course of restoration after its destruction during the Second World War. When the restoration is completed the altarpiece by Lucas Cranach the Elder (1539), one of his finest works, will be returned to the church.

Baroque buildings

Notable among the town's many Baroque buildings are two houses in Ernst-Schneller-Platz (Nos. 1 and 2) with stucco-decorated façades. The Fürstenplatz (1721) at Ernst-Schneller-Platz 4 has a middle section articulated by pilasters. The Bortenreuther-Haus (1724–25) in Rosa-Luxemburg-Platz also has pilasters and a handsome doorway.

Museum of Folk Art

The Museum of Folk Art, in a Baroque house in Obere Zobelgasse, illustrates the development of carving in the Erzgebirge from its beginnings to the present day; also silhouettes, pillow lace and pewterware.

Observatory

In Heinrich-Heine-Strasse is the Observatory, with a mini-planetarium.

Liebfrauenkirche

In the Neustädtel district stands the Late Gothic Liebfrauenkirche (Church of Our Lady), with two-storey galleries and a finely decorated interior.

Schwäbisch Gmünd   K 5

Land: Baden-Württemberg
Altitude: 321m/1053ft
Population: 60,000

Situation and characteristics

The old free imperial city of Schwäbisch Gmünd lies in the valley of the Rems, on the northern fringes of the Swabian Alb (see entry). It is noted for its goldsmith's and silversmith's work and for its glassware, an industry transferred here from Gablonz in Bohemia after the Second World War. Schwäbisch Gmünd was the birthplace of the 14th century master builder Peter Parler and the 16th century painter Hans Baldung Grien.

The Town

Markt

In the charming elongated Markt are the Town Hall (1783–85) and the important Late Romanesque St John's Church (1220–50; R.C.), with rich sculptural decoration. In front of the church can be seen the beautiful Marienbrunnen (fountain).

Cultural Centre

To the west of the church is a former Dominican monastery (remodelled in the 18th century by Dominikus Zimmermann; restored 1969–73), now housing the Prediger Cultural Centre and the Municipal Museum.

* Minster

To the south-west is the Gothic Minster of the Holy Cross (R.C.), built in the early 14th century by Heinrich Parler (father of Peter Parler, who built Prague Cathedral). This was one of the first large hall-churches in South Germany.

Fuggerei

South-east of the Minster is the Fuggerei, a Romanesque building with 15th century half-timbering.

South-west of the Minster stands the Town Church (Protestant), a former Augustinian church built in the 15th century and remodelled in Baroque style in the 18th (fine stucco decoration and ceiling paintings).
On the south side of the church are the conventual buildings (1732–49), now occupied by local government offices.

Town Church

A few towers belonging to the town's medieval fortifications (14th–15th c.) have been preserved.

Town walls

West of the town, beyond the railway station, is a Way of the Cross leading to the curious rock-cut pilgrimage chapel of St Salvator (1617–20; view).

St Salvator's Chapel

In the south-western district of Schirenhof are the excavated remains of Roman baths belonging to a small Roman fort of the 2nd century A.D.
In the nearby Rotenbach valley can be seen a remnant of the Rhaetian Wall, built by the Romans.

Roman baths

Surroundings of Schwäbisch Gmünd

9km/6 miles south rises the Rechberg (707m/2320ft; extensive views), with a ruined 12th century castle and a 17th century pilgrimage chapel.

Rechberg

Schwäbisch Hall

I 5

Land: Baden-Württemberg
Altitude: 270m/885ft
Population: 32,000

The former free imperial city of Schwäbisch Hall lies in the deeply indented valley of the Kocher on the north-eastern fringes of the Swabian Forest. The brine spring on the right bank of the Kocher brought the town prosperity at an early stage, and the *Häller pfennige* (heller) which were minted here, probably as early as the beginning of the 11th century, circulated widely and gave their name to coins minted elsewhere in Germany and Austria.

Situation and characteristics

The Town

In the Marktplatz, one of the most impressive of German market squares in the stylistic unity of its architecture, stands the Baroque Town Hall (1728–35).

*Marktplatz

An imposing flight of steps (on which festival performances are given in summer) leads up to St Michael's Church (15th c.; Protestant), with a notable interior (high altar of 1470). From the tower there are panoramic views.
Above the church are the Crailsheim Gate (1515) and the handsome "Neubau" ("New Building") or Grosses Büchsenhaus, built in 1527 as an arsenal (Great Hall).

St Michael's Church

In the nearby Untere Herrengasse, in the Keckenhof, is the Hall/Franconian Museum (Hällisch-Fränkisches Museum; geology, prehistory and early historical period, Middle Ages; special exhibitions).

Museum

Attractive old footbridges span the Kocher and the island of Unterwöhrd.

On the left bank of the Kocher, in the St Katharina district, are St Catherine's Church (choir of 1343 with fine stained glass) and the Pulverturm (Powder Tower; 1490).
On the west side of the town the old Hirtenscheuer houses the Fireworks Museum.

St Katharina

In the Unterlimpurg district, to the south of the Markt, can be found St Urban's Church (13th c.). From here a footpath leads to the scanty remains of Burg Limpurg, a 13th century castle which was later enlarged.

Unterlimpurg

*Hohenlohe Open-Air Museum

In Wackershofen (6km/4 miles north-west) is the Hohenlohe Open-Air Museum (Hohen-loher Freilandmuseum), with over 35 buildings from different parts of northern Württemberg. The museum is continually being extended.

**Comburg

In Unterlimpurg, on a conical hill above the right bank of the Kocher, stands the former Benedictine abbey of Comburg (Gross-Comburg), founded in 1075 and occupied from 1488 to 1802 by Augustinian canons. It is a magnificent example of a fortified Benedictine house dating from the heyday of the order.

Schwarza Valley   G 6

Land: Thuringia

The Schwarza ("Black Water"), a left-bank tributary of the Saale, rises at an altitude of 717m/2352ft in the Thuringian Hills, near Scheibe-Alsbach, emerging from a geological fault with a constant flow of water at a temperature of 6°C/43°F. After a course of 53km/33 miles it flows into the Saale at Schwarza (between Saalfeld and Rudolstadt), at an altitude of 203m/666ft.

*Landscape

Like many valleys on the north side of the Thuringian Hills, the Schwarza valley begins as a high trough valley, continues as a winding flat-bottomed valley and finally, near the edge of the hills, becomes a deeply indented canyon-like gorge. This last section of the valley, between Schwarzburg and Bad Blankenburg, is the most attractive part, with its steep wooded slopes and many rare plants.

Above the popular resort of Schwarzburg, the "Pearl of Thuringia", begins the section of the valley in which water power used to be the main source of energy, working numerous mills and forges. Place-names such as Blechhammer and Obstfelderschmiede, Schwarzmühle and Katzhütte, bear witness to this past industrial activity. Other early industries were glass-blowing and the manufacture of porcelain.

*View

From the Rennsteigwarte on the Eselsberg (841m/2759ft), near Masserberg, there are extensive views over the whole course of the Schwarza.

*Oberweissbach mountain railway

One of the sights of the Schwarza valley is the Oberweissbach mountain railway, the world's steepest normal-gauge cable railway. It climbs from Obstfelderschmiede to Lichtenhain (663m/2175ft), a height difference of 323m/1060ft, on a steel ramp 1400m/1530yds long, taking 18 minutes for the journey.

Schwarzenberg   G 8

Land: Saxony
Altitude: 475m/1558ft
Population: 16,800

Situation and characteristics

Schwarzenberg lies in a deep basin in the western Erzgebirge at the junction of the Schwarzwasser and the Mittweida. Surrounded by hills, it offers good walking, climbing and skiing.

Sights

*Schloss

The Late Gothic Schloss Schwarzenberg (1433) incorporates remains, including a keep, of an earlier 12th century castle; in 1555–58 it was converted into a hunting lodge by Elector Augustus of Saxony. It now contains a museum.

Sitzendorf, in the Schwarza valley

The exhibits in the Erzgebirge Iron and Tin Museum include a 19th century nailsmith's forge and products from foundries in the Erzgebirge.

*Museum

The parish church of St George (1690–99) is an aisleless Baroque church with a richly furnished interior (17th c. silver-plated crucifix, wrought-iron altar rails of 1737).

St George's Church

A covered wooden bridge over the Schwarzwasser links the districts of Untersachsenfeld and Neuwelt.

Schwedt

D 9

Land: Brandenburg
Altitude: 5m/16ft
Population: 51,500

Schwedt lies some 80km/50 miles north-east of Berlin at the junction of the river Welse with the Hohensaaten-Friedrichstal Waterway, a canal running parallel to the Oder. It has preserved only a few Baroque houses from the time when it was the seat of the Margraves of Brandenburg-Schwedt.

Situation and characteristics

Sights

Once the main avenue of the Baroque town, Vierradener Strasse is still the central feature of Schwedt, a pleasant street with fountains, sculpture and areas of grass.

Vierradener Strasse

The Baroque church of the French Reformed community, on an oval ground-plan, was built by Georg Wilhelm Berlischky in 1779. It is now used as a concert hall, known as the Berlischky Pavilion.

Berlischky Pavilion

The Municipal Museum (Am Markt 4) illustrates the history of the town down to 1945.   Museum

In Heinrichslust Park are an open-air theatre and a sundial of 1740 from the old   Heinrichslust
Schlosspark.   Park

Schweinfurt   H 5

Land: Bavaria. Altitude: 218m/715ft
Population: 51,000

This former free imperial city on the Main, founded by the Count of Henneberg in 1254, is   Situation and
now noted for the production of ball bearings, small motors and dyestuffs.   characteristics

The Town

In the Markt (pedestrian zone) is the handsome Town Hall (by Nikolaus Hofmann,   Markt
1570–72), a masterpiece of German Renaissance architecture. At the corner of Rückert-
strasse can be found the birthplace of the poet Friedrich Rückert (1788–1866); there is a
monument to him in the Markt.

To the north of the Markt stands St John's Church (originally Late Romanesque), with the   St John's Church
beautiful Brauttor (Bride's Doorway). Nearby, in Martin-Luther-Platz and Obere Strasse,
are the three sections of the Municipal Museum and Art Gallery (art of the 19th and 20th
c.; local history; cultural history).

Schwerin   C 6

Capital of the *Land* of Mecklenburg-West Pomerania
Altitude: 40m/130ft. Population: 130,000

Schlossinsel

There are numerous 18th and 19th century buildings in the old town, mostly designed by   *Schloss
the court architect, G. A. Demmler. On the Schlossinsel (Palace Island) is the Grand-
Ducal Palace (at present in course of restoration), which ranks as one of the finest 19th
century buildings in the region. It was given its present form, modelled on the French
château of Chambord, in 1843–57. Laid out on a pentagonal plan, with numerous towers
and turrets, it combines Gothic, Renaissance and Baroque features. The interior is
sumptuously appointed, with fine intarsia floors, silk wallpaper and richly gilded ornament. Particularly imposing, on the main floor, are the Throne Room, the Ancestral
Portrait Gallery, the Smoking Room and the Adjutants' Room.

In the wing facing the Burgsee is the Museum of Prehistory and the Early Historical   Museum of
Period. Among items of particular interest are finds from the Mesolithic settlement at   Prehistory
Hohen-Viecheln near Wismar and the Slav defensive rampart at Teterow.

In the north wing is the palace chapel (by J. B. Parr, 1560–63), a Renaissance building,   *Schlosskapelle
with a finely furnished interior, modelled on the palace chapel of Torgau.

South-west of the Burggarten with its tall beeches and old planes lies the Schlossgarten,   *Schlossgarten
laid out in the 18th century as a Baroque pleasure garden, with the Kreuzkanal, arcades
and copies of sculpture from the workshop of Balthasar Permoser. On the edge of the
gardens can be seen an old grinding-mill.

Old Town

North of the palace, in the Alter Garten, a square surrounded by imposing buildings,   *Theatre
stands the neo-Renaissance Mecklenburg State Theatre (Staatstheater; by G. Daniel,

◀ *Schloss Schwarzenberg*

1883–86). Near the theatre is a bust of Conrad Ekhof, who founded the first German academy of dramatic art in Schwerin in 1753.

*State Museum

On the east side of the Alter Garten is the State Museum (Staatliches Museum), a picture gallery in neo-classical style (by H. Willebrand, 1877–82). The façade, originally plain, was enriched during rebuilding with Italian Renaissance ornament. The collection includes large numbers of works by Flemish and Dutch masters of the 17th and 18th centuries, and modern art is also represented.

Altes Palais

On the west side of the Alter Garten, at Schloss-strasse 1, is the Altes Palais (Old Palace), a two-storey half-timbered building (1799) formerly used for the accommodation of members of the court; it is now occupied by offices.

Old Town Hall

The historic streets and squares of the old town, including the Markt, have been restored and rebuilt in recent years. At the south-east corner of the Markt stands the Old Town Hall (Altstädtisches Rathaus), the oldest parts of which date from the 14th century; it has a neo-Gothic façade (by G. A. Demmler, 1835). Behind it are four half-timbered gabled houses (17th c.).

Neues Gebäude

On the north side of the Markt is the so-called Neues Gebäude (New Building), built by J. J. Busch in 1783–85 as a row of shops. It has a massive porch with fourteen Doric columns.

Neustädtisches Palais

In the centre of the town are several old palaces and burghers' houses, including the Neustädtisches Palais (New Town Palace) at Puschkinstrasse 19–21. Originally built by J. J. Busch in 1776, it was rebuilt in French Renaissance style in 1878.

*Cathedral

The Cathedral (Dom; 14th–15th c.) is one of the finest examples of North German brick-built Gothic architecture. The most notable features of the interior are the Gothic altar (Lübeck work, c. 1440), two 14th century memorial brasses and the Gothic font.

St Nicholas's Church

The Baroque parish church of St Nicholas (Schelfkirche) in Schelfstrasse was built in 1708–11 on the site of an earlier medieval church.

Muess

In the Muess district is an open-air museum with examples of rural buildings of the 17th and 18th centuries, illustrating the life and work of the people of Mecklenburg.

Schweriner See (Lake Schwerin)

Situation and characteristics

The Schweriner See (area 65.5 sq.km/25 sq. miles), together with some 25 medium-sized lakes and numerous smaller ones, forms the most westerly part of the Mecklenburg lake district (see entry), a rolling area of morainic country lying at altitudes of between 50m/165ft and 100m/330ft. The lakes, within easy reach of Schwerin, offer abundant scope for bathing and water sports of all kinds and for pleasant walks along their wooded shores.

There are boat services between Schwerin and the most popular recreation areas – Zippendorf, Muess (see above) and the island of Kaninchenwerder.

Paulsdamm

Across the middle of the lake runs a causeway, the Paulsdamm (constructed in 1842), which separates the Binnensee (Inner Lake; maximum depth 43m/141ft) from the Aussensee (Outer Lake; maximum depth 51m/167ft). The causeway, which carries the main road from Schwerin to Güstrow and Neubrandenburg (B 104), is only a little above water level and affords magnificent views of the Aussensee (3–4km/2–2½ miles wide) and the Binnensee (up to 6km/4 miles wide).

Kaninchenwerder Ziegelwerder

In the Binnensee there are two islands of some size – Kaninchenwerder or Rabbit Island (nature reserve; outlook tower) and Ziegelwerder. The largest of the islands in the Aussensee is Lieps, a narrow island 2km/1¼ miles long.

Schwerin, with Cathedral

The Schweriner See has a natural outlet to the south by way of the river Stör to the Elbe and a man-made outlet to the north by way of the Wallensteingraben to the Baltic.

Seiffen

G 8

Land: Saxony
Altitude: 650m/2130ft
Population: 3500

The little holiday resort of Seiffen lies 40km/25 miles south-east of Chemnitz in the eastern Erzgebirge, under the south side of the Schwartenberg (788m/2585ft). Seiffen is the centre of Saxony's toy industry. In addition to its wooden toys it is also famed for its carved figures and a variety of other articles turned and carved from wood.

Situation and characteristics

Sights

Seiffen has a charming little Baroque village church (1779), an octagonal structure on a centralised plan, with galleries round the beautifully decorated interior.

*Church

At Ernst-Thälmann-Strasse 73 is the Erzgebirge Toy Museum, which illustrates the development of the Seiffen toy industry and the life of the villagers, who turned from mining to this cottage industry.

*Toy Museum

In a demonstration workshop at Bahnhofstrasse 12 visitors can watch the local craftsmen at work on the various processes of turning, carving and painting.

Demonstration workshop

On the east side of the town can be found the Erzgebirge Open-Air Museum, with a variety of old buildings, including a water-powered turning mill, which give an excellent impression of the life and work of the toy-makers and other craftsmen of the Erzgebirge.

Open-Air Museum

Seiffen

Selke Valley F 6

Land: Saxony-Anhalt

The river Selke, a right-bank tributary of the Bode, rises on the south side of the Ramberg (582m/1910ft), a granite massif in the Unterharz, near the old mining town of Harzgerode. The Selke valley is less deeply indented than that of the Bode, with considerable stretches of wide flat meadowland.

Many place-names (Selkemühle, Schneidemühle, Silberhütte, Stahlhammer, Kupferhammer, etc.) bear witness to the harnessing of the Selke in earlier days to provide water power for the smelting of metal ores and the production of hardware.

*Burg Falkenstein

A few kilometres above the river's emergence from the Harz, high above the valley, rises Burg Falkenstein. Here in the 13th century Eike von Repgow wrote the "Sachsenspiegel", the oldest German code of laws.

Selketalbahn

The Selketalbahn is a narrow-gauge steam railway running between Gernrode (see Quedlinburg, Surroundings) and Harzgerode.

Siegen G 3

Land: North Rhine-Westphalia
Altitude: 350m/1150ft
Population: 107,000

Situation and characteristics

Siegen, the ancestral seat of the Princes of Nassau-Orange, is attractively situated on both banks of the river Sieg in the centre of the Siegerland, an area rich in minerals, with wooded hills reaching right up to the outskirts of the town. It was the birthplace of the Flemish painter Peter Paul Rubens (1577–1640).

Old Town

The old town of Siegen lies on the slopes of a hill above the left bank of the Sieg. The Unteres Schloss, a large Baroque palace with three wings laid out round a courtyard, was built between 1695 and 1720 for Prince Frederick William of Nassau and became the seat of the Protestant branch of the house of Nassau-Siegen. Below the main wing of the palace is the princely burial vault; the rest of the building is occupied by local government offices.

Unteres Schloss

To the west of the palace stands the little church of St Martin, the oldest church in the Siegerland (founded in the 10th century and rebuilt in Gothic style in the early 16th century; Romanesque font).

St Martin's Church

To the east is the Markt, with St Nicholas's Church (13th c.; rebuilt in 17th c.), the burial church of the Counts of Nassau, with an unusual hexagonal ground-plan. It has a famous Peruvian font, still used in baptisms.

St Nicholas's Church

Farther south is the Baroque St Mary's Church (1702–25), with the New Burial Vault of the house of Nassau.

St Mary's Church

The Oberes Schloss originated as a hilltop stronghold of the 13th century; the present building dates from the 16th and 17th centuries. It now houses the Siegerland Museum (art and cultural history; 19th century domestic interiors; Rubens Room).

Oberes Schloss

Siegen-Eiserfeld

In the southern district of Eiserfeld is the Reinhard Forster mine (sunk in 1805), which has been open to visitors since 1982.

Show mine

Freudenberg

Freudenberg

*Townscape	15km/9 miles north-west of Siegen lies Freudenberg, a pretty little town, originally a mining settlement, which is famed for its half-timbered houses. Municipal Museum in the Alter Flecken; open-air theatre.

Siegerland-Wittgenstein   G 3

Land: North Rhine-Westphalia

Situation and characteristics	The Siegerland, an industrial region traversed by the beautiful valley of the Sieg, is bounded on the south by the Sauerland and the Westerland (see entries), on the west by the Bergisches Land (see entry). On the east it merges into the Wittgensteiner Land around Bad Berleburg, with which it has much in common.

Landscape

	This upland region of rounded hills rising to some 800m/2625ft is extensively covered with forest. In the hills are the sources of the Sieg, the Lahn and the Eder. There are many remains of the mines that were worked here for more than 2000 years; the last mines were closed in 1962. The chief town in the Siegerland is Siegen (see entry).
Bad Berleburg	The principal place in the Wittgensteiner Land is the spa of Bad Berleburg (Kneipp cure). Once the seat of the Princes of Sayn-Wittgenstein-Berleburg, it has an imposing Renaissance palace (16th and 18th c.). The Schlossmuseum has a collection of material of local interest, old arms and armour and uniforms. In Goetheplatz is the Wittgensteiner Heimathaus, with a regional museum. In the Arfeld district to the south-east is a Blacksmithing Museum, in the northern district of Girkhausen an old turner's workshop, in Riemland (south-west) a slate-mine open to the public.

Sigmaringen   L 4

Land: Baden-Württemberg
Altitude: 580m/1900ft
Population: 15,000

Situation and characteristics	The old Hohenzollern seat of Sigmaringen lies on the southern fringe of the Swabian Alb (see entry), here traversed by the romantic Danube valley (see entry). The town's economy is based on woodworking, engineering, electrical engineering, textiles, the clothing industry and the service trades.

Sights

*Schloss	On a hill rising steeply up from the river stands the imposing castle of the Princes of Sigmaringen-Hohenzollern. Originally a medieval stronghold, it was reconstructed in the 17th century. After being destroyed by fire in 1893 it was rebuilt in its present form between 1895 and 1908. The magnificently appointed interior is open to the public. The castle contains a variety of collections – weapons, miniatures, prehistoric antiquities, Swabian paintings, stained glass (15th and 16th c.) – and the Marstall (Court Stables) Museum.
St John's Church	To the south of the castle is the Roman Catholic parish church of St John (1757–58), with fine stucco decoration and wall paintings. In a chapel on the north side is the cradle of St Fidelis of Sigmaringen, a Capuchin friar who was martyred in 1611 and canonised in 1746.

Schloss, Sigmaringen

On the south side of the old town is the Runder Turm (Round Tower), a relic of the old fortifications which now houses the Heimatmuseum.

Runder Turm

On the Josefsberg is St Joseph's Chapel (17th c.), with a fine Baroque interior (1739).

Josefsberg

In the Hedingen district is the Baroque Hedinger Kirche (1680), with an 18th century Rococo chapel which contains the princely burial vault (1844).

Hedinger Kirche

Surroundings of Sigmaringen

14km/8½ miles east, in the Danube valley, is the little town of Mengen, with fine old half-timbered houses and a parish church remodelled in Baroque style.

Mengen

North-east of Mengen, at Hundersingen, above the steep bank of the Danube, is the Heuneburg (6th–5th c. B.C.), one of the largest fortified settlements of the Early Iron Age (Hallstatt period).

Heuneburg

Finds from the site, with dioramas, are displayed in the tithe barn of the Heiligkreuztal monastery (see below). Archaeological trail.

The monastery of Heiligkreuztal, to the north of the Heuneburg, is notable particularly for its 14th century stained glass.

Heiligkreuztal

*Through the Upper Danube Valley to Tuttlingen

There is an attractive trip from Sigmaringen to Tuttlingen through the upper Danube valley. The road follows the north bank of the river, passing the ruined castles of Gebrochen Gutenstein and Falkenstein and some extraordinary rock formations.

| Beuron | Beuron, a pilgrimage centre, has a monastery founded in the 11th century, secularised in 1802 and reoccupied by Benedictines in 1863. It has a notable Baroque church. |

The road continues via Fridingen (near which is the Kolbingen Cave) to Tuttlingen.

Soest

Land: North Rhine-Westphalia
Altitude: 98m/322ft
Population: 43,000

| Situation and characteristics | The old Westphalian town of Soest (pronounced as if it were spelt Soost) lies in the fertile Soester Börde on the northern edge of the Sauerland (see entry). It has a number of fine churches, half-timbered houses and an almost completely preserved ring of town walls. It has the oldest charter of municipal rights in Germany (c. 1120), which provided a model for other towns as far afield as the Baltic region. |

Old Town

*Cathedral	In the centre of the town stands the massive Cathedral (Dom) of St Patroclus (12th c.), one of the finest Early Romanesque churches in Westphalia. The choir has 12th century wall paintings and 13th century stained glass. The Cathedral Museum displays liturgical utensils, some of them dating from Romanesque times.
St Nicholas's Chapel	South-east of the Cathedral is St Nicholas's Chapel (Nikolaikapelle; 12th c.), which has 13th century wall and ceiling paintings and an altarpiece (c. 1500) by Master Konrad of Soest.
Wilhelm Morgner House	South of the Cathedral is the Wilhelm Morgner House (named after the Expressionist painter of that name, 1891–1917, a native of Soest), now a cultural centre, with the Municipal Art Gallery and a collection of works by the painter and engraver Heinrich Aldegrever, who died in Soest about 1555.
St Peter's Church	West of the Cathedral is St Peter's Church (St Petri; c. 1150), with a Romanesque west end and a Gothic choir.
Town Hall	The Town Hall (Rathaus; 1713–18), on the north side of the Domplatz, is the town's only surviving Baroque building. In the municipal archives are Soest's municipal charter and two copies of the "Sachsenspiegel", the oldest and most important collection of medieval German laws.
*Hohnekirche	In the north-east of the old town stands the Hohnekirche (St Maria zur Höhe; c. 1225), with some of the finest 13th century wall paintings in Germany and a ringed cross of about 1230.
*Wiesenkirche	Nearby is the Wiesenkirche (St Maria zur Wiese; 14th–15th c.), the finest Gothic building in Soest. In the north aisle is the "Westphalian Last Supper" (stained glass, c. 1500).
Osthofentor	On the east side of the old town is the Osthofentor (1523–26), a relic of the town's old fortifications. It now houses a museum (history of the town, old weapons).
Burghofmuseum	In the south of the old town can be found the Burghofmuseum (prehistory and the early historical period, art, folk art). Associated with the museum is the "Romanesque House" of about 1200.

Surroundings of Soest

| *Möhne Dam | 10km/6 miles south of Soest is the Möhne Dam, which was bombed by the RAF during the Second World War. The dam, 650m/710yds long and 40m/130ft high, forms a lake |

10km/6 miles long and up to 3.5km/2 miles across which is now a popular water sports area.

Solingen   F 2

Land: North Rhine-Westphalia
Altitude: 53m/174ft
Population: 162,000

The lively industrial town of Solingen, in the north-west of the Bergisches Land (see entry), is famed as a centre of the cutlery industry (mainly knives, scissors, etc.), and has a training school for the steelware industry.

Situation and characteristics

Sights

In an old monastery in the Gräfrath district is the German Sword Museum (Klingen-museum), with exhibits illustrating the development of cutting weapons from the Stone Age to the present day.

Sword Museum

On the eastern outskirts of the town the Wupper valley is spanned by the Müngsten Bridge, an arched lattice-girder bridge 506m/553yds long and 107m/351ft high – Germany's highest railway bridge.

Müngsten Bridge

To the south-east, beyond the Wupper, stands Schloss Burg (restored), once a seat of the Dukes of Berg. The castle was probably originally founded in the 12th century. It now houses the Bergisches Museum (weapons, tableware, furniture, etc., of the Middle Ages and Renaissance).

Schloss Burg

Farther west, on the banks of the Wupper, can be found the Balkhauser Kotten, an old tool-grinding mill (open to visitors).

Balkhauser Kotten

In the western district of Ohligs is the Rhineland Industrial Museum, housed in an old drop forge.

Rhineland Industrial Museum

Sonthofen   M 5

Land: Bavaria
Altitude: 750m/2460ft
Population: 22,000

Sonthofen, the most southerly town in Germany, lies in the wide valley of the Iller. The beauty of the surrounding country makes it a popular holiday resort both in summer and for winter sports.

Situation and characteristics

The Town

Notable features of the town are the parish church of St Michael (rebuilt 1891), the Marktplatz, with the Old Town Hall and the New Town Hall (1952), and the Heimathaus (museum).

Parish church
Heimatmuseum

On a hill terrace south-east of the town looms the "Ordensburg" built by the Nazis between 1935–41. It is now occupied by an army training school.

"Ordensburg"

On the eastern outskirts of the town rises the Kalvarienberg (Calvary), from which there are extensive views. At the foot of the hill is a military cemetery.

Kalvarienberg

Surroundings of Sonthofen

North-east of the town is the 1738m/5702ft high Grünten, the "watchman of the Allgäu", with views extending from the Zugspitze to Säntis.

Grünten

Grosser Alpsee

Immenstadt	7km/4½ miles north-west of Sonthofen, situated on the shores of the Grosser Alpsee at the foot of the steep Immenstädter Horn, lies the little town of Immenstadt. In the Marienplatz, in the old part of the town, are the Schloss (1620; fine Knights' Hall) and the Town Hall (1640). The Baroque parish church of St Nicholas has rich fresco decoration.
Grosser Alpsee	West of the town, at the foot of the Gschwendner Horn (1450m/4755ft), is the 3km/2 mile long Grosser Alpsee (water sports).
Oberstaufen	West of Sonthofen, on the Deutsche Alpenstrasse (see entry), is the scattered village of Oberstaufen, the most popular holiday resort in the western Allgäu. Heimatsmuseum; Bauernhofmuseum (Farm Museum) in Knechtenhofen district.
Hindelang	The eastern branch of the Deutsche Alpenstrasse leads to Hindelang, one of the best-known winter sports resorts in the Allgäu. In the district of Bad Oberdorf are the Luitpold Baths (mud baths, sulphur baths). From here there is an attractive drive on the winding Jochstrasse (fine views) to Oberjoch.

Spessart

H 4–5

Länder: Hesse, Bavaria

Situation and characteristics	The Spessart ("Woodpecker Forest") is an upland region of deciduous forest lying at an altitude of around 500m/1640ft, bounded on the west, south and east by the rectangular course of the Main (Hanau-Miltenberg-Wertheim-Gemünden) and extending in the north towards Schlüchtern in Hesse. The undulating plateau, with no individual peaks of dominating height, is broken up into a series of broad ridges by winding valleys between 150m/490ft and 200m/650ft deep with narrow strips of meadowland along the bottom.

Landscape

In the south of the area extends the Hochspessart, covered by magnificent natural forest of oak and beech, which reaches its highest point in the Geiersberg (585m/1919ft). North of a line from Aschaffenburg to Lohr is the Hinterspessart, in which afforestation since the 18th century has produced a predominance of pines. The Vorspessart, to the north, is a fertile region of sandstones, gneisses and micaceous schists, reaching a height of 437m/1434ft in the Hahnenkamm.

The most attractive spots in the Spessart are the picturesque moated castle of Mespelbrunn (see Aschaffenburg, Surroundings), the Rohrbrunn area and the old monastic house of Lichtenau, near which, in the Metzgergraben, are the finest stands of old oaks in Germany.

Mespelbrunn
Rohrbrunn
Lichtenau

See entry

Main valley

Speyer

I 3

Land: Rhineland-Palatinate
Altitude: 104m/341ft
Population: 43,000

Speyer, on the left bank of the Rhine, was the see of a bishop from the 7th century and a free imperial city from 1294 to 1797, the meeting-place of many Imperial Diets, including the famous one in 1529 at which the Reformed princes and estates made their protest against the anti-Reformation resolutions of the majority, giving rise to the term "Protestant".
The town's harbour on the Rhine makes a major contribution to its economy.

Situation and
characteristics

There are excursion boats on the Rhine during the summer months.

Rhine cruises

Sights

The six-towered Cathedral (Dom) of St Mary and St Stephen, the largest and most imposing cathedral of the High Romanesque period in Germany, was begun about 1030 by the Salian emperor Conrad II and consecrated in 1061. Between 1082 and 1125, in the reigns of Henry IV and V, a major rebuilding took place.
In the west porch are statues of the eight emperors and kings buried in the Cathedral.

**Cathedral

Features of the interior are the raised Royal Choir, the crypt (consecrated 1039) and the imperial burial vault, with the remains of the imperial tombs, some of which were plundered by the French in 1689. Among them are the tombs of Conrad II (d. 1039), Henry III (d. 1056), Henry IV (d. 1106), Henry V (d. 1125) and Rudolph of Habsburg (d. 1291).

In front of the Cathedral can be seen the Domnapf, a huge sandstone basin (1490) which was filled with wine at the induction of a new bishop.

To the south of the Cathedral is the Historical Museum of the Palatinate, with an outstanding collection of material from ancient, medieval and modern times. It also includes the Diocesan Museum and an interesting Wine Museum.

Historical
Museum

At the end of the nearby Judenbadgasse, in a little garden almost 10m/33ft below ground level, is the Jews' Bath (Judenbad; *c.* 1100), belonging to a synagogue which once stood here.

Jews' Bath

South-west of the Judenbad, at Allerheiligenstrasse 9, is the house in which the painter Anselm Feuerbach was born in 1829 (memorial museum; changing exhibitions).

Feuerbach House

From the Cathedral Maximilianstrasse, the town's wide main street, runs west to the Altpörtel, a handsome gate-tower of the 13th and 16th centuries (interior open to the public).

Altpörtel

In the north-west of the town, near the railway station (Bahnhof), is St Bernard's Church, the Peace Church, built jointly by Frenchmen and Germans in 1953–54.

St Bernard's
Church

Speyer Cathedral

Surroundings of Speyer

*Holiday Park

At Hassloch (14km/8½ miles north-west) is the Holiday Park, a leisure and amusement park (area 35 hectares/86 acres) with a Fairytale Park, a Lilliputian Town, a dolphinarium, a variety theatre, a cinema with a 180° screen and a wide range of other attractions.

Schwetzingen

See Heidelberg, Surroundings

Spreewald (Spree Forest)   E 9

Land: Brandenburg

Situation and characteristics

The Spreewald (Sorbian Blota, "marshland") is a charming area of woodland and water 100km/60 miles south of Berlin. Its uniqueness lies not only in the pattern of its landscape but also in the individuality of the Sorbs who make up the majority of the population (see Lusatia).

In the past the only means of transport in the Spreewald was by boat on the numerous little watercourses, and every farm had its own little harbour. Nowadays, with protection against flooding and regulation of the water supply, the Spreewald has become an area of intensively cultivated large farm holdings.

Boat trips

In 1908 a boatmen's association was founded at Lübbenau, the gateway to the Spreewald, and more than half a million visitors a year are now punted round the area by the local boatmen.

**Landscape

The Spreewald is a damp low-lying area traversed by numerous streams, with patches of sand and dunes. The scattered villages characteristic of the Spreewald developed on

In the Spreewald

these sand islands. The highest part, in the south, was built up from deposits laid down by the Spree during the last ice age.

The Oberspreewald begins at the little town of Burg. Between here and Lübben the Spree and its tributary the Malxe, with a fall of only 7m/23ft in a course of 34km/21 miles, split up into innumerable little streams. Here the trees lining the banks of the streams alternate with expanses of meadowland and patches of arable land and gardens.

Oberspreewald

In the Unterspreewald, below Lübbe, the Spree again divides into a number of different channels. This old glacier basin, filled up by deposits from the Spree, is now occupied by permanent grassland, fenwood and arable land. Those areas of the Spreewald which are safe from flooding have been settled since early times by Sorbs, with their own cultural traditions and characteristic costumes.

Unterspreewald

Stade

C 5

Land: Lower Saxony
Altitude: 7m/23ft
Population: 45,000

Stade lies on both banks of the navigable river Schwinge, which flows into the Elbe north-east of the town. The town, which first appears in the records in 994, was throughout the Middle Ages the most powerful town on the lower Elbe after Hamburg.

Situation and characteristics

The *Town

The charming old town of Stade, almost completely surrounded by the line of its old fortifications, now laid out as parks and gardens, has preserved large numbers of

Old Harbour, Stade

handsome half-timbered buildings. Particularly notable are Nos. 26 (1669) and 29 (1650) in Hökerstrasse and Nos. 3 (1590) and 21 (1539) in Bäckerstrasse. In the Pferdemarkt is the old Arsenal (Zeughaus; 1698).

St Willehad's Church	South-east of the Pferdemarkt is St Willehad's Church (Wilhadikirche), a brick-built Gothic church (13th–14th c.), several times destroyed and extensively rebuilt at the end of the 19th century.
Town Hall St Cosmas's Church	In Hökerstrasse stands the Town Hall (Rathaus), rebuilt in 1667 after a great fire (Ratskeller 1279). To the north is the Romanesque church of St Cosmas (12th c.), with a Baroque tower of 1684 (panoramic views). The church has the first organ built by Arp Schnitger. Nearby is the old monastery of St John (St Johannis; 17th c.).
Alter Hafen	Farther north lies the picturesque Alter Hafen (Old Harbour), with the Old Weigh-House (18th c.) and a reconstruction of the old wooden crane (Holzkran) of 1661. On Wasser West is Burgomaster Hintze's House (1621), a richly decorated sandstone building dating from the period of Swedish occupation. Nearby is the Schwedenspeicher (Swedish Granary; 1691), which now houses the Regional Museum.
Baumhaus Museum	On Wasser Ost, in a half-timbered house of 1775, is the privately owned Baumhaus Museum.
Museums	To the west of the Wallstrasse, at Inselstrasse 12, can be found the Heimatmuseum. Nearby, on an island in the Wallanlagen (the gardens on the site of the old fortifications), is an open-air museum.

Starnberger See   L 6

Land: Bavaria

Situation and characteristics	The Starnberger See or Würmsee, with the river Würm flowing out of its northern end, is a lake in the Alpine Foreland 25km/15 miles south-west of Munich. It occupies a basin

20km/12½ miles long and 2–5km/1¼–3 miles wide gouged out by a glacier and is surrounded by forest-covered morainic hills.

*Landscape

The lake, which on a fine summer day is dotted with sailing boats and excursion vessels, offers a varied pattern of great scenic beauty, with its wooded hills, the popular holiday and weekend resorts round its shores, its groups of villas and its beautiful parks and gardens, all set against the backdrop of the distant Alpine chain.

Rising in terraces above the northern tip of the lake is the attractive little town of Starnberg. Above the town stands a 16th century Schloss which belonged to the Dukes of Bavaria. The parish church (1765) has a fine Late Rococo interior.

Starnberg

Near the north end of the lake, on the east side, lies the village of Berg, with the little Schloss Berg. A cross in the lake marks the spot where King Ludwig II of Bavaria, accompanied by his doctor, was drowned in 1886.

Berg

From Starnberg a road leads along the west side of the lake to Possenhofen, which has a 16th century Schloss. Off to the right is the pretty little town of Pöcking.

Possenhofen

From Feldafing there is a fine view of the Alps.

Feldafing

In Tutzing, the second largest place on the lake, is the Evangelical (Protestant) Academy, occupying a Schloss set in a beautiful park.

Tutzing

From the Ilkahöhe (711m/2333ft), south-west of Tutzing, there are superb views of the lake and the Alps.

Ilkahöhe

The road continues from Tutzing to Bernried, with a former Augustinian monastery, and Seehaupt, at the south-west end of the lake.

Bernried
Seeshaupt

Stendal

D 7

Land: Saxony-Anhalt
Altitude: 33m/108ft
Population: 52,400

The old Hanseatic city of Stendal, the largest town in the Altmark (see entry), lies on the river Uchte some 60km/40 miles north of Magdeburg. It was the birthplace of the 18th century antiquarian and art historian Johann Joachim Winckelmann. The French novelist Henri Beyle (1783–1842), better known as Stendhal, took his pseudonym from the name of the town.

Situation and characteristics

Sights

The Town Hall (14th c., with much later alteration) is a gem of Gothic architecture with its stepped and curving gables. Nearby can be seen a monument to Winckelmann (1859).

*Town Hall

In front of the Town Hall is a figure of Roland, frequently found in North German towns as a symbol of municipal authority. The figure is a copy of the original (1525), which was destroyed in a violent storm in 1972.

Roland

Near the Town Hall stands the twin-towered parish church of St Mary, a hall-church consecrated in 1447. The most notable features of the interior are the groined vaulting, the beautiful choir screen and a fine altar of 1471. At the west end of the nave is an astronomical clock which is thought to date from the second half of the 15th century.

St Mary's Church

In the south of the town is the Cathedral of St Nicholas (1423–67), a Late Gothic hall-church with its original stained glass (scenes from the life of Christ and saints), fine

*Cathedral

choir-stalls (*c.* 1430–40) and thirteen sandstone figures (*c.* 1240–50) from the choir-screen of an earlier church on the site.

Altmark Museum

The surviving buildings of St Catherine's Convent (founded 1456) contain the Altmark Museum (early history of the area, Romanesque bronzes, wood sculpture, carved altars, faience and porcelain).

St James's Church

In the north of the town is St James's Church (1311–1477), with a fine interior (choir screen with a Triumphal Cross group, Late Gothic stalls and stained glass).

St Peter's Church

Also in the north of the town is the parish church of St Peter, Stendal's oldest church (end of 13th c.).

Winckelmann Museum

The birthplace of J. J. Winckelmann at Winckelmannstrasse 36 is now a museum.

*Uenglinger Tor Tangermünder Tor

Of the town's medieval fortifications there survive two gate-towers – the 15th century Uenglinger Tor on the north-west side of the old town, one of the finest brick-built town gates in North Germany, and the Tangermünder Tor (1220) to the south (stone-built, with a brick upper storey).

Stolpen

F–G 9

Land: Saxony
Altitude: 356m/1168ft
Population: 2100

Situation and characteristics

Stolpen, 20km/12½ miles east of Dresden, is noted for its medieval castle and for the fine basalt formations of the hill on which the castle stands.

Castle Stolpen

*Burg Stolpen

The castle, 220m/240yds long, consists of four wards or courtyards. A signposted route takes visitors round the main features of interest. A museum on the history of the castle and the town is housed in thirteen rooms and eight cellars.
The well in the fourth courtyard is the world's deepest basalt well (82m/269ft).

The round-topped hill on which the castle stands, with its striking octagonal basalt columns, is protected as a natural monument. The finest columns are to be seen on the west side of the castle; within the castle itself the columns have the appearance of organ pipes.

*Basalt formations

The Town

A striking feature of the town is the Markt, which is almost exactly square – a relic of the medieval settlement of this area. Beside the Town Hall is the Löwenapotheke (Lion Pharmacy; 1722), with a gilded coat of arms. The old Amtshaus (offices of a local government official), now occupied by a savings bank, has a fine coat of arms of the Electorate of Saxony dated 1673. In the new Amtshaus (also with the Electoral arms) Napoleon lodged in 1813.

Markt

Stralsund

B 8

Land: Mecklenburg-West Pomerania
Altitude: 5m/16ft
Population: 75,400

The former Hanseatic town of Stralsund, on the sound of the same name, is a treasure-house of historic buildings. The old town with its famous Town Hall, Gothic parish churches, old monasteries, fortifications and burghers' houses is surrounded by beautiful lakes and gardens.
Lying off Stralsund, linked with it by a causeway, lies the island of Rügen with its seaside resorts and the little port of Sassnitz (ferry to Trelleborg in Sweden).

Situation and characteristics

*Old Town

Stralsund has preserved considerable stretches of its old town walls, with a number of *wiekhäuser* (houses built into the town walls) on the Knieperwall and near the Johanniskloster, and two town gates, the Kütertor (1446; now a youth hostel) and the Kniepertor (early 14th c.; now a dwelling-house).

Fortifications

In the Alter Markt stands the Town Hall (Rathaus), begun in the 13th century, in brick-built Gothic style. The main front is one of the finest examples of secular brick-built Gothic architecture in North Germany.

*Town Hall

Immediately east of the Town Hall is St Nicholas's Church (Nikolaikirche; 1270–1350), also brick-built Gothic. Richly furnished interior (panel paintings).

St Nicholas's Church

North-east of the Alter Markt, in Schillstrasse, are the ruins of the Franciscan friary of St John (Johanniskloster; founded 1254), which have been left as a memorial to the destruction of the church in 1945. Concerts and other events are now held here. During restoration work fine medieval frescoes were brought to light.

Johanniskloster

Southern District

Two other notable churches are the Church of the Holy Ghost (Heiliggeistkirche) in Wasserstrasse, a Late Gothic brick-built hall-church (15th c.), with the Hospital of the Holy Ghost, and St James's Church (Jakobikirche), at the east end of Böttcherstrasse, a brick-built Gothic basilica (originally a hall-church, 14th–15th c.).

Church of Holy Ghost
St James's Church

View of the Stralsund from St Mary's Church

St Mary's Church	To the south of the Neuer Markt is St Mary's Church (Marienkirche), a massive brick-built Gothic church (from 1382, incorporating earlier work).
*Katharinenkloster (museums)	In Mönchstrasse, near the Knieperwall, can be found the old monastery of St Catherine (Katharinenkloster), a Dominican convent founded in 1251, which now houses two museums.
Museum of the Sea	The Museum of the Sea (Meeresmuseum) has one of Europe's largest aquariums for tropical fish (1984; tank with a capacity of 50,000 litres/11,000 gallons) and a variety of displays on life in the sea, fishing, the Baltic coast and beach flora and fauna.
Museum of Cultural History	The Museum of Cultural History (Kulturhistorisches Museum) displays a wide range of material (early medieval gold jewellery from the island of Hiddensee, medieval religious art, folk traditions, history of the town).

*Burghers' Houses

Alter Markt	The most notable of the burghers' houses in the Alter Markt are the Late Gothic Wulflammhaus (No. 5) and the former headquarters of the Swedish commandant (No. 14), a three-storey Baroque building.

Some characteristic old gabled houses can be seen in Mönchstrasse, Ossenreyerstrasse and Mühlenstrasse. At Mühlenstrasse 23 is the Kämpischer Hof, which belonged to the Neuenkamp monastery – an imposing range of buildings dating from different periods (the house is first mentioned in 1319). At Badenstrasse 17 is the Schwedenpalais, built in 1726–30 for the Swedish governor-general, and at Fährstrasse 23–24 the house in which the Swedish chemist C. W. Scheele (1742–86) was born.

Surroundings of Stralsund

*Putbus	24km/15 miles north-east of Stralsund is Putbus, a little princely residence and seaside resort, regularly planned and built in uniform style. Neo-classical theatre (1819–21).

Notable features of the Schlosspark are a game enclosure, old trees, the Marstall (Court Stables, 1821–24), the Orangery (1824) and the Garden House (now a café).

Straubing

Land: Bavaria
Altitude: 332m/1089ft
Population: 42,000

Straubing, an important agricultural market town, lies on the right bank of the Danube in a fertile plain (the Gäuboden) at the foot of the Bavarian Forest (see entry).

Situation and characteristics

New Town

In the centre of the new town, between Theresienplatz in the west and Ludwigsplatz in the east, rises the 68m/223ft high Stadtturm (14th c.; views). To the north of this is the Gothic Town Hall (1382), to the west the Tiburtius Fountain (1685) and the Trinity Column, set up in 1709 after the town had successfully withstood a siege.

To the north of Theresienplatz stands the massive St James's Church (15th–16th c.; designed by Hans Stethaimer), with an 86m/282ft tower and a fine interior (15th c. stained glass, pulpit of 1753, old tombs).

St James's Church

In Ludwigsplatz is St James's Fountain (1644). At No. 11 is the Löwenapotheke (Lion Pharmacy), in which the painter Karl Spitzweg worked as an apprentice in 1828–30.

Ludwigsplatz

From the centre of the square Fraunhofergasse runs north. No. 1 is the birthplace of the physicist Joseph Fraunhofer (1787–1826) and No. 9 is the Gäuboden Museum (prehistory, history of the town, folk traditions; the Straubing Treasure, a Roman hoard discovered in 1950).

Gäuboden Museum

A little way east are the Carmelite Church, built by Hans Stethaimer and remodelled in Baroque style in the 18th century (tomb of Duke Albrecht II, d. 1397, behind the high altar), and the sumptuous Ursuline Church (by the Asam brothers, 1738).

Carmelite Church
Ursuline Church

To the north, on the banks of the Danube, stands the 15th century Schloss.

Schloss

To the west of the new town is the Stadtpark (Municipal Park), laid out in 1905, with the Tiergarten (Zoo).

Stadtpark

Old Town

In the old town, to the east of the new town, is St Peter's Church (1180), a Romanesque basilica (towers built 1886), with a crucifix of about 1200 above the high altar. In the Kirchhof is the Agnes Bernauer Chapel (1436), with the grave-slab of Agnes Bernauer, the beautiful daughter of a burgher of Augsburg who became the wife of Duke Albrecht III against the wishes of his father, who then had her accused of witchcraft and drowned in the Danube. Nearby is the Totentanzkapelle (1486; ducal burial vault), with frescoes of the Danse Macabre (1763).

St Peter's
Church

Stuttgart

Capital of the *Land* of Baden-Württemberg
Altitude: 207m/679ft
Population: 561,000

In this guide the description of Stuttgart has been deliberately kept short, since a fuller account is provided in the "Stuttgart" guide in the same series.

N.B.

Stuttgart

Situation and characteristics

Stuttgart, capital of the *Land* of Baden-Württemberg, is beautifully situated in a basin enclosed by forest-covered hills, orchards and vineyards, open only on the east towards the Neckar. From the valley bottom, where the older part of the town and the historic buildings are to be found, the houses climb up the surrounding slopes; when these are too steep for streets they are reached by flights of steps or stepped lanes.

Stuttgart is an important fruit-growing and wine-producing centre. In the districts of Berg and Bad Cannstatt are the most productive mineral springs in Europe after those of Budapest.

Central Area

*Hauptbahnhof

In Arnulf-Klett-Platz (underground shopping arcade; late opening) is the Hauptbahnhof, Stuttgart's main railway station (by Paul Bonatz and E. F. Scholer, 1914–27), with a 58m/190ft high tower. Opposite the station is the Hindenburgbau (1927–28; extended 1951), and beyond this, in Lautenschlagerstrasse, are the Zeppelinbau (hotel) and Post Office Headquarters (1926–27).

Facing the station, on the left, can be found the Schlossgartenbau (hotel), originally built in 1960–61 as offices.

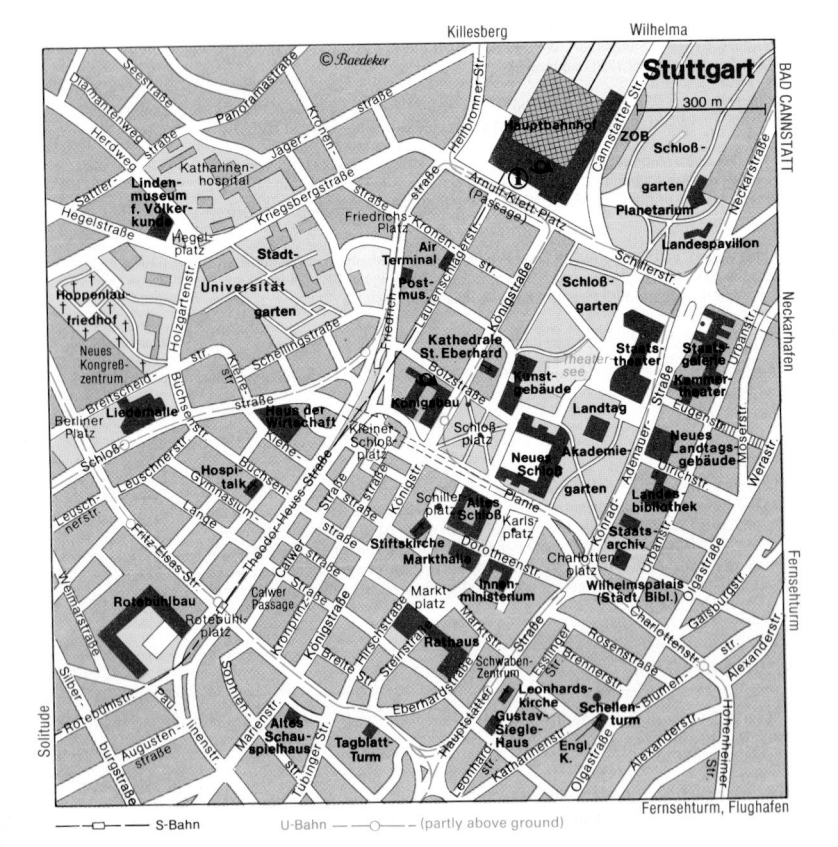

From the station Königstrasse, the town's main business and shopping street (pedestrian zone), runs south-west, past the Cathedral of St Eberhard (R.C.; rebuilt 1955), to the Schlossplatz, continuing to the Wilhelmsbau.

The spacious Schlossplatz is surrounded by buildings dating from the time when Stuttgart was a ducal and royal capital. In the centre of the gardens stands the Jubilee Column, erected in 1841 to commemorate King William I's 25 years of rule. Here too are a cast-iron bandstand (1871) and a number of pieces of modern sculpture (Calder, Hrdlička, Hajek). On the north-west side of the square is the Königsbau (1856–60; restored 1957–59), with a colonnade and a shopping arcade and to the south-west, on higher ground, the Kleiner Schlossplatz (1968), with shops and restaurants. At the north-east corner of the Schlossplatz is the Kunstgebäude (built 1912–13; rebuilt 1956–61), which houses the Municipal Art Gallery and periodic special exhibitions.

Dominating the square is the New Palace (Neues Schloss), with three wings built round a courtyard (1746–1807; rebuilt 1959–62), now occupied by the Ministries of Education and Finance.

To the south-west, on the Planie, is the massive bulk of the Old Palace (Altes Schloss; by A. Tretsch, 1553–78; rebuilt 1948–69), with a picturesque arcaded courtyard. It now houses the Württemberg Landesmuseum (medieval collection; applied art, religious and secular; the Württemberg crown jewels; watches and clocks, astronomical and musical instruments, costume of various periods, archaeological finds, etc.). In the south wing is the palace church (1560–62).

Flanking the Old Palace is Schillerplatz (underground car park), with a monument to Schiller by Thorvaldsen. On the north-east side of the square is the Alte Kanzlei (Old Chancery; c. 1500). On the north-west side is the Prinzenbau (begun in 1605 by Schickhardt, finished a hundred years later by Matthias Weiss), which during the reign of Duke Eberhard Ludwig (1677–1733) was the residence of his heir, Prince Friedrich Ludwig; it is now occupied by the Ministry of Justice. On the south-west side of the square is the old Fruchtkasten (Granary; 1390) and adjoining it is the choir of the Stiftskirche.

Schlossplatz, with the Old and New Palaces

Stuttgart

* Stiftskirche

The Stiftskirche (Protestant), with its two very different towers, was founded in the 12th century and rebuilt in Late Gothic style in the 15th century by Aberlin Jörg and others; reconsecrated in 1958 after the repair of heavy war damage. In the choir can be seen a magnificent series of eleven Renaissance figures of Counts of Württemberg by Simon Schlör (1576–1608).

Marktplatz

A little way south is the Marktplatz, with the Town Hall (Rathaus, 1956; carillon, Ratskeller, 61m/200ft high tower).

On the southern edge of the old town, in Eberhardstrasse, are the Tagblatt-Turm (1927–28; 61m/200ft high) and the "Kultur unterm Turm" cultural centre (theatre, periodic exhibitions).

Schwabenzentrum

To the south of the Tagblatt Tower lies the large complex of the Schwabenzentrum (Swabian Centre; 1980), with shops, shopping arcades and quiet little courtyards with restaurants. Beyond the broad Hauptstätter Strasse is St Leonard's Church (Leonhardskirche; 15th c.).

Writers' House

North of St Leonard's Church, just before Charlottenplatz, on right, is the Bohnenviertel, a part of the old town which has been rebuilt in modern style. At Kanalstrasse 4 is the Writers' House (Schriftstellerhaus), a forum for discussions between writers from Germany and other countries and for encounters between authors and readers.

Charlottenplatz
Konrad-Adenauer-Strasse

In Charlottenplatz, with its constant flow of traffic (underpass, on several levels, for road traffic, trams and pedestrians), is the Wilhelmspalais (built by Salucci in 1840, burned down 1944, rebuilt 1964–65), residence of the last king of Württemberg, William II, now housing a collection of material on the history of the town and the Municipal Library (Städtische Bibliothek). From here Konrad-Adenauer-Strasse runs north-east. On the right-hand side is the Landesbibliothek (Provincial Library; 1970), and farther along the street, on the left, are the Landtag (1960–61), the parliament of Baden-Württemberg (on the right, offices for members of the Landtag, 1984–87), and the State Theatre (Staatstheater), an effective group consisting of two buildings originally erected by Max Littmann in 1907–12. The Grosses Haus (opera) is still Littmann's building; the Kleines Haus (theatre) is a new building erected in 1960–62 to replace the original building destroyed during the war.

* State Gallery

On the right-hand side of the street, directly opposite the State Theatre, is the State Gallery (Staatsgalerie), with one of the finest art collections in Germany. It consists of the neo-classical Old Building (Altbau; 1838–42) and the New Building (Neubau; 1977–83), designed by the British architect Sir James Stirling. The Gallery has works by the older European masters (including 16th century Swabian painters), a department of modern art and a collection of graphic art.
Beyond the Old Building, to the right, can be seen the entrance to the 824m/900yd long Wagenburg Tunnel, which carries traffic to the eastern districts of the town.

Schlossgarten
* Planetarium

Along the west side of Konrad-Adenauer-Strasse and Neckarstrasse the Schlossgarten extends from the New Palace to the Neckar in Berg and Bad Cannstatt. In the Oberer Schlossgarten (Upper Garden), diagonally opposite the Wagenburg Tunnel, are the Landespavillon (exhibitions) and the Planetarium. Beyond this are pretty little lakes, sculptures and the "Berger Sprudler" (mineral spring).

North-west District

Haus der Wirtschaft

In the north-western part of the central area, near the Ministry of Economic Development, is the Haus der Wirtschaft (State Factory Inspectorate, Stuttgart Design Centre, etc.). In the Stadtgarten is the University of Technology.

Liederhalle
* Linden Museum

West of the Haus der Wirtschaft stands the Liederhalle, a concert hall. In nearby Hegelplatz is the Linden Museum of Ethnography (Museum für Völkerkunde).

Above the city to the north, near the Academy of Fine Art, is the Weissenhof, a pioneering and influential housing development, built in 1927 for an exhibition by the Werkbund, a group of leading international architects, including Le Corbusier, Mies van der Rohe and Gropius.

Weissenhof

Near the Weissenhof lies Killesberg Park, laid out from 1937 onwards, with exhibition halls used by the Stuttgart Trade Fair, a congress centre, a chair-lift and a summer theatre.

Killesberg Park

Stuttgart-Berg

In the Berg district on the left bank of the Neckar stands Schloss Rosenstein (1824–29), which together with the Museum am Löwentor (1984) houses the State Museum of Natural History.

Natural History Museum

Below Schloss Rosenstein is the Wilhelma Zoological and Botanic Garden (named after a little Moorish-style palace built in 1842–53), beautifully laid out, with hothouses, animal houses and enclosures and an aquarium.

*Wilhelma

Bad Cannstatt

On the right bank of the Neckar lies the old district of Bad Cannstatt, with the Kursaal (two mineral springs; restaurant) and the Kurpark. At Taubenheimstrasse 13 was the workshop of Gottlieb Daimler (memorial museum). On the Cannstatter Wasen (Meadows), the scene of the annual Spring and Folk Festival, are the large Neckar Stadium and the Hanns Martin Schleyer Hall, one of the most modern sports halls in Europe.

Outer Districts

South-west of the town is the Birkenkopf (511m/1677ft), a hill built up after the Second World War from the rubble of destroyed buildings (view).

*Birkenkopf

On the Hoher Bopser (481m/1578ft), a wooded hill in the south of the town, rises the Television Tower (Fernsehturm; 217m/712ft high including the aerial), with a restaurant at 150m/490ft and above it a viewing platform.

*Television Tower

In the eastern district of Untertürkheim is the Daimler-Benz Museum, which gives a comprehensive survey of the development of car manufacture. Between Untertürkheim and Obertürkheim extends the Neckar Harbour.

Untertürkheim

On the Württemberg, near Obertürkheim, can be found the burial chapel of Queen Katharina (d. 1819), a domed rotunda in neo-classical style; fine views.

*Württemberg

In the northern district of Zuffenhausen are the Porsche works (museum, with racing and sports cars).

Zuffenhausen

10km/6 miles west of the city centre stands Schloss Solitude, built for Duke Karl Eugen in 1763–67, with fine state apartments. An international art academy was established in the subsidiary buildings in 1990.

*Solitude

Suhl   G 6

Land: Thuringia
Altitude: 430–570m/1410–1870ft
Population: 56,000

The old Thuringian town of Suhl lies in the valley of the Lauter and the Hasel on the south-western fringes of the Thuringian Forest.

Situation and characteristics

Sights

Markt	In the Markt is the Town Hall (rebuilt in the early 20th c.). In the centre of the square is a fountain with the town's heraldic emblem, the Armourer of Suhl (1903).
St Mary's Church	To the south of the Markt stands St Mary's Church (17th c.; remodelled in Baroque style 1757–61), with a fine interior (altar; organ-case).
*Steinweg	In Steinweg, the old main street, are a number of handsome burghers' houses, some of them with Rococo façades. Particularly notable are No. 26, a Rococo house (1755–56) which belonged to an arms manufacturer named Steigleder, and No. 31 (sumptuously decorated interior), which belonged to another manufacturer named Spangenberg.
Kreuzkirche	At the end of Steinweg is the Kreuzkirche (Holy Cross Church; 1739), with a fine Baroque altar. Immediately adjoining the church is the Kreuzkapelle (1642).
*Arms Museum	The old Malzhaus (Malthouse; 1663) on the Herrenteich, one of the oldest and handsomest half-timbered buildings in the town, houses the Arms Museum.

Suhl-Heinrichs

*Town Hall	In the district of Heinrichs is the former Town Hall (1657), one of the finest half-timbered buildings in southern Thuringia. In this area are many well preserved half-timbered houses belonging to carriers and wine-dealers. The Marktplatz of Heinrichs is protected as a historic monument.

Schleusingen

*Schloss Bertholdsburg	20km/12½ miles south-east of Suhl is Schleusingen, a little town dominated by Schloss Bertholdsburg, a Renaissance castle flanked by four towers (Heimatmuseum, with a fine collection of toys). Until 1583 this was the seat of the powerful Princes of Henneberg.

Hildburghausen

	14km/8½ miles south of Schleusingen is Hildburghausen. In the idyllic Marktplatz are a number of burghers' houses of the 16th–19th centuries and the Late Gothic Town Hall, originally a moated castle belonging to the Henneberg family. Baroque estate office (18th c.); Baroque church, with unusual interior.

Sonneberg

*Toy Museum	Farther south-east (60km/37 miles from Suhl) is Sonneberg, which has been for centuries the leading doll and toy manufacturing town in Thuringia. The German Toy Museum at Beethovenstrasse 10 has a large and varied collection of dolls and toys from many parts of the world.

Kloster Vessra

*Agricultural Museum	9km/6 miles west of Schleusingen, near Themar, is Kloster Vessra, a house of Premonstratensian canons founded in 1131, with the Museum of Agricultural History: a collection of old peasants' houses which gives a vivid impression of country life in this area from the 17th century onwards.

Swabian Alb (Schwäbische Alb)   K–L 4–5

Land: Baden-Württemberg

Situation and characteristics	The Swabian Alb, an upland region of Jurassic limestone of about 700m/2300ft in height, extends for 210km/130 miles, varying in width between 15km/9 miles and 40km/25 miles,

from the south-eastern edge of the Black Forest (see entry), where it reaches a height of 1015m/3330ft in the Lemberg, to the Ries depression round Nördlingen. In the north-west the hills drop down to the valleys of the Neckar, the Fils and the Rems in a steep scarp some 400m/1300ft high, which is broken up by valleys reaching deeply into the hills and has a series of ruined castles perched on outlying crags. To the south-east the Alb slopes gently down to the Danube, in a gently undulating plateau of permeable limestone through which most surface water seeps away, forming caverns, swallo-wholes and dry valleys.

*Landscape

The great attraction of the Swabian Alb lies in the variety of its scenery – fertile fruit-growing valleys with trim villages and little towns containing treasures of art and architecture, rugged corries with abundant springs and huge caves, rocky hillsides with fine beech forests and numbers of ruined castles, and the austere beauty of the plateaux with their mountain pastures and lonely expanses of heath.

Among the areas most popular with visitors are the Honau valley, with Schloss Lichten-stein and two large caves, the Nebelhöhle and Bärenhöhle; the Erms valley; the Len-ningen valley, from which Teck and Hohenneuffen can be visited; the area between Göppingen and Schwäbisch Gmünd, with the Hohenstaufen and Hohenrechberg; and, to the south-west, the Zollernalb and the Heuberg, with the highest peaks.

Swabian Alb Route (Schwäbische Albstrasse)

The Swabian Alb Route, signposted by a stylised silver thistle on a bluish-green ground, runs along the hills from north-east to south-west for a distance of up to 260km/160 miles, depending on the starting and finishing points (Aalen-Nördlingen or Tuttlingen/Trossingen). The road, much of it improved since 1960, takes in interesting old towns, typical Alb villages and a range of attractive and varied scenery.

The north-eastern branch of the Swabian Alb Route leads south from Aalen over the "European watershed" between the valleys of the Kocher and the Brenz and down to Heidenheim.

North-eastern branch

The eastern branch runs south-west from Nördlingen and then pursues a winding course by way of the Härtsfeld and Neresheim to Heidenheim, on the Brenz.

Eastern branch

The main Swabian Alb Route goes west from Heidenheim to Geislingen an der Steige and from there continues via Bad Überkingen and Bad Ditzenbach to Bad Urach, It then climbs steeply up into the Hintere Alb, passing close to the Bärenhöhle near Engstingen; from there south-west to Albstadt and over the Grosser Heuberg. The main route ends at Dürbheim, from which there are continuations on the north-western and south-western branches.

Main route

The north-western branch runs from Dürbheim via Spaichingen to Trossingen, on the edge of the Baar.

North-western branch

The south-western branch runs from Dürbheim to the industrial town of Tuttlingen, on the young Danube.

South-western branch

See also Aalen, Albstadt, Blaubeuren, Göppingen, Hechingen, Kirchheim/Teck, Reut-lingen, Rottweil, Schwäbisch Gmünd, Tübingen and Villingen-Schwenningen.

Swabian Castle Country (Schwäbisches Burgenland)   I 5

Land: Baden-Württemberg

The "Swabian Castle Country" lies between Würzburg in the north and Heilbronn and Schwäbisch Hall in the south, broadly coinciding with the Hohenlohe area. It is a plateau

Situation and characteristics

slashed by the valleys of the Tauber, the Jagst and the Kocher with their old castles and picturesque little towns.

In the Tauber valley are the little wine town of Tauberbischofsheim (fine half-timbered houses, church with an altar by Tilman Riemenschneider, 16th c. Schloss of the Electors of Mainz), the well-known spa of Bad Mergentheim (see entry) and the world-famed medieval town of Rothenburg (see entry).

Tauber valley

The main places of interest in the Jagst valley are Schöntal monastery, the castles of Jagsthausen (home of Götz von Berlichingen) and the Langenburg area (castles).

Jagst valley

The road down the Kocher valley from Schwäbisch Hall (see entry) by way of Künzelsau to its junction with the Neckar at Bad Friedrichshall runs through a succession of picturesque little towns and villages. To the south, at the foot of the Waldenburg Hills, are the little towns of Neuenstein and Öhringen, with imposing castles of the Hohenlohe family. There are numbers of castles in the lower Neckar valley between Heilbronn and Heidelberg (see entries).

Kocher valley

To the south of the Hohenlohe plain is the Swabian Forest (Schwäbischer Wald), a wooded upland region with the Waldenburg, Löwenstein, Limburg and Ellwangen Hills and the Mainhardt, Murrhardt, Welzheim and Schur Forests.

Swabian Forest

Sylt

A 4

Land: Schleswig-Holstein
Area: 102 sq.km/39 sq. miles

The island of Sylt, a popular summer resort, is the most northerly German island and the largest of the North Frisian Islands (37km/23 miles long). It is shaped rather like a large pickaxe; its central portion is a sandy ridge mostly covered with heath. Its particular attractions are its dunes and its 40km/25 miles of wave-swept beach.

Situation and characteristics

The land route to Sylt is by rail over the 11km/7 mile long Hindenburg Causeway (Hindenburgdamm), built 1923–27 (cars carried between Niebüll and Westerland; about 1 hour), which cuts across the Wattenmeer (nature reserve).
There is an airstrip at Westerland.

Access
*Hindenburgdamm

Sights

Half way along the west coast, on the open sea, is the fashionable seaside resort of Westerland (founded 1857; pop. 10,000), the chief place on the island, with a long beach of fine sand, extensive treatment facilities, an indoor seawater pool with artificial waves, an aquarium and a casino. It has an old village church (17th–19th c.) with a sundial of 1789.

Westerland

Listland

From Westerland a road runs 18km/11 miles north to Wenningstedt (pop. 2200), with a long beach, treatment facilities and the "Hun's grave" (megalithic chamber tomb) of Denghoog.

Wenningstedt

Beyond Wenningstedt is the seaside resort of Kampen (pop. 1100), with reed-thatched houses, "Huns' graves", a bird-watchers' hide and the 4km/2½ mile long Rotes Kliff (Red Cliff), which falls sheer to the sea from a height of up to 27m/89ft. The road then continues through the Listland nature reserve (large dunes).

Kampen
*Rotes Kliff

On the east side of the island, near its northern tip, lies the resort of List (pop. 3200). It lies on the south side of the Königshafen (now silted up), which is enclosed on the north by

List

◄ *Lochen, near Balingen*

the 4km/2½ mile long strip of land known as the Ellenbogen ("Elbow"; two lighthouses). Car ferry to the Danish island of Rømø.

*Hörnum Peninsula

Rantum

From Westerland a road runs south through the beautiful dune landscape of the Hörnum peninsula to Rantum (pop. 600), with an 8km/5 mile long sandy beach on the west coast. North-east of the village is the large Rantumbecken bird sanctuary.

Hörnum

The road continues to the hamlet of Puan Klent and the little town of Hörnum (pop. 1400) at the southernmost tip of the island, with a powerful lighthouse, a harbour (boats to Amrum, Föhr and Heligoland: see North Sea Coast, North Frisian Islands) and good beaches.

Sylt-Ost

Tinnum
Keitum

The Sylt-Ost peninsula (mostly fenland) extends to the east of Westerland. A road (11km/7 miles) runs by way of Tinnum (pop. 1800), with the ring fort of Tinnumburg, to Keitum (pop. 6500) on the Wattenmeer, formerly the island's chief town. Typical Frisian houses (including the Altfriesisches Haus, 1739), the Sylt Heimatmuseum and the Late Romanesque church of St Severinus, standing on higher ground to the north.
7km/4½ miles south-east of Keitum is Morsum (12th c. church), near the eastern tip of Sylt, where the Hindenburgdamm begins.

Tangermünde   D 7

Land: Saxony-Anhalt
Altitude: 45m/148ft
Population: 12,000

Situation and characteristics

The old Hanseatic town of Tangermünde lies 50km/30 miles north of Magdeburg at the junction of the Tanger with the Elbe. It has largely preserved its medieval aspect, and the old town with its brick-built Gothic and half-timbered buildings is now protected as a historic monument.

Old Town

*Fortifications

Tangermünde's medieval fortifications are almost completely preserved – its town walls, mostly of brick (c. 1300), with *wiekhäuser* (houses built into the walls) and four towers, including the imposing Schrotturm at the north-west corner of the old town and two square towers on the Elbe front.

*Town gates

Of the old town gates there survive the Late Gothic Hühnerdorfer Torturm (15th c.), the Wassertor (Water Gate; 1470) and the Neustädter Tor (c. 1450).

*Half-timbered houses

There are many fine half-timbered houses (built after a fire in the 17th century), some of them with very handsome doorways. The largest and most richly decorated are in the town's two main streets, Kirchstrasse and the Lange Strasse.

*Town Hall

The Town Hall (Rathaus; c. 1430), which contains the Heimatmuseum, is a magnificent example of brick-built Gothic architecture, its gable richly decorated with filigree work.

*St Stephen's Church

The parish church of St Stephen (Stephanskirche; Late Gothic, brick-built; c. 1376 and early 16th c.) incorporates remains of an earlier Romanesque church. The most notable features of the interior are the pulpit (1619), the bronze font (by H. Mente, 1508), the organ (by H. Scherer the Elder, 1624) and a number of monuments of the 15th–19th centuries.

Town Hall, Tangermünde

The parish church of St Nicholas (Nikolaikirche; 12th c.), a fine Late Romanesque building of undressed stone, has a Late Gothic brick tower of about 1470.

St Nicholas's Church

St Elizabeth's Chapel (Elisabethkapelle) originally belonged to a hospital founded in the 13th century. After being used for many years as a salt store it was restored in 1891 and thereafter returned to the Roman Catholic church.

St Elizabeth's Chapel

Outside the south-west end of the old town are the remains of a Dominican monastery (Dominikanerkloster) founded in 1438: ruined church, east wing of the conventual buildings (barn), scanty remains of south wing, north gable, etc.

Dominican monastery

Burg

To the north of the town centre, close to the steep bank of the Elbe, can be found the remains of the Burg, a castle rebuilt by the Emperor Charles IV from 1373 onwards, altered in the 15th century, burned down in 1640 and rebuilt in 1902 in a reproduction of the original style. From the late medieval period date the remains of the battlemented curtain wall, the gatehouse (Burgtorturm) on the north-west side (*c.* 1480) and the outworks of the keep (1376) on the east side.

The only surviving building in the main part of the castle is the 14th century Kanzlei (Chancery), which has a hall with a beamed timber roof on the ground and first floors. The Baroque Amtshaus (now a hospital) was built in 1699–1701 on medieval foundations.

Jerichow

Jerichow, 9km/6 miles south-east of Tangermünde, beyond the Elbe, has a famous Late Romanesque brick-built monastic church (12th c.). The crypt has limestone columns with richly carved capitals. In the church itself is an Easter candelabrum in the form of a

**Church

Jerichow monastic church

column topped by a capital (12th c.). To the south of the church are remains of the conventual buildings.
In the Late Romanesque parish church is a fine epitaph of the Arnstedt family (1609).

Havelberg

**Cathedral

38km/24 miles north of Tangermünde is Havelberg, with the Cathedral of St Mary (consecrated 1170, rebuilt in Gothic style 1279–1330), with fine Gothic stained glass (14th–15th c.) and sculptural decoration (reliefs on rood screen and choir screen; 13th c. stone candelabrum). Other notable features are the choir-stalls (c. 1400), the Gothic Triumphal Cross groups (13th c.), the high altar (1700), the organ (1777) and the tomb of Bishop J. von Wöpelitz (1401). To the south of the Cathedral are the old conventual buildings.

Taunus   H 3–4

Land: Hesse

Situation and characteristics

The Taunus is a ridge of hills some 70km/45 miles long between the rivers Rhine, Main and Lahn and the Wetterau. It culminates in the Grosser Feldberg (881m/2891ft), the highest peak in the Rhenish Uplands. It is made up of slates, with beds of quartzite and a few rounded hills of volcanic origin. The higher levels are covered by fine beech and oak forests, with some conifers. On the side nearest Frankfurt the Taunus presents its steep southern slopes which, sheltered from the harsh north winds, have one of the mildest climates in Germany, producing excellent fruit, almonds and, at Kronberg, sweet chestnuts. The Taunus is also the region in Germany which is richest in mineral springs; the springs along the south side of the hills have led to the establishment of a series of famous spas.

Landscape

One of the most scenically attractive places in the Taunus is the little town of Königstein, with the ruins of its 13th century castle. From here a road runs up the Grosser Feldberg (telecommunications tower; superb views); there is also a road from Oberursel.

Königstein

In the north-western Taunus, near Wiesbaden, are the attractive little spas of Bad Schwalbach and Schlangenbad, from which the "Spa Highway" (Bäderstrasse, B 260) runs through the north-western foothills of the range to Bad Ems in the Lahn valley (see entry).

See entry

Bad Homburg

Tegernsee

L 7

Land: Bavaria

The beautiful Tegernsee (6.5km/4 miles long, up to 1.5km/1 mile wide, 72m/236ft deep), surrounded by a ring of hills with forest and Alpine meadows reaching high up their slopes, is one of the most popular altitude resorts and winter sports areas in Upper Bavaria. Round the lake are a series of little towns and villages offering good bathing and facilities for a variety of water sports.

Situation and characteristics

Landscape

The chief place on the lake is the little town of Tegernsee on its east side, with a Schloss which belonged to Duke Ludwig Wilhelm of Bavaria, a remnant of a Benedictine abbey founded in the 8th century, once a great centre of culture, which was dissolved in 1803. The original Romanesque church (with an 11th century crypt) was remodelled in Baroque style in 1684–94 and was given a new façade by Klenze in 1820.

Tegernsee

Rottach-Egern, on the Tegernsee

521

To the east of the Town Hall lies the Kurgarten, in which is the Olaf Gulbransson Museum.

Bad Wiessee

Beautifully situated on the west side of the lake is Bad Wiessee, with two productive mineral springs containing iodine and sulphur (drilled in 1909 and 1930) which are used in bathing, drinking and inhalation cures. The little town is in two parts – Wiessee-Nord, with the spa facilities and the Protestant church (1937), and Wiessee-Süd, with the prominently situated Roman Catholic church (1926).

Rottach-Egern

On the south-eastern shores of the lake is the double town of Rottach-Egern, in the centre of which stands its Late Gothic church (1466), topped by a slender tower. In the church-yard in Egern are the graves of the writers Ludwig Ganghofer (1855–1920) and Ludwig Thoma (1867–1921), the composer Heinrich Spoerl (1877–1955), the singer Leo Slezak (1873–1946) and Olaf Gulbransson (1873–1958), whose son built the Protestant church in Egern (1955).

Wallberg

There is a cableway up the Wallberg (1722m/5650ft; views).

Gmund

At the northern tip of the lake is the village of Gmund, with a parish church of 1688.

Schliersee

7km/4½ miles east of the Tegernsee, surrounded by hills, lies a smaller lake, the Schlier-see (2.5km/1½ miles long, up to 1.3km/1400yds across, 37m/121ft deep). This too is a popular holiday and winter sports area and a good base for walks and climbs in the hills.

Schliersee

At the northern tip of the lake is the little town of Schliersee, with a Baroque parish church (1714; fine interior), a 15th century Town Hall (rebuilt 1920) and a Heimatmuseum. The best view of the lake is to be had from the Weinbergkapelle above the parish church.

Spitzingsee

From the south end of the Schliersee the beautiful Spitzingstrasse (views) crosses the Spitzingsattel to the Spitzingsee, the smallest and highest of the three lakes.

Bayrischzell

From the Schliersee the Deutsche Alpenstrasse (see entry) runs south-east to the altitude resort and winter sports centre of Bayrischzell (fine Baroque church), surrounded by the peaks of the Wendelstein, the Kleiner Traithen and the Seeberg. The nearby Sudelfeld is a popular skiing area.

Wendelstein

The Wendelstein (1838m/6030ft), to the north of Bayrischzell, can be ascended either by mountain railway or on foot (2½ hours). In the summit area (extensive views) are a chapel (1718), a solar observatory and broadcasting transmitters.

Teutoburg Forest (Teutoburger Wald)   E 4

Länder: North Rhine-Westphalia, Lower Saxony

Situation and characteristics

The Teutoburg Forest extends along the north side of the Münster lowlands for some 100km/60 miles, beginning at the point where the Mittelland Canal joins the Dortmund-Ems Canal and rising from north-west to south-east to end in its highest peak, the Preussischer Velmerstot (468m/1536ft).

Landscape

The hills consist of Cretaceous limestones and sandstones, the difference between the two being reflected in the vegetation (beech forests on the limestone, spruces on

the sandstone). The principal beauty spots are the Dörenther Klippen at Brochterbeck, the Dörenberg (331m/1085ft) near Bad Iburg, the Ravensburg at Borgholzhausen, the Hermannsdenkmal and the Externsteine (see Detmold, Surroundings).
Other tourist attractions are the Safari Park at Stukenbrock, the Eagle Observatory at Detmold-Berlebeck and the Bird and Flower Park at Detmold-Heiligenkirchen.

There are numerous summer holiday resorts in these beautiful wooded hills – the picturesque little hill town of Tecklenburg, the spa of Bad Iburg (Kneipp cure), the brine spas of Bad Laer and Bad Rothenfelde, the gingerbread town of Borgholzhausen, the hill town of Oerlinghausen and many more.

See entry

Detmold

Immediately south of the Teutoburg Forest can be found the Eggegebirge, a 35km/ 22 mile long range of hills bounded on the south by the Diemel valley. In the Senne, an extensive area of heath and sand to the west, is Bad Lippspringe, while to the east of the hills are Bad Driburg and Willebadessen.

Eggegebirge

See entry

Paderborn

Thale   F 6

Land: Saxony-Anhalt
Altitude: 160–451m/525–1480ft
Population: 16,400

Thale lies in the wild and romantic Bode valley, on the north-eastern fringes of the Harz. The town's main sources of income are the tourist trade and iron and steelworking. It is also noted for the calcium chloride spring of the Hubertusbad, which has been used for medicinal purposes since 1836.

Situation and characteristics

Sights

The parish church of St Andrew (1540), within the precincts of a former nunnery, was rebuilt in 1786–90, incorporating remains of the conventual buildings. Notable features of the interior are a Baroque reredos (18th c.) and monuments of the 16th–18th centuries.

St Andrew's Church

South-east of the church stands a tower house of the 9th/10th century, the oldest secular building on the north side of the Harz – all that is left of a medieval castle, the site of which is now under cultivation.

Burg

At Rathausstrasse 1 is the Heimatmuseum (prehistoric material from the surrounding area) and also in the same street is the Works Museum of the local iron and steelworks.

Museums

At the Hubertusbrücke in the Bode valley a cabin cableway goes up to the Hexentanzplatz (see below). The cableway, 720m/785yds long, climbs 250m/820ft in 4 minutes (skis carried). There is also a chair-lift to the Rosstrappe (see below).

*Cableway

Surroundings of Thale

The Hexentanzplatz ("Witches' Dancing-Place") is a rock shelf (alt. 451m/1480ft) which falls steeply down into the Bode valley; fine views of the surrounding peaks. Nearby is an enclosure containing typical Harz animals.

*Hexentanzplatz

On the steep scarp of the Hexentanzplatz is the Harzer Bergtheater (Mountain Theatre; by E. Wachler, 1903), with seating for 1400. Beside the theatre stands the Walpurgishalle (museum), a timber building in the "Old German" style by the Berlin architect Sehring (1901), with paintings of scenes from the Faust legend.

*Harz
Mountain Theatre

Opposite the Hexentanzplatz is the Rosstrappe (403m/1322ft), from which there is a fine view of the Bode valley, with the Teufelsbrücke (Devil's Bridge).

The Hexentanzplatz and Rosstrappe were prehistoric cult sites. Stone and earth ramparts such as the Heidenwall on the Rosstrappe and the Sachsenwall on the Hexentanzplatz and finds of material ranging in date from the Neolithic to the Early Iron Age indicate that these sites were frequented over a very long period. In Christian times this was regarded as the abode of Satan, and legend had it that on Walpurgis Night (April 30th–May 1st) witches rode on broomsticks to the Brocken (Blocksberg) to make merry with the Devil.

Bode Valley

The source area of the Bode is the high moorland of the Upper Harz, an area of high rainfall (1000–1600mm/39–63in. annually) with a long period of snow cover (160 days in the year). The Kalte and the Warme Bode (Cold and Warm Bode) rise below the Brocken, the Rappbode farther south. They join at Wendefurth to form the Bode, which flows through Thale, Quedlinburg, Oschersleben and Stassfurt to join the Saale at Nienburg after a course of 169km/105 miles.

*Landscape

The deeply indented valley is caught between steep rock faces, with tumbles of boulders and detritus in the valley bottom. There is a particularly impressive stretch near Thale, where the valley emerges from the densely forested northern fringe of the Harz.

There are a number of dams on the Bode, creating reservoirs which supply water to the drier eastern foreland of the Harz (in particular the industrial concentrations around Halle, Leipzig and Magdeburg), provide protection from flooding and are harnessed to generate power.

Bode valley

Thuringian Forest (Thüringer Wald)   G–H 6

Land: Thuringia

The name of Thuringian Forest is generally applied to the upland region, still covered with great tracts of forest, which extends from Eisenach in the north-west to the upper Saale in the south-east. In the narrower sense it is the range of hills, 60km/37 miles long and 7–14km/4½–9 miles wide, between Hörschel an der Werra in the north-west and a line from Schleusingen to Gehren in the south-east, where it merges into the Thuringian Hills (Thüringer Schiefergebirge). Bounded as they are by fault lines, the hills of the Thuringian Forest rise directly out of the surrounding area in steep scarps 200–300m/650–1000ft high.

Situation and characteristics

The hills in the central Thuringian Forest mostly range between 800m/2600ft and 900m/2950ft. They consist largely of New Red Sandstone, with some volcanic rocks including porphyry. Around the edges are later deposits of limestones and sandstones.

The rounded hills which rise above the plateaux in the Thuringian Forest, such as the Grosser Beerberg (982m/3222ft), the Schneekopf (978m/3209ft) and the Grosser Inselsberg (916m/3005ft), are eroded masses of porphyry. The extent of the plateaux increases towards the south-east. Where granites and gneisses, less subject to erosion, lie on the surface this has led to the formation of basins, as at Suhl, Zella-Mehlis and Brotterode.

Grosser Beerberg
Schneekopf
Grosser Inselsberg

The Thuringian Forest is slashed by deeply indented valleys, often cutting into the rock to a depth of several hundred metres and enclosed between steep hillsides. A striking example is the Drachenschlucht ("Dragon's Gorge") near Eisenach. The scenic beauty of the Thuringian Forest lies in the contrasts between its forest-covered hills and its deep valleys.

The climate of the Thuringian Forest is cool, with a good deal of rain. The winters are long, with an abundance of snow, providing excellent conditions for winter sports. Spring comes late – several weeks later than in the surrounding foreland areas. In summer there are local differences in climate, depending on the topography of the area, exposure to the sun and the degree of exposure to, or shelter from, wind. In general the hills of the Thuringian Forest lie at an angle to the prevailing south-westerly winds, and their height tends to bring down rain.

Climate

The numerous streams flowing down from the Thuringian Forest are within the catchment area of the Werra on the south side of the hills and for the most part in that of the Saale on the north side. There are a number of small dams in the river valleys; the largest is the Ohra Dam, which has formed an artificial lake with a capacity of 18.4 million cu.m/4 billion gallons.

Rivers

Three-quarters of the area of the Thuringian Forest is under forest. The rest consists of arable and pasture land; but in general agriculture is of relatively minor economic importance.

Forestry and agriculture

The best-known resort is Oberhof (see entry), situated at a height of 825m/2707ft. Other climatically favoured resorts are Tambach-Dietharz, Finsterbergen and Friedrichroda.

Holiday resorts

Bad Tölz   L 7

Land: Bavaria
Altitude: 700m/2300ft
Population: 14,000

The spa of Bad Tölz lies on the river Isar, which here emerges into the Alpine foreland. On the right bank of the river is the picturesque old town, on the left bank the spa district, with water of high iodine content (springs drilled 1845).
Tölz is also famed for its Boys' Choir.

Situation and characteristics

Torgau

Old Town

Marktstrasse

The town's main street, the wide Markstrasse (pedestrian zone), runs up from the bridge over the Isar, and is lined by pretty gabled houses with painted façades. Behind the Town Hall can be found the Bürgergarten, from which there is a fine view of the Alps. Nearby is the parish church (originally Late Gothic). At the top end of the street are the Puppet Theatre and the Bürgerhaus (Heimatmuseum).

Kalvarienberg

Above the old town, to the north-west, rises the Kalvarienberg (Calvary), with a pilgrimage church (1726) and St Leonard's Chapel (1718), where on St Leonard's day (November 6th) the horses of the surrounding area are blessed.

Kurviertel (Spa District)

Set in beautiful gardens in the Kurviertel are the spa facilities and numerous hotels. In Herderstrasse is the Herderbad (Herder Baths; 1949–50); and farther west, in the Kurpark, the Kurhaus. In Herderpark are the Trinkhalle (pump room) and Wandelhalle (indoor promenade).

Torgau   F 8

Land: Saxony
Altitude: 85m/238ft
Population: 21,500

Situation and characteristics

Torgau lies on the west bank of the Elbe between the Dübener Heide and the Dahlener Heide. It was once the favourite residence of the Electors of Saxony after Dresden and an important stronghold in a strategic situation.

*Schloss Hertenfels

Schloss Hartenfels is a completely preserved Renaissance castle (1483–1622). Above the entrance, in the west wing, can be seen the Electoral coat of arms. In the courtyard is the Grosser Wendelstein (1532–34), a cantilevered spiral staircase by Conrad Krebs. From the Wächterturm (Watchman's Tower, 45m/148ft high) there is a fine view of the town and the Elbaue. In the Schlossgarten is a bear-pit.

Church and museum

In Wing B of the castle are the Schöner Erker ("Beautiful Oriel", 1544), the castle church (the prototype of a Protestant chapel, consecrated by Luther in 1544) and the District Museum (arms and armour). On the south front, facing the Elbe, are the Südturm (South Tower), the Hasenturm (Hare's Tower), the Jagdtor (Hunting Gate) and the Flaschenturm (Bottle Tower).
Below the castle, on the banks of the Elbe, can be seen a monument commemorating the meeting of American and Soviet troops here in 1945.

The Town

St Mary's Church

Near the castle stands St Mary's Church, a prominent landmark. It contains the tomb of Luther's wife Katharina von Bora (1499–1552). There is a commemorative plaque on the house at Katharinenstrasse 11 in which she died.

Markt

In the Markt are the Renaissance Town Hall (1561–77) and, in the Ratshof, St Nicholas's Church (mid 13th c.). Flanking the square are a number of handsome burghers' houses, including the Mohrenapotheke, the pharmacy at the sign of the Moor.

Trier   H 2

Land: Rhineland-Palatinate
Altitude: 330m/1085ft
Population: 100,000

Trier, Germany's oldest town, lies in a basin in the Mosel valley (see entry). Its importance in ancient times is attested by impressive Roman remains such as are found nowhere else north of the Alps. Numerous churches reflect its long-established status as the see of a bishop.

Situation and characteristics

During the summer months there are excursion ships on the Mosel (sometimes sailing as far as Luxembourg) and the Saar.

Boat trips

Sights

At the north entrance to the old town stands the massive Porta Nigra, a fortified gate in the Roman town walls (end of 2nd c. A.D.), whose age-blackened stones, held together by iron cramps, have earned it the name ("Black Gate") by which it has been known since the Middle Ages. It was converted into a church (St Simeon's) around 1040 and restored to its original state in 1804–17. In the adjoining Simeonstift (11th c.) is the Municipal Museum and close by the Kunsthandwerkerhof (craftsmen's workshops).

**Porta Nigra

North-east of the Porta Nigra, in Paulinstrasse, is St Paulinus's Church (by Balthasar Neumann, 1732–54; ceiling paintings by Thomas Scheffler), one of the finest Baroque buildings in the whole of the Rhineland.

*St Paulinus's Church

From the Porta Nigra Simeonstrasse (pedestrian zone; Dreikönigenhaus, c. 1230) runs south-west to the Hauptmarkt, with St Gangolf's Church (Late Gothic) and the Steipe (1430–83), the old banqueting house of the city councillors. A little to the west, in Dietrichstrasse, is the Frankenturm (11th c.), one of the earliest surviving dwelling-houses in Germany.

*Hauptmarkt

To the east of the Hauptmarkt stands the Cathedral (Dom; 4th, 11th and 12th c.; restored 1964–74), one of the oldest churches in Germany. Magnificent monuments of the 16th–18th centuries; rich treasury, including the portable St Andrew's Altar (10th c.), one of the great masterpieces of Ottonian art.

*Cathedral

Porta Nigra

*Liebfrauenkirche	Adjoining the Cathedral is the Liebfrauenkirche (Church of Our Lady; *c.* 1270), one of the earliest Gothic churches in Germany.
*Aula Palatina	South-east of the Hauptmarkt, in Konstantinplatz, are the Episcopal Museum and the Aula Palatina, a Roman basilica built in the time of the Emperor Constantine (who resided in Trier from 306 to 312), now restored and used as a church (Protestant). Adjoining is the old Electoral Palace (Kurfürstliches Palais; 17th and 18th c.), now occupied by local government offices.
*Rhineland Museum	To the south of the palace, beyond a stretch of the medieval town walls which bounds the palace gardens (Baroque sculpture), can be found the Rhineland Museum (Rheinisches Landesmuseum), with a collection of antiquities and works of art of prehistoric, Roman, Early Christian, Frankish and medieval times.
Imperial Baths	Farther south are the ruins of the Roman Imperial Baths (Kaiserthermen; 4th c. A.D.; converted into a fortified castle in medieval times; extensive complex of underground rooms and passages), one of the largest bathing establishments of Roman Imperial times. From here the Südallee leads west to the Barbarathermen (2nd c. A.D.). The nearby Römerbrücke over the Mosel still rests on Roman foundations.
Amphitheatre	From the Imperial Baths Olewiger Strasse runs east to the Roman Amphitheatre, built about A.D. 100, which had seating for some 25,000 spectators.
St Matthias's Church	On the southern outskirts of the town stands the 12th century pilgrimage church of St Matthias (with the remains of the Apostle Matthias), belonging to a Benedictine house (re-founded 1907) on the site of an Early Christian building.

Surroundings of Trier

Konz	At the junction of the Saar with the Mosel, 8km/5 miles south-west of Trier, is the little wine town of Konz (Wine Trail), with the Roscheiderhof folk and open-air museum.
*Igel Column	9km/6 miles south-west of Trier, on the left bank of the Mosel, lies the village of Igel, with the Igel Column, a funerary monument 22m/72ft high, with rich carved decoration, belonging to a Gallo-Roman family of the 3rd century A.D.
Nennig Roman villa	40km/25 miles south-west of Konz by way of Saarburg and Remich we reach the little town of Nennig, with the remains of a Roman villa discovered in 1852. The villa's mosaic pavement, measuring 10.30m/34ft by 15.65m/51ft, is one of the largest and finest mosaics north of the Alps.
Eifel	See entry

Tübingen   K 4

	Land: Baden-Württemberg Altitude: 515m/1690ft Population: 75,000
Situation and characteristics	The ancient and famous Swabian university town of Tübingen is attractively situated in the middle Neckar valley (see entry) north-west of the Swabian Alb (see entry). The picturesque old town lies on the steep slopes above the left bank of the river, between the Schlossberg and the Österberg. The best view of the river frontage of the town is to be had from the Platanenallee on the right bank of the Neckar.

*Old Town

Stiftskirche	In the Holzmarkt is the Late Gothic Stiftskirche (15th c.; Protestant), with handsome monuments commemorating members of the princely house of Württemberg, including Count Eberhard the Bearded and Duke Ludwig. The choir has 15th century stained glass.

View of Tübingen from the Stiftskirche

Beyond the church are the oldest parts of the Karl Eberhard University – the Alte Aula (Old Assembly Hall), the former Karzer (students' prison; open to visitors) and the fine Bursa, in which the Reformer Philip Melanchthon lectured in 1514–18.

University

Lower down, on the banks of the Neckar, stands the Hölderlin Tower (open to the public), in which the poet Friedrich Hölderlin lived from 1807 until his death in 1843.

River front

At the end of Bursagasse is the Stift (founded 1536), a Protestant theological seminary whose pupils included Kepler, Schelling, Hegel, Hölderlin, Mörike and Hauff. Higher up, at Neckarhalde 24, is the birthplace of the poet Ludwig Uhland (1787–1862). At No. 31, in the Theodor-Haering-Haus, is the Municipal Museum (new museum under construction).

Stift

In the nearby Markt stands the picturesque Town Hall (Rathaus), a half-timbered building of 1435. In front of it is the Market Fountain (1617).

Town Hall

From the Markt the Burgsteige runs steeply up, affording extensive views, to the 16th century Schloss Hohentübingen, built on the remains of an earlier castle of the Counts Palatine, with a handsome Renaissance doorway. There are frequent concerts in the castle courtyard. The Schloss now houses the collections of the Institutes of Ethnology, Prehistory and Cultural Studies.

Schloss

In Wilhelmstrasse, which leads north from the old town, are the Old Botanic Garden (Alter Botanischer Garten), the Neue Aula of the University and the University Library (Universitätsbibliothek), in the Old Building of which are displayed the figures carved from mammoth tusks, some 27,000 years old, which were discovered in the Lone valley in 1931.

Wilhelmstrasse

On the slopes of the Schnarrenberg are the University clinics. Higher up, on the Morgenstelle, are the new buildings of the Faculty of Science and the New Botanic Garden.

*Bebenhausen

5km/3 miles north is Bebenhausen Abbey, a Cistercian house founded about 1185 which ranks with Maulbronn (see Pforzheim, Surroundings) as one of the finest and best preserved monastic houses in Germany.

Überlingen   L 4

Land: Baden-Württemberg
Altitude: 409m/1342ft
Population: 15,000

Situation and characteristics

The old free imperial city of Überlingen, founded by the Emperor Frederick Barbarossa about 1180, is picturesquely situated on the Überlinger See, the north-western arm of Lake Constance (see entry), on the Upper Swabian Baroque Highway (see Upper Swabia). As a free imperial city it rose to considerable prosperity through its trade in salt, wine and corn.

The Town

Town Hall

In the square called the Hofstatt is the Town Hall (14th and 15th c.), with a handsome Council Chamber (carving).

Minster

Above the Town Hall stands the Gothic Minster of St Nicholas (14th–16th c.), with two towers, in the smaller of which is the unfinished Hosanna Bell, weighing over 6½ tons. Fine Renaissance and Baroque altars.

In Münsterplatz are the Municipal Archives (1600). To the north-west is the Late Gothic Franciscan Church (14th–15th c.; Baroque interior).

Heimatmuseum

North-east of the Minster a patrician house, which belonged to the Reichlin von Meldegg family, now houses the Heimatmuseum (prehistoric and Roman antiquities, history of the town, dolls' houses); fine view from the terrace.

Arsenal

South-west of the Minster is the Late Gothic Arsenal (Zeughaus), now housing a private collection.

Stadtgarten

On the west side of the old town lies the Stadtgarten (Municipal Park; rose garden, cactus garden, deer park). Farther south is the Kurgarten.

**Birnau

3km/2 miles south-east of Überlingen, high above Lake Constance, stands the Baroque pilgrimage church of St Mary (1746–50), which belonged to the monastery of Birnau, a daughter house of Salem (see Upper Swabia). It has a richly decorated Rococo interior (stucco work by Joseph Anton Feuchtmayr).
There is a pleasant walk on the Prälatenweg to Salem.

Uckermark   C 9

Land: Brandenburg

Situation and characteristics

The Uckermark – the area around Prenzlau, Angermünde and Templin, extending on both sides of the river Uecker between the upper Havel and the lower Oder – is a tract of partly wooded and partly open farming country, with numerous lakes. The name ("Mark" = "march", "borderland") reflects its situation on the borders between the historic territories of Brandenburg, Mecklenburg and Pomerania.

The northern part of the Uckermark, around Prenzlau (see entry), is an upland region with occasional rounded hills. It has good soil and is intensively cultivated (wheat, sugar-beet).

Northern area

In the wide Uecker valley are two lakes, the Oberueckersee and the Unterueckersee.

Ueckerseen

The southern part of the Uckermark, around Angermünde (pop. 11,500), is a hilly region with numbers of lakes of varying size, hollows and steep-sided valleys. There is much more forest in this area than in the northern Uckermark.

Southern area

Ulm   K 5

Land: Baden-Württemberg
Altitude: 479m/1572ft
Population: 100,000

The old imperial city of Ulm, on the left bank of the Danube, is the economic and cultural centre of Upper Württemberg and the starting-point of the Upper Swabian Baroque Highway (see Upper Swabia). It has long been an important commercial and industrial town, and it now also has a university (founded 1967).

Situation and characteristics

Old Town

In the centre of the town stands the Minster, Germany's largest Gothic church after Cologne Cathedral (1377–1529 and 1844–90; Protestant). The soaring spire (ascent recommended, but arduous; magnificent views, extending in clear weather to the Alps), begun by Ulrich von Ensingen in 1392 and finally completed in 1880–90 on the basis of a sketch left by Matthias Böblinger, is the tallest church spire in the world (161m/528ft, compared with Cologne Cathedral's 157m/515ft). In the interior are fine choir-stalls (1469–74) by Jörg Syrlin the Elder.
The Münsterplatz is being altered to a design by the American architect Richard Meier.

** Minster

To the south of the Minster, in the Marktplatz, is the handsome Gothic Town Hall (Rathaus; restored after wartime destruction), with frescoes of 1540. In front of the Town Hall can be seen the beautiful fountain known as the Fischkasten (fish tank), (by Jörg Syrlin the Elder, 1482).

Town Hall

On the east side of the Marktplatz (No. 9) is the Ulm Museum, which has the finest collection of Upper Swabian art and culture since the Middle Ages.

* Museum

Around the mouth of the river Blau, which flows into the Danube here, is the very picturesque and skilfully restored Fischerviertel, the old fishermen's and tanners' quarter.

Fishermen's quarter

Along the Danube a considerable stretch of the 15th century town walls has been preserved, with the Metzgerturm (Butchers' Tower), a leaning tower which is several feet off the vertical.

Town walls

In the south-west of the town, at Fürsteneckerstrasse 17, is the German Bread Museum (Deutsches Brotmuseum; history of bread and of baking).

Bread Museum

Between 1852 and 1867 the town was surrounded by a 9km/6 mile long ring of fortifications, with several forts and 41 major defensive works. The Oberer Kuhberg fort became a concentration camp during the Nazi period (memorial).

Fortifications

Wiblingen

In the southern district of Wiblingen is a large Benedictine monastery founded in the 11th century and dissolved in 1803, with a magnificent Baroque church (1780; sculpture by Januarius Zick) and a sumptuously decorated Library.

* Monastery

Neu-Ulm

	Land: Bavaria Altitude: 472m/1549ft Population: 48,000
Situation and characteristics	The Bavarian town of Neu-Ulm lies opposite Ulm on the right bank of the Danube. Founded only in 1811, it was until the First World War mainly a garrison town.
Edwin-Scharff-Haus	Set in gardens on the banks of the Danube (good view of Ulm) stands Edwin-Scharff-Haus, a cultural and congress centre (1977), with a small gallery of works by the artist Edwin Scharff (1877–1955). In front of the building is a reproduction of a Danube boat.
Heimatmuseum	In the town centre is the Heimatmuseum.

Surroundings of Ulm

Oberelchingen	10km/6 miles north-east of Ulm, on the southern fringe of the Swabian Alb, is Oberelchingen, with the remains of a monastery founded about 1000; fine church, remodelled in Baroque style.

Ulm, from the Danube

21km/13 miles down the Danube valley, at the junction with the Günz, lies the little town of Günzburg, with a large Renaissance Schloss (16th c.) and the beautiful Liebfrauen-kirche (by Dominikus Zimmermann, 1736–39).

Günzburg

See entry

Blaubeuren

Unstrut Valley

F 5–7

Länder: Saxony-Anhalt, Thuringia

The Unstrut rises at a height of 395m/1296ft in the limestone hills of the Eichsfeld, to the west of Dingelstädt. It is the principal tributary of the Saale, which it joins at Naumburg after a course of 192km/119 miles.

In its upper course the Unstrut cuts through the Muschelkalk limestone in a narrow, steep-sided valley, but opens out in the Keuper limestone of the Thuringian basin. In this part of its course it flows past Mühlhausen (see entry), the town of Thomas Müntzer, the spa of Bad Langensalza and the industrial town of Sömmerda.

At Heldrungen the Unstrut breaks through the Muschelkalk hills between Hainleite and Schmücke in a beautiful valley 400m/440yds wide. This "Thuringian Gate" was formerly protected by castles, the Sachsenburgen, of which only ruins remain.

At Artern the river turns south-east. In the Ried, the expanse of water meadows south-east of Artern, the Unstrut is joined by the Helme, which drains the Goldene Aue between the Harz and the Kyffhäuser Hills.

Between Memleben and the cathedral city of Naumburg (see entry) the river enters the Bunter sandstones and Muschelkalk limestones of northern Thuringia. In this part of its course narrow stretches of valley – for example above Nebra and below Karsdorf –

alternate with wider stretches, the south-facing slopes of which are covered with vineyards.

In the last narrow section of the valley is the town of Freyburg, a wine- and Sekt-producing centre. Near the town stands Schloss Neuenburg, originally Romanesque but much altered in later centuries. In the courtyard of the castle is a Late Romanesque double chapel (c. 1220; capitals with plant and animal ornament). The castle museum illustrates the story of wine-production in the Unstrut valley.

Freyburg
Schloss Neuenburg

Upper Swabia (Oberschwaben)

K 4 – M 6

Länder: Baden-Württemberg, Bavaria

Upper Swabia is bounded on the north by the Danube, on the west by the volcanic landscape of the Hegau and on the south by Lake Constance; in the east it extends to the river Lech. The landscape pattern was set by the deposits laid down during the Ice Age. Out of the gently undulating or rolling countryside individual hills rise to above 750m/2460ft; the highest is the Bussen (757m/2484ft), near Riedlingen on the Danube. Scattered over the region are numbers of small lakes, some of them reduced to bogs.

Situation and characteristics

Upper Swabia is traversed by two major tourist routes. The Upper Swabian Baroque Highway, with two variants, takes visitors through almost the whole of Upper Swabia; the Swabian Spa Route links Upper Swabia in Württemberg with the Alpine foreland area in Bavaria.

Tourist routes

**Upper Swabian Baroque Highway (Oberschwäbische Barockstrasse)

Main Route

Starting from Ulm (see entry), the route runs west to Blaubeuren)seen entry), with the beautiful Blautopf.

The main feature of interest in Ehingen, which lies on the Danube, is the Early Baroque Herz-Jesu-Kirche (1719), belonging to a seminary established here by the Benedictines of Zwiefalten. In the Heiliggeistspital (Hospital of the Holy Ghost) is an interesting Heimatmuseum.

Ehingen

10km/6 miles west is the imposing Schloss Mochental (1734), with a picture gallery and a Broom Museum.

The next place of interest on the route is Obermarchtal, with its Premonstratensian monastery perched high above the Danube. The church (1686–1701) has sumptuous stucco decoration.

*Obermärchtal

A few kilometres west of the Danube lies Zwiefalten, whose twin-towered Baroque Minster was built between 1744 and 1765 (fine ceiling paintings by Franz Joseph Spie-gler, stucco work by Johann Michael Feuchtmayr). 4km/2½ miles from the town can be found the Wimsener Höhle, a cave with a karstic resurgence.

*Zwiefalten

Riedlingen has preserved its medieval aspect, with some stretches of its old walls and numbers of half-timbered houses. The parish church of St George has remains of Late Gothic wall paintings.

Riedlingen

Bad Buchau lies on the Federsee, near which important prehistoric remains have been found (museum). On the north side of the town is a former house of Augustinian nuns (18th c. buildings).

Bad Buchau

◀ *Junction of the Unstrut and the Saale at Grossiena*

Upper Swabia

Just beyond this the western route (see below) branches off on the right.

**Steinhausen Off the main road on the left is Steinhausen, with what is claimed to be the world's most beautiful village church (1728–33), built on an oval plan by Dominikus Zimmermann, with paintings by his brother Johann.

Bad Schussenried At Bad Schussenried is a Premonstratensian abbey (1752–70), with ceiling paintings and stucco work by Johann Zick in the church, a sumptuous library and a museum. 2km/ 1¼ miles south-east is the Kürnbach open-air museum (Upper Swabian peasant houses).

Bad Waldsee At Bad Waldsee stands the former Stiftskirche of St Peter (originally Gothic; remodelled in Baroque style by Dominikus Zimmermann in 1766). Late Gothic Town Hall (1426).

Weingarten Weingarten Minster, the largest Baroque church in Germany (1715–24) has a finely proportioned interior, with beautiful ceiling frescoes by Cosmas Damian Asam, stucco work by Franz Schmuzer and choir-stalls by Joseph Anton Feuchtmayr; the organ, by Joseph Gabler, has 77 stops and 7041 pipes.

Ravensburg See entry

Friedrichshafen See entry

Tettnang Tettnang, once the seat of the Counts of Montfort, has a 16th century Town Hall, originally the Schloss, and the four-towered Neues Schloss (1712–20; interior decorated by Joseph Anton Feuchtmayr and Andreas Moosbrugger).

Wangen im Allgäu See entry

Kisslegg Kisslegg, attractively situated between two marshy lakes, has two castles of the Princes of Waldburg-Wolfegg and Wurzach-Zeil (16th and 18th c.) and a fine parish church by Johann Georg Fischer.
At Kisslegg the eastern route (see below) branches off on the right.

Wolfegg At Wolfegg can be found the imposing Renaissance Schloss (1578–86; rebuilt in 17th c.) of the Princes of Waldburg zu Wolfegg and Waldsee. Parish church by Johann Georg Fischer.

Bad Wurzach Bad Wurzach has a Baroque Schloss (1723–28; fine staircase hall), a neo-classical parish church (1775–77) and a pilgrimage chapel of 1709 on the Gottesberg. The Wurzacher Ried is a nature reserve.

Rot an der Rot The Premonstratensian abbey of Rot an der Rot was dissolved in 1803. The sumptuously furnished church (1777–86) was remodelled in neo-classical style later in the century. The parish church of St Martin in the nearby village of Tannheim was built by Franz Beer in 1702.

Ochsenhausen See Biberach, Surroundings

Biberach See entry

Gutenzell The monastic church at Gutenzell, originally Gothic, was remodelled in Baroque style by Dominikus Zimmermann. High altar and pulpit by Franz Xaver Feuchtmayr,

Laupheim The parish church of Laupheim was built in the 17th century by builders from northern Italy and remodelled in Baroque style at the turn of the 17th and 18th centuries. Built on to Schloss Grosslaupheim is a small Baroque building which now houses a museum.

From Laupheim the route returns to Ulm, passing through the Wiblingen district with its large Benedictine monastery.

Western Route

The western route branches off the main route just beyond Bad Buchau (see above).

Saulgau Saulgau has a noble Gothic church (14th c.). On the western outskirts of the town are attractive thermal baths. In the Siessen district (4km/2½ miles south-west) is a former convent of Dominican nuns, with a church rebuilt by Dominikus Zimmermann in 1726–27.

The principal feature of interest in Messkirch is its massive Renaissance Schloss (begun 1557). The parish church of St Martin, built in the 16th century, was remodelled in Baroque style in the 18th ("Adoration of the Kings" by the Master of Messkirch).	Messkirch
The old-world little town of Pfullendorf has preserved remains of fortifications dating from the time when it was a free imperial city. The parish church, originally Gothic, was altered in Baroque style in the 18th century.	Pfullendorf
Heiligenberg, on the edge of the plateau which falls steeply down to the Linzgau (fine views of Lake Constance and the Alps), has a Renaissance Schloss which belonged to the Princes Fürstenberg (magnificent Knights' Hall).	*Heiligenberg
Near Salem is the Salem monastery (boarding school), with a church built between 1299 and 1414 and remodelled in neo-classical style in the late 18th century.	Salem
See entry	Überlingen
See Überlingen, Surroundings	Birnau
See entry	Meersburg

At Friedrichshafen (see entry) the western route rejoins the main route.

Eastern Route

The eastern route branches off the main route at Kisslegg (see above).

The little town of Leutkirch in the Allgäu, once a free imperial city, has preserved some remains of its old fortifications. In the Marktplatz is the Town Hall (1741).	Leutkirch
See entry	Kempten
See entry	Memmingen
See Memmingen, Surroundings	Ottobeuren

At Rot an der Rot (see above) the eastern route rejoins the main route.

Swabian Spa Route (Schwäbische Bäderstrasse)

The Swabian Spa Route runs parallel to the fringes of the Alps, at some distance from them, taking in a series of spas in Upper Swabia and Bavarian Swabia.

See above, Upper Swabian Baroque Highway	Bad Buchau
See above, Upper Swabian Baroque Highway	Bad Schussenried
Aulendorf is a spa (Kneipp cure) in a hilly setting, with a Schloss of the 17th/18th century. The parish church was originally Romanesque, with later alterations.	Aulendorf
See above, Upper Swabian Baroque Highway	Bad Waldsee
See above, Upper Swabian Baroque Highway	Bad Wurzach
Grönenbach, an altitude resort and spa (Kneipp cure), has a Schloss of the 14th and 17th centuries.	Grönenbach
See Memmingen, Surroundings	Ottobeuren
See Landsberg, Surroundings	Bad Wörishofen

Usedom

Land: Mecklenburg-West Pomerania

Situation and characteristics

Usedom, the more westerly of the two large islands at the mouth of the Oder, has an area of 445 sq.km/172 sq. miles, of which 354 sq.km/137 sq. miles belong to Germany. The frontier with Poland runs to the east of the seaside resort of Ahlbeck in the north and to the east of Kamminke in the south.

The outer coast of Usedom, 42km/26 miles long, extends in an almost continuous straight line. The highest hills on this side of the island are the Streckelsberg (56m/184ft) near Koserow and the Langer Berg (54m/177ft) near Bansin. Covered with mixed and deciduous forest, they fall steeply down to the sea, with stretches of flat coast at intervals. Inland are tracts of mixed or coniferous forest. Along the whole coast are beaches of fine sand.

The coast on the inland side is broken up by two large inlets, the Achterwasser and the Krumminer Wiek, and these, combined with a series of peninsulas (Wolgaster Ort, Gnitz, Lieper Winkel, Usedomer Winkel), give the island a rather ragged coastline on this side. As a result considerable stretches of the coast are bordered by beds of reeds. Between Zemplin and Koserow the coast on the inland side comes within little more than 100m/110yds of the outer coast.

There are numbers of lakes on Usedom, particularly in the eastern part of the island; the largest are the Gothensee (609 hectares/1504 acres) and the Schmollensee (515 hectares/1272 acres).

The highest hills are in the centre of the island. Some, such as the Kükelsberg (58m/190ft), rise out of the surrounding arable land; others, including the Golm (59m/194ft) near Kamminke and the Kirchenberg (50m/164ft) near Morgenitz, are in areas of woodland. From the Weisser Berg (32m/105ft) on the Gnitz peninsula there are extensive views over the Achterwasser.

Seaside resorts

Until the middle of the 19th century the islanders' main source of income was fishing, and accordingly the old villages (now seaside resorts) almost all lie along the coast on the inland side of the island (Zinnowitz, Zempin, Koserow, Loddin, Ueckeritz, Bansin); the only exception is Ahlbeck. The holiday and tourist trade began to develop in the 1880s, and new settlements grew up along the outer coast. A typical 19th century resort is Heringsdorf with its tree-lined streets and guesthouses set in large gardens.

Usedom town

The town of Usedom (pop. 3000) occupies the site of an old Slav market settlement and fortress. At the Diet of Usedom in 1128 the Pomeranian nobles, under the influence of Bishop Otto of Bamberg, adopted the Christian faith (commemorative monument on the Schlossberg). In the 13th century Usedom developed into a town of craftsmen, traders, farmers and fishermen. A boost was given to the town's economy by the construction of the Zecherin Bridge in the 1930s, making it a port of call for holidaymakers on their way to the coastal resorts.

Wolgast

The administrative centre of the island and another transit point for road and rail traffic is Wolgast (pop. 17,000), on the west bank of the Peenestrom, on the mainland.

Verden

Land: Lower Saxony
Altitude: 23m/75ft
Population: 26,000

Situation and characteristics

The old episcopal and one-time free imperial city of Verden lies in a fertile depression on the west side of the Lüneburg Heath (see entry), near the junction of the Aller with the Weser. It is internationally known as a racing and equestrian centre.

Excursion ships ply on the Weser from May to September.   Boat trips

The Town

In the Lugenstein, a square in the south of the town with many old half-timbered houses,   Cathedral
stands the massive Cathedral (1270–1490), with a Romanesque tower and cloister.

To the south of the Cathedral is the little church of St Andrew, built before 1220. In the   St Andrew's
choir, to the right of the altar, can be seen the memorial brass of Bishop Yso (d. 1231), the   Church
oldest of its kind in Germany.

South of St Andrew's Church can be found the interesting Horse Museum. The horse   Horse Museum
training centre (racecourse) lies to the east of the town; visitors can watch the horses at
training.

In the old fishermen's quarter (restored), to the north of the Cathedral, is the Heimat-   Heimatmuseum
museum (local history and way of life; collection of birds).

From the Lugenstein the Grosse Strasse (pedestrian zone) runs north to the Town Hall   St John's Church
(1730) and St John's Church (brick-built; originally Romanesque, rebuilt in Gothic style
in 15th c.), with medieval wall and ceiling paintings and a stucco relief of the Last
Judgment.

To the north of the town centre is the Sachsenhain (Saxons' Grove), where Charlemagne   Sachsenhain
is said to have had 4500 defeated Saxons executed in 782. A path (2km/1¼ miles) runs
round the site, lined with 4500 travelled boulders set up here in 1934–35 to commemorate the event. On the south side of the grove is a "stork nursery" (visitors admitted).

At the Verden-Ost motorway link lies the Verden Leisure Park (fairytale forest, collection   Leisure park
of garden gnomes, dinosaur garden, etc.).

Villingen-Schwenningen   L 3–4

Land: Baden-Württemberg
Altitude: 750m/2460ft
Population: 76,000

The double town of Villingen-Schwenningen lies near the source of the Neckar at the   Situation and
point where the Baar hills merge into the Black Forest (see entry).   characteristics

Villingen

The central feature of the old town of Villingen, still surrounded by its walls and towers, is   Minster
the Minster of Our Lady (begun c. 1130; rebuilt in Gothic style after a great fire in 1271).

In Münsterplatz stands the Old Town Hall (first recorded 1306; rebuilt in Renaissance   Old Town Hall
style). Fine Council Chamber and Ratslaube (arcade); collection of antiquities.

In the north-west of the old town is the Benedictine church of St George (completed in   St George's
Baroque style in 1692).   Church

In the west of the old town the "Franziskaner" cultural centre, housed in a former   "Franziskaner"
Franciscan friary (fine church of 1292), incorporates the Franciscan Museum (Black
Forest collection; finds from a Celtic princely grave).

Schwenningen

In the centre of the town lies the attractive Muslenplatz, with the Protestant pastor's   Muslenplatz
house (1747) and the very interesting Heimat- and Clock Museum (which includes a
collection of glass). To the rear is the 15th century Town Church.

Aviation Museum | To the east of Schwenningen is the town's airfield, with a private Aviation Museum (some 30 aircraft).

Vogtland   G 7

Land: Saxony

Situation and characteristics
The Vogtland, long a zone of transit between north and south, is a densely settled upland region, partly wooded and partly open, lying on both banks of the Weisse Elster at the junction between the Thuringian Forest and the Erzgebirge. At the higher levels exposed to the prevailing strong winds the climate is harsh, but rainfall is low, thanks to the shelter of the hills.

Linen and other cloths were already being produced here in the Middle Ages, and textiles are still the main source of income in many parts of the area. At Plauen (see entry), the largest town in the Vogtland, the production of machine-made embroidery was introduced in the mid 19th century, and Plauen is also famed for its lace.

The rivers of the Vogtland have long been harnessed to provide power and water supply. The largest modern dam is the Pöhl Dam (1958–64) in the valley of the Trieb, north-east of Plauen. The lakes formed by this dam and the Pirk Dam, west of Oelsnitz, are now popular recreation areas.

Landscape

The undulating Vogtland plateau, slashed by deep, steep-sided winding valleys, rises from 450m/1475ft to over 650m/2130ft between Greiz in the north and Bad Brambach in the south.

Elstergebirge
In the Elstergebirge, along the frontier with Czechoslovakia, the hills rise to over 800m/2625ft (Grosser Rammelsberg, 963m/3160ft).

* Musikwinkel
The south-eastern Vogtland is known as the Musikwinkel ("Music Corner"). Musical instruments have been made in and around Klingenthal and Markneukirchen (see Klingenthal) since the 17th century.

* Bäderwinkel
The Vogtland also has a "Spa Corner" (Bäderwinkel) centred on Bad Elster and Bad Brambach. The most beautiful Vogtland village, famed for its richly decorated half-timbered houses, is Raun, south-east of Bad Elster.

Wangen im Allgäu   M 5

Land: Baden-Württemberg
Altitude: 556m/1824ft
Population: 24,000

Situation and characteristics
The former free imperial city of Wangen, on the Obere Argen, is the chief town of the Württemberg Allgäu and the centre of its dairying and cheese-making industry, with a dairying research and teaching institute. The whole of the old town, which has been preserved almost intact, was designated in 1976 as a protected national monument.

* Old Town

Marktplatz
In the Marktplatz stands the Town Hall, originally built in the 13th century; it preserves some 15th century work, but was largely rebuilt in Baroque style in 1719–21; to the left is a gate-tower known as the Ratloch. To the right of the Town Hall is the Late Gothic parish church of St Martin (13th c.; interior remodelled in Baroque style in 1684), with a 19th century altarpiece and ceiling paintings.

South of the Marktplatz is the Saumarkt, with St Anthony's Fountain (St Anthony surrounded by pigs).

From the Marktplatz Herrenstrasse (houses with painted façades) leads north to the Ravensburg Gate (1608; originally 13th c.), with a clock and sundial.

Ravensburg Gate

From the south corner of the Marktplatz the charming Paradiesstrasse runs west to the painted Martinstor (St Martin's Gate) or Lindau Gate (1608; originally 14th c.). Beyond the gate lies the Italian-style Old Cemetery (now a municipal park), with St Roch's Chapel (painted wooden ceiling).

Martinstor
Old Cemetery

From the Marktplatz, through the Ratloch, a street runs east to the picturesque Postplatz (Kornhausplatz, Kornmarkt), the main square of the lower town, with the Kornhaus (1595). From here Spitalstrasse leads north-east to the Altes Spital (Old Hospital), with the Spitalkirche (1719–32), and the Eselsmühle (Heimat- and Cheese-Making Museum).

Postplatz
Heimatmuseum

Near the Heimatmuseum are the Silesian Archives, with the Eichendorff Museum, a museum devoted to the novelist Gustav Freytag and the archives of the Silesian writer Hermann Stehr (1864–1940).

On the north-east and east sides of the old town, along the river Argen, extends a stretch of the old town walls, with the 15th century Pulverturm (Powder Tower).

Eichendorff Museum

1km/¾ mile south-west, on the Gehrenberg (582m/1910ft), is the large and attractively laid out St Wolfgang's Cemetery (New Cemetery), with St Wolfgang's Chapel (choir 15th c., nave 17th c.); magnificent views. The cemetery lies on the 16km/10 mile long ring road round the town, from which there are extensive views.

St Wolfgang's
Cemetery

Surroundings of Wangen

23km/14 miles north-east of Wangen is the former free imperial city of Leutkirch, on the Upper Swabian Baroque Highway (see Upper Swabia), which preserves remains of its old town walls. In the Marktplatz stands the Town Hall (1741). To the rear is the Bock (Heimatmuseum), with the Bockturm or Blaserturm.

Leutkirch

19km/12 miles east of Wangen (18km/11 miles south of Leutkirch) is Isny, which was also a free imperial city. Notable features are the slender Blaserturm in the Markt, the 17th century Town Hall in Wassertorstrasse and the Romanesque church of St Nicholas (1288). Higher up are St George's Church (1635–71; fine Rococo interior) and a 17th century Benedictine monastery.

Isny

11km/7 miles south-east of Wangen, on the Deutsche Alpenstrasse (see entry), is the town of Lindenberg. To the west of the parish church (1764) can be found the Hat Museum.

Lindenberg

Wasserburg am Inn

L 7

Land: Bavaria
Altitude: 427m/1401ft
Population: 11,000

Wasserburg is picturesquely situated on a peninsula almost completely enclosed by the Inn. It is a charming town, built in the style characteristic of the towns in the Inn and Salzach valleys.

Situation and
characteristics

The *Town

Wasserburg has preserved a number of fine buildings from its past as a prosperous trading town on the old Salt Road between Augsburg and Salzburg: the parish church of

Wasserburg am Inn

St James (by Hans Stethaimer, 1410), the Town Hall (1457–59, with much later alteration; concerts), the double church of St Michael (15th c.) and the Late Gothic Schloss.

Municipal Museum

In the Heimathaus in Herrengasse is the interesting Heimatmuseum (local crafts and guilds, religious art, history of the town, administration of justice, peasant domestic life).

Fire Service Museum

North of the old town centre (Im Hag 3) can be found the Fire Service Museum (fire-fighting since the 17th century).

Imaginary Museum

On the bridge over the Inn is the Imaginary Museum (copies of famous paintings and drawings).

Weimar
G 6

Land: Thuringia
Altitude: 240m/785ft
Population: 60,000

Situation and characteristics

Weimar, famed as the city of Goethe and the great centre of German classical literature, lies in the valley of the Ilm in the south-east of the Thuringian Basin, to the south of the Grosser Ettersberg.

Luther, Cranach and Bach all lived and worked in the town, but Weimar's great days began in the 18th century, when it was the home of Wieland, Goethe, Herder and Schiller. In the 19th century great musicians were attracted to the town, and the Art School founded in 1860 brought famous painters to Weimar.

Between 1902 and 1914 the Art School, now the College of Arts and Crafts, was directed by Henry van de Velde. From this college stemmed the Bauhaus, founded by Gropius in 1919, which in 1925 moved to Dessau (see entry).

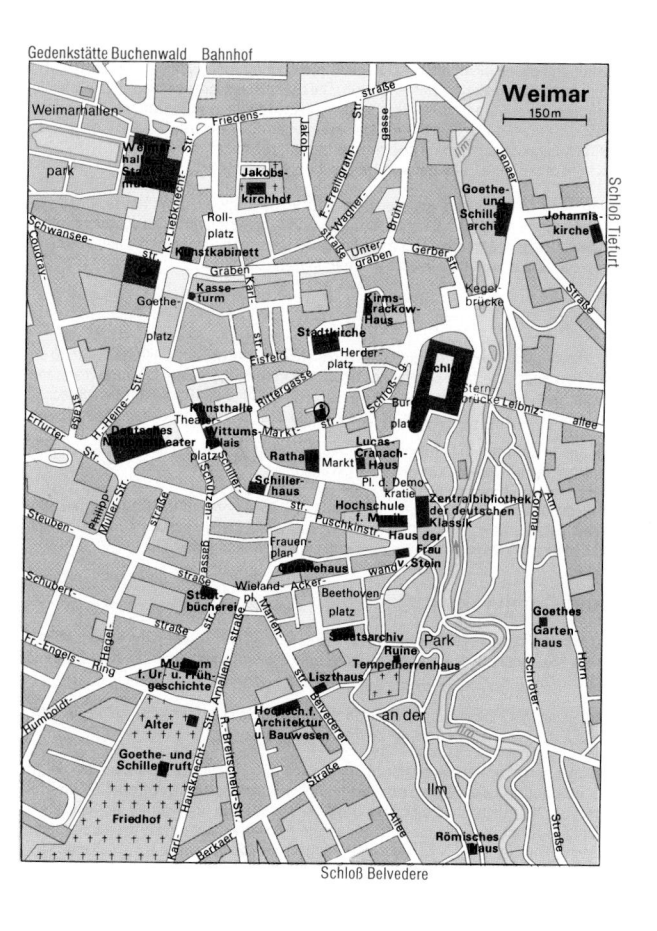

Gedenkstätte Buchenwald   Bahnhof

Schloß Belvedere

After the First World War the German National Assembly met in the National Theatre in Weimar and in 1919 adopted the constitution of the "Weimar Republic".

In 1920 Weimar became capital of the *Land* of Thuringia, formed by the amalgamation of many small territorial domains.

During the Nazi period the notorious Buchenwald concentration camp was established in the immediate vicinity of the town.

The Town

Herderplatz

The central feature of the old town (now protected as a national monument) is the Stadtkirche (Town Church) or Herder Church, a Late Gothic hall-church (1498–1500) dedicated to SS. Peter and Paul in which Johann Gottfried Herder, the great 18th century   *Herder Church writer and philosopher, officiated as court preacher for many years. In the west choir, under the organ gallery, is Herder's tomb. The church has a large winged altar (probably begun by Lucas Cranach the Elder and completed by Lucas Cranach the Younger in 1555), the grave-slab of Lucas Cranach the Elder (d. 1553) and a number of monuments of members of the Ernestine line (mostly 16th c.).

In front of the church is a statue of Herder (by L. Schaller, 1850).

*Kirms-Krackow House

North-east of the church, at Jakobstrasse 10, is the Kirms-Krackow House. Originally Late Gothic, it has a plain Baroque façade. Features of the interior are a courtyard with a wooden gallery, a garden with a tea-house and residential apartments and offices in neo-classical style. It now houses a Herder Museum.

Theaterplatz

*National Theatre

In Theaterplatz stands the German National Theatre. The present building, the third on the site, dates from 1907. Goethe was director of the original theatre for some years, and Franz Liszt and Richard Strauss were musical directors of its 19th century successor.

In front of the Theatre is a statue of Goethe and Schiller (by Ernst Rietschel, 1857).

Kunsthalle

Opposite the National Theatre is the neo-classical façade of the old Kulissenhaus (theatre store), now the Kunsthalle (art exhibitions).

*Wittumspalais

Adjoining the Kunsthalle is the Wittumspalais (1767), home of the Dowager Duchess Anna Amalia, which was a great centre of social and literary activity during Goethe's early years in Weimar. Period furniture; paintings; Wieland Museum.

Schiller House and Goethe House

*Schiller House

At Schillerstrasse 12 can be found the Schiller House (1777), in which the dramatist lived from 1802 until his death in 1805. The rooms are furnished in period style (restored 1986–87).

*Schiller Museum

Adjoining the Schiller House can be found the new Schiller Museum, opened in 1988, with a rich collection of material on his life and works.

**Goethe House

Farther south, in the Frauenplan, adjoining the historic old "White Swan" inn, is the Goethe House, a plain Baroque building (1709) in which Goethe lived from 1782 until his death in 1832. Furnished as it was in Goethe's time, with his pictures on the walls, it contains his art and scientific collections. Adjoining his work-room are the modest room in which he died and his library (5400 volumes). Behind the house is a small garden.

Museum

The upper floor of the house contains the Goethe National Museum, with a wide range of material on his life and work.

House of Frau von Stein

A short distance away, at Ackerwand 25, can be seen the house of Goethe's friend Frau von Stein.

Markt

*Lucas Cranach House

Among the old houses round the Markt (many of them rebuilt) is the Lucas Cranach House (1549), a handsome two-gabled Renaissance building in which Lucas Cranach the Elder spent the last year of his life.

North-Western District

St James's Church

There are a number of fine buildings around St James's Church (Jakobskirche; 1712), an aisleless Baroque church with a double row of windows; west tower with onion dome.

Churchyard

The churchyard (Jakobskirchhof) contains the vault in which Schiller was originally buried and the graves of Lucas Cranach the Elder, Goethe's wife Christiane and many other noted Weimar figures.

Goethe's house on the Frauenplan

Goethe's work-room

Weimar

Bertuchhaus
(Municipal Museum)

In Karl-Liebknecht-Strasse stands the Bertuchhaus (1802–06), a neo-classical building with a spacious hall and a double staircase, the home of F. J. Bertuch, an early 19th century Weimar businessman. It is now occupied by the Municipal Museum.

Kasseturm

In Goetheplatz, the hub of the town's traffic, from which a pedestrian boulevard runs south to Theaterplatz and Schillerstrasse, rises the Kasseturm, a round tower (rebuilt in the late 18th century) which formed part of Weimar's medieval fortifications. It now houses a student club.

Schloss

*Schloss

The Schloss, on the east side of the town, is a three-storey building with a neo-classical colonnade on the east side, facing the Ilm. Notable features of the interior are the staircase hall, the Great Hall and the Falcon Gallery (all in neo-classical style, 1801–03), the Luisenzimmer and the Goethe Gallery.

South-west of the Schloss are the medieval Schlossturm, with an elaborate Baroque top (1729–32) and the "Bastille" (basically Late Gothic, 15th c.).

*Art Collections

Housed in the Schloss are the Weimar Art Collections, which cover a wide range: German art of the Middle Ages and the Renaissance (Thuringian altars, works by Cranach the Elder, Baldung Grien and Bruyn); Italian painting of the 16th and 17th centuries (Veronese, Tintoretto, etc.); Dutch and Flemish painting of the 16th and 17th centuries (Rubens, Brouwer, Ostade, etc.); art of the Goethe period (Füssli/Fuseli, Kraus, Tischbein, Angelika Kaufmann, Graff, Hackert, Koball, Chodowiecki); the German Romantic period (Friedrich, Runge, Kersting, etc.), the Late Romantics and the Weimar school (Schwind, Preller, Blechen, Buchholz, Rohlfs, etc.); and German painting of the 19th and 20th centuries (Rayski, Böcklin, Liebermann, Beckmann, etc.). There are also a collection of graphic art (15,000 drawings, 50,000 sheets of printed graphic art) and a Coin Cabinet (1500 coins).

*Goethe and
Schiller Archives

On the far side of the Ilm, reached by way of the Kegelbrücke to the north of the Schloss, are the Goethe and Schiller Archives (built 1896), with the papers of some sixty German writers (including Wieland, Herder, Mörike, Hebbel, Otto Ludwig and Fritz Reuter), together with manuscripts in the hand of some 450 notable people from the 18th to the early 20th century – altogether almost 600,000 manuscripts.

Platz der Demokratie

To the south of the Schloss lies the Platz der Demokratie.

Fürstenhaus
(Academy of
Music)

On the south side of the square is the Fürstenhaus (1774), a three-storey Baroque building with a colonnade added in 1889. It is now occupied by the Academy of Music (Hochschule für Musik). In front of the building is an equestrian statue of Grand Duke Carl August (by A. von Donndorf, 1875).

*Grünes Schloss

On the east side of the square stands the Grünes Schloss (Green Castle), a Renaissance building of 1563 which was rebuilt in simplified form in the 18th century, with a magnificent library hall. It is now occupied by the Central Library of the German Classical Period (Zentralbibliothek der deutschen Klassik).

Rotes Schloss
Gelbes Schloss

On the west side of the square is the Rotes Schloss (Red Castle; 1574–76), with a Renaissance doorway. Nearby is the Gelbes Schloss (Yellow Castle), a two-storey Baroque building begun in 1702. In the courtyard is an amusing figure (by G. Elster) of the "Aktenmännchen" (civil servant).

*Park on the Ilm

The Park on the Ilm, the layout of which was planned by Goethe, is a beautiful landscaped park in which nature and art are happily combined.

Roman House, in the Park on the Ilm

On the east side of the Ilm can be seen Goethe's garden house, a plain 17th century building which was Goethe's home from 1776 to 1782 and which he frequently visited in later years. It contains the original furniture and other mementoes.

*Goethe's garden house

High above the west bank of the Ilm is the Roman House (Römisches Haus; 1791–97), designed by Goethe for Duke Carl August.

Roman House

In the Belvederer Allee, on the west side of the park, is the modest house originally occupied by the court gardener, in which Franz Liszt lived from 1869–86 (small exhibition of mementoes).

Liszt's house

At Humboldtstrasse 11, on the south side of the old town, can be found the Posecksches Haus, a plain patrician house of the Goethe period, now occupied by the Museum of Prehistory and the Early Historical Period (Museum für Ur- und Frühgeschichte).

Museum of Prehistory

Southern District

Immediately south of the Museum of Prehistory lies the Frauentor Cemetery, with the vault in which Goethe and Schiller are buried (Goethe- und Schillergruft). An avenue lined by fine old trees leads to a domed neo-classical chapel (by the court architect C. W. Coudray, 1825–27), under which is the vault containing the remains of Goethe, Schiller and Grand Duke Carl August.

*Frauentor Cemetery

South of this is the Russian Chapel (1862), in which Grand Duchess Maria Pawlowna is buried.

Also in the cemetery are the graves of other members of the Goethe family and many friends and associates of Goethe, including Charlotte von Stein, Johann Peter Eckermann (author of "Conversations with Goethe"), the composer Nepomuk Hummel and C. W. Coudray. There is also a striking monument (by Walter Gropius, 1921) to those who fell in the 1848 Revolution.

Ettersberg

To the north of Weimar rises the Ettersberg (478m/1568ft). Here in 1937 the Nazis established the notorious Buchenwald concentration camp in which 56,000 people died. It is now a memorial site (Gedenkstätte Buchenwald).

The memorial site, with the Grove of Honour and a bell-tower, was laid out between 1954 and 1958 on the southern slope of the hill, the site of the mass graves. On the site of the camp itself is a Museum of the Resistance.

Weissenfels   F 7

Land: Saxony-Anhalt
Altitude: 99–177m/325–581ft
Population: 28,700

Situation and
characteristics

Weissenfels, once capital of the duchy of Saxony-Weissenfels and now a centre of the shoe industry, lies on the Saale just before it emerges from the hills into the Saxon Lowland. On the slopes of the Saale valley around the town are the last vineyards in the Saale–Unstrut area.

Schloss Neu-Augustusburg

The town is dominated by Schloss Neu-Augustusburg, an Early Baroque palace of three wings laid out round a courtyard. On the central block is a tower topped by a dome and lantern.

*Chapel

Of the original interior there remains the chapel (by J. M. Richter the Elder, 1663–82; restored), with fine stucco work and a richly decorated reredos.

Museum

The Schloss contains the Weissenfels Museum, which includes a Shoe Museum (cultural history of the shoe; collection of shoes from all over the world; modern manufacturing methods).
The Schloss also has a Schütz memorial room commemorating the composer Heinrich Schütz (1585–1672), who lived at Nikolaistrasse 13 (see below).

The Town

Town Hall

Below the Schloss is the old market square, with the Town Hall, a Baroque building (1670), rebuilt in 1718–22 after a fire.

St Mary's Church

Adjoining the Town Hall stands St Mary's Church (consecrated 1303), an Early Gothic hall-church, with later alteration. Notable features of the interior are the reredos (1684), the pulpit (1674) and the font (1681).

*Geleitshaus

Near the Markt, at Grosse Burgstrasse 22, is the Geleitshaus, a richly decorated Renaissance building (1552), containing the room in which a post-mortem was carried out on King Gustavus Adolphus after the battle of Lützen and a diorama of the battle.

Heinrich-Schütz-
Haus

At Nikolaistrasse 13 is the Heinrich-Schütz-Haus (1550), in which the composer spent most of the last twenty years of his life.

Surroundings of Weissenfels

Lützen

15km/9 miles north-east of Weissenfels on B 87 is Lützen, with a fine 13th century castle (now a museum). On the road to Markranstädt can be found the Gustav-Adolf-Gedenkstätte, with a chapel (1807), a monument (1837) and a log cabin (museum) commemorating King Gustavus Adolphus of Sweden, who was killed in the battle of Lützen in 1632.

Gustavus Adolphus Monument, Lützen

Wernigerode   E 6

Land: Saxony-Anhalt
Altitude: 240m/790ft
Population: 36,000

Wernigerode lies at the junction of the river Holtemme and the Zillierbach, on the
northern fringes of the Harz. Above the town with its picturesque old half-timbered
buildings rears the Schloss. A popular attraction for visitors is a trip through the Harz on
the Harzquerbahn.

Situation and
characteristics

Sights

The medieval town centre is protected as a historical monument. It still preserves some
remains of its fortifications (13th–14th c.) – the Wallgraben, two round towers and the
Westerntor, a fortified gate.

Fortifications

On the south side of the Marktplatz is the Town Hall (Rathaus), Wernigerode's architectural gem. It first appears in the records in 1277 as the "Spelhus", a place of entertainment
for the Count of Wernigerode and a courthouse. A half-timbered upper storey in Late
Gothic style was added in 1492–97; then in 1543, after a fire, it was rebuilt as the Town
Hall. On the front are two oriels topped by steeples.

*Town Hall

Adjoining the Town Hall is the Weigh-House (Ratswaage; 16th c.), now occupied by
municipal offices. It is decorated with Carnival scenes and figures of saints.

Weigh-House

The town centre has preserved much of its medieval aspect, with many handsome old
half-timbered houses. In the Marktplatz is the Gothic House, which was originally similar
to the Weigh-House (enlarged in 1544).

*Half-timbered
houses

Wernigerode

Marktplatz and Town Hall, Wernigerode

Other interesting half-timbered buildings in the town centre are the Oldest House (Ältestes Haus; after 1400) at Hinterstrasse 48; the Smallest House (Kleinstes Haus; second half of 18th c.), barely 3m/10ft wide, at Kochstrasse 43; the Leaning House (Schiefes Haus; 1680) at Klintgasse 5 (behind the Town Hall), an old mill whose foundations have been undermined by water; the Krummelsches Haus (1674) at Breite Strasse 72, with fine Baroque carving; and the Krellsche Schmiede (1678) at Breite Strasse 95, with an interesting pattern of half-timbering.

Harz Museum

At Klint 10 (behind the Town Hall), in a house with a neo-classical gable, is the Harz Museum (medieval finds from castles in the surrounding area, documents on the history of half-timbered building, costumes of the northern Harz).

St Sylvester's Church

St Sylvester's Church (Sylvestrikirche), in the Klint, is an aisled Gothic basilica (first mentioned 1230; altered around 1500 and in 1881–85). Beautiful interior, with a fine carved altar (end of 15th c.).

Church of Our Lady

The aisleless Gothic church of Our Lady (Liebfrauenkirche), built on the site of an earlier Romanesque church, was remodelled in Baroque style in 1756–62. The altar has an altarpiece by B. Rode.

St John's Church

St John's Church (St Johanniskirche) was originally Romanesque (after 1265); nave and choir altered in 1497. It has a fine four-panel carved altar (1430–40).

*Schloss

On the Burgberg (350m/1150ft) stands the Schloss, now a museum. The present castle is essentially a 19th century reproduction of a medieval castle (by K. Frühling, 1862–93). The original castle of the Counts of Wernigerode was built in the 12th century, and there are some remains of medieval work in its successor (e.g. in the cellars of the north-eastern wing). Other remains of earlier work are the Hausmannsturm on the terrace, the

550

spiral ramp in the inner courtyard, the Hofstubenbau and parts of the chapel.The museum, with an alternation between rooms in period style and rooms devoted to particular fields, illustrates the history of the region.

The Orangery, in the terrace garden at the foot of the castle gardens, now houses the Magdeburg State Archives. Over the doorway on the garden side are the arms of the Counts of Wernigerode.

Orangery

*Harzquerbahn

The narrow-gauge Harzquerbahn between Wernigerode and Nordhausen (about 60km/37 miles) runs through a romantic landscape of hills and forests. There is a connection with the Selketalbahn in the Selke valley (see entry); at the Eisfelder Tal-mühle junction a branch line goes off to Gernrode (see Quedlinburg, Surroundings) via Hasselfelde or Stiege.

Blankenburg
E–F 6

The town of Blankenburg lies south-east of Wernigerode on the northern fringe of the Harz, enclosed by the Harz, the Regenstein and the Teufelsmauer (see below). Thanks to its agreeable climate and mineral springs (recommended for the treatment of rheumatism) it has developed into a spa and holiday resort.

Situation and characteristics

High above the town stands the Schloss (by H. Korb, 1705–18), an imposing Baroque building which incorporates some medieval work and a Renaissance wing (now occupied by a commercial college).
Near the Schloss are remains of the town's medieval fortifications.

Schloss

At the foot of the Burgberg (castle hill) is the Kleines Schloss, now occupied by the Heimatmuseum. The original Baroque half-timbered building was renovated in 1777. Beautiful Baroque garden.

Heimatmuseum

Below the Schloss is the parish church of St Bartholomew, a hall-church of 1585 (originally Romanesque) with an interesting interior (reredos, Triumphal Cross group) and monuments (15th–17th c.).

St Bartholomew's Church

The Town Hall is a two-storey Renaissance building of around 1546 incorporating some Gothic work, with a staircase tower and an ornamental gable. To the left of the entrance hangs an iron bar, the standard Blankenburg ell.

Town Hall

3km/2 miles west of the town, on the edge of the Harz, is Michaelstein Monastery (1147), now used for concerts and recitals. The surviving remains include the chapterhouse and refectory, the Early Gothic cloisters, the west wing of the conventual buildings and the gatehouse.

Michaelstein Monastery

2km/1¼ miles north are the ruins of Burg Regenstein, built in the 12th–14th centuries, with some earlier work. Strongly fortified in 1671, it was slighted in 1758. The picturesque ruins include the stump of a circular keep, various chambers hewn from the rock and the remains of 18th century casemates.

*Burg Regenstein

To the east of Blankenburg is the Teufelsmauer ("Devil's Wall"), a 4km/2½ mile long range of sandstone crags (nature reserve; waymarked footpaths, rock-climbing area).

Teufelsmauer

Rübeland

Rübeland lies in the narrow and deeply indented Bode valley in the central Harz. Its great attractions are its stalactitic caves.

The Baumannshöhle (discovered 1536) and the Hermannshöhle (discovered 1866) are among the finest natural caves in Germany, with striking stalactites and stalagmites.

*Baumannshöhle
Hermannshöhle

In the Baumannshöhle is the Goethe Hall (40m/130ft by 60m/200ft; Cave Theatre).
Evidence of Neolithic occupation (fragments of pottery, stone tools) were discovered in this cave.

Rübeland's great landmark is the "Cave Bear" of stone and concrete which stands outside the Hermannshöhle; from 1896 to 1969 it stood inside the cave.

Weserbergland   E 4

Länder: Hesse, North Rhine-Westphalia, Lower Saxony

Situation and characteristics	The Weserbergland (Weser Uplands) is made up of several ranges of hills on both sides of the Weser between Münden (Hannoversch Münden) and Minden. On the north it is bordered by the North German plain, while on the west it merges into the Lippe Uplands, on the east into the Leinebergland and on the south into the Hessian Uplands.

Landscape

Bramwald Solling	The Bramwald, to the east of the Weser, below Münden, reaches a height of 400m/1300ft in the Bramburg and 408m/1339ft in the Totenberg. Next come the Solling hills, a plateau of Bunter sandstone some 500 sq.km/195 sq. miles in extent with deciduous and coniferous forest, rising to 528m/1732ft in the Grosse Blösse, the highest hill in the Weser area.
Vogler Hils Ith	Between Stadtoldendorf and Bodenwerder lies the Vogler, a smaller massif of Bunter sandstone with flat-bottomed depressions and deeply indented valleys between the hills, which reaches its highest point in Ebersnacken (460m/1509ft; views). Beyond this are two beautifully wooded ridges of Jurassic limestone – the Hils ridge, with the Blosse Zelle (477m/1565ft) and the Grosser Sohl (472m/1549ft; views), and the long and often precipitous Ith ridge, with the Knüllbrink (439m/1440ft; views). To the north of the Hameln–Elze road (B 1) are the Osterwald (419m/1375ft) and the Saupark hills.
Deister Süntel	North-west of B 217 (Hameln-Springe-Hannover) are the Deister range, with the Annaturm (405m/1329ft), the Nordmannsturm (379m/1243ft), and the Süntel, with the Hohe Egge (437m/1434ft; views) and the magnificent limestone cliffs of the Hohenstein.
Wesergebirge Bückeberge	To the west are the Wesergebirge (Weser Hills), reaching a height of 320m/1050ft in the Amelungsberg, and the Bückeberge (367m/1204ft; sandstone quarries), farther north.
Reinhardswald	West of the Weser, below Münden, extends the Reinhardswald, the largest continuous area of forest in Lower Hesse (210 sq.km/81 sq. miles; 70 hectare/175 acre nature reserve around the Sababurg), reaching its highest point in the Staufenberg, a rounded basalt hill 472m/1549ft high.
Lippe Uplands Wiehengebirge	Between Höxter and Vlotho are the Lippe Uplands (Lippisches Bergland), with the Köterberg (497m/1631ft; television tower, Köterberghaus; wide views). Finally the northern limits of the Weserbergland are reached in the Wiehengebirge (Heidbrink and Wurzelbrink, 320m/1050ft), the continuation of the Wesergebirge to the west of the Porta Westfalica (see Minden).
Spas	Of the many spas in the Weserbergland the most notable are Bad Karlshafen, Bad Pyrmont (see Hameln, Surroundings), Bad Eilsen, Bad Münder, Bad Nenndorf, Bas Oeynhausen and Bad Essen.
Boat trips	Excursion ships ply on the Weser during the summer; the principal ports of call are Bodenwerder, Hameln, Höxter, Bad Karlshafen and Polle.

Weser Valley Road (Wesertalstrasse)

The most attractive route through the Weserbergland is the Weser Valley Road (Wesertalstrasse) between Münden (Hannoversch Münden) and Minden, with its ever-

The Weser breaks through the hills at the Porta Westfalica

changing scenery and numerous pretty villages and towns. See Münden, Höxter, Hameln and Minden.

A number of rewarding detours can be made from the Weser Valley Road: between Münden and Bad Karlshafen into the Reinhardswald, with the Sababurg; from Höxter to the Köterberg with its wide-ranging views and the climatic resort of Neuhaus in the Solling range; from Emmern to the imposing Hämelschenburg and Bad Pyrmont with its beautiful Kurpark.

Detours

The climax of a trip through the Weser valley is the Porta Westfalica (Westphalian Gate) to the south of Minden, where the Weser breaks through the hills, with the old princely capital of Bückeburg a few kilometres away.

*Porta Westfalica

Wetzlar

G 4

Land: Hesse
Altitude: 150m/490ft
Population: 36,000

The old free imperial city of Wetzlar is picturesquely situated on the Lahn above its junction with the Dill. Above the town stands the ruined 12th century castle of Kalsmunt. Wetzlar has optical and electronic as well as metalworking industries.

Situation and characteristics

Old Town

The old town on the slopes above the left bank of the Lahn, with its narrow lanes and handsome old burghers' houses, is dominated by the Cathedral (formerly the Stift-skirche of St Mary), a richly articulated building of the 12th–16th centuries.

Cathedral

Wetzlar

Reichskammer-
gericht

In the Fischmarkt, south-west of the Domplatz (Cathedral Square), are a number of houses of the 16th–18th centuries. A double eagle marks the building once occupied by the Reichskammergericht (German Supreme Court), where Goethe worked as a young lawyer in 1772.

Lottehaus

To the east of the Domplatz, at Lottestrasse 8, is the Lottehaus (Lotte's House), once the House of the Teutonic Order, home of Charlotte Buff, who won Goethe's heart during his stay in Wetzlar. The building now contains a collection of material on Goethe and Lotte, together with the Municipal Museum and the Industrial Museum.

Wiesbaden

H 3

Capital of the *Land* of Hesse
Altitude: 117m/384ft
Population: 268,000

Situation and
characteristics

Wiesbaden, capital of the *Land* of Hesse, lies at the foot of the wooded Taunus hills, extending with its suburbs to the Rhine. The town's 27 thermal springs (46–67°C/115–153°F), its mild climate and its beautiful surroundings make it a much frequented health resort. Wiesbaden is the seat of the Federal Criminal Department, the Federal Statistical Office and the Federation of the German Film Industry. There are a number of large Sekt-making establishments in the surrounding area.

* Kurbezirk (Spa District)

The town's main traffic artery is the wide Wilhelmstrasse, at the north end of which, to the right (east), is the Kurbezirk, bounded on the south by the Theatre Colonnade and the State Theatre (Staatstheater; 1892–94) and on the north by the Fountain Colonnade.

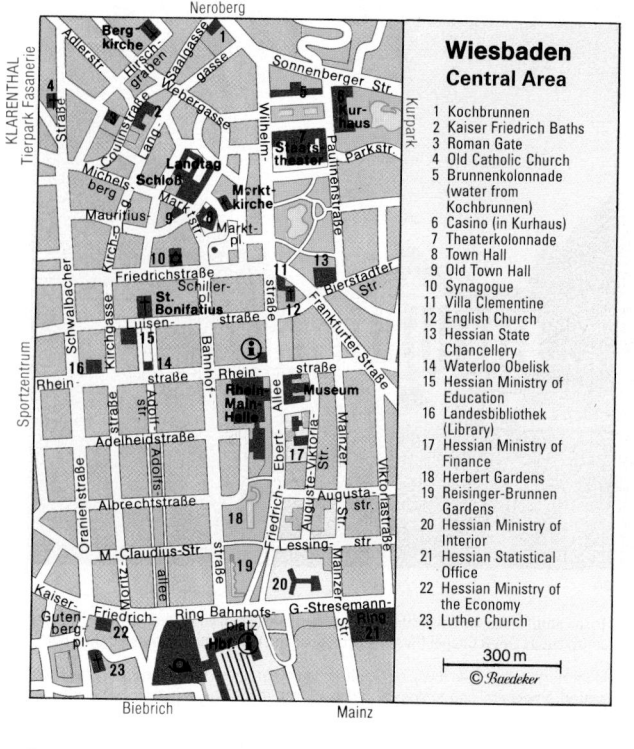

Wiesbaden
Central Area

1 Kochbrunnen
2 Kaiser Friedrich Baths
3 Roman Gate
4 Old Catholic Church
5 Brunnenkolonnade
   (water from
   Kochbrunnen)
6 Casino (in Kurhaus)
7 Theaterkolonnade
8 Town Hall
9 Old Town Hall
10 Synagogue
11 Villa Clementine
12 English Church
13 Hessian State
   Chancellery
14 Waterloo Obelisk
15 Hessian Ministry of
   Education
16 Landesbibliothek
   (Library)
17 Hessian Ministry of
   Finance
18 Herbert Gardens
19 Reisinger-Brunnen
   Gardens
20 Hessian Ministry of
   Interior
21 Hessian Statistical
   Office
22 Hessian Ministry of
   the Economy
23 Luther Church

300 m

© Baedeker

To the east stands the Kurhaus (by Friedrich von Thiersch, 1904–07), an imposing building with a massive Ionic portico. In the north wing is the Casino. Behind the Kurhaus extends the well groomed Kurpark.

Kurhaus

Beyond the Kurpark is the Aukammtal spa district (thermal baths, indoor and outdoor; clinics).

Aukammtal

To the east, on Aukamm-Allee, is the Indoor Bath. North-west of this can be found the Kochbrunnen (15 springs, 66°C/151°F), with the Kaiser Friedrich Baths (1910–13) a little way away to the south-west.

Kochbrunnen

To the north of the Kaiser Friedrich Baths, in Nerostrasse, is the Women's Museum (Frauenmuseum; temporary exhibitions, events of various kinds, seminars, etc.).

Women's Museum

Central Area

In the Schlossplatz, in the town centre (west of Wilhelmstrasse), is the Schloss (1837–41), now occupied by government offices. Between the Schlossplatz and the Marktplatz are the Town Hall (1884–88) and the Market Church (1852–62; Protestant).

Schloss

The Municipal Museum (Städtisches Museum), at the south end of Wilhelmstrasse (Friedrich-Ebert-Allee 2) has collections of antiquities and natural history and a picture gallery with the fine Jawlensky Collection. Opposite it is the Rhein-Main-Halle, a congress and exhibition centre.

Museum

Kurhaus, Wiesbaden

*Neroberg

To the north of the town rises the wooded Neroberg (245m/804ft; rack railway), with the conspicuous Greek Chapel (Russian Orthodox) and the beautifully situated Opel Baths.

Fasanerie

In the north-west of the town, on Schützenhausweg, can be found the Fasanerie (Pheasantry), a botanical and zoological park (red deer, moufflons, wild pigs, bison, etc.).

Wiesbaden-Biebrich

*Schloss

In the Biebrich district, 5km/3 miles south of the town centre is Schloss Biebrich (1698–1744), a Baroque palace which was a seat of the Dukes of Nassau.

Wildbad   K 4

Land: Baden-Württemberg
Altitude: 430m/1410ft
Population: 11,000

Situation and characteristics

Wildbad, in the deeply indented Enz valley, is second only to Baden-Baden in popularity among the spas of the northern Black Forest (thermal springs, 35–41°C/95–106°F).

The Town

Spa facilities

In the Kurplatz are the Graf Eberhard Baths (now protected as a historical monument), with a beautiful mosaic pool. To the rear is the terraced Treatment Centre (1977), close to the springs. In Olgastrasse are the Swimming Pool and Thermal Baths; farther upstream are the Kurtheater and the Pump Room and Promenade.

On the left bank of the Enz are the König Karl Baths and, beyond this, the Thermal Swimming Baths (two indoor and one outdoor pool); farther upstream can be found the Kurhaus (Kursaal). On both sides of the Enz are beautiful gardens.

Above the town to the west is the beautifully wooded Sommerberg (733m/2405ft), which can be ascended either by funicular or by road (2.8km/1¾ miles, gradient 16%). On the summit are numerous footpaths, including one leading to the Wildsee Moorland Nature Reserve.

Sommerberg

Surroundings of Wildbad

14km/8½ miles east of Wildbad, in the Nagold valley, is the altitude resort of Hirsau, with the picturesque ruins of a Benedictine monastery founded in 1059 (open-air theatre in summer) and the Early Romanesque church of St Aurelius (11th c.).

*Hirsau

3km/2 miles south of Hirsau is Calw, birthplace of Hermann Hesse (1877–1962; Hesse Museum). The old town, excellently restored, has handsome half-timbered houses and an interesting Municipal Museum.

Calw

Wilhelmshaven

C 3

Land: Lower Saxony
Altitude: 5m/16ft
Population: 95,000

Wilhelmshaven, situated on the west side of Jade Bay, a 5km/3 mile wide inlet on the North Sea coast, was until 1945 primarily a naval port. It is now an important oil terminal and has a variety of industry (chemicals, metalworking, engineering, textiles). It has a Marine Biological Research Station belonging to the Senckenberg Society (see Frankfurt am Main) and an Ornithological Institute.

Situation and characteristics

The Town

The Town Hall is a handsome building in clinker brick (by Fritz Höger, 1927–29). From the 49m/161ft high tower there are wide panoramic views.
To the east is the Kurpark.

Town Hall

On the north side of Rathausplatz is City-Haus, with the interesting Coast Museum (natural and cultural history of the North Sea coast, shipping; ship models).

Coast Museum

The extensive port installations lie to the south of the town. On Bontekai are a number of museum ships. On a disused section of railway track can be seen an old steam engine. Beyond this, on the South Beach, is a sea-water Aquarium.

Port

Wismar

B 6

Land: Mecklenburg-West Pomerania
Altitude: 14m/46ft
Population: 57,000

Wismar, a port, shipbuilding and industrial town, lies in Wismar Bay, which is sheltered by the island of Poel. The old town is a gem of medieval architecture.

Situation and characteristics

Sights

Of its medieval fortifications Wismar has preserved the Late Gothic Water Gate (mid 15th c.) on the Old Harbour, now occupied by the Club Maritim, and some remains of the old town walls. Of the defence works of the period of Swedish occupation (1648–1803) there survive the Baroque Provianthaus (1690), now a polyclinic, and the old Arsenal (Zeughaus; 1699) in Ulmenstrasse, which now houses the municipal archives.

Fortifications

Harbour, Wismar

*Marktplatz Town Hall	In the large Marktplatz (area 1 hectare/2½ acres) stands the neo-classical Town Hall (1817–19), designed by the court architect, Georg Barca. The court-room in the west wing and the vaulted cellars survive from an earlier (14th c.) building.
*Alter Schwede	On the east side of the square is the building known as the Alter Schwede (*c.* 1380), Wismar's oldest surviving burgher's house, which has been occupied since 1878 by a restaurant. The façade is charming, with its Gothic stepped gables articulated by pillars and relieved by openings and its glazed brick masonry.
*Water-Tower	On the south-east side of the Markt is the Wasserkunst (by Philipp Brandin, 1580–62), a water-tower in Dutch Renaissance style with a bell-shaped copper dome borne on twelve pillars which until 1897 supplied the town with water. Also in the Markt are a number of handsome gabled houses of the 17th and 18th centuries.
St Mary's Church	In an adjoining square rises the massive tower of St Mary's Church (1339; crypt 1270–80), which was destroyed in 1945. The Archidiakonat (pastor's house) of the mid 15th century was restored after the war.
St Nicholas's Church	On the north side of the old town is St Nicholas's Church (14th–15th c.), which was modelled on St Mary's. It has a 37m/121ft high nave and a fine interior (Late Gothic to Baroque); the font (*c.* 1335) came from St Mary's Church.
Other churches	Two other notable churches are the 14th century church of the Hospital of the Holy Ghost and the 15th century St George's Church (in ruins; rebuilding planned).
Fürstenhof	East of St George's Church we come to the Fürstenhof (1553–54), a three-storey Renaissance building which is now occupied by law courts and the municipal archives.
Schabbellhaus (Museum)	To the south of St Nicholas's Church, at Schweinsbrücke 8, is the Schabbellhaus, a building in Dutch Renaissance style (by Philipp Brandin, 1569–71) which is now occupied by a museum on the history of the town.

There are numbers of handsome old burghers' houses in Krämerstrasse (rebuilt; pedestrian zone) and neighbouring streets.

Krämerstrasse

On the Baumhaus (now the harbourmaster's office) can be seen two cast-iron heads known as the "Swedes' Heads" (Schwedenköpfe).

"Swedes' Heads"

Wittenberg

E 8

Land: Saxony-Anhalt
Altitude: 65–104m/213–341ft
Population: 54,000

The old university town of Wittenberg, famed as the starting-point of Luther's Reformation, lies on the north bank of the Oder in the southern foothills of the Fläming range.

Situation and characteristics

Central Area

The handsome Town Hall (Rathaus; 1524–40) has four Renaissance gables, Late Gothic windows, a balcony (by Georg Schröter, 1573) over the doorway and rich decoration (allegorical figures, columns; the goddess Justitia, with scales and sword).

*Town Hall

Immediately adjoining the Town Hall are the Market Fountain (1617) and bronze statues of Martin Luther (by Gottfried Schadow, 1821; iron canopy by K. F. Schinkel) and Philip Melanchthon (by Friedrich Drake, 1860; iron canopy by J. H. Strack).

Statues of Luther and Melanchthon

The oldest building in Wittenberg is the aisled Gothic church of St Mary (13th–15th c.), in which Luther is believed to have preached. The original twin spires of 1410 were pulled down and replaced in 1558 by octagonal towers in Renaissance style.

*St Mary's Church

Luther Room in the Luther House

The church was remodelled in neo-Gothic style in the 19th century by Carlo Ignazio Pozzi and others. Notable features of the interior are the winged altar by Lucas Cranach the Elder (1547), the richly decorated font by Hermann Vischer (1457), an organ noted for its fine tone, paintings by Lucas Cranach the Younger and Renaissance epitaphs and tombs, including that of the Reformer Johann Bugenhagen (1558).

Adjoining St Mary's Church is the Chapel of the Holy Body (Kapelle zum Heiligen Leichnam; 1377), in brick-built Gothic style, with a strikingly slender tower.

Chapel of the Holy Body

Schlossplatz

The Late Gothic Schlosskirche (by Conrad Pflüger, c. 1500), now known as the Reformation Memorial Church (altered by J. H. F. Adler, 1883–92), is closely bound up with the story of the Reformation. From the tower there are extensive views. It was to the wooden doors of this church that Luther nailed his 95 "Theses" in October 1517. The original doors were destroyed by fire during the Seven Years' War; the present bronze doors, bearing the Latin text of the Theses, were installed in 1858.

* Schlosskirche

In the church are life-size alabaster statues of Electors Frederick the Wise and John the Constant of Saxony-Wittenberg, the tombs of Luther and Melanchthon and the Early Renaissance monument of Elector Frederick III (1527) by the Nürnberg bronze-founder Peter Vischer the Younger, who was also responsible for the tombs of the knight Hans Hundt and Provost Henning Gode. The bronze monument of John the Constant was the work of Hans Vischer. On the columns of the nave are life-size figures of Luther, Melanchthon and other Reformers.

To the south of the church stands the Schloss, the old Electoral residence (by Claus Roder and Conrad Pflüger, 1490–1525), which suffered damage in 1760, during the Seven Years' War, and lost its original Late Gothic aspect during the subsequent rebuilding. It still preserves two staircases, balconies with friezes of coats of arms and a massive corner tower. The castle now houses the Julius Riemer Museum of Natural History and Ethnography, the Municipal Archives and a Museum on the History of the Town.

Schloss (Museums)

The Cranach House at Schloss-strasse 1 was the home of Lucas Cranach the Elder (1472–1553), who lived in Wittenberg from 1505 to 1547. Court painter to the Elector of Saxony, he also became burgomaster of Wittenberg and was the owner of a pharmacy in the town.

Cranach House

The house in which Martin Luther lived from 1508 to 1546 is in the south-east of the town. Built in 1504 as a house of Augustinian Hermits, it was altered in 1566; and between 1844 and 1900 it was converted into a Museum of the Reformation (Lutherhalle). In the room occupied by Luther, preserved in its original condition, are displayed Luther's writings, prints, medals, Luther's university lectern, his pulpit from St Mary's Church and a number of valuable pictures.

** Luther House (Museum)

The Augusteum (1564–83), adjoining the Luther House, originally belonged to the University. It was rebuilt in Baroque style in the 18th century.

Augusteum

Near the Luther House, at Collegienstrasse 60, is the Melanchthon House (1536), a three-storey building with Late Gothic windows and two Renaissance gables. The Reformer Philip Melanchthon (a Greek version of his original name, Schwarzerd) lived and worked here, dying in the house in 1560. It is now a memorial museum. Some features in the garden – the pump, the stone table, the herb garden, the old yew-trees, a stretch of the town walls – date from the 16th century.

* Melanchthon House

Wolfenbüttel

E 6

Land: Lower Saxony
Altitude: 75m/245ft
Population: 50,000

◀ *Schlosskirche, Wittenberg*

Wolfenbüttel

Situation and characteristics

The old town of Wolfenbüttel, from 1308 to 1753 the seat of the Dukes of Brunswick, lies between two arms of the river Oker, surrounded by attractive gardens on the line of the old fortifications. With its many fine half-timbered buildings it still preserves almost intact the aspect of a princely capital.

Since 1978 the old town has been thoroughly restored and rehabilitated.

The Town

Schloss

In the Schlossplatz is the Ducal Palace with its striking tower. Originally built in the 16th century, it was rebuilt in Baroque style in the early 18th century (façade by Hermann Korb, 1716). It now houses the Municipal and District Heimatmuseum (state apartments, domestic interiors).

Arsenal

On the north side of the square is the old Arsenal (Zeughaus, 1613–18), a handsome Renaissance building with a four-storey gable which now contains part of the Duke Augustus Library and a museum on the history of the book. To the west is the Lessing House (Museum), in which the great dramatist and critic lived from 1777.

Lessing House

∗∗Duke Augustus Library

Behind the Lessing House is the Duke Augustus Library (Herzog-August-Bibliothek), built 1882–87; the old library in which Leibniz and Lessing worked was pulled down in 1887. The Library possesses some 8000 manuscripts (including the 10th century Reichenau Gospels, a 12th century Gospel Book which belonged to Henry the Lion and a 12th century copy of the "Sachsenspiegel"), 4000 incunabula and over 450,000 volumes.

St John's Church

Some distance west of the Schlossplatz we come to St John's Church, a 17th century half-timbered building set in an idyllic churchyard.

Klein Venedig

To the east of the Schlossplatz is the last remnant of the old town moat, known as Klein Venedig ("Little Venice").

Stadtmarkt

In the Stadtmarkt, to the east of the Ducal Palace, is the Town Hall (*c.* 1600), a handsome half-timbered building with timber arcades. To the east is the Renaissance Kanzlei

Ducal Palace, Wolfenbüttel

(Chancery), until 1753 the seat of the provincial government, now housing the Museum of Prehistory.

To the south, in the centre of the town, is its principal church, St Mary's (by Paul Francke, 1607–23), a curious blend of Gothic layout and Renaissance forms and one of the major examples of early Protestant church-building in Germany. It has a Baroque high altar of 1618 with a Crucifixion group, a carved pulpit of 1623 supported on a figure of Moses, choir-stalls of 1625 and 16th century grave-slabs; Ducal burial vault.

St Mary's Church

Farther east is the Holzmarkt, with the Trinity Church, a strikingly unusual Baroque building (1719) flanked by two squat square towers.

Trinity Church

Wolfsburg

E 6

Land: Lower Saxony
Altitude: 60m/200ft
Population: 129,000

The town of Wolfsburg, on the Mittelland Canal, was established in 1938 together with the Volkswagen works. Originally consisting of two villages and the Schloss on the Aller, it developed into a single community only during the postwar reconstruction period from 1945 onwards.

Situation and characteristics

The Town

On the north side of the Mittelland Canal are the huge Volkswagen works, which employ some 65,000 people and have an output of 3600 cars a day. There are interesting conducted tours of the works.

Volkswagen works

Planetarium, Wolfsburg

Schloss	North-east of the Volkswagen works, beyond the Aller, is Schloss Wolfsburg (16th–17th c.), which now houses the Municipal Art Gallery and the Heimatmuseum. The Scheune Alt-Wolfsburg, an old barn, contains an Agricultural Museum.
Allerpark	Between the Aller and the Mittelland Canal lies the Allerpark, with the Allersee (bathing station), the Eispalast (an ice-rink) and the Badeland leisure centre (indoor and outdoor swimming pools).
Town Hall	The town's main street is Porschestrasse (partly pedestrianised). On its east side is the Town Hall (carillon), and adjoining this the Cultural Centre (by Alvar Aalto).
Klieversberg	To the south, on the Klieversberg, are the Theatre (by Hans Scharoun, 1973), the Planetarium (1983), the Congress Park and the Church of the Holy Ghost (by Alvar Aalto, 1962).
AutoMuseum	In the east of the town, at Dieselstrasse 35, is the AutoMuseum, with a comprehensive survey of the development of the Volkswagen, Audi, DKW, Horch, Wanderer and NSU marques.

Wörlitz   E 7

Land: Saxony-Anhalt
Altitude: 62m/203ft
Population: 2000

Situation and characteristics	Wörlitz, 20km/12½miles east of Dessau, is famed for its park, the first landscaped park in the English style to be laid out in Germany in the 18th century.

**Wörlitz Park

	Wörlitz Park, laid out between 1765 and 1810 to the design of Prince Franz of Anhalt-Dessau and his architect F. W. von Erdmannsdorff, contains a great variety of features – deciduous and coniferous trees in many different species, monuments, grottoes, canals, bridges, flowerbeds, groves of trees, vistas, a palm-grove, ferries, statues, reliefs and numerous small buildings.
*Schloss Wörlitz	Schloss Wörlitz (by Erdmannsdorff, 1769–73), modelled on Claremont House near London, contains a valuable art collection (pictures by Canaletto, grand pianos of 1810 and 1815, porcelain, glass, etc.); fine ceiling and wall paintings.
Synagogue	The Synagogue (by Erdmannsdorff, 1789–90) was partly destroyed in 1938 and restored in 1948.
Galerie am Grauen Haus	The Galerie am Grauen Haus (1790) is used for annual special exhibitions. The inn Zum Eichenkranz (Erdmannsdorf, 1785–87) is at present in course of restoration.
Georg Forster Museum	On the Eisenhart are two pavilions (1781–84) which now house the Georg Forster Museum. Georg Forster accompanied James Cook on his second voyage round the world, and the museum commemorates his work as a traveller, scientist and writer.
	On Rousseau Island is a memorial stone (1782) commemorating the 18th century writer and philosopher Jean-Jacques Rousseau.
*Gothic House	In Schochs Garten is the Gothic House (by G. C. Hesekiel, 1773–1813), which in its day was the largest neo-Gothic building in Germany. It contains a collection of South German and Swiss stained glass (15th–17th c.), Dutch paintings and pictures by Lucas Cranach the Elder.
	Other buildings in the park include the Nymphaeum (1767–68), the Temple of Flora (1796–98; said to be modelled on an ancient temple in Spoleto) and the Temple of Venus (1797), which is reminiscent of the Temple of the Sibyl at Tivoli.

Gothic House, Wörlitz Park

The "Golden Urn" of cast-iron and sandstone contains the remains of a Princess of Anhalt (d. 1769).

The Pantheon (1795–96) contains a collection of antique statues and busts, including the nine Muses.

The Herder Island (1788–94) commemorates Johann Gottfried Herder.

On the Amalieninsel, with the Amaliengrotte (1793), cann be seen herms symbolising the poets Sappho and Anacreon.

The Iron Bridge (Eiserne Brücke, 1791), modelled on the bridge over the Severn at Coalbrookdale in Shropshire, was the first of its kind on the European mainland.

Neue Anlage (New Gardens)

The Villa Hamilton (by Erdmannsdorff, 1791–94), named after the English antiquarian Sir William Hamilton, was built on the largest island in the park, modelled on the Bay of Naples.

Villa Hamilton

The Town

The town's principal landmark is the 66m/217ft high tower of St Peter's Church (originally Romanesque, 1196–1201; rebuilt in neo-Gothic style by G. C. Hesekiel in 1805–09). Remains of the Romanesque building are the doorway and the wall round the nave and tower.

St Peter's Church

The two-storey Town Hall (by Erdmannsdorf, 1792–95) is in the style of an English country house.

Town Hall

Surroundings of Wörlitz

At Oranienbaum (5km/3 miles south) are a Schloss and a park in Dutch Baroque style (1683 and 1798). Part of the park was laid out in Chinese style (c. 1800), with a Chinese

Oranienbaum

tea-house (1794–97) and a five-storey pagoda. In the left-hand wing of the Schloss is the District Museum, with a permanent exhibition on printing.

Coswig

In Coswig (5km/3 miles north-east) stands the Romanesque and Gothic church of St Nicholas (1150; rebuilt 1699–1708 and 1926), which has a finely carved organ-case (1713), a font by Giovanni Simonetti, Gothic choir-stalls, a "Last Supper" by Lucas Cranach the Younger, an epitaph by Lucas Cranach the Elder and stained glass of the Cranach school (1350).

The Schloss (1560 and 1667–77), an irregular structure of four wings round a central courtyard, was much altered in the 19th century.

Worms   I 3

Land: Rhineland-Palatinate
Altitude: 100m/330ft
Population: 74,000

Situation and characteristics

The cathedral city of Worms, on the left bank of the Rhine, is one of the oldest towns in Germany. It is a noted centre of the wine trade and a considerable industrial town.

Old Town

*Cathedral

In the centre of the town stands the Cathedral (Dom) of SS Peter and Paul (11th–12th c.; R.C.), with four towers and two domes, which ranks along with Speyer and Mainz Cathedrals as one of the finest achievements of the High Romanesque style. The nave is 27m/89ft high (domes 40m/130ft). In the north aisle are five fine Late Gothic sandstone reliefs from the demolished Gothic cloister; fine choir-stalls, Baroque high altar by Balthasar Neumann.

Worms Cathedral

To the east of the Cathedral, in the Marktplatz, can be found the Trinity Church (1709–25; fine interior) and the Town Hall (1956–58).

Trinity Church

To the north-east is St Paul's Church (Romanesque), with two round towers topped by domes.

South-west of the Cathedral are the Late Romanesque church of St Magnus (10th–14th c.; Protestant), the town's first church, with a spire, and the former St Andrew's Church (12th–13th c.), which along with the adjoining monastic buildings now houses the Municipal Museum (Roman antiquities, medieval art, Luther Room).

St Magnus's Church

North-west of the two churches, on the Andreasring, is the oldest and largest Jewish cemetery in Europe (gravestones dating back to the 11th and 12th centuries).

Jewish Cemetery

North of the Cathedral is the Heylshof (built in 1884 on the site of the old Bishop's Palace), an art gallery with a collection of paintings of the 16th–19th centuries, sculpture, stained glass, porcelain, etc.

Heylshof

Farther north, in Lutherplatz, can be seen the Luther Memorial (by Ernst Rietschel, 1868), commemorating Luther's appearance before the Diet of Worms in 1521.

In the north of the old town lies the well preserved (partly restored) old Jewish quarter, with the Romanesque Synagogue (destroyed 1938, rebuilt 1961), a ritual bath (*mikve*, 1186) and the Raschi-Haus (Jewish Museum). Nearby are remains of the old town walls.

Synagogue
Raschi-Haus

Near the road to Mainz (B 9), surrounded by vineyards, is the Liebfrauenkirche (Church of Our Lady; 13th–15th c.; R.C.), which has a fine tabernacle and a 15th century figure of the Virgin.

Liebfrauenkirche

On the banks of the Rhine, by the landing-stage, is a statue (1906) of Hagen sinking the treasure of the Nibelungs in the Rhine.

Hagen Monument

Alzey

25km/15 miles north-west of Worms is Alzey, the Roman Altiaia, an important wine-producing town and centre of the wine trade.

In the east of the old town is the Schloss (oldest parts 11th c.; much rebuilt 1902). In the Fischmarkt stands the Renaissance Town Hall (1586; carillon). In the Rossmarkt, to the north, is an unusual fountain. Farther north the old Amtshaus houses the Municipal Museum (history of the town, folk traditions, geology, palaeontology).

Wuppertal
F 2

Land: North Rhine-Westphalia
Altitude: 250m/820ft
Population: 380,000

The industrial city and university town of Wuppertal, finely situated in the Bergisches Land (see entry), consists principally of the districts of Barmen, Elberfeld and Vohwinkel, formerly separate towns, strung out along the narrow valley of the Wupper for a distance of some 20km/12½ miles.

Situation and characteristics

Barmen, Elberfeld and Vohwinkel are linked by the famous elevated railway (13.3km/8¼ miles long), constructed between 1898 and 1901.

* Elevated railway

Barmen

South-east of the Town Hall (Rathaus; 1913–22) is the House of Youth (Haus der Jugend), with the Municipal Library (periodic exhibitions). In Friedrich-Engels-Allee are the Opera

House and the Friedrich-Engels-Haus (documentation on Engels, the co-founder of socialism; museum of the early industrial period). To the west, on the Hardt, is the Missionshaus, with an ethnographic collection.

South of Barmen rises the Toelleturm, with fine views over the Wupper valley.

Elberfeld

Von der Heydt Museum

At Turmhof 8 is the Von der Heydt Museum (French Impressionism, 19th and 20th century German painting). To the east, at Poststrasse 11, is the Wuppertal Watch and Clock Museum (Uhrenmuseum).

On the Bundesallee is the Theatre (1966). On the Johannisberg, near the Stadthalle, is the striking modern Stadtbad (Municipal Baths, 1956).

Zoo

On the western outskirts of Elberfeld lies the Zoo (open enclosures, with some 3500 animals). To the south-east is the two-level Kiesberg Tunnel (upper carriageway 854m/934yds long, lower 1043m/1141yds).

Surroundings of Wuppertal

*Klütert Cave

In the Ennepe valley, 9km/6 miles east, is the Klütert Cave, one of the largest natural caves in Germany, with a total length of 5.2km/3¼ miles, which is used for the treatment of asthma.

*Müngsten Bridge

13km/8 miles south of Wuppertal is the Müngsten Bridge (see Solingen).

Würzburg   H 5

Land: Bavaria
Altitude: 182m/597ft
Population: 130,000

Situation and characteristics

The old Franconian episcopal city and university town of Würzburg, the main centre of the Franconian wine trade, is beautifully situated in a vineyard-fringed basin in the Main valley (see entry). High above the Main, dominating the scene, stands the medieval fortress of Marienberg.

The Town

* *Residenz

In the spacious Residenzplatz is the Residenz, the palace of the Prince-Bishops, one of the finest Baroque secular buildings in Germany (built 1719–44, mainly under the direction of Balthasar Neumann). The most notable features of the palace are the monumental staircase hall, with a huge fresco by Tiepolo, the White Hall, with Rococo stucco work, the sumptuously decorated Imperial Hall, the Hall of Mirrors and the beautiful Court Church. In the south wing is the Martin von Wagner Museum (collection of antiquities, picture gallery, print cabinet). Behind the Residenz is the Hofgarten (18th c.).

*Cathedral

To the west of the Residenz is the Cathedral (Dom; 11th–13th c.; interior destroyed by fire in 1945, restored in modern style). It contains a number of fine bishops' tombs, including those of Rudolf von Scherenberg and Lorenz von Bibra (both by Tilman Riemenschneider). In the north aisle is the Schönborn Chapel (by Balthasar Neumann, 1721–36).

Neumünsterkirche

Immediately north of the Cathedral is the Neumünsterkirche, with a Romanesque east end (11th and 13th c.) and a Baroque west end (1711–19). Under the dome are a figure of the Virgin and a crucifix, both by Riemenschneider. In the west crypt is the sarcophagus of the Irish monk St Kilian, the apostle of the Franks, who was murdered here in 689 along with his companions. In the former cloister (the "Lusamgärtlein") on the north side of the church can be seen a memorial stone commemorating Walther von der Vogelweide, the greatest German medieval poet, who is believed to have died in Würzburg about 1230.

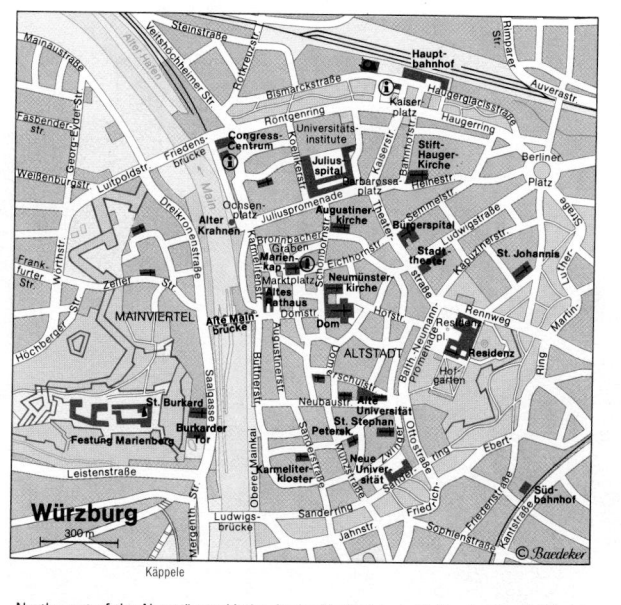

Würzburg

300m

Käppele

North-west of the Neumünsterkirche, in the Marktplatz, is St Mary's Chapel (Marienkapelle; 1377–1479; restored after 1945), the finest Late Gothic building in Würzburg, with magnificent doorways. Tomb of Balthasar Neumann (on the third pillar in the nave); monument of Konrad von Schaumberg (d. 1499) by Riemenschneider.

*St Mary's Chapel

Adjoining the chapel is the Haus zum Falken (House of the Falcon), with the finest Rococo façade in the town.

*Haus zum Falken

South-west of the Marktplatz, in Domstrasse, is the Old Town Hall (Altes Rathaus; 13th–19th c.).

Old Town Hall

On the Juliuspromenade stands the large Juliusspital, an 18th century hospital, and in nearby Theaterstrasse is the Bürgerspital, both with famous old wine-bars.

Juliusspital

On the south side of the old town is the Old University (Alte Universität; 1582–92). In the west wing is part of the University Library, in the east wing the University Church, one of the few major German Renaissance churches (now adapted for use as a concert hall, etc.). Farther south, on the Sanderring, is the New University (1892–96). Most of the University buildings lie to the east of the town.

University

The Old Main Bridge (Alte Mainbrücke), lined with Baroque statues of saints, leads to the districts on the left bank of the Main. From the bridge can be seen (to right, on the right bank of the river) the Alter Krahnen (Old Crane; 1773) and the Würzburg Congress Centre. On the left bank, below the Marienberg, are the parish church of St Burkard (11th, 12th and 15th c.) and the Burkarder Tor.

*Old Main Bridge

*Festung Marienberg

Above the banks of the Main rises the Marienberg (266m/873ft), crowned by the massive fortress which was the seat of the Prince-Bishops from the mid 13th century until the construction of the Residenz.

Residenzgarten   *In the Hofgarten, Veitshöchheim*

In the Arsenal of the fortress is the Museum of Eastern Franconia (Mainfränkisches   **Museum of
Museum), with works by artists who were either born in Franconia or worked there,   Western Franconia
including an important collection of work by Tilman Riemenschneider.

Near the keep is St Mary's Church, a Merovingian rotunda of 706. Fine views from the
Fürstengarten.

Upstream from the Marienberg is the Käppele, a picturesque pilgrimage chapel built by   *Käppele
Balthasar Neumann in 1747–50, with frescoes by Matthias Günther; beautiful views,
particularly in the evening.
From the banks of the Main a steep, shady stepped lane with Stations of the Cross leads
up to the chapel.

Along the northern outskirts of the town runs the Steinweinpfad, a wine trail through   Wine trail
some of the most famous Würzburg vineyards, with information tables and examples of
different types of vine.

Veitshöchheim

7km/4½miles north-west of Würzburg (accessible also by boat) is Schloss Veitshöchheim, a country palace of the Prince-Bishops of Würzburg (1682).

The Hofgarten, a French-style garden laid out between 1703 and 1774, is the best   *Hofgarten
preserved Rococo garden in Germany. The centrepiece of the gardens is a large artificial
lake with fountains and "Parnassus" (a sculptured group crowned by Pegasus). There is
much other Baroque sculpture in the gardens (ornamental vases, allegorical figures,
putti, etc.).

◄ *Festung Marienberg*

Xanten

Land: North Rhine-Westphalia
Altitude: 24m/79ft
Population: 17,000

Situation and
characteristics

The old town of Xanten on the Lower Rhine, originally a Roman fort, is referred to in the
"Nibelungenlied" as the birthplace of Siegfried.
It was from here that Varus set out with his three legions on the campaign which ended in
defeat in the Teutoburg Forest. In A.D. 100 Trajan founded the town of Ulpia Traiana to the
north of the original fort. The later town grew up to the south, around the graves of the
martyred St Victor and his companions.

The Town

*Cathedral

The Cathedral of St Victor (1190–1516) in the Markt, originally a monastic church, is, after
Cologne Cathedral, the finest Gothic church on the Lower Rhine. The most notable
feature of the interior is the large Altar of the Virgin (by H. Douvermann, 1525). There is a
fine cathedral treasury. On the north side of the Cathedral are the former conventual
buildings.

Regional Museum

To the south of the Cathedral, at Kurfürstenstrasse 7–9, can be found the Regional
Museum (history of the town and region).
A notable medieval building is the Gothic House at the corner of the Markt and
Kurfürstenstrasse.

*Archaeological Park

To the north of the town, beyond the main road, is the Archaeological Park, with
reconstructions of Roman buildings (amphitheatre, temple, hostelry). It is planned to

Archaeological Park and Cathedral, Xanten

extend the park to cover the whole area of the Roman settlement of Colonia Ulpia Traiana.

Zeitz

Land: Saxony-Anhalt
Altitude: 198m/650ft
Population: 43,500

The old episcopal city of Zeitz lies at the point where the Weisse Elster emerges from the hills into the Saxon Lowland.

Situation and characteristics

Sights

Schloss Moritzburg (1657–78), a Baroque palace built on the ruins of an earlier episcopal castle, is now a museum (history of the town; mining in the Zeitz–Weissenfels area; pictures, glass, pewter, porcelain, etc.).

Schloss Moritzburg

The palace church (originally a Romanesque basilica) has a 10th century crypt with the coffins of Dukes of Saxony-Zeitz, Early Gothic frescoes and the tomb of Georgius Agricola (1494–1555; physician, scientist, burgomaster of Chemnitz and the founder of mining science).

*Schlosskirche

The fine Late Gothic Town Hall (1505–09; extended 1909) has a richly decorated gable and a Ratskeller of 1505.

Town Hall

Perhaps the most interesting of the many fine Gothic and Renaissance burghers' houses in the town is the Seckendorffsches Palais (Am Brühl 11).

Seckendorffsches Palais

In Friedensplatz (the Alter Markt) stands St Michael's Church (12th c.; rebuilt in Early Gothic style *c.* 1300; restored in Late Gothic style in 1429 after a fire).

St Michael's Church

In the lower town is the Schlosskirche (originally the Cathedral, in Romanesque style; Gothicised in the 15th century and altered in the 17th century for use as the Schloss-kirche). The crypt dates from the Ottonian period (10th c.).

Schlosskirche

Of the town's old fortifications six towers (15th and 16th c.) and stretches of the town walls have survived. Under the medieval town is an extensive system of underground chambers and passages.

*Fortifications

Zittau

Land: Saxony
Altitude: 250m/820ft
Population: 40,200

Zittau (Sorbian Zitawa) lies in the "Dreiländereck" where the frontiers of Germany, Poland and Czechoslovakia meet. In the past a trading town situated on long-distance trade routes, it is now an important industrial and cultural centre.

Situation and characteristics

Sights

The signposted Zittauer Kulturpfad ("Cultural Trail") takes visitors round 51 features of interest in the old town.

"Cultural Trail"

In the Markt stands the Town Hall (Rathaus), in Italian Renaissance style (by K. F. Schinkel, 1840–45). Also in the square are the old inn Zur Sonne (*c.* 1710; Baroque), the

*Markt
Town Hall

In the Zittau Hills

Roland Fountain and Town Hall

Heffterbau

Rococo Fürstenherberge ("Prince's Lodging"; 1767) and the Noacksches Haus (1689), one of the finest Baroque patrician houses in the town.

On the west side of the square is the Roland Fountain or Mars Fountain (1585).

North-west of the Town Hall can be found the neo-classical St John's Church (by K. F. Schinkel, 1837). From the top of the tower there are fine views.

*St John's Church

In Johannisplatz is the Altes Gymnasium (Old Grammar School), with the tomb of Burgomaster Nikolaus Domspach. Close by is the Domspach-Haus (1553).

Altes Gymnasium
Domspach-Haus

In Innere Weberstrasse are a number of handsome merchants' houses. At the end of the street, outside the old town walls, is the Weberkirche (c. 1500), with a churchyard containing numbers of handsome tombs.

Weberkirche

Near the Post Office, opposite a monument to Burgomaster Ludwig Haberkom, rises the Constitution Column (Konstitutionssäule), commemorating the constitution granted to Saxony in 1831. The square is dominated by the neo-classical Johanneum, with a 56m/184ft high tower.

Constitution Column

Johanneum

South-east of the Johanneum we come to the Kreuzkirche (Holy Cross Church; 15th c.), a Late Gothic building which shows Bohemian influence in its architecture; wall paintings, Crucifixion group.

Kreuzkirche

On the Fleischerbastei (Butchers' Bastion) is a flower clock with a carillon of Meissen porcelain, a gift to the town from local craftsmen (1966).

Flower clock

In August-Bebel-Platz are the Marstall (Court Stables); the old Salt-House (1511), with a high mansard roof, now housing the Municipal Archives; the Swan, Hercules and Samaritan Woman's Fountains; and a number of handsome Renaissance and Baroque buildings, including the Sächsischer Hof.

August-Bebel-Platz

In Klosterplatz is the Klosterkirche, the former Franciscan church of SS Peter and Paul (Late Gothic, with remains of Romanesque work); reredos and pulpit of 1668, fine monuments.

Church of
SS Peter and Paul

In the cells of the Franciscan friary is the Municipal Museum (Stadtmuseum). In front of the Museum can be seen the Grüner Born, Zittau's most beautiful fountain.

Franciscan friary
Municipal Museum

On the other side of the friary building is the Heffterbau, with a superb Renaissance gable (1662). From 1699 it was used as a church for refugees who had been driven from their homes on religious grounds.

*Heffterbau

Zittauer Gebirge (Zittau Hills)

E 7

The Zittauer Gebirge, a range of sandstone hills, lies to the south of Zittau between the upper Neisse and the Lusatian Uplands. They are steeply scarped on the north side but slope gently down to the south, with a number of residual volcanic hills rising to heights of around 800m/2625ft (Lausche, 793m/2602ft; Hochwald, 749m/2457ft). There is heavy rainfall in the hills.

Situation

An old-world narrow-gauge steam railway, the Zittauer Bimmelbahn, runs between Oybin, Jonsdorf and Zittau.

*Zittauer
Bimmelbahn

Zwickau

G 7–8

Land: Saxony
Altitude: 263m/863ft
Population: 122,000

In the Schumann House

Situation and characteristics	Zwickau, birthplace of the composer Robert Schumann, lies on the river Mulde 40km/25 miles south-west of Chemnitz. The foundations of its prosperity from the Middle Ages onwards were cloth manufacture and silver-mining in the Erzgebirge.

Sights

Town Hall	In the Hauptmarkt is the Town Hall (built 1403, rebuilt in neo-Gothic style in 1862). The council chamber (originally St James's Chapel) dates from 1473–77.
*Gewandhaus	The Gewandhaus (Cloth Hall; 1522–25) is a Late Gothic building with some Renaissance features. From 1823 it was used as the municipal theatre.
Burghers' houses	There are numbers of fine burghers' houses in the Markt and in the old town. Notable among them are the Kräutergewölbe (early 16th c.) at Hauptmarkt 17–18, the Dünnebier-haus (1480; stepped gable) at Innere Dresdner Strasse 1 and the Schiffchen (c. 1485) at Münzstrasse 12.
*Schumann House	The birthplace of Robert Schumann (1810–56) at Hauptmarkt 5 is now a memorial museum and research centre.
*Cathedral	The Late Gothic Cathedral of St Mary (founded 1206; rebuilt from 1453 onwards after a number of fires) contains numerous art treasures, including a Late Gothic high altar (1479) with four scenes from the life of the Virgin by the Nürnberg artist M. Wolgemut, a portable Holy Sepulchre (1507), a Pietà by P. Breuer, an Early Renaissance pulpit (1538) and numerous monuments of the 16th and 17th centuries.
Schloss Osterstein	In the north-east of the old town stands the sombre Schloss Osterstein, built in 1590 on the site of an early 13th century castle. For many years it was used as a prison; among those confined here were Karl May, August Bebel and Rosa Luxemburg.

To the south of the Schloss is the parish church of St Catherine (founded between 1206 and 1219; rebuilt after a fire in the 14th c.), which has a fine winged altar from the Cranach workshop (1517). Thomas Müntzer preached in this church and in the Cathedral in 1520.

St Catherine's Church

At Lessingstrasse 1 is the Municipal Museum (history of the town and of coal-mining in the area, works of art and applied art; collections of minerals and fossils). In the same building are the Municipal Archives and Municipal Library (incunabula).

Municipal Museum

In the Planitz district can be found a Baroque Schloss, set in a park (tea-house, 1769). Also of interest is the village church (16th c.), with a rich interior.

Planitz

Practical Information from A to Z

Although the two parts of Germany, the Federal Republic and the former Democratic Republic, are now united, different conditions will continue to apply in certain services for a transitional period. Attention is drawn to such differences in the following notes. **N.B.**

Accommodation

See entry — Hotels

Accommodation in private homes on a bed and breakfast basis is now ubiquitous in Germany; it is particularly useful in the eastern *Länder,* where hotel accommodation is in short supply. Look for the sign "Zimmer frei" ("Room(s) free"). — Bed and breakfast

Lists of addresses can be obtained from offices of the German National Tourist Board (see Information) or regional tourist associations. — Farm holidays

Houses and flats, fully equipped for self-catering holidays, can be rented in all parts of the Federal Republic.
Further information is available from offices of the German National Tourist Board or regional tourist associations. — Self-catering

See entry — Camping and caravanning

See entry — Youth hostels

Air Travel

Germany is served by over 90 international airlines. The two national airlines, operating regular national and international services, are Lufthansa and Interflug (the former East German airline).

Germany's international airports are Berlin, Bremen, Cologne/Bonn, Dresden, Düsseldorf, Frankfurt am Main, Hamburg, Hannover, Leipzig, Munich, Münster/Osnabrück, Nürnberg, Saarbrücken and Stuttgart. — International airports

There is a wide range of services between German airports: — Domestic services
– regular services by Lufthansa, Interflug and Aero Lloyd;
– regular services to and from Berlin by Euro Berlin, Lufthansa, Interflug, Air France, Tempelhof Airways, TWA, Dan Air and British Airways;
– regular services operated by regional airlines under charter to Lufthansa;
– services with fixed departure times operated whenever there is a demand (e.g. from Frankfurt to Flensburg, Kiel, Lübeck, Münster, Kassel, Bayreuth and Hof; also summer services to the Frisian Islands, Heligoland, etc.);
– air taxi services linking all German civil airports, including regional and commercial airfields.

All German destinations served by Lufthansa from Frankfurt am Main are reached, on average, in 50 minutes; in most cases there are four flights a day. — Lufthansa services

The Lufthansa Airport Express provides rail connections between Bonn, Cologne, Düsseldorf and Frankfurt Airport and between Stuttgart and Frankfurt Airport. Meals and drinks are served to passengers at their seats and are included in the fare.

◀ *East end of Lake Constance, with the Nonnenhorn, Wasserburg and Lindau*

There is a regular airport bus transfer service between the two German airports, Schönefeld and Tegel.

Airport services

All German civil airports are linked with their local urban transport network; some also have their own feeder system (e.g. by coach) or a direct Metro service.

There are German Federal Railways offices at all airports, from which luggage can be despatched to any station.

Frankfurt Airport

Frankfurt Airport has its own station directly under the terminal building, providing excellent connections with the Federal Railways' InterCity network. There are direct services to and from 34 German and 45 European cities.

There are also direct InterCity services from Frankfurt's main railway station, which is linked to the Airport by Metro (trains every 10 minutes; journey time about 11 minutes). Tickets are issued by automatic machines (which give change).

Boat Services

Regular river, lake and coastal services are operated by various shipping lines.

Rivers and
lakes

There are river services on the Danube, Elbe, Main, Mosel, Neckar, Oder, Rhine, Saale and Weser, and lake services on Lake Constance and the Ammersee, Baldeneysee, Chiemsee, Königssee, Rursee and Starnberger See.

The KD German Rhine Line operates nineteen luxury passenger vessels on the Rhine, Main and Mosel, offering both short cruises with on-board entertainment and shore visits and longer cruises of several days' duration on the Rhine between Switzerland and Holland and on the Mosel. There are now also cruises on the Elbe. Information: G. A. Clubb Cruise Agency Ltd, 28 South Street, Epsom, Surrey KT18 7PF, tel. (0372) 742033.

On Lake Constance a fleet of some forty vessels operates regular services as well as excursions, special cruises and a car ferry service.

The "Weisse Flotte" ("White Fleet"), with headquarters in Dresden, operates scheduled services and pleasure cruises on the lakes and rivers around Berlin, cruises on the Elbe and Saale and trips round numerous lakes, particularly in the Mecklenburg lake district.

Coastal
services

There are services from Bremerhaven, Cuxhaven, Hamburg, Wilhelmshaven and other places on the North Sea coast to the Frisian Islands, and from Baltic ports along the coast of the Baltic and to the islands.

Bus Services

Bus services run jointly by the railway and postal services and by other operators supplement the rail network.
The Europa-Bus service runs regular trips for tourists along routes of particular interest. Information and booking: Deutsche Touring GmbH, Am Römerhof 17, 6000 Frankfurt am Main, tel. (069) 7 90 31.

Business Hours

See Opening Times

Camping and Caravanning

There are some 2600 camping sites in Germany with all necessary facilities, located in the most attractive and popular holiday areas. They are easily identified by blue boards carrying the international camping symbol of a black tent on a white background.

There are 400 special winter camping sites.

Allgemeiner Deutscher Automobil-Club (ADAC)
Am Westpark 8, 8000 Munich 70

Deutscher Camping-Club (DCC)
Mandlstrasse 28, 8000 Munich 40

Camping- und Caravanverband
Postfach 105, 1080 Berlin

Car Rental

Autohansa, Avis, Europa Service, Hertz, Severin, SU InterRent, Sixt-Budget and other
rental companies offer a wide range of cars for rental. There are booking offices at all
airports and main railway stations and in the larger towns.

Casinos

There are casinos (with roulette and baccarat played under international rules) at
Aachen, Bad Bentheim, Bad Dürkheim, Bad Harzburg, Bad Homburg, Bad Kissingen, Bad
Neuenahr, Bad Pyrmont, Bad Reichenhall, Bad Wiessee, Bad Zwischenahn, Baden-
Baden, Berlin, Dortmund, Garmisch-Partenkirchen, Hannover, Hittfeld (near Hamburg),
Konstanz, Lindau, Travemünde, Westerland and Wiesbaden.

Climate

The climate of Germany is temperate, and fluctuations in temperature are comparatively
slight. In winter the mountains have a deep covering of snow, and winter sports are
possible at heights from 500m/1650ft upwards. The average temperature in January (the
coldest month) is around freezing point; in the mountains it is about -10°C/+14°F. Winter
lasts from December to March, in the Alps until May.

In April skiing is still possible in the Alps, while the fruit-trees are already in blossom on
the Bergstrasse, in the Palatinate, in parts of the Black Forest and on Lake Constance.

In summer the average temperature in the valleys and plains is about 20°C/68°F. The best
time for bathing is between June and August.

Consulates

See Diplomatic and Consular Offices

Currency

The unit of currency is the German mark (DM), which consists of 100 pfennigs (Pf). There
are coins in denominations of 1, 2, 5, 10 and 50 pfennigs and 1, 2 and 5 marks and
banknotes for 5, 10, 20, 50, 100, 200, 500 and 1000 marks.

These fluctuate and current rates can be obtained from banks, exchange offices, tourist
offices and from the larger hotels. Exchange rates given by hotels are usually less
favourable than the official rates.

Customs Regulations

Import and export of currency There are no restrictions on the import or export of German marks or any other currency.

Travellers' cheques Eurocheques It is advisable to take money in the form of traveller's cheques or to use Eurocheques. Eurocheques can be cashed up to the equivalent of £100 per cheque.

Credit cards Most of the international credit cards are accepted in banks, frontier exchange offices and the larger hotels, restaurants and shops.

Loss of credit cards, etc. If credit cards, traveller's cheques, Eurocheques or a Eurocheque card are lost, the loss should be reported at once by telephone (confirmed in writing) to the issuing authority so that illicit payments can be stopped.

Customs Regulations

Personal effects, holiday equipment and sporting gear, food and fuel (including up to 10 litres in spare cans) for the journey can be taken into Germany without payment of duty. In addition visitors can take in, duty-free, specified amounts of alcoholic liquor, tobacco goods and perfumes. For goods obtained duty and tax paid within the European Community the permitted amounts are 1½ litres of spirits over 22% vol or 3 litres of spirits under 22% vol, fortified or sparkling wine; 5 litres of still wine; 90 cc of perfume; 375 cc of toilet water; and 300 cigarettes or 150 cigarillos or 75 cigars or 400 grams of tobacco. For goods obtained outside the European Community or from a duty-free shop within the Community the permitted amounts are 1 litre of spirits over 22% vol or 2 litres of spirits under 22% vol, fortified or sparkling wine; 2 litres of still wine; 60 cc of perfume; 250 cc of toilet water; and 200 cigarettes or 100 cigarillos or 50 cigars or 250 grams of tobacco. Other items (including foodstuffs) intended as gifts or for personal use or consumption may be taken in duty-free up to a value of DM810, including a maximum value of DM115 from non-Community countries.

Cycling

Bicycles for personal use may be taken into Germany duty-free and without an import licence.
In many resorts there are private bicycle hire firms. Bicycles can also be rented at some 260 stations of the Federal Railways; the charge for rail passengers is DM6 per day.

Diplomatic and Consular Offices

United Kingdom
Embassy:
Friedrich-Ebert-Allee 77, 5300 Bonn 1
Tel. (0228) 23 40 61

Embassy, Consular Section:
Uhlandstrasse 7, 1000 Berlin 12
Tel. (030) 3 09 52 92

Consulates:
Herrlichkeiten 6, Postfach 10 38 60, 2800 Bremen 1
Tel. (0421) 5 90 90

Yorckstrasse 19, 4000 Düsseldorf 30
Tel. (0211) 9 44 81

Bockenheimer Landstrasse 42, 6000 Frankfurt am Main 1
Tel. (069) 1 70 00 20

Buchenstrasse 4, 7803 Gundelfingen (Freiburg)
Tel. (0761) 58 31 17

Harvestehuder Weg 8A, 2000 Hamburg 13
Tel. (040) 44 60 71

Georgsplatz 1, 3000 Hannover 1
Tel. (0511) 1 03 22 20

United Baltic Corporation, Schleuse, P.O. Box 80 80, 2300 Kiel 17
Tel. (0431) 3 06 32

Amalienstrasse 62, 8000 Munich 40
Tel. (089) 3 81 62 80

Breite Strasse 2, 7000 Stuttgart 1
Tel. (0711) 1 62 69–0

Embassy: USA
Deichmanns Aue 29, 5300 Bonn
Tel. (0228) 33 91

Consulates:
Tempelhofer Damm 1–7, 1000 Berlin 42
Tel. (030) 8 19 64 75

Neustädtische Kirchstrasse 4–5, 1080 Berlin
Tel. (030) 2 20 27 41

Siesmayerstrasse 21, 6000 Frankfurt am Main
Tel. (069) 74 00 71

Alsterufer 27–28, 2000 Hamburg 36
Tel. (040) 44 10 61

Königinstrasse 5, 8000 Munich 22
Tel. (089) 2 30 11

Urbanstrasse 7, 7000 Stuttgart
Tel. (0711) 21 02 21

Embassy: Canada
Godesberger Allee 119, 5300 Bonn 2
Tel. (0228) 81 00 60

Consulates:
Europa-Center, 1000 Berlin 30
Tel. (030) 2 61 11 61

Immermannstrasse 3, 4000 Düsseldorf 1
Tel. (0211) 35 34 71

Maximiliansplatz 9, 8000 Munich 2
Tel. (089) 55 85 31

Electricity

Electricity supplies in Germany are 220–250 volts AC.

Power sockets are of the normal European type. Visitors from Britain, North America and other countries outside Europe should carry suitable adaptors for razors and other appliances.

Emergencies

Dial 110   Police
                                                                   Ambulance
Dial 112   Fire brigade

Events

The German National Tourist Board (GNTB) publishes a calendar of forthcoming events twice yearly, in April and October. This gives the dates of trade fairs and exhibitions, theatrical and musical performances, local and folk festivals, sporting events, conferences and congresses. It is available free of charge from GNTB offices.

Getting to Germany

By Air

There are numerous flights to German airports from many British and North American cities. Germany's busiest international airport is Frankfurt am Main, but there are also direct flights to Berlin, Cologne, Düsseldorf, Munich and other cities. From Frankfurt in particular there are excellent connecting services to other destinations.

By Car

Now that frontiers in eastern Europe have been opened up there is no difficulty about entering Germany from any side. For visitors coming from or via the United Kingdom, however, the normal point of entry will still be one of the Channel or North Sea ports. The most convenient routes to northern Germany are by way of the car ferry services to Hamburg and the Dutch and Belgian ports: Harwich to Hamburg (Scandinavian Seaways), Harwich to Hook of Holland (Sealink), Dover to Zeebrugge or Ostend (P & O European Ferries), Sheerness to Vlissingen (Olau Line), Felixstowe to Zeebrugge (P & O European Ferries), Hull to Zeebrugge or Rotterdam Europoort (North Sea Ferries). It is also possible to travel through France; the journey to southern Germany can be eased by using the Motorail service from Paris to Munich.

By Bus

In addition to numerous package tours by coach from Britain to Germany there are various regular bus services to many German towns.

Information
Eurolines
52 Grosvenor Gardens, London SW1
Tel. (071) 730 0202

By Rail

British Rail can issue tickets from main stations in Britain to main stations in Germany. Advance booking is advisable.

Information
European Rail Travel Centre
P.O. Box 303
Victoria Station, London SW1V 1JY

Hotels

Branch offices of the German National Tourist Board can supply the official German Hotel Guide (post and packing charge in Britain £3), which lists hotels and guest-houses (pensions) in Germany, with details of amenities and tariffs.

Hotels and local tourist associations publish their own lists of hotels and other accommodation.

For information about hotels in historic castles and country houses apply to German National Tourist Board offices, travel agents or the Association of German Castle Hotels:

Gast im Schloss e.V., 3526 Trendelburg 1

Room reservations can be made through the booking systems operated by hotel chains and airlines as well as through travel agencies. Many local tourist offices also run a hotel-booking system (Zimmerreservierung). The Allgemeine Deutsche Zimmer-reservierung (ADZ) operates a computerised reservation service based in Frankfurt:

ADZ
Corneliusstrasse 34, 6000 Frankfurt am Main 1
Tel. (069) 74 07 67, fax (069) 75 10 56

Information

German National Tourist Board

The central organisation responsible for the promotion of tourism in Germany is the German National Tourist Board:

Deutsche Zentrale für Tourismus (DZT)
Beethovenstrasse 69, 6000 Frankfurt am Main 1
Tel. (069) 75 72–0

The branch office of DZT in an English-speaking country is known as the German National Tourist Office.

German National Tourist Offices

German National Tourist Office
Nightingale House
65 Curzon Street
London W1Y 7PE
Tel. (071) 495 3990

German National Tourist Office
c/o German-American Chamber of Commerce
104 South Michigan Avenue, Suite 600
Chicago IL 60603
Tel. (312) 782 8557

German National Tourist Office
444 South Flower Street, Suite 2230
Los Angeles CA 90071
Tel. (213) 688 7332

German National Tourist Office
747 Third Avenue (33rd floor)
New York NY 10017
Tel. (212) 308 3300

German National Tourist Office
175 Bloor Street East
North Tower (6th floor)
Toronto, Ontario M4W 3R8
tel. (416) 968 1570

Local Tourist Offices

Aachen	Presse- und Werbeamt der Stadt Aachen, Haus Löwenstein, Am Markt 39, W-5100 Aachen, tel. (0241) 4 32 13 09
	Verkehrsverein Bad Aachen – Aachen Tourist Information, Postfach 2007, W-5100 Aachen, tel. (0241) 1 80 29 60
Alfeld	Stadtverwaltung, Rathaus, Marktplatz 1, W-3220 Alfeld (Leine), tel. (05181) 70 30
Alsfeld	Verkehrsbüro, Rittergasse 3, W-6320 Alsfeld, tel. (06631) 18 21 65
Altenberg	Stadtverwaltung Altenberg, Platz des Bergmanns, O-8242 Altenberg, tel. (052696) 42 61
Altenburg	Altenburg-Information, Markt/Weibermarkt 17, O-7400 Altenburg, tel. (0402) 31 11 45
Altötting	Verkehrsbüro, Kapellplatz 2A, W-8262 Altötting, tel. (08671) 80 68
Amberg	Verkehrsamt, Zeughausstrasse 1A, W-8450 Amberg, tel. (09621) 1 02 33
Anklam	Anklam-Information, Am Markt, Postfach 44, O-2140 Anklam, tel. (0994) 33 32/4
Annaberg-Buchholz	Reisebüro Annaberg-Buchholz, Ernst-Thälmann-Strasse 34, O-9300 Annaberg-Buchholz, tel. (0765) 26 53
Ansbach	Verkehrsamt, Martin-Lutherplatz, W-8800 Ansbach, tel. (0981) 5 12 43
Apolda	Apolda-Information, Heidenberg 41, O-5320 Apolda, tel. (0620) 53 20
Arnstadt	Arnstadt-Information, Markt 3, O-5210 Arnstadt, tel. (0618) 20 49
Arolsen	Verkehrsverwaltung, Prof.-Klapp-Strasse 14, W-3548 Arolsen, tel. (05691) 20 30
Aschaffenburg	Tourist-Information, Dalbergstrasse 6, W-8750 Aschaffenburg, tel. (06021) 3 04 26
Attendorn	Attendorner Reise- und Fremdenverkehrs GmbH, Kölner Strasse 12A, W-5952 Attendorn, tel. (02722) 30 91
Augsburg	Verkehrsverein, Bahnhofstrasse 7, W-8900 Augsburg, tel. (0821) 50 20 70
Aurich	Verkehrsverein, Am Pferdemarkt 2, W-2960 Aurich, tel. (04941) 44 64
Baden-Baden	Kurverwaltung, Augustaplatz 8, W-7570 Baden-Baden, tel. (07221) 27 52 00
Badenweiler	Kurverwaltung, Ernst-Eisenlohr-Strasse 4, W-7847 Badenweiler, tel. (07632) 7 21 10
Ballenstedt	Informationszentrum Ballenstedt, Ricarda-Huch-Strasse 13, O-4303 Ballenstedt, tel. (04 55 93) 2 63
Bamberg	Verkehrsamt, Hauptwachstrasse 16, W-8600 Bamberg, tel. (0951) 2 10 40
Bautzen	Bautzen-Information, Fleischmarkt 2–4, O-8600 Bautzen, tel. (054) 4 20 16
Bayreuth	Verkehrsverein, Luitpoldplatz 9, W-8580 Bayreuth, tel. (0921) 8 85 88
Berchtesgaden	Kurdirektion, Königseer Strasse 2, W-8240 Berchtesgaden, tel. (08652) 50 11
Berlin (West)	Verkehrsamt Berlin im Europa-Center, Budapester Strasse 45, W-1000 Berlin 30, tel. 2 62 60 31
	Verkehrsamt im Bahnhof Zoo, tel. 3 13 90 63/4
	Verkehrsamt im Flughafen Tegel (Haupthalle), tel. 41 01 31 45

(Dialling code from E. Germany and E. Berlin to W. Berlin 849; dialling code from W. Germany to W. Berlin 030; within W. Berlin no dialling code.)

Berlin-Information am Fernsehturm, Panoramastrasse 1, O-1020 Berlin, tel. (02) 2 12 46 25 and 2 12 45 12 — **Berlin** (East)

Bernburg-Information, Liebknechtplatz 1, O-4350 Bernburg, tel. (0447) 20 31 — **Bernburg**

Fremdenverkehrsstelle, Theaterstrasse 6, W-7950 Biberach an der Riss, tel. (07351) 5 14 36 — **Biberach**

Tourist-Information, Am Bahnhof 6, W-4800 Bielefeld 1, tel. (0521) 17 88 44 — **Bielefeld**

Stadtverwaltung, Rathaus, Karlstrasse 2, W-7902 Blaubeuren, tel. (07344) 1 30 — **Blaubeuren**

Verkehrsverein, Hauptbahnhof, Kurt-Schumacher-Platz, W-4630 Bochum 1, tel. (0234) 1 30 31 — **Bochum**

Tourist-Information, Münsterstrasse 20, W-5300 Bonn 1, tel. (0228) 77 34 66 — **Bonn**

Reisebüro Bottrop, Gladbecker Strasse 9, W-4250 Bottrop, tel. (02041) 2 70 11 — **Bottrop**

Stadtverwaltung Brandenburg, Auskunftsstelle, O-1800 Brandenburg, tel. (038) 3 00 — **Brandenburg**

Verkehrsverein, Hauptbahnhof, W-3300 Braunschweig, tel. (0531) 7 92 37 — **Braunschweig**

Verkehrsverein, Hillmannplatz 6, W-2800 Bremen 1, tel. (0421) 3 08 00–0 — **Bremen**

Verkehrsamt, Van-Ronzelen-Strasse 2, W-2850 Bremerhaven, tel. (0471) 5 90 22 43 — **Bremerhaven**

Stadtinformation, Am Alten Schloss 2, W-7520 Bruchsal, tel. (07251) 7 27 71 — **Bruchsal**

Verkehrsverein, Markt 6, W-3100 Celle, tel. (05141) 12 12 — **Celle**

Chemnitz-Information, Strasse der Nationen 3, O-9001 Chemnitz, tel. (071) 6 20 51; postal address Postfach 440, O-9010 Chemnitz — **Chemnitz**

Verkehrsamt, Herrngasse 4, W-8630 Coburg, tel. (09561) 7 41 80 — **Coburg**

Verkehrsamt, Unter Fettenhennen 9, W-5000 Cologne 1, tel. (0221) 2 21 33 45 — **Cologne**

Cottbus-Information, Altmarkt 29, O-7500 Cottbus, tel. (059) 2 42 54 — **Cottbus**

Stadtverwaltung, Grüner Weg 42, W-2190 Cuxhaven, tel. (04721) 1 20 — **Cuxhaven**

Verkehrsamt, Luisenplatz 5, W-6100 Darmstadt, tel. (06151) 13 27 80 — **Darmstadt**

Verkehrsverein, Verkehrspavillon am Bahnhof, W-2870 Delmenhorst, tel. (04221) 1 71 17 — **Delmenhorst**

Dessau-Information, Friedrich-Naumann-Strasse 12, Postfach 30, O-4500 Dessau, tel. (047) 46 61 — **Dessau**

Verkehrsamt, Rathaus, Lange Strasse, W-4930 Detmold, tel. (05231) 76 73 28 — **Detmold**

Verkehrsamt, Marktplatz, W-8804 Dinkelsbühl, tel. (09851) 9 02 40 — **Dinkelsbühl**

Verkehrsamt, Karlstrasse 58, W-7710 Donaueschingen, tel. (0771) 38 34 — **Donaueschingen**

Verkehrsamt, Rathausgasse 1, W-8850 Donauwörth, tel. (0906) 78 91 45 — **Donauwörth**

Verkehrsverein, Königswall 18, W-4600 Dortmund 1, tel. (0231) 54 22 21 64 — **Dortmund**

Dresden-Information, Prager Strasse 10–11, O-8010 Dresden, tel. (051) 4 95 50 25 — **Dresden**

Information

Duderstadt	Fremdenverkehrsamt, Rathaus, Marktstrasse 66, W-3408 Duderstadt, tel. (05527) 84 12 00
Duisburg	Duisburger Werbe- und Touristik GmbH, Königstrasse 53, W-4100 Duisburg, tel. (0203) 2 83 21 89
Düsseldorf	Verkehrsverein, Konrad-Adenauer-Platz (corner of Immermannstrasse), W-4000 Düsseldorf 1, tel. (0211) 35 05 05
Eberswalde-Finow	Eberswalde-Finow-Information, Wilhelm-Pieck-Strasse 26, O-1300 Oberswalde-Finow, tel. (0371) 2 31 68
Eichstätt	Verkehrsbüro, Domplatz 18, W-8078 Eichstätt, tel. (08421) 79 77
Eisenach	Eisenach-Information, Bahnhofstrasse 3–6, O-5900 Eisenach, tel. (0623) 48 95, 61 61 and 29 34
Eisenberg	Stadtverwaltung, Hauptamt, Postfach 63, Markt 27, O-6520 Eisenberg, tel. (0798) 4 04/5
Eisenhüttenstadt	Veranstaltungsbüro Eisenhüttenstadt, Fischerstrasse 15, O-1220 Eisenhüttenstadt, tel. (0375) 28 36
Eisleben	Eisleben-Information, Hallesche Strasse 6, O-4250 Eisleben, tel. (0443) 21 24
Emden	Verkehrsverein, Am Delft 30A, W-2970 Emden, tel. (04921) 3 25 28
Erfurt	Erfurt-Information, Bahnhofstrasse 37, Postfach 838, O-5020 Erfurt, tel. (061) 2 62 67
Erlangen	Verkehrsamt, Rathausplatz 1, W-8520 Erlangen, tel. (09131) 2 50 74
Essen	Verkehrsverein, Freiheit (in Hauptbahnhof, south side), W-4300 Essen 1, tel. (0201) 23 54 27 and 8 10 60 82
Esslingen	Kultur- und Freizeitamt, Marktplatz 16, W-7300 Esslingen, tel. (0711) 3 51 24 41
Ettal	Gemeindeverwaltung, Ammergauer Strasse 8, W-8107 Ettal, tel. (08822) 5 34
Flensburg	Verkehrsverein, Norderstrasse 6, W-2390 Flensburg, tel. (0461) 2 30 90
Frankfurt am Main	Tourist-Information, Hauptbahnhof (opposite Platform 23), W-6000 Frankfurt am Main, tel. (069) 21 23 88 49
	Verkehrsamt, Gutleut-Strasse 7–9, W-6000 Frankfurt am Main, tel. (069) 21 23 88 00
	Tourist-Information Römer, Römerberg 27, tel. (069) 21 23 87 08/09
	Tourist-Information Flughafen, Arrival Hall B, tel. (069) 69 31 53
Frankfurt an der Oder	Frankfurt-Information, Rosa-Luxemburg-Strasse 6, O-1200 Frankfurt an der Oder, tel. (030) 2 22 49
Freiberg	Freiberg-Information, Wallstrasse 24, O-9200 Freiberg, tel. (0762) 36 02
Freiburg im Breisgau	Verkehrsamt, Rotteckring 14, W-7800 Freiburg im Breisgau, tel. (0761) 2 16 32 89
Freising	Stadtverwaltung, Rathaus, Obere Hauptstrasse 2, W-8050 Freising, tel. (08161) 5 40
Freudenstadt	Kurverwaltung, Promenadenplatz 1, W-7290 Freudenstadt, tel. (07441) 86 40
Friedrichshafen	Tourist-Information, Friedrichstrasse 18, W-7990 Friedrichshafen, tel. (07541) 2 17 29
Fulda	Verkehrsbüro, Schloss-strasse 1, W-6400 Fulda, tel. (0661) 10 23 45

Verkehrsverein, Bahnhofplatz 8B, W-8510 Fürth, tel. (0911) 77 66 82 — **Fürth**

Kurverwaltung, Augsburger-Tor-Platz 1, W-8958 Füssen, tel. (08362) 70 77 — **Füssen**

Kurverwaltung, Stiftsfreiheit 12, W-3353 Bad Gandersheim, tel. (05382) 7 34 40 — **Bad Gandersheim**

Verkehrsamt, Bahnhofstrasse 34, W-8100 Garmisch-Partenkirchen, tel. (08821) 1 80 22 — **Garmisch-Partenkirchen**

Verkehrsverein, Hans-Sachs-Haus, Ebertstrasse, W-4650 Gelsenkirchen, tel. (0209) 2 33 76 — **Gelsenkirchen**

Gera-Information, Dr-Rudolf-Breitscheid-Strasse 1, Postfach I-146, O-6500 Gera, tel. (070) 2 48 13 and 2 64 32 — **Gera**

Verkehrsamt, Berliner Platz 2, W-6300 Giessen, tel. (0641) 3 06 24 89 — **Giessen**

Tourist-Information, Cardenap 1, W-3170 Gifhorn, tel. (05371) 8 81 75 — **Gifhorn**

Verkehrsamt, Marktstrasse 2, W-7320 Göppingen, tel. (07161) 6 52 92 — **Göppingen**

Görlitz-Information, Leninplatz 29, O-8900 Görlitz, tel. (055) 53 91 — **Görlitz**

Tourist-Information, Markt 7, W-3380 Goslar, tel. (05321) 28 46 — **Goslar**

Gotha-Information, Hauptmarkt 2, Postfach 109/110, O-5800 Gotha, tel. (0622) 40 36 — **Gotha**

Fremdenverkehrsverein, Altes Rathaus, Markt 9, W-3400 Göttingen, tel. (0551) 5 40 00 — **Göttingen**

Greifswald-Information, Strasse der Freundschaft 126, O-2200 Greifswald, tel. (0822) 34 60 — **Greifswald**

Greiz-Information, Alte Wache, Burgplatz, Postfach 231, O-6600 Greiz, tel. (0793) 65 37 — **Greiz**

Güstrow-Information, Gleviner Strasse 33, O-2600 Güstrow, tel. (0851) 6 10 23 — **Güstrow**

Verkehrsverein, Berliner Strasse 70, W-4830 Gütersloh, tel. (05241) 82 27 49 — **Gütersloh**

Verkehrsamt, Friedrich-Ebert-Platz, W-5800, tel. (02331) 1 35 78 — **Hagen**

Stadtverwaltung, Domplatz 16–17, O-3600 Halberstadt, tel. (0926) 5 83 16 — **Halberstadt**

Halle-Information, Kleinschmieden 6 (corner of Grosse Steinstrasse), Postfach 134, O-4010 Halle (Saale), tel. (046) 2 33 40 — **Halle**

Tourismus-Zentrale Hamburg, Burchardstrasse 14, W-2000 Hamburg 1, tel. (040) 3 00 51–242 — **Hamburg**

Other tourist information offices:
in Airport, tel. (040) 3 00 51–240;
on Harbour, tel. (040) 3 00 51–200;
in Hanseviertel, tel. (040) 3 00 51–220;
in Hauptbahnhof, tel. (040) 3 00 51–230

Verkehrsverein, Deisterallee, W-3250 Hameln, tel. (05151) 20 25 17 — **Hameln**

Städtisches Verkehrsbüro, Altstädter Markt 1, W-6450 Hanau, tel. (06181) 25 24 00 — **Hanau**

Verkehrsbüro, Ernst-August-Platz 8, W-3000 Hannover 1, tel. (0511) 1 68 23 19 — **Hannover**

Verkehrsamt, Marktplatz 1, W-7450 Hechingen, tel. (07471) 18 51 13 — **Hechingen**

Verkehrsverein, Friedrich-Ebert-Anlage 2, W-6900 Heidelberg, tel. (06221) 1 08 21 — **Heidelberg**

Information

Heilbronn	Verkehrsamt, Rathaus, W-7100 Heilbronn, tel. (07131) 56 22 70
Heiligenstadt	Heiligenstadt-Information, Kasseler Tor 18, O-5630 Heilbad Heiligenstadt, tel. (0629) 37 88
Heligoland	Kurverwaltung, Rathaus, Lung Wai 28, W-2192 Heligoland, tel. (04725) 8 08 50
Helmstedt	Verkehrsverein, Rathaus, Markt 1, W-3330 Helmstedt, tel. (05351) 1 73 33
Herford	Verkehrsamt, Fürstaustrasse 7, W-4900 Herford, tel. (05221) 5 14 15
Bad Hersfeld	Verkehrsbüro, Am Markt, W-6430 Bad Hersfeld, tel. (06621) 20 12 74
Hildesheim	Verkehrsverein, Am Ratsbauhof 1C, W-3200 Hildesheim, tel. (05121) 1 59 95
Hof	Stadtverwaltung, Rathaus, Klosterstrasse 1, W-8670 Hof (Saale), tel. (09281) 81 51
Bad Homburg	Verkehrsamt, Kurhaus, Louisenstrasse 58, W-6380 Bad Homburg, tel. (06172) 12 13 10
Höxter	Verkehrsamt, Am Rathaus 7, W-3470 Höxter, tel. (05271) 6 34 31
Hoyerswerda	Stadtverwaltung, Platz der Roten Armee 1, O-7700 Hoyerswerda, tel. (0582) 87 14
Husum	Verkehrsamt, Rathaus, Grasserstrasse 25, W-2250 Husum, tel. (04841) 66 61 33
Idar-Oberstein	Verkehrsamt, Bahnhofstrasse 13, W-6580 Idar-Oberstein, tel. (06781) 2 70 25
Ilmenau	Ilmenau-Information, Ernst-Thälman-Strasse 2, O-6300 Ilmenau, tel. (0672) 23 58
Ingolstadt	Verkehrsamt, Hallstrasse 5, W-8070 Ingolstadt, tel. (0841) 30 54 15
Iserlohn	Verkehrsamt, Konrad-Adenauer-Ring 15, W-5860 Iserlohn, tel. (02371) 1 32 33
Jena	Jena-Information, Neugasse 7, O-6900 Jena, tel. (078) 2 46 71
Kaiserslautern	Verkehrsamt, Neues Rathaus, W-6750 Kaiserslautern, tel. (0631) 8 52 23 17
Kamenz	Reisebüro Schindler, Pulsnitzer Strasse 10, O-8290 Kamenz, tel. (0525) 65 35
Karlsruhe	Verkehrsverein, Bahnhofplatz 6, W-7500 Karlsruhe, tel. (0721) 3 55 30
Kassel	Tourist-Information, in Hauptbahnhof, W-3500 Kassel, tel. (0561) 1 34 43
Kempten	Verkehrsamt, Rathausplatz 29, W-8960 Kempten, tel. (0831) 2 52 52 37
Kiel	Verkehrsverein, Sophienblatt 30, W-2300 Kiel, tel. (0431) 6 22 30
Kirchheim unter Teck	Verkehrsverein, Alleenstrasse 85, W-7312 Kirchheim unter Teck, tel. (07021) 30 27
Bad Kissingen	Kurverwaltung, Am Kurgarten 1, W-8730 Bad Kissingen, tel. (0971) 8 04 80
Kleinwalsertal	Verkehrsamt, Walserhaus, W-8985 Hirschegg, tel. (08329) 5 11 40
Kleve	Verkehrsamt, Kavarinerstrasse 20, W-4190 Kleve, tel. (0282) 8 42 67
Klingenthal	Fremdenverkehrsbüro, Kirchstrasse 6, O-9650 Klingenthal, tel. (07637) 24 94
Koblenz	Verkehrsamt, Pavillon am Hauptbahnhof, W-5400 Koblenz, tel. (0261) 3 13 04
Konstanz	Tourist-Information, Bahnhofplatz 13, W-7750 Konstanz, tel. (07531) 28 43 76
Köthen	Köthen-Information, Weintraubenstrasse 8, O-4370 Köthen, tel. (0445) 37 67

Stadtverwaltung, Markt 2, O-2602 Krakow, tel. (085197) 23 35 — **Krakow am See**

Verkehrsverein, Seidenweberhaus, Theaterplatz 1, W-4150 Krefeld, tel. (02151) 2 92 90 — **Krefeld**

Stadtverwaltung, Strasse des Friedens, O-1910 Kyritz, tel. (0365) 3 27 — **Kyritz**

Verkehrsamt, Hubert-von-Herkomer-Strasse, W-8910 Landsberg am Lech, tel. (08191) 12 82 46 — **Landsberg am Lech**

Verkehrsverein, Altstadt 315, W-8300 Landshut, tel. (0871) 2 30 31 — **Landshut**

Stadtverwaltung, O-4204 Bad Lauchstädt, tel. (044295) 2 05 — **Bad Lauchstädt**

Verkehrsbüro, Mühlenstrasse, W-2950 Leer, tel. (0491) 6 10 71 — **Leer**

Leipzig-Information, Sachsenplatz 1, O-7010 Leipzig, tel. (041) 7 95 90; Leipziger Messeamt (information about Trade Fairs), Markt 11–15, tel. 88 30; Reisebüro (room reservations), Hauptbahnhof (east side), tel. 7 92 12 95 and 7 92 12 97 — **Leipzig**

Verkehrsamt, Haus Wipperman, Kramerstrasse, W-4920 Lemgo, tel. (05261) 21 33 47 — **Lemgo**

Verkehrsamt, Hospitalstrasse 2, W-6250 Limburg an der Lahn, tel. (06431) 20 32 22 — **Limburg an der Lahn**

Verkehrsverein, Bahnhofplatz, W-8990 Lindau, tel. (08382) 50 22 — **Lindau**

Verkehrsverein, Lange Strasse 14, W-4780 Lippstadt, tel. (02941) 5 85 15 — **Lippstadt**

Löbau-Information, Rittergasse 2, O-8700 Löbau, tel. (0521) 7 11 76 — **Löbau**

Stadtverwaltung, O-7550 Lübben (Spreewald), tel. (0586) 1 31 — **Lübben**

Stadtverwaltung, O-7543 Lübbenau (Spreewald), tel. (05887) 81 01 — **Lübbenau**

Verkehrsverein, Breite Strasse 75, W-2400 Lübeck, tel. (0451) 7 23 00; Amt für Lübeck-Werbung und Tourismus, Beckergrube 95, tel. 1 22 81 00 (also information on Bremen and Hamburg) — **Lübeck**

Verkehrsamt, Wilhelmstrasse 12, W-7140 Ludwigsburg, tel. (07141) 91 02 52 — **Ludwigsburg**

Verkehrsverein, Pavillon am Hauptbahnhof, W-6700 Ludwigshafen am Rhein, tel. (0621) 51 20 35 — **Ludwigshafen am Rhein**

Stadtverwaltung, Wilhelm-Pieck-Strasse, O-2800 Ludwigslust, tel. (0852) 46 71 — **Ludwigslust**

Verkehrsverein, Marktplatz, W-2120, tel. (04131) 3 22 00 — **Lüneburg**

Magdeburg-Information, Alter Markt 9, O-3010 Magdeburg, tel. (091) 3 53 52 — **Magdeburg**

Verkehrsverein, Bahnhofstrasse 15, W-6500 Mainz, tel. (06131) 23 37 41 — **Mainz**

Verkehrsverein, Bahnhofplatz 1, W-6800 Mannheim 1, tel. (0621) 10 10 11 — **Mannheim**

Verkehrsamt (at Hauptbahnhof), Neue Kasseler Strasse 1, W-3550 Marburg, tel. (06421) 20 12 62 and 20 12 49 — **Marburg**

Kur- und Verkehrsverwaltung, Kirchstrasse 4, W-7758 Meersburg, tel. (07532) 8 23 83 — **Meersburg**

Stadtverwaltung, Postfach 291, O-6100 Meiningen, tel. (0676) 5 01 — **Meiningen**

Meissen-Information, An der Frauenkirche 3, O-8250 Meissen, tel. (053) 44 70 — **Meissen**

Verkehrsamt, Ulmer Strasse 9, W-8940 Memmingen, tel. (08331) 85 01 72 — **Memmingen**

Information

Bad Mergentheim	Verkehrsamt, Marktplatz 3, W-6990 Bad Mergentheim, tel. (07931) 5 71 35
Merseburg	Merseburg-Information, Bahnhofstrasse 17, O-4200 Merseburg, tel. (0442) 32 59
Miltenberg	Tourist-Information, Rathaus, Engelsplatz 69, W-8760 Miltenberg, tel. (09371) 40 01 19
Minden	Verkehrsamt, Grosser Domhof 3, W-4950 Minden, tel. (0571) 8 93 85
Mittenwald	Kurdirektion, Rathaus, Dammkarstrasse 3, W-8102 Mittenwald, tel. (08823) 3 39 81
Mönchengladbach	Verkehrsverein, Bismarckstrasse 23, W-4050 Mönchengladbach, tel. (02161) 2 20 01
Mühlhausen	Mühlhausen-Information, Görmarstrasse 57, O-5700 Mühlhausen, tel. (0625) 29 12
Mühlheim an der Ruhr	Verkehrsverein, Rathaus, Ruhrstrasse 32, W-4330 Mülheim an der Ruhr, tel. (0208) 4 55 90 16
Münden	Verkehrsverein, Rathaus, W-3510 Münden, tel. (05541) 7 53 13
Munich	Verkehrsamt, Sendlinger Strasse 1, W-8000 Munich 2, tel. (089) 2 39 11
Münster	Verkehrsverein, Berliner Platz 22, W-4400 Münster, tel. (0251) 51 01 80
Bad Nauheim	Stadtverwaltung, Friedrichstrasse 3, W-6350 Bad Nauheim, tel. (06032) 34 31
Naumburg	Naumburg-Information, Lindenring 38, O-4800 Naumburg (Saale), tel. (0454) 25 14
Neubrandenburg	Neubrandenburg-Information, Ernst-Thälmann-Strasse 35, O-2000 Neubrandenburg, tel. (090) 61 87
Neuruppin	Stadtverwaltung, Wichmannstrasse 8, O-1950 Neuruppin, tel. (0362) 24 38
Neuss	Verkehrsverein, Friedrichstrasse 40, W-4040 Neuss, tel. (02101) 27 98 17
Neustrelitz	Stadtverwaltung, Gewerbeamt, Markt 1, O-2080 Neustrelitz, tel. (0991) 49 21
Nordhausen	Nordhausen-Information, Zentraler Platz (postal address Töpferstrasse 42), O-5500 Nordhausen, tel. (0628) 84 33
Nördlingen	Verkehrsamt, Marktplatz 2, W-8860 Nördlingen, tel. (09081) 8 41 16
Nürnberg	Tourist-Information, Hauptbahnhof, W-8500 Nürnberg, tel. (0911) 23 36 32; Congress- und Tourismus-Zentrale, Verkehrsverein, Frauentorgraben 3, W-8500 Nürnberg 70, tel. 23 36–0
Oberammergau	Verkehrsbüro, Eugen-Papst-Strasse 9A, W-8103 Oberammergau, tel. (08822) 10 21
Oberhof	Oberhof-Information/Kurverwaltung, Haus der Freundschaft, O-6055 Oberhof, tel. (06682) 3 97
Oberstdorf	Verkehrsamt & Kurverwaltung, Marktplatz 7, W-8980 Oberstdorf, tel. (08322) 70 00
Offenbach am Main	Verkehrsbüro, Am Stadthof 17, W-6050 Offenbach am Main, tel. (069) 80 65 29 46
Offenburg	Verkehrsamt, Gärtnerstrasse 6, W-7600 Offenburg, tel. (0781) 8 22 53
Oldenburg	Verkehrsverein, Lange Strasse 3, W-2900 Oldenburg, tel. (0441) 2 50 96
Oranienburg	Stadtverwaltung, Strasse des Friedens 13, O-1400 Oranienburg, tel. (03271) 50 71
Osnabrück	Verkehrsamt, Markt 22, W-4500 Osnabrück, tel. (0541) 32 31
Paderborn	Verkehrsverein, Marienplatz 2A, W-4790 Paderborn, tel. (05251) 2 64 61

Stadtverwaltung, O-2100 Pasewalk, tel. (0995) 50 61 — Pasewalk

Fremdenverkehrsverein, Rathausplatz 3, W-8390 Passau, tel. (0851) 3 34 21 — Passau

Stadtinformation, Neues Rathaus, Marktplatz 1, W-7530 Pforzheim, tel. (07231) 39 21 90 — Pforzheim

Verkehrsamt, Vilstalstrasse, Ried, W-8962 Pfronten, tel. (08363) 50 44 — Pfronten

Verkehrsamt, Dankelsbachstrasse 19, W-6780 Pirmasens, tel. (06331) 8 44 45 — Pirmasens

Sächsische Schweiz-Information, O-8300 Pirna, tel. (056) 8 52 12 — Pirna

Plauen-Information, Rädelstrasse 2, O-9000 Plauen, tel. (075) 2 49 45 — Plauen

Potsdam-Information, Friedrich-Ebert-Strasse 5, O-1561 Potsdam, tel. (033) 2 30 12 — Potsdam

Uckermark-Information, Langer Markt 12, Postfach 20, O-2130 Prenzlau, tel. (0992) 27 81 — Prenzlau

Gemeindeverwaltung, Gemeindeplatz 1, O-2383 Ostseebad Prerow, tel. (08283) 2 26 — Prerow

Quedlinburg-Information, Markt 12, O-4300 Quedlinburg, tel. (0455) 28 66 (also information on Gernrode) — Quedlinburg

Stadtverwaltung, Leninplatz 1, O-4240 Querfurt, tel. (04430) 51 71 — Querfurt

Stadtverwaltung, Kaiserstrasse 91, W-7550 Rastatt, tel. (07222) 38 50 — Rastatt

Verkehrsamt, Marienplatz 54, W-7980 Ravensburg, tel. (0751) 8 23 24 — Ravensburg

Stadtverwaltung, Rathaus, W-4350 Recklinghausen, tel. (02361) 58 71 — Recklinghausen

Tourist-Information, Altes Rathaus, W-8400 Regensburg, tel. (0941) 5 07 21 41 — Regensburg

Kur- und Verkehrsverein, in Kurgastzentrum, Wittelsbacherstrasse 15, W-8230 Bad Reichenhall, tel. (08651) 30 03 — Bad Reichenhall

Verkehrsamt, Rathaus, W-5630 Remscheid, tel. (02191) 44 22 52 — Remscheid

Verkehrsamt, Rathaus, W-2370 Rendsburg, tel. (04331) 20 62 22 — Rendsburg

Verkehrsamt, Kronprinzenbau, Listplatz 1, W-7410 Reutlingen, tel. (07121) 30 35 26 — Reutlingen

Verkehrsamt, in Stadthalle, Kufsteiner Strasse 4, W-8200 Rosenheim, tel. (08031) 3 70 80 — Rosenheim

Rostock-Information, Schnickmannstrasse 13–14, O-2500 Rostock, tel. (081) 3 46 02 und 2 52 60; Auskunftstelle, Lange Strasse 5, tel. 2 26 19 — Rostock

Verkehrsamt, Marktplatz, W-8803 Rothenburg ob der Tauber, tel. (09861) 4 04 92 — Rothenburg

Verkehrsbüro, Altes Rathaus, Hauptstrasse 21, W-7210 Rottweil, tel. (0741) 49 42 80 — Rottweil

Saalfeld-Information, Blankenburger Strasse 4, O-6800 Saalfeld, tel. (0792) 39 50 — Saalfeld

Verkehrsverein, Rathausplatz, W-6600 Saarbrücken, tel. (0681) 3 69 01 — Saarbrücken

Bad-Salzungen-Information, Leninplatz, O-6200 Bad Salzungen, tel. (0673) 25 09 — Bad Salzungen

Reisebüro Salzwedel, Strasse der Freundschaft 41, O-3560 Salzwedel, tel. (0923) 23 01 — Salzwedel

Sangerhausen-Information, Göpenstrasse 19, Postfach 55, O-4700 Sangerhausen, tel. (0456) 25 75 — Sangerhausen

Information

Schleiz	Stadtverwaltung, O-6550 Schleiz, tel. (0794) 25 71
Schleswig	Touristbüro, Plessenstrasse 7, W-2380 Schleswig, tel. (04621) 81 42 26
Schliersee	Kurverwaltung, Bahnhofstrasse 11A, W-8162 Schliersee, tel. (08026) 40 69
Schmalkalden	Schmalkalden-Information, Mohrengasse 2, O-6080 Schmalkalden, tel. (0670) 31 82
Bad Schmiedeberg	Stadtverwaltung, Rathaus, O-4603 Bad Schmiedeberg, tel. (045195) 3 31
Schneeberg	Stadtverwaltung, Markt 1, O-9412 Schneeberg, tel. (076191) 22 51
Schwäbisch Gmünd	Verkehrsverein, Johannisplatz 3, W-7070 Schwäbisch Gmünd, tel. (07171) 6 62 44
Schwäbisch Hall	Informationsamt, Am Markt 9, W-7170 Schwäbisch Hall, tel. (0791) 75 12 46
Schwarzenberg	Stadtverwaltung, Strasse der Einheit 20, O-9430 Schwarzenberg, tel. (07618) 41 41
Schwedt	Schwedt-Information, Ernst-Thälmann-Strasse 30, O-1330 Schwedt, tel. (052597) 2 34 56
Schweinfurt	Verkehrsverein, Brückenstrasse 14, W-8720 Schweinfurt, tel. (09721) 5 14 98
Schwerin	Schwerin-Information, Markt 11, O-2750 Schwerin, tel. (084) 8 23 14
Seiffen	Fremdenverkehrsamt, O-9335 Kurort Seiffen, tel. (076692) 2 18
Siegen	Verkehrsamt, Rathaus, Markt 2, W-5900 Siegen, tel. (0271) 59 33 16
Sigmaringen	Verkehrsamt, Schwabstrasse 1, W-7480 Sigmaringen, tel. (07571) 10 62 23
Singen	Verkehrsamt, August-Ruf-Strasse 7, W-7700 Singen (Hohentwiel), tel. (07731) 8 54 73
Soest	Verkehrsamt, Am Seel 5, W-4770 Soest, tel. (02921) 10 33 23
Solingen	Stadtinformation, Potsdamer Strasse 41, W-5650 Solingen, tel. (0212) 2 90 23 33
Sonthofen	Verkehrsamt, Rathausplatz 3, W-8972 Sonthofen, tel. (08321) 7 62 91
Speyer	Verkehrsamt, Maximilianstrasse 11, W-6720 Speyer, tel. (06232) 1 43 95
Stade	Verkehrsamt, Bahnhofstrasse 3, W-2160 Stade, tel. (04141) 40 15 50
Starnberg	Verkehrsverband, Kirchplatz 3, W-8130 Starnberg, tel. (08151) 1 32 74
Stendal	Stendal-Information, Kornmarkt 8, O-3500 Stendal, tel. (0921) 21 61 86
Stolpen	Stadtverwaltung, Markt 1, O-8350 Stolpen, tel. (052893) 63 41 and 63 42
Stralsund	Stralsund-Information, Alter Markt 15, O-2300 Stralsund, tel. (0821) 24 39
Straubing	Verkehrsamt, Theresienplatz 20, W-8440 Straubing, tel. (09421) 1 63 07
Stuttgart	Verkehrsamt, Klett-Passage, Hauptbahnhof, W-7000 Stuttgart 10, tel. (0711) 2 22 82 40; Verkehrsamt, Lautenschlagerstrasse 3, W-7000 Stuttgart 10, tel. 22 28–0
Suhl	Suhl-Information, Steinweg 1, Postfach 141, O-6000 Suhl, tel. (066) 2 00 52
Sylt	See Westerland
Tangermünde	Stadtverwaltung, O-3504 Tangermünde, tel. (09218) 9 71–9 73
Tegernsee	Kuramt, in Haus des Gastes, Hauptstrasse 2, W-8180 Tegernsee, tel. (08022) 18 01 40

Thale-Information, Postfach 17, O-4308 Thale (Harz), tel. (04550) 25 97 — **Thale**

Kurverwaltung, Ludwigstrasse 11, W-8170 Bad Tölz, tel. (08041) 7 00 71 — **Bad Tölz**

Reisewelt-Reisebüro, Strasse der Opfer des Faschismus 9, Postfach 125, O-7290 Torgau, tel. (0407) 24 33 — **Torgau**

Tourist-Information, An der Porta Nigra, W-5500 Trier, tel. (0651) 4 80 71 — **Trier**

Verkehrsverein, an der Neckarbrücke (Eberhardsbrücke), W-7400 Tübingen, tel. (07071) 3 50 11 — **Tübingen**

Kurverwaltung, Landungsplatz 14, W-7750 Überlingen, tel. (07551) 40 41 — **Überlingen**

Verkehrsbüro, Münsterplatz 51, W-7900 Ulm, tel. (0731) 6 41 61 — **Ulm**

Verkehrsamt, Ostertorstrasse 7A, W-2810 Verden (Aller), tel. (04231) 1 23 17 — **Verden (Aller)**

Verkehrsamt, in Schwenningen, W-7730 Villingen-Schwenningen, tel. (07721) 8 23 11 — **Villingen-Schwenningen**

Gästeamt, in Rathaus, W-7988 Wangen im Allgäu, tel. (07522) 7 42 11 — **Wangen im Allgäu**

Verkehrsbüro, in Rathaus, W-8090 Wasserburg am Inn, tel. (08071) 1 05 22 — **Wasserburg am Inn**

Weimar-Information, Markt 15, O-5300 Weimar, tel. (0621) 7 22 33 — **Weimar**

Weissenfels-Information, Nikolaistrasse 37, O-4850 Weissenfels, tel. (0453) 30 70 — **Weissenfels**

Stadtverwaltung, Rathaus, Markt 1, O-3700 Wernigerode, tel. (0927) 35 40; Kurverwaltung, Klint 10, tel. 3 20 40; Reisebüro, Breite Strasse 35, tel. 3 21 46 — **Wernigerode**

Fremden-Verkehrs-Zentrale, Am Bundesbahnhof, W-2290 Westerland (Sylt), tel. (04651) 2 40 01 — **Westerland (Sylt)**

Verkehrsamt, Domplatz 8, W-6330 Wetzlar, tel. (06441) 40 53 38 — **Werzlar**

Verkehrsbüro, Rheinstrasse 15, W-6200 Wiesbaden, tel. (06121) 31 28 47 — **Wiesbaden**

Verkehrsbüro, König-Karl-Strasse 7, W-7547 Wildbad, tel. (07081) 1 02 80 — **Wildbad**

Wilhelmshaven-Information, Börsenstrasse 55B, W-2940 Wilhelmshaven, tel. (04421) 2 62 61 — **Wilhelmshaven**

Wismar-Information, Bohrstrasse 5A, O-2400 Wismar, tel. (0824) 29 58 — **Wismar**

Wittenberg-Information, Collegienstrasse 8, O-4600 Wittenberg, tel. (0451) 22 39 — **Wittenberg**

Verkehrsverein, Stadtmarkt 8, W-3340 Wolfenbüttel, tel. (05331) 2 75 93 — **Wolfenbüttel**

Tourist-Information, Pavillon Rathausvorplatz, W-3180 Wolfsburg, tel. (05361) 28 25 50 — **Wolfsburg**

Wörlitz-Information, Angergasse 131, O-4414 Wörlitz, tel. (04795) 2 16 — **Wörlitz**

Verkehrsverein, Neumarkt 14, W-6520 Worms, tel. (06241) 2 50 45 and 85 35 60 — **Worms**

Informationszentrum, Döppersberg, Elberfeld, W-5600 Wuppertal 1, tel. (0202) 5 63 22 70; Presse-und Informationsamt, Rathaus, Barmen, W-5600 Wuppertal 2, tel. 56 31 — **Wuppertal**

Fremdenverkehrsamt, Palais am Congress Centrum, W-8700 Würzburg, tel. (0931) 3 73 35 — **Würzburg**

Insurance

Insurance

General
Visitors are strongly advised to ensure that they have adequate holiday insurance including loss or damage to luggage, loss of currency and jewellery.

Medical Insurance
Under European Community regulations British visitors to Germany are entitled to medical care under the German social insurance scheme on the same basis as German citizens. Before leaving home they should apply to their local social security office for form E 111 and the accompanying leaflet on "How to get medical treatment in other European Community countries".

These arrangements may not cover the full cost of medical treatment, and it is advisable, therefore, even for EC citizens, to take out short-term health insurance. Visitors from non-EC countries should certainly do so.

Vehicles
Visitors travelling by car should ensure that their insurance is comprehensive and covers use of the vehicle in Europe

See also Travel Documents.

Language

German, like English, is a Germanic language, and the pronunciation of German usually comes more easily to English-speakers than does a Romance language like French. Much of the basic vocabulary, too, will be familiar to those whose native language is English, though they may have more difficulty with more complex terms incorporating native Germanic roots rather than the Latin roots so common in English. The grammar is not difficult, but has retained a much more elaborate system of conjugations and declensions than English.

Standard German (*Hochdeutsch*) is spoken throughout the country, although many Germans speak a strong local dialect as well.

Pronunciation
The consonants are for the most part pronounced broadly as in English, but the following points should be noted: *b, d* and *g* at the end of a syllable are pronounced like *p, t* and *k* (in some parts of Germany like the Scottish *ch* in "loch"); *c* (rare) and *z* are pronounced *ts; j* is pronounced like consonantal *y; qu* is somewhere between English *qu* and *kv; s* at the beginning of a syllable is pronounced *z; v* is pronounced *f;* and *w* is pronounced *v*. The double letter *ch* is pronounced like *ch* in "loch" after *a, o* and *u;* after *ä, e, i* and *ü* it is somewhere between that sound and *sh. Sch* is pronounced *sh,* and *th* (rare) *t.*

The vowels are pronounced without the diphthongisation normal in English; before a single consonant they are normally long, before a double consonant short. Note the following: short *a* is like the flat *a* of northern English; *e* may be either closed (roughly as in "pay"), open (roughly as in "pen") or a short unaccented sound like the *e* in "begin" or "father"; *ä* is like an open *e; u* is like *oo* in "good" (short) or "food" (long); *ö* is like the French *eu,* a little like the vowel in "fur"; *ü,* like the French *u,* can be approximated by pronouncing *ee* with rounded lips.

Diphthongs: *ai* and *ei* similar to *i* in "high"; *au* as in "how"; *eu* and *äu* like *oy; ie* like *ee.*

Numbers

0	null
1	eins
2	zwei
3	drei
4	vier
5	fünf
6	sechs
7	sieben
8	acht
9	neun
10	zehn
11	elf
12	zwölf
13	dreizehn
14	vierzehn
15	fünfzehn
16	sechzehn
17	siebzehn
18	achtzehn
19	neunzehn
20	zwanzig
21	einunzzwanzig
22	zweiundzwanzig
30	dreissig
40	vierzig
50	fünfzig
60	sechzig
70	siebzig
80	achtzig
90	neunzig
100	hundert
101	hundert und eins
153	hundert dreiundfünfzig
200	zweihundert
300	dreihundert
1000	tausend
1001	tausend und eins
1021	tausend einundzwanzig
2000	zweitausend
1,000,000	eine Million

Ordinals

1st	erste
2nd	zweite
3rd	dritte
4th	vierte
5th	fünfte
6th	sechste
7th	siebte
8th	achte
9th	neunte
10th	zehnte
11th	elfte
20th	zwanzigste
100th	hundertste

Language

Fractions

half	Hälfte
third	Drittel
quarter	Viertel
three-quarters	drei Viertel

Useful Expressions

Good morning	Guten Morgen
Good day	Guten Tag
Good evening	Guten Abend
Good night	Gute Nacht
Goodbye	Auf Wiedersehen
Do you speak English?	Sprechen Sie Englisch?
I do not understand	Ich verstehe nicht
Yes	Ja
No	Nein
Please	Bitte
Thank you (very much)	Danke (sehr)
The usual response to "Danke" is "Bitte" ("Not at all", "Don't mention it")	
Yesterday	Gestern
Today	Heute
Tomorrow	Morgen
Help!	Hilfe!
Have you a single room?	Haben Sie ein Einzelzimmer?
...a double room?	... ein Doppelzimmer?
...with twin beds?	... mit zwei Einzelbetten?
...with private bath?	... mit Bad?
What does it cost?	Was kostet das?
Please wake me at six	Wollen Sie mich bitte um sechs Uhr wecken?
Where is the lavatory?	Wo ist die Toilette?
Where is the bathroom?	Wo ist das Badezimmer?
Where is the chemist's?	Wo ist die Apotheke?
Where is the post office?	Wo ist das Postamt?
Where is there a doctor?	Wo gibt es einen Arzt?
Where is there a dentist?	Wo gibt es einen Zahnarzt?
Is this the way to the station?	Ist dies der Weg zum Bahnhof?

Months, Days of the Week and Festivals

Months	January	Januar
	February	Februar
	March	März
	April	April
	May	Mai
	June	Juni
	July	Juli
	August	August
	September	September
	October	Oktober
	Noevember	November
	December	Dezember

Days of the week	Sunday	Sonntag
	Monday	Montag
	Tuesday	Dienstag
	Wednesday	Mittwoch
	Thursday	Donnerstag
	Friday	Freitag

Saturday	Samstag, Sonnabend
Day	Tag
Public holiday	Feiertag

New Year	Neujahr
Easter	Ostern
Ascension	Christi Himmelfahrt
Whitsun	Pfingsten
Corpus Christi	Fronleichnam
Assumption	Mariä Himmelfahrt
All Saints	Allerheiligen
Christmas	Weihnachten
New Year's Eve	Silvester

Road and Traffic Signs

Abstand halten!	Keep your distance
Achtung!	Caution
Baustelle	Road works
Durchfahrt verboten	No thoroughfare
Einbahnstrasse	One-way street
Einordnen	Get into line
Gefahr	Danger
Halt!	Halt
Kurve	Bend
Langsam	Slow
Rollsplit	Loose stones
Stadtmitte	Town centre
Stop	Stop
Strasse gesperrt	Road closed
Vorsicht!	Caution
Zoll	Customs

Rail and Air Travel

Aircraft	Flugzeug
Airport	Flughafen
All aboard!	Einsteigen!
Baggage	Gepäck
Baggage check	Gepäckschein
Bus station	Autobushof
Bus stop	Haltestelle
Departure	Abfahrt (*train, bus*), Abflug (*aircraft*)
Flight	Flug
Halt (*railway*)	Haltestelle
Information	Auskunft
Lavatory	Toilette(n)
Line (*railway*)	Gleis
Luggage	Gepäck
Luggage trolley	Kofferkuli
Non-smoking	Nichtraucher
Platform	Bahnsteig
Porter	Gepäckträger
Restaurant car	Speisewagen
Sleeping car	Schlafwagen; Liegewagen (*couchettes*)
Smoking	Raucher
Station	Bahnhof
Stewardess	Stewardess
Ticket	Fahrkarte
Ticket collector	Schaffner
Ticket window	Schalter

Timetable	Fahrplan; Flugplan (*air*)
Train	Zug
Waiting room	Wartesaal
Window seat	Fensterplatz

At the Post Office

Address	Adresse
Express	Eilboten
Letter	Brief
Parcel	Paket
Post-box	Briefkasten
Postcard	Postkarte
Poste restante	Postlagernd
Postman	Briefträger
Post office	Postamt
Registered	Einschreiben
Small packet	Päckchen
Stamp	Briefmarke
Telegram	Telegramm
Telephone	Telefon
Telex	Fernschreiben

Topographical Terms

Allee	avenue, walk
Amt	office
Anlage	gardens, park
Anstalt	institution
Auskunft	Information
Aussicht	view
Aussichtsturm	outlook tower
Ausstellung	exhibition
Autobushof	bus station
Bach	brook, stream
Bahn	railway; lane (*in road*)
Bahnhof	railway station
Bau	building
Bauernhaus	farmhouse
Bauernhof	farm, farmstead
Becken	basin, pool
Berg	hill, mountain
Bergbahn	mountain railway
Bezirk	region (*an administrative subdivision of a* Land)
Bibliothek	library
Börse	(stock) exchange
Brücke	bridge
Brunnen	fountain
Bucht	bay, bight
Bundes-	Federal
Burg	(fortified) castle
Damm	causeway, dyke, breakwater
Denkmal	monument, memorial
Dom	cathedral
Dorf	village
Dreieck	triangle
Eingang	entrance
Einkaufszentrum	shopping centre
Eisenbahn	railway

Fähre	ferry
Fels	rock, crag
Fernmeldeturm	telecommunications tower
Fernsehturm	television tower
Feste, Festung	fortress, citadel
Flügel	wing
Flughafen	airport
Fluss	river
Förde	firth, fjord
Forst	forest
Freilichtmuseum	open-air museum
Fremdenverkehrsverein	tourist information office
Friedhof	cemetery
Furt	ford
Garten	garden
Gasse	lane, street
Gau	region
Gebäude	building
Gebirge	(range of) hills, mountains
Gelände	tract of land, grounds
Gemeinde	commune (*the smallest local government unit*)
Gericht	(law)court
Grab	tomb, grave
Graben	ditch, moat
Gut	estate, country house, farm
Hafen	harbour, port
Halbinsel	peninsula
Halde	hillside
Halle	hall
Hallenbad	indoor swimming pool
Hauptbahnhof	main railway station
Hauptpost(amt)	head post office
Hauptstrasse	main street
Haus	house
Heide	heath
Heim	home
Heimatmuseum	local or regional museum
Hochhaus	multi-storey building, tower block
Hochschule	higher educational establishment, university
Hof	courtyard; farm; (royal) court
Höhe	hill, eminence
Höhle	cave
Hospital	hospital, hospice
Hügel	hill
Hütte	hut; iron and steelworks, glassworks
Insel	island
Jagdschloss	hunting lodge
Jugendherberge	youth hostel
Kai	quay
Kammer	chamber, room
Kapelle	chapel
Keller	cellar
Kino	cinema
Kirche	church
Klamm	gorge
Klippe	cliff

Kloster	monastery, convent, religious house
Krankenhaus	hospital
Kreis	district (*an administrative subdivision of a Bezirk*)
Kurhaus	spa establishment
Kurort	spa, health resort
Kurverwaltung	spa management authority
Land	land; specifically, one of the *Länder* or provinces of the Federal Republic
Landkreis	rural district
Laube	arcade, loggia
Maar	small volcanic lake (in Eifel)
Markt(platz)	market (square)
Marstall	court stables
Mauer	wall
Meer	sea
Messe	trade fair
Moor	marsh(land)
Moos	moss, bog
Mühle	mill
Münster	minster, monastic church
Noor	coastal inlet, lagoon (*in North Germany*)
Nord	north
Ober-	upper
Oper	opera (house)
Ost	east
Palais, Palast	palace
Pfad	path, trail
Pfalz	(royal) palace, stronghold
Pfarrkirche	parish church
Pforte	doorway
Platz	square
Post(amt)	post office
Quelle	spring, source
Rasthaus, Raststätte	"rest-house" in motorway service area
Rathaus	town hall
Ratskeller	cellar (restaurant) of town hall
Reisebüro	travel agency
Rennbahn	race-track
Residenz	residence, seat of a ruling prince; princely capital
Ruine	ruin
Rundfunk	radio
S-Bahn, Stadtbahn	urban railway, tramway
Saal	hall, room
Säule	column
Schatzkammer	treasury
Schauspielhaus	theatre
Schlachthof	slaughterhouse
Schleuse	lock; sluice
Schloss (*plural* Schlösser)	castle, palace, country house (*usually designed for show rather then defence*)

Schlucht	gorge
Schnellweg	expressway
Schule	school
See	lake; sea
Seilbahn	cableway
Sperre	dam, barrage
Spielbank	casino
Spital	hospital
Staats-, staatlich	state, national
Stadt	town, city
städtisch	municipal
Standseilbahn	funicular
Stätte	place, spot
Stausee	lake formed by dam, reservoir
Steig	path
Steige	staircase; steep ascent
Stein	stone
Sternwarte	observatory
Stiege	staircase
Stift	religious house; chapter, college; foundation
Stiftskirche	collegiate church; monastic church
Strand	beach
Strasse	street, road
Strassenbahn	tramway
Strom	(large) river
Süd	south
Sund	sound, straits
Tal	valley
Teich	pond, small lake
Theater	theatre
Tiergarten, Tierpark	zoo, animal park
Tonhalle	concert-hall
Tor	gate(way)
U-Bahn	underground railway
Ufer	shore, coast
Unter-	lower
Verkehr	traffic, transport
Verkehrsamt, -büro, -verein	tourist information office
Veste	fortress, citadel
Viertel	quarter, district
Vogelpark	bird park
Vorort, Vorstadt	suburb, outer district
Wald	wood, forest
Wall	rampart
Wallfahrt	pilgrimage
Wand	wall
Wasser	water
Wasserburg, -schloss	moated castle
Weg	way, road
Weiler	hamlet
Weinstube	wine-bar, -house
Werder	small island in river
Werft	shipyard, wharf
West	west
Wildpark	game park, wild-life park
Zeughaus	arsenal
Zimmer	room
Zitadelle	citadel

Medical Assistance

German medical services are excellent and the country is well supplied with doctors, many of them able to speak English.

British visitors to Germany will find it helpful to obtain a free booklet prepared by the Department of Health, "The Traveller's Guide to Health", which gives information about health precautions and how to get urgent medical treatment when abroad.

See also Insurance.

Motoring in Germany

Roads

Germany has some 10,500km/6500 miles of toll-free motorways and a dense network of well maintained major and minor roads, though some of the roads in the eastern *Länder,* formerly in the German Democratic Republic, stand in need of improvement.

Traffic signs and road markings are in accordance with international standards.

Vehicles travel on the right, with overtaking on the left. Main road traffic has priority; at junctions of two main roads or two minor roads traffic from the right has priority. Traffic on motorways has priority over traffic entering or leaving the motorway.

Speed limits

Except in the *Länder* of the former GDR there is no compulsory speed limit for private cars on motorways (though a limit of 130km/81 miles p.h. is recommended); the limit outside built-up areas is 100km/62 miles p.h. and inside built-up areas 50km/31 miles p.h. The speed limit for cars with trailers, on both motorways and ordinary roads, is 80km/50 miles p.h.

In the ex-GDR *Länder* of Brandenburg, Mecklenburg-West Pomerania, Saxony, Saxony-Anhalt and Thuringia the speed limit for cars in 100km/62 miles p.h. on motorways and 80km/50 miles p.h. on ordinary roads outside built-up areas.

Safety belts

Safety belts must be worn by drivers and passengers in both front and rear seats. Children under 12 must not travel in the front seats of cars with rear seats unless special safety devices for children are fitted.

Lights

Dipped headlights must be used in darkness, fog, heavy rain or falling snow; driving on parking lights alone is prohibited.

Drink and driving

In the former GDR *Länder* there is an absolute ban on driving after drinking. In the rest of Germany the maximum permitted blood alcohol limit is 80mg/100ml.

Documents

Visitors to Germany may drive a car for up to a year if they have a national or international driving licence. National licences issued in Britain, other European Community countries and certain other countries are valid without further formality; in the case of visitors from other countries (including the USA and Canada) the national licence must be accompanied by a German translation.

Car registration documents from European Community countries are accepted; visitors from other countries are advised to have an "international certificate for motor vehicles".

Third party insurance is compulsory in Germany. Foreign motorists must therefore be covered by their own car insurance or must take out temporary insurance when entering Germany. Evidence of insurance cover is provided by the international insurance certificate ("green card"); and although British and other Community motorists are no longer under a legal obligation to carry a green card it is still advisable to have one, since it may save a great deal of inconvenience in the event of an accident.

Foreign vehicles must display a nationality plate on the rear.

Breakdown assistance

The German motoring organisation ADAC patrols motorways and major roads. Breakdown assistance is provided free of charge; only the cost of materials has to be reimbursed.

A patrol can be summoned from the emergency telephones on motorways: ask for "Strassenwachthilfe".

ADAC also provides a breakdown service in towns.

In the former GDR *Länder* a breakdown service is provided by the Auto Club Europa.

Motoring Organisations

Allgemeiner Deutscher Automobil Club
Am Westpark 8
8000 Munich 70
                                                                    ADAC

Automobilclub von Deutschland
Lyoner Strasse 16
6000 Frankfurt-Niederrad
                                                                    AvD

Deutscher Touring Automobil Club
Amalienburgstrasse 23
8000 Munich 60
                                                                    DTC

Auto Club Europa
Märkisches Ufer
1026 Berlin
                                                                    ACE

Opening Times

Opening times are not standard throughout Germany but may vary slightly in the
different *Länder*.

Banks are normally open on weekdays from 8.30am to 1pm and from 2.30 to 4pm   Banks
(Thursdays 5.30pm). They are closed on Saturdays and Sundays.

Chemists open during normal business hours. Information about chemists open at night   Chemists
and on Sundays is posted up at all pharmacies.

Doctors' consulting hours are normally 10am–noon and 4–6pm, except Wednesdays,   Doctors
Saturdays and Sundays.

Exchange offices at airports, railway stations and border crossing-points are normally   Exchange offices
open from 6am to 10pm.

Post offices are normally open Monday to Friday from 8am to 6pm, Saturday 8am to   Post offices
noon.

Shops are usually open from 9am to 6.30pm (in some cases until 8.30pm on Thursday),   Shops
on Saturday to 2pm (to 4pm on the first Saturday in the month); they are closed on
Sundays and public holidays.

Travel agencies are open Monday to Friday 9am to 6pm, Saturday 9am to noon. They are   Travel agencies
closed on Sundays and public holidays.

Post and Telephone

See Opening Times.   Post offices

Inland mail: letters (up to 20 grams) DM1, postcards DM0.60. The inland rate is charged   Postal
for mail to Britain and other European Community countries.   charges
Abroad: letters (up to 20 grams) DM1.40, postcards DM0.80.

In the *Länder* of Brandenburg, Mecklenburg-West Pomerania, Saxony, Saxony-Anhalt
and Thuringia the rates are:
Inland: letters up to 20 grams DM0.50, postcards DM0.30
Abroad: letters up to 20 grams DM0.70, postcards DM0.50.

Poste restante	Poste restante mail is issued on production of a passport or identity card.
Telephoning	Local and national calls may be made from all post offices and street call-boxes with coin-operated telephones (unit fee DM0.30).

Railways

There are two state railway systems in Germany, the Deutsche Bundesbahn (DB; Federal Railways), with a network of some 28,000km/17,400 miles, and the Deutsche Reichsbahn (DR) in the former GDR *Länder,* with some 15,000km/9,300 miles. These two main networks are supplemented by various privately owned railways and numerous services operated by regional bus companies.

Over 30,000 trains are run daily in the Federal Republic, and the InterCity network serves well over fifty cities and towns throughout Germany.

Tickets
Standard-fare tickets for journeys of up to 100km/62 miles are valid for the day of issue; for greater distances a single ticket is valid for four days and a return ticket for a month. Single and return tickets for distances of 51km/32 miles and over are valid for travel in long-distance expresses and fast trains without payment of any supplement. A special supplement of DM6 is payable for travel in the fast and luxurious EuroCity and InterCity trains.

Children
Children up to four years of age travel free of charge. For children between four and eleven and younger children occupying a reclining chair or sleeping berth half fares (and half any supplements) are payable.

Tourist tickets
Visitors who travel a minimum of 250km/155 miles by rail to their holiday destination can obtain, at very modest cost, tourist tickets (2nd class only) which allow unlimited travel on a local network of some 1000km/620 miles on any ten days during a period of three weeks.

Rail Pass
Youth Pass
The German Rail Pass and German Rail Youth Pass, obtainable only by persons normally resident outside Germany on presentation of a passport or other official identity document, also at very reasonable prices, are personal network tickets for travel on any five, ten or fifteen days with a period of a month. The adult Rail Pass can be bought for either first or second class travel, the Youth Pass (ages 12 to 26) only for second class.
Both passes are valid on DB and DR networks, including Metro services; on routes operated by regional bus companies; on all bus routes operated by the Deutsche Touring company (except on regular cross-border services) and on Europabus routes; on ships owned by the KD Rhine Line on the Rhine (between Mainz and Cologne) and Mosel (between Koblenz and Cochem); and on boats to Puttgarden.

Restaurants

Notes
Space does not permit the inclusion of restaurants in all places featured in this guide. The list below therefore only includes restaurants in the larger towns and in the principal tourist areas.
Restaurants in the former German Democratic Republic which bear the name of "Broiler" usually offer chickens or other poultry. Restaurants advertising a "Gastmahl des Meeres" will have a menu consisting predominantly of fish.

Aachen
*Gala and Palm Bistro (both in Casino), Monheimsallee 34, tel. 15 30 13; Le Canard, Bendelstrasse 28, tel. 3 86 63; La Bécasse, Hanbrucher Strasse 1, tel. 7 44 44; Elisenbrunnen, Friedrich-Wilhelm-Platz 13A, tel. 2 97 72; Im Moselhäuschen, Franzstrasse 40, tel. 2 95 34; Zum Schiffgen, Hühnermarkt 23, tel. 3 35 29.

Amberg
Casino Altdeutsche Stube, Schrannenplatz 8, tel. 2 26 64; Zum Kashansl, Salzstadlplatz 5, tel. 2 58 85.

Die Ecke, Elias-Holl-Platz 2, tel. 51 06 00; Agnes Bernauer Stuben, Ludwigstrasse 19, tel. 51 65 79; Fuggerei-Stube, Jakoberstrasse 26, tel. 3 03 70; Feinkost Kahn, Annastrasse 16, tel. 31 20 31; Sieben-Schwaben-Stuben, Bürgermeister-Fischer-Strasse 12, tel. 31 45 63. **Augsburg**

Stahlbad, Augustaplatz 2, tel. 2 45 69; Kurhausrestaurant, Kaiser-Allee 1, tel. 2 27 17; Palais Gagarin, Augustaplatz 1, tel. 2 58 38; Zum Nest, Rettigstrasse 1, tel. 2 30 76; La Terrazza im Goldenen Kreuz, Lichtentaler Strasse 13, tel. 3 27 27; Oxmox, Kaiser-Allee 4, tel. 2 99 00; Molkenkur, Quettigstrasse 19, tel. 3 32 57; Bellavista (Italian), in Römerpassage, Langestrasse 40–42, tel. 2 98 00. **Baden-Baden**
Cafés: Confiserie & Caféhaus König, Lichtentaler Strasse 12, tel. 2 35 73; Café in Holiday Inn Sporthotel, Falkenstrasse 2, tel. 21 90; Café in Hotel Kappelmann, Rotenbachtalstrasse 30, tel. 35 50.

Kurhaus-Restaurant, Schlossplatz 2, tel. Schwarzmatt, Schwarzmattstrasse 6A, tel. 60 42; Eckerlin, Römerstrasse 2, tel. 75 09 01. **Badenweiler**

An den Lohden, Heinestrasse 1, tel. 86 27; Schwarzer Bär, Rathausplatz 3, tel. 85 34; Weingaststätte Reblaus, Lindenallee 9, tel. 87 31; Weisses Ross, Poststrasse 88, tel. 85 45; Zum Brauberg, Am Brauberg, tel. 87 23. **Ballenstedt**

Weinhaus Messerschmitt, Lange Strasse 41, tel. 2 78 66; Würzburger Weinstube, Zinkenwörth 6, tel. 2 26 67; Brauerei-Ausschank Schlenkeria, Dominikanerstrasse 6, tel. 5 60 60; Spezial, Obere Königstrasse 10, tel. 2 43 04; Concordia im Böttingerhaus, Judenstrasse 14, tel. 5 40 74. **Bamberg**

Andena, Erich-Weinert-Strasse 31, tel. 2 20 37; Budysin, Reichenstrasse 7, tel. 4 43 20; Dom-Eck, Breitengasse 2, tel. 4 24 10; Exquisit, Postplatz 4, tel. 4 25 39; Gastmahl des Meeres, Steinstrasse 19A, tel. 4 41 07; Kaniga, Kurt-Pchalek-Strasse 1, tel. 4 79 13; Lipa, Karl-Marx-Strasse 5, tel. 4 25 82; Lubin, Wendischer Graben, tel. 51 11 14; Lusatia, Boleslaw-Bierut-Strasse 26, tel. 4 22 44; Radeberger Bierstuben, Goschwitzstrasse 3, tel. 4 44 29; Ratskeller, Innere Lauenstrasse 1, tel. 4 24 74; Stadt Bautzen, Steinstrasse 15, tel. 51 11 14; Wanoga, Töpferstrasse 30, tel. 53 92 39; Weisses Ross, Äussere Lauenstrasse 11, tel. 4 22 63; Zum Echten, Lauengraben 11, tel. 4 23 45; Zum Gerber, Taschenberg 2, tel. 4 39 17. **Bautzen**

Annecy, Gabelsbergerstrasse 11, tel. 2 62 79; Cuvée, Markgrafenallee 15, tel. 2 34 22; Provençale (French cuisine), Rathenaustrasse 28, tel. 5 70 58; Eule, Kirchgasse 8, tel. 6 43 46; Königsstuben in Hotel Königshof, Bahnhofstrasse 23, tel. 2 40 94; Zur Lohmühle, Badstrasse 37, tel. 6 30 31; Spiegelmühle, Kulmbacher Strasse 28, tel. 4 10 91; Mandarin (Chinese), Erlanger Strasse 2, tel. 6 19 11; Markgrafentor (Turkish), Markgrafenallee 17, tel. 2 44 62; Mexican Steakhouse, Friedrichstrasse 53, tel. 6 22 92; Peking, Casselmannstrasse 20, tel. 2 41 16; Schützenhaus, Am Schiesshaus 2, tel. 2 21 90; Weihenstefan, Bahnhofstrasse 5, tel. 2 02 03. **Bayreuth**
Cafés: Dippold, Maximilianstrasse 69, tel. 6 46 58; Händel, Dammallee 20, tel. 6 97 35; Jean-Paul-Café, Friedrichstrasse 10, tel. 6 78 76; Operncafé Zollinger, Opernstrasse 16, tel. 6 57 20; Neues Schloss, Eremitage, tel. 9 92 39; Piano-Café, Kulmbacher Strasse 12, tel. 5 41 77; Schweizer, Luitpoldplatz 20, tel. 2 05 96; restaurant and café in Schlosshotel Thiergarten, Obertiergärter Strasse 36, tel. 13 14.

Demming–Restaurant Le Gourmet, Sunklergässchen 2, tel. 50 21; Geiger, Stanggass, tel. 50 55; Post,, Maximilianstrasse 2, tel. 50 67. **Berchtesgaden**

Near the Kurfürstendamm: **Berlin (West)**
* Kempinski-Grill, Kurfürstendamm 27, tel. 88 43 40; Kräutergarten, in Hotel Mondial, Kurfürstendamm 47, tel. 88 41 10; Grand Cru, in Hotel Residenz, Meinekestrasse 9, tel. 88 28 91; Zlata Praha, Meinekestrasse 4, tel. 8 81 97 50; Am Fasanenplatz, Fasanenstrasse 42, tel. 8 83 97 23; Ernst-August, Sybelstrasse 16, tel. 3 24 55 76; Heinz Holl, Damaschkestrasse 26, tel. 3 23 14 04; Friesenhof, Uhlandstrasse 185, tel. 8 83 60 79; Hardtke, Meinekestrasse 27A, tel. 9 81 98 27; Kurpfalz Weinstuben, Wilmersdorfer Strasse 93, tel. 8 83 66 64.
Near the Zoo and Gedächtniskirche:
* Zum Hugenotten, in Hotel Inter-Continental, Budapester Strasse 2, tel. 2 60 20; * Park-Restaurant, in Steigenberger Hotel, Los-Angeles-Platz 1, tel. 2 10 80; Harlekin, in Grand

607

Restaurants

Hotel Esplanade, Lützowufer 15, tel. 26 10 11; Berlin-Grill, Lützowplatz 17, tel. 2 60 50; Grillrestaurant (with Fassbierstübli), in Hotel Schweizerhof, Budapester Strasse 21, tel. 2 69 20; La Réserve, in Palace Hotel, Budapester Strasse (in Europa-Center), tel. 25 49 70; Du Pont, Budapester Strasse 1, tel. 2 61 88 11; Bamberger Reiter, Regensburger Strasse 7, tel. 24 42 82; Bacco, Marburger Strasse 5, tel. 2 11 86 87; Mövenpick (with Café des Artistes), Budapester Strasse (in Europa-Center), tel. 2 62 70 77.
In Charlottenburg:
Apart, Heerstrasse 80, tel. 3 00 00 60; Au Lac, in Hotel Seehof, Lietzensee-Ufer 11, tel. 32 00 20; Schlossparkrestaurant, Heubnerweg 2A, tel. 3 22 40 61; Ponte Vecchio, Spielhagenstrasse 3, tel. 3 42 19 99; Alt-Luxemburg, Pestalozzistrasse 70, tel. 3 23 87 30; La Puce, Schillerstrasse 20, tel. 3 12 58 31; Funkturm-Restaurant, Messedamm 22, tel. 30 38 29 96; Ugo, Sophie-Charlotten-Strasse 101, tel. 3 25 71 10; Charlottenburger Ratskeller, Otto-Suhr-Allee 102, tel. 3 42 55 83; Trio, Klausenerplatz 14, tel. 3 21 77 82.
In Dahlem:
Forsthaus Paulsborn, Am Grunewaldsee, tel. 8 13 80 10; La Vernaccia, Breitenbachplatz 4, tel. 8 24 57 88; Alter Krug, Königin-Luise-Strasse 52, tel. 8 32 50 89.
In Grunewald:
*Grand Slam, Gottfried-von-Cramm-Weg 47, tel. 26 02 12 72; Hemingway's, Hagenstrasse 18, tel. 8 25 45 71; Chalet Corniche, Königsallee 5B, tel. 8 25 45 71; Hardtke, Hubertusallee 48, tel. 8 92 58 48.

Berlin (East)

Am Marstall, Marx-Engels-Forum 23, tel. 21 71 32 00; Ermelerhaus, Märkisches Ufer 10–12, tel. 2 79 40 28; Friedrichshof, in Köpenick, Bölschestrasse 56, tel. 6 45 50 74; Gastmahl des Meeres, Spandauer Strasse 4, tel. 2 12 32 86; Gaststätten am Fernsehturm, Panoramastrasse 1, tel. 2 10 40; Gaststätten in Palast der Republik, Marx-Engels-Platz, tel. 23 80; Lindencorso, Unter den Linden 17, tel. 2 20 24 61; Ratskeller, Rathausstrasse 14, tel. 2 15 53 01; Jade Restaurant, Märkisches Restaurant and Roti d'Or, in Palasthotel, Karl-Liebknecht-Strasse 5, tel. 2 41 22 45; Silhouette and Forellenquintett, in Grand Hotel, Friedrichstrasse 158–164, tel. 2 09 24 00.

Bielefeld

Ente, Niedernstrasse 18, tel. 55 54 55; Im Bültmannshof, Kurt-Schuhmacher-Strasse 17A, tel. 10 08 41; Sparrenburg, Am Sparrenberg 38A, tel. 6 59 39; Klötzer's Kleines Restaurant, Ritterstrasse 33, tel. 6 89 54; Nico's Restaurant, Wertherstrasse 58, tel. 6 12 44.

Bochum

Gastronomie im Stadtpark, Klinikstrasse 41, tel. 50 70 90; Torkelkeller im Plaza, Hellweg 20, tel. 1 30 85; Jägerstube, Hotel Ostmeier, Westring 35, tel. 6 08 15; Vitrine, Hotel Schmidt, Drusenbergerstrasse 164, tel. 33 39 60; Alt Nürnberg, Königsallee 16, tel. 31 16 98; Jacky Ballière, Wittener Strasse 123, tel. 33 57 60; Stammhaus Fiege, Bongardstrasse 23, tel. 1 26 43; Altes Bergamt, Schillerstrasse 20, tel. 5 19 55; Schindeldeele, Wasserstrasse 419, tel. 45 03 68; Arcade Treff, Universitätsstrasse 3, tel. 3 33 11.

Bonn

Majestic, Brasserie Kupferklause and Hofkonditorei Bierhoff, in Günnewig Hotel Bristol, Prinz-Albert-Strasse 2, tel. 2 69 80; La Couronne and Rhapsodie, in Scandic Crown Hotel, Berliner Freiheit 2, tel. 7 26 90; Felix Krull, in Hotel Domicil, Thomas-Mann-Strasse 24, tel. 72 90 90; Belle Epoque, in Pullmann-Hotel Königshof, Adenauerallee 9, tel. 2 60 10; Le Petit Poisson, Wilhelmstrasse 23A, tel. 63 38 83; Em Höttche, Markt 4, tel. 65 85 96; Zum Kapellchen, Brüdergasse 12, tel. 65 10 52; Grand'Italia, Bischofsplatz 1, tel. 63 83 33; Caminetto, Römerstrasse 83, tel. 65 42 27; Le Tastevin, Hohe Strasse 1, tel. 66 92 49; Im Bären, Acherstrasse 1, tel. 63 32 00.
In Bonn 2 (Bad Godesberg):
Restaurant Gobelin, in Rheinhotel Dreesen (with garden restaurant, terrace), Rheinstrasse 45, tel. 8 20 20; Halbedel's Gasthaus, Rheinallee 47, tel. 35 42 53; St Michael, Brunnenallee 26, tel. 36 47 65.

Brandenburg

Fontaneclub, Hauptstrasse 69, tel. 52 20 71; Gastmahl des Meeres, Hauptstrasse 42, tel. 52 27 49; Goldener Anker, Bäckerstrasse 32, tel. 52 28 32; Goldener Stern (also hotel), Genthiner Strasse 43, tel. 2 72 06; Jugendklubhaus, Steinstrasse 42, tel. 2 43 30; Märkische Bierstube, Magdeburger Strasse 12, tel. 2 39 49; Ratskeller, Markt 19, tel. 2 40 51; Theaterklause, Grabenstrasse 14, tel. 52 22 41; Treffpunkt, Molkenmarkt 26, tel. 52 23 09; Zum Bären (also hotel), Steinstrasse 60, tel. 2 41 79.

Rössli and Welfen-Stübli, in Mövenpick-Hotel, Jöddenstrasse 3, Welfenhof, tel. 4 81 70; **Braunschweig**
Zum Burglöwen, in Hotel Deutsches Haus, Burgplatz 1, tel. 4 44 22; Ritter St Georg and
Altes Haus, Alte Knochenhauerstrasse 12, tel. 1 30 39; Lessing-Hof, Okerstrasse 13,
tel. 4 54 55; Haus zur Hanse, Güldenstrasse 7, tel. 4 61 54; Gewandhaus-Keller, Altstadtmarkt 1, tel. 4 44 41; Löwen-Krone, Leonhardplatz, tel. 7 20 76.

*Park-Restaurant and Buten un Binnen, in Park-Hotel, Bürgerpark, tel. 3 40 80; Belvedere   **Bremen**
and Hillmanns Garden, in Bremen Marriott Hotel, Hillmannplatz 20, tel. 1 76 70; L'Orchi-
dée, Der Tingheter and Das Kachelstübchen, in Hotel zur Post, Bahnhofsplatz 11, tel.
3 05 90; Concordenhaus, Hinter der Holzpforte 2, tel. 32 53 31; Meierei Bürgerpark, in
Bürgerpark, tel. 3 40 86 19; Topaz, Violenstrasse 13, tel. 32 52 58; Das Kleine Lokal,
Besselstrasse 40, tel. 7 19 29; Ratskeller, Am Markt 1, tel. 3 29 09 10; Comturei, Ostertorstrasse 31, tel. 32 50 50; Flett, Böttcherstrasse 3, tel. 32 09 95; Al Carrello, Am Dobben 35,
tel. 70 41 42; Deutsches Haus am Markt, Marktstuben and Café, Am Markt 1, tel.
2 29 09 20; Paulaner im Schnoor, Tiefer 8, tel. 32 76 40; Grashoff's Bistro, Contrescarpe
80, tel. 1 47 40; Feinkost Hocke, Schlüsselkorb 17, tel. 32 66 51.

Waldschenke, in Parkhotel, Bürgerpark, tel. 2 70 41; Fischrestaurant in Hotel Am Theater-   **Bremerhaven**
platz, Schleswiger Strasse 3, tel. 4 26 20; Fischereihafen Restaurant Natusch, Am Fisch-
bahnhof 1, tel. 7 10 21; Miramare, Fritz-Reuter-Strasse 23, tel. 5 45 61; Seute Deern
(museum ship), Am Alten Hafen, tel. 41 62 64; Cap Horn, Am Baggerloch 3, tel. 7 38 79.

Endtenfang and Kutscherstube, in Hotel Fürstenhof Celle, Hannoversche Strasse 55, tel.   **Celle**
20 10; Heidrose, in Hotel Celler Hof, Stechbahn 11, tel. 2 80 61; Schifferkrug, Speicher-
strasse 9, tel. 70 15; Ratskeller, Marktstrasse 14, tel. 2 90 99; Schweine-Schulze, Neue
Strasse 36, tel. 2 29 44; Weinstube Utspann, Im Kreise 13, tel. 2 90 36.

Bijou and Erzgebirgsstube, in Hotel Chemnitzer Hof, Theaterplatz 4, tel. 68 40; Csarda,   **Chemnitz**
Sachsenring 48, tel. 7 10 09; Gockelbar, Hermannstrasse 10, tel. 4 27 15; Kongress-
restaurants Berlin and Jalta, in Hotel Kongress, Karl-Marx-Allee, tel. 68 30; Ratskeller,
Neumarkt 1, tel. 6 16 05; Roter Turm, Strasse der Nationen 5, tel. 6 29 49; Südblick,
Bruno-Granz-Strasse 26, tel. 22 41 21; Wolgograd, in Hotel Moskau, Strasse der Nationen
56, tel. 68 10; Zum Fass, Zwickauer Strasse 12, tel. 3 00 34.

Die Backstube, in Hotel Stadt Coburg, Lossaustrasse 12, tel. 77 81; Kräutergarten, in   **Coburg**
Hotel Blankenburg, Rosenauer Strasse 30, tel. 7 50 05; Traube-Stuben in der Goldenen
Traube, Am Viktoriabrunnen 2, tel. 98 33; Schaller, in Hotel Coburger Tor, Ketschendor-
fer Strasse 22, tel. 2 50 74; Loreley, Herrngasse 14, tel. 9 24 70.

*Hanse-Stube and Excelsior Keller, in Excelsior Hotel Ernst, Trankgasse 1, tel. 27 01;   **Cologne**
Etoile and Atelier am Dom, in Dom-Hotel, Domkloster 2A, tel. 2 02 40; Graugans,
Glashaus and Schälsick, in Hyatt Regency Hotel, Kennedy-Ufer 2A, tel. 8 28 12 34; Raffael
and Valentino, in Ramada Renaissance Hotel, Magnusstrasse 20, tel. 2 03 40; La Galerie,
Bellevue and Rotisserie, in Hotel Maritim, Heumarkt 20, tel. 2 02 70; Bergische Stube, in
Inter-Continental Hotel, Helenenstrasse 14, tel. 22 80; Le Bouquet and La Cave, in Holiday
Inn Crowne Plaza, Habsburgerring 9, tel. 2 09 50; Symphonie, in Pullmann-Hotel Mon-
dial, Kurt-Hackenberg-Platz 1, tel. 2 06 30; Quirinal, in Hotel Consul, Belfortstrasse 9, tel.
7 72 10; Brasserie, in Altea Hotel Severinshof, Severinstrasse 199, tel. 2 01 30; Viktoria, in
Haus Lyskirchen, Filzengraben 26, tel. 2 09 70; Restaurant Wintergarten, in Dorint Hotel,
Friesenstrasse 44, tel. 1 61 40; Coellner Stube, in Coellner Hof, Hansaring 100, tel.
12 20 75; Ambiance am Dom, in Europa Hotel am Dom, Am Hof 38, tel. 24 91 27;
restaurant in Senats-Hotel, Unter Goldschmied 9, tel. 2 06 20; Ascot Garden, Hohen-
zollernring 95, tel. 52 10 76; Rino Casati, Ebertplatz 3, tel. 72 11 08; Bado la Poêle d'Or,
Komödienstrasse 52, tel. 13 41 00; Chez Alex, Mühlengasse 1, tel. 23 05 60; Die Bastei,
Konrad-Adenauer-Ufer 80, tel. 12 28 15; Charrue d'Or, Hohenzollernring 20, tel. 21 76 10;
Alfredo, Tunisstrasse 3, tel. 24 43 01; Börsen-Restaurant (Maître, Börsen-Stube and
Börsen-Schänke), Unter Sachsenhausen 10, tel. 13 30 21; Wack (tel. 21 42 78) and D'r
Wackes (tel. 24 36 46), Benesisstrasse 57; Weinhaus Im Walfisch, Salzgasse 13, tel.
21 95 75; Ballarin, Ubierring 35, tel. 32 61 33; Frisée, Friesenstrasse 40, tel. 13 46 51; La
Baurie, Vorgebirgsstrasse 35, tel. 38 61 49; Soufflé, Hohenstaufenring 53, tel. 21 42 78;
Gaffel-Haus, Alter Markt 20, tel. 21 46 68; Gasthaus Adler, Friesenwall 74, tel. 21 71 93;
Alter Wartesaal, in Hauptbahnhof, tel. 13 30 61; Opernterrassen, with Offenbach's Café,

Restaurants

Brüderstrasse 2, tel. 23 32 91; Schwarzwald-Kamin, Martinstrasse 32, tel. 21 56 87; Em Krützche, Am Frankenturm 1, tel. 21 14 32; Chalet Suisse, Am Hof 20, tel. 23 38 91; Nüdelchen, Kleiner Griechenmarkt 23, tel. 21 45 12; Amabile, Görrestrasse 2, tel. 24 60 17; Alt-Köln Am Dom, Trankgasse 7, tel. 13 74 71; Le Moissonnier, Krefelder Strasse 25, tel. 72 94 79; Messeturm, Kennedy-Ufer, tel. 88 10 08.

Cottbus   Alte Welt, Karl-Liebknecht-Strasse 58A, tel. 3 37 09; Gastmahl des Meeres, Marktstrasse 7, tel. 2 47 95; Goldener Stern, Lieberoser Strasse 40, tel. 2 56 03; Haus des Handwerks, Altmarkt 12, tel. 2 37 15; Kavalierhaus Branitz, Branitzer Park, tel. 71 50 00; Lausitz, Berliner Strasse, tel. 3 01 51; Lipa, Wendenstrasse 2, tel. 2 52 50; Molle, Stadtpromenade 10, tel. 2 21 11; Spreewehrmühle and Freiluftgaststätte Spreewehrmühle, Am Grossen Spreewehr 3, tel. 71 41 74; Targowischte, Altmarkt 22, tel. 2 58 06; Tierparkgaststätte, Kiekebuscher Strasse, tel. 71 24 94; Zur Sonne, Taubenstrasse 9, tel. 2 25 00.

Darmstadt   Weinstuben and Taverne in Hotel Weinmichel, Schleiermacherstrasse 10, tel. 2 68 22; Orangerie, Bessunger Strasse 44, tel. 66 49 66; Ritter's Rustica, Platz der Deutschen Einheit 25, tel. 8 26 66; Zum Goldenen Anker, Landgraf-Georg-Strasse 25, tel. 2 08 25; Ristorante Vivarium, Schnampelweg 5, tel. 4 76 51.

Delmenhorst   Restaurant Château in Hotel Am Stadtpark, An den Graften 3, tel. 1 46 44.

Dessau   Drushba-Gaststätte, Paul-König-Platz, tel. 20 65; Jägerklause, Alte Leipziger Strasse 76, tel. 88 13 67; Ratskeller, Am Markt, tel. 46 92/22 46; Restaurant am Museum, Wilhelm-Pieck-Strasse 90, tel. 53 83; Stadt Dessau, Wilhelm-Pieck-Strasse 35, tel. 72 85; Waldbad Freundschaft, Am Schenkenbusch, tel. 88 10 56; Waldschenke im Lehrpark, Querallee 8, tel. 27 37.

Detmold   Le Gourmet, in Hotel Lippischer Hof, Hornsche Strasse 1, tel. 3 10 41; Ratskeller, Rosental, tel. 2 22 66.

Dinkelsbühl   Restaurant Zum kleinen Obristen and Weinkeller in Hotel Eisenkrug, Martin-Luther-Strasse 1, tel. 60 17; Goldener Hirsch, Weinmarkt 6, tel. 23 47; Weisses Ross, Steingasse 12, tel. 22 74; Zur Glocke, Weinmarkt 1, tel. 39 94.

Donauwörth   Zu den Drei Kronen, Bahnhofstrasse 25; Traube, Kapellstrasse 14; Tanzhaus-Restaurant, Reichsstrasse 34.

Dortmund   Rosenterrassen, Strobelallee 41; Hohe Zunft & Alte Gasse, Hohe Strasse 107; Krone am Markt (rôtisserie, bistro and café), Alter Markt; Mövenpick and Appenzeller Stube, Kleppingstrasse 9; SBB-Restaurant, Westfalendamm 166.

Dresden   Äberlausitzer Töpp'l, Strasse der Befreiung, tel. 5 56 05; Am Zwinger, Ernst-Thälmann-Strasse 24, tel. 4 95 12 81; Blockhaus, Neustädter Markt 19, tel. 5 36 30; Brauerei Mockritz, Gastrizer Strasse 30, tel. 47 75 33; Buri-Buri, in Hotel Bellevue (with Elbterrasse and Palais restaurants, Café Pöppelmann, Bierclub Nr 15, etc.), Köpckestrasse 15, tel. 5 66 20; Canaletto, tel. 5 66 27 37; Elbflorenz, in Hotel Astoria, Ernst-Thälmann-Platz, tel. 47 51 71; Haus Altmarkt, Ernst-Thälmann-Strasse 19–21, tel. 4 95 12 12; International, Prager Strasse 15, tel. 4 95 51 34; Kügelgenhaus, Strasse der Befreiung 11–13, tel. 5 27 91; Kurhaus Bühlau, Siegfried-Rödel-Platz 1, tel. 3 65 88; Le Gourmet, An der Frauenkirche 5, tel. 4 84 17 98; Leningrad, in Hotel Newa, Leningrader Strasse, tel. 4 96 71 12; Luisenhof, Bergbahnstrasse 8, tel. 3 68 42; Maygarten-Strassenbahnlinie 6, Schaufuss-strasse 24, tel. 3 02 68; Meissner Weinkeller, Strasse der Befreiung 1B, tel. 5 58 14; Ostrava (Czech specialities), Fetscher Strasse 30, tel. 4 59 31 31; Ratskeller, Dr-Wilhelm-Külz-Ring 19, tel. 4 95 25 81; Rebstock, Niederwaldstrasse 10, tel. 3 50 35; Rossini, An der Frauenkirche 5, tel. 4 84 17 41; Schillergarten (in Radeberg), Schillerstrasse 37, tel. 25 71; Semperoper, Theaterplatz 2, tel. 4 84 25 81; Szeged (Hungarian specialities), Ernst-Thälmann-Strasse 4–6, tel. 4 95 13 71; Turmhaus Cotta, Grillparzerstrasse 51, tel. 8 60 04; Weinrestaurant Bacchus, Clara-Zetkin-Strasse 15; Zum Grünen Baum, An der Frauenkirche 5, tel. 4 84 10.

Duisburg   * L'Escalier, in Steigenberger Hotel Duisburger Hof, König-Heinrich-Platz, tel. 33 10 21; Töpferstube, in Novotel, Landfermannstrasse 20, tel. 30 00 30; La Gioconda, in Hotel Regent, Dellplatz 1, tel. 2 72 02; Rôtisserie Laterne, Mülheimer Strasse 38 (in Klöckner-haus), tel. 2 12 98; La Provence, Hohe Strasse 29, tel. 2 44 53; Wilhelmshöhe, Am

Botanischen Garten 21, tel. 33 06 66; Mercatorhalle, König-Heinrich-Platz, tel. 33 20 66; Schwan, Alter Markt 7, tel. 2 21 33.

*Grill-Royal, Breidenbacher Eck and Trader Vic's, in Hotel Breidenbacher Hof, Heinrich-Heine-Allee 36, tel. 1 30 30; *Rôtisserie, in Steigenberger Parkhotel, Corneliusplatz 1, tel. 86 51; Benkay and Travellers, in Hotel Niko, Immermannstrasse 41, tel. 83 41; Duesseldorfer, in Holiday Inn, Graf-Adolf-Platz 10, tel. 3 87 30; La Grappa, in Hotel Majestic, Cantadorstrasse 4, tel. 36 70 30; Victorian and Victorian Lounge, Königstrasse 3A, tel. 32 02 22; Savini, Stromstrasse 47, tel. 39 39 31; Orangerie, Bilker Strasse 30, tel. 13 18 28; Café des Artistes, Locanda Ticinese and Café-Confiserie, Königsallee 60 (in Mövenpick in Kö-Galerie), tel. 32 03 14; Naschkörbchen, Königsallee 27 (in WZ-Center), tel. 32 95 50; La Terrazza, Königsallee 30 (in Kö-Center), tel. 32 85 53; Nachrichten Treff ("NT"), Königsallee 27 (in WZ-Center), tel. 13 23 11; Rib-Room, in Günnewig-Hotel Esplanade, Fürstenplatz 17, tel. 37 50 10; Weinhaus Tante Anna, Andreasstrasse 2, tel. 13 11 63; St Maximilian, Citadellstrasse 8, tel. 8 48 55; Benrather Hof, Steinstrasse 1, tel. 32 52 18. **Düsseldorf**

Stadt Eberswalde, Wilhelm-Pieck-Strasse 26, tel. 2 31 68; Ratskeller, Strasse der Jugend 44, tel. 2 25 90; Haus am Stadtsee, Angermünder Chaussee, tel. 2 24 81; Tierpark-Gaststätte, Am Wasserfall, tel. 2 24 04. **Eberswalde-Finow**

Domherrenhof, Domplatz 5, tel. 61 26; Gasthof Krone, Domplatz 3, tel. 44 06; Gasthof Zur Trompete, Ostenstrasse 3, tel. 16 13. **Eichstätt**

Broilerbar, Frauenberg 7, no tel.; Jägerrestaurant, Auf der Wartburg, tel. 51 11; Markt-schänke, Markt 19, tel. 34 61; Schlosskeller (fish), Esplanade, tel. 38 85; Schorschls Tagesbar, Georgenstrasse 19, tel. 7 27 39; Turmschänke, Wartburg-Allee 2, tel. 52 91; Zisterne, Jakobsplan 10, tel. 61 60; Zwinger, Bahnhofstrasse, tel. 52 91. **Eisenach**

Bärenschänke, Tiergarten, tel. 22 71; Kegelbahn, Goethestrasse, tel. 6 43 60; Trompeter-schlösschen, Ernst-Thälmann-Platz 11, tel. 22 13. **Eisenberg**

Aktivist, Karl-Marx-Strasse, tel. 4 33 30; Aufbau, Bahnhofstrasse 100, tel. 21 49; Bräus-tübl, Strasse des Komsomol 61, tel. 4 41 15; Club am Anger, Pionierweg 3, tel. 4 35 42; Diehloer Höhe, Diehloher Strasse, tel. 4 63 76; Friedensanker, Wilhelm-Pieck-Strasse, tel. 22 13; Fürstenberger Hof, Wilhelm-Pieck-Strasse, tel. 27 05; Halbzeit, Diehloher Strasse, tel. 4 60 22; Husch, Leninallee 1–3, tel. 4 60 26; Kastanienhof, Fischerstrasse, no tel.; Kosmos, Fröbelring, tel. 6 13 10; Mittelschleuse, Mittelschleuse, tel. 4 36 06; Schwarzer Adler, Buchwaldstrasse 42, tel. 27 32; Stadt-Mitte, Wilhelm-Pieck-Strasse, tel. 21 61; Unterm Schirm, Karl-Marx-Strasse, tel. 4 62 96; Unterschleuse, An der Unterschleuse, tel. 6 12 65; Zur Sonne, Thälmannstrasse, tel. 4 31 92. **Eisenhüttenstadt**

Schmidt, Friedrich-Ebert-Strasse 79, tel. 2 40 57; Goldener Adler, Neutorstrasse 5, tel. 2 40 55; Faldernpoort, Courbièrestrasse 6, tel. 2 10 75; restaurant in Heerens-Hotel, Friedrich-Ebert-Strasse 67, tel. 2 37 40; Deutsches Haus, Neuer Markt 7, tel. 2 20 48. **Emden**

Alter Schwan, Gotthardstrasse 27, tel. 2 91 16; Berolina, Berliner Platz, tel. 72 20 50; Caponniere, iga-Gelände, tel. 2 64 95; Drushba, Anger 19–20, tel. 2 13 16; restaurants in Erfurter Hof, Am Bahnhofsvorplatz, tel. 5 11 51; Gastmahl des Meeres, Bahnhofstrasse 45, tel. 2 23 84; Gildehaus, Fischmarkt 13–16, tel. 2 32 73; Hohe Lilie, Domplatz 31, tel. 2 25 78; International, Neuwerkstrasse 31–32, tel. 2 25 61; Lowetsch, Walkmühlstrasse 13, tel. 2 40 47; Presseklub, Dalbersweg, tel. 2 23 16; Stadt Berlin, Berliner Platz, tel. 72 10 02; Stadt Moskau, Moskauer Platz, tel. 77 31 18; Stadt Vilnius, Vilniuser Strasse, tel. 72 11 02; Winzerkeller, Bahnhofstrasse 5, tel. 5 11 51; Zur Alten Stadtmauer, Juri-Gagarin-Ring, tel. 2 64 20. **Erfurt**

Bayerischer Hof, Schuhstrasse 31, tel. 81 10; Le Bistro and Ratsstüberl, in Transmar Kongress-Hotel, Beethovenstrasse 3, tel. 80 40; Frankenkrug, Neuer Markt, tel. 2 58 82; Altmann's Stube, Theaterplatz 9, tel. 2 40 82; Da Pippo, Paulistrasse 12, tel. 20 73 94; Fischküche Silberhorn, Wöhrstrasse 13, tel. 2 30 05; A'Petit Theater-Restaurant, Theater-strasse 6, tel. 2 42 39; Schoppenweinstube Zur Kanne, Goethestrasse 25, tel. 2 10 31; Weinhaus Kach, Kirchenstrasse 2, tel. 2 23 72; Gasthaus Oppelei, Halbmondstrasse 4, tel. 2 15 62; Fränkischer Hof, Goethestrasse 34, tel. 2 20 12; Drei Husaren, Apfelstrasse 8, tel. 1 17 50. **Erlangen**

Restaurants

Essen

Restaurant am Park, in Sheraton Hotel, Huyssenallee 55, tel. 2 09 51; Au Premier and Le Bistro, in Hotel Handelshof-Mövenpick, Am Hauptbahnhof 2, tel. 1 70 80; Essener Hof, Teichstrasse 2, tel. 2 09 01; Barrelhouse, in Hotel Assindia, Viehofer Platz 5, tel. 23 50 77; Le Point de Rencontre, in Hotel Arcade, Hollestrasse 50, tel. 2 42 80; La Grappa, Rellinghauser Strasse 4, tel. 23 17 66; Rôtisserie im Saalbau, Huyssenallee 53, tel. 22 18 66; Bonne Auberge, Witteringstrasse 92A, tel. 78 39 99.

Esslingen

Distel, in Hotel Am Schelztor, Schelztorstrasse 5, tel. 35 30 51; Rosenau, Plochinger Strasse 65, tel. 31 63 97; Kupferschmiede, Mittlere Beutau 43, tel. 35 37 21; Dicker Turm, Auf der Burg, tel. 35 50 35.

Ettal

Klosterhof, in Hotel Ludwig der Bayer, Kaiser-Ludwig-Platz 10, tel. 66 01; Poststubn and Café, Kaiser-Ludwig-Platz 18, tel. 5 96.

Flensburg

Bei Petuh, in Flensburger Hof, Süderhofenden 38, tel. 1 73 20; Stadtrestaurant, Bahnhofstrasse 15, tel. 2 35 66; Borgerforeningen, Holm 17, tel. 2 33 85; Piet Henningsen, Schiffbrücke 20, tel. 2 45 76.

Frankfurt am Main

* Français, Hofgarten, Frankfurter Stubb and Bistro Kaiserbrunnen, in Steigenberger Hotel Frankfurter Hof, Am Kaiserplatz, tel. 2 15 02; * Rôtisserie, Brasserie and Bierstube, in Hotel Intercontinental, Wilhelm-Leuschner-Strasse 43, tel. 2 60 50; Hessischer Hof, Friedrich-Ebert-Anlage 40, tel. 7 54 00; La Truffe and Mövenpick, in Parkhotel, Wiesenhüttenplatz 28, tel. 2 69 70; Geheimratsstube and Bäckerei, in Marriott-Hotel, Hamburger Allee 2, tel. 7 95 50; Pullman Hotel Savigny, Savignystrasse 14, tel. 7 53 30; Altea Hotel Residenz an der Messe, Voltastrasse 29, tel. 7 92 60; Savoy and Rhapsody, in Scandic Crown Hotel, Wiesenhüttenstrasse 42, tel. 27 39 60; Conti, in Continental Hotel, Baseler Strasse 56, tel. 23 03 41; Bastei im Palmenhof, Bockenheimer Landstrasse 89, tel. 7 53 00 60; Le Midi, Liebigstrasse 47, tel. 72 14 38; * Weinhaus Brückenkeller, Schützenstrasse 6, tel. 28 42 38; Mövenpick-Gastronomie: Baron de la Mouette, Orangerie, Rob-Roy and Boulevard Opera, Opernplatz 2, tel. 2 06 80; Gastronomie in der Alten Oper: Jacques Offenbach, Opernkeller and Café Im Alten Foyer, Opernplatz, tel. 1 34 03 80; Villa Leonardi, Zeppelinallee 18, tel. 74 25 35; Alte Kanzlei, Niedenau 50, tel. 72 14 24; Da Claudio, Zum-Jungen-Strasse 10, tel. 56 54 71; Charlot, Opernplatz 10, tel. 28 70 07; Zum Schwarzen Stern, Römerberg 6, tel. 29 19 79; Da Mario, Moselstrasse 12, tel. 25 11 94; Schildkröte, Grosse Eschenheimer Strasse 41, tel. 28 10 36; Casa del Pittore, Zeisselstrasse 20, tel. 59 91 34; Da Bruno, Elbestrasse 15, tel. 23 34 16; Börsenkeller, Schillerstrasse 11, tel. 28 11 15; Aubergine, Alte Gasse 14, tel. 28 78 43; Incontro, Kettenhofweg 64, tel. 72 58 81; Da Lucio e Mario, Feuerbachstrasse 23, tel. 72 54 80; Intercity-Restaurant, in Hauptbahnhof, tel. 27 39 50; Zum Bitburger, Hochstrasse 54, tel. 28 03 02; Rosa, Grüneburgweg 25, tel. 72 13 80; Entrecôte, Reuterweg 61, tel. 72 45 98; Bindingbräu, Friedensstrasse 2, tel. 28 52 12; Löffel, Mainzer Landstrasse 374, tel. 73 33 60; Apfelwein Klaus, Meisengasse 10, tel. 28 28 64.

Frankfurt an der Oder

Broilereck, Tunnelstrasse 1, tel. 2 79 91; Gastmahl des Meeres, Kleine Oderstrasse, tel. 32 71 75; Grillbar im Hochhaus, tel. 38 15 43; Grillbar and restaurant in Hotel Stadt Frankfurt, Karl-Marx-Strasse 193, tel. 38 90; Grünhof, August-Bebel-Strasse 54, tel. 2 71 84; Haus der Einheit, Gubener Strasse 13–14, tel. 2 26 11; Haus des Handwerks, Bahnhofstrasse 13, tel. 32 45 73; Oderland, in Hochhaus, tel. 38 15 86; Polonia, Wilhelm-Pieck-Strasse 296, tel. 2 26 95; Ratskeller, in Rathaus, tel. 32 70 05; Stadtwappen, Ernst-Thälmann-Strasse 32, tel. 32 63 05; Wintergarten am Alten Wasserturm, Mühlenweg, tel. 4 26 69; Witebsk, Karl-Marx-Strasse 169, tel. 32 50 63.

Freiberg

Bergglöckchen, Ulrich-Rülein-Strasse 13, tel 33 70; Brauhof, Körnerstrasse 2, tel. 32 81; Erbisches Tor, Karl-Marx-Strasse 16, tel. 4 80 96; Euchler, Berthelsdorfer Strasse 7, tel. 4 77 55; Gastmahl des Meeres, Karl-Marx-Strasse 3, tel. 4 71 08; Gastronom, Karl-Kegel-Strasse, tel. 60 35; Gold-Broiler, Obermarkt, tel. 4 75 88; Klosterschänke, Pfarrgasse 35, tel. 30 20; Ofenblase, Stollengasse 5, tel. 35 67; Peterstor, August-Bebel-Strasse 14, tel. 34 67; Ratskeller, Obermarkt 16, tel. 33 22; Sächsischer Hof, Berthelsdorfer Strasse 23, tel. 30 82; Schlosskeller, Otto-Nuschke-Platz, tel. 38 04; Schloss-schänke, Prüferstrasse 8, tel. 22 06; Seilerberg, Thomas-Mann-Strasse 18, tel. 6 75 95; Stadt Dresden, Dresdener Strasse 4, tel. 27 87.

Falkenstube and Zirbelstube, in Colombi-Hotel, Rotteckring 16, tel. 3 14 15; Wolfshöhle, Konviktstrasse 8, tel. 3 03 03; Alte Weinstube Zur Traube, Schusterstrasse 17, tel. 3 21 90; Victoria, Eisenbahnstrasse 54, tel. 3 18 81; Oberkirchs Weinstuben, Münsterplatz 22, tel. 3 10 11; Zum Roten Bären, Oberlinden 12, tel. 3 69 13; Badische Winzerstube, in Schwarzwälder Hof, Herrenstrasse 43, tel. 3 23 86; Markgräfler Hof, Gerberau 22, tel. 3 25 40; Kolpinghaus, Karlstrasse 7, tel. 3 19 30; Rappen, Münsterplatz 13, tel. 3 13 53; Kleiner Meyerhof, Rathausgasse 27, tel. 2 69 41; Grosser Meyerhof, Grünwälderstrasse 1, tel. 2 25 52.

Freiburg im Breisgau

Jagdhorn and Im Schnokeloch restaurants in Steigenberger Hotel, Karl-von-Hahn-Strasse 129, tel. 8 10; Kurhaus Palmenwald, Lauterbadstrasse 56, tel. 40 01; restaurant in Schwarzwaldhotel Birkenhof, Wildbader Strasse 95, tel. 40 74; Weinstube in Hotel Hohenried, Zeppelinstrasse 5, tel. 24 14; Golfhotel Waldlust, Lauterbadstrasse 92, tel. 40 51; Sonne Exquisit and Sonnenstüble, in Kurhotel Sonne am Kurpark, Turnhallestrasse 63, tel. 60 44; Kur- und Sporthotel Eden, Im Nickentäle 5, tel. 70 37; Luz Posthotel, Stuttgarter Strasse 5, tel. 24 21; Bären, Lange Strasse 33, tel. 27 29; Gasthof Warteck, Stuttgarter Strasse 14, tel. 74 18; Gasthof Schwanen, Forststrasse 6, tel. 22 67; Ratskeller, Marktplatz 8, tel. 26 93; Bärenschlössle, Christophstal 29, tel. 78 50.

Freudenstadt

Kurgartenrestaurant, Olgastrasse 20 (in Graf-Zeppelin-Haus), tel. 7 20 72; Buchhorner Hof, Friedrichstrasse 33, tel. 20 50; Föhr, Albrechtstrasse 73, tel. 2 60 66; City-Krone, Schanzstrasse 7, tel. 2 20 86.

Friedrichshafen

Dianakeller, in Hotel Maritim Am Schlossgarten, Pauluspromenade 2, tel. 28 20; restaurant in Romantik-Hotel Goldener Karpfen, Simpliziusplatz 1, tel. 7 00 44; Zum Kurfürsten, Schloss-strasse 2, tel. 7 00 01; Prälat im Kolpinghaus, Goethestrasse 13, tel. 7 60 52; Bachmühle, Künzeller Strasse 133, tel. 3 40 01; Corniche de France, Kanalstrasse 3, tel. 7 02 00; Dachsbau, Pfandhausstrasse 7, tel. 7 40 30 (Weinstube tel. 7 41 12).

Fulda

Rauchkuchl, in Hotel Bavaria, Nürnberger Strasse 54, tel. 77 49 41; Baumann, Schwabacher Strasse 131, tel. 77 76 50; Alter Nachtwächter, Marienstrasse 11, tel. 77 59 51; Kupferpfanne, Konigstrasse 85, tel. 77 12 77.

Fürth

Café in Hotel Sonne, Reichenstrasse 37, tel. 60- 61.
In Bad Faulenbach:
Kur-Hotel Ruchti, Alatseestrasse 38, tel. 40 42; Alpen-Schlössle, Alatseestrasse 28, tel. 40 17.
In Hopfen am See:
Landhaus Enzensberger, Höhenstrasse 53, tel. 40 61; Alpenblick, Uferstrasse 10, tel. 5 05 70.
In Weissensee:
Bergruh, Alte Steige 16, tel. 77 42.

Füssen

In Garmisch:
*Terrasse and Post-Hörnd'l, in Clausings Posthotel, Marienplatz 12, tel. 70 90; Blauer Salon and Zirbelstube in Grand-Hotel Sonnenbichl, Burgstrasse 97, tel. 70 20; Rôtisserie Mühlenstube and Zum Mühlradl in Hotel Obermühle, Mühlstrasse 22, tel. 70 40; Alpina Stuben, Alpspitzstrasse 12, tel. 5 50 31; Alpenhof, Bahnhofstrasse 74, tel. 5 90 55.

In Partenkirchen:
Reindl's Partenkirchner Hof, Bahnhofstrasse 15, tel. 5 80 25; Alte Posthalterei and café in Posthotel Partenkirchen, Ludwigstrasse 49, tel. 5 10 67; Zirbelstube, Bayernland and Almstadl, in Dorint Sporthotel, Mittenwalder Strasse 59, tel. 70 60; Bayerische Botschaft restaurant in Queens Hotel Résidence, Mittenwalder Strasse 2, tel. 75 61; restaurant and café in Hotel Mercure Königshof, St-Martin-Strasse 4, tel. 72 70; Leiner, Wildenauer Strasse 20, tel. 5 00 34; Gasthof Fraundorfer, Ludwigstrasse 24, tel. 21 76; Werdenfelser Hof, Ludwigstrasse 58, tel. 36 21.

Garmisch-Partenkirchen

Parkrestaurant, in Hotel Maritim, Am Stadtgarten 1, tel. 17 60; Ibis, Bahnhofsvorplatz 12, tel. 1 70 20; Freudenstein am Zoo, Bleckstrasse 47, tel. 8 56 60; Hirt, Arminstrasse 14, tel. 2 32 35.

Gelsenkirchen

Restaurants

Gera
Bierhöhler, in Hotel Gera, Strasse der Republik 30, tel. 2 29 91; Gastmahl des Meeres, Zschochernstrasse 4, tel. 2 31 93; Gastronom, Strasse der Republik, tel. 2 62 28; restaurant in Sports and Leisure Centre, Naulitzer Strasse 28, Gera-Leumnitz, tel. 2 34 88; Haus des Handwerks, Puschkinplatz, tel. 2 40 41; Jagdhof, Schlossallee, tel. 2 32 88; Quisisana, Neue Strasse 2, tel. 2 35 10; Ratskeller, Markt, tel. 2 66 80; Sliven (Bulgarian specialities), Kornmarkt, tel. 2 65 22; Theaterrestaurant, Dimitroffallee, tel. 2 69 03; Thüringen Grill, Haus der Kultur, Strasse des 7. Oktober, tel. 61 92 83; Wernesgrüner Bierstube, Kornmarkt, tel. 2 39 53.

Görlitz
Berggaststätte Landskrone, Görlitz-Biesnitz, tel. 7 80 15; Bürgerstübl, Neiss-strasse 27, tel. 47 22; Burghof, Promenadenstrasse 96, tel. 7 80 98; Destille, Nikolaistrasse 6, tel. 55 32; Deutsches Haus, Reichenbacher Strasse 61, tel. 7 82 41; Gastmahl des Meeres, Struvestrasse 2, tel. 46 29; Goldener Baum, Untermarkt 4–5, tel. 62 68; Landskronbierstuben, Berliner Strasse 50, tel. 49 14; Stadthalle, Strasse der Freundschaft, tel. 44 60; Taverne, Platz der Befreiung, tel. 43 25; Touristenheim, Promenadenstrasse 120, Görlitz-Biesnitz, tel. 7 88 58.

Goslar
Altdeutsche Bierstube, in Hotel Der Achtermann, Rosentorstrasse 20, tel. 2 10 01; Die Worth, in Hotel Kaiserworth, Markt 3, tel. 2 11 11; Schwarzer Adler, Rosentorstrasse 25, tel. 2 40 01; Das Brusttuch, Hoher Weg 1, tel. 2 10 81; Goldene Krone, Breite Strasse 46, tel. 2 27 92; Burgrestaurant im Zwinger, Thomasstrasse 2, tel. 2 20 77; Crêperie and Weinstube Bei Bernard, Worthstrasse 11, tel. 2 96 79.

Gotha
Alte Sternwarte, Kleiner Seeberg, tel. 5 26 05; Berggarten, In der Klinge, Galbergweg 16, tel. 5 44 75; Düppel, Seebergen (reached via Wechmar), tel. 4 42; Feldschlösschen, Waltershäuser Strasse, tel. 5 43 32; Freundschaft, Wilhelm-Pieck-Platz, tel. 5 85 14; Gastmahl des Meeres, Schwabhäuser Strasse 47, tel. 5 29 55; Gockel-Grill, Hauptmarkt 26, tel. 5 32 54; Orangerie, Karl-Marx-Strasse 8, tel. 5 36 51; Parkpavillon, Puschkinallee 3, tel. 5 21 44; ; Schlossgaststätte, Schloss Friedenstein, tel. 5 23 31; Tanne, Jüdenstrasse, tel. 5 24 50; Thüringer Hof, Hüttenstrasse 8, tel. 5 25 48; Zur Wartburg, Waltershäuser Strasse 43, tel. 5 20 66.

Göttingen
Gebhards, Goetheallee 22, tel. 4 96 80; Schwarzer Bär, Kurze Strasse 12, tel. 5 82 84; Junkernschänke, Barfüsserstrasse 5, tel. 6 73 20; Eden Stube, Reinhäuser Landstrasse 22A, tel. 7 60 07; Kasseler Hof, Rosdorfer Weg 26, tel. 7 20 81.

Güstrow
Altdeutsche Bierstuben, Am Berge 11, tel. 6 26 17; Fischerklause, Lange Strasse 9, tel. 6 44 38; Freundschaft, Wilhelm-Pieck-Strasse 2, tel. 6 35 66; Haus des Handwerks, Strasse der Befreiung 1, tel. 6 20 51; Kurhaus, Inselsee, tel. 6 30 06; Marktkrug, Markt 14, tel. 62 34–0; Schlossgaststätte, Franz-Parr-Platz 1, tel. 6 30 30; Stadt Güstrow, Markt 2–3, tel. 48 41; Weinstuben, Markt 27–28, tel. 6 26 12; Zum Jägerstübchen, Schloss-strasse 1–2, tel. 6 18 13; Zum Kaland, Mühlenstrasse 21, tel. 6 32 32; Zum Ratskeller, Markt 10, tel. 6 41 83.

Gütersloh
Restaurant and Brasserie in Parkhotel, Kirchstrasse 27, tel. 87 70; Busch, Carl-Bertelsmann-Strasse 127, tel. 18 01; Stadt Hamburg, Feuerbornstrasse 9, tel. 5 89 11; Appelbaum, Neuenkirchener Strasse 59, tel. 5 11 76; Zur Deele and Apostel-Weinstube, Kirchstrasse 13, tel. 1 40 17; Bockskrug, Parkstrasse 44, tel. 5 43 70.

Hagen
Felsengarten, in Queens Hotel, Wasserloses Tal 4, tel. 39 10; Rustika, in Hotel Lex, Elberfelder Strasse 71, tel. 3 20 30; Zum Bauernhaus, Feithstrasse 141, tel. 8 17 43.

Halle
Alchimistenklause, Reilstrasse 47, tel. 2 42 72; Böllberger Gaststätte, Katowicer Strasse, tel. 4 10 46; Eissporthalle, tel. 64 20 35; Freyburger Weinstuben, Rathausstrasse 7, tel. 2 49 93; Haus am Leipziger Turm, Waisenhausring 16, tel. 2 63 91; Intermezzo, Rathausstrasse 9, tel. 2 96 65; Krug zum Grünen Kranze, Talstrasse 37, tel. 3 00 49; Market Snack, Grosse Steinstrasse 74, tel. 2 90 83; Moritzburg-Weinkeller, Friedemann-Bach-Platz 5, tel. 2 93 39; Panorama, Grosse Ulrichstrasse 6–8, tel. 2 31 64; Pirouette, Gimritzer Damm, tel. 64 20 54; Ratsgaststätte, Marktplatz 2, tel. 2 46 50; Roland, Marktplatz, tel. 2 41 91; Schellenmoritz, An der Moritzkirche 1, tel. 2 37 13; Silberhöhe, Strasse der Neuerer 19, tel. 70 20 13; Tallinn, Rigaer Strasse, tel. 4 53 45; Ufa (Russian specialities), in Hotel Stadt Halle, Ernst-Thälmann-Platz 17, tel. 3 80 41.

*Haerlin, Jahreszeiten-Grill, Spät-Restaurant Jahreszeiten-Keller and Café Condi, in **Hamburg** Hotel Vier Jahreszeiten, Neuer Jungfernstieg 9, tel. 3 40 40; *Dachgarten-Restaurant Fontenay-Grill and Hulk-Brasserie, in Hotel Inter-Continental, Fontenay 10, tel. 41 41 50; Atlantic-Grill and Atlantic-Mühle, in Atlantic Hotel Kempinski, An der Alster 72, tel. 2 88 80; Noblesse, in Hotel Ramada Renaissance, Grosse Bleiche, tel. 34 91 80; Sea Grill, in Marriott Hotel, ABC-Strasse 52, tel. 34 91 80; Vierländer Stuben, in SAS Plaza Hotel Hamburg, Marseiller Strasse 2, tel. 3 50 20; La Mer, in Hotel Prem, An der Alster 9, tel. 24 17 26; Schümanns Austernkeller, Jungfernstieg 34, tel. 34 62 65; Il Ristorante, Gross Bleichen 16, tel. 34 33 35; Peter Lembcke, Holzdamm 49, tel. 24 32 90; Petit Délice, Grosse Bleichen 21 (in Galleria), tel. 34 34 70; Zum Alten Rathaus, Börsenbrücke 10, tel. 36 75 70; Galerie-Stuben, Krayenkamp 11, tel. 36 58 00; Deichgraf, Deichstrasse 23, tel. 36 42 08; Café des Artistes, Backstube, Weinkeller Bistro à Vin and Espresso, in Mövenpick, Grosse Bleiche 30 (Hanse-Galerie), tel. 3 41 00 32; Im Finnlandhaus, Esplanade 41, tel. 34 41 33; Ratsweinkeller, Grosse Johannisstrasse 2, tel. 36 41 53; Old Commercial Room, Englische Planke 10, tel. 36 63 19; Mövenpick Spitaler Brücke, Backstube and Café Veneto, Spitaler Strasse 9, tel. 32 14 61; Vitell, Wexstrasse 38, tel. 34 50 30; Dominique, Karl-Muck-Platz 11, tel. 34 45 11; Nikolaikeller, Cremon 36, tel. 36 61 13; Zur Schlachter-börse, Kampstrasse 42, tel. 43 65 43.
In Altona:
*Fischereihafen-Restaurant, Grosse Elbstrasse 143, tel. 38 18 16.

Brochette and Alt Hameln, in Dorint Hotel Weserbergland, 164er Ring 3, tel. 79 20; Zur **Hameln** Krone, Osterstrasse 30, tel. 74 11; Reckzeh's Restaurant Alte Marktstube, Alte Markt-strasse 31, tel. 4 46 64; Seehof, Tönebönweg 3, tel. 4 17 22; Rattenfängerhaus, Oster-strasse 28, tel. 38 88.

La Fontana, in Brüder-Grimm-Hotel, Kurt-Blaum-Platz 6, tel. 30 60; Königs-Stuben, in **Hanau** Hotel Royal, Salzstrasse 14, tel. 2 41 57; Zur Linde, Steinheimer Vorstadt 31, tel. 65 90 71.

*Ammans Restaurant, Hildesheimer Strasse 185, tel. 83 08 18; Prinz Taverne, Wilhelm- **Hannover** Busch-Stube and Café am Kamin, in Hotel Inter-Continental, Friedrichswall 11, tel. 3 67 70; Schu's Restaurant and Gourmets' Buffet, in Hotel Schweizerhof, Hinüberstrasse 6, tel. 3 49 50; Luisenstube and Luisenpub, in Kastens Hotel Luisenhof, Luisenstrasse 1, tel. 3 04 40; Le Cordon Rouge, in Hotel Maritim, Hildesheimer Strasse 34, tel. 1 65 31; Bristol Grill and Kanzleistube, in Congress-Hotel am Stadtpark, Clausewitzstrasse 6, tel. 2 80 50; Four Seasons, in Plaza Hotel, Fernroder Strasse 9, tel. 3 38 80; Kastanie, in Hotel Mercure, Am Maschpark 3, tel. 8 00 80; Brunnenhof, in Central-Hotel Kaiserhof, Ernst-August-Platz 4, tel. 3 68 30; Loccumer Hof, Kurt-Schumacher-Strasse 16, tel. 32 60 51; Lützower Jäger, in Hotel Körner, Körnerstrasse 24, tel. 1 46 66; Milano, in Hotel Am Funkturm, Hallerstrasse 34, tel. 31 70 33; Intercity-Restaurant, Ernst-August-Platz 1, tel. 32 74 61; Am Rathaus, Friedrichswall 21, tel. 32 62 68; Baron de la Mouette, Backstube and Mövenpick-Café Kröpcke, Georgstrasse 35, tel. 32 62 85; Lila Kranz, Kirchwender Strasse 23, tel. 85 89 21; Stern's Sternchen, Marienstrasse 104, tel. 81 73 22; Clichy, Weissekreuzstrasse 31, tel. 31 24 47; Hindenburg-Klassik, Gneisenaustrasse 55, tel. 85 85 88; A la Lune, Marktstrasse 41, tel. 32 22 29; Ratskeller, Schmiedestrasse 1, tel. 1 53 63; Wein-Wolf, Rathenaustrasse 2, tel. 32 07 88; Budweiser Hof, Adenauerallee 10, tel. 81 45 46; Prager Hof, Gellertstrasse 26, tel. 81 57 83; Limandes, Raschplatz 3, tel. 31 86 05; Rôtisserie Helvetia, Georgsplatz 11, tel. 1 48 41; Altdeutsche Bierstube, Lär-chenstrasse 4, tel. 34 49 21; Kartoffelhaus, An der Lutherkirche 13, tel. 70 25 33; Roma, Goethestrasse 24, tel. 32 06 45; Vater und Sohn, Warmbüchenstrasse 30, tel. 32 12 76; Brauhaus Ernst August, Schmiedestrasse 13, tel. 30 60 30; Wiener Sophie, Königstrasse 12, tel. 35 54 38; Broyhan-Haus, Kramerstrasse 24, tel. 32 39 19.

Kurfürstenstube and Caféteria Europa-Treff, in Hotel Europäischer Hof-Hotel Europa, **Heidelberg** Friedrich-Ebert-Anlage 1, tel. 51 50; Globetrotter, in Penta Hotel, Vangerowstrasse 16, tel. 90 80; Palatina and Atrium, in Holiday Inn City Center, Kurfürstenanlage 1, tel. 91 70; Brasserie in Rega-Hotel, Bergheimer Strasse 63, tel. 50 80; Holländer Hof, Neckarstaden 66, tel. 1 20 91; restaurant in Romantik-Hotel Zum Ritter St Georg, Hauptstrasse 178, tel. 2 02 03; Zur Herrenmühle, Hauptstrasse 237, tel. 1 29 09; Simplicissimus, Ingrimstrasse 16, tel. 1 33 36; Scheffeleck, Friedrich-Ebert-Anlage 51, tel. 2 61 72; Schönberger Hof, Untere Neckarstrasse 54 (opposite Stadthalle), tel. 2 26 15; Goldener Hecht, Steingasse 2, tel. 16 60 25; Piccolo Mondo, Klingenteichstrasse 6, tel. 1 29 99.

Restaurants

Heilbronn
Royal and Schwäbisches Restaurant, in Insel-Hotel, Friedrich-Ebert-Brücke, tel. 63 00; Götz, Moltkestrasse 52, tel. 15 50; Burkhardt, Lohtorstrasse 7, tel. 6 22 40; Moustache, in Hotel Urbanus, Urbanstrasse 13, tel. 8 13 44; Wirtshaus Am Götzenturm, Allerheiligenstrasse 1, tel. 8 05 34; Haus des Handwerks, Allee 76, tel. 8 44 68; Heilbronner Winzerstüble, Ludwig-Pfau-Strasse 14, tel. 8 40 42; Münch's Beichtstuhl, Fischergasse 9, tel. 8 95 86.

Heiligenstadt
Berg's Gasthaus, tel. 27 70; Bistro St Martin (Eichsfeld specialities), Wilhelmstrasse 22, no tel.; Eichsfelder Hof, Karl-Marx-Strasse 56, tel. 26 75; Forsthaus, tel. 27 64; restaurant in Kreiskulturhaus, Aegidienstrasse 11, tel. 35 70; Goldener Löwe, Karl-Marx-Strasse 75, tel. 34 44; Haus des Handwerks, Marktplatz 8, tel. 30 51; Herget's Pizzeria, Schönbach, no tel.; Liethen-Treffpunkt, Bruno-Leuschner-Strasse 70, tel. 25 23; Neun Brunnen, Flinsberger Strasse, tel. 26 75; Norddeutscher Bund, Friedrich-Engels-Strasse 25, tel. 26 48; Schwarzer Adler, Wilhelmstrasse 2, tel. 22 50; Stadion, Am Leinberg 2, tel. 27 83; Thüringer Hof, Geislader Tor 8, tel. 36 61; Zum Brauhaus, tel. 29 22.

Heligoland
In Unterland:
Schwan, Am Südstrand 17, tel. 77 51; Deutsches Haus, Siemensterrasse 149, tel. 3 94.

In Oberland:
Zum Hamburger, Am Falm 304, tel. 4 09; Störtebeker, Steanakerstrasse 365, tel. 6 22.

Herford
Dohm-Klause, Lörstrasse 4, tel. 5 33 45; Die Alte Schule, Holland 39, tel. 5 40 09.

Hildesheim
Stadtschänke and Gildehaus in Forte Hotel, Am Markt 4, tel. 30 00; Im Potte restaurant in Gollarts Hotel Deutsches Haus, Bischof-Janssen-Strasse 5, tel. 1 59 71; Alex, in Hotel Schweizerhof, Hindenburgplatz 6, tel. 3 90 81; Bürgermeisterkapelle, Rathausstrasse 8, tel. 1 40 21; Ratskeller, Markt 1, tel. 1 44 41; Marco Polo, Sedanstrasse 10, tel. 13 24 24; Weinstube Schlegel, Am Steine 4, tel. 3 31 33; Zum Knochenhauer (with café), Markt 1, tel. 3 23 23.

Bad Homburg
Parkrestaurant and Bürgerstube in Kurhaus-Hotel Maritim, Ludwigstrasse, tel. 2 80 51; Hardtwald, Philosophenweg 31, tel. 8 10 26; Oberle's, Obergasse 1, tel. 2 46 62; Table, Kaiser-Friedrich-Promenade 85, tel. 2 44 25; Schildkröte, Mussbachstrasse 19, tel. 2 33 07; Assmann's, Kisseleffstrasse 27 (in Kurpark), tel. 27 10; Da Giovanni, Louisenstrasse 126, tel. 4 52 11; La Mamma, Dorotheenstrasse 18, tel. 2 47 28; Wasserweibchen, Am Mühlberg 57, tel. 2 98 78; Taverne Kavala, An der Weed, tel. 2 98 59.

Jena
Forelle, Holzmarkt 14, tel. 2 21 60; Fuchsturm, tel. 2 24 17; Jenzighaus, Am Jenzig 99, tel. 2 27 74; Kiosk Planetarium, Saalbahnhofstrasse 12, tel. 2 45 82; Kulturhaus Lobeda, Karl-Marx-Allee, tel. 3 40 74; Lodeburgklause, tel. 3 21 85; Ratzeise, Markt 1, tel. 2 39 11; restaurant in University Tower, Schillerstrasse, tel. 8 22 84 79.

Kaiserslautern
Alte Post, Mainzer Tor 3, tel. 6 43 71; Weinrestaurant Hans Hexenbäcker, Am Fackelrondell, tel. 7 29 20; Uwe's Tomate, Schillerplatz 4, tel. 9 34 06; Foyer, Mühlstrasse 31, tel. 7 84 88; Rathaus, Maxstrasse 1 (on 21st floor of New Town Hall), tel. 6 89 71.

Karlsruhe
Zum Markgrafen and Zum Brigande, in Ramada Renaissance Hotel, Mendelssohnplatz, tel. 3 71 70; La Résidence and Schwarzwaldstube, in Schlosshotel, Bahnhofplatz 2, tel. 35 40; Mövenpick, Ettlinger Strasse 23, tel. 3 72 70; Sam's, in Hotel National, Kriegsstrasse 90, tel. 6 09 50; Residence, Bahnhofplatz 14, tel. 3 71 50; Kaiserhof, Karl-Friedrich-Strasse 12, tel. 2 66 15; Rio, Hans-Sachs-Strasse 3, tel. 84 50 61; Hasen, Gerwigstrasse 47, tel. 61 50 76; Unter den Linden, Kaiserallee 71, tel. 84 91 85; Oberländer Weinstube, Akademiestrasse 7, tel. 2 50 66; Adria, Ritterstrasse 19, tel. 2 06 65; O'Henry's Spezialitätenrestaurant, Breite Strasse 24, tel. 38 55 51; Blüthner's, Gutenbergstrasse 5, tel. 84 22 28; Kommödchen, Marienstrasse 1, tel. 69 64 45; Goldenes Kreuz, Karlstrasse 21A, tel. 2 20 54; Moninger, Kaiserstrasse 142, tel. 2 48 19.

Kassel
Alt Cassel and Hessenklause, in Dorint Hotel Reiss, Werner-Hilpert-Strasse 24, tel. 7 88 30; Domus, Erzbergerstrasse 1, tel. 10 23 85; Ratskeller, Obere Königsstrasse 8, tel. 1 59 28; Weinstuben Boos, Wilhelmshöher Allee 97, tel. 2 22 09.

Kempten
Le Tzigane, Mozartstrasse 8, tel. 2 63 69; Sir Alexander, Haslacher Berg 2, tel. 2 83 22; Fürstenhof, Rathausplatz 8, tel. 2 53 60; Peterhof, Salzstrasse 1, tel. 2 55 25; Cambodu-

num, in Hotel Bayerischer Hof, Füssener Strasse 96, tel. 7 84 81; Gasthof Waldhorn, Steufzger Strasse 80, tel. 8 31 76; Sonnenhang, Mariaberger Strasse 78, tel. 9 37 56; Hummel (with café), Immenstädter Strasse 2, tel. 2 22 86.

Fayence and Hansa-Pavillon, in Hotel Conti-Hansa, Schlossgarten 7, tel. 5 11 50; Restaurant im Park, in Hotel Kieler Kaufmann, Niemannsweg 102, tel. 8 50 11; Kieler Yacht-Club, Hindenburgufer 70, tel. 8 50 55; Hotel Astor, Am Holstenplatz 1, tel. 9 30 17; Consul, Walkerdamm 11, tel. 6 30 15; Claudio's Ristorante, Königsweg 46, tel. 67 68 67; Restaurant im Schloss, Am Wall 80, tel. 9 11 58; September, Alte Lübecker Chaussee 27, tel. 68 06 10; Normandie, Schützenwall 1, tel. 67 34 24.   **Kiel**

Kurhaus-Restaurant and Kissinger Stüble, in Steigenberger Kurhaus-Hotel, Am Kurgarten 3, tel. 8 04 10; Bristol, Bismarckstrasse 8, tel. 82 40; Rixen, Frühlingstrasse 1, tel. 82 30; restaurant in Laudensacks Parkhotel, Kurhausstrasse 28, tel. 12 24; Vier Jahreszeiten, Bismarckstrasse 25, tel. 20 78; Bayerischer Hof, in Kurheim Dösch, Maxstrasse 9, tel. 52 70; Weinhaus Schubert, Kirchgasse 2, tel. 26 24.   **Bad Kissingen**

Le Gourmet and Rhapsody, in Scandic Crown Hotel, Julius-Wegeler-Strasse 6, tel. 13 60; Warsteiner Stuben, in Hotel Continental Pfälzer Hof, Bahnhofsplatz 1, tel. 3 30 73; Stresemann, Rheinzollstrasse 8, tel. 1 54 64; Wacht am Rhein, Rheinzollstrasse 6, tel. 1 53 13.   **Koblenz**

Seerestaurant and Dominikaner-Stuben in Steigenberger Inselhotel, Auf der Insel 1, tel. 2 50 11; restaurant in Parkhotel am See, Seestrasse 25, tel. 5 10 77; Ganter, in Hotel Seeblick, Neuhauser Strasse 14, tel. 5 40 18; Siber, in Seehotel, Seestrasse 25, tel. 6 30 44; Zum Nikolai Torkel, Eichhornstrasse 83, tel. 6 48 02; Goldener Stern, Bodanplatz 1, tel. 2 52 28; Casino-Restaurant, Seestrasse 21, tel. 6 36 15.   **Konstanz**

L'Escargot, Rôtisserie im Park and Niederrheinische Altbierstube, in Parkhotel Krefelder Hof, Uerdinger Strasse 245, tel. 58 40; restaurant in Hansa-Hotel, Am Hauptbahnhof, tel. 82 90; König-Stube in City Hotel Dahmen, Philadelphiastrasse 63, tel. 6 09 51; Koperpot, Rheinstrasse 30, tel. 6 48 14; Aquilon, Ostwall 199, tel. 80 02 07; Le Crocodile, Uerdinger Strasse 336, tel. 50 01 10; Gasthof Korff/Zum Königshof, Kölner Strasse 256, tel. 31 17 89; Seidenweberhaus, Theaterplatz 1, tel. 18 16; Poststuben, Dampfmühlenweg 58, tel. 2 46 56.   **Krefeld**

*Arabeske, in Hotel Merkur, Gerberstrasse 15, tel. 79 90; *Auerbachs Keller, Grimmaische Strasse 2–4, tel. 20 91 31; Barthels Hof, Markt 8, tel. 20 09 75; Bodega, Peterstrasse 15, Messehof, tel. 20 94 90; Burgkeller, Naschmarkt 1–3, tel. 29 56 39; Csárda, Schulstrasse 2, tel. 28 14 20; Falstaff, Georgiring 9, tel. 28 64 03; Fürstenhof, in Hotel International, Tröndlinring 8, tel. 7 18 80; Galerie, in Hotel Astoria, Platz der Republik, tel. 7 22 20; Gastmahl des Meeres, Dr-Kurt-Fischer-Strasse 1, tel. 29 11 60; Journalistenclub, Neumarkt 26, tel. 20 95 60; Kaffeebaum, Kleine Fischergasse 4, tel. 20 04 52; Parkgaststätte Markkleeberg, Agra-Gelände, tel. 32 61 47; Paulaner, Klostergasse 3, tel. 20 99 41; Pragers Biertunnel, Nürnberger Strasse 1, tel. 29 47 89; Rhapsodie, in Hotel Am Ring, Karl-Marx-Platz, tel. 7 95 20; Ratskeller, Lotterstrasse 1, tel. 7 91 35 91; Sachsen-Bräu, Hainstrasse 17–19, tel. 28 11 48; Spreewaldgaststätte, Fichtestrasse 25, tel. 31 15 71; Stadtpfeiffer, Am Markt, tel. 71 32; Thüringer Hof, Burgstrasse 19–23, tel. 20 98 84; Varadero, Barfussgässchen 8, tel. 28 16 86; *Vignette, in Hotel Stadt Leipzig, Richard-Wagner-Strasse 1–5, tel. 28 88 14; Wildpark-Gaststätte, Koburger Strasse, tel. 31 16 13; Zills Biertunnel and Weinstube, Barfussgässchen 9, tel. 20 04 46; Zum Löwen, Rudolf-Breitscheid-Strasse, tel. 7 22 30.   **Leipzig**

Bayerischer Hof, Seepromenade (on Hafenplatz), tel. 50 55; Reutemann, with Seegarten, Ludwigstrasse 23, tel. 50 55; Lindauer Hof, Dammgasse 2, tel. 40 64; Beaujolais, Ludwigstrasse 7, tel. 64 49; Spielbank-Restaurant, Oskar-Groll-Anlage 2, tel. 52 00; Helvetia, Seepromenade, tel. 40 02.   **Lindau**

Yachtzimmer in Ringhotel Jensen, An der Obertrave 4, tel. 7 16 46; Schabbelhaus, Mengstrasse 48, tel. 7 20 11; Wullenwever, Beckergrube 71, tel. 70 43 33; L'Etoile and Le Bistro, Grosse Petersgrube 8, tel. 7 64 40; Lübecker Hanse, Kolk 3, tel. 7 80 54; Die   **Lübeck**

Restaurants

Gemeinnützige, Königstrasse 5, tel. 7 38 12; Stadtrestaurant in Hauptbahnhof, Am Bahnhof 2, tel. 8 40 44; Das Kleine Restaurant, An der Untertrave 39, tel. 70 59 59; Haus der Schiffergesellschaft, Breite Strasse 2, tel. 7 67 76; Spökenkieker, in Hotel Alter Speicher, Beckergrube 91, tel. 7 10 45.

Ludwigsburg
Rhapsody, in Forum am Schlosspark, Stuttgarter Strasse 33, tel. 2 57 61; Favorit, Gartenstrasse 18, tel. 9 00 51; Schiller-Hospiz, Gartenstrasse 17, tel. 2 34 63; Alte Sonne, Bei der Katholischen Kirche 3 (on Marktplatz), tel. 2 52 31; Post-Cantz, Eberhardstrasse 6, tel. 2 35 63; Ratskeller, Wilhelmstrasse 13, tel. 2 70 60; Zum Justinus, Marktplatz 9, tel. 2 48 28.

Ludwigshafen
Bibliothek im Landhaus, Landhaus and Löwenbräu restaurants, in Ramada Hotel Ludwigshafen, Pasadena-Allee 4, tel. 51 93 01; Windrose, in Europa Hotel, Am Ludwigsplatz 5, tel. 58 70.

Lüneburg
Wellenkamp, Am Sande 9, tel. 4 30 26; Zum Heidkrug, Am Berge 5, tel. 3 12 49; Bremer Hof, Lüner Strasse 13, tel. 3 60 77; Ratskeller, Am Markt 1, tel. 3 17 57; Kronen-Brauhaus (with brewery museum), Heiligengeiststrasse 39, tel. 71 32 00.
In spa district:
Die Schnecke, in Hotel Residenz, Mustermannskamp 10, tel. 4 50 47; Seminaris, with Palmengarten, Soltauer Strasse 3, tel. 71 30; Heiderose, Uelzener Strasse 29, tel. 4 44 10; Am Kurpark, Uelzener Strasse 41, tel. 4 80 78.

Magdeburg
Bördegrill, Leiterstrasse, tel. 3 27 10; Bötelstube, Alter Markt, tel. 34 44 09; Buttergasse, Alter Markt, tel. 34 47 48; Donezk, Hegelstrasse 42, tel. 34 42 50; Fischerufer-Gastmahl des Meeres, Jakobstrasse 20, tel. 3 57 80; Moskwa, in Hotel International, tel. 38 40; Pliska (Bulgarian specialities), Karl-Marx-Strasse 115, tel. 115, tel. 5 11 62; Postkutsche, Leiterstrasse 6, tel. 3 19 12; Ratskeller, Alter Markt 5, tel. 3 21 02; Savarin, Breiter Weg 226, tel. 34 47 10; Stadt Prag, Karl-Marx-Strasse 20, tel. 34 46 72; Teestube Aserbaidshan, Karl-Marx-Strasse 20, tel. 3 59 35; Wildbrettstübel, Karl-Marx-Strasse 113, tel. 5 19 06; Zentral, Karl-Marx-Strasse, tel. 5 83 01.

Mainz
Rheingrill, Römische Weinstuben and Le Bistro, in Hotel Hilton International Mainz, Rheinstrasse 68, tel. 24 50; La Poularde and Moguntia-Stube, in Europahotel, Kaiserstrasse 7, tel. 63 50; Kaiserkeller, in Hotel Mainzer Hof, Kaiserstrasse 98, tel. 23 37 71; Bierkutsche, in Favorite Parkhotel, Karl-Weiser-Strasse 1, tel. 8 14 16; L'Echalote, in Central Hotel Eden, Bahnhofsplatz 8, tel. 61 43 31; Mainzer Weinkeller, in Hotel Stadt Mainz, Frauenlobstrasse 14, tel. 67 22 50; Zum Leininger Hof, Weintorstrasse 6, tel. 22 84 84; Drei Lilien and Drei Lilien-Keller, Ballplatz 2, tel. 22 50 68; Walderdorff, Karmeliterplatz 4, tel. 22 25 15; Haus des Deutschen Weines, Gutenbergplatz 3, tel. 22 86 76; Gebert's Weinstuben, Frauenlobstrasse 94, tel. 61 16 19; Rats- und Zunftstuben Heilig Geist, Rentengasse 2, tel. 22 57 57.

Mannheim
Restaurant and Holzkistl, in Steigenberger Hotel Mannheimer Hof, Augusta-Anlage 4, tel. 4 50 21; Park-Restaurant and Weintruhe, in Maritim Parkhotel, Friedrichsplatz 2, tel. 4 50 21; Le Pavillon, in Holiday Inn, Kurfürstenarkade, N 6, 3–7, tel. 1 07 10; Le Petit Restaurant and Mannemer Stubb, in Hotel Augusta, Augusta-Anlage 43, tel. 41 80 01; restaurant in Novotel, Auf dem Friedensplatz, tel. 41 70 01; Wartburg, F 4, 4, tel. 2 89 91; Intercity-Restaurant and Bürgerstube, in Intercity-Hotel Mannheim, Hauptbahnhof (East Wing), tel. 1 59 50; Da Gianni, R 7, 34, tel. 2 03 26; Blass, Friedrichsplatz 12, tel. 44 80 04; L'Epi d'Or, H 7, 3, tel. 1 43 97; Kopenhagen, Friedrichsring 2A (at Water-Tower), tel. 1 48 70; Altdeutsche Bierstube, Seckenheimer Strasse 4, tel. 22 41 46.

Marburg
Atelier, in Hotel Europäischer Hof, Elisabethstrasse 12, tel. 6 40 44; Waldecker Hof, Bahnhofstrasse 23, tel. 6 00 90; Hostería del Castello, Markt 19, tel. 2 58 84; Gasthaus Zur Sonne, Markt 14, tel. 2 60 36.

Meersburg
Winzerstube Zum Becher, Höllgasse 4 (at Neues Schloss), tel. 90 09; Weinstube Löwen, Marktplatz 2, tel. 60 13; Bären, Marktplatz 11, tel. 60 44; Seerestaurant Stärk, Seestrasse 7, tel. 77 28; restaurant and café in Hotel-Pension Off, Uferpromenade 51, tel. 3 33; Droste, Seestrasse 9, tel. 92 00.

Meissen
Am Burgberg, Meisastrasse 1, tel. 35 02; Bauernhäusel, Oberspaarer Strasse 20, tel. 33 17; Burgkeller, Domplatz 11, tel. 30 37; Domkeller, Domplatz 9, tel. 20 34; Gambrinus,

Wilhelm-Walkhoff-Platz, tel. 24 77; Goldener Löwe, Rathenau-Platz 6, tel. 33 04; Hamburger Hof, Dresdner Strasse 9, tel. 21 18; Meissner Hof, Lorenzgasse 7, tel. 24 96; Ratskeller, Markt 1, tel. 21 77; Sächsischer Hof, Hahnemannplatz 17, tel. 30 28; Stadtparkhöhe, Stadtparkhöhe 2, tel. 29 25;

Parkrestaurant, Fränkische Hofstube, Götz-Keller and Café Rosengarten, in Maritim Park Hotel, Lothar-Daiker-Strasse 6, tel. 53 90; Zirbelstuben and Tiroler Stuben, in Hotel Victoria, Poststrasse 2, tel. 59 30; Bundschu, Cronbergstrasse 15, tel. 30 43.　　**Bad Mergentheim**

Restaurant in Kruses Parkhotel, Marienstrasse 108, tel. 4 60 33; Bad Minden, Portastrasse 36, tel. 5 10 49; Alt Minden, Hahler Strasse 38, tel. 2 22 08; Lord Nelson, Stiftsallee 124, tel. 4 82 80; Domschänke, Kleiner Domhof 14, tel. 2 78 53.　　**Minden**

Post, Obermarkt 9, tel. 10 94; Rieger, Dekan-Karl-Platz 28, tel. 50 71; Gaststube and Josefikeller der Alpenrose, Obermarkt 1, tel. 50 55; Jägerstuben, in Jägerhof, Partenkirchner Strasse 35, tel. 10 41; Gasthof Mühlhauser, Partenkirchner Strasse 53, tel. 15 90; Arnspitze, Innsbrucker Strasse 68, tel. 24 25; La Toscana, Obermarkt 54, tel. 39 94; Postkeller and Alte Braustuben, Innsbrucker Strasse 13, tel. 17 29.　　**Mittenwald**

Brabanter Stuben, in Ambassador Hotel, Geroplatz, tel. 30 70; Parkrestaurant and Bierstube in Dorint Hotel, Hohenzollernstrasse 5, tel. 8 60 60; restaurant in Quality Inn Hotel Dahmen, Aachener Strasse 120, tel. 30 60; Burgund, Kaiserstrasse 85, tel. 2 01 55; Mike's, Weiherstrasse 51, tel. 1 25 40; Bohemia, Regentenstrasse 35, tel. 2 26 82; Tho Penningshof, Eickener Strasse 163, tel. 18 10 00.　　**Mönchengladbach**

*Restaurant in Hotel Vier Jahreszeiten Kempinski, Maximilianstrasse 17, tel. 23 03 90;　　**Munich**
*Aubergine, Maximiliansplatz 5, tel. 59 81 71; *Königshof, Karlsplatz 25, tel. 55 13 60;
*Tantris, Johann-Fichte-Strasse 7, tel. 36 20 61; La Mer, Schraudolphstrasse 24, tel. 2 72 24 39; Hilton-Grill and Isar-Terrassen, in Park Hilton Hotel, Am Tucherpark 7, tel. 3 84 50; Grill, Trader Vic's and Palais-Keller, in Bayerischer Hof, with Palais Montgelas, Promenadeplatz 2, tel. 2 12 00; Hubertus, in Excelsior Hotel, Schützenstrasse 11, tel. 55 13 70; Ambiente, in Arabella Westpark-Hotel, Garmischer Strasse 2, tel. 5 19 60; restaurant in Intercity-Hotel, Bahnhofplatz 2, tel. 55 85 71; Zirbelstube, in Eden-Hotel-Wolff, Arnulfstrasse 4, tel. 55 11 50; Alt Württemberg, in Hotel Erzgiesserei Europe, Erzgiesserei 15, tel. 18 60 55; Löwencorner, in Hotel Drei Löwen, Schillerstrasse 8, tel. 55 10 40; Regent, Seidlstrasse 2, tel. 55 15 90; Gundel, in Hungar Hotel, Paul-Heyse-Strasse 24, tel. 51 49 00; Belvedere, in Austrotel Deutscher Kaiser, Arnulfstrasse 2, tel. 5 38 60; Budapest, Schwanthaler Strasse 36, tel. 55 11 10; Le Gourmet, Ligsalzstrasse 46, tel. 50 35 97; Sabitzer, Reitmorstrasse 21, tel. 29 85 84; Weinhaus Neuner Restaurant Krukenberg, Herzogspitalstrasse 8, tel. 2 60 39 54; Weinhaus Schwarzwälder, Hartmannstrasse 8, tel. 22 72 16; Toula, Sparkassenstrasse 5, tel. 29 28 69; Hunsinger, Hans-Sachs-Strasse 10, tel. 26 68 77; Zum Alten Markt, Dreifaltigkeitsplatz 3, tel. 29 99 95; Chesa Rüegg, Wurzerstrasse 18, tel. 29 71 14; Zum Bürgerhaus, Petterkoferstrasse 1, tel. 59 79 09; La Vie, Ottostrasse 5, tel. 59 34 83; Dallmayr, Dienerstrasse 14 (1st floor), tel. 2 13 51 00; Austernkeller, Stollbergstrasse 11, tel. 29 87 87; Halali, Schönfeldstrasse 22, tel. 28 59 09; Boettner, Theatinerstrasse 8, tel. 22 12 10; Gasthaus Glockenbach, Kapuzinerstrasse 29, tel. 53 40 43; Bistro Chablis, Stollbergstrasse 2, tel. 29 84 84; Csarda Piroschka, Prinzregentenstrasse 1 (in Haus der Kunst), tel. 29 54 25; Hundskogel, Hotterstrasse 18, tel. 25 42 72; Spatenhaus, Residenzstrasse 12, tel. 22 78 41; Rothof, Denninger Strasse 114, tel. 91 50 61; Donisl, Weinstrasse 1, tel. 22 01 84.
Beer halls (mostly with beer-garden or garden restaurant):
Hofbräuhaus, Platzl 9, tel. 22 16 76; Zum Pschorrbräu, Neuhauser Strasse 11, tel. 2 60 30 01; Mathäser Bierstadt, Bayerstrasse 5, tel. 59 28 96; Hofbräukeller, Innere Wiener Strasse 19, tel. 48 94 89; Augustiner-Keller, Arnulfstrasse 52, tel. 59 43 93; Augustiner Grossgaststätten, Neuhauser Strasse 16, tel. 55 19 92 57; Salvator-Keller, Hochstrasse 77, tel. 48 32 74.

Rössli and Mövenpick, in Hotel Mövenpick, Kardinal-von-Galen-Ring 65, tel. 8 90 20;　　**Münster**
Zur Guten Stube, Mecklenbecker Strasse 80, tel. 7 71 79; Central, Aegidiistrasse 1, tel. 4 03 55; Feldmann, Klemensstrasse 24, 4 33 09; Martinihof, Hörsterstrasse 25, tel. 4 00 73; Kleines Restaurant im Oerschen Hof, Königsstrasse 42, tel. 4 20 61; Kiepenkerl,

Restaurants

Spiekerhof 45, tel. 4 03 35; Stuhlmacher, Prinzipalmarkt 6, tel. 4 48 77; Wielers, Spieker-hof 47, tel. 4 34 16; Pinkus Müller, Kreuzstrasse 4, tel. 4 51 51; Alter Gasthof Homann, Wolbecker Strasse 154, tel. 31 42 25; Altes Gasthaus Leve, Alter Steinweg 37, tel. 4 55 95.

Neuss

*Alfredo's and Petit Paris, in Hotel Rheinpark-Plaza, Rheinallee 1, tel. 15 30; Herzog von Burgund, Erftstrasse 88, tel. 2 35 52; Bölzke, Michaelstrasse 29, tel. 2 48 26; Giesskanne, in Hamtor-Hotel, Hamtorwall 17, tel. 22 20 02; Em Hahnekörfke, in Haus Hahn, Berg-heimer Strasse 121, tel. 4 90 51; Zum Stübchen, Preussenstrasse 73, tel. 8 22 16.

Nürnberg

Die Auster and Nürnberger Stuben, in Hotel Maritim, Frauentorgraben 11, tel. 2 36 30; Zirbelstube, in Altea-Hotel Carlton, Eilgutstrasse 13, tel. 2 00 30; restaurant in Grand Hotel, Bahnhofstrasse 1, tel. 20 36 21; Merkur Stuben, Pillenreuther Strasse 1, tel. 44 02 91; Senator, Landgrabenstrasse 25, tel. 4 19 71; Holzkistl, Theatereck and Bocks-beutelkeller, in Hotel Deutscher Hof, Frauentorgraben 29, tel. 20 38 21; Reichshof, Johannesgasse 16, tel. 20 37 17; restaurant in Ibis Hotel, Steinbühler Strasse 2, tel. 2 37 10; Badische and Pfälzer Weinstube, in Hotel Steichele, Knorrstrasse 2, tel. 2 03 77; Essigbrätlein, Weinmarkt 3, tel. 22 51 31; Goldenes Posthorn, Glöckleinsgasse 2, tel. 22 51 53; Nassauer Keller, Karolinenstrasse 2, tel. 22 59 67; Zum Weissgerber, Weiss-gerbergasse 18, tel. 20 88 00; Zum Sudhaus, Bergstrasse 20, tel. 20 43 14; Böhms Herrenkeller, Theatergasse 19, tel. 22 44 65; Da Claudio, Hauptmarkt 16, tel. 20 47 52; Bratwurstglöcklein (typical Nürnberg grilled sausages), Am Königstor (in Handwerker-hof), tel. 22 76 25; Bratwursthäusle bei St Sebald, Rathausplatz 1, tel. 22 76 95; König-shof, Zirkelschmiedsgasse 28, tel. 20 96 55.

Oberammergau

Restaurant in Parkhotel Sonnenhof, König-Ludwig-Strasse 12, tel. 10 771; Alois Lang, St-Lukas-Strasse 15, tel. 10 01; Böld, König-Ludwig-Strasse 10, tel. 30 21; Ammergauer Stubn, in Hotel Wittelsbach, Dorfstrasse 21, tel. 10 11; Turmwirt, Ettaler Strasse 2, tel. 30 91; Hafner-Stuben, Dorfstrasse 1, tel. 30 71; Friedenshöhe, König-Ludwig-Strasse 31, tel. 5 98; Wenger, Ludwig-Lang-Strasse 20, tel. 47 88.

Oberstdorf

Jagdstübchen, in Parkhotel Frank, Sachsenweg 11, tel. 55 55; Filser, Freibergstrasse 15, tel. 70 80; Exquisit, Prinzenstrasse 17, tel. 10 34; Wittelsbacher Stube, Prinzenstrasse 24, tel. 10 18; Alpenhof, Zweistapfenweg 6, tel. 30 95; Grün's Restaurant, Nebelhornstrasse 49, tel. 24 24; Baur, Marktplatz 5, tel. 20 91; Adler, Fuggerstrasse 1, tel. 30 50; Mohren, Marktplatz 6, tel. 30 05; Fuggerhof, Speichackerstrasse 2, tel. 47 32; Sieben Schwaben, Pfarrstrasse 9, tel. 38 70; Bacchus-Stuben, Freibergstrasse 4, tel. 47 87.

Offenbach am Main

Jacques Offenbach and Rhapsody, in Scandic Crown Hotel, Kaiserleistrasse 45, tel. 8 06 10; Le Grill, in Novotel, Strahlenberger Strasse 12, tel. 81 80 11; Il Calderone, Berliner Strasse 74, tel. 88 88 88; Ottavio, Löwenstrasse 26, tel. 81 84 84; Ristorante Italiano Alt-Offenbach, Domstrasse 39, tel. 88 71 19; Die Terrine, Luisenstrasse 53, tel. 88 33 39.

Oldenburg

Kiebitz-Stube and café in City-Club-Hotel, Europaplatz 4, tel. 80 80; Heidekate, in Hotel Heide, Melkbrink 49, tel. 80 40; Wieting, Damm 29, tel. 2 72 14; Schützenhof Eversten, Hauptstrasse 38, tel. 5 00 90; Le Journal, Wallstrasse 13, tel. 1 31 28.

Osnabrück

Hohenzollern, Heinrich-Heine-Strasse 17, tel. 3 31 70; Kulmbacher Keller, Schlosswall 67, tel. 2 78 44; Walhalla, Bierstrasse 24, tel. 2 72 06; Le Ballon, in Ibis Hotel, Blumenhaller Weg 152, tel. 4 04 90; Altes Landhaus, Lange Strasse 19, tel. 8 88 78; Welp, Natruper Strasse 227, tel. 12 33 07; Klute, Lotter Strasse 30, tel. 4 50 01; Der Landgraf, Domhof 9, tel. 2 23 72; Artischocke, Buersche Strasse 2, tel. 2 33 31; Alte Posthalterei, Hakenstrasse 4A, tel. 2 22 92; Ellerbrake, Am Neumarkt, tel. 2 28 11; Bürgerbräu, Blumenhaller Weg 41, tel. 4 58 22.

Paderborn

Walliser Stuben, in Hotel Arosa, Westernmauer 38, tel. 20 00; Schweizer Haus, War-burger Strasse 99, tel. 7 80 05; Ratskeller, Rathausplatz, tel. 2 57 53; restaurant in Hotel Ibis, Paderwall 1, tel. 2 50 31; Bistro Le Mans, Hathumarstrasse 1, tel. 2-851; Ahorn-Restaurant and Klause, Ahornallee, tel. 10 39 89.

Passau

Batavia, in Holiday Inn, Bahnhofstrasse 24, tel. 5 90 00; Weisser Hase, Ludwigstrasse 23, tel. 3 40 66; Passauer Wolf, Rindermarkt 6, tel. 3 40 66; Kaiserin Sissi and café in Hotel Wilder Mann, Rathausplatz, tel. 3 50 71; Altstadt, Bräugasse 27, tel. 3 34 51; Dreiflüssehof, Danziger Strasse 42, tel. 5 10 18; Heilig-Geist-Stiftsschenke, Heilig-Geist-Gasse 4, tel. 26 07.

Alte Wache, Bäckerstrasse 6, tel. 2 14 84; Altes Jagdschloss, Jagdhausstrasse, tel. 62 13 44; Am Stadttor, Brandenburger Strasse 1–3, tel. 2 17 29; Asiatisches Restaurant, Berliner Strasse 133, tel. 2 46 07; Auerochs, Schilfhof 26, tel. 8 22 19; Bolgar, Brandenburger Strasse 35–36, tel. 2 25 05; Charlottenhof, Geschwister-Scholl-Strasse, tel. 9 28 77; Die Rebe, Feuerbachstrasse 1, tel. 2 40 02; Drachenhaus, Maulbeerallee, tel. 2 15 94; Froschkasten, Kiezstrasse 4, tel. 2 13 15; Gastmahl des Meeres, Brandenburger Strasse 72, tel. 2 18 54; Gemütliche Klause, Berliner Strasse 133, tel. 2 46 07; Haus der Freundschaft, Strasse der Jugend 52, tel. 2 25 86; Havelgarten, Auf dem Kiewitt 30, tel. 9 23 16; Havellandgrill, in Hotel Potsdam, Lange Brücke, tel. 46 31; Historische Mühle, Park Sanssouci, tel. 2 31 10; Kahn der Fröhlichen Leute, Drewitz, tel. 62 20 42; Klosterkeller, Friedrich-Ebert-Strasse 94, tel. 2 12 18; Klub der Künstler und Architekten Eduard Claudius, Am Karl-Liebknecht-Forum 3, tel. 2 15 06; Klubgaststätte in Kulturbundhaus Bernhard Kellermann, Mangerstrasse 34–36, tel. 2 15 72; Minsk, Am Brauhausberg, tel. 2 36 36; Orion, Johannes-Kepler-Platz, tel. 62 30 67; Pegasus, Am Karl-Liebknecht-Forum 3, tel. 2 15 06; Plantagenklause, Rudolf-Breitscheid-Strasse 85, tel. 7 79 25; Seerose, Wilhelm-Külz-Strasse 24, tel. 2 34 90; Strandterrassen, Park Babelsberg, tel. 7 51 56; Templiner Eck, Leipziger Strasse 28, tel. 2 10 93; Teufelsklause, Waldstadt II, Werner-Wittig-Strasse, tel. 8 02 25; Theaterklause, Zimmerstrasse 10, tel. 2 23 64; Ufergaststätte, Auf dem Kiewitt, tel. 2 41 32; Weberschänke, Karl-Liebknecht-Strasse, tel. 7 88 47; Weinkeller, Am Alten Markt, tel. 2 31 35; Wohngebietsklub Zur Weide, Erlenhof 57, tel. 8 20 91; Zum Atlas, Heinrich-Rau-Allee 53, tel. 2 52 46; Zum Kahleberg, Fritz-Perlitz-Strasse, tel. 8 22 87; Zum Keller, Waldstadt I, Friedrich-Wolf-Strasse, tel. 8 21 91.

Westfalenstube, in Hotel Engelsburg, Augustinessenstrasse 10, tel. 2 50 66; Scirocco, Dortmunder Strasse 20, tel. 4 44 06; Die Weisse Brust, Münsterstrasse 4, tel. 2 99 04; Auerbach's Keller, Heilig-Geist-Strasse 3, tel. 18 28 18.

Historisches Eck, Watmarkt 6, tel. 5 89 20; Zum Krebs, Krebsgasse 6, tel. 5 58 03; Bischofshof, Krauterer Markt 3, tel. 5 90 86; Taverne, in Hotel Karmeliten, Dachauplatz 1, tel. 5 43 08; Kaiserhof am Dom, Kramgasse 10, tel. 5 40 27; Gänsbauer, Keplerstrasse 10, tel. 5 78 58; Ratskeller, Rathausplatz 1, tel. 57 77; Bischofshof Braustuben, Dechbettener Strasse 5, tel. 2 14 73; Münchner Hof, Tändlergasse 9, tel. 5 82 62; Wiendl, Universitätsstrasse 9, tel. 9 04 16; Alte Münz, Fischmarkt 7, tel. 5 48 86; Der Treff, in Hotel Arcade, Hernauerstrasse 2, tel. 5 69 30; Winklhofer-Weinwirt, Spiegelgasse 3, tel. 5 17 93; Beim Dampfnudel-Uli, Watmarkt 4, tel. 5 32 97.

Parkrestaurant and Axel-Stüberl, in Steigenberger Hotel Axelmannstein, Salzburger Strasse 2, tel. 40 01; Luisenbad-Restaurant and Die Holzstub'n, in Kurhotel Luisenbad, Ludwigstrasse 33, tel. 60 40; St-Zeno-Stuben and Kutscherstube, in Hotel Residenz Bavaria, Am Münster 3, tel. 50 16; Panorama, Baderstrasse 3, tel. 6 10 01; Bayerischer Hof, Bahnhofsplatz 14, tel. 60 90; Tiroler Hof, Tiroler Strasse 12, tel. 20 55; Hofwirt, Salzburger Strasse 21, tel. 6 20 21; Salzburger Hof, Mozartstrasse 7, tel. 20 62; Schweizer Stuben, in Kirchberg-Schloss, Thumseestrasse 11, tel. 27 60.

Landgraf, in Fürstenhof Hotel, Kaiserpassage 5, tel. 31 80; Stadt Reutlingen, Karlstrasse 55, tel. 4 23 91.

Restaurant in Parkhotel Crombach, Kufsteiner Strasse 2, tel. 1 20 82; Bonaparte, in Goldener Hirsch, Münchner Strasse 40, tel. 1 20 29; Zum Santa, Max-Josefsplatz 20, tel. 3 41 21.

Alte Münze, Am Ziegenmarkt 3, tel. 2 25 17; Alter Hafen, Strandstrasse 24, tel. 3 42 26; Alter Markt, Alter Markt 8, tel. 2 20 84; Alte Schänke, Rungestrasse 17, tel. 2 31 61; Am Bussebart Imbisszentrum, Am Bussebart, tel. 2 29 87; Am Ulmenmarkt, Fiete-Schulze-Strasse 74, tel. 2 24 86; Bierstube Helms, Doberaner Strasse 107, tel. 2 51 62; Bierstube Stauer, Wokrenter Strasse 36, tel. 2 99 82; Blauer Turm, Schnickmannstrasse 3, tel. 3 41 80; Bräustübl, Kröpeliner Strasse 18, tel. 2 92 61; Broilerstube, Doberaner Strasse 20, tel. 2 20 80; Fährhufe, Fährberg, no tel.; Fritz-Reuter-Stuben, Fritz-Reuter-Strasse 17, tel. 2 52 02; Fünfgiebelhaus, Universitätsplatz, tel. 2 26 60 and 2 21 62; Gastmahl des

Potsdam

Recklinghausen

Regensburg

Bad Reichenhall

Reutlingen

Rosenheim

Rostock

Restaurants

Meeres, August-Bebel-Strasse 112, tel. 2 23 01; Goldbroiler, Kröpeliner Strasse 80, tel. 3 44 07; Hallenschwimmbad, Kopernikusstrasse 17, tel. 3 49 83; Hansa, Fiete-Schulze-Strasse 51, tel. 2 26 68; Haus der Freundschaft, Doberaner Strasse 21, tel. 2 39 51; Hier is'n Krog, Stampfmüllerstrasse 9, tel. 2 93 32; Jägerhütte, Barnstorfer Wald 2, tel. 2 34 57; Klause Strempelstrasse 1, tel. 2 31 90; Klub des Kulturbundes, Hermannstrasse 19, tel. 3 43 96; Kosmos, Südring, tel. 4 11 71; Kulturhaus der Neptunwelt, Werftstrasse, tel. 3 45 85; Lindeneck, Liskowstrasse 14, tel. 2 20 82; Lindenhof, Fährstrasse 2, tel. 3 46 59; Malmö, in Hotel Warnow, Hermann-Duncker-Platz 4, tel. 3 73 81; Mitropa, Hauptbahnhof, tel. 2 36 80; Neue Münze, Klement-Gottwald-Strasse 58, tel. 2 33 29; Nordland, Steinstrasse 7, tel. 2 37 06; Onkel Toms Hütte, Amtsstrasse 9, tel. 2 50 39; Ostseegaststätte, Lange Strasse 9, tel. 3 42 20; Pizza-Buffet, Doberaner Platz, tel. 2 21 34; Platz der Jugend, Barndorfer Wald, tel. 3 47 88; Ratsweinkeller, Neuer Markt, tel. 2 35 77; Reifer Eck, Hermannstrasse 23, tel. 2 71 25; restaurant in Haus der Chemiearbeiter, Platz der Freundschaft, tel. 4 29 48; Rostocker Bierstuben, Lohgerberstrasse 33, tel. 2 37 29; Schnells Bierstuben, Grosse Scharrenstrasse 2, tel. 2 26 76; Sport- und Kongresshalle, Bierstube with bowling alley and bar), Südring, tel. 40 01 30; Stralsunder, Wismarsche Strasse 22, tel. 3 49 00; Tannenweg, Tannenweg 6, tel. 2 63 43; Taun Vagel Grip, Neuer Markt, tel. 2 39 53; Trotzenburg, Tiergartenallee 1, tel. 3 47 11; Weinkeller Zum Alten Gewölbe, Kröpeliner Strasse 76, tel. 2 66 33; Zoologischer Garten, Zoologischer Garten, tel. 3 71 11-128; Zum Frosch, Neue Werderstrasse 42, tel. 2 11 69; Zum Goldenen Anker, Strandstrasse 35, no tel.; Zum Greif, Budapester Strasse 57, tel. 2 50 19; Zum Kartoffelkeller (vegetarian), Friedrichstrasse 38, no tel.; Zum Kugelfisch, Kröpeliner Strasse 78, tel. 2 50 01; Zum Weissen Ross, Gertrudenstrasse 9, tel. 2 99 56; Zur Börse, Margaretenplatz, tel. 3 47 69; Zur Gemütlichkeit, Faule Strasse 7, tel. 2 23 88; Zur Kogge, Wokrenter Strasse 27, tel. 3 44 93; Zur Möwe, Schröderstrasse 35, tel. 2 64 05; Zur Wappenklause, Doberaner Strasse 15, tel. 2 21 73; Zur Quelle, Fiete-Schulze-Strasse 26, tel. 2 28 05; Zum Stauer, Wokrenter Strasse, tel. 2 99 82.

Rothenburg ob der Tauber

Eisenhut, Herrngasse 3, tel. 7 05 01; Die Blaue Terrasse and Café, in Hotel Goldener Hirsch, Untere Schmiedgasse 16, tel. 70 80; Bärenwirt, Hofbronnengasse 9, tel. 60 33; Tilman Riemenschneider, Georgengasse 11, tel. 20 86; Baumeisterhaus, Obere Schmiedgasse 3, tel. 34 04; Mittermeier, Vorm Würzburger Tor 9, tel. 50 41; Gasthof Rappen, Vorm Würzburger Tor 10, tel. 60 71; Klosterstüble, Heringsbronnengasse 5, tel. 67 74; Glocke, Am Plönlein 1, tel. 30 25; Reichs-Küchenmeister, Kirchplatz 8, tel. 20 46; Gasthof Zum Klingentor, Mergentheimer Strasse 14, tel. 34 68; Bayerischer Hof, Ansbacher Strasse 21, tel. 34 57.

Saarbrücken

Handelshof, Wilhelm-Heinrich-Strasse 17, tel. 5 69 20; Légère, Cecilienstrasse 17, tel. 3 59 00; Pullman, Hafenstrasse 8, tel. 3 06 91; Grill, in Novotel, Zinzinger Strasse 9, tel. 5 86 30; Provence, in Bauer Hotel Rodenhof, Kalmanstrasse 47, tel. 4 77 22; Le Jardin, in Park-Hotel, Deutschmühlental 4, tel. 58 10 33; Zum Stiefel, Am Stiefel 2, tel. 3 12 46; Gasthaus Horch, Mainzer Strasse 2, tel. 3 44 15.

Schwerin

Altschweriner Schankstuben, Schlachtermarkt, tel. 8 30 58; Casino, Pfaffenstrasse 3, tel. 8 60 43; Gambrinus, Tallinner Strasse, tel. 37 50 20; Haus der Kultur, Wilhelm-Pieck-Strasse 8, tel. 8 37 63; Jagdhaus Schelfwerder, Güstrower Strasse 109, tel. 86 32 51; Klubgaststätte Lankow, Dr-Joseph-Herzfeld-Strasse 42, tel. 4 20 83; Martins Bierstuben, Ernst-Thälmann-Strasse 19, tel. 8 31 74; Panorama, Johannes-Brahms-Strasse 65, tel. 8 32 06; Seewarte, Pauldamm 21, tel. 86 15 54; Tallinn, Puschkinstrasse 19, tel. 86 48 89; Uns Hüsing, Bischofstrasse 3, tel. 86 46 55; Weinhaus Uhle, Schusterstrasse 13–15, tel. 86 44 55; Wernesgrüner Bierstuben, Lennéstrasse 4, tel. 81 23 63.

Siegen

Restaurant in Park-Hotel, Koblenzer Strasse 135, tel. 3 38 10; restaurant in Queens Hotel Am Kaisergarten, Kampenstrasse 83, tel. 5 40 72; Kochs Ecke, Koblenzer Strasse 53, tel. 5 20 23.

Soest

Biermann's Restaurant and Bistro, Thomästrasse 47, tel. 1 33 10; Andernach Zur Börse, Thomästrasse 31, tel. 40 19; Börde-Stuben, in Wilder Mann, Markt 11, tel. 1 50 11; Pilgrim Haus, Jakobistrasse 75, tel. 18 28; Im Zuckerberg, Höggenstrasse 1, tel. 28 68.

Solingen

Atlantic, Goerdelerstrasse 9, tel. 1 60 01; Zum Goldenen Spiess, Entenpfuhl 1, tel. 1 08 95; Gasthaus Schultz, Werwolf 62, tel. 20 41 24; Goldener Löwe, Heinestrasse 2, tel. 1 20 30; Landhaus Schmalzgrube, Mangenberger Strasse 356, tel. 1 80 03.

Backmulde, Karmeliterstrasse 11, tel. 7 15 77; restaurant in Graf's Hotel Löwengarten,   Speyer
Schwerdstrasse 14, tel. 7 10 51; Zum Alten Engel, in Hotel Goldener Engel, Mühlturm-
strasse 1A, tel. 7 67 32; Trutzpfaff, Webergasse 5, tel. 7 83 99.

Alte Schleuse, Hansestrasse 14, tel. 30 63; Vier Linden, Schölischer Strasse 63, tel.   Stade
4 40 11; Schwedenkrone, Richeyweg 15, tel. 8 11 74; Inselrestaurant, Auf der Insel 1, tel.
20 31; Zur Einkehr, Freiburger Strasse 82, tel. 23 25.

Romagna, in Hotel Seehof, Bahnhofsplatz 4, tel. 60 01; Allodi's Restaurant, Söckinger   Starnberg
Strasse 39, tel. 1 27 88; Weinpresse, Kaiser-Wilhelm-Strasse 2, tel. 44 66; Seerestaurant
Undosa, Seepromenade 1, tel. 89 21; Tutzinger Hof, Tutzinger-Hof-Platz 7, tel. 30 81;
Starnberger Alm Illguth's Gasthaus, Schlossbergerstrasse 24, tel. 1 55 77.

Pfau, in Hotel Heimer, Schlesische Strasse 131, tel. 6 10 91; Seethaler, Theresienplatz 25,   Straubing
tel. 1 20 22; Mirage, Regensburger Strasse 46, tel. 20 51; Alte Post, Seminargasse 4, tel.
24 68; Röhrl, Theresienplatz 7, tel. 1 02 29; Wenisch, Innere Passauer Strasse 159,
tel. 2 20 66.

*Les Continents, Classico Lounge, Neckarstube and Piazzetta Wulle, in Hotel Inter-   Stuttgart
Continental, Neckarstrasse 60, tel. 2 02 00; Graf Zeppelin, Zeppelin-Stüble, Maukenescht
and Zepp 7, in Steigenberger Hotel Graf Zeppelin, Arnulf-Klett-Platz 7, tel. 29 98 81;
Schlossgarten-Restaurant, Zirbelstube and Café am Schlossgarten, in Hotel am Schlossgarten, Schillerstrasse 23, tel. 2 02 60; Alte Post, Friedrichstrasse 43, tel. 29 30 79;
Mövenpick-Gastronomie: Rôtisserie Baron de la Mouette and Chesa, Kleiner Schlossplatz 11, tel. 2 26 89 34; Villa Berg and Radio-Stüble, in Parkhotel, Villastrasse 21, tel.
28 01 61; Sympathie, in Hotel Ketterer, Marienstrasse 3, tel. 2 03 90; Royal, Sophien-
strasse 35, tel. 62 50 50; Logo, Willi-Bleicher-Strasse 19, tel. 22 50 02; Ruff, Friedhof-
strasse 21, tel. 2 58 70; Intercity, Arnulf-Klett-Platz 2, tel. 29 49 46; Am Feuersee,
Johannesstrasse 2, tel. 62 61 03; Zur Weinsteige, in Hotel Wörtz, Hohenheimer Strasse
30, tel. 24 06 81; Alter Simpl, Hohenheimer Strasse 64, tel. 24 08 21; Gaisburger Pas-
tetchen, Hornbergstrasse 24, tel. 48 48 55; Goldener Adler, Böheimstrasse 38, tel.
6 40 17 62; Délice, Hauptstätter Strasse 61, tel. 6 40 32 22; Come Prima, Steinstrasse 3, tel.
24 34 22; Da Franco, Calwer Strasse 23, tel. 29 15 81; Incontro, Rotebühlstrasse 50,
tel. 62 62 32; Martins Stuben, in Engelhorn Hotel, Neckarstrasse 119, tel. 26 16 31;
Bäckerschmiede, Schurwaldstrasse 44, tel. 46 60 35; Bellevue, Schurwaldstrasse 44, tel.
48 10 10; Lausterer, Bärenstrasse 3, tel. 24 23 80; Wirtshaus Hasen, Gablenberger
Hauptstrasse 91, tel. 46 47 00; Weinstube Kachelofen, Eberhardstrasse 10, tel. 24 23 78;
Wartburg-Hospiz, Lange Strasse 49; Das Lokal, in Hotel Münchner Hof, Neckarstrasse
170, tel. 28 30 86; Zur Kiste, Kanalstrasse 2, tel. 24 40 02.

Bayern, Neureuthstrasse 23, tel. 18 20; restaurant in Seehotel Zur Post, Seestrasse 3, tel.   Tegernsee
39 51; Leeberghof, Ellinger Strasse 10, tel. 39 66; Fischerstüberl am See, Seestrasse 51,
tel. 46 72.

Forelle, Karl-Marx-Strasse 84, tel. 27 57; Gaststätte Georgshöhe, tel. 27 38; Hexentanz-   Thale
platz, tel. 22 12; Rosstrappe, tel. 30 11; Wilder Jäger, Ernst-Thälmann-Strasse, tel. 24 17.

Residenz, Stefanie-von-Strechine-Strasse 16, tel. 80 10; Jodquellenhof, Ludwigstrasse   Bad Tölz
13, tel. 50 90; Schwaighofer, Marktstrasse 17, tel. 27 62; Terrassenhotel Kolbergarten,
Fröhlichgasse 5, tel. 90 67; restaurant in Posthotel Kolberbräu, Marktstrasse 29, tel.
91 58; Gästehaus Pichler, Angerstrasse 23, tel. 96 72; Bruckfeld, Ludwigstrasse 24, tel.
21 55.

Pfeffermühle, Zurlaubener Ufer 76, tel. 1 61 33; Porta and Salong, in Dorint Hotel Porta   Trier
Nigra, Porta-Nigra-Platz 1, tel. 2 70 10; Römertreff, in Europa Parkhotel Mövenpick,
Kaiserstrasse 29, tel. 7 19 50; La Brochette, in Scandic Crown Hotel, Zurmaiener Strasse
164, tel. 14 30; restaurant in Nell's Parkhotel, Dasbachstrasse 12, tel. 2 80 91; Alte Kate,
Matthiasstrasse 71, tel. 3 07 33; Lenz Weinstuben, Viehmarktstrasse 4, tel. 4 53 10.

Krone, with Uhland-Stube, Uhlandstrasse 1, tel. 3 10 36; Stadt Tübingen, Stuttgarter   Tübingen
Strasse 97, tel. 3 10 71; Museum, Wilhelmstrasse 3, tel. 2 28 28; Landgasthof Rosenau, at
New Botanic Garden, tel. 6 64 66; Weinstube Forelle, Kronenstrasse 8, tel. 2 29 38;
Barbarina, Wilhelmstrasse 94, tel. 2 60 48.

Restaurants

Überlingen

Restaurant and café in Parkhotel St Leonhard, Obere St-Leonhard-Strasse 71, tel. 80 80; Ochsen, Münsterstrasse 48, tel. 40 67; restaurant in Romantik-Hotel Hecht, Münsterstrasse 8, tel. 6 33 33; Walter, Seepromenade 13, tel. 48 83; Gasthof Bürgerbräu, Aufkircher Strasse 29, tel. 6 34 07.

Ulm

Neuthor, Neuer Graben 23, tel. 1 51 60; Stern, Sterngasse 17, tel. 6 30 91; Ulmer Spatz, Münsterplatz 27, tel. 6 80 81; Goldener Bock, Bockgasse 25, tel. 2 80 79; Weinstube Pflugmerzler, Pfluggasse 6, tel. 6 80 61; Forelle, Fischergasse 25, tel. 6 39 24; Lochmühle, Gerbergasse 6, tel. 6 73 05; Zunfthaus der Schiffleute, Fischergasse 31, tel. 6 44 11; Drei Kannen, Hafenbad 31, tel. 6 77 17.

Wangen im Allgäu

Restaurant in Romantik-Hotel Alte Post, Postplatz 2, tel. 40 14; Mohren-Post, Herrenstrasse 27, tel. 2 10 76; Fidelisbäck, Paradiesstrasse 3, tel. 7 95 90; Altdeutsche Weinstube Zum Kornhausmeister, Bindstrasse 29, tel. 23 83.

Weimar

Elephantenkeller, Markt 19, tel. 6 14 71; Gastmahl des Meeres, Herderplatz 16, tel. 47 21 and 45 21; Grabenschänke, Am Graben 8, tel. 6 21 07; Ratskeller, Stadthaus, Markt, tel. 41 42; Stadt Weimar, in Hotel Elephant, Markt 19, tel. 6 14 71; Scharfe Ecke, Eisfeld 2, tel. 24 30; Schlossgaststätte Belvedere, Schloss Belvedere, tel. 26 04; Schwanseebad, Herbststrasse 2, tel. 28 74; Theater-Kasino, Theaterplatz 1, tel. 32 09; Waldgaststätte Fasanerie, tel. 21 91; Waldschlösschen, Jeaner Strasse 56, tel. 37 08; Weimarhalle, Karl-Liebknecht-Strasse 3, tel. 23 41; Weinstube Alt-Weimar, Prellerstrasse 2, tel. 20 56; Am Dichterweg, Bodelschwingstrasse, tel. 21 72; Zum Birkenhaus, Leibnizallee 27, tel. 45 56; Zum Fiaker, Oberweimar, tel. 28 48; Zum Siechenbräu, Ferdinand-Freiligrath-Strasse 17, tel. 33 87; Zum Weissen Schwan, Am Frauenplan, tel. 6 17 15.

Wiesbaden

*Die Ente vom Lehel, Bistro, Orangerie and Entenkeller, in Hotel Nassauer Hof, Kaiser-Friedrich-Platz 3, tel. 13 30; Steigenberger Kurhaus-Restaurant *La Belle Epoque and Le Bistro, Kurhausplatz 1, tel. 52 69 37; Elisabeth and Nostalgisches Caféhaus, in Hotel Schwarzer Bock, Kranzplatz 12, tel. 15 50; Rosenpark, Imari and Bier-Kathdrälsche, in Aukamm-Hotel, Aukammallee 31, tel. 57 60; De France, Taunusstrasse 49, tel. 5 12 51; Maurice, in Holiday Inn, Bahnhofstrasse 10, tel. 16 20; Globetrotter, in Penta Hotel, Auguste-Viktoria-Strasse 15, tel. 37 70 41; Friesenstube, in Forum-Hotel, Abraham-Lincoln-Strasse 17, tel. 79 70; Klee am Park, Parkstrasse 4, tel. 30 50 61; Oranien, Platter Strasse 2, tel. 52 50 25; Alte Münze, Kranzplatz 5, tel. 52 48 33; Alte Krone, Sonnenberger Strasse 82, tel. 56 39 47; Mövenpick-Gastronomie: Möpi and La Chesa, Sonnenberger Strasse 2, tel. 52 40 05; Zum Dortmunder, Langgasse 34, tel. 30 20 96; Bobbeschänkelche, Röderstrasse 39, tel. 52 79 59.

Wildbad

Restaurant Graf Eberhard and café, in Badhotel, Kurplatz 5, tel. 17 60; Bären, Kurplatz 4, tel. 16 81; Valsana am Kurpark, Kernerstrasse 182, tel. 13 25; Kurhotel Post, Kurplatz 2, tel. 16 11; Weingärtner, Olgastrasse 15, tel. 1 70 60; Goldenes Lamm, Wilhelmstrasse 1, tel. 20 33; Kurpark-Restaurant, in Kurpark, tel. 25 86.

Wilhelmshaven

Alkoven, in Hotel Am Stadtpark, Friedrich-Paffrath-Strasse 116, tel. 86 21; Kaiser, Rheinstrasse 128, tel. 4 20 04; Maris, Werftstrasse 54, tel. 20 20 96; Ratskeller, Rathausplatz 1, tel. 2 19 64; Mon Abri, in Hotel Jacobi, Freiligrathstrasse 163, tel. 6 00 51; Artischocke, Paulstrasse 6, tel. 3 43 05.

Wittenberg

Friedrichstadt, Strasse der Befreiung 102, tel. 8 11 26; Goldener Adler, Markt 7, tel. 20 53 and 20 54; Haus des Handwerks, Collegienstrasse 54A, tel. 29 87; Kosmos, Ernst-Thälmann-Strasse, tel. 8 10 87; Ratsschänke, Markt 14, tel. 43 51; Schlosskeller, Schloss, tel. 23 27; Weinkeller, Markt 7, tel. 20 53 and 20 54; Wittenberger Hof, Collegienstrasse 56, tel. 35 94.

Wolfsburg

Zille-Stube, in Holiday Inn Wolfsburg, Rathausstrasse 1, tel. 20 70; Kellerklause, in Parkhotel Steimkerberg, Unter den Eichen 55, tel. 50 50; Primas, Büssingstrasse 18, tel. 2 00 40; Goyastuben, Poststrasse 34, tel. 2 30 66; Alter Wolf, Schloss-strasse 21, tel. 6 10 15.

Bacchus, in Domhotel, Obermarkt 10, tel. 69 13; Tivoli, Adenauerring 4B, tel. 2 84 85;
Bistro Léger, Siegfriedstrasse 2, tel. 4 62 77.

Palais and Weinstube, in Maritim Hotel Würzburg, Pleichertorstrasse 5, tel. 5 08 31;
Rebstock, Neubaustrasse 7, tel. 3 09 30; Walfisch-Stube, Am Pleidenturm 5, tel. 5 00 55;
Amberger, Ludwigstrasse 17, tel. 5 01 79; Klosterschänke in Hotel Franziskaner, Fran-
ziskanerplatz 2, tel. 1 50 01; Würtzburg, in Hotel Strauss, Juliuspromenade 5, tel. 3 05 70;
Gasthof Zur Stadt Mainz,Semmelstrasse 39, tel. 5 31 55; Weinhaus Zum Stachel, Gres-
sengasse 1, tel. 5 27 70; Ratskeller, Langgasse 1, tel. 1 30 21; Backöfele, Ursulinengasse
2, tel. 5 90 59.

Astoria, Poetenweg 6, tel. 35 70; Baikal, Marchlewskistrasse 1, tel. 78 10 86; Burg-
schenke, Alter Steinweg 2, tel. 27 69; Freundschaft, Leninstrasse 94, tel. 78 11 05;
Historische Weinstube, Neuberinplatz, tel. 4 18 64; Kosmos, Scheffelstrasse, tel. 7 42 51;
Kulturhaus, Marienthaler Strasse 120, tel. 7 20 26; Lindenhof, Marienthaler Strasse 3, tel.
7 33 90; Neue Welt, Leipziger Strasse 182, tel. 25 83; Park Eckersbach, Trillerplatz 1, tel.
7 55 72; Parkgaststätte, Bahnhofstrasse 1, tel. 33 33; Ringgaststätte, Dr-Friedrichs-Ring
21A, tel. 25 96; Windberghaus, Werdauer Strasse 152, tel. 72 95 66; Zur Waldschänke,
Königswalder Strasse 12, tel. 7 32 43.

Time

Germany observes Central European Time, one hour ahead of Greenwich Mean Time.
Summer Time (two hours ahead of GMT and one hour ahead of British Summer Time) is
in force from the last Sunday in March to the last Sunday in September.

Travel Documents

British nationals require only a valid passport (or British Visitor's Passport) for entry to   Personal
Germany. Holders of United States, Canadian and other Commonwealth passports do   documents
not require a visa for a visit of up to three months unless they are taking up employment
in Germany.

See Motoring in Germany   Car documents

Youth Hostels

There are some 600 excellently equipped youth hostels in Germany, open to holders of
the international youth hostel card (which is obtainable from national youth hostel
associations). There is no age limit except in Bavaria, where hostellers have to be under
27.
The German youth hostel association is the Deutsches Jugendherbergswerk, Bismarckstrasse 8, 4930 Detmold, tel. (05231) 7 40 10, which publishes a list of German youth
hostels (DM6.50).
In the *Länder* of Brandenburg, Mecklenburg-West Pomerania, Saxony, Saxony-Anhalt
and Thuringia accommodation in youth hostels can be booked through the following
organisations:

Jugendtourist GmbH
Alexanderplatz 5
1026 Berlin
Tel. 2/2 40 62 50

Jugendherbergsverband
Postfach 105
1080 Berlin
Tel. 2/2 26 60

Index

Index

Index

Index

The Principal Sights at a Glance

Continued from page 6

Source of illustrations

Aalto-Theater Essen, p. 203; Kloster Andechs, p. 61 (two); Anthony/Büth, p. 52 (left); Anthony/Jogschiess, p. 206; Fremdenverkehrsamt Aschaffenburg, p. 67; Kurverwaltung Bad Kissingen, pp. 310, 311; Kurbetriebsgesellschaft Bad Zwischenahn, p. 423; Baedeker-Archiv, p. 500; Bartholdt, p. 251 (right); Baumann, p. 49; Baumgarten, p. 460; Fremdenverkehrsamt Bodenwerder, p. 265; Presseamt Bonn, p. 117; Borowski, pp. 123 (two), 135, 263 (two), 269, 285 (two), 327, 335, 542, 554, 562, 563; Verkehrsverein Bremen, p. 125; Presse- und Werbeamt Bremerhaven, p. 127; Cabos, pp. 89, 90, 91, 94, 105, 113, 466, 511; Cambodunum/Kempten, p. 306; Verkehrsverein Celle, p. 129; Fremdenverkehrs- und Kongressbetrieb Coburg, p. 137; Verkehrsverein Darmstadt, p. 150; Verkehrsverein Detmold, p. 154 (two), Verkehrsamt Diez, p. 323; Informations- und Presseamt Dortmund, p. 161; Dreier, p. 251 (left); Werbe- und Wirtschaftsförderungsamt Düsseldorf, p. 178; Eisenschmid, pp. 103, 343; Fix, p. 502; Frässdorf, pp. 442 (right), 444, 509; Stadt Freudenberg, p. 495; Kur- und Fremdenverkehrsgesellschaft Goslar, p. 239; Graf-Zeppelin-Haus Friedrichshafen, p. 225; Grill, p. 159; Haberstock, p. 86; Tourismus-Zentrale Hamburg, pp. 255, 260; Verkehrsverein Heidelberg, p. 276; Kurverwaltung Helgoland, p. 280; Herold, pp. 301, 356, 360, 370, 468 (two); Hinze, p. 175; Hoffmann, p. 503; Huber, p. 81; Ihlow, p. 574 (top); Fremdenverkehrsverein Ingolstadt, p. 294; Jürgens, pp. 181, 508, 558; Keidel, p. 274; Tourist-Info Kiel, p. 308; Kienberger, p. 229; Verkehrsamt Kleinwalsertal, p. 311; Klöppel, pp. 218 (right), 367, 471; Köln-Düsseldorfer Deutsche Rheinschiffahrt, p. 459 (two); König, pp. 120 (right), 163, 188, 191 (right), 218 (left), 241, 244, 299, 340, 351, 367, 398, 418, 442 (left), 470, 559, 574 (right); Korff, p. 332; Krumbholz, p. 404; Kühn, pp. 197, 473, 545 (two), 565; Lade, pp. 52 (right), 221, 228, 229, 362; Landesbildstelle Württemberg, p. 516; Leser, p. 448; Limmer, p. 77 (two); Fremdenverkehrsamt Lüneburg, p. 347; Mader, pp. 342, 414 (two), 452; Mainau-Verwaltung, p. 317 (left); Magistrat Michelstadt, p. 420; Fremdenverkehrsamt Miltenberg, p. 373; Stadtverwaltung Minden, p. 374; Kuverwaltung Mittenwald, p. 376; Verkehrsverein Münster, pp. 393, 394; Musewald, pp. 247, 405; Nahm, pp. 177, 205, 400, 403, 529, 571 (two); Nathke, pp. 331, 560; Stadtverwaltung Neresheim, p. 408; Neubert, p. 489; Nitschke, pp. 57, 549; Verkehrsverein Nonnenhorn, p. 578; Verkehrs- und Reisebüro Oberammergau, p. 417; Kurverwaltung Oberstdorf, p. 419; Fremdenverkehrsverband Ostbayern, pp. 148, 450; Fremdenverkehrsverein Passau, p. 430; Pellmann, pp. 132, 133, 145, 165, 166–67, 194–95, 434, 435, 481, 482, 490, 494, 576; Kurverwaltung Plön, p. 286; Ponti, p. 497; Fremdenverkehrsamt Porta Westfalica, p. 553; Prenzel, pp. 386, 391; Stadtverwaltung Rastatt, p. 447; Fremdenverkehrsamt Ratzeburg, p. 326; Reiter, 391; Stadtverwaltung Rendsburg, p. 454; Stadt Reutlingen, p. 455 (two); Fremdenverkehrsverband Rheinland-Pfalz, p. 379; Röding, pp. 182, 463, 465, 493, 520, 547; Rothe, p. 401 (two); Kuramt Rottach-Egern, p. 521; Rudolph, pp. 152, 364–65; Stadtamt Saarbrücken, p. 476; Schmidt, pp. 445, 574 (left); Schuster, pp. 426, 427; Schütze-Rodemann, pp. 74, 191 (left), 252, 345, 524, 534, 550; Sieber, p. 223; Sperber, pp. 211, 214; Fremdenverkehrsamt Stade, p. 504; Kurverwaltung Tönning, p. 291; Tourist-Verlag, p. 8; Verkehrsamt Trier, p. 527; Verkehrsamt Ulm, p. 533; Vetter, pp. 172, 506; Verkehrsamt Volkach, p. 355; Wanke, pp. 120 (left), 440, 441; Kurbetriebe Wiesbaden, p. 556; Stadtinformation Worms, p. 566; Wurlitzer, p. 187; Fremdenverhrsamt Würzburg, p. 570; Freizeit und Fremdenverkehr Xanten, p. 572.

Notes